DATE DUE

OVERDUE FINE
$0.10 PER DAY

Elegant Glass

Early, Depression, & Beyond

Revised & Expanded 2nd Edition

Debbie and Randy Coe

Schiffer Publishing Ltd

4880 Lower Valley Road, Atglen, PA 19310 USA

Printed in China

Dedication

This book is dedicated to our dear Lord above, who has truly blessed
us with wonderful family and friends. In His infinite wisdom, He has
now provided us with the ability to do this revision.

Library of Congress Cataloging-in-Publication Data

Coe, Debbie.
Elegant glass : early, depression, & beyond / by Debbie and Randy Coe.— Rev. & expanded 2nd ed.
p. cm.
ISBN 0-7643-2028-9 (hardcover)
1. Depression glass—Collectors and collecting—Catalogs. 2. Glassware—United
States—History—20th century—Catalogs. I. Coe, Randy. II. Title.
NK5439.D44C63 2004
748.2'0973'075—dc22
2004009799
Revised price guide: 2004

Designed by "Sue"
Type set in Shelley Allegro BT/Humanist 521 BT

ISBN: 0-7643-2028-9
Printed in China
1 2 3 4

Published by Schiffer Publishing Ltd.
4880 Lower Valley Road
Atglen, PA 19310
Phone: (610) 593-1777; Fax: (610) 593-2002
E-mail: Info@schifferbooks.com
Please visit our web site catalog at **www.schifferbooks.com**

In Europe, Schiffer books are distributed by Bushwood Books
6 Marksbury Avenue Kew Gardens
Surrey TW9 4JF England
Phone: 44 (0) 20-8392-8585; Fax: 44 (0) 20-8392-9876
E-mail: info@bushwoodbooks.co.uk
Free postage in the UK. Europe: air mail at cost.

This book may be purchased from the publisher.
Include $3.95 for shipping. Please try your bookstore first.
We are always looking for people to write books on new and related subjects.
If you have an idea for a book please contact us at the above address.
You may write for a free catalog.

Contents

Acknowledgments, 4
Preface, 5
What is Elegant Glass?, 6
Measurements, 7
Value Guide, 7
Information Request, 7
The Patterns – Arranged Alphabetically, 8
　　American, 8
　　American Lady, 12
　　Apple Blossom, 13
　　Ardith, 17
　　Baroque, 20
　　Black Forest, 23
　　Buttercup, 26
　　Candlelight, 27
　　Candlewick, 30
　　Canterbury, 39
　　Cape Cod, 42
　　Caprice, 48
　　Caribbean, 54
　　Cascade, 56
　　Century, 58
　　Chanticleer, 59
　　Chantilly, 60
　　Cherokee Rose, 65
　　Chintz, 66
　　Cleo, 68
　　Coin, 71
　　Colonial Dame, 73
　　Colony, 73

Coronet, 76
Crests, 77
Crown, 82
Crow's Foot, 83
Crystollite, 85
Cupid, Fostoria, 89
Cupid, Paden City, 90
Dancing Nymph, 92
Decagon, 93
Deerwood, 94
Delilah Bird, 95
Della Robbia, 97
Diamond Optic, 99
Diane, 101
Elaine, 106
Empress/Queen Anne, 111
Fairfax, 113
First Love, 115
Flanders, 118
Florentine, 120
Fuchsia, Fostoria, 121
Fuchsia, Tiffin, 122
Gloria, 124
Golf Ball, 127
Gothic Garden, 128
Heather, 130
Heirloom, 131
Hermitage, 133
Hobnail, 135
Holly, 142

Imperial Hunt, 143
Ipswich, 145
Jamestown, 146
Jenny Lind, 147
Jubilee, 148
June, 149
June Night, 151
Lafayette, 152
Lariat, 153
Lido, 155
Lincoln Inn, 157
Mayfair, 158
Mayflower, 160
Meadow Rose, 161
Midnight Rose, 163
Minuet, 164
Moondrops, 165
Morgon, 168
Morning Glory, 170
Mount Vernon, 171
Navarre, 173
Oak Leaf/Oak Wood, 176
Old Colony, 178
Old Sandwich, 180
Orchid, Heisey, 181
Orchid, Paden City, 185
Peacock and Rose, 187
Plantation, 189
Pleat and Panel, 191
Plymouth, 192

Portia, 193
Prelude, 197
Radiance, 200
Ridgeleigh, 202
Romance, 205
Rosalie, 207
Rose, 209
Rose Point, 211
Ruba Rombic, 219
Sandwich, 220
Shirley, 222
Spiral Flutes, 223
Sunray, 224
Sunrise Medallion, 226
Tally Ho, 227
Teardrop, 229
Terrace, 232
Trojan, 233
Twist, 236
Vernon, 238
Versailles, 240
Wildflower, 243
Willowmere, 248
Collector Organizations, 250
Replacing Items, 251
Glass Museums, 251
Bibliography, 252
Glossary, 254

Acknowledgments

Everyone has been so generous. So many collectors and dealers have continued to give us their support on this project. This book is the end result of all the information that has been gathered and the generosity of people to let us photograph their glass. We can compile any information but we need the continued input of people in the market to truly give an accurate reflection of the market place across the country. We can't be everywhere. No matter how simple the fact, if we don't have it to include in this edition, then it means we still need it. Don't just assume someone else will give us the information; we need all of your help.

Through personal correspondence we gained additional information to include in this edition. A great many of the dealers provided us with different prices and also opened up their inventory records to show us when and where items sold. We are so grateful to the many people who opened up their entire homes to us. They provided access to all their glass and inventory records. Everyone also informed us about other collectors that had glass we need. We were provided with old catalogs, ads, brochures, and newsletters to compliment what we already had in our files. At several different glass shows we were given a special room so we could photograph the pieces we found there. Several people were extremely helpful with the proofing. We were encouraged and given great recommendations for this project.

This definitely is a comprehensive project that would not have happened without all the support we received. This book belongs to all glass enthusiasts.

A special place in our hearts belongs to our two daughters, Myra & Tara. Since our last edition, they have both: graduated from college, obtained jobs in their respective fields, gotten married, and written books in their particular collecting areas. Their love of glass collecting has continued with them in their adult lives and is now shared with their husbands. They both collect elegant glass. From their collections, we were able to photograph several unique pieces and get various sizes. We are so thankful to have Myra & Stephen Hixson and Tara & Jeff McRitchie enrich our lives.

Janine, Joanne, & Dale Bender are long time Fostoria collectors and dealers. They were a real bonus to have when working on all the Fostoria patterns. They opened up their inventory records to us. This information indicated what patterns were receiving the most attention and the prices being actually paid. We could easily see a trend and understand why.

Darlene & Gordon Cochran, long-time Heisey collectors, were a huge help in furnishing some much need facts. Gordon is a former member of the Heisey board. They are a true plus to the collecting world since they are so willing to share what they know. They give a whole new meaning to sharing. We greatly appreciate all they shared with us.

John Fallihee, of Blue Ribbon Photography, provided us with some photographs we were missing that we wanted to include in this edition. It was great to have him to rely on.

Robert Henicksman & Larry Hamilton, also Heisey collectors, were another huge help on Heisey information. They really took extra time to help us correct some overlooked mistakes in our last edition and to provide information on the addition of Heisey patterns.

Pat & Sue McGrain are longtime Fostoria dealers, that still travel the different parts of the country doing shows. They provided a lot of help in determining the requests of customers and prices being paid.

Dean Six has been a true inspiration to the importance of researching accurate information and sharing it with others. He is a great glass enthusiast and a super person to know and talk with about preserving our glass heritage.

Bill and Sandy Walker, longtime Paden City collectors and dealers, were invaluable in providing information about patterns from this company. Their extensive knowledge helped identify some errors in the previous edition.

Kent Washburn deserves a special note of appreciation. He was the first of many to invite us to be guests at his show in Texas. Sadly, this occurred just two weeks after September 11. We made our commitment to go and Kent made a commitment that he felt the show should still happen. Kent went out of his way to make this show a great distraction to the world events going on around us. A beautiful patriotic display greeted the public as they entered the building. We had a super time. There were several dealers we were already acquainted with and others we got to meet for the first time. At this show we were able to photograph so many neat pieces of glass. Our seminars were well attended and collectors had so many questions that, hopefully, we answered to their satisfaction. Everyone was so appreciative that they could even get out and have a chance to visit with others.

The West Virginia Museum of American Glass has provided such a tremendous amount of help in locating older company information. They have such a wealth of information that is cataloged for research purposes. All the board members are a great group to know and get to work with. We thank you for all your ongoing educational projects.

Juanita Williams, a long time friend and author of the new Fostoria books by Schiffer, was of immense help in furnishing Fostoria information. We were both working on books at the same time and we were continually bouncing ideas off each other. She is such a valuable support to have.

The following people were also of great help to this project, either letting us photograph their glass and/or providing us with information about many of the patterns. Our heartfelt thanks goes out to the following people: David & Linda Adams, Lou Bauman, James & Phyllis Booth, Neila & Tom Bredehoft, Jeff Burton, Carol & Al Carder, Bob Carlson, Bonnie & Bruce Catton, Ann Christianson, Darlene & Gordon Cochran, Larry Cook, Robin & Tim Cook, Elizabeth Cooper, Cynthia & Karla Cronkhite, Carolyn Crow, Vicky Cumpston, Chris Damson, Penny Drucker, Victor Elliott, Susan Farwell, Frank M. Fenton, Dallas & Kathy Figley, Dick & Marcia Floyd, Cindy & John Frank, Barbara Grey, Bev & Ed Groshen, Dan & Delene Haake, Bill Harmon, Dennis Headrick, James Horine, Darlene Horn, Jozell Johnson, Helen & Bob Jones, Dale & Jan Kreiger, Lafayette Schoolhouse Mall, Debbie & Ed Lane, Kay & Swede Larsson, William Line, Susan Mahoney, Arnie Masoner, Bea & Terry Martin, Donna & Ron Miller, Robby Miller, Iris Natividad, Mark Nye, Dave & Barbara Ownbey, Dick Ponti, Lana & Ted Renner, Dave Renner, Penny Renner, Bill & Wanda Rice, Jaime Robinson, Carlotta & Jim Roecker, Karin & Tom Sanders, Jon Saffell, Jackie Shirley, Jack & Jackie Skaw, Tom Smith, Ronda & Steve Stone, Cecil & Sharyn Taylor, Llynn Thompson, Rosemary Trietsch, Bob Van Aken, John Walk, Deen Warren, Fred Wilkerson, Jevena Word, Leegh & Michael Wyse.

Our job has been made so much easier by being able to photograph at several glass shows. We were able to contact so many dealers all at once. Our thanks goes out to: The Pacific Northwest Fenton Association for their All American Glass Shows in Oregon; Southern Oregon Antique & Collectible Club shows in Oregon; McGrain Productions in Florida & Louisiana, and Washburn Productions in Texas.

Suburban Photo in Beaverton, Oregon, has provided us with great customer service. Their staff has been invaluable in helping us to select the photography equipment we need and remained committed to assisting us with answers to continuing questions. Every time we go in, they are ready to help.

Our last special thank you has to go to our editors, Jean Cline and Jeff Snyder, for their help with this revision. They have been of enormous help in answering questions. Putting together a revision is much different than the actual book. Several different steps were involved and we value their assistance.

We really appreciate all of your help!

Who could have known, since our last edition came out, that there would be so many changes in the collecting market. September 11 tested our country's strength, followed by a decline in our stock markets. So many people used their investments to purchase glassware. Two longtime publications, *The Daze* and *Glass Digest,* ceased operations.

Most of the Cambridge patterns have suffered the biggest declines. We assume this is because of those collectors relying on their investments and not many younger collectors looking for these particular patterns. The Fostoria patterns have fared the best. Most of the patterns were made for longer periods and some continued to be made up until Fostoria closed. All of this has contributed to younger collectors being attracted to the various Fostoria patterns. There is a silver lining in this situation though that, as prices have come down, new collectors hopefully will be attracted to many of these patterns and in turn contribute to an increase in value again. Every collectible has an up and down cycle.

As the collector has gotten more sophisticated, we noticed some trends happening. Today, the collector seems to be buying only one style of stemware in their pattern, if more than one is offered. They select the style they like the best and go with it. Everyone is limited on space and time to collect. To set an elegant table, the collector is also focusing on what they would use on their own tables. Most everyone wants a large wine glass and, thus, is now using the water goblet as their stem of choice. The original wine goblet is too small for most people. The other sizes of stems are not that important to a lot of collectors and are not used on most tables. The fast and furious buying of cordials has ended. A few people were buying them as special collections because they were small. Prices also increased dramatically and now those collectors that have them are not buying more of the same. This has allowed the market to settle back down. Many of the etched patterns had increased too dramatically and many of the collectors turned to the plain blank patterns to now collect or to supplement their original collections. Many of the later issue Fostoria patterns are attracting new collectors to the market since they are still affordable to the budget. The future of this market definitely depends on attracting younger people to this world of collecting. Everyone needs to work on making them feel welcome and answering all their many questions. We have all learned by exposure and growing up around glass. Utilize that valuable expertise and share it.

J.R. Schonscheck, in December 2001, bucked the odds and started a new glass publication called *Glasstown USA.* He thought things would eventually improve and that there was still a place for this type of publication. He was right! Advertisers continue to be attracted to his newsletter, and so do collectors. In Spring 2003, the West Virginia Museum of American Glass decided to expand on their quarterly publication of the *Glory Hole.* They too felt the need to reach more glass collectors. Various glass experts were contacted to be contributing advisors to the new magazine, *All About Glass.* This author was one of them. We are proud to be part of this new publication to further educate all glass enthusiasts, no matter what they collect. We greatly encourage all of you to subscribe and thus ensure the continuation of these valuable publications.

Collectors also need to be aware of another occurrence that happened in the summer of 2003. After several years of languishing in a warehouse at Lancaster Colony, many original prominent cast iron glass moulds have found a new home at the Fenton Art Glass Company. The Lancaster Colony Company made a decision to no longer produce any handmade glass at their facilities and decided to sell the moulds that they had obtained through acquisitions. Lancaster Colony owned moulds from: Imperial, Cambridge, Indiana, and Fostoria. Some were previously used in the Tiara home party line. Several thousand moulds were purchased and are now in the safe hands of Fenton. Of the Fostoria line, some of the identified moulds include: American, Baroque, Colony, Coin, and Crown. There are several Cape Cod moulds from Imperial, along with Everglades moulds from Cambridge. Whenever Fenton issues any of these items, they will be made in an entirely new color along with being marked with the Fenton logo. Even if Fenton never uses some of the moulds, no foreign importer will ever be able to unscrupulously reproduce these items.

We have attempted to address more of the needs of collectors in this book. Many of the suggestions provided to us concerning ways to improve this type of book were definitely used. More patterns have been added to this edition. We have expanded on the descriptions of the items to make the text more user friendly. A detail of each etched pattern is given so you will know for sure which pattern it is. There are also some pressed patterns that caused confusion, so we have included details of those as well. Many of the items normally sold only as sets, such as cup & saucer, cheese & cracker, mayonnaise, are now listed that way to end the frustration of totaling the individual pieces. Pattern numbers and etching numbers are given whenever we could supply that information. Captions include all the colors, numbers, and sizes for ease in identifying the actual piece. This edition contains the most requested elegant glass patterns. Many collectors furnished us input and we continue to welcome others to do the same. The book can only improve with added information furnished by all collectors and dealers. Don't feel that someone else probably has already provided us with the information; we value having many sources. Also, if you find a mistake, **please,** let us know. Don't assume someone has already told us. Many hands touch the book before it even gets to the hardback form you are able to purchase. We value everyone's feedback, no matter what it is.

A full century of American's finest glass making is included in this book. Patterns range from American by Fostoria, first introduced in 1915 to Cranberry Opalescent Hobnail still made by Fenton in the late 1990s. Some patterns are full lines of dinnerware while others are small companion lines or glass for the bedroom, bath, or decorating your home. We have included the size in inches on most items and capacity in ounces on all the stemware and tumblers.

We would love to hear about any new discoveries that are made in any of the patterns. The book can only improve with continuing input from our readers. If you would like to have any other patterns included in an elegant listing, please let us know. If you would like to share your collection with us, we would welcome that gesture. We encourage everyone to give us feedback, and if you have a size that we do not list, let us know.

In striving to get accurate information, we are always looking for old glass catalogs, reprints, and original advertising. If you have any of these you would like to share or sell, we would be very interested in obtaining them.

What is Elegant Glass?

The term "elegant glass" was developed by noted glass author Gene Florence, in order to distinguish better-made glass from the less expensive machine-made glass of the American depression era. Collectors eagerly accepted this term and now all the better-made glass is referred to as "elegant."

Elegant glass is handmade, either pressed, blown or a combination of the two processes. The glass is first heated in a glory-hole opening in the hot furnace and put in a mould, either by pressing or blowing. After removing it from the mould, the piece can have special crimping, flaring or cupping done to it. Handles, feet or special ornamentation can also be applied. In some cases, with heat sensitive glass, after working it to a desired shape, it is put back into the glory-hole to establish its final color.

One of the final steps in the glass-making process is to fire polish the piece. In this step, the glass is reheated to remove any mould seams and to give it extra clarity. The final step is to grind and polish the bottom of the piece to allow it to have a smooth surface. Not every piece in a pattern was ground nor did every company do this.

Elegant glass was sold in fine department and jewelry stores that also carried many china and silver patterns, allowing customers to mix and match the selections with their own preferences. All these patterns remained open stock items for several years. Open stock meant that after you selected a particular pattern, you could go back to that store to purchase additional items to add to your set. Many of these patterns were very extensive and ran for many years, even several decades. Not every piece was available every year as different items were periodically added and dropped from the line. Some items were only available for very short time periods, making them hard to find today and usually expensive.

Etched Glass

For making etched pieces, there were many labor-intensive steps following the glass-making process. Skilled workers needed to be trained to ensure every step was properly followed to end up with a correctly finished product.

The patterns that were etched were usually found on several types of blanks. The styles of blanks with the same etching give the collector a wide range of choices if only trying to build a specific place setting. Collectors trying to obtain everything made in a pattern will spend years and vast amounts of money.

The Companies

The companies that made elegant glassware in the early years and are mentioned in this book include: Cambridge, Central, Consolidated, Duncan & Miller, Fenton, Fostoria, Heisey, Imperial, Morgantown, New Martinsville, Paden City, Tiffin, Viking, and Westmoreland. Gradually, through the years, most of these have now been closed.

The first of these to close was Central Glass Works in 1939. In the 1940s, New Martinsville reorganized and was given the new name of Viking so it could have a fresh start. During the 1950s, Cambridge, Duncan & Miller, Heisey, and Paden City all closed. This was a tremendous loss in the number of companies making elegant glass.

Tiffin (U.S. Glass) closed in the early 1960s before being bought by employees. A few years later it was sold to Continental Can. In 1968 it was sold to Interpace, who owned Franciscan China. In 1979 Tiffin was sold again to Towle Silversmiths before finally closing in 1980.

Consolidated closed in 1964. Fostoria purchased Morgantown in 1965 but allowed them to operate under their own name. The Morgantown plant was sold in 1972 to Bailey Glass with the Morgantown name disappearing.

In the 1980s several more companies closed: Fostoria, Imperial, Viking, and Westmoreland. Viking was purchased several years later by Kenneth Dalzell, who reopened it under the Dalzell-Viking name. Kenneth Dalzell is a former Fostoria employee. Then, Lancaster Colony purchased Fostoria. They continue to utilize the moulds but have eliminated the high quality finish work on their glass that was done at Fostoria. Dalzell-Viking closed in the late 1990s.

The only company left standing today that continues to make elegant glass is the Fenton Art Glass Company. They have survived by continuing to adapt their products to meet the needs of today's consumers. They are still family-owned with fourth generation family members now working within the company.

Measurements

All of our initial measurements came from original company catalogs or reprints. Different companies included different information. On the stemware and tumblers, some only gave ounces while others also gave inches. Whenever possible, when we obtained actual measurement, that is what we used.

- On stemware and tumblers, the height measurement is given first; following the description will be the ounces.
- Liquid measurement was determined by filling the item to the top rim.
- Serving bowls and mayonnaise bowls are measured according to their diameter.
- If there is a handle, measurement is made without the handle.
- Compotes are measured by height, then width.
- Creamers, sugars, cups, pitchers, decanters, cruets, bottles, and cocktail shakers are all measured by height, and then ounces are given.
- Plates and platters are measured straight across, unless otherwise noted.
- Cake plates and serving trays are measured by the diameter without handles.
- Candlesticks are measured first by height and then by spread of the arms, if they hold two or three candles.

Value Guide

All values given in this book are for glassware in **mint condition** only. Items that are scratched, chipped, and cracked will only bring a small portion of the given amount. Pieces that have been repaired should reflect a below-normal value, the amount of that depreciation dependant on their appearance.

There are of course regional differences. More collectors in a particular area may be looking for the same pattern, causing the supply to be depleted. In another area there may be many pieces of the pattern, but no collectors there to seek it. Some patterns were more prevalent in certain areas, depending on the salesmen placing orders for the stores at the time the glass was made. Certain patterns were just shipped to specific areas.

All values have been derived from many sources including dealers' actual sales, what collectors have paid, show prices, national publications, and eBay. Collectors and dealers alike were consulted to try to obtain a true analysis of the market. We are not here to set prices but to deliver a reflection of what is going on in the market place. Each of you can then determine for yourselves what price you would be willing to pay for an item.

This book is intended to be only a guide when determining what an item is worth. You, the collector, will ultimately decide what you want to pay for a specific item.

Neither the authors nor the publisher assume any responsibility for transactions that may occur because of this book.

Information Request

We are continually looking for more people, especially on the East Coast, that actively deal in certain patterns to give us feedback. The constant search for which patterns are selling and what prices are being realized is a huge undertaking. We can't be everywhere and have to depend on the diligence of a lot of dealers. The information compiled within these pages is the result of information we were given. Also, if you were to see something different, please contact us.

Likewise, to all collectors who are actively seeking a pattern, we are also looking for your feedback. You know your own pattern best. You can provide us with missing items, missing sizes, better descriptions of the items, and the prices you are paying. We want all the listings to be a true reflection of the individual pattern.

Our address and email are:

Coe's Mercantile
P. O. Box 173
Hillsboro, OR 97123
email: elegantglass@aol.com.
web site: coesmercantile.com

On the email, please provide brief information in the subject line (such as the pattern name) describing what your message is about. We receive so much email that frequently items get deleted if there is no reference to what a message concerns. We would like to be of assistance to all of you.

Tom & Jerry Punch bowl 12", footed, 1.75 gallon

Left: Candlestick 2-lite 6.5", footed, bell shape. **Right:** Candlestick 2-lite 4.4", footed, flat arm 8.3" spread

Left: Syrup w/chrome cover w/bakelite handle 5.25", flat, 6.5 oz. **Right:** Bottle 6.75", ketchup round w/stopper (6 sided & flat on top) 8.5 oz.

AMERICAN

Fostoria Glass Company   Blank #2056   1915-86
Main Color: Crystal
Other Colors: Amber, Blue, Ebony (black), Canary, Green, Milk Glass, and Ruby

American continues to be one of Fostoria's most popular patterns. It is the single most asked for pattern by name. This pattern seems to offer many things to all collectors. A beginning collector can still afford many of the items for an elegant place setting for their table. For the advanced collector there are still many unique pieces that are expensive and will take lots of time to find by searching all parts of this country. The big advantage of this pattern is that it was offered continuously for sixty-six years. This fact alone gives us an idea of just how successful this pattern was when it was first produced. Since it was still being offered when the doors of Fostoria closed, it was still obviously very popular. Not all pieces were produced the entire time. However, a variety of pieces were made during each year.

Collectors at times seem overwhelmed with all of the unusual pieces that can be collected in American. Prices on a lot of these items have been reserved for only the most dedicated collector. Some of these items include a banana split dish, biscuit jar, dinner bell, glove box, molasses can, pickle jar with a glass top, straw jar, and water bottle. Dinner plates with a large center are not always the plates of choice by collectors, because of the small surface area. Many collectors turn to using the 10.5" torte plate because of its size; yet it only comes with a small center.

The pattern was originally only made in Crystal, although there were several pieces made in colors. Davidson of England made some items that closely resembled American but they had three handles on them. This has caused some confusion, especially when some of these items were made in an opaque green that resembled the Jade color. For awhile these items were passed off as rare American Jade but soon the collectors learned to tell the difference. There were several items that were later reproduced by Dalzell Viking. Indiana also produced a variant of the American pattern, which they called American Whitehall. The mould seams on these items are easily visible and the clarity of this glass is lacking, since it wasn't fire polished like American.

Since this was primarily a crystal pattern and most collectors only look for that color, the value are only given for crystal. There were some colored pieces made in this pattern, but not enough on a consistent basis to determine values for the colored items.

AMERICAN

	Crystal
Ashtray 2.8", square, shallow	6
Ashtray 5", square, deep	50
Ashtray 5.5", oval	8
Ashtray 5.5", oval w/match box holder	15
Banana split 9", oblong w/1-tab handle	600+
Basket 9", oval, 2 sides turned up w/woven reed handle	95
Basket 10.5", 3-toed, crimped (ruffled) w/applied handle	195
Bell, dinner (pressed)	350+
Biscuit jar w/cover 6", metal lid & handle	850+
Bonbon 6", 3-toed, tri-corn	15
Bonbon 7", 3-toed, cupped	12
Bottle w/chrome tube 4.6", square, bitters, 4.5 oz.	68
Bottle w/chrome tube 4.6", frosted name plate 4.5 oz.	195
Bottle w/stopper 5.75", cologne, 6 oz.	85
Bottle w/stopper 7.25", cologne, 8 oz.	75
Bottle w/stopper 7.25", square, cordial, 9 oz.	85
Bottle w/stopper 7.25", square, cordial, plain label, 9 oz.	98
Bottle w/stopper 7.25", square, cordial, embossed (bourbon, gin, rye or scotch), 9 oz.	165
Bottle w/stopper 9.25", square, decanter, 24 oz.	98
Bottle w/stopper 9.25", square, decanter, plain label, 24 oz.	110
Bottle w/stopper 9.25", square, decanter, embossed (bourbon, gin, rye or scotch), 24 oz.	175
Bottle w/wood stopper 9.25", flat, water carafe, 44 oz.	750+
Bottle 6.75", ketchup, round w/stopper (6-sided & flat on top) 8.5 oz.	195
Bowl 3.75", oval, almond	20
Bowl 4" to 4.4", straight sided or flared, baby	60
Bowl 4.4", oval (large almond)	24
Bowl 4.5", regular nappy	10
Bowl 4.5", straight sided w/1 handle, round or square (2 styles)	12
Bowl 4.75", flared, fruit	16
Bowl 5", tri-corn nappy w/1 handle	12
Bowl 5", regular nappy	12
Bowl w/cover 5", regular nappy	32
Bowl 5.5", flared, round nappy w/1 handle	15
Bowl 5.5", shallow, ice cream, turned up edge	45
Bowl 6", regular or flared nappy (2 styles)	16
Bowl 6.5", 2 piece, sponge bowl w/drain	2,500+
Bowl 7", flared nappy	24

Bowl 7", regular or cupped (2 styles)	35
Bowl 8", deep nappy, cupped or regular (2 styles)	45
Bowl 8", flared nappy	28
Bowl 8", footed, handled, oval, trophy	125
Bowl 8.5", flat, handled, oval, trophy	85
Bowl 9", crimped top nappy	195
Bowl 9", flared nappy	35
Bowl 9", oval, straight sided	60
Bowl 9", flat, flared, handled	48
Bowl 9.25", oval, flared, vegetable	45
Bowl 9.5", flared centerpiece	45
Bowl 10", deep salad, 4.4" high	45
Bowl 10", footed	45
Bowl 10", oval, 2 sections, vegetable	45
Bowl 10", oval, straight sided, floating garden	40
Bowl 10.25", 3-toed, flared	40
Bowl 11", flared centerpiece	48
Bowl 11", 3-toed, tri-corn, centerpiece	45
Bowl 11.5", oval, straight sided, floating garden	65
Bowl 11.5", rolled edge	65
Bowl 11.75", oval vegetable (2 styles)	50
Bowl 12", flat, shallow lily pond, cupped edge	58
Bowl 13", flat, shallow lily pond, cupped edge	60
Bowl 15", large, flared, centerpiece	175
¹ Bowl 16", footed, low fruit, turned up edge	185
Box w/cover 1", square, rouge	495+
Box w/cover 2", square, pomade	495+
Box w/cover 3", round, cosmetic, 2.6" wide	1200
Box w/cover 3", square, puff	250
Box w/cover 3", square, hair receiver (hole in lid)	850+
Box w/cover 3.5", oblong, hair pin	400
Box w/cover 4.5", square, large puff	950+
Box w/cover 4.75" long, 3.5" wide, oblong cigarette	40
Box w/cover 4.85" long, 3.4" wide, 3.7" tall, soap box	2500
Box w/cover 5.5" long, 4.25" wide, oblong handkerchief	375
Box w/cover 5.5" long, 2.25" wide, oblong jewel	275
Box w/cover 9.5" long, 3.5" wide, oblong glove	600+
Butter dish w/cover 7.25", round, dome lid	135
Butter dish w/cover 7.5", rectangular, .25 lb.	35
Cake plate 10", handled	32
Cake stand 12", 3-toed, flat top	35
Cake salver 10", pedestal footed, square top	175
Cake salver 10", pedestal footed, round top	125
¹ Cake salver 11.4", pedestal footed, low, round top (new style)	50
Candelabra 2-lite 6.75", footed, bell shape w/bobeches/prisms, pair	395
Candle lamp 8.5" (candlestick, #26 adapter & necked top chimney) each	175
Candlestick 1-lite 2", handled, chamber, pair	125
Candlestick 1-lite 3", footed, short stem, pair	30
Candlestick 1-lite 6", footed, octagonal, pair	65
¹ Candlestick 1-lite 7", 2 step square, columned, pair	145
Candlestick 1-lite 8.25", Eiffel tower shape, pair	195
Candlestick 2-lite 4.4", footed, flat arm 8.3" spread, pair	95
Candlestick 2-lite 6.5", footed, bell shape, pair	195
Candy w/cover 7", hexagon foot	40
Candy box w/cover 6.1", flat, 3 sections, tri-corn	95
Cheese & cracker: comport 4", short stem, 5.75" wide; plate 12"	48
Cheese or sugar shaker 5.25", flat w/chrome top	75
Coaster 3.75", round (3 styles)	12
Comport 5", plain stem, 5" wide	15
Comport 6.5", bell footed, 8" wide, (Tom & Jerry shape)	275
Comport w/cover 9", plain stem 5" wide	35
¹ Cookie jar w/cover 8.9", straight sided, pretzel or cracker	375
Cream soup & liner: bowl 4.8", footed, handled, 10 oz.; liner w/indent 7.5"	75
Creamer 2.25", flat, individual w/handle, 4 oz.	10
Creamer 2.75", flat, regular w/handle, 6 oz.	8
Creamer, 3.25" tall, flat, hexagon shape w/handle	995
Creamer 4.25", flat, large w/handle, 9.5 oz.	12
Cruet w/stopper 6.5", flat, oil bottle w/handle, 5 oz.	38
Cruet w/stopper 7", flat, oil bottle w/handle, 7 oz.	42
Crushed fruit w/cover 10", straight sided, domed lid	2,000+
Crushed fruit spoon 9", long (flat arrow shape)	495+
Cup 2", flat, handled punch (4 styles) 6 oz.	6
Cup & saucer, coffee: cup 2.5", footed (2 styles) 7 oz.; saucer w/indent 6", smooth rim	8
Finger bowl & liner: bowl 4.5", cupped; plate 6.5"	85
Flower pot w/perforated cover 9.5" x 5.5", flat, flared	2,000+
Goblet 4.4", hexagon footed, wine, 2.5 oz.	12
Goblet 3.6", oyster cocktail, 4.5 oz.	8
Goblet 3.5", sherbet w/handle, 4.5 oz.	145
Goblet 4.5", hexagon footed, dessert, 4.75 oz.	8

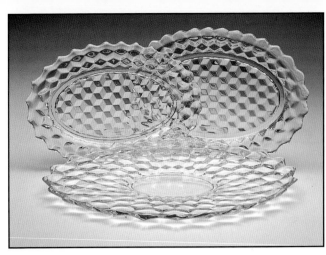

Back left: Platter 10.5", oval, patterned center. **Back right:** Platter 12", oval, patterned center. **Front center:** Platter 13.75", oval torte, plain center.

Back row: Tumbler 4.75", footed juice, 5 oz.; Tumbler 5.75", footed, ice tea, 12 oz.; Goblet 6.8", hexagon footed, water, 10 oz.; Tumbler 5", flat, straight sided ice tea, 12 oz.; Goblet 3.25", flared sherbet 5 oz. **Front row:** Tumbler 2.9", cone footed cocktail, 3 oz.; Goblet 3.5", cupped sherbet 5 oz.; Goblet 3.6", oyster cocktail, 4.5 oz.; Tumbler 2.5", flat whiskey, 2 oz.

Left: Pitcher 8", flat water, loop handle w/o ice lip, 48 oz. **Right:** Pitcher 8.25", flat, straight sided, water w/ice lip, 72 oz.

Back left: Cake salver 10", pedestal footed, square top. **Back right:** Tray 6.75", tab handled, for cream/sugar. **Front Left:** Butter dish w/cover 7.5", rectangular, .25 lb. **Front center:** Creamer 2.75", flat, regular w/handle, 6 oz. **Front right:** Sugar 2.75", flat, regular, handled, 6 oz.

Left: Jam Pot w/metal lid 4.25"; necked rose bowl, flat, spherical, 4" wide. **Right:** Honey jar w/cover (metal) 5.4" high.

Left: Spooner 3.75", straight sided. **Right:** Wedding bowl w/cover 8", footed (lid fits on outside rim of bowl).

Goblet 3.25" to 3.5", sherbet, flared or cupped (2 styles) 5 oz.	6
Goblet 4.4" to 5", saucer champagne (3 styles) 5 oz.	8
Goblet 3.1", sundae, 6 oz.	6
Goblet 4.9", claret, 7 oz.	40
Goblet 5.6", lunch water, 9 oz.	14
Goblet 6.8", hexagon footed, water, 10 oz.	15
Goblet (or tumbler) 5.75", footed, ice tea, 12 oz.	18
Hat 1.5" high, top hat shape, ashtray	15
Hat 2.5" high, top hat shape	25
Hat 3" high, top hat shape	28
Hat 4" high, top hat shape	38
Honey jar w/cover (metal) 5.4" high	495
Humidor w/metal cover 5", flat, straight sided, cigar	395
Humidor w/wood cover, flat, straight sided, tobacco	295
Hurricane lamp 12", short base w/tall crimped chimney, each	245
Ice bowl 10", cracked ice, deep, straight sided, hotel 1.25 gallon	1,200+
Ice bucket 3.75", tab handled	58
Ice bucket 4.5", tab handled	68
Ice bucket 4.5", chrome handle	75
Ice cream 3.5", square w/1-tab handle	35
Ice dish 3", bowl w/3-tabs to hold inserts, 5" wide	45
Ice dish liner 2.75" #2451, crab meat, 4 oz.	24
Ice dish liner 1.9" #2451, fruit cocktail, 5 oz.	28
Ice dish liner 3.5" #2451, tomato juice, 5 oz.	18
Jam Pot w/metal lid 4.25"; necked rose bowl, flat, spherical, 4" wide	495
Jam Pot w/cover 4.5", high	54
Jelly w/cover 7", footed, short stem	35
Jelly 3.5", footed, short stem, flared	18
Jelly 4.25", footed regular	18
Lemon w/cover 5.25", round, shallow, tab handled	50
Lemon 5.25", round, shallow, tab handled (no lid)	25
Marmalade w/cover 5.5", collar foot w/metal spoon	145
Mayonnaise 3 piece: bowl 3" flared; liner w/indent 6"; ladle 5.75"	48
Mayonnaise 2 piece: bowl 4.6", hexagon foot, short stem; ladle 5.75"	48
Mayonnaise 3 piece: bowl 6.25", salad dressing; 2 ladles 5.75"	60
Molasses can 6.75", flat, applied handle w/metal top, 11 oz. (syrup shape)	600+
Mug 3.25", straight sided, Tom & Jerry or baby, 5.5 oz.	35
Mug 4.5", flat, flared base, beer tankard, 12 oz.	60
Mustard w/cover 3.75", collar foot w/spoon	50
Napkin ring 2", (originally 4 in a set) each	18
Pickle jar w/domed glass cover 6", straight sided, 12 oz.	495+
Pickle jar w/metal cover (E.P.N.S.) 5", straight sided, 12 oz.	175
Picture frame, tab footed, oval	14
Pitcher 5.4", flat cereal, loop handle w/o ice lip, 16 oz.	49
Pitcher 7.25", flat juice, loop handle w/o ice lip, 32 oz.	68
Pitcher 8", flat water, loop handle w/o ice lip, 48 oz.	65
Pitcher 6.5", flat water, loop handle w/ice lip, 48 oz.	70
Pitcher 8.1", flat water, w/o ice lip, 64 oz.	98
Pitcher 7.75", flat, straight sided, water w/o ice lip (flat top) 72 oz.	295
Pitcher 8.25", flat, straight sided, water w/ice lip, 72 oz.	98
Plate 6", bread & butter, small center	6
Plate 7", salad, small center	10
Plate 7", 3-toed, flat, tidbit	15
Plate 7.5", crescent salad	68
Plate 8.5", salad, large center	18
Plate 9", sandwich, small center	14
Plate 9.5", dinner, large center	30
Plate 10.5", sandwich, small center	20
Plate 11.5", sandwich, small center	24
Plate 14", small center, turned up edge, cabaret or salad bowl liner	40
Plate 18", chop or torte	95
Plate 20", chop or torte	135
Platter 10.5", oval, patterned center	48
Platter 12", oval, patterned center	60
Platter 13.5", oblong, ice cream, large center	350
Platter 13.75", oval torte, plain center	50
Preserve w/cover 4", 2-handled, shallow	98
Punch bowl 12", footed, Tom & Jerry, 1.75 gallon	265
Punch bowl 14", flat, round, 2 gallon	195
Punch bowl 18", flat, round, 3.75 gallon	295
Punch bowl base 3.75", 10" wide, w/rays (low style)	40
Punch bowl base 4.5", w/o rays (also use as a bowl)	50
Punch bowl base 7", high style (also use as a vase)	95
Relish 6", oval olive	16
Relish 8", oval pickle	18
Relish 8.5", tab handled, oval, boat shape	15
Relish 8.5", tab handled, oval, 2 sections, boat shape	20
Relish 9" long, 6" wide, oblong, 3 equal sections & celery section	38
Relish 9.5", oval, 3 sections, diagonally divided	38
Relish 10.25", oval celery	24

Relish 10.8", square, 3 equal sections & celery section	175
Relish 11", oval, 2 equal sections & celery section	48
Relish 11.75", tab handled, oval, boat shape	24
Relish 11.75", tab handled, oval, 2 sections, boat shape	28
Salt dip 2.15" wide, 1" tall, round	10
Sandwich server 10.5", center chrome handle	35
Sandwich server 12", center handled server	45
Sauce 2 piece: bowl 6.75", flared, oval; plate w/indent, oval 8"	60
Shaker 2.4", individual, square, chrome top, pair	20
Shaker 3", small tapered, round, pair	18
Shaker 3", straight sided, round, pair	20
Shaker 3.75", large tapered, round, pair	18
Shrimp & dip bowl 12.25", (all one piece)	450+
Spooner 3.75", straight sided	32
Straw jar w/glass cover 10", flat, straight sided	275
Sugar 2.25" tall, flat, hexagon shape, 4.5" wide	795
Sugar 2.4", flat, individual, handled, 4 oz.	10
Sugar 2.75", flat, regular, handled, 6 oz.	8
Sugar 3.25", flat, regular, handled 7 oz.	12
Sugar 6.25", flat, regular, no handles 7 oz.	48
Sugar w/cover 5.25", flat, large, handled, 10 oz.; lid w/knob finial	35
Sugar cuber w/chrome cover (tongs are part of lid)	350
Sugar shaker chrome top 4.75", large opening (old style)	125
Sugar shaker chrome top 4.75", small opening (new style)	85
Syrup w/fancy metal lid 5.25", flat, handled, 6 oz.	495+
Syrup w/chrome cover 5.25", flat, Sani-cut/Dripcut, 6.5 oz. 2 styles of tops	65
Syrup w/chrome cover w/bakelite handle 5.25", flat, 6.5 oz.	125
Syrup w/cover 3 piece: 5.25", pitcher 10 oz.; 6" liner w/indent; cover/lid	195
Toothpick holder 2.25", flat, straight sided	24
Tray 4", oblong, for individual s & p	20
Tray 5.5" long, 4.5" wide, oblong pin	175
Tray 6", tab handled, 7.8" counting handles, oval pin	35
Tray 6.75", tab handled, for cream/sugar	15
Tray 9", tab handled, cloverleaf (shaped) condiment	195
Tray 9.5", utility w/handles turned up	35
Tray 10", muffin w/handles turned up	45
Tray 10", square, patterned bottom	175
Tray 10", tab handled, oval condiment	45
Tray 10.5", oblong ice cream (holds 6 ice cream inserts) tray only	90
Tray 10.5", smooth tab handled, oval, comb/brush	50
Tray 10.5", 2 tier, tidbit w/metal handle	125
Tray 12", round, raised rim around edge w/patterned bottom	175
Tumbler 2.5", flat whiskey, 2 oz.	15
Tumbler 2.9", cone footed cocktail, 3 oz.	10
Tumbler 3", flat (smooth border) baby	145
Tumbler 3.6", flat, straight sided juice, 5 oz.	16
Tumbler 4.75", footed juice, 5 oz.	14
Tumbler 3.4", flat old fashion, 6 oz.	16
Tumbler 3.9", flat, straight sided water, 8 oz.	16
Tumbler 4.1", flat, flared water, 8 oz.	14
Tumbler 4.4", footed water, 9 oz.	15
Tumbler 5", flat, straight sided ice tea, 12 oz.	20
Tumbler 5.25", flat, flared ice tea, 12 oz.	18
Tumbler 5.75", footed, ice tea, 12 oz.	14
Tumbler 5.75", footed, ice tea w/handle, 12 oz.	250
Vase 3.5", flat, spherical, rose bowl (smooth border)	18
Vase, necked rose bowl 4.1", flat, spherical	295
Vase 4.6", flat, deep, flared sweet pea 7.1" wide	75
Vase 5", flat, spherical, rose bowl (smooth border)	28
Vase 6", hexagon footed w/cupped or flared top, bud vase	18
Vase 6", flat, straight sided, celery shape	38
Vase 6", flat, squat, flared out top	28
Vase 6.5", smooth square footed & square tapered urn top	40
Vase 7", flared base w/large flared out top	48
Vase 7.5", smooth square footed & square tapered urn top	40
Vase 8", footed, straight sided, celery	50
Vase 8", straight sided w/flared top	58
Vase 8" to 10", small porch (swung) 5" to 6" wide at top	250
Vase 8" to 10", large porch (swung) 7" to 8" wide at top	300+
Vase 8.5", hexagon footed w/cupped or flared top, bud vase	24
Vase 9", square footed, large, flared (no pattern on foot)	50
Vase 9.5", large, flared	50
Vase 10", cupped top w/wide smooth border	245
Vase 10", flat, necked in w/wide smooth border at top	900+
Vase 10", flat, straight sided, celery shape	85
Vase 10", flat, straight sided, slightly flared top	95
Vase 12", flat, straight sided, celery shape	135
Vase 14" to 16", flat, concave sided, swung	275
Vase 18" to 20", flat, concave sided, swung	350+
Vase 23" and higher, flat, concave sided, swung	500+

Left: Basket 9", oval, 2 sides turned up w/woven reed handle. **Right:** Tray 10.5", 2 tier, tidbit w/metal handle.

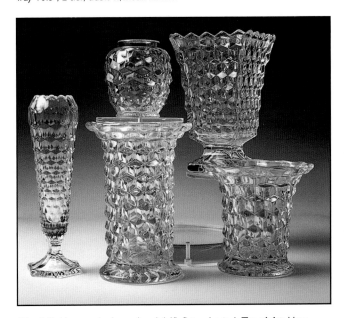

Top left: Vase, necked rose bowl 4.1", flat, spherical. **Top right:** Vase 7.5", smooth square footed & square tapered urn top. **Bottom left:** Vase 8.5", hexagon footed w/cupped or flared top, bud vase. **Bottom center:** Vase 8", straight sided w/flared top. **Bottom right:** Vase 6", flat, squat, flared out top.

Pickle jar w/domed glass cover 6", straight sided, 12 oz.

Left: Sugar cuber w/chrome cover (tongs are part of lid).
Right: Box w/cover 3", square, puff.

Washbowl set, 16" washbowl & 11.5" pitcher 1.25 gallon, hotel	3,000+
¹ Wedding bowl w/cover 8", footed (lid fits on outside rim of bowl)	125
¹ Wedding bowl 5.25", small (bottom only)	50
¹ Wedding lid, Note same lid fits on both, small & large wedding bowls	75
Wedding bowl w/cover, footed (lid fits on the inside lipped rim of the bowl)	750+

¹ Items have been reproduced.

Left: Banana split 9", oblong w/1-tab handle.
Center: Box w/cover 4.85" long, 3.4" wide, 3.7" tall, soap box. **Right:** Tumbler 5.75", footed, ice tea w/handle, 12 oz.

Left: Goblet 3.1", cordial (w/o optic), 1 oz., Burgundy (amethyst) bowl w/crystal stem/foot. **Center:** Goblet 4.1", sherbet (w/o optic), 5.5 oz., Regal Blue (cobalt) bowl w/crystal stem/foot. **Right:** Goblet 6.1", water (w/o optic), 10 oz., Regal Blue (cobalt) bowl w/crystal stem/foot.

Left: Tumbler 4.1", footed juice (w/o optic), 5 oz., Regal Blue (cobalt) bowl w/crystal foot. **Right:** Tumbler 5.5", footed, ice tea (w/o optic), 12 oz., Burgundy (amethyst) bowl w/crystal foot.

AMERICAN LADY
Fostoria Glass Company Blank #5056 1933–73
Colors: Crystal, Crystal foot with colored bowl of Burgundy (amethyst), Empire Green or Regal Blue (cobalt)

American Lady, the companion pattern to American, was only offered as a blown glass stemware line. The pressed American foot makes a striking contrast to the plain blown bowl. This is fine, delicate stemware that can be used to dress up your table for special occasions, especially when you consider the two-tone colored pieces. An elusive piece to find is the water lamp, which was only produced in Crystal. The water lamp is made from a goblet before the top blow-over was removed. This enabled a metal cap to be mounted that would hold the electrical fixture. The goblet was meant to be filled with water to make it more stable. Most of the time these lamps will have a cut pattern on them.

AMERICAN LADY	Crystal	Colors
Goblet 3.1", cordial (w/o optic), 1 oz.	30	58
Goblet 4.1", wine (w/o optic), 2.5 oz.	15	28
Goblet 4.6", claret (w/o optic), 3.5 oz.	15	28
Goblet 4", liquor cocktail (w/o optic), 3.5 oz.	12	20
Goblet 3.5", oyster cocktail (w/o optic), 4 oz.	10	18
Goblet 4.1", sherbet (w/o optic), 5.5 oz.	10	18
Goblet 6.1", water (w/o optic), 10 oz.	16	30
Tumbler 4.1", footed juice (w/o optic), 5 oz.	15	28
Tumbler 5.5", footed, ice tea (w/o optic), 12 oz.	18	35
Water lamp 6.5", footed, cupped top w/metal cap for electric socket	225	

APPLE BLOSSOM
Cambridge Glass Company   **Etching #744**   **1930-40**
Colors: Amber, Crystal, Gold Krystol (yellow), Green, Moonlight Blue, and Peach Blo/Dianthus (pink)
Other Color: Emerald Green and Heatherbloom

This is one of most beautiful etched flower patterns of Cambridge. Being made in five colors, this pattern is sought by a variety of collectors. While the colored pieces of amber, yellow, pink, and green can get pricey, the crystal has low prices to attract the beginning collector. A number of different blanks can be found with the Apple Blossom etching. This allows for a great variety of shapes to be collected and to stay within your own price range.

Pieces in Moonlight Blue are the hardest to assemble, while the Gold Krystol are the easiest. Gold Krystol items with gold colored metal ormolu are so outstanding that when you see them they always attract a lot of attention and usually go home with a collector of Art Deco. It is a shame that they do not show up more often. Amber items are harder to find but collectors do not have very much interest in them.

The boudoir collectors generally will pay more to have the cologne and puff boxes. This is a pretty etching and collectors of other things have a few pieces of this tucked into their collections. There are many unusual items that are available with different colors and treatments. The nude stems allow the advanced collector something to look for and not to be shocked by the price whenever they do turn up. Some of the other hard to find items include the following: after dinner cup/saucer, butter dish, cocktail shaker, decanter, pitcher, refractory bowl, and rectangular vase.

Few Heatherbloom items in this etching have shown up and we haven't found consistent prices so far to list a fair market value here.

Pattern detail, Apple Blossom.

APPLE BLOSSOM	Crystal	Amber Yellow	Green Pink	Blue
Bonbon 5.5" #3400/1179, handled	22	30	36	45
Bowl 2.75" #3400/71, 4-footed, tab handled, nut	52	72	80	98
Bowl 5.25" #3400/1180, handled, sweetmeat	24	34	40	50
Bowl 5.5" #3400/56, shallow, fruit	20	25	30	40
Bowl 6" #3400/53, cereal	28	35	40	50
Bowl 10" #1185, open handled, flared	54	78	90	115
Bowl 10" #3400/51, oval vegetable	58	85	94	118
Bowl 11" #3400/3, footed, low, flared	58	85	94	118
Bowl 11" #3400/1188, handled, flared, fruit	60	80	95	125
Bowl 11.25" #3400/33, mushroom shape	56	80	90	115
Bowl 11.75" #3400/32, flat, flared	56	80	90	115
Bowl 12" #3400/4, 4-footed, flared	60	85	95	120
Bowl 12" #3400/5, footed, rolled edge	52	75	84	110
Bowl 12" #3400/1240, 4-footed, oval, refractory	125	185	225	295
Bowl 12.5" #3400/2, mushroom shape	62	88	100	130
Bowl 13" #3400/1, flared	52	85	94	118
Box w/cover 4.5" #3400/94, puff w/keyhole finial	150	195	250	300
Box w/cover 4.5" #3400/95, tilt ball, puff w/key hole finial	175	225	275	325
Butter w/cover 5.5" #3400/52, handled	225	375	500	600
Candlestick 1-lite 4" #627, round foot, faceted ball stem, pair	50	68	80	100
Candlestick 1-lite 5" #3400/646, keyhole, pair	48	75	85	110
Candlestick 2-lite 6" #3400/647, pair	60	95	125	150
Candlestick 3-lite 7" #3400/638, pair	74	115	150	195
Candy w/cover 6.5" #3400/9, 4-footed, tab handled, 7" wide; dome lid w/finial	90	145	175	225
Cheese & cracker: comport 3" #3400/7, short stem, 5.5" wide; plate 11.5" #3400/8, tab handled	78	110	120	145
Cigarette box w/cover 3.6" #616, rectangle, 3.1" wide	68	95	125	165
Cigarette holder 4.6" #1066, oval, short stem, w/ashtray foot	60	85	110	145
Cocktail shaker w/glass cover #3400/78, flat, applied handled	300	395	425	550
Cocktail shaker 12" #1020, flat sided, chrome top, 34 oz.	200	375	400	500

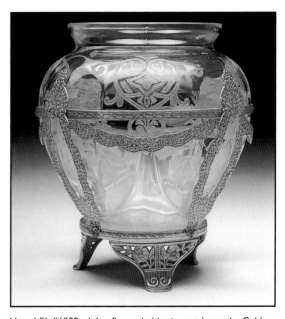

Vase 4.5" #1309, globe, flower holder in metal ormolu, Gold Krystol (yellow).

Decanter w/stopper, 7.75" #3400/46, oval bottle, 3.5" wide, cabinet flask, 12 oz., Amber.

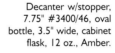

Moonlight Blue grouping: **Left:** Candlestick 1-lite 5" #3400/646, keyhole. **Center:** Bowl 12.5" #3400/2, mushroom shape; Flower frog 8.75" #518, draped lady (non-etched).

Left: Mayonnaise bowl #3400/13 bowl 5.8", 4-toed, flared, tab handled, Green w/Gold encrusted. **Right:** Bowl 11" #3400/3, footed, low, flared, Gold Krystol (yellow). **Front:** Bowl 10" #1185, open handled, flared, Gold Krystol w/Gold trim.

Gold Krystol (yellow) grouping: **Left:** Cup & saucer, coffee #3400/54. **Center:** Sandwich server 11" #3400/10, center handled server. **Right:** Candlestick 1-lite 5" #3400/646, keyhole.

Comport 7.5" #3400/14, fancy stem, flared, 7" wide, Green.

Cologne w/keyhole stopper 2.5" #3400/97: tilt bottle, 2 oz.; stopper w/long dauber	195	275	350	450
Comport #3400/15, shallow, 4" wide	30	40	50	65
Comport 7.5" #3400/14, fancy stem, flared, 7" wide	48	70	85	100
Comport 7.75" #3011, banquet size nude stem, 6.6" wide	850			
Cream soup & liner: bowl 4.75" #3400/55, 2-handled, 9 oz.; liner 7" #3400/55	40	54	65	80
Creamer 3.8" #3400/68, regular, scalloped foot, 4.75 oz.	20	28	32	40
Creamer #3400/16, footed, cone shape, 6 oz.	22	30	35	45
Cup & saucer, after dinner #3400/83: cup 2.25", 2 oz.; saucer w/indent (square) 4"	75	95	120	175
Cup & saucer, coffee #3400/54: cup 2.4", 6 oz.; saucer w/indent 5.5"	20	34	40	50
Decanter w/stopper, 7.75" #3400/46, oval bottle, 3.5" wide, cabinet flask, 12 oz.		695		
Decanter w/stopper #1070, pinch, 36 oz.	275	375	450	600
Finger bowl & liner: bowl #3025, (blown); plate w/indent	45	60	72	85
Finger bowl & liner: bowl #3130, (blown); plate w/indent	40	55	68	78
Finger bowl & liner: bowl #3135, (blown); plate w/indent	40	55	68	78
Flower frog 8.75" #518, draped lady (non-etched)	148	185	225	295
Goblet #1066, one ball stem, brandy, .75 oz.	52	80	96	125
Goblet 4.9" #1066, one ball stem, cordial, 1 oz.	68	110	165	195
Goblet #1066, one ball stem, pousse-cafe, 1 oz.	62	98	145	175
Goblet 4.25" #3130, cordial, 1 oz.	65	100	150	185
Goblet #1066, one ball stem, sherry, 2 oz.	35	50	60	78
Goblet 5.1" #1066, one ball stem, wine, 3 oz.	15	28	34	45
Goblet 5.25" #3130, liquor cocktail, 3 oz.	16	30	36	48
Goblet 4.9" #3135, liquor cocktail, 3 oz.	15	28	34	45
Goblet 4.25" #1066, one ball stem, liquor cocktail, 3.5 oz.	18	32	38	50
Goblet 7.6" #3011, regular table nude stem, cocktail, 3.5 oz.	400			
Goblet 7.6" #1066, one ball stem, claret, 4.5 oz.	32	45	55	70
Goblet #3025, oyster cocktail, 4.5 oz.	18	25	30	38
Goblet 3.5" #1066, ball stem, oyster cocktail, 5 oz.	20	28	35	42
Goblet #1066, ball stem, cafe parfait, 5 oz.	30	75	95	110
Goblet 5.6" #3130, saucer champagne, 5 oz.	18	30	55	45
Goblet 4.25" #3130, sherbet, 6 oz.	15	22	26	32
Goblet 4.25" #3135, sherbet, 6 oz.	15	22	26	32
Goblet 5.6" #3135, saucer champagne, 6 oz.	18	30	35	45
Goblet #3011, regular table size nude stem, champagne, 7 oz.	450			
Goblet 4.75" #1066, one ball stem, sherbet, 7 oz.	16	30	35	42
Goblet #3025, sherbet, 7 oz.	15	24	30	36
Goblet #1066, one ball stem, saucer champagne, 7 oz.	18	32	38	45
Goblet #3025, saucer champagne, 7 oz.	20	32	36	45
Goblet 7.25" #3130, water, 8 oz.	22	32	45	55
Goblet 7.25" #3135, water, 8 oz.	22	32	45	55
Goblet #3400, lunch water, 9 oz.	24	35	48	58
Goblet 6.1" #1066, one ball stem, water, 11 oz.	20	32	38	48
Goblet #3025, water, 10 oz.	24	35	48	58
Goblet 6.1" #1066, ball stem, water, 11 oz.	22	34	36	50
Goblet 9.25" #3011, large banquet size nude stem, water, 11 oz.	750			
Goblet 8.9" #3011, regular table nude stem, water, 11 oz.	500			
Gravy boat & liner: #1091 Decagon, sauce bowl, 11 oz.; plate w/indent	145	225	275	375
Ice bucket 5.75" #3400/851, flat, scalloped top w/chrome handle	100	165	225	275
Mayonnaise 2 piece #3400: #13 bowl 5.8", 4-toed, flared, tab handled; #11 liner w/indent 5"	50	70	85	110
Pitcher #3400, footed, water jug, 50 oz.	180	275	325	400
Pitcher #3130/1205, footed, water, 64 oz.	195	295	350	425
Pitcher 8.75" #935, flat, oval, water w/o ice lip, 64 oz.	195	295	350	425
Pitcher #3400/27, flat, water w/ice lip, 67 oz.	225	325	375	475
Pitcher w/cover #3135/711, footed jug 76 oz.	245	375	495	650
Pitcher 9" #3400/38, ball jug w/ice lip 80 oz.	265	425	525	695
Plate 6" #3400/60, bread & butter (6 sided)	10	12	15	18
Plate 6" #3400/1174, square, bread & butter	12	14	18	20
Plate 6" #3400/1181, 2 open handled lemon server	14	22	28	35
Plate 7.5" #3400/61, salad (6 sided)	12	20	26	32
Plate 8.5" #3400/62, lunch (6 sided)	14	22	28	35

Plate 8.5" #3400/1176, square salad	13	20	26	30
Plate 9.5" #3400/63, dinner (6 sided)	55	85	100	135
Plate 9.5" #3400/1177, square dinner	60	95	115	145
Plate 10" #3400/66, grill/club lunch	38	60	70	85
Plate 10.5" #3400/1178, square service	32	42	50	60
Plate 12.5" #3400/1186, oblong, open handled sandwich	35	55	60	75
Platter 11.5" #3400/57, tab handled, oval	58	90	110	125
Platter 13.5" #3400/58, tab handled, oval	70	125	195	245
Relish 6" #3400/1093, 2 sections, center handled	26	40	48	60
Relish 8.75" #3400/862, center plume handled, oblong, 4 sections	48	65	78	95
Relish 9" #3400/59, oval pickle	32	50	58	65
Relish 12" #3400/67, 4 equal sections & celery section	48	75	85	110
Sandwich server 11" #3400/10, center handled server	38	58	70	90
Shaker 4.5" #3400/18, footed w/chrome top, pair	58	95	125	150
Sugar #3400/16, footed, cone shape, 6 oz.	22	28	32	40
Sugar 4" #3400/68 regular, scalloped foot, 6 oz.	22	28	32	40
Tray 6" #3400/1182, handled mint, turned up edge	24	35	42	48
Tumbler 2.1" #3400/92, flat, barrel shaped, whiskey, 2.5 oz.	40	68	85	110
Tumbler 2.6" #3400, cone footed, whiskey, 2.5 oz.	35	60	75	95
Tumbler 2.75" #3130, footed whiskey, 2.5 oz.	28	50	65	85
Tumbler 3.8" #3025, footed juice, 4 oz.	18	28	30	36
Tumbler 4" #3130, footed juice, 4.5 oz.	16	25	28	32
Tumbler 4" #3135, footed, juice, 5 oz.	16	25	28	32
Tumbler #3400, cone footed, sherbet, 6 oz.	18	26	30	35
Tumbler 4.75" #3130 or #3135, footed water (lunch) 8 oz.	22	30	35	42
Tumbler #3400, cone footed, water, 9 oz.	24	32	38	45
Tumbler 4.8" #3130, footed water (dinner) 9.5 oz.	24	35	40	50
Tumbler 5.25" #3025 or #3135, footed water, 10 oz.	24	35	40	50
Tumbler 5.25" #3130, footed beverage, 11 oz.	30	40	48	58

Heatherbloom bowl w/crystal stem/foot grouping: **Left:** Goblet 7.6" #3011, regular table nude stem, cocktail, 3.5 oz. **Right:** Goblet 8.9" #3011, regular table nude stem, water, 11 oz.

Left: Goblet 5.6" #3135, saucer champagne, 6 oz., Moonlight Blue. **Left center:** Goblet 5.6" #3130, saucer champagne, 5 oz., Moonlight Blue. **Center:** Goblet 6.1" #1066, ball stem, water, 11 oz., Gold Krystol (yellow). **Right center:** Goblet 7.25" #3135, water, 8 oz., Moonlight Blue. **Right:** Goblet 7.25" #3130, water, 8 oz., Moonlight Blue.

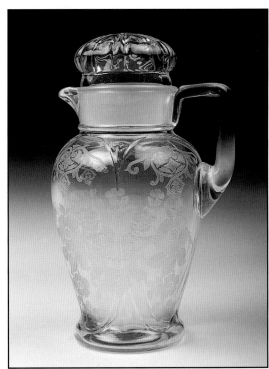

Cocktail shaker w/glass cover #3400/78, flat, applied handled.

Moonlight Blue grouping: **Back left:** Ice bucket 5.75" #3400/851, w/ chrome handle. **Back right:** Plate 12.5" #3400/1186, handled sandwich. **Front left:** After dinner cup & saucer #3400/83. **Front center:** Coffee cup & saucer #3400/54. **Front right:** Pitcher 8.75" #935, flat, oval water w/o ice lip, 64 oz.

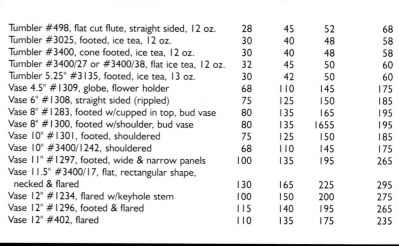

Tumbler #498, flat cut flute, straight sided, 12 oz.	28	45	52	68
Tumbler #3025, footed, ice tea, 12 oz.	30	40	48	58
Tumbler #3400, cone footed, ice tea, 12 oz.	30	40	48	58
Tumbler #3400/27 or #3400/38, flat ice tea, 12 oz.	32	45	50	60
Tumbler 5.25" #3135, footed, ice tea, 13 oz.	30	42	50	60
Vase 4.5" #1309, globe, flower holder	68	110	145	175
Vase 6" #1308, straight sided (rippled)	75	125	150	185
Vase 8" #1283, footed w/cupped in top, bud vase	80	135	165	195
Vase 8" #1300, footed w/shoulder, bud vase	80	135	1655	195
Vase 10" #1301, footed, shouldered	75	125	150	185
Vase 10" #3400/1242, shouldered	68	110	145	175
Vase 11" #1297, footed, wide & narrow panels	100	135	195	265
Vase 11.5" #3400/17, flat, rectangular shape, necked & flared	130	165	225	295
Vase 12" #1234, flared w/keyhole stem	100	150	200	275
Vase 12" #1296, footed & flared	115	140	195	265
Vase 12" #402, flared	110	135	175	235

Moonlight Blue grouping: **Back left:** Plate 10" #3400/66, grill/club lunch. **Back right:** Relish 12" #3400/67, 4 equal sections & celery section. **Front left:** Relish 8.75" #3400/862, center plume handle, 4 sections. **Front right:** Candy w/ cover 6.5" #3400/9, 4-footed, tab handled, 7" wide; dome lid w/finial.

Gravy boat & liner: #1091 Decagon, sauce bowl, 11 oz.; plate w/indent, Gold Krystol (yellow).

Gold Krystol (yellow) grouping: **Left:** Cigarette box w/cover 3.6" #616, rectangle, 3.1" wide. **Center:** Cologne w/keyhole stopper 3.5" #3400/97, tilt ball w/dauber, 2 oz. **Right:** Box w/ cover 5" #3400/95, tilt ball, puff w/keyhole finial. Note, all in gold color metal ormolu.

Vase 11.5" #3400/17, flat, rectangular shape, necked & flared, Moonlight Blue.

Moonlight Blue grouping: **Left:** Tumbler 5.25" #3135, footed, ice tea, 13 oz. **Left center:** Tumbler 4" #3130, footed juice, 4.5 oz. **Right center:** Tumbler 4.8" #3130, footed water (dinner) 9.5 oz. **Right:** Tumbler 5.25" #3130, footed beverage, 11 oz.

Left: Shaker 4.5" #3400/18, footed w/chrome top, Moonlight Blue. **Right:** Vase 11" #1297, footed, wide & narrow panels, Emerald Green bowl w/crystal stem/foot.

ARDITH

Paden City Glass Company   Etching #511   mid-1930s-40s
Colors: Amber, Crystal, Cheriglo (pink), Ebony (black), Green, Ruby, and Topaz (Yellow)

The arrangement of cherry blossoms now known as Ardith was first identified in Jerry Barnett's book, *Paden City*, in 1977. At the 1999 L.G. Wright auction, many Paden City etching plates were discovered and sold to the West Virginia Museum of American Glass. The etching plates for Ardith were part of this group.

We were the first to give a full listing of this etching in our premier edition of *Elegant Glass*. Many collectors since have commented on how pretty this etching is and how nice it was to finally get a list of the items. Collectors like to know what was made so they can have an idea of what type of set they could build.

Most items are found on the #411 Mrs. "B" line. There are a few of the items found on the #210 Regina line along with Crow's Foot. The dinner plate and 6.5" tall vase seem a little harder to find.

Ardith is mostly found in Paden's delicate yellow color known as Topaz. Crystal and amber items will bring substantially less than the pastel colored pieces. For more information you can refer to the book *Paden City Glass Company* by William P. Walker, Melissa Bratkovich, and Joan C. Walker.

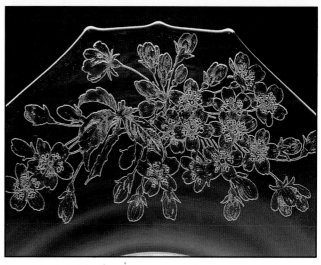

Pattern detail, Ardith.

ARDITH	Pastel Colors	Ebony	Ruby
Biscuit Jar 5.5", embossed plume base w/wicker handle	80	125	
Bowl 8.25" #411 Mrs. "B", deep, handled	60	72	90
Bowl 9" #411 Mrs. "B", footed, flared	68	80	100
Bowl 9" #412 Crow's Foot (square), footed, flared	68	80	100
Bowl 9.25" #411 Mrs. "B", footed, rolled edge, console	85	95	120
Bowl 9.5" #411 Mrs. "B", cupped w/center handle	85	100	125
Bowl 9.75" #411 Mrs. "B", 2 open handled	85	125	145
Bowl 10.75" #411 Mrs. "B", shallow, flared	85	95	120
Bowl 10.75" #411 Mrs. "B", rolled edge, console	85	95	120
Bowl 11.25" #411 Mrs. "B", flat top	75	80	100
Bowl 12.5" #211 Spire, flat, round, console	85		
Cake salver 9.25" #411 Mrs. "B", footed, 1.9" high	100	115	135
Cake salver 11.25" #300 Archaic, short stem w/ scalloped edge, 2" high	110	130	165
Candlestick 1-lite 2.5" #221 Maya, pair	85		
Candlestick 1-lite 2.5" #411 Mrs. "B", footed, mushroom shape, pair	85	100	125
Candlestick 1-lite 2.5" #412 Crow's Foot (square), dome footed, oval cupped & flared, 4" wide, pair	95	125	145
Candlestick 1-lite 5.25" #411 Mrs. "B", square dome footed, keyhole stem, pair	85	100	125
Candy jar w/cover 6" #701 Triumph, footed, (round bottom) square lid w/ball finial	125	150	185
Candy box w/cover 6.5" #411 Mrs. "B", flat, square, 2 or 3 sections	100	120	150
Candy jar w/cover 7" #701 Triumph bottom w/#411 Mrs. "B" lid, footed, round w/keyhole finial	145	165	210
Candy box w/cover 7" #412 1/2 Crow's Foot (square), flat, 3-lobe sides, 3 equal sections, w/keyhole finial	110	130	165
Comport 4.5" #411 Mrs. "B", cupped & flared, oval, 7.5" wide	80	95	120
Comport 6.5" #300 Archaic, tall stem, flared w/scalloped edge, 8" wide	60	75	95
Comport 6.6" #411 Mrs. "B", flared, 7" wide	65	80	100
Comport 7.25" #411 Mrs. "B", oval, cupped & flared, 8.25" wide	85	110	130
Cookie or biscuit jar w/cover 6.5" (Lady Fingers), flat, embossed plume base w/wicker handle	195	210	245
Creamer 3" #412 Crow's Foot (square), flat, regular, 7 oz.	50	60	75
Creamer 3.5" #411 Mrs. "B", flat, deco handle, 6 oz.	45	54	68
Cup & saucer, coffee #412 Crow's Foot (square): cup 2.1", 6 oz.; saucer w/indent 5.75"	60	70	85
Decanter w/stopper 5.5", rectangular, 10 oz., 5.75" wide	150	150	195
Decanter w/stopper 10.5", 2 pinch sides, 32 oz.; mushroom or paneled shape stopper	175	195	245
Decanter w/stopper 13.25" #410, tall, slender, bell shaped, 32 oz.	175	225	270
Ice bucket 5.8" #902, flat, straight sided, w/chrome handle	85	110	130
Mayonnaise 2 piece #411 Mrs. "B": footed bowl 5.75", rolled edge; liner w/indent 7.25"	80	95	120
Pitcher 7.75" #179, flat, spherical w/o ice lip, 82 oz.	250	295	375
Plate 5.75" #411 Mrs. "B", bread & butter	20	24	28
Plate 8.5" #411 Mrs. "B", lunch	35	45	52
Plate 8.5" #412 Crow's Foot (square), lunch	45	55	68
Plate 10", dinner	60	68	75
Plate 10" #411 Mrs. "B", dinner	60	68	75
Plate 10" #411 Mrs. "B", handled	75	85	95
Plate 10.25" #210 Regina, dinner	68	75	85
Plate 11", handled, diagonal, service	60	72	90

Back left: Plate 10", dinner Ebony (black). **Front left:** Comport 6.5" #300 Archaic, tall stem, flared w/scalloped edge, 8" wide, Yellow. **Right:** Pitcher 7.75" #179, flat, spherical w/o ice lip, 82 oz., Yellow.

Yellow grouping: **Back left:** Plate 8.5" #412 Crow's Foot (square), lunch. **Back right:** Sandwich server 10.25" #412 Crow's Foot (square), center handled tray. **Front top left:** Creamer 3" #412 Crow's Foot (square), flat, regular, 7 oz. **Front bottom left:** Sugar 2.6" #412 Crow's Foot (square), flat, regular, 6 oz. **Center:** Cup & saucer, coffee #412 Crow's Foot (square): cup 2.1", 6 oz.; saucer w/indent 5.75".

Bowl 9" #412 Crow's Foot (square), footed, flared, Ruby.

Platter 12" #411 Mrs. "B", open handled, oblong	85	95	110
Sandwich server 10" #411 Mrs. "B", center handled tray	85	100	125
Sandwich server 10.25" #412 Crow's Foot (square), center handled tray	95	125	145
Sugar 2.6" #412 Crow's Foot (square), flat, regular, 6 oz.	50	60	75
Sugar 3.5" #411 Mrs. "B", flat, deco handled, 6 oz.	45	55	68
Vase 5.1" #182-5, flat, squat (pillow shape)	120	135	150
Vase 6.5" #210-7 Regina, flat, 3 rings on base & neck shouldered, flared	200	250	300
Vase 8" O'Kane, spherical bottom, narrow flared neck		250	
Vase 8" O'Kane, spherical bottom, narrow flared neck & rolled edge		250	
Vase 8" #184-8, flat, spherical bottom, flared	145	175	225

Back: Platter 12" #411 Mrs. "B", open handled, oblong, Ebony (black).
Front: Bowl 9.75" #411 Mrs. "B", 2 open handled, Yellow.

Cheriglo (pink) grouping: **Top left:** Comport 7.25" #411 Mrs. "B", oval, cupped & flared, 8.25" wide. **Top right:** Bowl 10.75" #411 Mrs. "B", shallow, flared. **Bottom left:** Bowl 9.75" #411 Mrs. "B", 2 open handled. **Bottom Right:** Vase 6.5" #210-7 Regina, flat, 3 rings on base & neck shouldered, flared.

Crystal grouping: **Left:** Vase 5.1" #182-5, flat, squat (pillow shape). **Left:** Ice bucket 5.8" #902, flat, straight sided, w/chrome handle.

Yellow grouping: **Top left:** Mayonnaise 2 piece #411 Mrs. "B": footed bowl 5.75", rolled edge; liner w/indent 7.25". **Top right:** Comport 6.6" #411 Mrs. "B", flared, 7" wide. **Bottom left:** Sugar 3.5" #411 Mrs. "B", flat, deco handled, 6 oz. **Center:** Bowl 9.5" #411 Mrs. "B", cupped w/center handle. **Bottom right:** Creamer 3.5" #411 Mrs. "B", flat, deco handle, 6 oz.

Decanter w/stopper 10.5", 2 pinch sides, 32 oz.; paneled shape stopper, Cheriglo (pink).

Left: Cookie or biscuit jar, missing cover 6.5" (Lady Fingers), flat, embossed plume base w/wicker handle, Ebony (black).
Right: Candy box w/cover 6.5" #411 Mrs. "B", flat, square, 2 sections, Ebony (black) lid.

Yellow grouping: **Back row:** Cake salver 11.25" #300 Archaic, short stem w/scalloped edge, 2" high. **Front left:** Candy box w/cover 6.5" #411 Mrs. "B", flat, square, 2 sections. **Front center:** Candlestick 1-lite 2.5" #411 Mrs. "B", footed, mushroom shape, pair. **Front right:** Candy jar w/ cover 7" #701 Triumph bottom w/#411 Mrs. "B" lid, footed, round w/keyhole finial.

Green grouping: **Left:** Candlestick 1-lite 5.25" #411 Mrs. "B", square dome footed, keyhole stem, pair. **Top center:** Comport 4.5" #411 Mrs. "B", cupped & flared, oval, 7.5" wide. **Bottom center:** Sandwich server 10" #411 Mrs. "B", center handled tray. **Right:** Candy jar w/cover 6" #701 Triumph, footed, (round bottom) square lid w/ball finial.

Ebony (black) grouping: **Left:** Vase 6.5" #210-7 Regina, flat, 3 rings on base & neck shouldered, flared. **Right:** Vase 8" #184-8, flat, spherical bottom, flared.

Topaz (yellow) grouping: **Left:** Comport 4.75", fancy flame stem, 5.5" wide. **Left:** Vase 8", large, flared w/flame handles.

Azure (blue) grouping: **Back row:** Plate 14", small center, turned up edge, cabaret or salad bowl liner. **Front left:** Sugar 3.6", collar footed, regular, 7.5 oz. **Front center:** Creamer 3.75", collar footed, regular, 7.5 oz. **Front right:** Pitcher 7", collar footed w/ice lip, 48 oz.

Crystal grouping: **Left:** Candelabra 1-lite 7.75" #2484, flame stem w/8 prisms. **Right:** Candelabra 2-lite 8.25" #2484, flame center, bobeches/prisms, 10" spread.

BAROQUE

Fostoria Glass Company   **Blank #2496**   **1936-66**

Main Colors: Azure (blue), Crystal, Gold Tint, and Topaz (yellow)
Other Colors: Burgundy (Amethyst), Empire Green, and Regal Blue (cobalt)

An embossed "fleur-de-lis" design on plain, wide panels make this an elegant but simple pattern. Azure was the most collected color, for many years while the prices kept increasing. Now Topaz and Gold Tint (both Yellow) are steadily attracting many new collectors. The Topaz color, a bright yellow, was offered from 1936 to 1938. After 1938 the formula was changed slightly and renamed Gold Tint. This color of Baroque was used until 1944. We do not see any difference in the colors. Fine collectors and dealers alike only refer to the yellow color as Topaz and not Gold Tint. We like the name Topaz, named after the natural stone, much better and it makes us wonder why Fostoria would have renamed it Gold Tint.

The Baroque blank in Crystal was used for several of Fostoria's etched patterns including Chintz, Lido, Meadow Rose, and Navarre. The Durgin Silver Company, a division of Gorham, produced the sterling "fleur-de-lis" pattern. When setting a table, this pattern goes nicely with your Baroque. The 3-lite candlestick can be found in several of Fostoria's dark colors.

Four Flame items were produced and listed as the #2484 line number, yet were part of the Baroque line. These items are the 10.75" wing handled bowl, single candelabra, 2-lite candelabra, and 3-lite candelabra. The following items can be difficult in locating: bowls, candelabras (in colors), cigarette set, cream soups, cruets, flat tumblers, mustard, pitcher, and punch bowl.

After Fostoria closed, the Baroque moulds continued to be used by Lancaster Colony in their Tiara line but the name was changed to Eve. Lancaster Colony contracted with Fenton Art Glass to make the items in their Dusty Rose color, which resembles the Fostoria Wisteria color, but is not dichromatic (changes color under different light). Recently, as stated in this book's preface, Lancaster Colony sold all of their hand-worked moulds to Fenton. The three section candy box mould has been reworked to remove the inner dividers. It will be issued in a new color with the Fenton logo. Be aware that as time goes on there may be other pieces in this pattern that could be reissued by Fenton.

BAROQUE	Crystal	Topaz	Azure
Ashtray 3.75", individual	12	20	30
Bonbon 7.4", 3-toed, flared or crimped	20	26	38
Bowl 4", 3-toed, square, mint w/1 handle	24	40	48
Bowl 4.25", 3-toed, round, mint w/1 handle	22	36	45
Bowl 4.6", 3-toed, tri-corn w/1 handle	24	40	48
Bowl 5", flared, fruit	18	28	38
Bowl 5", round, flared w/1 handle	20	32	40
Bowl 6", flared, cereal	48	60	75
Bowl 6", 4-toed, tab flame handled, square, sweetmeat	24	38	48
Bowl 6", 3-toed, cupped	28	40	60
Bowl 6.25", 3-toed, flared	28	40	60
Bowl 6.9", 3-toed, crimped, nut	28	40	60
Bowl 7", deep (spherical) cupped	42	60	85
Bowl 8.5", 2-tab flame handled, flared, vegetable	48	64	100
Bowl 9.5", oval, vegetable	70	85	125
Bowl 10", oval, tab flame handled	38	75	145
Bowl 10", 4-tab feet, rectangle, tab flame handled, shallow, floating garden	62	72	95
Bowl 10.5", deep, cupped, salad	78	90	145
Bowl 10.75", 4-tab feet, oval, wing flame handled	48	75	95
Bowl 10.75" #2484, oval, large wing handled	45	64	90
Bowl 11", round, rolled edge	45	55	85
Bowl 12", flat, round, flared	40	50	70
Cake plate 10.25", 2-tab flame handled	35	48	75
Candelabra 1-lite 7.75" #2484 Baroque, flame stem w/8 prisms, pair	145	275	325
Candelabra 2-lite 8.25" #2484 Baroque, flame center, bobeches/prisms, 10" spread, pair	245	325	400
Candelabra 3-lite 9.5" #2484, flame center, bobeches/prisms, 12.4" spread, pair	325		495
Candlestick 1-lite 4", cornucopia flame shape, pair	46	68	110
Candlestick 1-lite 5.5", fancy stem, pair	68	78	125
Candlestick 2-lite 5.25", flame arms, 8" spread, pair	78	98	145
Candlestick 2-lite 8" #2484 Baroque, flame center, 9.5" spread, pair	145	225	300
Candlestick 3-lite 6", flame arms, 8.25" spread, pair	95	145	250
Candlestick 3-lite 9" #2484 Baroque, flame center, 11.5" spread, pair	175		345
Candy w/cover 6.25", triangular, 3 equal sections w/flame finial	65	100	160
Cigarette set 5.5" x 3.5": box w/attached part holding 4 ashtrays; cover	98	125	195
Cheese & cracker: comport 3.25", short stem, 5.25" wide, plate 11"	49	75	95
Comport 4.75", fancy flame stem, 5.5" wide	28	40	58
Comport 5.75", fancy flame stem, 6.5" wide	32	46	65
Cream soup & liner: bowl footed w/2 handles, 9 oz.; saucer w/indent 7"	58	95	135
Creamer 3.1", footed, individual, 4 oz.	10	20	30

Item			
Creamer 3.75", collar footed, regular, 7.5 oz.	12	22	32
Cruet w/clear paneled stopper 5.75", flat oil bottle, 3.5 oz.	75	295	575
Cup & saucer, coffee: cup 2.4", footed, 6 oz., saucer w/indent 5.6"	12	22	32
Cup 2.5", flat, punch, 6 oz.	16		38
Goblet 3", cone liquor cocktail, 3.5 oz.	15	22	32
Goblet 3.9", cone shaped sherbet, 5 oz.	14	20	28
Goblet 6.75", cone dinner water, 9 oz.	26	32	50
Ice bucket 4.5", flat, squat chrome handle, 6.5" wide	70	95	145
Jelly 5", fancy flame stem, cupped w/scalloped edge	35	45	68
Jelly w/cover 7.5", fancy flame stem & finial	68	85	145
Mayonnaise 2 piece: bowl 5", flared, crimped, 3.5" high; liner w/indent 6.5"	54	78	110
Mustard set 3.75", 3 piece (jar, lid & spoon)	75	95	125
Pitcher 6.5", collar footed w/o ice lip, 48 oz.	115	425	750
Pitcher 7", collar footed w/ice lip, 48 oz.	125	395	695
Plate 6", bread & butter	7	12	16
Plate 7.25", salad	12	15	20
Plate 8.5", lunch	16	22	26
Plate 9.5", dinner	38	50	75
Plate 14", small center, turned up edge, cabaret or salad bowl liner	42	50	85
Platter 11", oval	62	95	110
Platter 12.5", oval	65	100	125
Punch bowl 13.25", footed, flared, 1.5 gallon	450		1,450+
Relish 6" (or sweetmeat), tab flame handled, 2 equal sections, square	24	38	48
Relish 8", oval pickle	20	28	38
Relish 10", 4-tab feet, tab flame handled, oblong, 2 equal sections & celery section	32	40	48
Relish 10", 4-tab feet, tab flame handled, oblong, 4 equal sections	50	75	125
Relish 10.75", oval celery	28	38	50
Sauce 2 piece: bowl 6.5", oblong, tab flame handled; liner 6.75"	76	105	135
Shakers 2", individual, straight sided w/clear glass top, pair	85	150	225
Shakers 2.75", regular, straight sided w/clear glass top, pair	75	135	175
Sugar 2.9", footed, individual, 4 oz.	10	20	30
Sugar 3.6", collar footed, regular, 7.5 oz.	12	22	32
Tray 6.5", tab flame handled, for individual creamer & sugar	20	30	40
Tray 8", tab flame handled, oblong	25	50	60
Tray 8.25", flat, 3-toed, tidbit w/turned up edge	28	35	55
Tumbler 3.9", flat, straight sided, juice, 5 oz.	22	32	55
Tumbler 3.4", flat, straight sided, old fashion, 6.5 oz.	25	50	65
Tumbler 4.25", flat, straight sided, water, 9 oz.	30	50	75
Tumbler 5.9", flat, straight sided, ice tea, 14 oz.	45	65	95
Vase 3.5", round, rose bowl	48	65	85
Vase 7", flared w/flame handles	85	125	145
Vase 8", large, flared w/flame handles	98	145	195

Crystal grouping: **Left:** Candy w/cover 6.25", triangular, 3 sections, lid w/ flame finial. **Right:** Cruet w/clear paneled stopper 5.75", flat oil bottle, 3.5 oz.

Topaz (yellow) grouping: **Left:** Bonbon 7.4", 3-toed, crimped. **Right:** Bowl 5", round, flared w/1 handle.

Topaz (yellow) grouping: **Left:** Candlestick 1-lite 5.5", fancy stem, pair. **Right:** Bowl 12", flat, round, flared.

Azure (blue) grouping: **Back left:** Tray 8.25", flat, 3-toed, tidbit w/turned up edge. **Back right:** Cake plate 10.25", 2-tab flame handled. **Front left:** Bowl 6", 3-toed, cupped. **Front right:** Bowl 6.25", 3-toed, flared.

Azure (blue) grouping: **Left:** Goblet 3", cone liquor cocktail, 3.5 oz. **Center:** Goblet 3.9", cone shaped sherbet, 5 oz. **Right:** Goblet 6.75", cone dinner water, 9 oz.

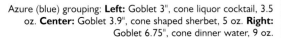

Topaz (yellow) grouping: **Left:** Ice bucket 4.5", flat, squat chrome handle, 6.5" wide. **Center:** Shaker 2", individual, straight sided w/clear glass top. **Right:** Cruet w/clear paneled stopper 5.75", flat oil bottle, 3.5 oz.

Azure (blue) grouping: **Back left:** Tray 8.25", flat, 3-toed, tidbit w/turned up edge. **Back right:** Plate 9.5", dinner. **Front:** Sauce 2 piece: bowl 6.5", oblong, tab flame handled; liner 6.75".

Topaz (yellow) grouping: **Left:** Candlestick 3-lite 9", flame center, 11.5" spread. **Right:** Candlestick 1-lite 5.5", fancy stem.

Crystal grouping: **Left:** Cup 2.25", flat, punch, 6 oz. **Left:** Punch bowl 13.25", footed, flared, 1.5 gallon.

Azure (blue) grouping: **Top center:** Bowl 4.6", 3-toed, tri-corn w/1 handle. **Bottom left:** Bowl 4.25", 3-toed, round, mint w/1 handle. **Bottom right:** Bowl 4", 3-toed, square, mint w/1 handle.

Azure (blue) grouping: **Back:** Bowl 10", 4-tab feet, rectangle, tab flame handled, shallow, floating garden. **Front left:** Tumbler 3.4", flat, straight sided, old fashion, 6.5 oz. **Front center:** Candlestick 1-lite 4", cornucopia flame shape. **Front right:** Tumbler 5.9", flat, straight sided, ice tea, 14 oz.

BLACK FOREST

Paden City Glass Company Etching #517 1928-30s
Main Colors: Cheriglo (pink), Crystal, Ebony (black), and Green
Other Color: Amber

Black Forest was correctly identified as being made by Paden City in our premier *Elegant Glass* book. This etching has caused some confusion over the years. The problem came because of old ads, which only listed Van Deman of New York, not Paden City, in connection with the etching. It is our opinion that since Van Deman was only a distribution company, Paden City must have made this etching exclusively for them to sell. Since this etching is found primarily on the Paden City "Regina" line #210, it was easy to make the association between the two.

Later, the L.G. Wright Glass Company obtained the Black Forest etching plates and made several items under their line, which they called Forest. There were water and whiskey goblets along with a comport with the Daisy & Cube pattern that were etched with the Forest etching. Also used with this etch were four goblets (cordial, sherbet, wine, and water) and a finger bowl, all with the Kings Crown pattern. All of these were sold under the L.G. Wright name from 1965 to 1984. These L.G. Wright items can be found in crystal and several colors. These are nice go-along pieces, but are not part of the original etching line. They are often priced considerably higher by dealers not knowing this etching since they think the items are rare and unlisted. This is another reason to work hard to know the glass you collect.

Some of the most difficult items for collectors to find are the following: cocktail shaker, cup/saucer, decanter, dinner plate, nite set, and pitcher. The versatility of using one mould to make something else can be seen in the 74 oz. pitcher. It is made from the large vase, with a handle that was applied and spout pulled out of one side.

New collectors will sometimes confuse this etching with Deerwood (Tiffin). Take time to compare the close up photos of each of these etchings to see the differences between them.

All colors are the same price, except Crystal (deduct 50% off price), and some dealers price black a little higher. Only a few ruby pieces are reported and they would bring 25% higher. Amber is a hard color to find, but not many collectors seem to be drawn to it. For more information, you can refer to the book *Paden City Glass Company* by William P. Walker, Melissa Bratkovich & Joan C. Walker.

Pattern detail, Black Forest.

BLACK FOREST

	Colors
Bowl 8.25" #210 Regina, tab handled	110
Bowl 9.25" #210 Regina, flat, w/2 open handles, shallow & flared	135
Bowl 10" #210 Regina, footed, short stem, rolled edge	175
Bowl 10.75" #210 Regina, deep, flared	135
Bowl 12" #210 Regina, rolled edge, console	145
Bowl 12.5" #220 Largo, flat, round, console	145
Bowl 14" #210 Regina, mushroom-shaped, console	175
Cake plate 11" #210 Regina, round w/2 open handles	125
Cake salver 11" #210 Regina, footed, short stem	145
Candlestick 1-lite 2.75" #210 Regina, flat w/flared top rim, 4.5" wide, pair	145
Candlestick 1-lite 5" #210 Regina, footed, mushroom w/rolled top edge, pair	165
Candy w/cover #210 Regina, flat	185
Candy w/cover 6.4", short stem, 6.4" wide #503 Vermilion bottom & #210 Regina lid	225
Cocktail shaker #210 Regina, flat w/chrome top	225
Comport 5" (Daisy & Cube blank by L.G. Wright), flared, 4.5" wide	28
Comport 5.5" #210 Regina, rolled edge, 7.5" wide	125
Creamer 4" #210 Regina, footed w/deco handles, 6.5 oz.	60
Creamer, Loaf, 2 piece #323: creamer, straight sided, 6 oz.; sugar wafer tray, round, square open handled, w/center indent for creamer	135
Cup & saucer, coffee #210 Regina: cup 2.4", flat, coffee, 6 oz.; saucer w/indent 6"	115
Cup & saucer, coffee #991 Penny Line: cup, 6 oz.; saucer w/indent 5.75"	125
Decanter w/stopper 8.5", bulbous center, 28 oz.	375
Decanter w/stopper 11" #210 Regina, flat, 24 oz.	300
Egg cup 4.4" #210 Regina, footed	145
Goblet 3.75" (Kings Crown blank by L.G. Wright), whiskey, 2 oz.	50
Goblet 4" #991 Penny Line, wine, 3 oz.	125
Goblet 5.6" (Daisy & Cube blank by L.G. Wright) water, 8 oz.	24
Ice tub 4" #210 Regina, flat, tab handled, 6" wide	200
Mayonnaise 2 piece #881 Gadroon: bowl 5.5", flat deep, 4.5" wide; liner w/indent 6.5"	145
Mayonnaise 2 piece #210 Regina: bowl 6.25", footed, rolled edge, 3.75" high; liner w/indent 7.25"	185
Nite set 8" #210 Regina, flat, handled, jug & flat tumbler w/flared base	500+
Pitcher #210 Regina, flat jug w/applied handle, 12 oz.	250+
Pitcher #210 Regina, flat jug w/applied handle, 18 oz.	275+
Pitcher #210 Regina, flat jug w/applied handle, 30 oz.	325+
Pitcher #210 Regina, flat jug w/applied handle, 47 oz.	375+
Pitcher #210 Regina, flat jug w/applied handle, 62 oz.	400+
Pitcher 10.25" #210 Regina, flat, 3 rings on base & neck shouldered, jug w/applied handle, 74 oz.	500+
Plate 6.3" #210 Regina, bread & butter	35
Plate 8.25" #210 Regina, lunch	65
Plate 10.25" #210 Regina, dinner	125
Relish w/cover 10.5", pedestal footed, 5 sections (only lid etched)	900+
Sandwich server 10.75" #210 Regina, center handled tray	95
Sugar 4" #210 Regina, footed w/deco handles, 6.5 oz.	60
Tumbler 3.5" #191 1/2 party Line, flat juice, 4.5 oz.	100

Back: Cake salver 11" #210 Regina, footed, short stem, Ebony (black).
Front: Cake salver 11" #210 Regina, footed, short stem, Green.

Candy w/cover 6.4", short stem, 6.4" wide #503 Vermilion bottom & #210 Regina lid, Green.

Back: Sandwich server 10.75" #210 Regina, center handled tray, Ebony (black). **Front:** Candlestick 1-lite 2.75" #210 Regina, flat w/flared top rim, 4.5" wide, pair, Crystal (right one turned on side).

Left to right: Goblet 5.6" (<u>Daisy & Cube blank by L.G. Wright</u>) water, 8 oz., in the following colors: Amber; Crystal; Blue; Ebony (black). **Note:** goblets pictured here are <u>**not**</u> **Paden City.**

Amber grouping: **Left:** Bowl 9.25" #210 Regina, flat, w/2 open handles, shallow & flared. **Right:** Sandwich server 10.75" #210 Regina, center handled tray.

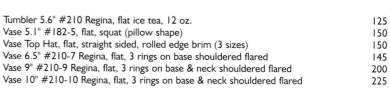

Tumbler 5.6" #210 Regina, flat ice tea, 12 oz.	125
Vase 5.1" #182-5, flat, squat (pillow shape)	150
Vase Top Hat, flat, straight sided, rolled edge brim (3 sizes)	150
Vase 6.5" #210-7 Regina, flat, 3 rings on base shouldered flared	145
Vase 9" #210-9 Regina, flat, 3 rings on base & neck shouldered flared	200
Vase 10" #210-10 Regina, flat, 3 rings on base & neck shouldered flared	225

Top left: Vase 6.5" #210-7 Regina, flat, 3 rings on base shouldered flared, Ebony (black). **Top right:** Creamer & sugar #210 Regina, footed w/deco handles, 6.5 oz., Green. **Front left:** Egg cup 4.4" #210 Regina, footed, Green. **Front center left:** Tumbler 3.5" #191 1/2 party Line, flat juice, 4.5 oz., Cheriglo (pink). **Front center right:** Decanter w/stopper 11" #210 Regina, flat, 24 oz., Cheriglo (pink). **Front right:** Ice tub 4" #210 Regina, flat, tab handled, 6" wide, Ebony (black).

Cheriglo (pink) grouping: **Top left:** Ice tub 4" #210 Regina, flat, tab handled, 6" wide. **Top right:** Cake plate 11" #210 Regina, round w/2 open handles. **Bottom left:** Bowl 8.25" #210 Regina, tab handled. **Bottom right:** Bowl 10" #210 Regina, footed, short stem, rolled edge.

Vase 6.5" #210-7 Regina, flat, 3 rings on base shouldered flared, Cheriglo (pink).

Back left: Plate 8.25" #210 Regina, lunch, Ebony (black). **Back right:** Plate 6.3" #210 Regina, bread & butter, Ebony (black). **Front left:** Goblet 5.6" (<u>Daisy & Cube blank by L.G. Wright</u>) water, 8 oz., Crystal. **Front right:** Goblet 3.75" (<u>Kings Crown blank by L.G. Wright</u>), whiskey, 2 oz., Crystal. **Note:** goblets pictured here are **not Paden City.**

Mayonnaise 2 piece #881 Gadroon: bowl 5.5", flat deep, 4.5" wide; liner w/indent 6.5", Crystal.

Green grouping: **Left:** Tumbler 5.6" #210 Regina, flat ice tea, 12 oz. **Right:** Pitcher 10.25" #210 Regina, flat, 3 rings on base & neck shouldered, jug w/applied handle, 74 oz.

Nite set 8" #210 Regina, flat, handled, jug & flat tumbler w/flared base, Green.

Left: Mayonnaise 3 piece #210 Regina: bowl 6.25", footed, rolled edge, 3.75" high; liner w/ indent; ladle, Ebony (black) w/Gold encrusted. **Right:** Vase 10" #210-10 Regina, flat, 3 rings on base & neck shouldered flared, Green.

Pattern detail, Buttercup.

Left to right: Goblet 3.6" #6030 Astrid, oyster cocktail, 4 oz.; Goblet 4.25" #6030 Astrid, sherbet, 6 oz.; Goblet 5.8" #6030 Astrid, claret/wine, 3.5 oz.; Goblet 5.6" #6030 Astrid, saucer champagne, 6 oz.; Tumbler 6" #6030 Astrid, footed, ice tea, 12 oz.; Goblet 7.8" #6030 Astrid, dinner water, 10 oz.

Left: Plate 9.5" #2337, dinner. **Right:** Plate 11" #2364 Sonata, small center, sandwich or 9" salad bowl liner.

BUTTERCUP
Fostoria Glass Company   Etching #340   1941-60
Color: Crystal

Imagine a summer day with a field of golden flowers waving in the breeze and you can visualize how the idea for this etching may have come to a designer. World War II was going on and Fostoria was looking for ways to revitalize their sales. Buttercup was designed to harmonize with the Spode China and Gorham silver patterns of the same name. This made for a real selling power at the fine department stores that were set up with all three patterns. Brides had an excellent opportunity to mix and match when registering their pattern at the department store. Since the stems were typically purchased to go with a china set, there seems to be an abundance of them and not accessory items.

The Sonata #2364 blank is used for most of the accessory pieces in this etching. The stemware will be found on the Astrid #6030 blank.

Some of the hard to find items today that were only produced for a few years during the war are: salad dressing bottle, candy dish, cigarette holder, and Sani-cut syrup. These were only made from 1941 to 1943 and it is easy to understand that not many are now available to collectors.

BUTTERCUP	Crystal
Ashtray 2.6" #2364 Sonata, (blown) round	24
Bottle w/flat stopper 6.5" #2083, flat, salad dressing, 7 oz.	275
Bowl 6" #2364 Sonata, rim baked apple	24
Bowl 9" #2364 Sonata, shallow, salad	45
Bowl 9" #6023, (blown) footed, short stem	85
Bowl 10" #2594, plume handled, oval, console (13.5" overall)	95
Bowl 10.5" #2364 Sonata, deep, salad	55
Bowl 12" #2364 Sonata, flat, flared	45
Bowl 12.5" #2364 Sonata, flat, shallow lily pond, cupped edge	49
Bowl 13" #2364 Sonata, shallow, fruit	49
Bowl 13.5" #2594, plume handled, oval	68
Candlestick 1-lite 4" #2324, short wafer stem, pair	45
Candlestick 1-lite 5.5" #2594, plume stem, pair	68
Candlestick 1-lite 6" #2324, plain stem, pair	68
Candlestick 2-lite 5.5" #6023, plain "U" stem, pair	85
Candlestick 3-lite 8" #2594, plume stems, 6.5" spread, pair	125
Candy w/cover 4" #2364 Sonata, (blown) 3.75" wide	135
Cheese & cracker: comport 2.9" #2364 Sonata, short stem, 5.75" wide; plate 11.25"	68
Cigarette holder 2" #2364 Sonata, (blown) flat, round	34
Comport 5" #6030 Astrid, plain stem, cupped	38
Comport 8" #2364 Sonata, lady leg stem & flared	48
Creamer 3.25" #2350 1/2, footed, regular, 7 oz.	15
Cup & saucer, coffee #2350 1/2: cup 2.6", footed, coffee, 6 oz.; saucer w/indent 5.75"	18
Finger bowl 4.1" #1769, (blown)	30
Goblet 3.9" #6030 Astrid, cordial, 1 oz.	35
Goblet 5.25" #6030 Astrid, liquor cocktail, 3.5 oz.	16
Goblet 5.8" #6030 Astrid, claret/wine, 3.5 oz.	25
Goblet 3.6" #6030 Astrid, oyster cocktail, 4 oz.	18
Goblet 4.25" #6030 Astrid, sherbet, 6 oz.	14
Goblet 5.6" #6030 Astrid, saucer champagne, 6 oz.	16
Goblet 6.4" #6030 Astrid, lunch water, 10 oz.	20
Goblet 7.8" #6030 Astrid, dinner water, 10 oz.	24
Mayonnaise 3 piece #2364 Sonata: bowl 5", deep; liner w/indent 6.75"; ladle 5.75"	62
Pitcher 8.9" #6011, water w/o ice lip, 53 oz.	245
Plate 6" #2337, bread & butter	6
Plate 7.25" #2337, salad	10
Plate 7.25" #2364 Sonata, crescent salad (kidney)	45
Plate 8.5" #2337, lunch	16
Plate 9.5" #2337, dinner	45
Plate 11" #2364 Sonata, small center, sandwich or 9" salad bowl liner	38
Plate 14" #2364 Sonata, torte or 10.5" salad bowl liner	58
Plate 16" #2364 Sonata, torte or service	75
Relish 6.5" #2364 Sonata, tab handled, oval, 2 sections	28
Relish 8" #2350, oval, rim pickle	22
Relish 10" #2364 Sonata, tab handled, oval, 3 sections	40
Relish 11" #2350, oval, rim celery	28
Sandwich server 11.5" #2364 Sonata, center plume handled	48
Shaker 2.25" #2364 Sonata, w/glass top, pair	85
Shaker 2.6" #2364 Sonata, w/metal top, pair	65
Sugar 3.1" #2350 1/2, footed, regular, 7 oz.	15
Syrup 5.5" #2586, flat, chrome Sani-cut top, 9 oz.	295
Tumbler 4.6" #6030 Astrid, footed juice, 5 oz.	18
Tumbler 6" #6030 Astrid, footed, ice tea, 12 oz.	25
Vase 6" #4143, footed, large, flared top	125
Vase 6" #6021, footed, necked, flared, bud vase	90
Vase 7.5" #4143, footed, large, flared top	160
Vase 10" #2614, flat w/bulging ring near bottom, flared top	215

Back left: Bowl 12.5" #2364 Sonata, flat, shallow lily pond, cupped edge. **Back right:** Sandwich server 11.5" #2364 Sonata, center plume handled. **Front left:** Relish 11" #2350, oval, rim celery. **Front right:** Relish 8" #2350, oval, rim pickle.

CANDLELIGHT
Cambridge Glass Company   **1936-50**
Main Color: Crystal
Other Color: Crown Tuscan

The Candlelight etching features a glowing candle that radiates out in a circle surrounded by beautiful scroll work. Cambridge obviously wanted to highlight the importance of candles in our lives before the introduction of electricity in our homes. Now it seems all the rage to have different colored and scented candles as part of our decor.

The following three different stemware lines were used for Candlelight: #3111, #3114, and #3776. Line #3114 was only offered through the 1940s while the other two continued until the etching was discontinued. The accessory items are mostly found on the #3400 Ball or #3900 Corinth lines. It is primarily a Crystal pattern, but 22 pieces were offered in Crown Tuscan. A number of the items can be found with gold encrusting. For items made in Crown Tuscan and gold encrusted, add 80% to Crystal prices.

Candlelight is a difficult etching to find and you need to be a seasoned collector to have the patience to find it. Some of the hardest to find pieces include: several pitchers, cocktail shaker, hurricane lamps, toast cover, flat tumblers, and a few vases.

Pattern detail, Candlelight.

CANDLELIGHT	Crystal
Bonbon 5.25" #3400/1180, handled	48
Bowl 2.5" #3400/71, tab handled, 4-footed, nut	60
Bowl 5.75" #3900/130, footed, tab handled, sweetmeat	45
Bowl 8.5" #381 Pristine, rim soup	125
Bowl 9.5" #3400/34, handled	85
Bowl 10" #3400/1185, handled, deep	125
Bowl 10" #3900/54, 4-footed, flared	75
Bowl 10.5" #3400/168, flat, flared	85
Bowl 11" #1399, deep salad, scalloped edge	85
Bowl 11" #3400/48, 4-footed shallow ruffled edge	95
Bowl 11" #3900/34, handled, flared	85
Bowl 10.5" #3900/28, footed, tab handled, flared	75
Bowl 12" #3400/4, 4-footed, square, flared edge	85
Bowl 12" #3400/1240, 4-footed, oval, refractory	245
Bowl 12" #3400/160, 4-footed, oblong, crimped	95
Bowl 12" #3900/62, 4-footed, flared	75
Bowl 12" #3900/65, handled, 4-footed, oval	95
Bowl 13" #1398, shallow, fruit	85
Butter w/cover 5.5" #3400/52, round, 2 open handles	295
Cake plate 13.5" #3900/35, handled	85
Candelabra 1-lite 5.5" #648, keyhole stem, etched bobeches & prisms, pair	195
Candelabra 2-lite 6" #3400/1268, keyhole stem, bobeches & prisms, pair	275
Candlestick 1-lite 3.5" #628 Pristine, w/wafer stem, pair	75
Candlestick 1-lite 4.4" #3900/68, bell footed, skirted, pair (also is a comport)	98
Candlestick 1-lite 5" #3400/646, keyhole stem, pair	95
Candlestick 1-lite 5" #3900/67, pair	90
Candlestick 2-lite 6" #3400/647, keyhole stem, pair	145
Candlestick 2-lite 6" #3900/72, pair	135
Candlestick 3-lite 6" #3900/74, pair	165
Candlestick 3-lite 6.25" #3400/1338, tiered (looks like ocean waves) 7" spread, pair	225
Candlestick 3-lite 7" #3400/638, keyhole stem, pair	175
Candy w/cover 5.4" #1066/4, blown w/fancy ball stem, plain finial	295
Candy w/cover 6.5" #3400/9, 4-footed, tab handled, 7" wide; dome lid w/finial	165
Candy w/cover 8" #3500/57 Gadroon, 3 open handled, 3 equal sections	145
Candy w/cover 8" #3900/138, footed, wafer stem, dome lid w/finial (optic)	145
Candy box w/cover 7" #3900/165	150
Cheese & cracker: comport 3" #3400/7, short stem, flared, 5.5" wide; plate 11.5" #3400/6, tab handled	75
Cheese & cracker: comport, 3.5" #3900/135, short stem, 5" wide; plate 13.5"	125
Cheese dish w/cover 5" #980, (blown) flat	400+
Cigarette holder #1066, oval, short stem w/ashtray foot	150
Cocktail icer 4.2" #187 Pristine, footed, 2 piece w/non-etched insert	75
Cocktail icer 4.2" #3600, footed, 2 piece w/non-etched insert	80
Cocktail icer 4.6" #968, footed, 2 piece w/non-etched insert	85
Cocktail shaker (Pristine) #99, sham base w/chrome top	175
Cocktail shaker 9.8" #101 Pristine, sham spouted w/glass top ball finial 32 oz.	250
Comport 5" #1066, (blown) w/1 ball stem, 5.4" wide	85
Comport 5" #3114, (blown) cupped, 6" wide	75
Comport 5.25" #3111, (blown) cupped, 5.5" wide	80
Comport 5.75" #3776, (blown) 5.4" wide, straight stem w/wafers at top	68
Comport 6.1" #3121/2, (blown) tall stem, 5.4" wide	75
Comport 7" #3114/1, (blown) cupped 6" wide	95
Comport 7.5" #3400/14, fancy wafer stem, flared, 7" wide	75
Comport 7.5" #3900/136, scalloped edge, 7.25" wide	60
Creamer 2.6" #3900/40, footed, individual, 3.5 oz.	24
Creamer 3" #3900/41, footed, regular, 6 oz.	20
Creamer 3.8" #3400/68, regular, scalloped foot, 4.75 oz.	28
Cruet w/stopper #3400/161, footed, handled, 6 oz.	225
Cruet w/stopper 6" #3900/100, flat, spherical, 6 oz.	115
Cup & saucer, coffee #3400/54: cup 2.4", 6 oz.; saucer w/indent 5.5"	35

Plate 8.5" #3400/62, lunch (6-sided).

Candy w/cover 8" #3500/57 Gadroon, 3 open handled, 3 equal sections, Crown Tuscan w/Gold encrusted.

Hurricane lamp 17" #1613, bobeche w/prisms & etched large chimney.

Cup & saucer, coffee #3900/17: cup 2.5", 7 oz.; saucer w/indent 5.5"	32
Decanter w/flat stopper 11" #1321, footed, 28 oz.	295
Epergne 4 piece #3900/75, etched 3-lite candlestick w/plain arm & 2 vases	175
Finger bowl & liner: bowl #3111 (blown); plate w/indent	48
Goblet #3111, ball & ribbed stem, cordial, 1 oz.	75
Goblet #3114, plain stem, cordial, 1 oz.	68
Goblet #3776, cordial, 1 oz.	75
Goblet 5" #7966, flared, cone shape cordial, 1 oz.	125
Goblet 5.25" #7966, flared, cone shaped sherry, 2 oz.	75
Goblet #3111, ball & ribbed stem, wine, 2.5 oz.	45
Goblet #3114, plain stem, wine, 2.5 oz.	42
Goblet #3776, wine, 2.5 oz.	42
Goblet #3111, ball & ribbed stem, liquor cocktail, 3 oz.	35
Goblet #3114, plain stem, liquor cocktail, 3 oz.	30
Goblet #3776, liquor cocktail, 3 oz.	28
Goblet #7801 Pristine, plain stem, liquor cocktail, 4 oz.	30
Goblet #3111, ball stem, oyster cocktail, 4.5 oz.	35
Goblet #3114, short stem, oyster cocktail, 4.5 oz.	30
Goblet #3776, oyster cocktail, 4.5 oz.	25
Goblet #3111, ball & ribbed stem, claret, 4.5 oz.	45
Goblet #3114, plain stem, claret, 4.5 oz.	45
Goblet #3776, claret, 4.5 oz.	45
Goblet #3111, ball & ribbed stem, sherbet, 7 oz.	20
Goblet #3114, plain stem, sherbet, 7 oz.	18
Goblet #3776, sherbet, 7 oz.	18
Goblet #3111, ball & ribbed stem, saucer champagne, 7 oz.	28
Goblet #3114, plain stem, saucer champagne, 7 oz.	26
Goblet #3776, saucer champagne, 7 oz.	26
Goblet #3776, water, 9 oz.	38
Goblet #3111, ball & ribbed stem, water, 10 oz.	38
Goblet #3114, plain stem, water, 10 oz.	35
Hurricane lamp 9" #1617, skirted/etched chimney, each	295
Hurricane lamp 11.5" #1603, keyhole, bobeche/prisms & etched chimney, each	345
Hurricane lamp 17" #1613, bobeche w/prisms & etched large chimney, each	495+
Ice bucket 5.75" #3400/851, flat, scalloped top w/chrome handle	135
Ice bucket #957, chrome handle	110
Ice bucket 5.75" #3900/671, chrome handle	160
Mayonnaise 2 piece #1532 Pristine: bowl 4.5" (blown), spherical, 3" high; liner w/indent 6.75"	90
Mayonnaise bowl 4" #3900/19, footed, ball shape, 4.1" high	48
Mayonnaise 2 piece #3900: #127 bowl 5", flared; #128 liner w/indent 6.5"	60
Mayonnaise comport 6" #3900/137, footed, wafer stem, flared w/optic	68
Mayonnaise 2 piece #3900/111: bowl 5.25", salad dressing; liner w/indent 6.75"	65
Mayonnaise bowl 5.75" #1402/95 Tally Ho, footed, salad dressing	75
Mayonnaise bowl 5.75" #1402/133, footed, salad dressing, 4.75" high	85
Mayonnaise bowl (Tally Ho) #1402/137, 2 part, salad dressing, 2 spouted	90
Mayonnaise 2 piece #3400: #13 bowl 5.8", 4-toed, flared, tab handled; #11 liner w/indent 5"	78
Nite set #103, flat, handled, jug & flat tumbler w/flared base	350+
Pitcher #3900/117, flat, jug w/ice lip, 20 oz.	250
Pitcher #3900/114, flat, martini jug w/ice lip, 32 oz.	325
Pitcher #3900/118, flat, jug w/ice lip, 32 oz.	300
Pitcher 7.75" #3400/152, Doulton style, 76 oz.	450
Pitcher #3900/115, flat, water jug w/ice lip (optic), 76 oz.	295

Left: Bowl 5.75" #3900/130, footed, handled, sweetmeat. **Center left:** Comport 5.75" #3776, (blown) 5.4" wide, straight stem w/ wafers at top. **Center right:** cocktail #968 non-etched insert. **Right:** Cocktail icer 4.6" #968, footed, 2 piece w/non-etched insert.

Pitcher 9" #3900/116, ball w/ice lip, 80 oz.	250	Sugar 2.4" #3900/40, footed, individual, 3.5 oz.	24
Pitcher 8.1" #3400/141, water jug w/o ice lip, 80 oz.	275	Sugar 3" #3400/68 regular, scalloped foot, 5 oz.	28
Plate 6" #3400/60, bread & butter (6 sided)	12	Sugar 2.75" #3900/41, regular footed, 6 oz.	20
Plate 6" #3400/1181, 2 open handled, lemon server	30	Toast cover 4.5" #1533, (blown) w/finial	475+
Plate 6.5" #3900/20, bread & butter	14	Tumbler 2.4" #321, sham, whiskey, 2 oz.	60
Plate 7.5" (Pristine) 555, dessert	16	Tumbler #498, flat, cut flute, straight sided, whiskey, 2 oz.	60
Plate 7.5" #3400/176, square, salad or dessert	18	Tumbler #3111, footed, whiskey, 3 oz.	45
Plate 8" #3900/22, salad	20	Tumbler #3114, footed, whiskey, 3 oz.	40
Plate 8" #3900/131, handled lemon server, 9.25" counting handles	35	Tumbler #321, sham, tapered juice, 5 oz.	40
Plate 8.5" #3400/62, lunch (6 sided)	25	Tumbler #498, flat, cut flute, straight sided juice, 5 oz.	35
Plate 10.5" #3900/24, dinner	78	Tumbler #3111, footed juice, 5 oz.	28
Plate 11" #3400/35, handled	50	Tumbler #3114, footed, juice, 5 oz.	28
Plate 11.5" #3400/8, tab handled, sandwich	50	Tumbler #3776, footed juice, 5 oz.	28
Plate 12" #3900/26, 4-footed, service	65	Tumbler #3900/117, footed, juice, 5 oz.	28
Plate 12.5" #3400/1186, oblong, open handled sandwich	78	Tumbler #321, sham, old fashion, 8 oz.	45
Plate 13" #3900/33, 4-footed, torte	70	Tumbler #498, flat, cut flute, straight sided, 8 oz.	35
Plate 13.5" #1396 Pristine, flat, torte/service	75	Tumbler #497, sham, straight sided, 9 oz.	40
Plate 13.5" #1397 Pristine, small center, turned up edge, cabaret	80	Tumbler #498, flat, cut flute, straight sided, 10 oz.	38
Plate 14" #3400/65, torte or chop, large center	95	Tumbler #3111, footed, water, 10 oz.	35
Plate 14" #3900/166, small center, turned up edge, cabaret	75	Tumbler #3114, footed, water, 10 oz.	35
Relish 6" #3400/90, handled, 2 sections	35	Tumbler #497, sham, straight sided, 11 oz.	40
Relish 7" #3900/123, 4-toed, tab scroll handled, oblong pickle	35	Tumbler #498, flat, cut flute, straight sided, 12 oz.	45
Relish 7" #3900/124, 4-toed, tab scroll handled, 2 equal sections, oblong	40	Tumbler #3111, footed, ice tea, 12 oz.	45
Relish 8" #3500/57 Gadroon, 3 sections, 3 handled (candy bottom)	60	Tumbler #3114, footed, ice tea, 12 oz.	45
Relish 9" #3900/125, handled, oblong, 3 sections	48	Tumbler #3776, footed, ice tea, 12 oz.	45
Relish 10" #3500/64 Gadroon, 4-toed, handled, 2 equal sections & celery section	75	Tumbler #497, sham, straight sided, 13 oz.	48
Relish 11" #3500/152 Gadroon, handled, rectangular, 3 equal sections & celery section	125	Tumbler #3400/115, bellied ice tea, 13 oz.	50
		Tumbler 4.1" #3900/115, flat barrel, 13 oz.	48
Relish 12" #3400/67, 4 equal sections & celery section	95	Vase 4.5" #1309, globe, flower holder	125
Relish 12" #3500/67 Gadroon, round, 5 inserts & tray w/scalloped edge	225	Vase 5" #3400/102, globe, short neck	95
Relish 12" #3900/120, oblong, 4 equal sections & celery section	95	Vase 6" #6004, footed, one ball stem	48
Relish 12" #3900/126, handled, oblong, 3 sections	65	Vase 8" #1430, large, flat, flared flip	95
		Vase 8.4" #6004, footed, one ball stem	60
Relish 15" #3500/112 Gadroon, handled, oval, 2 equal sections & celery section	150	Vase 9" #1237, footed, keyhole stem, flared	100
		Vase 9" #575 Pristine, footed, smooth top, cornucopia, each	175
Sandwich server 11" #3400/10, center handle	85	Vase 10" #274, footed, tapered out to top, bud vase	175
Shaker 2.25" #1468, egg shaped w/glass square base, pair	95	Vase 10.5" #3400/1242, flat, shouldered, flared	245
Shaker #1470, small, round w/square glass base, pair	95	Vase 11" #278, large, footed, flared top	145
Shaker #1471, large, round w/square glass base, pair	90	Vase 11.5" #1299, footed, urn shape, ball stem	195
Shaker 3.5" #3900/1177, flat w/chrome top, pair	55	Vase 12" #1238, footed, keyhole stem, flared	125
Shaker 3.75" #3400/77, footed w/glass top, pair	75	Vase 13" #279, footed, flared	150

Relish 10" #3500/64 Gadroon, 4-toed, handled, 2 equal sections & celery section, Crystal w/Gold encrusted.

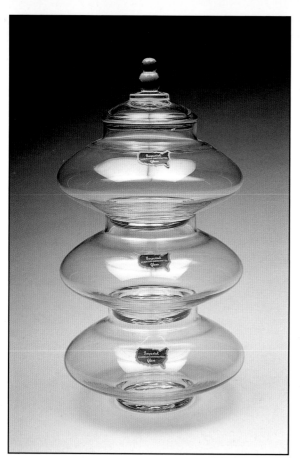

Jar set w/cover 10.75" #655: 3 ovoid ball jars, 6" wide; w/lid 2 bead finial, 5.75" wide, 4 piece – shown w/original labels.

CANDLEWICK
Imperial Glass Company   **Blank #400**   **1936-82**
Main Color: Crystal
Other Colors: Amethyst, Black, Cartel Slag, Cranberry, Emerald Green, Nut Brown, Ritz Blue, Ruby, Sunshine Yellow, Verde Green, and Viennese Blue

The name Candlewick comes from a sewing technique that originated in Colonial America. With a shortage of material, the women utilized the cotton wick that was used in candle making, for doing embroidery work. Unbleached muslin was generally used, in which a series of French knots were used to make a design. This was primarily employed on bedspreads and pillows.

Imperial's President Newton was seeking ideas to rejuvenate his company. He purchased a piece of French glass with a bead design. He took the piece back to the factory, to develop a mould. Thus, a new line of glassware was produced that would be named after the Colonial sewing technique.

Candlewick became Imperial's most prolific line of glassware. It was a household word with women in America for many years. This wonderful pattern can be found in a vast array of shapes with many colored items. To collect everything made in this pattern would be a life-long goal.

Between all of the items produced, unusual shapes, colors, cuttings, etchings, sand carvings, and decorated pieces, collectors of Candlewick could fill an entire house with this one pattern if enough time and money were available. At almost every show we go to, there are pieces we have never seen before. The possibilities are almost endless with this pattern.

To expand on the items that were made in Candlewick, we searched through the catalogs for special items made for Irice and DeVilbiss. We have included all of those items here since they typically show up in displays of Candlewick for sale.

During the last few years, several items have been reproduced in Delphite, Jade, and Vaseline. There are also round three section relishes that have come from Czechoslovakia that resemble Candlewick. Be aware of all of these items if you collect Candlewick.

Not many colored pieces in this pattern have shown up on a consistent basis, making it impossible to list a fair market value here.

CANDLEWICK

	Crystal
Adapter w/peg 4" #152, adds chimney to candlestick	75
Ashtray #118, w/tab for match holder	90
Ashtray #118, w/tab for one cigarette	12
Ashtray 2.75" #19, individual, round	12
Ashtray 3.25" #651, individual, square	50
Ashtray 4" #440, round w/large beads	8
Ashtray 4.25" #134, oblong w/large beads	8
Ashtray 4.5" #652, square	48
Ashtray 5" #133, round (2 styles)	11
Ashtray 5.75" #653, square	50
Ashtray 6" #60, round w/raised center	175
Ashtray 6" #150, beaded edge (large beads) round	10
Ashtray 6.5" #1776/1, Eagle at top, 3.75" wide	65

Left back: Bowl 7.5" #62B, handled, sweetmeat, Ruby.
Top right: Bowl 8.5" #74B, 4-footed, Black. **Front left:** Shaker 5" #190, high, bell beaded foot & chrome top, pair, Crystal. **Bottom right:** Dealer sign, 5.25" oblong calendar embossed "Hand Made Imperial U.S.A. Candlewick Crystal", Crystal.

Atomizer 2.75" #96, (made for DeVilbiss Co.) round, beaded foot	95
Atomizer 4" #247, (made for DeVilbiss Co.) straight sides, beaded foot	85
Atomizer 4.5" #247, (made for DeVilbiss Co.) tear drop shape, beaded foot	75
Banana stand 10" #67D, w/I bead stem	2,500+
Banana stand 10" #103E, w/3 bead stem	2,500+
Basket 5" #273, beads on handle	350
Basket 6.5" #40/0, handled	52
Basket 11.75" wide, 7.5" tall, #73/0, applied handle, 7.5" tall	300
Bell 4" #179, handle w/4 graduated beads	200
Bell 5" #108, handle w/4 graduated beads	93
Bottle w/chrome tube #117, bitters, 4 oz.	100
Bottle w/stopper 5" #E130/E121, (made for Irice Co.) 2 bead stopper, cologne	75
Bottle w/stopper 6.5" #E408, (made for Irice Co.) beaded foot, 4 bead stopper, cologne	125
Bottle w/stopper 6.5" #277 salad dressing, embossed with oil & vinegar 8 oz.	300
Bowl 4" #33, round w/small beads, individual jelly	15
Bowl 4.5" #206, 3-toed	80
Bowl 4.75" #42B, handled fruit	15
Bowl 5" #1F, round, shallow	15
Bowl 5" #231, square shape	155
Bowl 5.25" #23B, fruit or mayonnaise	15
Bowl 5.5" #53, crimped	16
Bowl 5.5" #243, deep, sauce	75
Bowl 5.8" #3F, round fruit	16
Bowl 5.8" #183, 3-toed	89
Bowl 6" #51, round, shallow, mint w/handle	25
Bowl 6" #51C, round, shallow, crimped, candy w/handle	40
Bowl 6" #52, handled, 2 sections, jelly	30
Bowl 6" #53X, baked apple	33
Bowl 6" #85, deep, cottage cheese	60
Bowl 6" #232, square	165
Bowl 6.5" #52B, handled, round	24
Bowl 6.5", #52C crimped, six points	40
Bowl 7" #5F, round	35
Bowl 7" #62B, flared, handled	20
Bowl 7" #74J, deep, flared w/4 ball feet	250
Bowl 7" #233, square	185
Bowl 7.5" #75N, flat, shallow lily pond, cupped edge	500+
Bowl 7.5" #127B, belled (console base)	350
Bowl 8" #7F, round	35
Bowl w/cover 8" #65/1, vegetable	325
Bowl 8.5" #69B, vegetable	45
Bowl 8.5" #72, handled, 2 sections	112
Bowl 8.5" #72B, handled	35
Bowl 8.5" #74B, 4-footed	125
Bowl 8.5" #182, 3-toed	150
Bowl 9" #10F, round	50
Bowl 9" #74SC, ruffled, 4-footed	88
Bowl 10" #13F, round	55
Bowl 10" #113A, handled, deep	175
Bowl 10" #128B, straight sided, punch base	200
Bowl 10" #145B, handled	55
Bowl 10" #205, 3-toed	200
Bowl 10.5" #63B, flared	40
Bowl 10.5" #75B, vegetable	55
Bowl 11" #13B, console	113
Bowl 11" #75F, cupped, float	50
Bowl 11" #114A, 2 sections, handled, deep dessert scalloped or plain edge on divider	700+
Bowl 11" #124A, oval vegetable	300
Bowl 11" #125A, oval, 2 sections, vegetable	350
Bowl 12" #92B or #92F, flared or cupped float	55
Bowl 12" #106B, flared	50
Bowl 12" #113B, handled	160
Bowl 12.5" #17F, round	100
Bowl 13" #92L, mushroom shape	100
Bowl 13" #101, straight sided, float	250
Bowl 14" #104B, flared	150
Bowl 14" #131B, deep, oval	400
Butter w/cover 5.5" #144, round, handled	50
Butter w/cover #161, .25 lb., beads on top	50
Butter w/cover #276, 6.7" California (short) plain top 4.1" wide	195
Butter w/cover #276, 6.7" California (short) graduated beads on top 4.1" wide	165
Cake plate 14" #160, flat, birthday (72 candle holes)	600+
Cake salver 10" #67D, footed w/I bead stem	88
Cake salver 11.25" #103D, footed w/3 bead stem	145
Candelabra 1-lite 6.5" #1752, footed, 3 bead stem w/bobeches & prisms, pair	700+
Candle bowl 1-lite 4.5" #207, 3-toed, pair	250
Candle bowl 1-lite 5" #40C, ruffled, pair	80

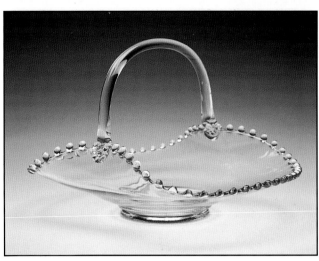

Basket 11.75" wide, 7.5" tall, #73/0, handled, 7.5" tall.

Back: Bowl 11" #13B, console, Viennese Blue. **Front left:** Goblet 5.5" #3400, four bead stem, wine, 4 oz., Nut Brown. **Front center:** Goblet 7.5" #3400, four bead stem, water, 9 oz., Crystal. **Front right:** Goblet 7.75" #3400, four bead stem, water, 10 oz., Nut Brown.

Banana stand 10" #103E, w/3 bead stem.

Cake plate 14" #160, flat, birthday (72 candle holes), floral cutting.

Hurricane lamp 3 piece 14" #152, candlestick/adaptor/chimney
(crimped), shade only, 10.5" tall, 4.75" tall for insert and candle holder.

Candle bowl 1-lite 5" #40CV, ruffled, w/miniature 4.6" peg vase	125
Candle bowl 1-lite 5" #40HC, handled, heart, pair	300
Candle bowl 1-lite 6" #40F, cupped, pair	100
Candle bowl 1-lite 6.5" #40S, square shape, pair	180
Candlestick 1-lite 3.5" #79B, flat, pair	150
Candlestick 1-lite 3.5" #79R, turned up edge, pair	46
Candlestick 1-lite 3.5" #80, bell footed, small beads, pair	40
Candlestick 1-lite 3.5" #81, handled, bell footed, small beads, pair	130
Candlestick 1-lite 3.5" #170, bell footed, large beads, pair	45
Candlestick 1-lite 3.5" #280, flat, no beads on base pair	600
Candlestick 1-lite 4" #155, rayed stem, beaded base, pair	550
Candlestick 1-lite 4.5" #66C, footed, ruffled, pair	210
Candlestick 1-lite 4.5" #66F, footed, cupped, pair	200
Candlestick 1-lite 5" #86, mushroom shape, pair	65
Candlestick 1-lite 5" #90, beaded handle, beaded turned up edge, pair	125
Candlestick 1-lite 5.5" #224, arched tri-stem, pair	500
Candlestick 1-lite 6" #129R, footed, urn, pair	500
Candlestick 1-lite 6.5" #175, 3 bead stem, pair	300
Candlestick 1-lite 9" #196FC, footed, ruffled bowl, pair	475
Candlestick 2-lite 4.75" #100, beads form a circle between candle cups, 5.6" spread, pair	50
Candlestick 3-lite #115, oval, 7.5" spread, pair	275
Candlestick 3-lite #147, one bead stem, pair	72
Candy w/cover 6" #656, (blown) ovoid 5.25" tall	400
Candy w/cover 6.4" tall #140, footed, bead stem; lid w/2 bead finial	325
Candy w/cover 6.5" #59, round, 2 bead finial	50
Candy w/cover 6.5" #59, round, knob finial	80
Candy w/cover 6.5" #245, square base; lid round w/2 bead finial	500
Candy w/cover 7" #110, round, 2 sections	150
Candy w/cover 7" #158, 3 sections	450
Candy w/cover 7" #259, shallow	135
Candy w/cover 7" wide #260, deep, beaded edge, 3 sections; lid w/2 bead finial	250
Candy w/cover 8" #65, round, 2 sections	250
Candy w/cover 8.75" tall #140, bell footed (.5" lipped edge), 2 sections, 8.5" wide; lid w/2 bead finial	1,500+
Cheese & cracker 2 piece: comport 2.5" #88, short stem, 5.5" wide; plate 10" #72D, 2-handled	68
Cheese & cracker 2 piece: comport #157, short stem, 4.75" wide; plate 12" #145, 2-handled plate	95
Cheese & cracker 2 piece: comport #157, short stem, 4.75" wide; plate 14" #92D, flat torte	95
Cheese, cover & cracker 2 piece: comport #66B, short stem, 5.5" wide; plate 14" #92D	95
Cheese, cover & cracker 3 piece: comport #157, short stem, 4.75" wide; cover #144; plate 14" #92D	195
Chip & dip 14" #228, one piece of glass, divided center	750+
Cigarette box w/cover 5.25" #134, oblong w/large beads	50
Cigarette holder 3" #44, collar footed w/small beads on foot	60
Cigarette holder, 4", #1950/776, footed, embossed eagle, Not Candlewick, but a-go-with	25
Clock 4" #M79 (#400/440), ashtray round w/large beads, w/metal works (made for Irice Co.)	250
Clock 4.5" #E109 (#400/34), plate w/metal works (made for Irice Co.)	250
Coaster 4.5" #78, five raised rays	75
Coaster 4.5" #78, beaded edge (small beads) ten raised rays	12
Coaster #226, with spoon rest	24
Comport 4" #66B, bead stem, 5.5"	30
Comport 4" #66B, plain stem, 5.5"	45
Comport 5" #45, flared, 4 bead stem, 5.5" wide	35
Comport 5" #220, 3 beaded open stems, 5.6" wide	150
Comport 5.75" #45, cupped, 4 bead stem, 5.5" wide	85
Comport #48F, cupped, 4 bead stem, 8" wide	100
Comport #48F, cupped, 5 bead stem, 8" wide	300
Comport #67B, 8 panels, dome foot, one bead stem, 9" wide	175
Comport #67C, ruffled, w/1 bead stem, 9" wide	250
Comport #103C, footed, 3 bead stem, ruffled, 10" wide	225
Comport #103F, footed, 3 bead stem, cupped in, 10" wide	295
Comport #137, large, bell footed, oval, 11" wide	2,000+
Cream soup & liner 5.25" #50: bowl handled, 10 oz.; liner 8" plate	75
Creamer #122, individual, beads on handles, 3.5 oz.	20
Creamer 2.25" #126 (same as #153), regular, beads on handles, 6 oz.	50
Creamer #18, (blown) bell bead footed, regular, 6 oz.	100
Creamer 2.75" #30, flat, regular, beads on handles, 6 oz. (old style)	12
Creamer 3.5" #30, flat, regular, beads on handles, 6 oz.	10
Creamer 5" #31, footed, regular, beads on handles, 6 oz.	18
Creamer #31, footed, plain handle w/beads on base, 6 oz.	35
Cruet w/stopper #177, beaded foot, oil & vinegar, 2 oz.	65
Cruet w/stopper #70, handled, oil & vinegar, 4 oz.	100
Cruet w/stopper #164, beaded foot, oil & vinegar, 4 oz.	60
Cruet w/stopper #274, oil & vinegar, 3 spout, 4 oz.	75

Cruet w/stopper #278, handled, oil & vinegar, 3 spout, 4 oz.	85
Cruet w/stopper #71, handled, oil & vinegar, 6 oz.	125
Cruet w/stopper 7.8" #119, oil & vinegar, 6 oz.	35
Cruet w/stopper #121, etched w/oil or vinegar, 6 oz.	85
Cruet w/stopper #166, beaded foot, oil & vinegar, 6 oz.	95
Cruet w/stopper 6.8" #275, oil & vinegar, 3 spouted, 6 oz.	65
Cruet w/stopper #279, handled, oil & vinegar, 3 spouted, 6 oz.	95
Cup & saucer, after dinner: cup #77, 3.5 oz.; saucer 5" w/indent	20
Cup & saucer, tea: cup #35, 6 oz.; saucer 5.75" w/indent	10
Cup #211, punch, round beaded handle, 5 oz.	50
Cup & saucer, coffee: cup 2.8" #37, 6 oz.; #35 saucer 5.75" w/indent	12
Cup bouillon #126: cup 2-handled, 8 oz.; #35 saucer 5.75" w/indent	54
Dealer sign, 5.25" oblong calendar embossed "Imperial Candlewick Crystal"	275
Decanter w/3 bead stopper #82/2, cordial, beaded foot, 15 oz.	1,000+
Decanter w/3 bead stopper 10.75" #82, handled, cordial, beaded foot, 15 oz.	750+
Decanter w/3 bead stopper #18, cordial, beaded foot, 18 oz.	1,000+
Decanter/163 w/stopper 12.25" #163, beaded foot, 26 oz.	500+
Eagle peg 5.5" candlestick adapter #777/1	350
Eagle peg 5.5" figural adapter #777/2	150
Eagle bookend, 9.25" figural adapter on columned & ribbed base #777/3, 5" wide, each	350
Epergne 5.5" #196, 2 piece, ruffled bowl w/1 8.5" lily (horn)	350
Epergne #40CV, 2 piece, candle bowl w/1 lily (horn)	135
Finger bowl 4" #3400, footed, plain	35
Finger bowl 4.25" #3800, footed, plain	85
Goblet #190, bell beaded foot, cordial, 1 oz.	125
Goblet 4.5" #3400, 4 bead stem, cordial, 1 oz.	40
Goblet #3800, two bead stem, cordial, 1 oz.	65
Goblet #3800, brandy, 1 oz.	145
Goblet 3.25" #4000, two bead stem, cordial, 1.25 oz.	65
Goblet #195, hollow stem, wine, 2 oz.	250
Goblet #3800, two bead stem, wine, 2 oz.	35
Goblet #190, high, bell beaded foot, seafood cocktail (lipped edge)	95
Goblet #3800, two bead stem, cocktail, 3.5 oz.	25
Goblet #190, bell beaded foot, cocktail, 4 oz.	30
Goblet #195, hollow stem, cocktail, 4 oz.	250
Goblet 3.4" #3400, oyster cocktail, 4 oz.	20
Goblet 3.4" #3400, oyster cocktail, 4 oz. (optic)	50
Goblet 4.5" #3400, four bead stem, cocktail, 4 oz.	30
Goblet 5.5" #3400, four bead stem, wine, 4 oz.	28
Goblet #4000, 3 bead stem, cocktail, 4 oz.	35
Goblet 5.4" #190, bell beaded foot, wine, 5 oz.	35
Goblet 6.1" #3400, four bead stem, claret, 5 oz.	55
Goblet #3800, two bead stem, claret, 5 oz.	45
Goblet #4000, 3 bead stem, wine, 5 oz.	40
Goblet 4.25" #190, bell beaded foot, sherbet, 6 oz.	22
Goblet #195, hollow stem, dessert, 6 oz.	250
Goblet #195, hollow stem, juice, 6 oz.	250
Goblet 5" #3400, four bead stem, saucer champagne, 6 oz.	19
Goblet #3800, one bead stem, sherbet, 6 oz.	35
Goblet #3800, two bead stem, saucer champagne, 6 oz.	50
Goblet #3800, two bead stem, saucer champagne, 6 oz. (optic)	150
Goblet #4000, 3 bead stem, saucer champagne, 6 oz.	35
Goblet #195, hollow stem, old fashion, 9 oz.	250
Goblet 7.5" #3400, four bead stem, water, 9 oz.	25
Goblet 7.5" #3400, four bead stem, flared water, 9 oz. (optic)	130
Goblet #3800, two bead stem, water, 9 oz.	45
Goblet #3800, two bead stem, water, 9 oz. (optic)	200
Goblet 7.75" #3400, four bead stem, water, 10 oz. (not made in crystal)	
Goblet #195, hollow stem, water, 11 oz.	300
Goblet 6" #4000, 3 bead stem, water, 11 oz.	50
Goblet #195, hollow stem, ice tea, 14 oz.	300
Gravy boat & liner: bowl #169, oval, sauce (no beads); liner #169, oval, plate w/indent	175
Heart shape 4.5" #201, handled, bonbon	75
Heart shape 5" #40H, handled, bonbon, 5.75" long	33
Heart shape 5" #49/1, fruit bowl, 4.75" long	23
Heart shape 6" #51H, handled, shallow, bonbon	35
Heart shape 6" #51T, center handled, wafer	35
Heart shape 5.5" #53H, nappy	28
Heart shape 5.5" #173, nut dish	11
Heart shape 5.5" #202, handled, bonbon	85
Heart shape 6.5" #203, handled, bonbon	95
Heart shape 9" #49H, salad bowl, 9.5" long	175
Heart shape 9" #73H, handled salad	225
Hospitality tray 6.5" #269, triangle shaped w/beads on one edge (6 form circle) each	450+
Hurricane lamp 2 piece 11.5" #178, candle base & chimney, each	750
Hurricane lamp 2 piece 12" #14994, candlestick & chimney, each	125
Hurricane lamp 2 piece 13.5" #79, high, candlestick & chimney, each	200

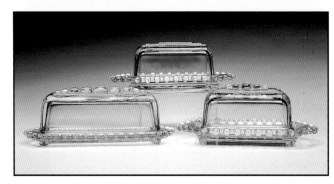

Top: Butter w/cover #276, 6.7" California (short) plain top 4.1" wide. **Bottom left:** Butter w/cover #161, .25 lb, beads on top. **Bottom right:** Butter w/cover #276, 6.7" California (short) graduated beads on top 4.1" wide.

Relish 10.5" #262, tab handled, 3 sections, butter/jam, 7" wide.

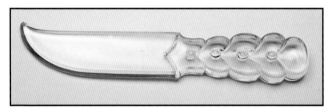

Knife, butter 8.5" #4000, pattern on handle (4 half beads on each side).

Toast w/cover 7.75" #123, lid (no pattern) beaded edge on liner, 4.5" tall.

Top: Bowl 5" #231, square shape. **Bottom left:** Bowl 6" #53X, baked apple. **Bottom right:** Bowl 5.5" #53, crimped.

Back left: Candle bowl 1-lite 5" #40C, ruffled. **Top center:** Candlestick 2-lite 4.75" #100, beads form a circle between candle cups, 5.6" spread. **Top right:** Candlestick 3-lite #115, oval, 7.5" spread. **Bottom left:** Candlestick 1-lite 3.5" #79R, turned up edge. **Bottom center:** Candle bowl 1-lite 5" #40CV, ruffled, w/miniature 4.6" peg vase. **Back right:** Candle bowl 1-lite 6" #40F, cupped. **Front right:** Candlestick 1-lite 5" #86, mushroom shape.

Top center: Sugar 2.75" #30, flat, regular, beads on handles, 6 oz.; Creamer 2.75" #30, flat, regular, beads on handles, 6 oz.; both w/floral cutting. **Far left:** Sugar 4.25" #31, footed, regular, beads on handles, 6 oz., floral cutting. **Far right:** Creamer 5" #31, footed, regular, beads on handles, 6 oz., floral cutting. **Bottom center:** Sugar 2.25" #126 (same as #153), regular, flared, beads on handles, 6 oz.; Creamer 2.25" #126 (same as #153), regular, beads on handles, 6 oz., both floral w/Gold encrusted; Tray 6.5" #29, oblong for cream/sugar.

Back left: Tumbler 5.25" #19, straight sided, beaded foot, water, 10 oz. **Back center:** Marmalade 4 piece #89: jar, lid, liner, ladle. **Back right:** Tumbler 2" #19, ball footed sherbet, 5 oz., 3.75" wide. **Front left:** Cigarette holder 3" #44, collar footed w/small beads on foot. **Front center:** Nut cup 2.75" #64, individual almond or sugar dip. **Front right:** Tumbler 2.1" #19, beaded foot, low, cocktail, 3 oz.

Hurricane lamp 3 piece 14" #152, candlestick/adaptor/chimney (crimped) each	295
Hurricane lamp 3 piece 14" #152R, candlestick, adaptor & chimney (plain) each	325
Hurricane lamp 2 piece 14" #14996, candlestick & chimney, each	125
Hurricane lamp 3 piece 15" #142K/HL, rose bowl, adapter & chimney, each	500+
Hurricane lamp 3 piece 16" #32, ribbed (Lightolier) base/adaptor/chimney, each	800+
Hurricane lamp 3 piece #26, kerosene base, adaptor & chimney, each	2,000+
Hurricane lamp 2 piece #76, handled, candlestick & chimney, each	450+
Hurricane lamp 2 piece #264, black out light, 3 stem w/beads & chimney, each	300+
Hurricane lamp 5 piece #680, 2-lite candlestick, 2 adapters & w chimneys, each	2,000+
Hurricane lamp 3 piece #1753, candlestick #175, adaptor/prisms & chimney, each	600+
Ice bucket 7-8" #63, 5.5" deep	150
Ice bucket 7" #168, tab handled, deep	275
Ice dish 5.5" #53C, 3-tab risers (hold inserts)	125
Ice dish insert #530, fruit cocktail, 5.5 oz.	35
Ice dish insert #530, tomato juice, 5.5 oz.	60
Jar set w/cover 10.75" #655: 3 ovoid ball jars, 6" wide; w/lid 2 bead finial	700+
Jelly w/cover #157, footed, one bead stem	125
Knife, butter 8.5" #4000, pattern on handle (4 half beads on each side)	450+
Ladle 4.75" #130, 3 bead handle, jam or marmalade	20
Ladle 5.75" #165, 3 bead handled, mayonnaise	16
Ladle 6.5" #135, two bead handle, mayonnaise	18
Ladle 9.5" #255, small size punch, 2 spouted, no beads	150
Ladle 9.5" #139, covered punch	55
Ladle 13" #91, (blown) large punch	70
Lazy susan 3 piece: 10" #1503, tray, ball bearing ring & 4" ashtray	300
Marmalade 2 piece #89: jar; dimple on lid (no finial)	80
Marmalade 3 piece #89: jar; lid 2 bead finial; ladle	60
Marmalade 3 piece 3.5" #289: jar, heavy base; lid; ladle	60
Marmalade 3 piece #1989: straight sided, beads on base; lid; ladle	85
Marmalade 3 piece #8918: 4.5" tall, belled, beads on base; lid; ladle	145
Marmalade 4 piece #89: jar; lid; liner; ladle	70
Mayonnaise 6.25" #84, salad dressing	32
Mayonnaise 2 piece #23: bowl; liner w/indent	38
Mayonnaise 3 piece #40: bowl; liner w/indent; ladle	58
Mayonnaise 3 piece #42/3: bowl; handled liner w/indent; ladle	47
Mayonnaise 3 piece #49: heart bowl; liner w/indent; ladle	45
Mayonnaise 3 piece #52/3: bowl; handled liner w/indent; ladle	60
Mayonnaise 3 piece #496: bowl, heart shape; liner triangular w/indent; ladle	500+
Mayonnaise 4 piece #84: divided bowl; liner w/indent; 2 ladles	100
Mirror 4.25", (made for Irice Co.) question mark handle	150
Mirror 6.5" #1776/3, w/eagle at top	75
Mirror #E55, upright, dome beaded foot, peg to fit in ferrule, swivel (made for Irice Co.)	250
Mirror 8.75" #E129, hand, 5 beads on handle (made for Irice Co.)	150
Muddler 4.5" #19	25
Mustard/cover 4" #156, beaded foot, 2.5" wide, lid w/2 bead finial	95
Nut cup 2.75" #64, individual almond or sugar dip	12
Picture frame 6.5" #1776/2, w/eagle	100
Pitcher #330, rum pot (no beads) 14 oz.	400
Pitcher 6" #16, flat, handle w/beads 16 oz.	275
Pitcher 6.75" #19, beaded foot, Lilliputian, 16 oz.	325
Pitcher #416, handle (plain) 20 oz.	125
Pitcher 9.75" #18, footed, handled, Manhattan, 40 oz.	350
Pitcher #19, flat, handled, cocktail, 40 oz.	295
Pitcher 9.25" #419, handle (plain) 40 oz.	125
Pitcher #24, flat, handle w/beads, 64 oz.	450
Pitcher #424, handle (plain) 64 oz. or 80 oz. (2 sizes)	85
Pitcher 10" #18, beaded foot, handled, 80 oz.	345

Pitcher #24, flat, handle w/beads, 80 oz.	225
Plate 4.5" #34, individual butter	11
Plate 5.5" #42D, 2-handled	14
Plate 6" #1D, bread & butter	10
Plate 6" #39, off center 2.5" indent (seat), canape	18
Plate 6.25" #36, off center 2" indent (seat), canape	23
Plate 6.75" #52C, 2-handled, ruffled	45
Plate 7" #3D, salad	11
Plate 7" #52E, 2-handled, sides turned up	50
Plate 7.5" #52D, 2-handled	18
Plate 8" #5D, salad	12
Plate 8.5" #62C, 2 handles turned up, ruffled	40
Plate 8.5" #62D, 2-handled	15
Plate 8.5" #120, crescent salad	80
Plate 8.75" #7D, luncheon	18
Plate 9" #38, oval salad	60
Plate 9.5" #98, oval snack w/off center indent	25
Plate 10" #72C, 2-handled, ruffled	50
Plate 10.5" #10D, dinner	50
Plate 12" #145D, 2-handled	45
Plate 12" #13D, service	38
Plate 12" #145C, 2-handled, ruffled	75
Plate 12" #75V, small center, turned up edge, cabaret	35
Plate 12.5" #124, oval	95
Plate 13.5" #92V, small center, turned up edge, cabaret	55
Plate 14" #17D, torte	55
Plate 14" #113D, 2-handled	65
Plate 17" #20D, flat edge torte or punch bowl liner	65
Plate 17" #20V, cupped, torte or punch bowl liner	65
Platter 13" #124D, oval	105
Platter 16" #131D, oval	250
Powder box & cover #E409, (made for Irice Co.) beaded foot; lid w/3 bead finial	125
Punch 15 piece #20, 12 cups, liner & ladle	300
Punch 15 piece #128, 12 cups, base & ladle	450
Punch bowl w/cover #139/2, beaded foot, lid w/2 bead finial (family)	1,100+
Punch 11 piece #139/77, covered family eight cups, bowl, lid, & ladle	1,250+
Punch 15 piece #210, w/high base 12 cups, liner & ladle	1,200+
Relish 6.5" #54, tab handled, 2 sections, round	20
Relish 7" #234, square, 2 sections (diagonal divided)	195
Relish 7.5" #57, oval pickle	45
Relish 8" #268, tab handled, oval, 2 sections	30
Relish 8.5" #55, 4-tab handles, round, 4 sections	25
Relish 8.5" #58, oval, pickle or celery	25
Relish 10" #208, 3-toed, irregular shaped, 3 sections w/curved dividers	130
Relish 10" #213, oblong, tab handled, 4 sections	95
Relish 10" #213, oblong, tab handled (not divided)	400+
Relish 10" #217, pickle w/curled handles	40
Relish 10.5" #56, round, 3 sections	65
Relish 10.5" #56, five tab handles, 5 sections, round	50
Relish 10.5" #256, tab handled, oval, 2 sections	45
Relish 10.5" #262, tab handled, 3 sections, butter/jams, 7" wide	195
Relish 11" #46, oval celery, irregular shaped	100
Relish 12" #215, tab handled, 3 equal sections & celery section	95
Relish w/cover 12" #216, tab handled, oblong	500+
Relish 13" #102, round, 4 equal sections & celery section	110
Relish 13.5" #105, celery w/curled handles	50
Relish 13.5" #209, round, 5 sections (starfish shaped divider)	500+
Salad fork/spoon 9" #75, six beads form handle, set	40
Salt dip 2" #61, deep	14
Salt dip 2.25" #19, shallow	12
Sandwich server 11.75" #68D, w/heart shaped center handle	50
Shaker 2.25" #109, individual, beaded foot/chrome top, pair	24
Shaker 2.25" #109, individual, beaded foot/plastic top, pair	22
Shaker 2.75" #96, beaded foot w/chrome or plastic top, pair	20
Shaker 4" #247, straight sided, beaded foot w/chrome top, pair	30
Shaker 4.5" #167, beaded foot w/chrome top, pair	24
Shaker #116, one bead stem w/plastic top, pair	195
Shaker 5" #190, high, bell beaded foot & chrome top, pair	75
Snack jar w/cover 6.25" #139/1, beaded foot, 5" wide	750+
Spoon 2.6" #4000, salt size	30
Spoon 2.7" #616, salt size	30
Sugar #122, individual, beads on handles, 3.5 oz.	20
Sugar #126 (same as #153), regular, flared, beads on handles, 6 oz.	50
Sugar #18, (blown) bell beaded foot, regular, 6 oz.	100
Sugar 2.75" #30, flat, regular, beads on handles, 6 oz. (old style)	12
Sugar 3.25" #30, flat, regular, beads on handles, 6 oz.	10
Sugar 4.25" #31, footed, regular, beads on handles, 6 oz.	18
Sugar 4.25" #31, regular, plain handled, beaded foot, 6 oz.	35
Tidbit 2 tier bowls #17TB, (5" & 7.5") w/wood center handle	225

Top back center: Plate 4.5" #34, individual butter; Mustard/cover 4" #156, beaded foot, lid w/2 bead finial, 2.5" wide. **Top left:** Shaker 2.75" #96, beaded foot w/chrome top. **Center left:** Cruets w/stoppers 7.8" #119, oil & vinegar, 6 oz.; Shaker 2.75" #96, beaded foot w/chrome top; Tray 9" #159, oval, plain center. **Center right:** Cruets w/stoppers 6.8" #275, oil & vinegar, 3 spouted, 6 oz.; Shaker 2.75" #96, beaded foot w/chrome top; Tray 9" #159, oval, plain center. **Front left:** Shaker 4" #247, straight sided, beaded foot w/chrome top. **Front center:** Salt dip 2" #61, deep; Nut cup 2.75" #64, individual almond or sugar dip. **Front right:** Shaker 4" #247, straight sided, beaded foot w/chrome top, shown w/silver band at top.

Left: Decanter w/stopper 12.25" #163, beaded foot, 26 oz. **Right:** Decanter w/3 bead stopper 10.75" #82, handled, cordial, beaded foot, 15 oz.

Left: Candy w/cover 7" wide #260, deep, beaded edge, 3 sections; lid w/2 bead finial. **Center:** Candy w/cover 8.75" tall #140, bell footed (.5" lipped edge), 2 sections, 8.5" wide; lid w/2 bead finial. **Right:** Candy w/cover 6.4" tall #140, footed, bead stem; lid w/2 bead finial.

Candy w/cover 6.5" #245, square base; lid round w/2 bead finial.

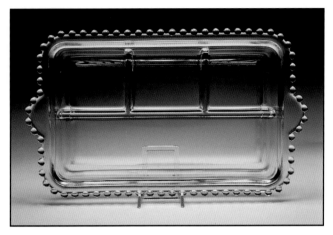

Relish 12" #215, tab handled, 3 equal sections & celery section.

Left: Cigarette holder, 4", #1950/776, footed, embossed eagle, not Candlewick, but a go with. **Right:** Ashtray 6.5" #1776/1, Eagle at top, 3.75" wide, shown w/original label.

Tidbit 2 tier bowls #2701, (7.5" & 10.5") cupped edge w/chrome handle	125
Tidbit 2 tier plates #73TB, (7.5" & 10.5") w/wood center handle	275
Tidbit 3 tier bowl set #18TB, (5", 6" & 7") w/wood center handle	275
Toast w/cover 7.75" #123, lid (no pattern) beaded edge on liner	450
Tray 5" #96T, oblong for s & p	22
Tray 5.5" #42E, 2-handled, mint, sides turned up	35
Tray 5.5" #221, 3 patterned stems center handle, lemon server	55
Tray 6" #51M, flat, handled, round, card	195
Tray 6.5" #29, oblong for cream/sugar, 3.75" wide	23
Tray 8" #169, oval	50
Tray 8" #171, (keyhole shape)	52
Tray 8" #222, 3 arched patterned stems form center handle	350+
Tray 8.5" #62C, handles turned up, crimped	35
Tray 8.5" #62E, handles turned up	35
Tray 9" #149D, center heart handled, mint	38
Tray 9" #159, oval, plain center	40
Tray 9" #M152, oval mirror, curved lines on underside (made for Irice Co.)	60
Tray 9.25" #148, condiment w/indents	200
Tray 10" #72E, muffin w/handles turned up	65
Tray 10" #151, round (graduated circles pattern in base)	58
Tray 10.5" #68F, center heart handled, fruit w/turned up edge	275
Tray 11" #E666, round mirror, beaded edge (made for Irice Co.)	55
Tray 11.5" #145E, handles turned up	45
Tray 11.5" #145H, handles turned up, muffin	400+
Tray 11.5" #154, deviled egg server w/heart shaped center handle	195
Tray 14" #113E, handles turned up, muffin	175
Tumbler #19, straight sided, beaded foot, wine, 3 oz.	45
Tumbler 2.1" #19, beaded foot, low, cocktail, 3 oz.	30
Tumbler #18, beaded foot, cocktail, 3.5 oz.	80
Tumbler #3400, 2 piece, seafood cocktail w/insert, 4 oz.	125
Tumbler #3800, 2 piece, fruit cocktail/insert, 4 oz.	80
Tumbler #18, bell beaded foot, juice, 5 oz.	125
Tumbler 2" #19, bead footed sherbet, 5 oz., 3.75" wide	18
Tumbler #19, straight sided, beaded foot, juice, 5 oz.	15
Tumbler 3.9" #3400, footed, w/1 bead, sherbet, 5 oz.	20
Tumbler 4.75" #3400, footed, w/1 bead, juice, 5 oz.	25
Tumbler #3800, one bead stem, juice, 5 oz.	40
Tumbler #15, beaded foot, juice, 6 oz.	195
Tumbler #18, beaded foot sherbet, 6 oz.	80
Tumbler #19, beaded foot, large beads, egg cup, 6 oz.	60
Tumbler #19, bell beaded foot, small beads, egg cup, 6 oz.	95
Tumbler 6.25" #3400, footed, one bead stem, parfait, 6 oz.	75
Tumbler #18, bell beaded foot, hi ball, 7 oz.	85
Tumbler #18, bell beaded foot, parfait, 7 oz.	125
Tumbler #19, straight sided, beaded foot, old fashion, 7 oz.	40
Tumbler #195, old fashion, 8 oz.	300
Tumbler #18, bell beaded foot, water, 9 oz.	85
Tumbler 5.75" #3400, footed, one bead stem, water, 9 oz.	45
Tumbler 5.75" #3400, footed, one bead stem, flared, lunch water, 9 oz. (optic)	200
Tumbler #3800, one bead stem, water, 9 oz.	35
Tumbler #15, beaded foot, water, 10 oz.	225
Tumbler 5.25" #19, straight sided, beaded foot, water, 10 oz.	18
Tumbler 5.9" #3400, footed w/1 bead stem, water, 10 oz.	30
Tumbler #3800, two bead stem, water, 10 oz.	40
Tumbler #18, bell beaded foot, ice tea, 12 oz.	85
Tumbler 5.4" #19, straight sided, beaded foot, ice tea, 12 oz.	23
Tumbler #195, footed, brandy sniffer, 12 oz.	300
Tumbler 6.5" #3400, footed w/1 bead stem, ice tea, 12 oz.	24
Tumbler #3800, one bead stem, ice tea, 12 oz.	35
Tumbler #3800, one bead stem, ice tea, 12 oz. (optic)	175
Tumbler #4000 bead stem, straight sided, ice tea, 12 oz.	40
Tumbler #15, beaded foot, ice tea, 13 oz.	225
Tumbler 6" #19, straight sided, beaded foot, ice tea, 14 oz.	25
Tumbler #195, beaded foot, jumbo, 16 oz.	250
Vase 3.75" #25, beaded foot, spherical & necked w/ruffled top	65
Vase 5.75" #107, bell beaded foot, small beads, mini bud vase	85
Vase 5.75" #107, beaded foot, large beads, crimped	75
Vase 6" #138B, footed, one bead stem, flared w/beads on top edge	245
Vase 6" #198, beads on top rim	450
Vase 6" #242, bell, flat, necked & flared/beads on top edge, w/frog insert	600+
Vase 6" #287C, beads on sides, crimped	75
Vase 6" #287F, beads on sides, fan	75
Vase 7" #87R, beads on handles & rolled top edge	50
Vase 7" #87R, beads on 2 smooth handles & rolled edge	70
Vase 7" #142K, rose bowl w/beads at top	300+
Vase 7" #185, bell beaded foot, hour glass shape	200
Vase 7" #186, bell beaded foot, shouldered	400
Vase 7" #187, bell beaded foot (2 steps up on bowl of vase)	500+
Vase 7" #188, bell beaded foot, ivy bowl (brandy sniffer shape)	265

Vase 7.25" #132C, bell beaded foot, rose bowl, crimped top — 500+
Vase 7.5" #132, bell beaded foot, rose bowl, plain top — 500+
Vase 8" #87C, beads on sides, crimped top — 48
Vase 8" #87C, beads on handles, crimped top — 70
Vase 8" #87F, beads on handles & top edge, fan top — 35
Vase 8" #87F, beads on handles, fan top — 45
Vase 8" #143A, round, flip, beads on top — 350
Vase 8" #143C, flip, beads top — 145
Vase 8.5" #21, bell beaded foot, flared — 325
Vase 8.5" #27, beaded foot, tapered — 425
Vase 8.5" #28, beaded foot, spherical, round top — 250
Vase 8.5" #28C, beaded foot, spherical, crimped — 145
Vase 8.5" #227, beaded foot, (ewer) handled — 500+
Vase 9" #189, high, bell beaded foot, 2 graduated steps up on bowl of vase — 275
Vase 10" #22, beaded foot & straight sided — 300
Vase 10" #192, bell beaded foot, 2 graduated steps up on bowl of vase — 500+
Vase 10" #193, bell beaded foot, 3 graduated steps up on bowl of vase — 500+
Vase 10" #194, bell beaded foot, necked in & flared — 500+

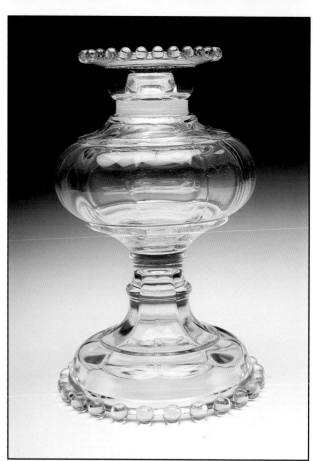

Hurricane lamp 3 piece #26, kerosene base, adaptor, shown missing chimney.

Left: Hurricane lamp 2 piece 13.5" #79, high, candlestick & chimney hand painted pink flowers. **Right:** Hurricane lamp 2 piece 13.5" #79, high, candlestick & chimney hand painted gold flowers.

Punch bowl w/cover #139/2, beaded foot, lid w/2 bead finial (family).

Left: Vase 10" #192, bell beaded foot, 2 graduated steps up on bowl of vase. **Right:** Vase 10" #194, bell beaded foot, necked in & flared.

Left: Pitcher 10" #18, beaded foot, handled, 80 oz. **Center:** Pitcher 6.75" #19, beaded foot, Lilliputian, 16 oz. **Right:** Pitcher 9.75 #18, footed, handled, Manhattan, 40 oz.

Back left: Bell 5" #108, handle w/4 graduated beads. **Back center:** Eagle bookend, 9.25" figural adapter on columned and ribbed base, #777/3 5" wide. **Back right:** Comport 5" #220, 3 beaded open stems, 5.6" wide. **Front left:** Bowl 6" #183, 3-toed, 5.6" wide. **Front center:** Tray 5.5" #221, lemon server, 3 patterned stems center handle. **Front right:** Comport 5" #45, flared, 4 bead stem, 5.5" wide.

Top left: Vase 8.5" #28C, beaded foot, spherical, crimped. **Top right:** Vase 8" #87C, beads on handles, crimped top. **Bottom left to right:** Vase 3.75" #25, beaded foot, spherical & necked w/ruffled top; Vase 8" #87C, beads on sides, crimped top, floral cut; Vase 6" #287F, beads on sides, fan; Vase 8" #87F, beads on handles, fan top; Vase 6" #287C, beads on sides, crimped; Vase 8.5" #21, bell beaded foot, flared.

CANTERBURY
Duncan & Miller
1938-55

Blank #115 & Blown items #5115

Main Color: Crystal
Other Colors: Amberina, Cape Cod Blue, Chartreuse, Ebony (black), Jasmine Yellow, Milk Glass, Ruby, and Shell Pink

During World War II, with a shortage of Crystal glassware coming into this country, Duncan & Miller designed Canterbury. Most pieces will have six bulging, petal-like panels. When looking at the bottom of these pieces, you will see what looks like the outline of a flower. Even on the stems, when looking at the base of the bowl connected to the stem, you will find this flower outline. This fact makes it easy to recognize. Made primarily in Crystal, a few pieces were also made in colors. Later, after Duncan closed, the moulds were transferred to Tiffin, where a variety of colors were made. The following colors were produced by them: Copen Blue, Citron Green, Desert Red, Greenbriar, Golden Banana, Smoke, and Twilight. It is difficult to get any item in the Twilight color, because the collectors of this color tend to drive the prices up. Twilight imitates the rare earth color of the gem stone Alexandrite. It changes color under different lighting sources.

Elusive to collectors are the following items: applied handle mugs, martini pitcher, and candelabras. The basket measurement used does not include the handle on this pattern.

Since it is primarily a crystal pattern, we are only giving those values. Occasionally colored pieces in this pattern do appear, but not in large enough quantities to build a set. This is an excellent pattern for a new collector to start with since pieces are plentiful and reasonable in price.

CANTERBURY	Crystal
Ashtray 3" #93, deep, club, 1.75" high	5
Ashtray 3" #99, or lid to cigarette jar	14
Ashtray 3.5" #96, rectangular	4
Ashtray 4.5" #94, deep, club, 2.5" high	9
Ashtray 4.5" #97, rectangular	5
Ashtray 5", flat, crimped, bowl shape	14
Ashtray 5.5" #95, deep, club, 3" high	12
Ashtray 6.5" #98, rectangular	7
Basket 3", deep, oval w/applied handle	24
Basket 3", high, deep, crimped w/applied handle	28
Basket 3.5", deep, oval w/applied handle	26
Basket 3.5", high, deep, crimped w/applied handle	30
Basket 4.5", deep, oval w/applied handle	30
Basket 4.5", high, deep, crimped w/applied handle	35
Basket 10" #91, deep, tall, crimped w/applied handle	60
Basket 10" #92, low, oval w/applied tall handle	65
Basket 11.5" #92, low, oval w/applied tall handle	68
Bowl 4.5", sherbet, crimped	10
Bowl 5" #84, fruit nappy	7
Bowl 5.5", sherbet, crimped	9
Bowl 5.5" #85, (heart, round, star or square shape) 4 styles w/1-tab handle	12
Bowl 6" #86, round 2-tab handles, nappy	12
Bowl 6" #86, 2-tab handles, star shape, sweetmeat	15
Bowl 7.5", crimped	17
Bowl 7.5", shallow, gardenia	20
Bowl 8", crimped shallow fruit or flared vegetable (2 styles)	24
Bowl 9" #107, shallow fruit or gardenia (2 styles)	28
Bowl 9", oval, 2 sides turned up	26
Bowl 10", deep, salad	35
Bowl 10" #109, deep, oval, 2 sides turned up	30
Bowl 10.5" #108, shallow, crimped, fruit	30
Bowl 11.5" #115, oval, shallow w/2 sides pulled up	30

Back left: Goblet 6" #1, dinner water, 9 oz. **Back right:** Decanter w/ stopper 12", cylindrical w/2 rings on neck, 32 oz. **Front left:** Goblet 4.5" #2, saucer champagne, 6 oz. **Front center:** Goblet 3.75" #10, sherbet, 8 oz. **Front right:** Goblet 3.8" #7, sea food/oyster cocktail, 4.5 oz.

Comport 5.5" #87, flared, 6" wide, Rockwell sterling silver encapsulated (the Rockwell shield mark on bottom of foot).

Back row: Comport 5.5" #87, flared, 6" wide, Ruby. **Back center:** Cruet w/stopper 5.6" #73, spherical, 3 oz., Crystal. **Back right:** Basket 4.5", high, deep, crimped w/applied handle, Blue Opalescent. **Front left:** Tray 8" #63, tab handled, for individual cream/sugar or used for #73 cruets, Crystal. **Front center:** Cigarette box w/cover 4.75" #99, rectangular, Crystal. **Front right:** Basket 10" #92, low, oval w/applied tall handle, Crystal.

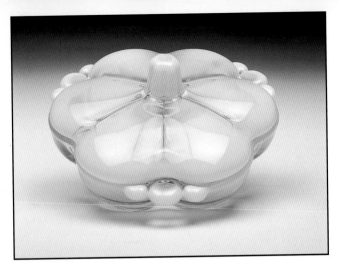

Candy w/cover 8" #89, flat, 3-tab handled, 3 equal sections, cylindrical, paneled finial, Pink Opalescent.

Left: Candy w/cover 5.75", flat, domed top w/tear drop finial, Crystal.
Right: Pitcher 9.25" #79, handled, martini mixer w/ice lip, 32 oz., Crystal.

Relish 8" #89, 3-tab handled, 3 sections (candy bottom), Ruby.

Bowl 12", oval, flared	35
Bowl 12", (deep, crimped salad, gardenia, shallow salad) 4 styles	35
Bowl 13", oval, crimped, fruit	38
Bowl 13" #110, deep, oval, flared, center piece	38
Bowl 15", shallow, salad or flower	40
Candelabra 1-lite 6.5", fancy stem bobeche & prisms, pair	80
Candelabra 2-lite 6.75" #123, leaf arms, bobeches/prisms, pair	195
Candelabra 3-lite 7", two open arms 2 bobeches/prisms 11" spread, pair	195
Candelabra 3-lite 7", two open arms 3 bobeches/prisms 11" spread, pair	245
Candlestick 1-lite 3" #121, low, footed, wafer stem, pair	24
Candlestick 1-lite 6", fancy leaf stem, pair	38
Candlestick 2-lite 6.5" #122, leaf arms w/center leaf, pair	65
Candlestick 3-lite 6", fancy leaf stem w/2 open arms 10" spread, pair	80
Candy w/cover 5.75", flat, domed top w/tear drop finial	40
Candy w/cover 8" #89, flat, 3-tab handled, 3 equal sections, cylindrical, paneled finial	32
Candy w/cover 9" #90, footed, ball stem, domed top w/tear drop finial	45
Cheese & cracker: comport 3.5" #82, short stem, 5.75" wide; plate 11", tab handled	40
Cigarette box w/cover 4.75" #99, rectangular	25
Cigarette holder 3", top hat, 2 sides rolled over	18
Cigarette jar w/cover 4", round, cylinder	35
Comport 4" #83, shallow mint	15
Comport 4.75", crimped, 6" wide	18
Comport 5.5" #87, flared, 6" wide	18
Comport 5.5" #88, shallow, crimped, 7.5" wide	18
Creamer 2.6" #62, flat, individual, open handle, 3 oz.	6
Creamer 3.75" #66, flat, regular, open handle, 7 oz.	8
Cruet w/stopper 5.6" #73, spherical, 3 oz.	30
Cup & saucer, coffee or tea #32: cup 2.6", flat, 6 oz.; saucer w/indent 6"	10
Decanter w/stopper 12", cylindrical w/2 rings on neck, 32 oz.	85
Finger bowl 4.25" #16, or dessert dish, 2" high	10
Goblet 4.25", (blown) cordial, 1 oz.	25
Goblet 5.25", (blown) liquor cocktail, 3 oz.	12
Goblet 4.25" #3, liquor cocktail, 3.5 oz.	10
Goblet 6", (blown) wine, 3.5 oz.	16
Goblet 5" #4, claret/wine, 4 oz.	16
Goblet 3.8" #7, sea food/oyster cocktail, 4.5 oz.	8
Goblet 5.5", (blown) ice cream, 5 oz.	9
Goblet 5.5", (blown) saucer champagne, 5 oz.	10
Goblet 6.75", (blown) claret, 5 oz.	18
Goblet 4.5" #2, saucer champagne, 6 oz.	10
Goblet 3.75" #10, sherbet, 8 oz.	7
Goblet 5.5" #9, lunch water, 9 oz.	14
Goblet 6" #1, dinner water, 9 oz.	16
Goblet 7.25", (blown) water, 10 oz.	18
Ice bucket 6", straight sided, no handle (also a vase)	28
Ice bucket 7", straight sided, no handle (also a vase)	30
Marmalade & liner: bowl 4.5" #48, flat, crimped; liner w/indent 6"	24
Mayonnaise 3 piece: bowl 5", flat; liner w/indent 8.5"; ladle	34
Mayonnaise 4 piece: bowl 5", flat, salad dressing; liner w/indent 8.5"; 2 ladles	45
Mayonnaise 3 piece: bowl 5.5" #50, flat, crimped; liner w/indent 7.5"; ladle	38
Mayonnaise 4 piece: bowl 5.5" #51, flat, flared, salad dressing; liner w/indent 7.5"; 2 ladles	48
Mayonnaise 3 piece: bowl 6", flat; liner w/indent 8.5"; ladle	45
Mayonnaise 4 piece: bowl 6", flat, salad dressing; liner w/indent 8.5"; 2 ladles	58
Mug 5.6", straight sided, beverage w/applied handle, 11 oz.	48
Mug 6.25" #11, straight sided, ice tea w/applied handle, 13 oz.	60
Pitcher 4.75" #80, squat, milk jug, 16 oz.	24
Pitcher 9.25" #79, martini mixer w/ice lip, 32 oz.	65
Pitcher 9.25" #79, handled, martini mixer w/ice lip, 32 oz.	78
Pitcher 7.75" #115/81, handled, water w/ice lip, 64 oz.	125
Plate 6" #25, bread & butter	5
Plate 7.5" #26, salad or dessert	8
Plate 7.5" #30, tab handled, lemon server	12
Plate 8.5" #27, lunch	10
Plate 11" #28, large dinner or service	20
Plate 11.5" #31, tab handled, sandwich	20
Plate 14" #29, torte or service (small center)	26
Relish 6", oval, tab handled, olive	12
Relish 6" #52, tab handled, 2 sections, round or star shape	14
Relish 7", oval, tab handled, 2 sections	16
Relish 7", oval, 3 sections	18
Relish 8.6", oblong, 2 sections, two 3-ball tab handles	20
Relish 8", oblong pickle	12
Relish 8" #89, 3-tab handled, 3 equal sections (candy bottom)	16
Relish 9" #53, tab handled, oblong, 2 sections	20
Relish 9" #54, 3-tab handled, 3 sections, flared	22
Relish 10.5", tab handled, 2 sections w/curved divider, celery	28
Relish 10.5" #5, tab handled, 2 equal sections & celery section	28
Relish 11" #56, oblong celery	16

Relish 11" #57, oblong, 2 equal sections & celery section	20
Relish 12" #58, round, 4 equal sections & celery section	35
Shaker 3.75" #70, flat, spherical, chrome top, pair	18
Sugar 2.5" #61, flat, individual, open handles, 3 oz.	7
Sugar 3.25" #65, flat, regular, open handles, 7 oz.	9
Tray 6" #72, tab handled, for individual shakers	10
Tray 8" #63, tab handled, for individual cream/sugar or used for #73 cruets	12
Tray 9" #76, tab handled, holds 2 shakers/cruets	12
Tray 10" #67, tab handled, for regular cream/sugar	14
Tumbler 2.5" #15, flat, straight sided, whiskey, 1.5 oz.	12
Tumbler 3.25", (blown) footed, oyster cocktail, 4 oz.	8
Tumbler 2.5", (blown) footed, ice cream, short stem, 5 oz.	8
Tumbler 3.75" #13, flat, straight sided, orange juice, 5 oz.	9
Tumbler 4.25" #6, footed orange juice, 5 oz.	10
Tumbler 4.25", (blown) footed orange juice, 5 oz.	12
Tumbler 3.25" #14, flat, straight sided, old fashion, 7 oz.	8
Tumbler 4.5" #12, flat, straight sided, water, 9 oz.	12
Tumbler 4.5", (blown) footed water, 10 oz.	16
Tumbler 5.75", (blown) footed, ice tea, 12 oz.	18
Tumbler 6.25" #11, flat, straight sided, ice tea, 13 oz.	18
Tumbler 6.25" #5, footed, ice tea, 13 oz.	20
Vase 3", flared & crimped, violet	12
Vase 3", tri-corn, crimped, clover leaf	12
Vase 3" #106, flat, rose bowl, cupped, 5" wide	18
Vase 3.5", crimped, flared, violet	12
Vase 3.5", oval, flared, 2 sides turned up	12
Vase 3.5", straight sided, flared, crimped top	12
Vase 3.5", tri-corn, crimped, clover leaf	12
Vase 4", crimped, flared, violet	15
Vase 4", oval flared, 2 sides turned up	16
Vase 4", rose bowl, cupped, 6" wide	18
Vase 4", straight sided, flared, crimped top	16
Vase 4", tri-corn, crimped, clover leaf	15
Vase 4.5", crimped, flared, violet	16
Vase 4.5", tri-corn, crimped, clover leaf	16
Vase 5", oval, flared, 2 sides turned up	16
Vase 5", tri-corn, crimped, clover leaf	18
Vase 5" #111, straight sided, flared, crimped top	18
Vase 5.5", tight crimped, flower arranger	20
Vase 5.5" #112, tight or wide crimped (2 styles) flower arranger	20
Vase 6.5", tri-corn, crimped, clover leaf	28
Vase 7", straight sided, flared, crimped top	28
Vase 7", tight or wide crimped, flower arranger (2 styles)	30
Vase 8", straight sided, crimped, flared	35
Vase 8.5", tri-corn, crimped, clover leaf	35
Vase 8.5" #113, flat, tall crimped, flower arranger	35
Vase 9" #114, straight sided, slightly flared	38
Vase 10", straight sided, crimped & flared	38
Vase 10.5", crimped, flared, flower arranger	38
Vase 10.5", tri-corn, crimped, clover leaf	38
Vase 12", straight sided, slightly flared	45

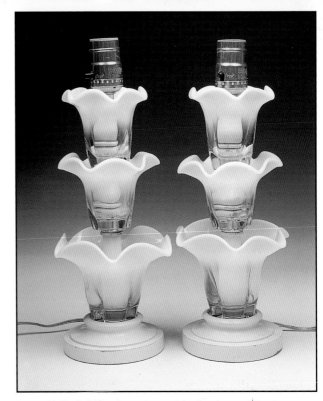

Lamp, 11.1" tall, 5.5" wide, made up of the flared, crimped violet vases: top, 3"; center 3.5"; and bottom 4"; Special order for lamp company; Pink Opalescent ($225 each – we found them priced this).

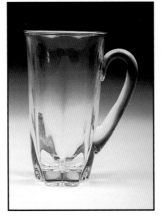

Mug 5.6", straight sided, beverage w/applied handle, 11 oz., Crystal.

Vase 9" #114, straight sided, slightly flared, Blue Opalescent.

Left: Relish 12" #58, round, 4 equal sections & celery section. **Right:** Relish 8.6", oblong, 2 sections, two 3-ball tab handles.

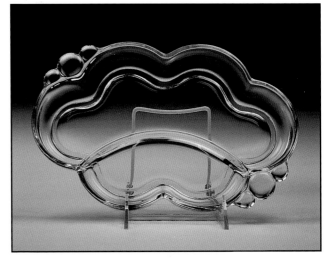

Relish 10.5", tab handled, 2 sections w/1 curved divider, celery, Crystal.

Pattern detail, Cape Cod.

Bowl 4.5" #197, I lug/tab handle, dessert.

CAPE COD

Imperial Glass Company   Blank #160   1932-83

Main Color: Crystal

Other Colors: Amber, Antique Blue, Azalea (pink), Black, Ritz Blue (cobalt), Evergreen (dark green), Heather, Marigold Carnival, Milk Glass, Purple Slag, Ruby Flashed, Ruby, Sunshine Yellow, and Verde Green (olive)

Cape Cod was the first pattern made by the Sandwich Glass Company. Located in Cape Cod, Massachusetts, Sandwich honored the town by naming its first pattern after it. Pairpoint continued making the pattern, after Sandwich closed, in both a cut and pressed version. Then after Pairpoint closed, Imperial acquired the rights and began making the pressed version.

This pattern was made for over 50 years and today's collector can easily build a set. Quite a few of the pieces are under $20 and you can't say that about too many patterns. This is an excellent pattern for the beginning collector since it is still reasonable in price and quite plentiful. One problem for this pattern is the over-abundant supply of stemware, especially the #160 wafer stem pieces. It is mainly a crystal pattern but several pieces can be found in a variety of colors. Amber can range from light to quite dark, depending on the piece. The 1/4 lb. butter dish in this pattern is hard to spot because the pattern is split between the top and bottom.

Like Candlewick, Cape Cod is also a pattern where a large collection of production items, unusual pieces, colors, and decorated examples could be amassed. Collectors can fill an entire house with this one pattern. Some of the hard to find items are the following: Aladdin lamp type candle bowl, basket, bar bottle, birthday cake plate, ceiling lamp, cookie jar, crescent salad plate, toast cover, two-tier tidbit, and urns. Ritz Blue (cobalt) and Ruby items, other than stems, are always in very high demand.

Stemware presents its own set of problems. When looking at the photo showing goblets, you will see the difference between line numbers. Notice the #160 will have a wafer stem, while #1600 & #1602 both have fancy stems, with a bowl shape that is not the same. The Avon produced a dinnerware by the same name but that is where the similarity ends. The Avon Cape Cod has a completely different look and was only made in ruby. For further reading on this pattern, please refer to our book, *Avon Cape Cod*, to learn more about this pattern of the same name.

One of the most frequently asked questions on Cape Cod would be "what is a spider?" A spider is a skillet-shaped bowl with its origins in a cast iron piece looking similar, except the cast iron piece had three long legs and was used in a fireplace, enabling you to cook. Imperial used the shape, but without the legs. To pioneers, this shape with legs would have looked like a spider. However, now with Cape Cod using this term, its name no longer brings up the right image.

In the 1980s three pieces of Cape Cod were reproduced for the Tiara line in non-Imperial colors. These pieces were the footed bud vase, spider, and butter dish.

This is primarily a crystal pattern and a complete set can be assembled. Colored pieces in this pattern do not show up in large enough quantities to build a set.

CAPE COD	Crystal
Ashtray 4" #134/1, I cigarette rest	10
Ashtray 5.5" #150, 2 cigarette rests	14
Basket 9" #221/0, ruffled w/applied handle	200

Back left: Candlestick 1-lite 6" #48BC, large comport shape, Crystal (red candle). **Back center:** Candlestick 1-lite 5.4" #80, fancy square ball stem, Crystal. **Back right:** Candlestick 2-lite 5.75" #100, square foot 6.75" spread, Crystal. **Center of photo:** Candlestick 1-lite 4.5" #90, handled, Aladdin lamp shape, Crystal (white candle). **Front left:** Candlestick 1-lite 3" #170, plain short stem, Verde Green. **Front center left:** Candlestick 1-lite 4.25" #81, fancy 1 ball stem, Crystal. **Front center right:** Candlestick 1-lite 4.5" #16880, spider (2" wide indent for candle), Crystal (2" wide yellow candle). **Front right:** Candlestick 1-lite 5.25" #45B, small comport shape, Crystal (blue candle).

Basket 10.5" #40, flared (oval top) w/applied handle	165
Basket 11" #40, footed, flared w/applied handle	110
Basket 11" #73/0, shallow w/applied handle	185
Bottle w/chrome tube 5" #235, bitters, 3 oz.	58
Bottle w/stopper 6.25" #177, oil & vinegar, 3 oz.	35
Bottle w/chrome tube 6.75" #224, footed bitters, 5 oz.	64
Bottle w/stopper 8" #241, footed oil & vinegar, 5 oz.	56
Bottle w/top 8.25" #237, ketchup, 12 oz. (listed as 14 oz.)	175
Bottle w/stopper 13" #244, straight sided w/long neck bar 26 oz.	200
Bowl 3" #33, individual jelly	10
Bowl 4.5" #1W, fruit	12
Bowl 4.5" #197, 1 lug/tab handle, dessert	28
Bowl 4.5" #1604 1/2A, straight sided, finger	14
Bowl 5" #49H, heart shaped, mint	18
Bowl 5" #1602, flared, finger, 2.25" tall	12
Bowl 5.5" #23B, flared	10
Bowl 5.5" #198, 1 lug/tab handle, soup	24
Bowl 5.75" #51H, w/1 handle pulled to center, heart shape	60
Bowl 6" #3F, cupped, shallow	12
Bowl 6" #40H, handled, heart shaped	26
Bowl 6" #51F, handled (finger) round, mint	25
Bowl 6" #51T, handled (finger) shallow, heart shape	12
Bowl 6" #53X baked apple	35
Bowl 6.5" #199, 1 lug/tab handle, sweetmeat	32
Bowl 6.75" #5W, flared	20
Bowl 7" #5F, cupped, shallow	22
Bowl 7" #5X, shape of baked apple	18
Bowl 7.5" #7F, cupped, shallow	20
Bowl 7.5" #62B, handled, sweetmeat	26
Bowl 8.75" #10F, cupped, shallow	32
Bowl 9" #67F, bell footed, cupped, fancy short stem	68
Bowl 9.5" #145B, handled, flared, vegetable	42
Bowl 9.5" #221C, ruffled, fruit	110
Bowl 9.5" #221F, shallow, float	65
Bowl 10" #137B, footed, flared, fancy short stem	85
Bowl 10" #221, elliptical, vegetable w/wide edged handles	75
Bowl 11" #10A, salad w/1.5" smooth edge	130
Bowl 11" #124 or #125, oval or divided vegetable	85
Bowl 11" #1608A, salad w/.5" smooth edge	120
Bowl 11" #1608X, oval, flanged, vegetable	150
Bowl 11.25" #1602, oval vegetable	78
Bowl 11.5" #1608X, flanged lip w/.5" smooth edge	130
Bowl 12" #131B, oval, flared	100
Bowl 12" #131C, oval, ruffled	175
Bowl 12.5" #16010B, flared w/1.5" smooth edge	90
Bowl 13" #16010R, rolled edge w/1.5" smooth edge	65
Bowl 13.25" #160/75L, low mushroom shape	45
Bowl 14" #92F, shallow, float	55
Butter w/cover 5" #144, handled (skillet shape)	45
Butter w/cover 7.5" #161, oblong .25 lb.	78
Cake plate 10" #220, square w/4-tab feet	125
Cake plate 13" #72, flat, birthday (72 candle holes)	395
Cake salver 10.5" #67D, footed w/pattern	45
Cake salver 11.5" #103D, footed, skirted (patterned top)	85
Cake salver 11.5" #103D, footed, skirted (plain top)	95
Candle bowl 1-lite 4.5" #175, single, pair	45
Candle bowl 1-lite 4.5" #16880, spider (2" wide indent for candle) pair	90
Candle bowl 3-lite #100, footed w/1 removable peg (price for 1)	395
Candlestick 1-lite 3" #170, plain short stem, pair	38
Candlestick 1-lite 4.25" #81, fancy 1 ball stem, pair	58
Candlestick 1-lite 4.5" #90, handled, Aladdin lamp shape, pair	250
Candlestick 1-lite 5.25" #45B, small comport shape, pair	125
Candlestick 1-lite 5.4" #80, fancy square ball stem, pair	58
Candlestick 1-lite 5.5" #45N, goblet shape, pair	200
Candlestick 1-lite 6" #48BC, large comport shape, pair	150
Candlestick 2-lite 5.75" #100, square foot 6.75" spread, pair	200
Candy w/cover 6.5" #194, straight sided w/wicker handle, 4.5" wide	90
Cigarette box w/cover 4.5" #134, w/1 handle	48
Cigarette lighter 3.5" #1602, cordial w/insert (4" total height)	28
Coaster 3" #85, square	38
Coaster 3.4" x 4.6" #76, round w/spoon or cigarette rest	15
Coaster 4" #78, round	20
Cologne w/stopper 6.25" #1601, flat, 7 oz.	48
Comport 4" #160F, cupped w/wafer stem, 6" wide	26
Comport 4.4" #45, flat rim, fancy square ball stem, 5.75" wide	26
Comport 4.5" #160X, flat rim, wafer stem, 5.75" wide	30
Comport 5.75" #1602, oval, fancy square ball stem, 11.25" wide	135
Comport 7.25" #48B, large, fancy square ball stem, 7" wide	40
Comport w/cover 6.2" #140, fancy square ball stem, 6.25" wide	90

Top left: Decanter w/shot glass top 8.75" #260, sq. 26 oz., marked "Rye", Crystal. **Top right:** Decanter w/stopper 10" #163, spherical, 30 oz., Verde Green. **Bottom left:** Decanter w/stopper 13" #185, footed, handled, wine carafe, 26 oz., Crystal. **Bottom center left:** Decanter w/ stopper 8.75" #212, square, 26 oz., Crystal. **Bottom center right:** Decanter w/stopper 11" #256, urn shaped, cordial, 18 oz., Crystal. **Bottom right:** Bottle w/stopper 13" #244, straight sided w/long neck bar 26 oz., Crystal.

Back row, left to right: Goblet 6.4" #1602, fancy ball stem, ice tea, 11 oz., Amber; Goblet 5.4" #1602, fancy ball stem, claret/wine, 5 oz., Antique Blue; Goblet 3.5" #1602, fancy ball stem, cordial, 2 oz., Purple Slag; Cigarette lighter 3.5" #1602, fancy ball stem, Black; Goblet 5" #1602, fancy ball stem, saucer champagne, 7 oz., Azalea (pink); Goblet 5.8" #1602, fancy short stem, parfait, 6 oz., Crystal. **Front row, left to right:** Goblet 5.25" #160, wafer stem water, 8 oz., Ritz Blue (cobalt); Goblet 3.5" #1602, fancy short stem, oyster cocktail, 3 oz., Crystal; Goblet 3.25" #160, wafer stem sherbet, 6 oz., Ruby; #1600 liquor cocktail 4 oz.; Goblet 5.75" #1600, fancy ball stem, water, 11 oz., Ruby Flashed; Goblet 6.5" #1600, plain ball stem, Hoffman House beer, 16 oz., Evergreen (dark green).

Back row: Creamer w/covered sugar & tray (4 piece) #25, square shape. **Front left:** Creamer & sugar #190, footed, no stem, handled, regular, 6 oz. **Front right:** Creamer & sugar #31, footed, regular, handled, wafer stem, 6 oz.

Back left: Plate 8.25" #5D, salad, Antique Blue. **Back right:** Plate 10" #10D, dinner, Crystal. **Center:** Butter w/cover 7.5" #161, oblong .25 lb, Ritz Blue (cobalt). **Front row:** Teacup 2.5" #35 w/rounded sides, 6 oz., Crystal; Shaker 3.75" #117, flat, straight sided, Azalea (pink); Shaker 2.75" #236, pepper mill/chrome grinder, Amber; Shaker 4" #116, sham footed, tapered, Evergreen (dark green); Cup 2.6" #37, flat, 6 oz. & saucer 5.5" #37, Ruby.

Back row: Hurricane lamp 2 piece #1604, 7.5" (total height) base/chimney, Crystal; Platter 13.5" x 9.75" #124D, oval, Crystal; Tray 6.6" #455, square, condiment, Crystal. **Front row:** Nut cup 3" #183, handled (or s & p tray), Azalea (pink); Cologne w/stopper 6.25" #1601, flat, 7 oz., Ruby Flashed; Horseradish w/stopper 4" #226, flat, 5 oz., Crystal; Hurricane lamp 2 piece #79, 13.5" (total height) base/chimney, Crystal.

Comport w/cover 6.5" #110, fancy short stem, candy 1 lb., 5" wide	75
Cookie jar w/cover #195, 9" straight sided, wicker handle, 6.25" wide	300
Creamer 3.5" #30, flat 6 sided base, regular, handled, 6 oz.	12
Creamer 4.75" #31, footed, regular, handled, wafer stem, 6 oz.	9
Creamer 4.75" #31, footed, regular, handled, fancy short stem, 6 oz.	18
Creamer 4" #190, footed, no stem, handled, regular, 6 oz.	12
Creamer 3.25" #25, footed, square, 7 oz.	45
Creamer w/covered sugar & tray (4 piece) #25, square shape	165
Cruet/stopper 5.25" #119, spherical, handled, 4 oz.	30
Cruet/stopper 7.25" #70, straight sided w/pointed handle, 6 oz.	35
Cruet/stopper 7.5" #70, straight sided w/round handle, 6 oz.	35
Cup & saucer, tea: cup 2.5" #35, tea w/rounded sides, 6 oz.; saucer 5.75"	10
Cup & saucer, coffee (punch w/o sau) cup 2.6" #37, flat, 6 oz.; saucer 5.5"	9
Cup 1.75" #250, handled, bouillon, 7 oz. (4.1" wide)	28
Decanter w/stopper 9" #82, cordial, ruffled top, 16 oz.	275
Decanter w/stopper 11" #256, urn shaped, cordial, 18 oz.	125
Decanter w/stopper 8.75" #212, square, 26 oz.	85
Decanter w/shot glass top 8.75" #260, sq 26 oz., marked "Scotch, Bourbon & Rye"	165
Decanter w/stopper 8.75" #160, sq 26 oz., marked "Scotch, Bourbon, Rye & Gin	145
Decanter w/stopper 10" #163, spherical, 30 oz.	75
Decanter w/stopper 13" #185, footed, handled, wine carafe, 26 oz.	175
Eagle candlestick adapter #777/1 (Candlewick #) fits any candlestick	350
Egg cup 4.6" #225, bell footed, 5 oz.	38
Epergne 2 piece #196, 12" bowl/horn no pattern	275
Goblet 3.5" #1602, fancy ball stem, cordial, 2 oz.	15
Goblet 4" #1602, fancy ball stem, sherry, 2.5 oz.	20
Goblet 3.5" #160, wafer stem cocktail, 3 oz.	6
Goblet 3.5" #1602, fancy short stem, oyster cocktail, 3 oz.	9
Goblet 3.75" #160, wafer stem wine, 3 oz.	5
Goblet 4.5" #1600, fancy ball stem wine, 3 oz.	18
Goblet 4.5" #1602, fancy ball stem wine, 3 oz.	10
Goblet 4.6" #1602, fancy ball stem, liquor cocktail, 3.5 oz.	9
Goblet 4.25" #1600, fancy ball stem, liquor cocktail, 4 oz.	14
Goblet 4.25" #1602, fancy short stem, oyster cocktail, 4 oz.	6
Goblet 5.4" #1602, fancy ball stem, claret/wine, 5 oz.	14
Goblet 3.25" #160, wafer stem sherbet, 6 oz.	4
Goblet 4.8" #1600, fancy ball stem, sherbet, 6 oz.	12
Goblet 4" #1602, fancy ball stem, sundae, 6 oz.	8
Goblet 5.8" #1602, fancy short stem, parfait, 6 oz.	14
Goblet 5" #1602, fancy ball stem, saucer champagne, 7 oz.	9
Goblet 5.25" #160, wafer stem water, 8 oz.	7
Goblet 5.4" #1602, fancy ball stem, lunch water, 9 oz.	14
Goblet 5.75" #1600, fancy ball stem, water, 11 oz.	18
Goblet 6.4" #1602, fancy ball stem, ice tea, 11 oz.	16
Goblet 6.5" #1600, fancy ball stem, ice tea, 14 oz.	14
Goblet 6.5" #1600, plain ball stem, Hoffman House beer, 16 oz.	48
Gravy boat & liner: sauce 3.75" #202, footed, handled, 22 oz., 5.5" wide; liner 8" #203, cupped, under plate	90
Horseradish w/stopper 4" #226, flat, 5 oz.	68
Hurricane lamp 2 piece #1604, 7.5" (total height) base/chimney, each	85
Hurricane lamp 2 piece #79, 13.5" (total height) base/chimney, each	115
Ice bucket 6.5" #63, w/wicker handle, 6.25" wide	195
Ice dish 2 piece #53/3, bowl & plain insert (2 styles)	50
Ketchup jar w/cover #252, flat round base w/ball finial lid	125
Ladle 4.1" #130 (Candlewick) 2 ball handle	20
Ladle 5.75" #615, plain handle	12
Ladle #165 (Candlewick) 1 ball handle	18
Ladle 6" #130 (Candlewick) 3 ball handle	18
Ladle #91 (blown) large punch	45
Lamp 8.5", cylindrical ceiling w/metal bands 5" wide (cookie jar shape)	375
Lamp 31.5", table size, made from (glass measures 8") #160 decanter w/prisms	195
Mantle lustre 10.75", footed, urn shape w/12 prisms	450
Marmalade w/cover & liner: jar 3.5" #89, flat w/ball finial lid, 3.25" wide: liner 5.75"	48
Mayonnaise 2 piece: bowl 3.75" #208/9, footed, handled, 7 oz.; liner w/indent 6"	65
Mayonnaise 2 piece: bowl 4.5" #205/6, footed, handled, 13 oz., 3.4" wide; liner w/indent 7"	50
Mayonnaise 2 piece: bowl 5" #52, heart shaped, 2" tall; liner w/indent 7"	42
Mayonnaise 2 piece: bowl 5.5" #23, round, 1.9" tall; liner w/indent 7" #1601D	35
Mayonnaise 2 piece: bowl 5.5" #1604 1/2B, round; liner w/indent 7" #1600D	35
Muddler #701, tight ringed handle	28
Mug 2.8" #200, handled, Tom & Jerry, 6.5 oz.	15
Mug 4.75" #188, handled, stein, 14 oz.	68
Mug w/cover 4.75" #210, handled, straight sided, peanut jar, 14 oz.	95
Mustard w/cover 3.5" #156, 6 sided foot w/ball finial	45
Nut cup 3" #183, handled (or s & p tray)	22
Nut cup 4" #184, handled (or s & p tray)	26
Peanut jar w/cover 5.25" #193, straight sided w/wicker handle, 3.5" wide	100
Pitcher 6" #240, footed milk w/ice lip, 16 oz.	65
Pitcher 5.75" #160, flat top w/ice lip, 32 oz. (made 1932 only)	225

Pitcher 9.25" #19, footed jug w/ice lip, 38 oz.	80
Pitcher 10" #178 (blown) martini w/ice lip, 44 oz.	275
Pitcher 8" #239, jug w/ice lip, 56 oz.	125
Pitcher 9.6" #24, footed, jug w/ice lip, 52 oz.	100
Pitcher 9.75" #176 (blown) w/ice lip, 76 oz.	225
Plate 4.5" #34, individual butter/coaster (round)	10
Plate 6.5" #1D, bread & butter	5
Plate 7" #3D, dessert	8
Plate 8" #12, crescent salad (kidney shape)	100
Plate 8.25" #5D, salad	9
Plate 8.5" #62D, handled lemon server	28
Plate 9" #7D, lunch	18
Plate 10" #10D, dinner	38
Plate 11.5" #145D, handled service	38
Plate 12.25" #222, elliptical, bread w/wide edged handles	80
Plate 13.5" #1608F, torte	40
Plate 13.5" #1608V, small center, turned up edge, cabaret	45
Plate 14" #75D, chop w/plain ring at edge	36
Plate 14" #75D, torte w/pattern to edge	40
Plate 16" #20V, small center, turned up edge, cabaret or punch bowl liner	55
Plate 17" #20D, chop w/plain ring at edge	58
Plate 17" #20D, torte or punch bowl liner	50
Platter 12.25" x 8.4" #124D, oval	85
Platter 13.5" x 9.75" #124D, oval	95
Puff box w/cover 4.5" #1601, low w/fancy finial, 2.1" tall	75
Punch bowl 12.5" #10B, flared, 1 gallon	80
Punch bowl 11" #120B, footed, Tom & Jerry, 1.15 gallon, 9.25" tall	275
Punch bowl 13" #20B, flared, 1.5 gallon	100
Relish 8" #105/105, oval celery	38
Relish 8.25" #192, footed (6 sided) fancy short stem, 2 sections, oblong, mint	195
Relish 8.5" #233, rectangle, w/1 handle, 2 sections mint (also cigarette server)	40
Relish 9.4" #55, oval, 3 sections, plain rim	26
Relish 9.4" #55, oval, 3 sections, patterned rim	30
Relish 9.5" #56, tab handled, 4 sections, round	48
Relish 10.5" #189, oval celery	42
Relish 10.5" #191, oval, 2 sections, pickle/olive	60
Relish 10.5" #191, oval, 2 sections, radish/celery (divided 1/3 & 2/3)	50
Relish 11" #102, round, 5 sections	60
Relish 11.25" #1602, oval, 3 sections	90
Salad bowl 12" #75B, flared salad	48
Salad bowl liner 14" #75V, or small center, turned up edge, cabaret plate	42
Salad fork 9.5" #701, plumed handle	28
Salad spoon 9.4" #701, plumed handle	28
Salt dip 2.25" #61, footed, round, 1.25" tall	25
Salt dip 3 piece 4.75" (long) #219, dip, pepper & spoon	58
Shaker 2.25" #109, short, flat, square, pair	30
Shaker 2.5" #251, round ball, pair	25
Shaker 2.75" #236, pepper mill/chrome grinder	30
Shaker 2.75" #238, salt shaker w/chrome	20
Shaker 3.25" #96, flat, straight sided, pair	20
Shaker 3.75" #117, flat, straight sided, pair	30
Shaker 4" #116, sham footed, tapered, pair	24
Shaker 4" #247, footed, straight sided, pair	32
Shaker 5" #243, footed, fancy ball stem, pair	50
Shaker set #213, individual, s & p, handled (nut) tray	45
Shaker set #216, footed, s & p, handled (nut) tray	50
Spider 4.5" #180, handled (skillet shape)	25
Spider 5.5" #181, handled (skillet shape)	30
Spider 6.25" #182, handled (skillet shape)	35
Spider 6.25" #187, 2 sections, handled (skillet shape)	40
Sugar 3.5" #190, footed, no stem, handled, regular, 6 oz.	12
Sugar 3.5" #30, flat, 6 sided base, regular, handled 6 oz.	12
Sugar 4.25" #31, footed, regular, handled, fancy short stem, 6 oz.	18
Sugar 4.25" #31, footed, regular, handled, wafer stem, 6 oz.	9
Sugar w/cover 3.25" #25, footed, square, 7 oz.	65
Tidbit 2 tier #2701 flat plates w/wood or chrome handle	150
Toast w/cover #123, cover not patterned	300
Tray 3" #183, handled, oval, nut, 1.1" high	22
Tray 4" #184, handled, oval, nut, 1.25" high	24
Tray 5.5" #242, oblong, for shakers	16
Tray 6" #26, rectangle, for square cream/sugar	45
Tray 6.6" #455, square, condiment	150
Tray 7" #29, oval, pattern in bottom only	28
Tray 8" #149D, center handled server, snack	34
Tray 11" #68D, center handled server, pastry	48
Tray 12" #93, multi server 1 piece w/center bowl	90
Tumbler 2.5" #160, flat whiskey, 3 oz.	10
Tumbler 4.25" #160, flat juice, 5 oz.	9
Tumbler 5.1" #1600, footed, juice, fancy short stem, 6 oz.	12

Back row: Salad bowl liner 14" #75V, or small center, turned up edge, cabaret plate, Ruby; Cake plate 13" #72, flat, birthday (72 candle holes), Crystal. **Center row:** Basket 10.5" #40, flared (oval top) w/applied handle, Crystal; Imperial dealer sign ($195 – we found this priced this), Crystal w/part satin; Bowl 4.5" #1604 1/2A, straight sided, finger, Crystal Satin (in metal ormolu). **Front row:** Salt dip 2 piece 4.75" (long) #219, dip, pepper, Crystal; Whimsy hat vase, Crystal ($125); Cake salver 11.25" #103D, footed w/3 ball stem, Crystal; Heart shape 6" #51H, handled, shallow, bonbon, Crystal.

Back row: Plate 12.25" #222, elliptical, bread w/wide edged handles, Crystal; Bottle w/top 8.25" #237, ketchup, 12 oz., Crystal. **Center row:** Cruet/stopper 7.5" #70, straight sided w/round handle, 6 oz., Marigold Carnival; Imperial dealer sign, Crystal w/part satin ($195 – we found it priced this). **Front row:** Cruet/stopper 7.25" #70, straight sided w/pointed handle, 6 oz., Crystal; Cruet/stopper 5.25" #119, spherical, handled, 4 oz., Sunshine Yellow; Bottle w/stopper 6.25" #177, oil & vinegar, 3 oz., Crystal; Bottle w/chrome tube 6.75" #224, footed bitters, 5 oz., Crystal; Bottle w/stopper 8" #241, footed oil & vinegar, 5 oz., Crystal.

Bowl 12.5" #16010B, flared w/1.5" smooth edge.

Top left: Relish 8.5" #233, rectangle, w/1 handle, 2 sections mint (also cigarette server). **Top center:** Peanut jar w/cover 5.25" #193, straight sided w/wicker handle, 3.5" wide. **Top right:** Mustard/cover 4" #156, beaded boot, lid w/2 bead finial. **Bottom left:** Relish 8.25" #192, footed (6 sided) fancy short stem, 2 sections oblong, mint. **Bottom center:** Candy w/cover 6.5" #194, straight sided w/wicker handle, 4.5" wide, Milk Glass. **Bottom right:** Cookie jar w/cover #195, 9" straight sided w/wicker handle, 6.25" wide.

Top left: Pitcher 8" #239, jug w/ice lip, 56 oz. **Top center:** Pitcher 10" #178 (blown) martini w/ice lip, 44 oz. **Top right:** Pitcher 9.75" #176 (blown) w/ice lip, 76 oz. **Bottom left:** Pitcher 9.25" #19, footed jug w/ ice lip, 38 oz. **Bottom center:** Pitcher 6" #240, footed milk w/ice lip, 16 oz. **Bottom right:** Pitcher 5.75" #160, flat top w/ice lip, 32 oz., non production Teal Green.

Tumbler 4" #1601, collar footed, no stem, juice, 6 oz.	12
Tumbler 5.2" #1602, footed, juice, fancy short stem, 6 oz.	9
Tumbler 5.1" #1602, footed, juice, plain short stem, 6 oz.	5
Tumbler 3.4" #160, flat, small, old fashion, 8 oz.	9
Tumbler 4" #160, flat water, 8 oz.	12
Tumbler 4.75" #1601, collar footed, no stem, water, 9 oz.	14
Tumbler 5" #160, flat water, 10 oz.	12
Tumbler 5.6" #1602, footed, water, fancy short stem, 10 oz.	10
Tumbler 3.8" #160, flat, large, old fashion, 11 oz.	16
Tumbler 4.8" #160, flat ice tea, 11 oz.	10
Tumbler 6" #1602, footed, fancy short stem, ice tea, 11 oz.	12
Tumbler 5.25" #1601, collar footed, no stem, ice tea, 12 oz.	16
Tumbler 6" #1602, footed, fancy short stem, ice tea, 12 oz.	7
Tumbler 6.1" #1600, fancy short stem, ice tea, 12 oz.	16
Tumbler 6.5" #160, flat beverage, 14.5 oz.	20
Tumbler 6.4" #160, flat, jumbo beverage, 16 oz.	26
Urn w/cover 10" #133, footed (8 sided foot) Pokal	145
Urn w/cover 11" #128, footed (4 sided foot) Pokal	165
Urn w/cover 15.5" #132, footed (4 sided foot) Pokal	100
Vase 6.5" #22, flared w/8 sided foot	36
Vase 6.5" #110B, fancy short stem (comport shape)	75
Vase 6.75" #27, flared, high, ridged stem, bud vase	40
Vase 7.5", swung, crimped top	125
Vase 7.5" #22, flared w/8 sided foot	46
Vase 8.25" #143, flip shape	72
Vase 8.5" #28, straight sided, flared, high ridged stem	55
Vase 8.5" #87F, fan shape w/fancy short stem	96
Vase 10" #192, straight sided, celery	95
Vase 10.5" #186, handled, urn shape w/fancy short stem	150
Vase 11" #1603, flip shape w/ridged stem	110
Vase 11.25" #21, straight sided, flared, high ridged stem	85
Vase 15.75", square footed, 1 ball stem, swung, bud vase	110

Top left: Vase 7.5", swung, crimped top. **Top center:** Vase 8.5" #87F, fan shape w/fancy short stem. **Bottom left:** Vase 8.25" #143, flip shape. **Bottom center:** Vase 7.5" #22, flared w/8 sided foot. **Right:** Vase 15.75", square footed, 1 ball stem, swung, bud vase.

Top left: Mug 4.75" #188, handled, stein, 14 oz., Milk Glass. **Top center:** Mug 2.8" #200, handled, Tom & Jerry, 6.5 oz., Crystal. **Bottom left:** Egg cup 4.6" #225, bell footed, 5 oz., Crystal. **Bottom center left:** Tumbler 6" #1602, footed, fancy short stem, ice tea, 12 oz., Verde Green. **Bottom center right:** Tumbler 5.2" #1602, footed, juice, fancy short stem, 6 oz., Azalea (pink). **Bottom right:** Tumbler 6.1" #1600, fancy short stem, ice tea, 12 oz., Ruby Flashed.

Left: Mantle lustre 10.75", footed, urn shape w/12 prisms. **Right:** Urn w/cover 15.5" #132, footed (4 sided foot), Pokal.

Top left: Tumbler 2.5" #160, flat whiskey, 3 oz., Ritz Blue (cobalt). **Top center:** Tumbler 3.4" #160, flat, small, old fashion, 8 oz., Crystal. **Top right:** Tumbler 3.8" #160, flat, large, old fashion, 11 oz., Crystal. **Bottom left:** Tumbler 4.25" #160, flat juice, 5 oz., Sunshine Yellow. **Bottom center left:** Tumbler 5" #160, flat water, 10 oz., Marigold Carnival. **Bottom center right:** Tumbler 4.8" #160, flat ice tea, 11 oz. **Bottom right:** Tumbler 6.4" #160, flat, jumbo beverage, 16 oz., Evergreen (dark green).

Left: Vase 6.75" #27, flared, high, ridged stem, bud vase, Crystal. **Left center:** Vase 8.5" #28, straight sided, flared, high ridged stem, Crystal. **Right center:** Vase 6.75" #27, flared, high, ridged stem, bud vase, Light Blue (Tiara item). **Right:** Vase 11.25" #21, straight sided, flared, high ridged stem, Crystal.

Punch bowl 14.75" #478, footed, bellied, flared, 1.5 gallon.

CAPRICE

Cambridge Glass Company   **Blank #3550**   **1936-57**

Main Colors: Crystal, and Moonlight Blue
Other Colors: Amethyst, Cobalt, Emerald Green, La Rosa (pink), Mandarin Gold (yellow), Milk Glass, Mocha (light amber), and Pistachio (light green)

    Caprice was a popular pattern when it was introduced and today continues to attract many collectors. Its immense number of pieces offers the collector a wide selection for setting a table. The swirled effect of the pattern gives it a rich look. The majority of Crystal and Moonlight Blue items can be found with the Alpine decoration. Alpine used an acid etching, satin finish on part of the pattern, leaving a striking combination between the glossy and frosted surfaces. None of the blown vases have been found with the Alpine decoration. In the pastel colors, only a lunch set can be assembled; add 25% to the blue color prices.

    Collectors of Caprice have more things to choose from than most budgets would ever allow. You can pick and choose the items that will fit with your budget. No one has room for all the pieces anyway. Large sets of Crystal and Moonlight Blue can be collected, with the latter taking patience and money in order to complete the task. Some of the hard to find items are: basket, bitters bottle, cake plate, candle reflector, cracker jar, decanter, Doulton pitcher, punch bowl, blown mustard, and blown vase.

    Some of the dark colors of Amethyst and Emerald Green can be used to accent the crystal on a table. In addition, a few pieces of Milk Glass have also shown up.

CAPRICE	Crystal	Blue
Almond cup 2" #95, 4-footed, round	24	60
Almond cup 2.5" #93, square, tab handled	20	50
Almond cup 2.5" #94, tab handled, 2 sections, nut/mint	24	60
Ashtray 2.75" #213, 3 shell footed, cupped w/card slot, shell shape	14	28
Ashtray 3" #206, triangle shape	12	25
Ashtray 3" #213, flared, 3 shell footed, shell shape	8	16
Ashtray 3" #214, round (nesting #1)	6	14
Ashtray 4" #215, round (nesting #2)	8	18
Ashtray 4.5" #210, triangle shape	14	30
Ashtray 5" #216, round (nesting #3)	10	22
Basket 4" #146, square w/tab handles turned up	15	35
Basket 5" #153, shallow, tab handles turned up	16	38
Basket 7" #134, low, footed, crimped, 2-handled	25	60
Basket 10.1", footed w/applied handle, 8.75" tall	1,500+	
Bonbon 4" #147, tab handled w/4 sides turned up	16	38
Bonbon 4.5" #148, shallow, tab handled, crimped	16	38
Bonbon 6" #133, footed, tab handled w/4 sides turned up	22	48
Bonbon 6" #154, tab handled w/4 sides turned up	18	45
Bonbon 6" #155, handled, oval	24	52
Bonbon 6.25" #132, footed, tab handles turned up	22	48
Bottle w/chrome tube 6" #186, bitters	245	550+
Bowl 4.25" #144, square, tab handled, slightly flared, jelly	15	38
Bowl 5" #18, shallow, cupped, fruit	28	78

Top left: Candlestick 2-lite 7.1" #69, w/shell bobeches, 2 prisms, 9.25" spread. **Top center:** Candlestick 5-lite 6" #1577, tiered, base like ocean waves, 11.5" spread, centerpiece. **Top right:** Candlestick 1-lite 7.25" #70, shell foot, curved high stem w/1 prism. **Center of photo:** Candlestick 1-lite 2.5" #67, no stem. **Bottom left:** Candlestick 2-lite 6" #72, footed plume arms, 8" spread. **Bottom center:** Candle reflector 1-lite 6.5" #73, high shell backdrop, 90 degree angle to base. **Bottom right:** Candlestick 3-lite 4" #74, oval base, 7.5" spread.

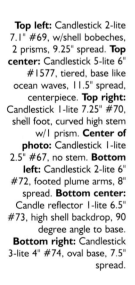

Item		
Bowl 5.1" #19, flared crimped, fruit	32	98
Bowl 5.25" #151, square, tab handled, jelly	14	38
Bowl 6", (5 shape styles) #169 heart, #170 club, #171 diamond, #172 spade, #173 clover leaf	38	100
Bowl 7" #135, footed, low, crimped, tab handled, jelly	20	50
Bowl 8" #49, 4-footed, deep, salad	45	115
Bowl 8.5" #50, 4-footed, square, crimped	58	145
Bowl 9" #64, 4-footed, deep, oval, closed handled	65	160
Bowl 9.5" #51, 4-footed, deep	48	125
Bowl 9.5" #52, 4-footed, deep, crimped	60	135
Bowl 10" #57, 4-footed, deep, salad	50	125
Bowl 10" #58, 4-footed, square, crimped	65	150
Bowl 10.5" #53, 3-footed, crimped, flared	35	
Bowl 10.5" #53, 4-footed, crimped, flared	40	110
Bowl 10.5" #54, 3-footed, flared	38	
Bowl 10.5" #54, 4-footed, flared	40	95
Bowl 11" #59 or #60, 4-footed, deep, crimped or slightly flared (2 styles)	58	145
Bowl 11" #83, shallow, crimped	45	
Bowl 11.25" #65, 4-footed, oval, flared w/tab handles	45	115
Bowl 11.5" #81, 3-footed, cupped, shallow, gardenia	45	
Bowl 11.5" #81, 4-footed, cupped, shallow, gardenia	50	125
Bowl 12.25" #61, 3-footed, deep, flared & crimped	40	
Bowl 12.25" #61, 4-footed, deep, flared & crimped	42	110
Bowl 12.75" #62, 3-footed, flared	45	
Bowl 12.75" #62, 4-footed, flared	45	120
Bowl 13" #66, 4-footed, shallow, crimped, tab handled	48	130
Bowl 13" #80, shallow, cupped, salad	75	195
Bowl 13.25" #82, 4-footed, cupped, shallow, gardenia	75	195
Bowl 13.5" #82, 3-footed, cupped, shallow, gardenia	65	
Bowl 13.5" #66A, 4-footed, oval, 2 sides turned up	125	295
Bowl 15" #84, shallow, float	75	195
Butter w/cover #52, oblong .25 lb.	195	
Cake plate 13" #36, 3-tab feet, scalloped edge	150	400+
Cake salver 13" #31, 3-toed plate w/pedestal (2 piece)	225	600+
Candle block 5" #68, triangle, pair	300+	700+
Candle reflector 1-lite 6.5" #73, high shell backdrop, 90 degree angle to base, pair	700+	
Candelabra 2-lite 6" #78, 2 bobeches (2 styles) w/prisms, 8.5" spread, pair	225	395
Candlestick 1-lite 2.5" #67, no stem, pair	35	85
Candlestick 1-lite 5" #68, (Cascade pattern), pair	98	
Candlestick 1-lite 7.25" #70, shell foot, curved high stem w/ 1 prism, pair	75	145
Candlestick 2-lite 6" #72, footed plume arms, 8" spread, pair	85	200
Candlestick 2-lite 7" #69, w/bobeches (2 styles) 2 prisms, 9.1" spread, pair	350	800+
Candlestick 2-lite 7.1" #69, w/shell bobeches, 2 prisms, 9.25" spread, pair	450+	1,200+
Candlestick 2-lite 7.5" #71, w/2 bobeches, 10 prisms, pair	375	900+
Candlestick 3-lite 4" #74, oval base, 7.5" spread, pair	95	225
Candlestick 3-lite 6.25" #1338, cascading (like ocean waves) 7" spread, pair	95	225
Candlestick 5-lite 6" #1577, tiered, base like ocean waves, 11.5" spread, centerpiece, each	225	
Candy w/cover 6" #167, footed, tab handled	85	195
Candy w/cover 6" #168, footed, 2 sections, tab handled	100	225
Candy w/cover 6.25" #165, 3-footed, round	68	185
Cigarette holder 2.25" #205, triangle shape, 2.1" tall	28	60
Cigarette holder 3" #204, triangle shape, 3" tall	30	65
Cigarette box/cover 3.75" x 2.5" #207, 4-footed, oblong	35	75
Cigarette box/cover 5" x 4" #208, 4-footed, oblong	40	95
Cigarette box/cover 5" x 4" #209, w/plain bottom (no pattern)	30	65
Coaster (or ashtray) 3.5" #13, round, scalloped edge	14	32
Comport 2.75" #130, low, tab handled, 7" wide	20	48
Comport 5" #136, shallow, cheese, 6.75" wide	45	125
Comport 5.5" #136, tall stem, cupped top, 6.25" wide	40	95
Cracker jar/cover 5.5" #202, 4-footed w/chrome handle, 6" wide cover (candy lid) total 8.25" high	450+	1,250+
Creamer 2.5" #40, 4-footed, individual, 2.5 oz.	12	28
Creamer 3.25" #38, 4-footed, medium, 5 oz.	10	24
Creamer 4.25" #41, 4-footed, large, 5 oz.	14	30
Cruet w/stopper 3.5" #98, tilt ball, 3 oz.	34	85
Cruet w/stopper 4.4" #101, solid tab handle, 3 oz.	45	110
Cruet w/stopper 4.75" #117, open angle handle, 3 oz.	50	125
Cruet w/stopper 6" #100, upright shape, 5 oz.	95	225
Cup & saucer, footed coffee: cup 2.5" #17, 6 oz., saucer w/indent 5.5"	18	38
Decanter w/stopper 7.5" #187, tilt ball, applied handle 35 oz.	195	500+
Epergne #75, 4 piece #74 3-lite, arm w/2 vases	125	295
Epergne #76, 5 piece #74 3-lite, arm, bobeche w/prisms & 2 vases	150	350

Top left: Cruet w/stopper 4.4" #101 solid tab handle, 3 oz. **Top center:** Mustard w/cover 3.25" #87, (blown); Marmalade w/cover 4.25" #89, (blown); Tray 7.75" #42, oblong, condiment. **Top right:** Cruet w/ stopper 6" #100, upright shape, 5 oz. **Bottom left:** Shakers 2.75" #96, flat on Tray 5.75", oblong, center plume handle. **Bottom center:** Shaker 2.1" #90, flat, individual, ball shape w/square glass lid for base; Shaker 2.25" #92, individual, triangle w/glass lid. **Bottom right:** Cruet w/ stopper 3.5" #98, tilt ball, 3 oz., oblong, center plume handle.

Moonlight Blue grouping: **Top left:** Cigarette box/cover 5" x 4" #208, 4-footed, oblong. **Top right:** Bowl 13.25" #82, 4-footed, shallow, cupped. **Front left:** Ice bucket 5.8" #201, 4-footed w/chrome handle, 5.4" wide. **Front center:** Tumbler 4.75" #184, (blown) ice tea, 12 oz. **Front right:** Cruets w/stoppers 4.4" #101, solid tab handle, 3 oz.; Shakers 2.25" #92, individual, triangle w/glass lid on Tray 7.75" #42, oblong, condiment.

Moonlight Blue grouping: **Left:** Vase 5.5" #345, squat, short neck, scalloped top. **Right:** Candlestick 1-lite 7.25" #70, shell foot, curved high stem w/1 prism.

Grouping of blown goblets: **Top row:** Oyster cocktail, 3.5" #300, 4.5 oz.; Cordial, 3.6" #301, plain stem, 1 oz.; Cordial, 4.4" #300, 1 oz. **Front row:** Parfait, 6.25" #300, 5 oz.; Claret, 6.25" #300, 4.5 oz.; Wine, 5.75" #300, 2.5 oz.; Liquor cocktail, 5.4" #300, 3 oz.; Sherbet, 4.25" #300, 6 oz.; Saucer champagne, 5.6" #300, 6 oz.; Water, 7.75" #300, 9 oz.

Grouping of pressed goblets: **Left to right:** Claret, 5" #5, 4.5 oz.; Wine, 4.75" #6, 3 oz.; Liquor cocktail, 4.1" #3, 3.5 oz.; Seafood cocktail, 4" #7, 4.5 oz.; Sherbet, 3.75" #4, 5 oz.; Saucer champagne, 4.4" #2, 7 oz.; Dinner water, 6.6" #1, 10 oz.

La Rosa (pink) grouping: **Top left:** Sugar & creamer #38, 4-footed, medium, 5 oz., on Tray 7.75" #42, oblong, condiment. **Top right:** Plate 11.5" #26, 4-footed, service/torte. **Front left:** Bowl 12.25" #61, 3-footed, deep, flared & crimped. **Front center:** Shakers 2.75" #96, flat, on Tray 5.75", oblong, center plume handle. **Front right:** Candy w/ cover 6.25" #165, 3-footed, round.

Item		
Finger bowl & liner: bowl 4.5" #16, round, deep cupped; plate w/indent 6.1"	40	95
Finger bowl & liner: bowl #300 (blown) round, flared; plate w/indent	45	110
Flower block 4" #1502, shell shaped holes, fits 6" rose bowl	48	145
Flower block 4.75" #1502, shell shaped holes, fits 8" rose bowl	50	165
Goblet 4.4" #300, (blown) cordial, 1 oz.	60	145
Goblet 3.6" #301, (blown) cordial, plain stem, 1 oz.	40	
Goblet #200, wine, 2.5 oz.	24	50
Goblet 5.75" #300, (blown) wine, 2.5 oz.	30	72
Goblet #301, (blown) wine, plain stem, 2.5 oz.	28	
Goblet 4.75" #6, pressed wine, 3 oz.	35	95
Goblet #200, liquor cocktail, 3 oz.	15	32
Goblet 5.4" #300, (blown) liquor cocktail, 3 oz.	24	54
Goblet #301, (blown) liquor cocktail, plain stem, 3 oz.	22	
Goblet 4.1" #3, pressed liquor cocktail, 3.5 oz.	22	48
Goblet 5" #5, pressed claret, 4.5 oz.	75	150
Goblet 3.5" #300, (blown) oyster cocktail, 4.5 oz.	18	40
Goblet 4" #7, pressed seafood cocktail, 4.5 oz.	25	65
Goblet 6.25" #300, (blown) claret, 4.5 oz.	75	195
Goblet #301, (blown) claret, plain stem, 4.5 oz.	38	
Goblet 3.75" #4, pressed sherbet, 5 oz.	22	48
Goblet 6.25" #300, (blown) parfait, 5 oz.	95	245
Goblet #200, sherbet, 6 oz.	15	32
Goblet 4.25" #300, (blown) sherbet, 6 oz.	14	30
Goblet 5.6" #300, (blown) saucer champagne, 6 oz.	15	32
Goblet #301, (blown) sherbet, plain stem, 6 oz.	14	
Goblet 4.4" #2, pressed saucer champagne, 7 oz.	16	35
Goblet #400, pressed saucer champagne, 7 oz.	22	45
Goblet #200, water, 9 oz.	20	50
Goblet 7.75" #300, (blown) water, 9 oz.	18	48
Goblet #301, (blown) water, plain stem, 9 oz.	16	
Goblet 6.6" #1, pressed dinner water, 10 oz.	28	60
Goblet #400, pressed water, 10 oz.	35	75
Ice bucket 5.8" #201, 4-footed w/chrome handle, 5.4" wide	98	245
Marmalade w/cover 4.25" #89, (blown), Note blue has clear lid	85	245
Mayonnaise 2 piece: bowl 5.25" #127, flat sauce, 2.5" tall; #128 liner w/indent 6.25"	45	100
Mayonnaise 2 piece: bowl 6" #105, footed, deep, tab handled, 3.1" tall; liner w/indent 8.6"	55	125
Mayonnaise bowl 6.1" #110, footed, tab handled, salad dressing	60	135
Mayonnaise 8" #112, footed, oval, salad dressing w/center handle	195	450+
Mustard w/cover 3.25" #87, (blown), Note blue has clear lid	75	145
Pitcher 6.8" #179, tilt ball, juice jug, 32 oz.	150	395
Pitcher 9.25" #178, Doulton jug w/o ice lip, 80 oz.	850+	4500+
Pitcher 9.25" #183, tilt ball, water w/ice lip, 80 oz.	175	400+
Plate 5" #145, tab handled, lemon server	12	30
Plate 5.5" #20, used as coaster	10	25
Plate 6" #152, tab handled, lemon server	16	38
Plate 6.5" #21, bread & butter	10	25
Plate 7.5" #23, dessert or small salad	14	30
Plate 8" #131, footed, shallow, tab handled	20	45
Plate 8.5" #22, salad or lunch	16	35
Plate 9.5" #24, dinner	60	195
Plate 11" #32, 3-footed, small center, turned up edge, cabaret	25	
Plate 11" #32, 4-footed, small center, turned up edge, cabaret	28	75
Plate 11.5" #26, 3-footed, service/torte	30	
Plate 11.5" #26, 4-footed, service/torte	35	80
Plate 14" #28, 3-footed, service/torte	35	
Plate 14" #28, 4-footed, service/torte	38	100
Plate 14" #33, 3-footed, small center, turned up edge, cabaret	40	
Plate 14" #33, 4-footed, small center, turned up edge, cabaret	45	110
Plate 16" #30, service/torte	54	125
Plate 16" #35, small center, turned up edge, cabaret	58	145
Punch bowl 14.75" #478, footed, bellied, flared, 1.5 gallon	2,500+	
Relish 5.5" #119, shallow, flared, tab handled, 2 sections	25	58
Relish 6" #115, shallow, crimped, diamond shape, 2 sections	32	78
Relish 6.75" #120, tab handled, 2 sections	25	68
Relish 8" #122, 3-tab handles, tri-corn, 3 equal sections	22	48
Relish 8.5" #124, oblong, 2 equal sections & celery section	25	60
Relish 9" #102, tab handled, oval, shallow pickle	24	58
Relish 12" #125, 4-footed, tab handled, 2 equal sections & celery section	60	145

Top left: Mayonnaise 2 piece: bowl 6" #105, footed, deep, tab handled, 3.1" tall; liner w/indent 8.6". **Bottom left:** Mayonnaise 2 piece: bowl 5.25" #127, flat sauce, 2.5" tall; #128 liner w/indent 6.25". **Bottom right:** Mayonnaise 8" #112, footed, oval, salad dressing w/ center handle.

Relish 12.75" #103, tab handled, oblong (3 sphere shape) celery	75	195
Relish 12.75" #126, tab handled, oblong (3 sphere shape) 4 sections	85	225
Salad fork/spoon set #609, pattern on handle	40	
Shaker 2.1" #90, flat, individual, ball shape w/square glass lid for base, pair	65	165
Shaker 2.25" #92, individual, triangle w/glass lid, pair	45	125
Shaker 2.6" #91, flat, regular, ball shape w/square glass lid for base, pair	60	145
Shaker 2.75" #96, flat w/chrome, plastic or glass top, pair	35	80
Sugar 2.5" #40, 4-footed, individual, 3 oz.	12	28
Sugar 3" #38, 4-footed, medium, 5 oz.	10	24
Sugar 3.4" #41, 4-footed, large, 6 oz.	14	30
Tray 5.75", oblong, center plume handle, w/2 indents	45	95
Tray 6.1" #37, oblong, tab plume handled	18	40
Tray 7.75" #42, oblong, condiment	25	58
Tumbler 2.75" #188, (blown), flat whiskey, 2 oz.	30	75
Tumbler #300, (blown), footed whiskey, 2.5 oz.	60	195
Tumbler 4.25" #12, pressed, footed cocktail, 3 oz.	30	75
Tumbler 4.8" #11, pressed, footed juice, 5 oz.	25	60
Tumbler 3.6" #180, (blown), flat juice, 5 oz.	25	60
Tumbler #200, footed juice, 5 oz.	20	38
Tumbler 4.1" #300, (blown), footed juice, 5 oz.	16	36
Tumbler #301, (blown), footed juice, plain stem, 5 oz.	14	
Tumbler 3.75" #310, (blown), flat juice, 5 oz.	30	75
Tumbler 3.25" #310, (blown), flat old fashion, 7 oz.	48	145
Tumbler 4.1" #14, flat water, straight sided, 9 oz.	35	85
Tumbler #301, (blown), footed cocktail, low, 9 oz.	20	
Tumbler 6" #10, pressed lunch water, 10 oz.	20	48
Tumbler 5.1" #300, (blown), footed water, 10 oz.	18	45
Tumbler 3.8" #310, (blown), flat lunch water, 10 oz.	34	80
Tumbler 4.5" #310, (blown), flat dinner water, 10 oz.	35	85
Tumbler 6.5" #9, pressed ice tea, 12 oz.	24	58
Tumbler 5.4" #15, flat, straight sided, ice tea, 12 oz.	36	90
Tumbler 4.75" #184, (blown) ice tea, 12 oz.	28	62
Tumbler 5.4" #200, footed, ice tea, 12 oz.	28	60
Tumbler 6.25" #300, (blown), footed, ice tea, 12 oz.	26	58
Tumbler 6.25" #300, (blown), footed w/stem ice tea, 12 oz.	28	62
Tumbler #301, (blown), footed, ice tea, 12 oz.	18	
Tumbler 5.25" #310, (blown), flat ice tea, 12 oz.	45	125
Vase 3.25", short, squat neck, plain top	65	145
Vase 3.5" #249, spherical base, flared top	75	195
Vase 3.5" #250, flat, shouldered, flared top	68	175
Vase 4" #256, rose bowl/ivy ball w/o neck	70	175
Vase 4.25" #341, short neck, scalloped top	70	175
Vase 4.25" #344, squat, short neck, scalloped top	60	145
Vase 4.4" #251, (blown) necked in at top & bottom	95	225
Vase 4.5" #237, ringed neck, plain top	68	165
Vase 4.5" #241, short neck, plain top	58	130
Vase 4.5" #244, squat, short neck, plain top	60	145
Vase 4.5" #252, (blown), shouldered, short neck	80	165
Vase 4.5" #253, ball, short neck, plain top	65	145
Vase 4.5" #337, ringed neck, scalloped top	62	135
Vase 4.6" #235, rose bowl, 4-footed (flat top) 6" wide	80	175
Vase 4.75" #232, rose bowl/ivy ball w/o neck	95	225
Vase 5.5" #245, squat, short neck, plain top	80	165
Vase 5.5" #345, squat, short neck, scalloped top	95	225
Vase 6" #236, rose bowl, 4-footed (flat top) 8" wide	85	195
Vase 6" #242, short neck, plain top	95	225
Vase 6" #342, short neck, scalloped top	90	210
Vase 6.5" #238, ringed neck, plain top	80	175
Vase 6.5" #338, ringed neck, scalloped top	135	275
Vase 7.5" #246, squat, short neck, plain top	135	275
Vase 7.5" #346, squat, short neck, scalloped top	145	295
Vase 8.5" #239, ringed neck, plain top	135	275
Vase 8.5" #243, short neck, plain top	145	295
Vase 8.5" #343, short neck, scalloped top	160	325
Vase 8.5" #339, ringed neck, scalloped top	160	325
Vase 9.25" #240, ringed neck, plain top	170	345
Vase 9.25" #340, ringed neck, scalloped top	225	450

Top left: Comport 5" #136, shallow, cheese, 6.75" wide. **Top right:** Comport 5.5" #136, tall stem, cupped top, 6.25" wide. **Front row:** Almond cup 2.5" #93, square, tab handled; Almond cup 2" #95, 4-footed, round; Decanter w/stopper 7.5" #187, tilt ball, applied handle 35 oz.; Cigarette holder 2.25" #205, triangle shape, 2.1" tall; Ice bucket 5.8" #201, 4-footed w/chrome handle, 5.4" wide.

Emerald Green grouping: **Top left:** Candlestick 3-lite 6.25" #1338, cascading (like ocean waves) 7" spread. **Top right:** Bonbon 6.25" #132, footed, tab handles turned up. **Bottom left:** Vase 4.5" #241, short neck, plain top. **Bottom right:** Bowl 11.25" #65, 4-footed, oval, flared w/tab handles.

Top left: Relish 8" #122, 3-tab handles, tri-corn, 3 equal sections. **Top right:** Relish 12.75" #103, tab handled, oblong (3 sphere shape) celery. **Bottom left:** Finger bowl 4.5" #16, round, deep, cupped. **Bottom center:** Bowl 5" #18, shallow, cupped, fruit. **Bottom right:** Bowl 5.1" #19, flared & crimped, fruit.

Alpine (crystal w/part satin finish) grouping: **Left:** Pitcher 9.25" #183, tilt ball, water w/ice lip, 80 oz. **Center:** Pitcher 6.8" #179, tilt ball, juice jug, 32 oz. **Right:** Pitcher 9.25" #178, Doulton jug w/o ice lip, 80 oz.

Moonlight Blue grouping: **Top left:** Bowl 11.25" #65, 4-footed, oval, flared w/tab handles. **Bottom left:** Mayonnaise bowl 6.1" #110, footed, tab handled, salad dressing, liner w/indent, 8.6". **Bottom right:** Pitcher 9.25" #183, tilt ball, water w/ice lip, 80 oz.

Top row: Tumbler 6.25" #300, (blown), footed w/stem ice tea, 12 oz.; Tumbler 5.1" #300, (blown), footed water, 10 oz.; Tumbler 4.1" #300, (blown), footed juice, 5 oz.; Tumbler 3.6" #180, (blown), flat juice, 5 oz. (Alpine). **Bottom row:** Tumbler 6.5" #9, pressed ice tea, 12 oz.; Tumbler 6" #10, pressed lunch water, 10 oz.; Tumbler 4.8" #11, pressed, footed juice, 5 oz.; Tumbler 3.75" #310, (blown), flat juice, 5 oz.; Tumbler 4.5" #310, (blown), flat dinner water, 10 oz.; Tumbler 5.25" #310, (blown), flat ice tea, 12 oz.

Top left: Vase 4.75" #232, rose bowl/ivy ball w/o neck. **Top center left:** Vase 4.4" #251, (blown) necked in at top & bottom. **Top center right:** Vase 4.5" #252, (blown), shouldered, short neck. **Top right:** Vase 6" #236, rose bowl, 4-footed (flat top) 8" wide. **Bottom left:** Vase 6" #242, short neck, plain top. **Bottom center:** Flower block 4.75" #1502, shell shaped holes, fits 8" rose bowl. **Bottom right:** Vase 4.6" #235, rose bowl, 4-footed (flat top) 6" wide.

Amethyst grouping: **Top left:** Vase 4.5" #237, ringed neck, plain top. **Top right:** Vase 5.5" #245, squat, short neck, plain top. **Bottom left:** Vase 3.25", short, squat neck, plain top. **Bottom center:** Vase 8.5" #239, ringed neck, plain top. **Bottom right:** Vase 4.5" #244, squat, short neck, plain top.

Moonlight Blue grouping: **Top left:** Bowl 11.25" #65, 4-footed, oval, flared w/tab handles (Alpine). **Top right:** Bowl 12.75" #62, 4-footed, flared (Alpine). **Center row:** Plate 7.5" #23, dessert or small salad; Creamer 2.5" #40, 4-footed, individual, 2.5 oz. **Front row:** Tray 6.1" #37, oblong, tab plume handled; dealer sign, celluloid ivory color ($65 – we found it priced this); Sugar 2.5" #40, 4-footed, individual, 3 oz.; Goblet 5" #5, pressed claret, 4.5 oz.; Candlestick 1-lite 7.25" #70, shell foot, curved high stem w/1 prism (Alpine), this one has the wrong prism.

Top left: Cruet w/stopper 4.75" #117, open angle handle, 3 oz., Milk Glass. **Top center left:** Tumbler 2.75" #188, (blown), flat whiskey, 2 oz., Amethyst. **Top center right:** Tumbler 2.75" #188, (blown), flat whiskey, 2 oz., Emerald Green. **Top right:** Decanter w/stopper 7.5" #187, tilt ball, applied handle 35 oz., Cobalt. **Front row:** Creamer 3.25" #38, 4-footed, medium, 5 oz., La Rosa (pink); Almond cup 2.5" #94, tab handled, 2 sections nut/mint, Moonlight Blue; Sugar 3" #38, 4-footed, medium, 5 oz., Pistachio (light green); Ashtray 3" #213, flared, 3 shell footed, shell shape, Mocha (light amber); Ashtray 3" #213, flared, 3 shell footed, shell shape, Mandarin Gold (yellow).

Top left: Relish 6.75" #120, tab handled, 2 sections La Rose (pink). **Top right:** Plate 8.5" #22, salad or lunch, Mocha (light amber). **Center right:** Bowl 4.25" #144, square, tab handled, slightly flared, jelly, Moonlight Blue. **Bottom left:** Bowl 5.25" #151, square, tab handled, jelly, Mandarin Gold (yellow). **Bottom right:** Cup & saucer, footed coffee: cup 2.5" #17, 6 oz., saucer w/indent 5.5", Pistachio (light green).

Sapphire Blue grouping: **Back:** Bowl 9.25", tab handled, flared, vegetable. **Front:** Vase 5.75" tall, flared top, 7.75" wide.

Sapphire Blue grouping: **Left:** Cruet 4.5", flat, spherical w/angled handle, 3 oz.; Tray, 7.5", center handle, 6.5" tall, for holding cruets. **Right:** Cruet 4.5", flat, spherical w/angled handle, 3 oz. ($350 set).

Sapphire Blue grouping: **Left:** Goblet 4.75", ball stem, liquor cocktail, 3.5 oz. **Right:** Goblet 5.75", ball stem, water, 8 oz.

CARIBBEAN

Duncan & Miller Glass Co. **Blank #112** **1936-55**
Main Colors: Crystal and Sapphire Blue
Other Colors: Amber, Cobalt, and Ruby

Caribbean was designed by James E. Duncan III & Robert A. May, and was meant to imitate the rippling waves in the Caribbean. When initially advertised, this pattern was listed as Wave and then the name was changed later.

Many collectors are initially attracted to the Sapphire Blue pieces. With rising prices and short supply on the blue, however, collectors are now turning to crystal. Some of the pieces can be mixed with some blue to create a nice accent on the table. The punch cups can be found in plain Crystal and in Crystal with applied handles in Amber, Cobalt, and Ruby. These usually run about $18.

Note, the cylindrical vase is being reproduced by the Gillinder Glass Company in yellow and green at this time. These new vases are only marked with a paper label. The vase mould is on loan from the Davis Lynch Co. There could be other colors made in the future, so one needs to be wary of any non-standard colors.

Most collectors are actively searching for the candelabra, cocktail shaker, epergne, and pitcher. Add 50% more for Cobalt and Ruby item prices. Generally, Amber is the same price as Crystal, but not many customers even want it. This puts those customers in a real advantage when they are buying.

CARIBBEAN	Crystal	Blue
Almond 2.5", round	14	30
Ashtray 3", round (also lid to cigarette jar)	12	26
Ashtray 6", round	14	34
Bowl 5", fruit, tab handled	12	30
Bowl 6.5", soup	15	40
Bowl 7", tab handled	20	45
Bowl 7.25", footed, tab handled, grapefruit	18	48
Bowl 8.5", vegetable	28	78
Bowl 9", salad	28	78
Bowl 9.25", tab handled or flared (2 styles) vegetable	30	80
Bowl 9.5", tab handled, shallow, console	38	98
Bowl 10.75", oval, tab handled, flower	36	95
Bowl 12", flared, console	48	125
Candelabra 1-lite 8", flared base w/ball under candle cup, prisms, pair	195	395
Candlestick 2-lite 4.75", footed, "U" shape stem, pair	85	195
Candy w/cover 7", flat, round	50	125
Cheese & cracker: comport 3.5", ball stem, crimped, 4.5" wide; plate 11", tab handled	50	110
Cigarette jar w/cover 3.5", cylindrical; lid makes an ashtray	45	98
Cocktail shaker 10.5", flat, straight sided, 32 oz.	98	295
Creamer, flat, 6 oz.	10	24
Cruet 4.5", flat, spherical w/angled handle, 3 oz.	55	125
Cup 2.25", flat, punch w/applied handle, 5 oz.	10	24
Cup & saucer, coffee w/pressed handle: cup 2.25", footed, 6 oz.; saucer w/indent 6"	18	60
Finger bowl 4.5", flat	14	34
Goblet 3", ball stem, cordial, 1 oz.	65	195
Goblet 3.5", ball stem, wine, 3 oz.	20	48
Goblet 4.75", ball stem, liquor cocktail, 3.5 oz.	22	55
Goblet 4.4", ball stem, sherbet, 6 oz.	10	28
Goblet 5", ball stem, champagne, 6 oz.	12	30
Goblet 5.75", ball stem, water, 8 oz.	20	48
Ice bucket 6.5", flat, handled	85	195
Mayonnaise 2 piece: bowl 5.75", flat; liner w/indent 8"	30	65
Mayonnaise 2 piece: bowl 5.75", flat, salad dressing; liner w/indent 8"	32	75
Mustard w/cover 4", flat, cylindrical (notch in lid)	35	75
Pitcher 4.75", juice, 16 oz.	100	295
Pitcher 9", water w/ice lip, 72 oz.	200	600+
Plate 6", handled lemon server	10	24
Plate 6.25", bread & butter	5	14
Plate 7.25", rolled edge	6	16
Plate 7.5", salad	8	20
Plate 8.5", lunch	16	38
Plate 10.5", dinner	60	165
Plate 12", small center, turned up edge, cabaret	24	60
Plate 13.5", small center, turned up edge, cabaret	30	85
Plate 16", torte	38	115
Punch bowl 6" deep, flat, cupped, 1.5 gallon	100	500+
Punch bowl liner 18", small center, turned up edge, w/indent (or cabaret)	50	125
Punch ladle, w/patterned bowl, plain applied handle	60	125
Relish 6", round, 2 sections	15	32
Relish 6", round, 2 sections, tab handled	18	35
Relish 9.5", oblong, 4 sections	34	75
Relish 12.75", round, 4 equal sections & celery section	45	110
Relish 12.75", round, 7 sections	50	125
Shaker 3", w/chrome top, pair	35	95
Shaker 5", w/chrome top, pair	45	125

Sugar, flat, 6 oz.	10	24
Syrup 5", flat, chrome drip-cut top, 9 oz.	125	275
Tray, 7.5", center handle, 6.5" tall, for holding cruets	75	100
Tumbler 3.6, cone footed & cone bowl, whiskey, 2.5 oz.	24	50
Tumbler 3.5", flat, juice, 5 oz.	15	40
Tumbler 4.25", flat, old fashion, 8 oz.	20	45
Tumbler 5.5", footed, water, 8.5 oz.	24	50
Tumbler 6.5", footed, ice tea, 11 oz.	26	58
Tumbler 5.25", flat, ice tea, 11.5 oz.	24	50
Vase 3", squat w/rolled edge, 7" wide	50	125
Vase 4", flat, hat shape w/2 sides rolled over	24	50
Vase 5.75", footed, crimped	25	65
Vase 5.75" flared top, 7.75" wide	45	125
Vase 6.5", cylindrical	35	85
Vase 7.25", footed, ball stem, flared	35	75
Vase 7.5", footed, spherical bottom, flared top	35	75
Vase 8", footed, cylindrical	45	100
Vase 9", footed, crimped	60	175
Vase 10", footed	50	145

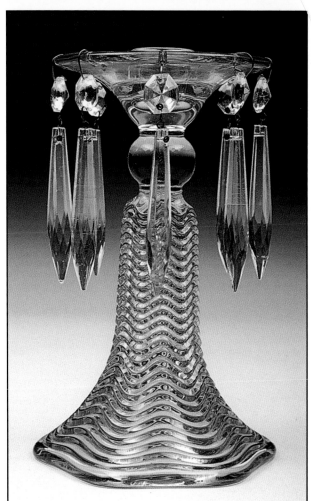

Candelabra 1-lite 8", flared base w/ball under candle cup, prisms, Sapphire Blue.

Cobalt grouping: **Left & center:** Ashtrays 3", round (also lid to cigarette jar). **Right:** Cigarette jar w/cover 3.5", cylindrical; lid makes an ashtray.

Candy w/cover 7", flat, round, 4" tall, Sapphire Blue.

Sapphire Blue grouping: **Left:** Pitcher 4.75", juice, 16 oz. **Right:** Syrup 5", flat, missing chrome top, 9 oz.

Vase 3", squat w/rolled edge, 7" wide, Sapphire Blue.

Left: Plate 8.5" #22, lunch. **Right:** Cup & saucer, coffee: cup 2.4" #17, collar footed, 6 oz.; saucer w/indent 5.5".

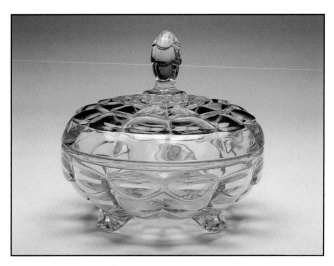

Candy w/cover 5.8" #165, 3-footed, low, round, 5.5" tall, Mandarin Gold (yellow).

Ice bucket 4.75" #671, tab handled.

CASCADE
Cambridge Glass Company   **Blank #4000**   **1949-50s**
Main Color: Crystal
Other Colors: Bluebell Blue, Crown Tuscan, Emerald Green, Mandarin Gold (yellow), and Milk Glass

Original ads show streams cascading over flat rocks, which shows the origins of this pattern. Even though it is a small line, this pattern is continuing to attract new collectors because of reasonable prices. About half of the pieces are $20 or less. This is a real advantage to beginning collectors.

The candlesticks are hard to spot because the cascade part of the pattern is only found on the candle cup, which may cause you to overlook them. Candlestick collectors love to find these. It is interesting to note that even though this is a small pattern, there are two different styles of stems on the goblets. Collectors desire to have the 2-lite candlesticks and candy in their various collections.

Several of the pieces were purchased by the Abel Wasserburg Company in the 1940s to decorate as part of their Charleton line. This company purchased items from several different companies to paint with their special decorations of roses. Many collectors just look for Charleton decorated pieces.

Even though Cascade was made in Bluebell, Crown Tuscan, Emerald Green, and Mandarin, very few examples of these pieces in this pattern have shown up. Therefore, it is impossible to list the fair market value.

CASCADE	Crystal
Ashtray 4.5" #214, round, small nesting	6
Ashtray 6" #215, round, medium nesting	10
Bowl 4.5" #16, shallow, fruit	10
Bowl 6" #164, footed, low, round, candy bottom	16
Bowl 7" #130, footed, handled, sweetmeat	18
Bowl 10" #54, 4-footed, flared, fruit	30
Bowl 10.5" #81, 4-footed, shallow, cupped	32
Bowl 12" #65, oval, 4-footed, fruit	38
Bowl 12.5" #62, 4-footed, flared, fruit	34
Bowl 13.25" #82, 4-footed, shallow, cupped	36
Candlestick 1-lite 5" #67, footed, fancy stem, pair	38
Candlestick 2-lite 6" #72, fan center, pair	56
Candy w/cover 5.8" #165, 3-footed, low, round	45
Cigarette w/cover 4" #616, rectangle	38
Comport 7" #136, high, cupped, 5.5" wide	20
Creamer 3" #41, footed regular, 6 oz.	10
Cup 2.4" #488, handled punch, 4.5 oz.	8
Cup & saucer, coffee: cup 2.4" #17, collar footed, 6 oz.; saucer w/indent 5.5"	14
Goblet 3.8" #3, liquor cocktail, 3.5 oz.	12
Goblet 4" #2, sherbet, 5 oz.	10
Goblet 5.6" #1, water, 9 oz.	16
Ice bucket 4.75" #671, tab handled	38
Mayonnaise 2 piece: bowl 6.75" wide #129, footed tab handled, liner w/indent	30
Plate 6.5" #21, bread & butter	6
Plate 8" #131, footed, handled, lemon server	16
Plate 8.5" #22, lunch	12
Plate 11.5" #26, 4-footed, small center, torte	28
Plate 14" #26, 4-footed, small center & turned up edge, torte	35
Plate 21" #479, punch bowl liner or Sunday evening supper torte	48
Punch bowl 15" #478, cupped, 2.5 gallon	98
Punch bowl base 8" #216, or large nesting ashtray	20
Relish 6.5" #89, footed, oblong pickle	14
Relish 6.5" #89, footed, oblong, 2 sections	18
Relish 10" #64, footed, oblong, 2 equal sections & celery section	24
Shaker #96, flat, squat w/glass top, pair	26
Sugar 2.75" #41, footed regular, 6 oz.	10
Tumbler #15, flat juice, 5 oz.	14
Tumbler 4" #11, footed juice, 5 oz.	14
Tumbler #14, flat ice tea, 12 oz.	16
Tumbler #9, footed, ice tea, 12 oz.	16
Vase 9.5" #573, cylindrical, straight sided	40
Vase 9.5" #574, cylindrical, flared, oval at top	45

Left: Tumbler 4" #11, footed juice, 5 oz. **Center:** Goblet 4" #2, sherbet, 5 oz. **Right:** Goblet 5.6" #1, water, 9 oz.

Vase 9.5" #573, cylindrical, straight sided, Emerald Green.

Candlestick 1-lite 5" #67, footed, fancy stem, Milk Glass.

Mayonnaise bowl 6.75" wide #129, footed tab handled.

Candy w/cover 5.8" #165, 3-footed, low, round, Emerald Green (Charleton decoration).

CENTURY
Fostoria Glass Company **Blank #2630** **1949-86**
Color: Crystal

Fostoria needed a new pattern to jump start their department store sales at the end of World War II. Century featured flowing raindrops as its design and was selected as the new crystal pattern. This was a popular pattern, ranking only behind American and Colony. It proved to be a good seller upon its introduction and remained so until Fostoria closed.

The Century blank was used for the popular Camellia, Heather, and Lacy Leaf etchings. This was a pressed pattern; but, if you wanted some blown stemware, the Rhapsody pattern has a stem that is very similar to Century and these could be used. The cake stand is hard to spot because the pattern is stretched out on the edge, so it does not show up very well.

Some of the more elegant looking items in this pattern are the candlesticks (with all of their curves), center handled tray, cruet, and pitchers. The hardest piece to locate is the footed 3 pint pitcher with ice lips. This piece was only made for a short period of time from 1950 to 1952.

CENTURY	Crystal
Ashtray 2.5", rectangle, individual w/2 cigarette rests	15
Basket 10.25", oval w/reed handle	110
Bonbon 7.1", 3-toed, tri-corn, cupped	24
Bonbon 7.25", 3-toed, round, flared	20
Bowl 3.5", deep, footed, snack	42
Bowl 4.5", one handled nappy	20
Bowl 5", fruit or berry	20
Bowl 6", flared cereal	30
Bowl 8", deep, cupped or w/slightly flared	48
Bowl 8.5", deep, cupped, salad	50
Bowl 8.5", handled vegetable, flared, 10" counting handles	45
Bowl 9", flat, shallow lily pond, cupped edge	65
Bowl 9.5", flat, oval vegetable, 6.5" wide	58
Bowl 10.5", deep, cupped, salad	68
Bowl 10.5", handled, oval utility	45
Bowl 10.75", footed, flared, fruit (sherbet shape)	60
Bowl 11", footed, rolled edge, console	70
Bowl 11.25", flat, shallow lily pond, cupped edge	75
Bowl 12", flared, shallow, fruit	55
Butter w/cover 7.5", handled, oblong .25 lb.	50
Cake plate 9.5", handled	40
Cake salver 12.25", low pedestal	110
Candlestick 1-lite 4.5", curled stem, pair	45
Candlestick 2-lite 7", w/curled "C" stems, 6.6" spread, pair	95
Candlestick 3-lite 7.75", w/1 curled "C" arm over a leaning S arm, 7.5" spread, pair	115
Candy jar w/cover 6.75": footed, short stem; curlicue finial	68
Cheese & cracker: comport 2.5", short stem, 5.4" wide; plate w/indent 10.75"	48
Comport 4.3", flared, 4.75" wide	24
Creamer 3.5", footed, individual, 3.5 oz.	12
Creamer 4.25", footed, regular, 7 oz.	10
Cruet w/stopper 6", flat, oil bottle, 5 oz.	65
Cup & saucer, coffee: cup 2.5", footed, 6 oz.; saucer w/indent 6"	16
Goblet 4.1", liquor cocktail, 3.5 oz.	14
Goblet 4.5", wine, 3.5 oz.	20
Goblet 3.6", oyster cocktail, 4.5 oz.	14
Goblet 4.25", sherbet, 5.5 oz.	12
Goblet 5.75", water, 10.5 oz.	20
Ice bucket 4.8", chrome handle, 7.3" wide	95
Mayonnaise 3 piece: bowl 3.25", footed, flared; liner w/indent 7"; ladle 5"	56
Mayonnaise 4 piece: bowl 3.25", footed, salad dressing; liner w/indent 7"; 2 ladles 5"	68
Mustard 3 piece 4": footed jar, cover, & spoon	68
Pitcher 6.1", cereal (milk) w/no ice lip, 16 oz.	85
Pitcher 7.1", water w/o ice lip, 48 oz.	145
Pitcher 9.5", water w/large ice lip, 48 oz.	215
Plate 6", bread & butter	10

TOP TO BOTTOM:

Top left: Tray 10", tidbit w/center metal handle. **Top right:** Cake plate 9.5", handled. **Bottom left:** Ashtray 2.5", rectangle, individual w/2 cigarette rests. **Bottom center:** Cake salver 12.25", low pedestal. **Bottom right:** Bowl 4.5", one handled nappy.

Left: Mayonnaise 3 piece: bowl 3.25", footed, flared; liner w/indent 7"; ladle 5". **Right:** Cruet w/stopper 6", flat, oil bottle, 5 oz.

Left: Goblet 4.5", wine, 3.5 oz. **Center left:** Goblet 4.25", sherbet, 5.5 oz. **Center right:** Goblet 5.75", water, 10.5 oz. **Right:** Tumbler 5.9", ice tea, 12 oz.

Left: Pitcher 6.1", cereal (milk) w/no ice lip, 16 oz. **Right:** Pitcher 9.5", water w/large ice lip, 48 oz.

Left: Butter w/cover 7.5", handled, oblong .25 lb. **Right:** Vase 7.5", flat, flared, 2 handled.

Plate 7.25", salad or dessert	14
Plate 7.5", crescent salad (kidney shape)	65
Plate 8.25", Party round w/off center indent	18
Plate 8.1", 3-toed, round, tidbit	18
Plate 8.5", lunch	20
Plate 9.5", small dinner	28
Plate 10.25", large dinner	45
Plate 10.5", flat, small center, turned up edge, cabaret	32
Plate 12.75", flat, small center, turned up edge, cabaret	38
Plate 14", torte (small center)	48
Plate 16", torte (small center)	60
Platter 12", oval	65
Preserve w/cover 6", footed	55
Relish 7.4", handled, oval, 2 sections	28
Relish 8.75", oval pickle	24
Relish 11.1", handled, oval, 2 equal sections & celery section	35
Sandwich server 11.25", center S shaped handle	45
Shakers 2.4", individual w/chrome top, pair	30
Shakers 3.25", regular w/chrome top, pair	24
Sugar 3.4", footed, individual, 3.5 oz.	12
Sugar 4", footed, regular, 7 oz.	10
Tray 4.25", rectangle, for individual s & p	20
Tray 7.1", for cream/sugar or oil/vinegar	30
Tray 9.1", handled, cupped, utility	38
Tray 9.75", handles turned up, muffin	48
Tray 10", tidbit w/center metal handle	30
Tray 2 tier 10.25", plates w/chrome center handle	85
Tumbler 4.75", juice, 5 oz.	24
Tumbler 5.9", ice tea, 12 oz.	34
Vase 6", footed, short stem, bud vase	30
Vase 7.5", flat, flared, 2-handled	85
Vase 8.5", flat, oval shape	95

Left: Vase 6", footed, short stem, bud vase. **Right:** Candlestick 2-lite 7", w/curled "C" stems, 6.6" spread.

Bowl 8.5", handled vegetable, flared, 10" counting handles.

CHANTICLEER
Duncan & Miller Glass Company   1920s-30s
Colors: Amber, Blue Opalescent, Cobalt, Crystal, Green, and Ruby

The Lalique influence can be seen in the heavily sculptured roosters walking together. The Paris Exposition attracted many designers from the United States, hoping to get some ideas to imitate the expensive glass. Duncan & Miller introduced Chanticleer as their attempt at sculptured art glass, like Consolidated & Phoenix had extensively done earlier. This was the only design to feature chickens as the pattern. Chanticleer was Duncan's most popular line of bar ware and was one of their smallest lines. The same mould would be used to make several different pieces. All the small vases were adapted from the whiskey tumbler, while the large vase came from the cocktail shaker mould.

You find the following colors in this pattern: Amber, Cobalt, Crystal, Green Opalescent, and Ruby. Transparent and frosted tumblers are easy to find. All the other pieces will take some patience in order to find them.

CHANTICLEER	Amber Crystal	Blue Opal	Green	Ruby Cobalt
Cocktail shaker, straight sided, chrome top, 16 oz.	165	325	350	495
Cocktail shaker 8" (total 10.75"), straight sided, chrome top, 32 oz.	165	325	350	495
Martini mixer, straight sided, chrome top, 16 oz.	98	195	225	295
Toothpick 3.75", straight sided	42	85	100	125
Tumbler 3", flat, whiskey, 3 oz.	20	38	45	60
Tumbler 3.25", flat, whiskey, 6 oz.	24	48	55	75
Tumbler 3.5", flat, old fashion, 7 oz.	36	72	85	110
Vase 3.25", mini, tri-corn crimped	48	95	110	145
Vase 3.25", mini, flared & crimped, 4.25" wide	45	90	100	135
Vase, medium, flared & crimped	85	175	200	250
Vase 8", large, flared & crimped	110	245	275	325

Pattern detail, Chanticleer.

Left: Tumbler 3", flat, whiskey, 3 oz., Crystal Satin. **Right:** Cocktail shaker 8" (total 10.75"), straight sided, chrome top, 32 oz., Cobalt.

Left: Tumbler 3.5", flat, old fashion, 7 oz., Crystal Satin. **Center:** Cocktail shaker 8", straight sided (missing top), Crystal Satin. **Right:** Tumbler 3.25", flat, whiskey, 6 oz., Crystal.

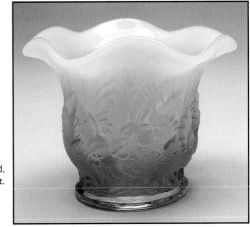

Vase 3.25", mini, flared & crimped, 4.25" wide, Blue Opalescent.

Pattern detail, Chantilly.

Left: Cocktail icer 4.6" #968, footed, 2 piece w/non-etched insert. **Right:** Ice bucket 4.75" #671 Pristine, sham base, graduated deco tab handled w/sterling silver foot.

Left: Mayonnaise bowl 4.5" #1532 Pristine (blown), spherical, 3" high w/sterling silver foot. **Center:** Sugar 2.75" #252 Martha, footed, regular, 6 oz. **Right:** Goblet 4.75" #3600, sherbet, 7 oz.

Left to right: Goblet 3.75" #3775, oyster cocktail, 5 oz.; Goblet 5.9" #3600, saucer champagne, 7 oz.; Goblet 4.75" #3600, sherbet, 7 oz.; Goblet 6.75" #3625, claret, 5 oz.; Goblet 7.1" #3775, water, 10 oz.; Tumbler 7.5" #3625, footed, ice tea, 12 oz.

CHANTILLY
Cambridge Glass Company   1936-58
Color: Crystal

Chantilly spent over 20 years in the Cambridge line. Since there were six different stemware lines, you choose the style you liked the best. The #3600 line was later discontinued and replaced with the #3900 Corinth line. Several items can also be found that were gold encrusted.

Numerous contract pieces were made, primarily for Farber Bros. of New York. Of all the Cambridge patterns, Chantilly was found most often mounted on sterling silver bases. You can add 10% to the listed price. Gorham's Chantilly sterling pattern matches the design on the glass and is a nice compliment to a place setting.

Besides the stemware listed above, Cambridge used the #3080 blown line on which to etch Chantilly. These stems have a bowl with the stem pulled down from it on a plain, straight shaft. There are not enough of these found to determine the market value at this time. You may find a plain lady leg stem #3138 with the Chantilly etching.

Collectors are on the hunt for the following: butter dish, candy dish, candelabras, cheese dish, crescent salad plate, decanters, dinner plate, epergne, French dressing bottle, hurricane lamp, fruit icer, nite set, pitcher, punch bowl, and toast cover. The epergne and candelabras are also favorites among designers and are both in short supply.

CHANTILLY	Crystal
Basket 6" #55 Pristine, footed, low, 2 handles turned up	40
Basket 6.5" #326 Martha, 2 handles turned up	38
Bell 6.5" #3265, dinner	85
Bottle w/stopper 6.5" #1263, flat, French dressing, 8 oz.	245
Bonbon 5.5" #324 Martha, handled	28
Bonbon 6" #54 Pristine, footed, low, 2-handled	30
Bonbon 6" #325 Martha, handled	30
Bonbon 6" #3400/205, 4-footed, flared	35
Bowl 2.5" #3400/71, tab handled, 4-footed, nut	42
Bowl 5" #1534, cupped (blown)	50
Bowl 5.25" #3400/1180, handled, sweetmeat	40
Bowl 5.4" #177 Martha, flared, shallow, fruit	25
Bowl 5.75" #3900/130, footed, tab handled, sweetmeat	42
Bowl 6" #181 Martha, flared, cereal	30
Bowl 6" #444 Martha, crimped, pulled up 4-footed (handkerchief shape)	65
Bowl 7.5" #435 Pristine, deco tab handle	75
Bowl 9" #420 Martha, vegetable	58
Bowl 9.5" #225 Pristine, blown, 2 sections	250
Bowl 9.5" #426 Martha, deep, belled, flared	60
Bowl 9.5" #454 Martha, footed, cupped, cone shape	65
Bowl 10" #427 Pristine, sham base, deep, salad	75
Bowl 10" #3900/54, two styles (3 or 4-footed) flared	55
Bowl 10.5" #222 Pristine, round, deep, 3 sections	195
Bowl 10.5" #435 Martha, handled, dessert	50
Bowl 10.5" #1351 Pristine, crimped, flared	45
Bowl 10.5" #1359 Pristine, tab footed, smooth edge, flared	65
Bowl 10.5" #3900/28, footed, tab handled, flared	85
Bowl 11" #425 Martha, wide, flared	50
Bowl 11" #427 Martha, low, cupped, salad	50
Bowl 11" #428 Martha, basket w/turned up sides	65
Bowl 11" #446 Martha, 4-footed, deep, crimped	75
Bowl 11" #449 Martha, deep, salad	78
Bowl 11" #453 Martha, footed, cone shape, flared	75
Bowl 11" #3400/48, 4-footed, shallow, ruffled edge	80
Bowl 12" #3400/4, 4-footed, square, flared, edge	70
Bowl 12" #440 Martha, wide, flared	60
Bowl 12" #430 Pristine, sham base, belled & flared	58
Bowl 12" #1349 Pristine, tab footed, crimped edge, flared	65
Bowl 12" #3400/160, 4-footed, oblong, crimped	70
Bowl 12" #3900/62, (3 or 4-footed) flared	60
Bowl 12" #3900/65, 4-footed, handled, oval	75
Bowl 12.5" #445 Martha, 4-footed, deep, square, flared	70
Bowl 12.5" #447 Martha, 4-footed, deep, crimped	75
Bowl 13" #436 Martha, handled, dessert	68
Bowl 13" #442 Martha, low, cupped, salad	65
Bowl 13" #448 Martha, shallow	60
Bowl 13.5" #443 Martha, basket w/turned up sides	75
Butter w/cover 5.5" #506, round, tab handled	250
Butter w/cover 5.5" #3400/52, handled	375
Cake plate 13.5" #3900/35, 2-handled	75
Cake salver 13" #170 Martha, tab footed, scalloped edge	175
Canape set #693/3000, plate/cocktail #3000 footed cocktail, 3.5 or 5 oz.	195
Candelabra 1-lite 5.5" #648, keyhole stem, bobeches (plain) & prisms, pair	125
Candelabra 2-lite 6" #1268, keyhole stem, bobeches (plain) & prisms, pair	195
Candelabra 2-lite 6.5" #496 Martha, w/#19 bobeches & prisms, pair	245
Candlestick 1-lite 4" #494 Martha, skirted, pair	85
Candlestick 1-lite 5" #3400/646, keyhole, pair	75
Candlestick 1-lite 5" #3900/67, skirted, pair	72
Candlestick 1-lite 6" #3500/31 Gadroon, column stem, pair	75
Candlestick 2-lite 5.75" #495 Martha, plume arms & ball center, 8.25" spread, pair	145

Candlestick 2-lite 6" #3400/647, keyhole stem, pair	100
Candlestick 2-lite 6" #3900/72, pair	98
Candlestick 3-lite 6" #3900/74, pair	125
Candlestick 3-lite 6.25" #3400/1338, tiered (looks like ocean waves) 7" spread pair	165
Candlestick 3-lite 7" #3400/638, keyhole stem, pair	125
Candy w/cover 5.5" #311 Martha, 4-footed, domed lid, pointed finial	125
Candy w/cover 5.4" #1066/4, blown w/fancy ball stem, plain finial	175
Candy w/cover 5.4" #3600/3, (blown) tall, fancy stem, ball finial	225
Candy w/cover 5.4" #3600/4, (blown) low, fancy stem, ball finial	195
Candy w/cover 7" #103, flat, 3 sections, ball finial	100
Candy w/cover 7" #3900/165, flat	95
Candy w/cover 8" #3500/57 Gadroon, 3 open handled, 3 equal sections	85
Candy w/cover 8" #3900/138, footed, wafer stem, dome lid w/finial (optic)	175
Cheese & cracker: comport, 3.5" #3900/135, short stem, 5" wide; plate 13.5"	85
Cheese & cracker: comport 3.75" #462 Martha, short stem, 6" wide; plate 12.5"	90
Cheese & cracker: comport 5.75" #463 Martha, scalloped edge, 6" wide; plate 11"	99
Cheese dish w/cover 5" #980, (blown)	500+
Cigarette urn 3.1" (blown) Pristine, w/sterling silver foot	50
Cocktail icer 4.2" #187 Pristine, footed, grapefruit, 2 piece w/non-etched insert	75
Cocktail icer 4.2" #3600, footed, 2 piece w/non-etched insert	65
Cocktail icer 4.6" #968, footed, 2 piece w/non-etched insert	60
Cocktail shaker #97, small, #9 chrome lid	350
Cocktail shaker #98, large, #10 chrome lid	195
Cocktail shaker 9.8" #101 Pristine, sham spouted w/glass top ball finial 32 oz.	145
Cocktail shaker #3400/175, #10 chrome lid	150
Comport 4.75" #2496 Baroque, fancy flame stem, flared, 5.5" wide	45
Comport 5" #1066, (blown) w/1 ball stem, 5.4" wide	50
Comport 5" #3600/2, (blown) fancy stem, 5.4" wide	60
Comport 5.5" #3600/1, (blown) fancy stem, 5.4" wide	65
Comport 6.1" #3121/2 (blown) tall stem, 5.4" wide	68
Comport 7" #3500/148 Gadroon, high fancy stem, 6" wide	50
Comport 7.5" #469 Martha, high, scalloped edge, 7" wide	60
Comport 7.5" #3900/136, scalloped edge, 5.75" wide	48
Creamer 2.25" #252 Pristine, flat, individual, plain handle, 3.5 oz.	20
Creamer 2.6" #3900/40, footed, individual, 3.5 oz.	20
Creamer 2.5", sham base w/fancy handle, 4 oz.	30
Creamer 3" #252 Martha, footed, regular, 6 oz.	20
Creamer 3" #3900/41, footed, regular, 6 oz.	20
Cruet/stopper #3400/161, footed w/handle, 6 oz.	165
Cruet w/stopper 6" #3900/100, flat, spherical, 6 oz.	135
Cup 2.5" #488 Martha, punch w/fancy handle, 5 oz.	28
Cup & saucer, coffee #101 Martha: cup 2.6", flat, 6 oz.; saucer w/indent 6"	28
Cup & saucer, coffee #3900/17: cup 2.5", 7 oz.; saucer w/indent 5.5"	24
Decanter w/stopper #3400/119, tilt ball, cordial, 12 oz.	225
Decanter w/flat stopper 11" #1321, footed, 28 oz.	245
Decanter w/stopper 6.25" #3400/92, tilt ball, 32 oz.	295
Epergne 4 piece #645, etched 3-lite candlestick w/plain arm & 2 vases	125
Epergne 4 piece #3900/75, etched 3-lite candlestick w/plain arm & 2 vases	145
Finger bowl & liner: bowl #3600 (blown); plate w/indent	35
Goblet 5.4" #3600, cordial, 1 oz.	60
Goblet 5.6" #3625, cordial, 1 oz.	68
Goblet 4.6" #3775, cordial, 1 oz.	58
Goblet #3779, cordial, 1 oz.	78
Goblet 5.25" #7966, flared, cone shaped, sherry, 2 oz.	80
Goblet 6.2" #3600, wine, 2.5 oz.	30
Goblet 5.5" #3625, wine, 2.5 oz.	30
Goblet #3775, wine, 2.5 oz.	30
Goblet #3779, wine, 2.5 oz.	30
Goblet 5.6" #3600, liquor cocktail, 2.5 oz.	25
Goblet 4.4" #3625, liquor cocktail, 3 oz.	35
Goblet 4.9" #3775, liquor cocktail, 3 oz.	30
Goblet #3779, liquor cocktail, 3 oz.	30
Goblet #7801 Pristine, plain stem, liquor cocktail, 4 oz.	35
Goblet 4.5" #3600, oyster cocktail, 4.5 oz.	16
Goblet 4.4" #3625, oyster cocktail, 4.5 oz.	16
Goblet #3779, oyster cocktail, 4.5 oz.	16
Goblet 6.6" #3600, claret, 4.5 oz.	48
Goblet 5.6" #3775, claret, 4.5 oz.	48
Goblet #3779, claret, 4.5 oz.	50
Goblet 3.75" #3775, oyster cocktail, 5 oz.	16
Goblet 6.75" #3625, claret, 5 oz.	50
Goblet 4.25" #3775, sherbet, 6 oz.	15
Goblet #3779, sherbet, 6 oz.	18
Goblet 5.6" #3775, saucer champagne, 6 oz.	20
Goblet #3779, saucer champagne, 6 oz.	20
Goblet 4.75" #3600, sherbet, 7 oz.	16

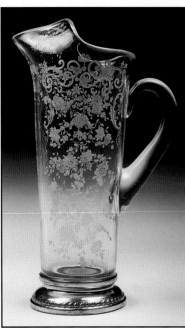

Pitcher 9.25" #100 Pristine, handled, martini mixer, 32 oz., w/ sterling silver foot.

Top left: Cigarette urn 3.1" (blown) Pristine, w/sterling silver foot. **Top right:** Marmalade w/cover 5.4" #147 Pristine, (blown) 8 oz., w/sterling silver foot. **Bottom:** Candy w/cover 7" #103, flat, 3 sections ball finial, w/sterling silver trim on finial.

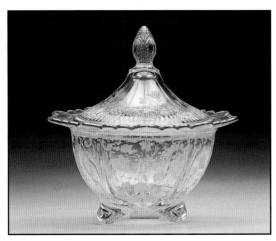

Candy w/cover 5.5" #311 Martha, 4-footed, domed lid, pointed finial.

Top left: Shaker 2.5" #3400, flat, tilt, applied handle, w/chrome top.
Top right: Shaker 3.75" #3400, flat, applied handle, w/chrome top, pair.
Bottom left: Sugar 2" #252 Pristine, flat, individual, plain handles, 4 oz.
Bottom right: Creamer 2.25" #252 Pristine, flat, individual, plain handle, 3.5 oz.

Bowl 10.5" #222 Pristine, round, deep, 3 sections.

Hurricane lamp 17" #1613, bobeche w/prisms & etched large chimney.

Goblet 4.6" #3625, sherbet, 7 oz.	16
Goblet 5.9" #3600, saucer champagne, 7 oz.	20
Goblet 5.8" #3625, saucer champagne, 7 oz.	20
Goblet #3779, lunch water, 9 oz.	30
Goblet #3779, dinner water, 9 oz.	34
Goblet 7.75" #3600, dinner water, 10 oz.	34
Goblet 7.6" #3625, dinner water, 10 oz.	34
Goblet 7.1" #3775, water, 10 oz.	32
Hurricane lamp 8" #1601, short stem, bobeche, prisms & etched chimney, each	195
Hurricane lamp 9" #1617, skirted w/etched chimney, each	225
Hurricane lamp 11.5" #1603, keyhole stem, bobeche, prisms & etched chimney, each	245
Hurricane lamp 17" #1613, bobeche w/prisms & etched large chimney, each	400+
Ice bucket 4.75" #671 Pristine, sham base, graduated deco tab handled	165
Ice bucket 5.75" #3900/671, chrome handle	145
Ice bucket 6" #674 Martha, chrome handle	175
Icer fruit #188 Martha, scalloped edge fits into the Pristine #427 deep salad	245
Marmalade w/cover 5.4" #147 Pristine, (blown) 8 oz.	95
Mayonnaise 2 piece #1532 Pristine: bowl 4.5" (blown), spherical, 3" high; liner w/indent 6.75"	60
Mayonnaise bowl 4" #3900/19, footed, ball shape, 4.1" high	45
Mayonnaise 2 piece #278 Martha: bowl 4.5", flat, cupped; #279 liner w/indent 6.5"	65
Mayonnaise 2 piece #3900: #127 bowl 5", flared; #128 liner w/indent 6.5"	50
Mayonnaise 2 piece #3900/111: bowl 5.25", salad dressing; liner w/indent 6.75"	58
Mayonnaise 2 piece #276 Martha: bowl 5.5", footed, short stem, deep, flared; liner w/indent 7"	68
Mayonnaise 2 piece #328 Martha: bowl 5.5", handled, flared; liner w/indent 7", handled	68
Mayonnaise 2 piece #1491 Pristine: bowl 5.5", flared, salad dressing; liner w/indent 6.4"	65
Mayonnaise comport 6" #3900/137, footed, wafer stem, flared w/optic	60
Mustard w/cover 3" #151 Pristine, (blown) spherical, 3 oz.	115
Nite set #103, handled, jug & flat tumbler w/flared base	500+
Pitcher #3900/117, milk jug w/ice lip, 20 oz.	195
Pitcher 9.1" #3900/118, flat jug/ice lip 32 oz.	245
Pitcher 9.25" #100 Pristine, handled, martini mixer, 32 oz.	300
Pitcher 10.25" #3900/114, martini jug w/ice lip, 32 oz.	275
Pitcher #3900/115, water jug w/ice lip (optic), 76 oz.	250
Pitcher 9.25" #3400/152, Doulton style w/o ice lip, 76 oz.	450
Pitcher 9" #3900/116, ball w/ice lip, 80 oz.	225
Pitcher 8.1" #3400/141, water jug w/o ice lip, 80 oz.	195
Pitcher 9" #3400/38, tilt ball w/ice lip, 80 oz.	245
Pitcher #119, high w/ice lip, 83 oz.	400
Pitcher #1561, ball w/ice lip, 86 oz.	300
Plate 6" #121 Martha, bread & butter	10
Plate 6.5" #3900/20, bread & butter	8
Plate 7" #131 Pristine, (blown) salad/coupe	75
Plate 7" #327 Martha, handled, lemon server	28
Plate 7.5" #122 Martha, dessert/salad	15
Plate 7.5" #555 Pristine, dessert	12
Plate 8" #3900/22, salad or lunch	16
Plate 8" #56 Pristine, handled, lemon server	30
Plate 8" #3900/131, handled lemon server, 9.25" counting handles	32
Plate 8.5" #123 Martha, salad or lunch	18
Plate 9.5" #124 Martha, dinner	95
Plate 9.5" #485 Pristine, crescent salad	125
Plate 10.5" #125 Martha, service or torte	75
Plate 10.5" #162 Martha, small center, turned up edge, cabaret	65
Plate 10.5" #3900/24, dinner	80
Plate 11" #3400/35, open handled, sandwich	50
Plate 12" #3900/26, 4-footed, service	54
Plate 12" #138 Martha, handled, sandwich	48
Plate 12" #164 Martha, small center, turned up edge, cabaret	65
Plate 12.5" #165 Martha, torte w/small center	52
Plate 13" #3900/33, rolled edge, 4-footed, torte	65
Plate 13.5" #126 Martha, service or torte	70
Plate 13.5" #1397 Pristine, small center, turned up edge, cabaret	48
Plate 14" #166 Martha, turned up edge, cabaret, small or large (#128) center (2 styles)	60
Plate 14" #167 Martha, torte w/small center	50
Plate 14" #130 Pristine, (blown) torte	195
Plate 14" #3900/166, small center, turned up edge, cabaret	65
Plate 14.5" #127 Martha, torte w/large center	60
Plate 14.5" #139 Martha, handled, sandwich	50
Punch bowl 15" #478 Martha, footed, deep, scalloped edge, 2.5 gallon	2450+
Punch bowl liner 18" #129 Martha, scalloped edge	300
Relish 6" #203 Martha, handled, round, 2 sections	30
Relish 6.25" #3500/69 Gadroon, 3 equal sections, scalloped edge	35
Relish 6.5" #3400/90, 2 open handles, 2 equal sections	32
Relish 7" #3900/123, 4-toed, tab scroll handled, oblong pickle	35

Relish 7" #3900/124, 4-toed, tab scroll handled, 2 equal sections, oblong   38
Relish 8" #3500/57 Gadroon, 3 sections, 3 handled (candy bottom)   35
Relish 8.5" #235 Martha, oval pickle   32
Relish 8.5" #236 Martha, oval, 2 sections (diagonal divided)   36
Relish 8.5" #353 Martha, handled, oval pickle or cream/sugar tray   24
Relish 8.75" #209 Martha, irregular shape, 3 sections, celery w/4 fan shape
   tab handles   58
Relish 9" #3900/125, handled, 3 sections, oblong   38
Relish 9.5" #464 Pristine, crescent salad shape, 3 sections   145
Relish 9.5" #477 Pristine, oblong w/tab feet, oval pickle or corn   50
Relish 10" #3500/64 Gadroon, 4-toed, handled, 2 equal sections & celery section   65
Relish 11" #246 Martha, oval, celery   38
Relish 11" #247 Martha, oval, 2 sections (diagonal divided)   40
Relish 11" #248 Pristine, narrow oblong, celery   35
Relish 11" #3400/200, handled, 4-toed, curved divider 2 equal sections &
   celery section   68
Relish 12" #215 Martha, oblong, 4 equal sections & celery section   85
Relish 12" #3900/120, oblong, 4 equal sections & celery section   75
Relish 12" #3900/126, handled, oblong, 3 sections   50
Sandwich server 11" #143 Martha, chrome center handle   45
Shaker 2.25" #1956/105, flat, spherical w/tapered neck, chrome top, pair   60
Shaker 2.5" #360 Pristine, flat, spherical, metal top, pair   65
Shaker 2.5" #3400, flat, tilt, applied handle, w/chrome top, pair   40
Shaker 3.25" #3400/76, footed, w/glass top, pair   65
Shaker, 3.5" #3900/1177, flat, w/chrome or glass top, pair   42
Shaker 3.75" #3400, flat, applied handle, w/chrome top, pair   60
Shaker 3.75" #3400/77, footed w/glass top, pair   75
Sugar 2.4" #3900/40, footed, individual, 3.5 oz.   20
Sugar 2" #252 Pristine, flat, individual, plain handles, 4 oz.   20
Sugar 2.25", sham base w/fancy handle, 4 oz.   30
Sugar 2.75" #252 Martha, footed, regular, 6 oz.   20
Sugar 2.75" #3900/41, regular footed, 6 oz.   20
Toast cover 4.5" #1533, (blown) w/finial   450+
Tray 8.5" #3900/37, regular cream/sugar   20
Tray 2 tier 10.5" #144 Martha, center metal handled, tidbit   85
Tray 12" #437 Martha, handles turned up, muffin   48
Tumbler #3400/1344, flat, cordial, 1 oz.   60
Tumbler 2.1" #3400/92, flat, barrel, whiskey, 2.5 oz.   65
Tumbler #3775, footed, whiskey, 2.5 oz.   50
Tumbler #3000, footed, cone cocktail, (3.5 oz. or 5 oz.) use with canape   24
Tumbler 5.6" #3600, footed, juice, 5 oz.   18
Tumbler 5.75" #3625, footed, juice, 5 oz.   18
Tumbler #3775, footed, juice, 5 oz.   16
Tumbler #3779, footed, juice, 5 oz.   20
Tumbler #3900/117, footed, juice, 5 oz.   22
Tumbler #7801, footed juice, 5 oz.   30
Tumbler 7" #3625, footed, lunch water, 10 oz.   25
Tumbler 5.25" #3775, footed, lunch water, 10 oz.   24
Tumbler #498, flat, cut flute, straight sided, 12 oz.   38
Tumbler #3400/38, flat ice tea, 12 oz.   65
Tumbler 7.5" #3600, footed, ice tea, 12 oz.   28
Tumbler 7.5" #3625, footed, ice tea, 12 oz.   28
Tumbler 6" #3775, footed, ice tea, 12 oz.   25
Tumbler #3779, footed, ice tea, 12 oz.   30
Tumbler #7801, footed, ice tea, 12 oz.   50
Tumbler #3400/115, bellied ice tea, 13 oz.   60
Tumbler 4.1" #3900/115, flat, barrel, 13 oz.   40
Vase 4.5" #1309, globe, flower holder   115
Vase 5" #3400/102, globe, flower holder   100
Vase 6" #6004, footed, flared, 1 ball stem, bud vase, flared   48
Vase 6.5" #3400/103, globe, short neck   110
Vase 7.8" #797, flip shape   175
Vase 8" #6004, footed, 1 ball stem, flared   50
Vase 9" #1237, footed, keyhole stem, flared   65
Vase 10" #274, footed, tapered out to top, bud vase   125
Vase 10" #575 Pristine, footed, smooth top, cornucopia, each   125
Vase 10" #1528, spherical bottom, bud vase   100
Vase 10.5" #3400/1242, shouldered, flared   185
Vase 11" #278, large, footed, no stem, flared top   145
Vase 11.5" #1299, footed, ball stem, urn shape   175
Vase 12" #1238, footed, keyhole stem, flared   98
Vase 13" #279, footed, no stem, flared   165

Pitcher #3900/115, 9.1", water jug w/ice lip (optic), 76 oz., Crystal w/ sterling silver base.

Left: Cigarette urn 3.1" (blown) Pristine, w/sterling silver foot. **Center:** Relish 12" #3900/120, oblong, 4 equal sections & celery section. **Right:** Relish 7" #3900/124, 4-toed, tab scroll handled, 2 equal sections, oblong.

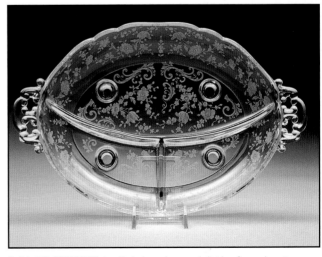

Relish 11" #3400/200, handled, 4-toed, curved divider, 2 equal sections & celery section.

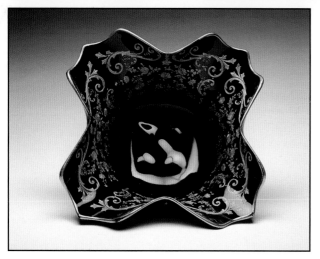

Bowl 12" #3400/160, 4-footed, oblong, crimped, Ebony (black) w/Gold encrusted.

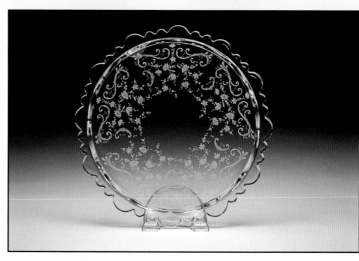

Cake salver 13" #170 Martha, tab footed, scalloped edge.

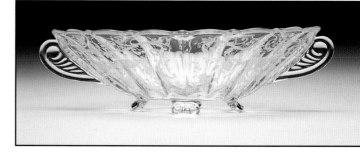

Bowl 12" #3900/65, 4-footed, handled, oval.

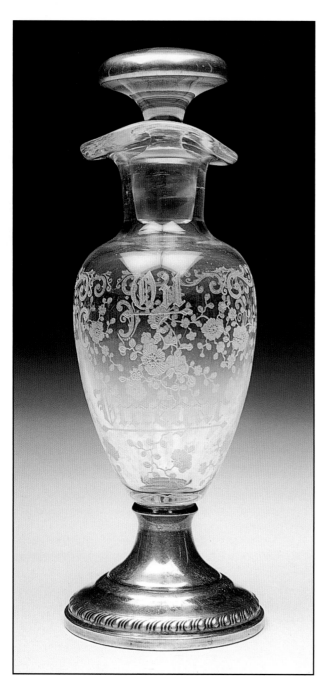

Vase 11" #278, large, footed, no stem, flared top, Crystal w/ sterling silver base.

Bottle w/stopper 6.5" #1263, flat, French dressing, 8 oz., 8", Crystal w/ sterling silver base.

CHEROKEE ROSE
Tiffin Glass Company   **1941-50s**
Color: Crystal

Pattern detail, Cherokee Rose.

New collectors sometimes confuse Cherokee Rose etching with Rose Point. It would be helpful to take time to compare the close-up shots of each etched pattern. This etching is very similar in that Rose Point has roses inside a medallion while Cherokee Rose has an urn inside a medallion. There is an S-shaped garland of roses on each side of the urn. An earlier pattern, Queen Anne was modified to make this pattern. For many years this was one of Tiffin's top selling patterns. There are two other Tiffin patterns that feature the Cherokee Rose etching. The Talisman has a simple gold band at the top of the stem. The Gold Medallion pattern features Cherokee Rose and a band of gold encrusted leaves at the top. These patterns both compliment the plain Crystal Cherokee Rose. For items that are gold encrusted, add 25% to the listed price.

Some of the hard to find items are the bell, 2-lite candlesticks, pitcher, and tub-shaped vase.

CHEROKEE ROSE	Crystal
Bell 5.75" #9743, dinner, 7 graduated beads on handle	65
Bell 6.25" #9742, dinner, 7 graduated beads on handle	75
Bowl 6" #5902, cupped, nut	30
Bowl 7.25" #5902, shallow, flared, soup or salad	36
Bowl 10" #5902, cupped, salad	68
Bowl 12" #5902, crimped, centerpiece	65
Bowl 12.6" #5902, flared, centerpiece	68
Bowl 13" #5902, cone, flared, centerpiece	72
Bowl 13" #5902, crimped, centerpiece	78
Candlestick 2-lite 5.6" #5902, plume center, 7.5" spread, pair	95
Comport 6.25" #15082, 6 beads on stem, cupped, 6.5" wide	58
Creamer 3.4" #5902, regular w/beaded handle, 6 oz.	18
Finger bowl 4.6" #14196 (blown), flat, 12 oz.	24
Goblet 5.3" #17399, cordial, 1 oz.	50
Goblet 5.5" #17399, sherry, 2 oz.	32
Goblet 5.1" #17399, liquor cocktail, 3.5 oz.	20
Goblet 5.6" #17399, wine, 3.5 oz.	28
Goblet 6.25" #17399, claret, 4 oz.	38
Goblet 3.25" #17399, oyster cocktail, 4.5 oz.	18
Goblet 6.5" #17399, parfait, 4.5 oz.	45
Goblet 4.1" #17399, sherbet or sundae, 5.5 oz.	16
Goblet 6.2" #17399, saucer champagne, 5.5 oz.	18
Goblet 8" #17399, water, 9 oz.	28
Mayonnaise 2 piece #5902: bowl 4.4", cupped; liner w/indent 6.25"	48
Pitcher 8" #5859, flat, jug w/o ice lip, 64 oz.	195
Pitcher 8" #14194, footed, jug w/o ice lip, 64 oz.	350
Pitcher w/cover 9.4" #14194, footed w/o ice lip, 64 oz.	495
Plate 6" #5902, bread & butter	6
Plate 8.25" #5902, salad or lunch	12
Plate 13.5" #5902, small center, turned up edge, cabaret	40
Plate 14.6" #5902, sandwich, small center	50
Relish 6.4" #5902, round, 3 sections	30
Relish 10.5" #5902, rectangle, celery	42
Relish 12.5" #5902, tab handled, oblong, 2 equal sections & celery section	48
Sugar 3.25" #5902, regular w/beaded handle, 8 oz.	18
Tray 12.5" #5902, center beaded handle	48
Tumbler 5.3" #17399, footed, juice, 5 oz.	20
Tumbler 6" #17399, footed, water, 8 oz.	24
Tumbler 6.75" #17399, footed, ice tea 10.5 oz.	30
Vase 6.5" #14185, footed, tapered, bud vase	24
Vase 8.25" #14185, footed, tapered, bud vase	30
Vase 8.5" #5856, footed, tear drop shape	85
Vase 9.25" #17350, footed w/1 ball stem (tub shape)	100
Vase 10.5" #14185, footed, tapered, bud vase	42
Vase 10.9" #15082, footed w/6 bead stem, flared, bud vase	60
Vase 11" #5943, footed, urn w/1 large ball stem	125
Vase 12" #5855, footed, short stem, flared	135

Back: Plate 8.25" #5902, salad or lunch. **Front:** Goblet 4.1" #17399, sherbet or sundae, 5.5 oz.

Vase 10.5" #14185, footed, tapered, bud vase.

Pattern detail, Chintz.

Back left: Plate 6" #2496 Baroque, bread & butter. **Back center:** Plate 9.5" #2496 Baroque, dinner. **Front left:** Shaker 2.6" #2364 Sonata, flat, egg shape w/chrome top, pair. **Front center:** Comport 4.75" #2496 Baroque, fancy flame stem, flared, 5.5" wide. **Front right:** Cup & saucer, coffee #2496 Baroque: cup 2.4", footed, 6 oz.; saucer w/indent 5.6".

Left: Goblet 4.25" #6026 Greenbriar, sherbet, 6 oz. **Center left:** Goblet 5.5" #6026 Greenbriar, saucer champagne, 6 oz. **Center right:** Goblet 6.2" #6026 Greenbriar, lunch water, 9 oz. **Right:** Goblet 7.6" #6026 Greenbriar, dinner water, 9 oz.

Left: Goblet 3.6" #6026 Greenbriar, oyster cocktail, 4 oz. **Center:** Tumbler 4.75" #6026 Greenbriar, footed juice, 5 oz. **Right:** Tumbler 6.1" #6026 Greenbriar, footed ice tea, 13 oz.

CHINTZ
Fostoria Glass Company   **Etching #338**   **1940-76**
Color: Crystal

    Chintz etching was Fostoria's answer to compete with the Johnson Brothers' Rose Chintz china pattern, which also incorporated small roses. The petite roses trail on a small branch. This etching is most often found on the Baroque #2496 blank, unless otherwise noted. The stemware is found on the Greenbriar #6026 line.

    In 1980, Fostoria decided to bring back some of its previous best selling patterns under the heading of the Nostalgia line. Six stems from the original Chintz line were selected to be produced. Only as the stems were ordered were they made. This policy enabled customers to replace stemware that had been previously broken. The promotion ended in 1982 but sparked new interest in collecting this etched pattern.

    Some of the hardest to find items are those that were only produced for a few years during the war. These include: vegetable bowl, cigarette box, cruet, platter, salad dressing bottle, Sani-cut syrup, shakers, and 7.5" footed vase.

CHINTZ	Crystal
Bell 6.75" #6014, dinner	175
Bonbon 7.4" #2496 Baroque, 3-toed, flared or crimped	32
Bottle w/flat stopper 6.5" #2083, flat, salad dressing, 7 oz.	500+
Bowl 4" #2496 Baroque, 3-toed, square w/1 handle, mint	32
Bowl 4.25" #2496 Baroque, 3-toed, round w/1 handle, mint	30
Bowl 4.6" #2496 Baroque, 3-toed, tri-corn w/1 handle	32
Bowl 5" #2496 Baroque, flared, fruit	35
Bowl 6" #2496 Baroque, 4-toed, tab flame handled, square, sweetmeat	34
Bowl 8.5" #2496 Baroque, 2-tab flame handled, flared, vegetable	90
Bowl 9" #6023, footed, short stem (blown)	175
Bowl 9.5" #2496 Baroque, oval, vegetable	165
Bowl 10.75" #2484 Baroque, oval, large wing handled	125
Bowl 10.75" #2496 Baroque, 4-toed, oval, flame handled	110
Bowl 12" #2496 Baroque, flat, round, flared	80
Cake plate 10.25" #2496 Baroque, 2-tab flame handled	60
Candlestick 1-lite 4" #2496 Baroque, cornucopia flame shape, pair	78
Candlestick 1-lite 5.5" #2496 Baroque, fancy flame stem, pair	98
Candlestick 2-lite 5.25" #2496 Baroque, flame arms, 8" spread, pair	125
Candlestick 2-lite 5.5" #6023, plain "U" shape stem, 6" spread, pair	145
Candlestick 3-lite 6" #2496 Baroque, flame arms, 8.25" spread, pair	150
Candy w/cover 6.25" #2496 Baroque, triangular, 3 sections, lid w/flame finial	145
Cheese & cracker #2496 Baroque: comport 3.25", short stem, 5.25" wide; plate w/indent 10.75"	98
Cigarette box w/cover 4.25" x 5.5", etched on lid only	195
Comport 4.75" #2496 Baroque, fancy flame stem, flared 5.5" wide	45
Cream soup & liner #2496 Baroque: bowl 4.75", footed w/2 handles, 9 oz.; saucer w/indent 7.5"	90
Creamer 3.1" #2496 Baroque, footed, individual, 4 oz.	22
Creamer 3.75" #2496 Baroque, collar footed, regular, 7.5 oz.	18
Cruet w/clear paneled stopper 5.75" #2496 Baroque, flat oil bottle, 3.5 oz.	175
Cup & saucer, coffee #2496 Baroque: cup 2.4", footed, 6 oz.; saucer w/indent 5.6"	24
Finger bowl & liner: bowl 4.6" #869, blown, 8 oz.; plate 6" w/indent	60
Goblet 4" #6026 Greenbriar, cordial, 1 oz.	58
Goblet 3.6" #6026 Greenbriar, oyster cocktail, 4 oz.	18
Goblet 5.1" #6026 Greenbriar, liquor cocktail, 4 oz.	24
Goblet 5.4" #6026 Greenbriar, wine or claret, 4.5 oz.	45
Goblet 4.25" #6026 Greenbriar, sherbet, 6 oz.	18
Goblet 5.5" #6026 Greenbriar, saucer champagne, 6 oz.	20
Goblet 6.2" #6026 Greenbriar, lunch water, 9 oz.	35
Goblet 7.6" #6026 Greenbriar, dinner water, 9 oz.	42
Ice bucket 4.5" #2496 Baroque, flat, squat, chrome handle, 6.5" wide	155
Jelly 5" #2496 Baroque, fancy flame stem, cupped w/scalloped edge	40
Jelly w/cover 7.5" #2496 Baroque, fancy flame stem & finial	85
Mayonnaise 3 piece #2496 Baroque: bowl 5", flared, crimped, 3.5" high; liner w/indent 6.5"; ladle 5.75"	78
Mayonnaise 4 piece #2496 Baroque: bowl 6.5", salad dressing, oblong, handled; liner 6.75"; 2 ladles 5.75"	135
Pitcher 6.9" #2666 Contour, flat, applied handle, ice lip, 32 oz.	375
Pitcher 9.75" #5000, footed, applied handle, water w/o ice lip, 48 oz.	495
Plate 6" #2496 Baroque, bread & butter	10
Plate 7.25" #2496 Baroque, salad	16
Plate 8.5" #2496 Baroque, lunch	24
Plate 9.5" #2496 Baroque, dinner	68
Plate 14" #2496 Baroque, small center, turned up edge, cabaret	95
Plate 16" #2364 Sonata, small center, turned up edge, cabaret	120
Platter 12.5" #2496 Baroque, oval	145
Relish 6" (or sweetmeat) #2496 Baroque, 4-tab feet, tab flame handled, 2 sections, square	34
Relish 8" #2496 Baroque, oval pickle	32
Relish 10" #2496 Baroque, 4-tab feet, tab flame handled, oblong, 2 equal sections & celery section	49
Relish 10.75", oval celery	55
Relish 13.25" #2419 Mayfair, irregular shape, 4 equal sections & celery section	95
Sauce 2 piece #2496 Baroque: bowl 6.5", oblong, tab flame handled; liner 6.75"	98
Sandwich server 11" #2375 Fairfax, center "fleur-de-lis" handle	75
Shaker 2.6" #2364 Sonata, flat, egg shape w/chrome or glass top, pair	95

Shakers 2.75" #2496 Baroque, regular straight sided, clear glass top, pair — 145
Sugar 2.9" #2496 Baroque, footed, individual, 4 oz. — 22
Sugar 3.6" #2496 Baroque, collar footed, regular, 7.5 oz. — 18
Syrup 5.5" #2586, chrome Sani-cut top, 9 oz. — 600+
Tray 6.5" #2496 Baroque, rectangle, tab flame handled, for individual cream/sugar — 28
Tray 8" #2496 Baroque, tab flame handled, oblong — 42
Tray 8.25" #2496 Baroque, flat, 3-toed, turned up edge, tidbit — 28
Tumbler 4.75" #6026 Greenbriar, footed juice, 5 oz. — 24
Tumbler 6.1" #6026 Greenbriar, footed, ice tea, 13 oz. — 35
Vase 5" #4121, symmetrical, necked & flared — 135
Vase 5" #4128, flared, flip w/regular optic — 145
Vase 6" #4143, footed, large, flared top — 160
Vase 7.5" #4143, footed, large, flared top — 325
Vase 8" #2660, flip shape w/o optic — 225
Vase 9.5" #2470, footed, w/fancy 3 scroll stem, flared — 275

Back: Relish 13.25" #2419 Mayfair, irregular shape, 4 equal sections & celery section. **Front left:** Candlestick 1-lite 5.5" #2496 Baroque, fancy flame stem. **Front center:** Candlestick 2-lite 5.5" #6023, plain "U" shape stem, 6" spread. **Front right:** Candlestick 1-lite 4" #2496 Baroque, cornucopia flame shape.

Top left: Bowl 9.5" #2496 Baroque, oval, vegetable. **Top right:** Bowl 10.75" #2496 Baroque, 4-tab footed, oval, flame handled. **Center:** Bowl 10.75" #2484 Baroque, oval, large wing handled. **Bottom left:** Finger bowl 4.6" #869, blown, 8 oz. **Bottom center:** Bowl 4.25" #2496 Baroque, 3-toed, round w/1 handle, mint. **Bottom right:** Bowl 8.5" #2496 Baroque, 2-tab flame handled, flared, vegetable.

Left: Ice bucket 4.5" #2496 Baroque, flat, squat, chrome handle, 6.5" wide. **Center:** Bell 6.75" #6014, dinner. **Right:** Pitcher 9.75" #5000, footed, applied handle, water w/o ice lip, 48 oz.

Left: Relish 6" (or sweetmeat) #2496 Baroque, 4-tab feet, tab flame handled, 2 equal sections, square. **Center:** Sandwich server 11" #2375 Fairfax, center "fleur-de-lis" handle. **Right:** Cup & saucer, coffee #2496 Baroque: cup 2.4", footed, 6 oz.; saucer w/indent 5.6".

Left: Vase 5" #4128, flared, flip w/regular optic. **Center:** Vase 7.5" #4143, footed, large, flared top. **Right:** Vase 9.5" #2470, footed, w/fancy 3 scroll stem, flared.

Back left: Bottle w/flat stopper 6.5" #2083, flat, salad dressing, 7 oz. **Back right:** Cruet w/clear paneled stopper 5.75" #2496 Baroque, flat oil bottle, 3.5 oz. **Front left:** Candy w/cover 6.25" #2496 Baroque, triangular, 3 sections, lid w/flame finial. **Front center:** Shakers 2.75" #2496 Baroque, regular straight sided, clear glass top, pair. **Front right:** Jelly w/cover 7.5" #2496 Baroque, fancy flame stem & finial.

Vase 5" #4121, symmetrical, necked & flared.

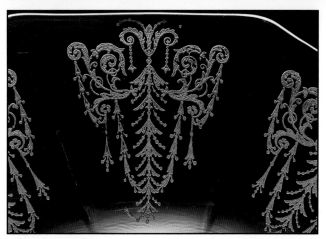

Pattern detail, Cleo.

Peach Blo/Dianthus (pink) grouping: **Back left:** Creamer, 3" #960 Aero optic, flat, regular, high handle 7 oz. **Back center:** Plate 9" #811 Decagon, dinner. **Back Right:** Sugar 3.25" #960 Aero optic, flat, regular, high handles. **Center of photo:** Creamer 2.5" #979 Decagon, flat, handled, 7 oz. **Front left:** Cream soup & liner: bowl 2" #1075 Decagon, 4.75" wide 10 oz., saucer w/indent 6.3". **Front center:** Sugar 2.4" #979 Decagon, flat, handled, 7 oz. **Front right:** Cup & saucer, coffee: cup 2.5" #865 Decagon, flat, 7 oz.; saucer w/indent 5.6".

Pitcher w/cover 13" #3077/10, footed, tall cone shaped, 63 oz., Peach Blo/Dianthus (pink).

CLEO
Cambridge Glass Company   1921-45
Main Colors: Amber, Emerald Green, Gold Krystol (yellow), Peach Blo/Dianthus (pink), and Willow Blue
Other Colors: Amethyst and Royal Blue

The majority of Cleo pieces can be found on the Decagon blank. Stemware will be found on lines #3060, #3077, and #3115. Most collectors don't want every type of stem in the three lines but will choose the style they like the best. With limited budgets and space to store the glassware, collectors are now only selecting a water goblet for their table. This larger size of goblet fits in more with the needs of today's collector. A luncheon set in Green with a few accessory pieces can be found. In 1934, the Peach Blo name was changed to Dianthus, even though no change was made to the original color.

A new style of candlestick to surface since our last edition was the 1-lite plain column stem candlestick. It had not appeared in any of the catalogs or reprints we had. Now it is one to add to the list since we could physically see it and make measurements. A few pieces of Amethyst, and Cobalt pieces, can be found, but not enough in any great quantities to build a set.

The sugar sifter, with the original glass lid, is extremely hard to find. Other challenging items include the gravy boat with liner, toast cover, covered pitcher, cruet, and covered vegetable.

CLEO	Amber	Green Yellow	Pink	Blue
Basket 7" #760 Decagon, 2 handles turned up	20	45	65	74
Basket 11.25" #977 Decagon, 2 handles turned up	38	75	95	115
Bonbon 6.25" #749 Decagon, handled, flared	20	34	50	58
Bowl 2.5" #611 Decagon, footed, individual, almond	32	54	80	90
Bowl 3.75" #1101 Decagon, flared or #1102 flat rim, cranberry	22	38	55	68
Bowl 5.4" #1010 Decagon, flared, fruit	15	25	36	42
Bowl 5.5" #758 Decagon, 5.5" handled, sweetmeat	22	38	55	68
Bowl 5.75" #1098 Decagon, flat rim or #1099 rolled edge, cereal	20	34	50	58
Bowl 5.8" #3400/13, 4-toed, tab handled, flared	26	55	70	80
Bowl 6" #1011 Decagon, flared, cereal	20	34	50	58
Bowl 8.5" #971 Decagon, flat, deep, oval, handled	32	65	78	92
Bowl 8.5" #1012 Decagon, flared soup	28	48	72	84
Bowl w/cover 8.6" #910, oval w/open finial, vegetable	175	325	400+	
Bowl 9.5" #1087 Decagon, oval vegetable	42	78	100+	125+
Bowl 10" #984, flared, open handled	38	85	98	125
Bowl 10" #1013 Decagon, flared, berry	38	85	98	125
Bowl 10.5" #877 Decagon, footed, short stem & flared	75	125	175	195
Bowl 11" #856 Decagon, rolled edge, console	36	78	98	110
Bowl 12" #747, bell footed, rectangular, flared, console	42	92	110	135
Bowl 14.25" #676, rolled edge, mushroom shape, console	42	92	110	135
Cake plate 11" #972 Decagon, small center, open handled	34	78	100	125
Candlestick 1-lite 3" #747, bell footed, rectangular, pair	40	75	95	115
Candlestick 1-lite 3.5" #878 Decagon, wafer stem, pair	38	68	80	100
Candlestick 1-lite 4" #627, round foot, faceted ball stem, pair	38	68	80	100
Candlestick 1-lite 4.25", plain column stem, pair	60	125	145	185
Candlestick 2-lite 6" #3400/647, keyhole stem, pair	72	160	180	225
Candy w/cover 5.75" #104, flat, round, straight sided, ball finial	100	175	225	295
Candy w/cover 6" #864, 3-footed, egg shape	100	175	225	295
Candy w/cover 9.75" #88; footed, short stem; lid w/pointed finial	110	200	250	325
Cigarette box w/cover 3.75" #430, flat, rectangular, 2.75" wide	48	90	100	145
Comport 3.5" #608 Decagon, short stem, 6.5" wide	35	65	75	115
Comport 5.5" #981, short stem, 6" wide	26	55	70	80
Comport 6.75" #1089, short stem	35	65	95	115
Comport 7" #1090 Decagon, tall stem, 7" wide	38	70	80	125
Cream soup & liner: bowl 2" #1075 Decagon, 4.75" wide 10 oz., saucer w/indent 6.3"	30	62	72	90
Creamer 3.5" #1096 Decagon, footed, individual, lightning handle, 4 oz.	22	38	55	68
Creamer 6" #816, footed, tall slim, 5 oz. (use with sugar sifter)	64	145	160	200
Creamer, 3" #960 Aero optic, flat, regular, high handle 7 oz.	24	42	58	72
Creamer 2.5" #979 Decagon, flat, handled, 7 oz.	16	24	34	40
Creamer 4" #867 Decagon, footed (ball shape) 9.5 oz.	15	25	36	42

Peach Blo/Dianthus (pink) grouping: **Back left:** Cigarette box w/cover 3.75" #430, flat, rectangular, 2.75" wide. **Back right:** Cake plate 11" #972 Decagon, small center, open handled. **Center left:** Candy w/cover 5.75" #104, flat, round, straight sided, ball finial. **Center:** Syrup w/chrome top 4.5" #170, flat, squat shape, 9 oz. **Center right:** Candlestick 1-lite 3.5" #878 Decagon, wafer stem. **Front left:** Toast w/cover 9" #951; dome lid w/open finial, plate w/tab handles. **Front right:** Bowl w/cover 8.6" #910, oval w/open finial, vegetable.

Willow Blue grouping: **Left:** Tumbler 5.25" #3077, cone footed, dinner water, 10 oz. **Right:** Goblet 5.5" #3077, saucer champagne, 5.5 oz.

Peach Blo/Dianthus (pink) grouping: **Top left:** Bowl 10.5" #877 Decagon, footed, short stem & flared. **Top right:** Sandwich server 10.75" #870 Decagon, center keyhole handle. **Front:** Bowl 14.25" #676, rolled edge, mushroom shape, console.

Amber grouping: **Left:** Tray 9.1", tab handled, square. **Right:** Plate 6" #809 Decagon, bread & butter.

Cruet w/stopper #193 Decagon, short, oil, 6 oz.	175	325	360	450
Cruet w/stopper #197 Decagon, high, oil, 6 oz.	198	375	450	550+
Cup & saucer, bouillon: cup 2.4" #866 Decagon, handled, 9 oz.; saucer w/indent 6"	30	60	70	85
Cup & saucer, coffee: cup 2.5" #865 Decagon, flat, 7 oz.; saucer w/indent 5.6"	14	27	32	35
Finger bowl & liner: bowl #3077 (blown), sherbet; plate w/indent 6.5"	24	50	60	70
Finger bowl & liner: bowl #3115 (blown); plate w/indent	22	45	54	65
Goblet 4.6" #3077, cordial, 1 oz.	70	165	195	245
Goblet 4.5" #3060, wine, 2.5 oz.	24	50	60	
Goblet 4.5" #3077, wine, 2.5 oz.	32	65	80	98
Goblet 4.9" #3060, liquor cocktail, 2.5 oz.	18	38	42	
Goblet 4.9" #3077, liquor cocktail, 2.5 oz.	28	54	65	76
Goblet 6.1" #3115, paneled stem, liquor cocktail, 3.5 oz.	18	38	42	

Whipping pail 3.3" #847, or ice tub, chrome handle, 5.4" wide, Green.

Peach Blo/Dianthus (pink) grouping: **Back left:** Basket 11.25" #977 Decagon, 2 handles turned up. **Back right:** Pitcher w/cover 11" #124, flat, lemonade, 68 oz. **Front left:** Sugar sifter 6.75" #813, footed w/ glass top. **Front right:** Creamer 6" #816, footed, tall slim, 5 oz. (use w/ sugar sifter).

Peach Blo/Dianthus (pink) grouping: **Back row:** Platter 15.5" #1079/15 Decagon, oval. **Center:** Sugar basket 4.5" #1169, flat w/chrome handle & tongs. **Front left:** Candy w/cover 9.75" #88; footed, short stem; lid w/pointed finial. **Front center:** Gravy boat & liner #917/1167 Decagon: bowl 5.75", handled w/2 spouts; oval tab handled, 9" plate. **Front left:** Vase 11.75" #1130/1, footed (Nautilus design) flared top.

Candlesticks 1-lite 4.25", plain column stem, pair – shown w/1 laying down, Peach Blo/Dianthus (pink).

Item			
Goblet 3.75" #3060, oyster cocktail, 4.5 oz.	18	38	42	
Goblet 5.6" #3077, claret, 4.5 oz.	34	68	80	100
Goblet 6.5" #3060, parfait, 5 oz.	26	50	60	
Goblet 5.5" #3077, saucer champagne, 5.5 oz.	16	24	32	38
Goblet 6.5" #3077, parfait, 5.5 oz.	28	58	70	80
Goblet 4.25" #3077, sherbet, 6 oz.	14	20	28	34
Goblet 4.75" #3115, paneled stem, sherbet, 6 oz.	12	18	25	
Goblet 5.6" #3060, saucer champagne, 6 oz.	14	20	28	
Goblet 6.5" #3115, paneled stem, saucer champagne, 6 oz.	14	20	28	
Goblet 4.25" #3060, fruit salad or sherbet, 7 oz.	12	18	25	
Goblet 7.1" #3060, water, 9 oz.	24	45	55	
Goblet 7.1" #3077, water, 9 oz.	28	54	65	76
Goblet 8.3" #3115, paneled stem, water, 8 oz.	24	45	55	
Gravy boat & liner #917/1167 Decagon: bowl 5.75", handled w/2 spouts; oval tab handled, 9" plate	125	225	295	395
Gravy boat & liner: #1091 Decagon, sauce bowl, 11 oz.; plate w/indent	115	200	275	375
Ice bucket 5.75" #3400/851, flat, scalloped top w/chrome handle	70	165	195	250
Ice tub 3.25" #1147, low w/open handles	58	110	125	175
Mayonnaise 2 piece #871 Decagon: bowl 5.5", footed, flared; liner w/indent 7"	58	110	125	175
Mayonnaise 2 piece #960 Aero Optic: bowl 6.5", footed; liner w/indent 7"	70	165	195	250
Pitcher w/cover #3077, cereal open finial, 22 oz.	75	165	195	250
Pitcher w/cover #955, footed, water, 62 oz.	165	225	375	495
Pitcher w/cover 13" #3077/10, footed, tall cone shaped, 63 oz.	250	450	700	950+
Pitcher w/cover 11" #124, flat, lemonade, 68 oz.	165	225	375	495
Plate 6" #809 Decagon, bread & butter	5	8	10	14
Plate 7" #759 Decagon, handled lemon server	16	20	30	40
Plate 7.25" #815 Decagon, salad	10	16	22	25
Plate 8" #698 Decagon, salad or lunch	14	22	30	38
Plate 8.4" #597 Decagon, lunch	16	25	36	42
Plate 9" #811 Decagon, dinner	48	98	120	150
Plate 10.5" #812 Decagon, large dinner	72	150	175	225
Platter 12" #1078 Decagon, oval, service	58	125	150	200
Platter 15.5" #1079/15 Decagon, oval	95	195	225	295
Relish 6" #3400/90, handled, 2 sections	16	32	40	48
Relish 9" #1082 Decagon, oval pickle	30	60	70	90
Sandwich server 10.75" #870 Decagon, center keyhole handle	40	85	100	125
Sugar 3.3" #1096 Decagon, footed, individual, lightning handled, 4 oz.	22	38	55	68
Sugar 2.4" #979 Decagon, flat, handled, 7 oz.	16	24	34	40
Sugar 3.25" #960 Aero optic, flat, regular, high handles 7.5 oz.	24	42	58	72
Sugar 4" #867 Decagon, footed, ball shape, 9.5 oz.	15	25	36	42
Sugar basket 4.5" #1169, flat w/chrome handle & tongs	48	90	100	145
Sugar sifter 6.75" #813, footed w/glass top	250	600	700	850+
Sugar sifter 6.75" #813, footed w/chrome top	150	400	475	600
Syrup w/chrome top 4.5" #170, flat, squat shape, 9 oz.	175	325	375	450
Toast w/cover 9" #951; dome lid w/open finial, plate w/tab handles	200	400	550	700+
Tray 8" #1096 Decagon, center lightning handle	30	66	78	95
Tray 9.1", tab handled, square	32	72	80	100
Tray 13" #1084 Decagon, round, open handled	72	160	180	250
Tumbler 2.75" #3115, cone footed, whiskey, 2.5 oz.	25	50	60	
Tumbler 2.8" #3060, footed whiskey, 3 oz.	14	22	30	
Tumbler 2.75" #3077, cone footed, whiskey, 3 oz.	24	45	60	68
Tumbler #3060, footed juice, 5 oz.	20	36	45	
Tumbler #3077, cone footed, juice, 5 oz.	16	32	40	48
Tumbler 5.75" #3115, cone footed, juice, 5 oz.	20	36	45	
Tumbler 2.5" #3077, cone footed, fruit salad, 6 oz.	16	24	32	38
Tumbler 4.25" #3115, cone footed, fruit salad, 6 oz.	20	36	45	
Tumbler #3077, cone footed, lunch water, 8 oz.	22	40	48	60
Tumbler 6" #3115, cone footed, lunch, 8 oz.	15	30	38	
Tumbler 5.25" #3077, cone footed, dinner water, 10 oz.	24	45	60	68
Tumbler 6.5" #3115, cone footed, dinner, 10 oz.	22	40	48	
Tumbler 6" #3060, footed, ice tea, 12 oz.	22	40	48	
Tumbler 6" #3077, cone footed, ice tea, 12 oz.	32	66	78	95
Tumbler 7.1" #3115, cone footed, ice tea, 12 oz.	25	50	60	
Tumbler #9403, flat, straight sided, ice tea, 12 oz.	25	50	60	
Vase 6" (blown), concave w/2 rings in center, regular optic, flared	85	195	245	300
Vase 11.75" #1130/1, footed (Nautilus design) flared top	125	225	275	400
Whipping pail 3.3" #847, or ice tub, chrome handle, 5.4" wide	50	100	125	165

COIN

Fostoria Glass Company　　　　**Blank #1372**　　　　**1957-82**
Colors: Amber, Blue, Crystal, Emerald Green, Olive Green, and Ruby

Wedding bowl w/cover 8.25", footed, 5.25" wide, Crystal w/ Gold Coin decoration.

The Coin pattern is based on an earlier U. S. Glass pattern. The glass features embossed coins as the pattern. In addition to the colors, a special Gold Coin decoration was put on crystal items. Decoration #646 featured gold gilding being applied to the crystal coins. The Gold Coin decoration was only put on the candy jar, covered cigarette box, decanter, and wedding box. Prices are three times as much as crystal. The gold was soft on the coins and tended to wear easily. Items that are worn will bring the same price as crystal.

The cigarette urn can be found most commonly with a slight flare or less often flared out to almost 90 degrees. The Crystal lamp is very hard to locate. We sometimes concentrate so much on the colors, that we overlook the hard to find Crystal pieces.

It is important to remember that there are two other versions of Coin. This glass can also be found with different Avon and Canada coin emblems. Avon Coin was produced by Fostoria for the Avon Company as awards for their representatives. The pieces were all made in Crystal. Designs on the coins were: a lady with a rose; door knocker; Avon insignia, tree, key, Script A, and North & South America on a globe. The Canadian Coin was designed by Fostoria to celebrate Canada's 100th Year Commemoration from 1867 - 1967. The coins featured: a flying goose, a howling wolf, a walking bobcat, and a flying bird. These animals appeared on the Canadian coins at the same time. Canadian items were also only made in Crystal. Both the Avon and Canadian pieces were made by changing Fostoria's normal design on the coins in their regular line items.

After the closure of Fostoria, Lancaster Colony reissued many of the pieces for sale at their outlet stores. The colors were slightly different than the originals and all of them had heavy sand blasted coins that appeared almost white. The original coins were satinized by the use of acid. In the fall of 2003 Lancaster Colony sold their hand worked glass moulds to the Fenton Art Glass Company. See the preface for more detail. Among these moulds were the Coin moulds. At this time Fenton has not decided to use any of these moulds. If they do in the future, the items will be made in a different color and will be marked with the Fenton logo. Just this fact alone should safe guard collections in existence and put aside the worries that more reproduction Coin could be on the market.

Fred Wilkerson of Wilkerson Glass is currently making commemorative Coin paperweights. They are being made utilizing the original sugar bowl lid and pouring the glass solid. Across the top, where the knob would have been, the surface is flat. On that surface is etched the Fostoria factory with a flag flying over the factory. The Wilkerson mark (a W) is on the flag. Frosted coins go around the edge. These paperweights were not made originally and are a new item by Wilkerson. We have seen several of these being sold as rare Fostoria on eBay, which in fact they are not. Retail on these is $60. As with any collectible, be aware of any new issues that may come out.

Left: Vase 8", footed, bud vase, Emerald Green. **Center:** Candlestick 1-lite 4.5", short plain stem, Blue. **Right:** Candlestick 1-lite 8", tall stem w/ coins, Ruby.

COIN	Olive	Crystal	Amber	Blue	Red	Emerald
Ashtray 3.5", individual, round		20	20	25		30
Ashtray 4", rectangle	8	10	15	20		25
Ashtray 5", round w/1 coin	8	18	15	25	25	30
Ashtray 7.5", round w/1 raised coin	12	25	20		25	
Ashtray 7.5", round w/4 coins	16	25	25	40	40	50
Ashtray 10", round w/4 raised coins	12	25	25	40		50
Bowl 4.1", flat, round, fruit		45				
Bowl 4.5", round		25				
Bowl 5.4", round w/handle	8	15	15	25	30	35
Bowl 8", deep, round	16	30	30	45	45	65
Bowl 8.9", deep, oval	18	30	30	50	50	65
Cake salver 10", pedestal	45	95	95	175		275
Candlestick 1-lite 4.5", short plain stem, pair	20	40	30	50	50	60
Candlestick 1-lite 8", tall stem w/ coins, pair	28	50	45		110	
Candy box w/cover 4", low, flat, 6.25" wide	18	24	25	60	60	75
Candy jar w/cover 6.5", flat, 4" wide	20	28	30	55	60	85
Cigarette box w/cover 5.75", rectangle		45	50	75		100
Cigarette jar w/cover 4.75", (lid is individual ashtray)		45	50	75	75	95
Cigarette urn 3.4", footed	18	20	25	45	40	50
Comport open 6.5", large, 8.25" wide	26	45	45	85	70	100
Comport w/cover 10.25", large, 8.25" wide		65	65	145		195
Cream pitcher 3.5", flat, 7 oz.	8	10	10	16	18	28
Cruet w/stopper 6", oil bottle, 7 oz.	35	55	60	120		185
Cup 3.5", handled punch, 6 oz.		20				
Decanter w/stopper 10.5", flat, 16 oz.	65	95	95	185		295
Goblet 5", wine, 5 oz.	18	30			65	
Goblet 5.1", sherbet, 9 oz.	18	30			60	
Goblet 6.5", water, 10 oz.	22	35			85	
Jelly dish 3.75", footed, cupped, 4.5" wide	8	15	15	25	25	30
Lamp 9.75", courting w/handle - oil or electric			95	145		
Lamp 13.5", coach, 8 flat sided - oil or electric		175	145	225		
Lamp 16.6", high, patio - oil or electric		225	165	245		

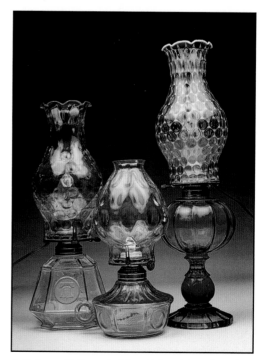

Left: Lamp 13.5", coach, 8 flat sided – electric, Crystal.
Center: Lamp 9.75", courting w/handle – oil, Blue.
Right: Lamp 16.6", high, patio – electric, Amber.

Pitcher 6.6", flat, water, 32 oz.	30	45	50	125	145	165
Plate 8", lunch	12	20			40	
Punch bowl 14", capacity, 1.5 gallon		195				
Punch base 5.5", pedestal		75				
Shaker 3.25", chrome top, pair	24	40	50	60	85	115
Sugar bowl w/cover 5.4", flat, 8 oz.	14	25	28	42	48	68
Tray, condiment 9.1", oval, tab handled	25	30	30	60		
Tumbler 3.6", flat, Juice, 9 oz.		20				
Tumbler 4.25", flat, water, 9 oz.		30				
Tumbler 4", flat, old fashion, 10 oz.	12	20			48	
Tumbler 5.25", flat, ice tea, 12 oz.		35				
Tumbler 5.5", flat, ice beverage, 14 oz.	20	35			75	
Urn & cover 12.75", footed, 5.4" wide	40	75	60	125	100	195
Vase 8", footed, bud vase	15	18	20	35	35	50
Vase 10", footed, bud vase		45				
Wedding bowl w/cover 8.25", footed, 5.25" wide	30	55	60	85	85	135

CANADIAN COIN

	Crystal
Bowl 5.4", round w/handle nappy	25
Candlestick 1-lite 4.5", low, pair	48
Jelly dish 3.75", footed, cupped, 4.5" wide	20
Shaker 3.25", chrome top, pair	45
Vase 8", footed, bud vase	28

AVON COIN

	Crystal
Bowl 8", deep, round	18
Candlestick 1-lite 4.5", low, pair	30
Comport open 9", large, 8.25" wide	25
Cruet w/stopper 6", oil bottle, 7 oz.	50
Jelly dish 3.75", footed, cupped, 4.5" wide	10
Shaker 3.25", chrome top, pair	30
Wedding bowl w/cover 8.25", footed, 5.25" wide	48

TOP TO BOTTOM:

Back row: Tumbler 5.5", flat, ice beverage, 14 oz., Crystal; Tumbler 5.25", flat, ice tea, 12 oz., Crystal; Tumbler 4.25", flat, water, 9 oz., Crystal; Tumbler 3.6", flat, Juice, 9 oz., Crystal. **Front row:** Decanter w/stopper 10.5", flat, 16 oz., Gold Coin decoration; Goblet 5", wine, 5 oz., Crystal; Goblet 5.1", sherbet, 9 oz., Olive Green; Goblet 6.5", water, 10 oz., Olive Green; Pitcher 6.6", flat, water, 32 oz., Amber.

Back left: Urn & cover 12.75", footed, 5.4" wide, Amber. **Back center:** Wedding bowl w/cover 8.25", footed, 5.25" wide, Emerald Green. **Back right:** Comport w/cover 10.25", large, 8.25" wide, Blue. **Front left:** Candy jar w/cover 6.5", flat, 4" wide, w/Gold Coin decoration. **Front right:** Candy box w/cover 4", low, flat, 6.25" wide, Ruby.

Top Left: Shaker 3.25", chrome top, pair, Olive Green; Cruet w/stopper 6", oil bottle, 7 oz., Olive Green; Tray, condiment 9.1", oval, tab handled, Olive Green. **Top right:** Plate 8", lunch, Crystal; Nappy 5.4", round w/handle, Emerald Green. **Front left:** Sugar bowl w/cover 5.4", flat, 8 oz., Amber. **Front right:** Cream pitcher 3.5", flat, 7 oz., Blue. **Front right:** Jelly dish 3.75", footed, cupped, 4.5" wide, Ruby.

Top left: Cake salver 10", pedestal, Amber. **Top center:** Bowl 4.1", flat, round, fruit, Crystal. **Top right:** Comport open 6.5", large, 8.25" wide, Ruby. **Bottom left:** Bowl 8", deep, round, Emerald Green. **Bottom right:** Bowl 8.9", deep, oval, Blue.

Top left: Ashtray 7.5", round w/1 raised coin, Ruby. **Top right:** Ashtray 10", round w/4 raised coins, Amber. **Front left:** Cigarette urn 3.4", footed, Olive Green. **Front center left:** Ashtray 3.5", individual, round, Crystal. **Front center right:** Cigarette jar w/cover 4.75", (lid is individual ashtray), Blue. **Front right:** Cigarette box w/cover 5.75", rectangle, Crystal.

Paperweight, 3.25" long, 2" across the top. New commemorative being made by Wilkerson Glass. On the top is an etched Fostoria Glass factory w/a flag flying over the factory. There are frosted coins around the bottom. 2003 ($60 each). **Top left:** Vaseline. **Top right:** Blue. **Bottom left:** Cobalt. **Bottom right:** Purple.

COLONIAL DAME
Fostoria Glass Company   **Blank #5412**   **1948-86**
Colors: Crystal and Crystal stem/foot with Empire Green bowl

Colonial Dame was a companion pattern to Colony that was only offered as a blown lead glass stemware line. The pattern is on the foot with a plain bowl. It is a nice, delicate stemware that could be used to dress up your table for special occasions, especially in the two-tone colored pieces. The two-tone pieces have the Empire Green bowl & clear stem/foot.

Collectors do not seem to care as much for this companion pattern, which is surprising. Due to this lack of interest, it is still an inexpensive pattern. It makes a delightful addition to any of the dark green colored patterns that don't have stems or ones with stems that have gotten too expensive.

COLONIAL DAME

	Crystal	Empire Green
Goblet 3.25", cordial, 1 oz.	24	45
Goblet 4", liquor cocktail, 3.5 oz.	12	20
Goblet 4.6", claret/wine, 3.75 oz.	22	32
Goblet 3.9", oyster cocktail, 4.5 oz.	8	20
Goblet 4.2", sherbet, 6 oz.	10	20
Goblet 4.75", saucer champagne, 6.5 oz.	14	22
Goblet 5.6", lunch water, 10 oz.	20	30
Goblet 6.4", dinner water, 11 oz.	24	36
Tumbler 4.6", footed juice, 5 oz.	14	25
Tumbler 6", footed, ice tea, 12 oz.	24	36

TOP RIGHT: Crystal foot w/Empire Green bowl grouping: **Left to right:** Goblet 3.25", cordial, 1 oz.; Goblet 3.9", oyster cocktail, 4.5 oz.; Goblet 4.6", claret/wine, 3.75 oz.; Goblet 4.75", saucer champagne, 6.5 oz.; Goblet 6.4", dinner water, 11 oz.

CENTER RIGHT: Crystal foot w/Empire Green bowl grouping: **Left to right:** Goblet 3.9", oyster cocktail, 4.5 oz.; Tumbler 4.6", footed juice, 5 oz.; Tumbler 6", footed, ice tea, 12 oz.

COLONY
Fostoria Glass Company   **Blank #2412**   **1938-82**
Color: Crystal
Other Color: Milk Glass

Colony has its roots in the early pattern of Queen Anne, which Fostoria produced at the turn of the century. The simple swirled effect lent itself to many different types of entertaining themes. This large pattern was offered for many years. This pattern ran a close second in popularity to the American pattern also offered by Fostoria.

You can find some items with only a pattern on the rim that looks like a rope edge. When you look at the edge, the thin repeating pattern resembles the coils on a rope. The same lid fits both styles of covered comports and covered urns. One style has a pattern on the bowl, while the much harder to find style has a plain bowl. The nesting ashtrays can be found in both round and square, which may add a small amount of confusion. The large 18" torte plate is another item that is almost always missing from collections.

In 1982, Colony was reintroduced into the line and renamed Maypole. Instead of being made in Crystal, it was now offered in Blue, Yellow, and Pink. Also, a few items were made in Milk Glass and Ruby for the outlet stores. New collectors may think these pieces are rare. With the closing of Fostoria, the Colony moulds were kept in production by Lancaster Colony for their Tiara line. Colony was renamed Colony Gardens with pieces being made in Lilac and Mint Green Opalescent. These were made by the Fenton Art Glass Company for the Tiara line.

In the fall of 2003 Lancaster Colony sold their hand worked glass moulds to the Fenton Art Glass Company; among these were the Colony moulds. See the preface for more detail. At this time Fenton has not decided to use any of these moulds. If they do use the moulds in the future, the items will be made in a different color and will be marked with the Fenton logo. There are some reproduction crystal Colony candle holders coming from Taiwan. They are seedy and there is a slight stippling around the middle. The example we saw still had the original paper label that said: Biedermann Made in Taiwan. The candle holder was 3" tall and 4.5" across the base. Just be aware that there could be other pieces.

Colony collectors do not seem to be interested in the Milk Glass items, so all these pieces go into Milk Glass collections.

Left: Punch bowl 13.25", collar base deep w/slightly flared, 8.25" tall, 2 gallon. **Right:** Cup 2.9", footed punch, 5.25 oz.

COLONY

	Crystal
Ashtray 3", individual, square (pattern on rim) nesting #1	14
Ashtray 3", individual, round (pattern on rim) nesting #1	12
Ashtray 3.5", square (pattern on rim) nesting #2	18
Ashtray 4.5", round (pattern on rim) nesting #2	16
Ashtray 4.5", square (pattern on rim) nesting #3	20
Ashtray 6", round (pattern on rim) nesting #3	18
Bonbon 5" x 6", tab handles turned up	10
Bonbon 7", 3-toed, round, shallow, flared	15
Bonbon 7", 3-toed, shallow, tri-corn shape	14
Bowl 2.6", collar footed, oval, almond	28

Bowl 11", collar footed, oval, console, Crystal.

Left: Candlestick 1-lite 7", tall stem. Top center: Candlestick 2-lite 6.5", center spire, 8.25" spread. Bottom center: Candlestick 1-lite 3.25", low, no stem. Right: Candlestick 1-lite 9" (Not Colony – Note, made by McKee & sometimes mistaken for Colony).

Back left: Tray 6.75", for individual cream/sugar (pattern on rim). Back right: Cruet w/matching stopper 5.9", flat, 4.5 oz. Front left: Creamer 3.25", footed, individual, 4.25 oz. Front right: Sugar bowl 2.9", footed, individual, 4.25 oz.

Vase 6", footed w/wafer stem, flared, bud vase.

Candelabra, 1-lite 14", lustre, 10 prisms.

Candelabra 2-lite 13" #15, w/2 bobeches, 16 prisms, 14" spread.

Bowl 3" #112, flat, sponge	28
Bowl 4.5", round nappy	12
Bowl 4.75", finger bowl, deep w/slightly flared	18
Bowl 5", round nappy	16
Bowl 5", tab handled, shallow, sweetmeat	18
Bowl 5.5", shallow, square shaped, ice cream	45
Bowl 5.6", 3-toed, round, cupped, nut	15
Bowl 8", deep, cupped (rose bowl like)	48
Bowl 8.25", collar base, deep w/slightly flared	45
Bowl 8.5", open handled, shallow, vegetable	48
Bowl 9", flat, shallow lily pond, cupped edge	40
Bowl 9", deep, rolled edge, console	45
Bowl 9.75", deep, cupped, salad	75
Bowl 10", flat, shallow lily pond, cupped edge	40
Bowl 10", low, flared, fruit	45
Bowl 10.5", footed, short stem (comport like) 5.6" high	100
Bowl 10.5" footed, tall stem (comport like) 8.25" high	150
Bowl 10.5", shallow, oval, vegetable	65
Bowl 10.5", shallow, oval, 2 sections, vegetable	60
Bowl 10.5", deep, cupped, fruit or salad	45
Bowl 11", collar footed, oval, console	85
Bowl 11", deep, flared	48
Bowl 11", pedestal footed, flared, centerpiece	125
Bowl 13", flat, shallow lily pond, cupped edge	42
Bowl 13.75", shallow w/rolled edge, centerpiece	58
Bowl 14", low, cupped, fruit	70
Butter w/cover 7.5", tab handled, oblong .25 lb.	50
Cake plate 10", open handled (12.1" overall)	35
Cake salver 12", low, pedestal w/turned up edge	125
Candelabra 1-lite 6" #2412 1/2, lustre, bobeche, 3 B (fat) prisms, pair	195
Candelabra 1-lite 7.5", lustre, bobeche, 8 prisms, pair	175
Candelabra 1-lite 9.75" #10, lustre, bobeche, 10 prisms, pair	225
Candelabra 1-lite 14" #1103, lustre, bobeche, 10 prisms, pair	350
Candelabra 2-lite 6.25", center spire, w/2 bobeches, 8 B (fat) prisms, pair	195
Candelabra 2-lite 13" #15, w/2 bobeches, 16 prisms, 14" spread, pair	395
Candelabra 6-lite 24.5", w/5 arms, center stem, bobeches & prisms, 15" spread, each	795
Candlestick 1-lite 3.25", low, no stem, pair	34
Candlestick 1-lite 7", tall stem, pair	75
Candlestick 1-lite 9", tall stem, pair	85
Candlestick 2-lite 6.5", center spire, 8.25" spread, pair	95
Candy box w/cover 6.5", low, flat, round	60
Cheese & cracker: comport 3.5", short stem, 5.25" wide; plate 12.5"	65
Cigarette box w/plain cover 6", oblong (pattern on rim) 4.75" wide	85
Comport 3", shallow, tidbit, 7.3" wide	25
Comport 3", shallow, tidbit, plain bowl (no pattern/optic) 7.3" wide	95
Comport 3.8", plain bowl (no pattern/optic) 6.25" wide	90
Comport 4.1", tall stem, 5" wide	20
Comport w/cover 6.4", footed, 6.25" wide	45
Comport w/cover 6.4", plain bowl (no pattern/optic) 6.25" wide	145
Creamer 3.25", footed, individual, 4.25 oz.	6
Creamer 3.9", footed regular, 7 oz.	8
Cream soup 5", collar footed, handled, 9 oz.	65
Cruet w/matching stopper 5.9", flat, 4.5 oz.	65
Cup 2.9", footed punch, 5.25 oz.	20
Cup & saucer, coffee: cup 2.5", footed, 6 oz.; saucer w/indent 5.75"	8
Goblet 4.25", wine, 3.25 oz.	18
Goblet 3.8", liquor cocktail, 3.5 oz.	10
Goblet 3.4", wafer stem, oyster cocktail, 4 oz.	9
Goblet 3.6", sherbet, 5 oz.	5
Goblet 5.25", water, 9 oz.	11
Ice tub 6.25", deep, bowl, 4.5" wide	95
Ice tub 4", deep, bowl w/plain lip at top, 7.25" wide	275

Jelly w/cover 6.8", footed w/tall stem	55
Mayonnaise 3 piece: bowl 4.75", collar footed, flared, 3.4" high; liner w/indent 6.9"; ladle	68
Mayonnaise 3 piece: bowl 5.75", deep, plain bowl w/pattern on rim; liner 7.25" (pattern on rim); ladle	145
Pitcher 5.8", footed cereal w/o ice lip, 16 oz.	145
Pitcher 8.5", footed w/ice lip, 48 oz.	225
Pitcher 7.9", blown, ball shape (plain rim at top) w/ice lip, 64 oz.	145
Plate 6", bread & butter	8
Plate 6.5", tab handled, lemon server	16
Plate 7", salad	12
Plate 7.4", salad (pattern on rim)	38
Plate 8.25", lunch	18
Plate 9", dinner	38
Plate 10.5", snack tray, turned up edge	32
Plate 13", small center, turned up edge, cabaret or salad bowl liner	38
Plate 15", small center, turned up edge, cabaret	65
Plate 18", small center, turned up edge, cabaret	125+
Platter 12.5", oval, serving	60
Punch bowl 13.25", collar base deep w/slightly flared, 2 gallon	850
Relish 6.25", oval olive	15
Relish 6.5", rectangular (pattern on rim) olive	48
Relish 7", oval olive	16
Relish 7", open handled, oval, 2 sections	20
Relish 7.25", rectangular, 2 sections, divided diagonally (pattern on rim)	80
Relish 8", rectangular, 2 sections (pattern on rim) sweetmeat	75
Relish 8", rectangular (pattern on rim) pickle	60
Relish 8", oval pickle	22
Relish 9.5", oval pickle	28
Relish 9.6", oval celery	30
Relish 10", rectangular, 3 sections, divided diagonally (pattern on rim)	95
Relish 10.75", open handled, oval, 2 equal sections & celery section	38
Relish 10.5", rectangular (pattern on rim) celery	72
Relish 11.5", oval celery	35
Sandwich server 11.5", center "question mark shape" handle	45
Shaker 1.9", individual, squat w/glass top, pair	34
Shaker 2.4", individual, tapered w/chrome top, pair	20
Shaker 2.75", regular, squat w/glass top, pair	38
Shaker 3.6", regular, tapered w/chrome top, pair	24
Sugar bowl 2.9", footed, individual, 4.25 oz.	6
Sugar bowl 3.4", footed, regular, 7 oz.	8
Tray 4.25", tab handled, for individual salt & pepper	20
Tray 6.75", for individual cream/sugar (pattern on rim)	24
Tray 7.5", 3-toed, flat, tidbit w/turned up edge	12
Tray 8.4" x 9.75", handles turned up, muffin	58
Tumbler 3.7", flat straight sided, juice, 5 oz.	32
Tumbler 4.5", footed, wafer stem, juice, 5 oz.	16
Tumbler 3.9", flat, straight sided, water, 9 oz.	28
Tumbler 4.9", flat, straight sided, ice tea, 12 oz.	54
Tumbler 5.6", footed, wafer stem, ice tea, 12 oz.	20
Urn w/cover 8.9", footed w/all over pattern	125
Urn w/cover 8.9", footed w/plain bowl (no pattern/optic)	225
Vase 6", collar base, cupped, rose bowl	24
Vase 6", footed w/wafer stem, flared, bud vase	18
Vase 7", footed, short fat stem w/cupped in top	60
Vase 7.5", footed, short fat stem w/flared top	70
Vase 9.25", footed, cornucopia w/curled tail	145
Vase 12", straight side, flared at top	195
Vase 14", straight side, flared at top	225
Whip cream bowl 4.75", flat, cupped, tab handled	18

Top row: Goblet 3.6", sherbet, 5 oz.; Tumbler 3.7", flat straight sided, juice, 5 oz.; Tumbler 4.5", footed, wafer stem, juice, 5 oz. **Bottom row:** Goblet 4.25", wine, 3.25 oz.; Goblet 3.4", wafer stem, oyster cocktail, 4 oz.; Goblet 3.8", liquor cocktail, 3.5 oz.; Goblet 5.25", water, 9 oz.; Tumbler 5.6", footed, wafer stem, ice tea, 12 oz.

Left: Ice tub 4", deep, bowl w/plain lip at top, 7.25" wide. **Right:** Comport w/cover 6.4", plain bowl (no pattern/optic) 6.25" wide.

Left: Ashtray 3", individual, square (pattern on rim) nesting #1. **Right:** Cigarette box w/plain cover 6", oblong (pattern on rim) 4.75" wide.

Back row: Platter 12.5", oval, serving. **Front left:** Cream soup 5", collar footed, handled, 9 oz. **Front right:** Candlestick 1-lite 6", lustre, 3 B (fat) prisms.

Top left: Urn w/cover 8.9", footed w/all over pattern. **Top center:** Pitcher 5.8", footed cereal w/o ice lip, 16 oz. **Top right:** Pitcher 7.9", blown, ball shape (plain rim at top) w/ice lip, 64 oz. **Bottom center:** Mayonnaise 3 piece: bowl 4.75", collar footed, flared, 3.4" high; liner w/indent 6.9"; ladle. **Bottom right:** Bowl 3" #112, flat, sponge.

Left: Vase 6", footed w/wafer stem, flared, bud vase. **Right:** Vase 7.5", footed, short fat stem w/flared top.

Left: Sugar 3", footed, individual, 4 oz. **Right:** Creamer 3.25", footed, individual, 3.5 oz.

Back left: Plate 7.5", salad or dessert. **Back center:** Plate 9.5", dinner. **Front left:** Vase 3.75" #2560 Coronet, footed, cupped in top, pansy. **Front center:** Mayonnaise 4 piece: bowl 6.75", footed, salad dressing, 3.5" high liner 7.1"; 2 ladles 5.75". **Front right:** Cup & saucer, coffee: cup 2.75", footed, 5.5 oz.; saucer w/indent 5.75".

Left: Candlestick 1-lite 4.25", graduated plume handled. **Right:** Candlestick 2-lite 5.1", w/plume center, 9" spread.

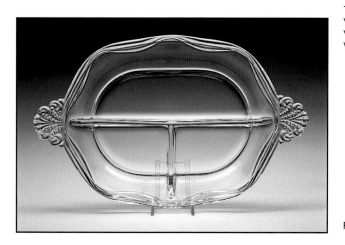

CORONET
Fostoria Glass Company   **Blank #2560**   **1939-60**
Color: Crystal

    Coronet looks like rippling waves at the edge of each piece. The Mayflower and Willowmere etchings are found on this blank. This pattern is unusual in that no stemware or tumblers were made to go with the pattern. Collectors can use any number of blanks to go with this pattern. Coronet came out a year after Colony and shares some similarities. Both center handled trays utilize the exact same handle. The handles on the 1-lite candlestick, creamer, cup, cruet, and sugar are all rope-like and resemble Colony.

    The candlesticks are hard to spot, because the cascade part of the pattern is only found on the drip edge of the candle cup. Therefore, this may cause you to overlook them.

    In the early years, some of the items were made for a short time and are much harder to find now. They include: cheese & cracker, ice bucket, four & five section relishes, and the handled vase.

CORONET	Crystal
Bonbon 6.25", flat, tab plume handles turned up	12
Bonbon 7.25", 3-toed, flared	14
Bonbon 8.25", flat, 3-toed, tidbit	16
Bowl 5", rim fruit	12
Bowl 5.5", flat, tab plume handled, sweetmeat	14
Bowl 5.9", 3-toed, cupped, nut	16
Bowl 6", rim cereal, flared	18
Bowl 8.5", flat, tab plume handled, vegetable	35
Bowl 10", deep salad	45
Bowl 11", plume handled, flared	35
Bowl 12", deep, crimped, fruit	28
Bowl 12", round, flared	24
Bowl 12.75", shallow, flared, fruit	22
Cake plate 10.5", tab plume handled	20
Candlestick 1-lite 4" #2560 1/2, column stem w/drip ring on candle cup, pair	38
Candlestick 1-lite 4.25", graduated plume handled, pair	48
Candlestick 2-lite 5.1", w/plume center, 9" spread, pair	65
Cheese & cracker: comport 2.8" #2560, short stem, 5.25" wide; plate 11"	35
Comport 4.6", flared w/plain stem, 6" wide	18
Creamer 3.25", footed, individual, 3.5 oz.	8
Creamer 4.1", footed regular, 7 oz.	7
Cruet w/stopper 4.5", footed, oil bottle, 3 oz.	48
Cup & saucer, coffee: cup 2.75", footed, 5.5 oz.; saucer w/indent 5.75"	9
Ice bucket 4.9", footed w/chrome handle	65
Mayonnaise 3 piece: bowl 5.5", footed, 3.25" high liner w/indent 7.1"; ladle 5.75"	45
Mayonnaise 4 piece: bowl 6.75", footed, salad dressing, 3.5" high liner 7.1"; 2 ladles 5.75"	58
Plate 6", bread & butter	5
Plate 6.25", flat, handled, lemon server	14
Plate 7.5", salad or dessert	8
Plate 8.5", lunch	10
Plate 9.5", dinner	25
Plate 14", torte or salad bowl liner	28
Relish 6.5", flat, tab plume handled, 2 sections	14
Relish 6.75", oval olive	14
Relish 8.75", oval pickle	16
Relish 10", tab plume handled, 2 equal sections & celery section	30
Relish 10", tab plume handled, 3 equal sections & celery section	38
Relish 11", oval celery	18
Relish 13.25", oval, 4 equal sections & celery section	42
Sandwich server 11.25", center "question mark shape" handle	24
Shaker w/stopper 2.9", footed w/chrome top, pair	38
Sugar 3", footed, individual, 4 oz.	8
Sugar 3.5", footed, regular, 7 oz.	7
Tray 7.5", rectangle, for individual cream & sugar	18
Tray 10", tab plume handles turned up, muffin	24
Vase 3.75" #2560 Coronet, footed, cupped in top, pansy	28
Vase 6", handled	45
Whip cream bowl 5", flat, tab plume handled	18

Relish 10", tab plume handled, 3 equal sections & celery section.

CRESTS

Fenton Art Glass Company　　　　　**1941-92**

Colors: Aqua Crest, Emerald Crest, and Silver Crest

Fenton's crests are one of their most identifiable trademarks. This pattern was one of the most requested to be added to this edition. These pieces of glass have also been known as Petticoat glass. A thin stream of transparent glass is applied to the milk glass. This special edging is applied by Fenton's skilled craftsman after the piece has been shaped. The molten glass is evenly applied by using only a steady hand and skilled eye. The applied handles and stoppers correspond to the particular crest. In Silver Crest there are some exceptions while normally the handles on the baskets are crystal, some have shown up with milk glass handles.

Aqua Crest was introduced in 1941 and discontinued at the end of 1943. Fenton purchased some of the Barcelona moulds from Dugan Diamond and added crests to the shapes. Barcelona was an old Spanish style of glass with irregular lines and edges. In 1948 Aqua Crest was brought back in new shapes and then was discontinued at the end of 1953.

Silver Crest was introduced in 1943. By 1976, when a lamp was introduced to the Silver Crest line, there were only 39 items left being produced. In 1979, the count dropped to 31. One of the shortest run pieces was the wheat vase. It was introduced in 1983 and discontinued before June 1985. After 43 years of being in Fenton's line, Silver Crest was discontinued at the end of 1986. With a newly embossed pattern of Spanish Lace, Silver Crest returned in 1989. Silver Crest was again discontinued at the end of 1992 and has not yet returned to the line.

Emerald Crest was introduced in 1949. That first year it was called Green Crest. The following year was renamed Emerald Crest. It was discontinued at the end of 1955

Originally Fenton used a two or three digit number to identify the whole line and not an individual piece. For the July 1, 1952 catalog, this system was replaced. Fenton changed any previous items that were continuing to be made from a two or three digit number to a four digit number. This new number would also individually identify the item.

Aqua Crest grouping: **Back:** Plate 8.5" #7217 (680), crimped. **Front left:** Vase 4.5" #36, footed, cone shape, oval, double crimped. **Right:** Bowl 10" #7224 (1522), double crimped.

Epergne #1522, four piece, 10" DC bowl, frog, crimped horn & swirl base, Aqua Crest.

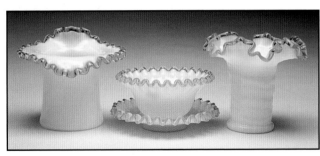

Aqua Crest grouping: **Left:** Vase 5" #1924, hat shape, tulip crimped. **Center:** Mayonnaise & liner #7203: bowl, 5.5" wide, 2.5" tall, crimped, deep; plate 6" w/small indented, crimped. **Right:** Vase 6" #187, Barcelona, straight sides, double crimped.

CRESTS	Aqua	Emerald	Silver
Ashtray 6.75" #7377, round, raised center with 4 indents, crimped			24
Banana Bowl, #5824, low footed, embossed Spanish Lace pattern			50
Banana Bowl, #5824, low footed, exterior ribbed pattern			50
Banana Bowl, #7324, high pedestal footed			75
Basket 2.5" #37, miniature, crimped, 4 styles (fan, flared, oval, square)	145		115
Basket 4.5" #36, footed, cone shape, crimped			65
Basket 5" #1924, hat shape, crimped	60		45
Basket 5" #7236, (680) deep, crimped	125	95	45
Basket 6.25" #36, footed, cone shape, crimped	85		60
Basket 6.5" #7336, shallow, double crimped			40
Basket 6.5" #7436, deep, crimped			35
Basket 7" #192, Melon	85		
Basket 7" #203, cupped upward, crimped, special issue	165		
Basket 7" #711, Beaded Melon	125	195	75
Basket 7" #1923, hat shape, crimped	85		65
Basket 7" #1925, crimped	145		
Basket 7" #7237 (203), flared, crimped	85	125	45
Basket 8" #1502, double crimped	175		
Basket 8" #6833, Ribbed			35
Basket 8" #7339, curved divided center, flared, shallow, crimped			95
Basket 8.5" #3538, embossed Spanish Lace pattern, double crimped			60
Basket 8.5" #6730, embossed Paisley pattern			49
Basket 8.75" #3132, Melon			30
Basket 10" #201, crimped	125		100
Basket 10" #3537, embossed Spanish Lace pattern, flared, crimped			125
Basket 10.5" #192, Melon, crimped	125		100
Basket 10.5" #711, Beaded Melon			125
Basket 11" #7434, deep, cone shape, embossed outer rib pattern			95
Basket 12" #7234, double crimped, shallow			95
Basket 13" #7233 (1523), flared, shallow, crimped	350		145
Bell 6" #3567, embossed Spanish Lace pattern			35
Bell 7" #6761, embossed Paisley pattern			24
Bonbon 4.5" #36, flared	12		
Bonbon 5.5" #36, double crimped, 3 styles (oval, square, triangle)	15		12
Bonbon 5.5" #7225 (36), shallow bowl, flared, double crimped	28	28	10
Bonbon 8" #7428, shallow bowl, double crimped			18
Bonbon, 2 tier, #7497, 5.5" & 8" bonbons with center metal handle, double crimped			45
Bonbon 8" #7498, center metal handle, shallow, double crimped			20
Bowl #7316, shallow, straight sided, crimped			48
Bowl #7330, square, high footed, double crimped, compote shape		250	85

Aqua Crest grouping: **Back:** Plate 11.5" #7212, crimped. **Front:** Bowl 10" #7220 (680), salad, flared, crimped.

Aqua Crest grouping: **Left:** Vase 6.25" #7356 (36), cone, footed, paneled, double crimped. **Center:** Vase 4.5" #36, cone footed, tulip, double crimped. **Right:** Vase 6.5" #4517, flat, urn shape, double crimped.

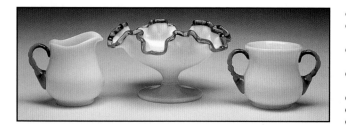

Emerald Crest grouping: **Left:** Sugar 3.25" #7231 (680), flat, no crest on edge, applied emerald handle. **Center:** Compote 4" #7329, low footed, double crimped, 7" wide. **Right:** Creamer 3.25" #7261 (680), flat, no crest on edge, applied emerald handle.

Bowl #7427, high footed, double crimped, compote shape			45
Bowl 4" #202, dessert or finger, crimped	24		18
Bowl 4.5" #203, flared cup	24		20
Bowl 5" # 7221 (680), deep, dessert or mayonnaise, flared, crimped	35	38	28
Bowl 5" #7222 (680), shallow, dessert, crimped	32	32	24
Bowl 5.5" #7320 (680), soup, flared, crimped	40	45	24
Bowl 7" #203, crimped, 4 styles (flared, oval, square, triangle)	28		24
Bowl 7" #711, Beaded Melon, double crimped		48	35
Bowl 7" #7227 (203), double crimped		30	24
Bowl 7" #7335, serving, double crimped		48	60
Bowl 7.5" #7425, footed, crimped, cone shape			38
Bowl 8.5" #205, flared, crimped	38		30
Bowl 8.5" #205, double crimped, 3 styles (round, square, triangle)	40		25
Bowl 8.5" #680, flared, crimped	75	48	28
Bowl 8.5" #7338, double crimped, deep, lamp shade shape			45
Bowl 9" #3524, embossed Spanish Lace pattern			45
Bowl 9.5" #201, triangle, double crimped	65		
Bowl 9.5" #682, flared, crimped	60		
Bowl 9.5" #7423, double crimped			45
Bowl 10" #1522, triangle, double crimped	75		45
Bowl 10" #3524, embossed Spanish Lace pattern, double crimped			45
Bowl 10" #7220 (680), salad, flared, crimped	85	75	55
Bowl 10" #7224 (1522), double crimped	75	125	48
Bowl 10" #7316, shallow, straight sides, crimp			65
Bowl 10.5" #192, Melon, double crimped			45
Bowl 11" #5823, footed, deep cone shape, exterior ribbed pattern			60
Bowl 11" #6721, Paisley interior pattern, ribbed outer pattern, footed			48
Bowl 11.5" #7321, shallow, double crimped			49
Bowl 13" #1523, rolled rim	165		
Bowl 13" #1523, triangle, double crimped	145		
Bowl 13" #7223 (1523), double crimped			85
Bowl #7317, punch, seven quart			400
Bowl 14" #7323, shallow, straight sides, crimped			65
Cake Plate 11" #3510, footed, embossed Spanish Lace pattern			65
Cake Plate 12.25" #5813, low footed, crimped		145	45
Cake Plate 12.25" #6710, embossed Paisley pattern on top, ribbed pattern underneath			40
Cake Plate 13" #7213 (680), high pedestal footed, crimped	95	165	65
Candlestick 1-lite #192, Melon, squat, each	35		24
Candlestick 1-lite #680, flat, small stem, crimped base, each	65	125	45
Candlestick 1-lite #3570, embossed Spanish Lace pattern each			22
Candlestick 1-lite #7270 (1523), crimped top with 2 ball stem & wafer base, each	75		45
Candlestick 1-lite 3.5" #7271, ball center, dome foot, crimped edge, each			24
Candlestick 1-lite #7272, double crimped bowl top with ringed base, compote shape, each			45
Candlestick 1-lite #7274 (951), cornucopia, crimped top, each	48		38
Candlestick 1-lite 6" #1523, hollow base with 2 oval ball stem, each	55	60	
Candlestick 1-lite 6" #7474, urn shape stem, crimped foot, each			35
Candy box w/cover #3580, footed, embossed Spanish Lace pattern			65
Candy box w/cover #7280, footed, pointed finial on lid			75
Candy Jar w/cover #192, Melon			65
Candy Jar w/cover #206, footed, covered, round finial with blue wafer, crest on lip of base	250		
Candy Jar w/cover #711, Beaded Melon, crystal lid			75
Chip & Dip, #7303, 14" shallow bowl w/indent: nut dish sets in center indent			85
Chip & Dip, #7402, 10" shallow bowl w/indent: nut dish set in center indent			85
Compote 6" #206, plain stem, round or triangle, double crimped	35		
Compote 6" #206, plain stem, flared or flat, crimped	35		
Compote #3522, embossed Spanish Lace pattern			29
Compote #7228 (680), low footed, double crimped	40	48	30
Compote 4" #7329, low footed, double crimped, 7" wide		45	35
Compote #7429, high footed, flared, double crimped			38
Compote #7430, high footed, flared, crimped			45
Compote 6.5" #9229, embossed Empress pattern, double crimped			28
Creamer 3.25" #7261 (680), flat, no crest on edge, applied colored handle, 2 styles	35	48	25

Item			
Creamer 4" #711, Beaded Melon			65
Creamer 5" #1924, straight sides, applied handle	49		40
Cruet #7269 (680), opal oil bottle, flat, applied colored handle & stopper	150	145	85
Cup & saucer, coffee: cup #7248 (680), flat, applied colored handle; saucer 5.5" #7218 (680), crimped	48	65	34
Cup #7249, footed, applied handle, plain opal			25
Cup #7247, punch, plain opal with interior panels			15
Epergne #1522, four piece, 10" DC bowl, frog, crimped horn & swirl base	275		175
Epergne 9.5" #4801, embossed Diamond Lace pattern, double crimped bowl with 3 horns			195
Epergne #7200, 3 piece set		300	145
Epergne #7202, 2 piece, single horn in compote, hollow base, wafer stem		300	95
Epergne #7301, two piece, large single horn in double crimped bowl			175
Epergne 13" #7305, five piece, double crimped bowl with 3 horns & large center horn, 11.75" wide			250
Epergne #7308, four piece, double crimped bowl with 3 horns			145
Epergne #7402, two piece, single horn in large double crimped compote			350
Hurricane Lamp #7290, two piece, crimped top, applied handle base			175
Lamp 18" #6505, Student, plain			175
Lamp 24" #3509, Gone with the Wind, embossed Spanish Lace pattern			245
Lamp 23" #9219, Gone with the Wind, embossed Roses pattern			295
Mayonnaise & liner #7203: bowl 5.5" wide, 2.5" tall, crimped deep; plate 6" w/small indented, crimped	60	75	45
Nut dish #7229 (680), footed, flared, crimped, compote shape	28	35	20
Pedestal #7378, punch bowl, crimped on bottom of base			175
Perfume 4.6" #192A: Melon shape, small squat, hobnail stopper, color matches crest	65		45
Perfume 4.9" #192A: Melon shape, small squat, ribbed stopper, color matches crest	65		45
Perfume 4.9" #711, Beaded Melon, small squat, ribbed stopper, color matches crest			45
Perfume 5.5" #711, Beaded Melon, ribbed stopper, color matches crest			75
Perfume 6.25" #192, Melon, large squat, hobnail or ribbed stopper, color matches crest	98		65
Perfume 6.75" #192: Melon shape; hobnail stopper, color matches crest	85		45
Perfume 7.25" #192: Melon shape; ribbed stopper, color matches crest	85		45
Perfume 9.1" #192, Melon, long neck, hobnail or ribbed stopper color matches crest	125		75
Pitcher 2" #37, miniature	175		150
Pitcher 5.5" #192, Melon, Squat	195		95
Pitcher 5.5" #192, Melon, crimped			30
Pitcher 5.5" #711, Beaded Melon		75	45
Pitcher 6" #192, Melon, bulbous base	60		34
Pitcher 6" #7166 (711), Beaded Melon		85	45
Pitcher 8" #192, Melon, bulbous base	125		55
Pitcher 8" #711, Beaded Melon			125
Pitcher 9" #192A, Melon, slender ewer shape			85
Pitcher 9" #711, Beaded Melon			95
Pitcher, 9.5" #6575, Apple Tree			125
Pitcher #1353, 70 oz.	395		
Pitcher #7467, flat, 70 oz., applied handle, crimped top edge, no ice lip			375
Planter #680, 3 tier, 5.5", 8.5" & 10" bowls, deep, flared, center metal handle		125	75
Plate #7312, low footed		95	40
Plate 5.5" #680		15	6
Plate 6.5" #7219 (680), wide center, crimped	14	18	12
Plate 8.5" #7217 (680), crimped	30	30	20
Plate 9" #681, crimped	28		24
Plate 10" #682, crimped	60		
Plate 10.5" #7210 (680), crimped	65	65	40
Plate 11.5" #7212, crimped		75	45
Plate 12" #600, salver	65		
Plate 12" #682, crimped	75		48
Plate 12.5" #7211 (680), crimped	75	75	45
Plate 16" #7216, small center, crimped		85	60
Pot & saucer, one piece w/drainage hole in pot #7299			75
Puff Box & cover 4.4", #192-A, Melon, hobnail finial on lid, cover color determines crest		85	45

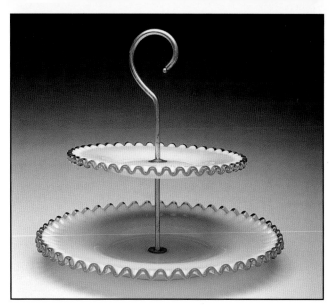

Tray, 2 tier, #7294, tidbit, 8.5" and 12.5" flat plates w/center metal handle, Emerald Crest.

Emerald Crest grouping: **Left:** Vase 4.5" #36, footed, cone shape, oval, double crimped. **Right:** Vase 6.5" #1923, double crimped.

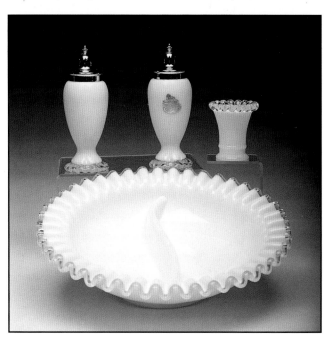

Silver Crest grouping: **Top left:** Shaker 4.8" #7206, egg shape, footed, crimped bottom. **Top right:** Vase 2" #37, miniature, crimped, flared. **Bottom:** Relish 8" #7334, round, 2 sections w/curved divider, flared.

Vase 4.5" #36, footed, cone shape, oval, crimped, Silver Crest.

Silver Crest grouping: **Left:** Basket 7" #1923, hat shape, crimped w/milk handle. **Center:** Vase 12" #7262, fan shape, footed, crimped. **Right:** Vase 6.25" #7232, footed ivy ball, crimped top, cupped in, wafer stem.

Puff Box & cover 4.6", #192-A, Melon, ribbed finial on lid, cover color determines crest	85	45
Puff Box & cover 4.6" #711, Beaded Melon, ribbed finial on, crystal lid		45
Relish 8" #7334, round, 2 sections w/curved divider, flared		55
Relish 8.5" #7333, heart shape, applied handled, crimped	75	35
Sandwich server 10.5" #7291, crimped, center metal handle		48
Shakers #3508, embossed Spanish Lace pattern, footed, crimped on base, pair		45
Shakers 4.8" #7206, egg shape, footed, crimped bottom, pair		125
Shakers #7406, footed, crimped bottom, pair		150
Sherbet 7226 (680), footed, crimped top	24 28	20
Shrimp & Dip, #7403, same as chip & dip but with metal toothpick holder hanging on edge		125
Sugar 3.25" #7231 (680), flat, no crest on edge, applied colored handle	35 48	35
Tray, 2 tier, #7294, tidbit, 8.5" & 12.5" flat plates with center metal handle	65	45
Tray, 2 tier, #7296, tidbit, 5.5" & 8.5" flat plates with metal center handle, crimped	65	45
Tray, 2 tier, #7297 (680), tidbit, 8.5" & 12" plates with metal handle	85 85	45
Tray, 2 tier, #7394, tidbit, 8" & 11.5" bowls, double crimped with metal center handle		45
Tray, 3 tier, #7295, tidbit, 5.5", 8.5" & 12.5" plates with metal center handle	95	65
Tray, 3 tier, #7298 (680), tidbit, 5.5", 8.5" & 12" plates with metal center handle	98 98	60
Tray, 3 tier, #7397, tidbit, 8.5", 11.5" & 16.5" plates with metal center handle, crimped edge		65
Tumbler #711, Beaded Melon, 5 ounce		45
Tumbler #1353, 10 ounce	35	
Tumbler #7342, footed, cone shaped, crimped bottom edge		85
Vase 2" #37, miniature, crimped, 3 styles (fan, flared, oval)	145	120
Vase 2" #37, miniature, double crimped, square or triangle	175	145
Vase 2" #37, miniature, tulip, double crimped	175	195
Vase 3.75" #711, miniature, Beaded Melon, crimped or triangle	45	30
Vase 4" #711, miniature, Beaded Melon, tulip		40
Vase 4" #711, Beaded Melon, double crimped		25
Vase 4" #711, Beaded Melon, cupped crimped		45
Vase 4" #711, Beaded Melon, rose bowl		65
Vase 4" #3554, embossed Spanish Lace pattern, cone shape		20
Vase 4.5" #36, footed, cone shape, oval, double crimped, 3 styles (oval, square, triangle)	24	
Vase 4.5" #36, cone footed, tulip, double crimped	30	
Vase 4.5" #203, rose bowl shape, cup flared, crimped	26	18
Vase 4.5" #203, rose bowl shape, double crimped, square or triangle	30	20
Vase 4.5" #203, rose bowl shape, footed, tulip, crimped	32	24
Vase 4.5" #7254 (203), bulbous, no neck, double crimped	30	20
Vase 4.5" #7354 (36), cone, footed, paneled, double crimped	22 26	16
Vase 4.5" #7355 (36), cone, footed, fan	28 30	24
Vase 5" #192, Melon, double crimped, 3 styles (round, square, triangle)	40	16
Vase 5" #192, Melon, squat, cupped oval, crimped	38	
Vase 5" #201, double crimped, bulbous	38	18
Vase 5" #201, cupped oval, bulbous		20
Vase 5" #201, bulbous, double crimped, square or triangle	42	24
Vase 5" #711, Beaded Melon, crimped, rose bowl	55	35
Vase 5" #1924, crimped, hat shape	35 60	28
Vase 5" #1924, hat shape, double crimped	38 50	30
Vase 5" #1924, hat shape, double crimped, 3 styles (square, triangle, tulip)	45	35
Vase 5" #7292, top hat, sides turned down, crimped		45
Vase 5.5" #192, melon		20
Vase 5.5" #711, Beaded Melon, double crimped	45	40
Vase 5.5" #711, Beaded Melon, triangle, double crimped		35
Vase 5.5" #711, Beaded Melon, tulip, double crimped	60	45
Vase 5.5" #835, double crimped	95	
Vase 5.5" #835, triangle, double crimped	110	
Vase 6" #951, cornucopia		35
Vase 6" #187, Barcelona, straight sides, double crimped, 4 styles (flared, square, triangle, tulip)	55	
Vase 6" #1923, top hat, crimped	60	
Vase 6" #192, Melon, ringed neck, regular, bottle shape		24
Vase 6" #192, Melon, ringed neck, double crimped, 4 styles (flared, square, triangle, tulip)	65	24
Vase 6" #711, Beaded Melon, double crimped, flared or tulip	60	35

Item			
Vase 6" #1925, triangle, double crimped	75	75	45
Vase 6" #7156, Beaded Melon, double crimped			20
Vase 6" #7157, tulip, crimped			45
Vase 6", #7451, Melon, double crimped			30
Vase 6.25" #36, double crimped, square or triangle	45		24
Vase 6.25" #7232, footed ivy ball, crimped top, cupped in, wafer stem			45
Vase 6.25" #7356 (36), cone, footed, paneled, double crimped	24	30	18
Vase 6.25" #7357 (36), cone, footed, fan, crimped	30	38	24
Vase 6.5" #1923, double crimped, triangle or tulip	48		
Vase 6.5" #1925, double crimped	55		
Vase 6.5" #1925, triangle, double crimped	65		
Vase 6.5" #4517, flat, urn shape, double crimped		65	35
Vase, 6.5" #9252, roses			28
Vase 7" #7455, flat, double crimped top, domed lamp shade style			50
Vase 7.75" #9752, embossed Daffodil pattern, double crimped			40
Vase 8" #186, bulbous bottom with long neck, double crimped, square or triangle	50	55	35
Vase 8" #192, double crimped, melon	69		32
Vase 8" #192, double crimped, Melon, 3 styles (square, triangle, tulip)	75		36
Vase 8" #711, Beaded Melon, double crimped, flared or tulip			45
Vase 8" #3551, embossed Spanish Lace pattern, double crimped			49
Vase 8" #1502, double crimped	75		
Vase 8" #5858, Wheat, sheaf of wheat shape		65	
Vase 8" #7258 (186), bulbous base with long neck, double crimped	65	65	30
Vase 8" #7293, top hat, crimped, sides turned down			100
Vase 8" #7453, Melon, double crimped			45
Vase 8.5" #7458, flat, double crimped top, domed lamp shade style			75
Vase 9" #1353, double crimped, flared or triangle	135		
Vase 9" #192A, Melon, double crimped	80		35
Vase 9" #192A, Melon, square, double crimped, 3 styles (square, triangle, tulip)			38
Vase 9" #711, Beaded Melon, double crimped, flared or tulip			65
Vase 9" #7454, shouldered with flared top, crimped			75
Vase 9" #7459, double crimped, long neck			60
Vase 9.5" #6575, Apple Tree, crimped			85
Vase 10" #189, double crimped, flared or tulip	125		
Vase 10" #192, double crimped, Melon, 4 styles (flared, square, triangle, tulip)			40
Vase 10" #7450, flat, double crimped top, domed lamp shade style			100
Vase 10" #7450, flat, Melon, double crimped			75
Vase 11" #193, hand shape	250		195
Vase 11" 4517, flat, urn shape, double crimped		165	65
Vase 11" #7458, Melon, crimped			80
Vase 12" #191, double crimped, flared or triangle	165		
Vase 12" #7262, fan shape, footed, crimped			145

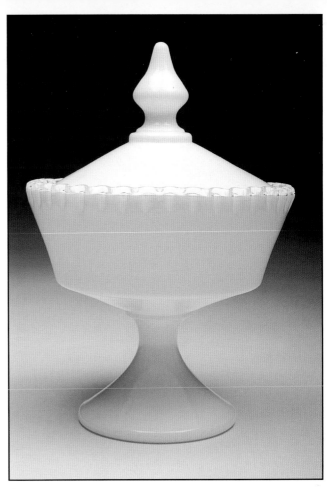

Candy box w/cover #7280, footed, pointed finial on lid, Silver Crest.

Epergne #7305, 13" tall, 5 piece, double crimped bowl w/3 horns & large center horn, 11.75" wide, Silver Crest.

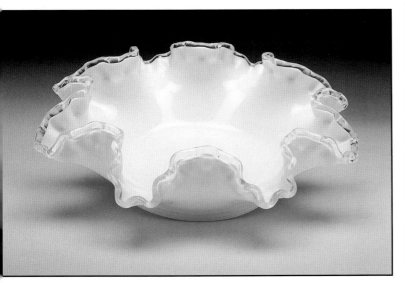

Bowl 11.5" #7321, shallow, double crimped, Silver Crest.

Windsor, Chalice w/cover 8.5"
#386, footed candy, Gold.

Navarre, Bowl & cover 9" wide #203,
footed pedestal, 12.1" tall, Gold.

Navarre, Bowl 9" wide #195, flat, 4.5" high, Ruby.

Hapsburg, Candy w/cover 5.75" #676, flat, Ruby.

CROWN
Fostoria Glass Company Blank #2749 - #2750
- #2751 - #2766 1960-65

Colors: Crystal, Gold, Regal Blue (cobalt), and Ruby

Crown consists of four different types of crowns: #2749 Windsor Crown, #2750 Hapsburg Crown, #2751 Navarre Crown, and #2766 Luxembourg Crown. This was a unique design for Fostoria. The pattern was based on the different types of crowns from royal families in Europe.

The dark Green baskets are sometimes listed as Fostoria Crown, but are in fact Tiara items. Collectors like to have them go with their collections, but it does not bring a Fostoria price. The covered candies in Cobalt and an odd grayish Blue color with poor quality are also Tiara. The Cobalt candy is the only piece that can be found in an old or new version. The original Fostoria pieces will be fire polished and have better detail.

In the Windsor Crown line you will find the elusive cologne bottle. Along with the Crown collectors are perfume collectors, who also want this item and are more willing to pay higher to obtain it. All three colors in the Luxembourg Crown candle bowls are hard to locate. The Navarre Crown large 9" covered bowl is a very impressive piece of glass. When you see it, its appearance makes it seem even larger.

In the fall of 2003 Lancaster Colony sold their hand worked glass moulds to the Fenton Art Glass Company; among these were the Crown moulds. See the preface for more detail. At this time Fenton has not decided to use any of these moulds. If they do use them in the future the items will be made in a different color and will be marked with the Fenton logo.

HAPSBURG CROWN #2750	Crystal	Gold	Blue	Ruby
Candy 3.75" #677, open, flat	25	35	45	50
Candy w/cover 5.75" #676, flat	45	60	70	75
Chalice 7.25" #388, open, footed candy	35	50	60	60
Chalice w/cover 9.25" #386, footed candy	58	75	85	95
LUXEMBOURG CROWN #2766				
Candle Bowl 3-lite 4.75" high #311, footed centerpiece, 7.25" wide	70	85	98	98
NAVARRE CROWN #2751				
Bowl 9" wide #195, flat, 4.5" high	45	65	75	85
Bowl w/cover 9" wide #198, 8.1" high	65	85	95	115
Bowl 9" wide #199, footed pedestal, 8.25" high	70	85	115	125
Bowl & cover 9" wide #203, footed pedestal, 12.1" high	125	135	195	225
WINDSOR CROWN #2749				
Bottle w/stopper #133; cologne 4.75", flat, short	98	125	145	
Candlestick 1-lite 3.5" #314, pair	85	110	135	
Candy 3.75" #677, open, flat	25	35	45	50
Candy w/cover 5.5" #676, flat	45	60	70	75
Chalice 6.75" #388, open, footed candy	35	50	60	65
Chalice w/cover 8.5" #386, footed candy	58	75	85	95

Windsor, Candlestick 1-lite 3.5" #314, pair, Gold.

Left: Luxembourg, Candle Bowl 3-lite 4.75" high #311, footed centerpiece, 7.25" wide, Gold. **Right:** Luxembourg, Candle Bowl 3-lite 4.75" high #311, footed centerpiece, 7.25" wide, Ruby.

CROW'S FOOT
Paden City Glass Company   **Blank #412 & #890**   **1930s**
Main Colors: Crystal, Cobalt, Ebony (black), and Ruby
Other Colors: Amber, Amethyst, Forest Green, Green, and Opal (milk glass)

Crow's Foot has two versions of this pattern and possibly three or four variants. The #412 line is referred to as a square shape. All colors were produced in #412 during the 1930s. The #890 line is referred to as round and was only produced in a few colors in the early 1940s. Line #890 normally has six fans that touch the edge with a trail of tear drops alternating beneath every other one and darts in half of its fans. Handles for the center servers and plates incorporate the fans on the handles. Line #412 normally has four fans with tear drops beneath each one and darts within all of its fans. The number of fans reveal the line, not the shape. On the handles for trays and plates there is a scroll look. In plates, the round seem to be much harder to locate than the square.

Ruby is the color of choice by most collectors, with Cobalt being close behind. Amber is around, but we do not see much interest shown by collectors. Both transparent Green and Opal colors are hard to find; however, collectors only pay big prices for Opal.

The 2-tier tray is a combination of the round and square plates. The 2-lite and 3-lite candlesticks with the fan shaped center attract a lot of attention at shows. The punch bowls in Ruby and Cobalt are hard enough to come by.

There have been very few Forest Green, Green, and Opal pieces in this pattern to show up, which makes it impossible to list the fair market value. For more information you can refer to the book *Paden City Glass Company* by William P. Walker, Melissa Bratkovich & Joan C. Walker.

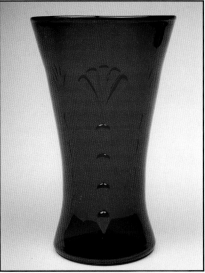

Vase 8" #412-8 (square), flat, concave sided w/slightly flared, Ruby.

CROW'S FOOT	Amber Crystal	Amethyst Ebony	Cobalt	Ruby
Bowl 5" #412 (square), shallow, flared	8	25	26	30
Bowl 6" #412 (square), crimped	12	28	30	35
Bowl 6" #412 (square), flared	15	24	30	35
Bowl 7" #412 (square), flat, 2 spouted nappy, cupped & flared	32	65	70	75
Bowl 7.25" #890 (round), footed, deep, w/flat, rim edge	24	45	54	60
Bowl 8.5" #412 (square), flared	20	40	45	50
Bowl 8.5" #412 (square), open handled, flared	25	52	58	65
Bowl 9" #412 (square), footed, flared	24	45	54	60
Bowl 9.6" #890 (round), oval, flared, vegetable	32	60	68	75
Bowl 9.75" #412 (square), footed w/flat rim edge	30	60	68	75
Bowl 10" #412 (square), oval	36	72	85	95
Bowl 10" #890 (round), 3-toed, flared	40	60	75	85
Bowl 10" #890 (round), footed, deep, flared	36	60	75	85
Bowl 10.25" #412 (square), handled, flared	32	65	72	80
Bowl 10.25" #412 (square), handled, crimped	48	95	110	125
Bowl 11" #412 (square), deep, flared	28	60	68	75
Bowl 11" #412 (square), rolled edge, console	28	60	68	75
Bowl 11.75" #412 (square), rolled edge, console	36	72	80	90
Bowl 11.75" #412 (square), deep flared	36	72	80	90
Bowl 11.75" #412 (square), deep w/flat rim edge, console	36	72	80	90
Bowl 12" #412 (square), flared, console	36	78	85	95
Bowl 12" #412 (square), footed w/flat rim edge, console	36	78	85	95
Bowl 12" #890 (round), 3-footed, shallow, flared, console	40	90	100	115
Cake salver 9.5" #412 (square), low, footed, 2" high	60	120	130	145
Cake salver 12.5" #890 (round), low, footed	78	165	180	195
Candlestick 1-lite 2.5" #412 (square), dome footed, mushroom-shaped, 4" wide, pair	40	80	95	100
Candlestick 1-lite 2.5" #412 (square), dome footed, oval cupped & flared top, 4" wide, pair	65	145	160	175
Candlestick 1-lite 5.25" #412 (square), bell footed, keyhole stem, pair	40	80	90	100
Candlestick 1-lite 7" #890 (round), footed w/tall fancy stem, pair	78	135	150	165
Candlestick 2-lite 5" #890 (round), fan center, 8.25" spread, pair	78	150	175	200
Candlestick 3-lite 6.4" #890 (round), fan shaped, 8.25" spread, pair	100	200	225	250
Candy box w/cover 7" #412 Crow's Foot (square), flat, square, 2 equal sections, lid w/keyhole finial	80	150	175	200
Candy box w/cover 7" #412 1/2 Crow's Foot (square), flat, 3-lobe sides, 3 equal sections, lid w/keyhole finial	95	175	200	225
Cheese & cracker: comport 2.25" #412 (square), short stem, 5" wide; plate 10.25"	42	90	100	110
Cheese & cracker: comport 2.25" #890 (round), short stem, 5" wide; plate 10.4"	45	90	100	115
Comport 3.75" #412 (square), short stem, flared, 6.5" wide	15	36	40	42
Comport 3.75" #412 (square), short stem, crimped,				

Plate 11.75" #412 (square), open handled, sandwich, Cobalt.

Ruby grouping: **Back left:** Plate 5.75" #412 (square), bread & butter. **Back center:** Plate 8.5" #412 (square), lunch. **Front left:** Cream soup 4.5" #412 (square), 2 handled, 11 oz. **Front right:** Cup & saucer, coffee #412 (square): cup 2.1", 6 oz.; saucer w/indent 5.75".

Ruby grouping: **Back left:** Plate 9.25" #890 (round), dinner. **Back right:** Bowl 12" #412 (square), footed w/flat rim edge, console. **Front center:** Sandwich server 10.25" #412 (square), center handled tray.

Ruby grouping: **Left:** Candy box w/cover 7" #412 Crow's Foot (square), flat, square, 2 sections, lid w/keyhole finial. **Right:** Candy box w/cover 7" #412 1/2 Crow's Foot (square), flat, 3-lobe sides, 3 sections, lid w/ keyhole finial.

Back row: Comport 6.5" #412 (square), tall stem, flared, 7" wide, Ruby; Plate 11.75" #412 (square), open handled, sandwich, Ruby; #412 tall cupped comport. **Center row:** Bowl 9.6" #890 (round), oval, flared, vegetable, Ruby; Sugar 2.6" #412 (square), flat, regular, 6 oz., Ruby. **Front row:** Candlestick 1-lite 5.25" #412 (square), bell footed, keyhole stem, Ruby; Candlestick 1-lite 2.5" #412 (square), dome footed, oval cupped & flared top, 4" wide, Crystal; Creamer 3" #412 (square), flat, regular, 7 oz., Ruby.

Top left: Bowl 7.25" #890 (round), footed, deep, w/flat, rim edge, Cobalt. **Top right:** Cake salver 9.5" #412 (square), low, footed, 2" high, Cobalt. **Bottom center:** Cake salver 12.5" #890 (round), low, footed, Ruby.

Back row: Platter 11" #412 (square), oval, Ruby. **Center left:** Relish 11.5" #890 (round), oval, celery, Green. **Center right:** Tray 2 tier, 7.5" plate #412 (square) & 11" plate #890 (round) w/chrome handle, Opal. **Front left:** Sugar 2.6" #412 (square), flat, regular, 6 oz., Opal decorated; Creamer 3" #412 (square), flat, regular, 7 oz., Opal decorated. **Front center:** Bowl 7" #412 (square), flat, 2 spouted nappy, cupped & flared.

Item				
6.5" wide	18	40	45	48
Comport 4.25" #412 (square), short stem, oval cupped & flared, 7.5" long, sauce	32	65	70	75
Comport 6.5" #412 (square), tall stem, cupped, 6" wide	34	68	75	80
Comport 6.5" #412 (square), tall stem, flared, 7" wide	26	50	65	70
Comport 6.75" #412 (square), tall stem, oval cupped, 5.5" wide	40	98	110	120
Comport 7.25" #412 (square), tall stem, 8" wide	32	65	70	75
Cream soup 4.5" #412 (square), 2-handled, 11 oz.	12	20	24	28
Creamer 2.75" #890 (round), flat, regular, 5.5 oz.	10	18	22	24
Creamer 3" #412 (square), flat, regular, 7 oz.	8	15	18	20
Cup & saucer, coffee #412 (square): cup 2.1", 6 oz.; saucer w/indent 5.75"	12	20	24	28
Cup & saucer, coffee #890 (round): cup 3.5", 6 oz.; saucer w/indent 5.75"	14	24	28	32
Mayonnaise #412 Crow's Foot (square): footed, rolled edge; liner w/indent	38	85	95	110
Mayonnaise 2 piece #890 (round): bowl 3.75", footed, flared; liner w/indent 7.25"	30	60	75	85
Mayonnaise 2 piece #890 (round): bowl, footed, salad dressing; liner w/indent 7.25"	35	68	85	98
Mayonnaise bowl 4.5" #890 (round), deep, flared, 3-footed	36	82	90	95
Plate 5.75" #412 (square), bread & butter	6	12	14	16
Plate 6.25" #890 (round), bread & butter	8	15	18	20
Plate 7.5" #412 (square), salad or sherbet	9	20	22	25
Plate 8.5" #412 (square), lunch	9	20	22	25
Plate 9.25" #890 (round), dinner	20	40	45	50
Plate 9.5" #890 (round), open handled	28	60	68	74
Plate 10.5" #412 (square), open handled	30	64	72	76
Plate 11" #412 (square), service	27	64	68	74
Plate 11" #890 (round), service	36	80	85	90
Plate 11.75" #412 (square), open handled, sandwich	30	64	72	76
Platter 11" #412 (square), oval	30	60	68	75
Punch bowl 8.5" #890, w/chrome ring (for tumblers), cover & ladle, 1.2 gallon	275	400	450+	500+
Relish 11.5" #890 (round), oval, celery	18	40	48	48
Relish 11.5" #890 (round), oval, 2 sections	20	42	50	50
Sandwich server 10.25" #412 (square), center handled tray	26	48	58	65
Sandwich server 10.25" #890 (round), center handled tray	24	45	54	60
Sugar 2.4" #890 (round), flat, regular, 5 oz.	14	22	28	34
Sugar 2.6" #412 (square), flat, regular, 6 oz.	12	20	25	30
Tray 2 tier, 7.5" plate #412 (square) & 11" plate #890 (round) w/chrome handle	36	100	125	145
Tumbler 2.5", flat, blown, roly poly (goes with punch bowl) 5 oz.	6	15	16	18
Tumbler 4.25" #890 (round), flat, straight sided	36	95	120	135
Vase 4.6" #412-5 (square), footed, flared, rose bowl	32	75	85	95
Vase 4.6" #412-5 (square), footed, cupped, ivy ball	32	85	110	125
Vase 8" #412-8 (square), flat, concave sided, cupped top	48	150	185	195
Vase 8" #412-8 (square), flat, concave sided w/ slightly flared	40	125	160	175
Vase 10" #412-10 (square), flat, concave sided, cupped top	45	125	140	155
Vase 10.25" #412-10 (square), flat, concave sided w/slightly flared	36	120	150	165
Vase 11.75" #412-12 (square), flat, concave sided, cupped top	60	175	225	245
Vase 11.75" #412-12 (square), flat, concave sided, flared	60	175	200	225

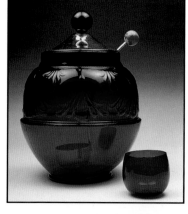

Cobalt grouping: **Left:** Punch bowl 8.5" #890, (shown missing chrome ring, for tumblers), 1.2 gallon. **Right:** Tumbler 2.5", flat, blown, roly poly (used w/punch bowl) 5 oz.

CRYSTOLITE

A. H. Heisey & Company   **Blank #1503**   **1937-57**

Color: Crystal

Crystolite is a simple design of curved panels that has attracted many collectors. The simple fact that there are quite a few pieces under $30 also lends itself well to new collectors. It is mainly a pressed pattern; but, there are some blown items that add variety to this pattern. All the #5003 blank items are blown. Blown accessory items other than the pitcher are all very hard to find.

Catalogs show that the cologne bottle came with or without a long dauber. It is our opinion that it is really a cologne bottle when it has no dauber, yet when found with a dauber it would be a perfume bottle. The point to remember is that the dauber makes it a much more valuable item.

A nice addition to find is the pictured dresser set that came with a metal ormolu. The ornate tray is marked Apollo on the bottom. We have found no information about this company and can only assume it was a distributor that bought glass from various glass companies and sold them under their label with accessory pieces.

CRYSTOLITE	Crystal
Ashtray 3", small, round	15
Ashtray 3.5", square	8
Ashtray (coaster) 4", shell shape	45
Ashtray (coaster) 4" x 6"	60
Ashtray 4.5", square	10
Ashtray 5", book match	75
Bonbon 7.5", shell shaped, 3-toed, slightly cupped	26
Bonbon 6.25", 2-tab handles turned up	24
Bottle 4.5", bitters w/chrome tube (5.75" total) 4 oz.	125
Bowl 4.5", fruit	20
Bowl 5", round or tri-corn, one handled, jelly, 2" deep	20
Bowl 5.5", cereal	25
Bowl 6", tab handled, jelly	24
Bowl 6", tab handled, 2 equal sections, jelly	30
Bowl 6", oval, tab handled, 4-footed, jelly	48
Bowl 8.25", deep, dessert/sauce	35
Bowl 8.5", flat, floral Touraine, high, slightly cupped in	85
Bowl 10", deep, salad	75
Bowl 10", flared, centerpiece	45
Bowl 10", square, shallow	125
Bowl 10.75", shell shape	225
Bowl 10.75", shell shape, raised curved divider, combination salad & salad dressing	250
Bowl 11.5", flared, centerpiece	45
Bowl 12", deep, cone shape	50
Bowl 12", oval, shallow, floral or gardenia	50
Bowl 12", shallow, floral or gardenia	58
Bowl 12.75", 4-tab feet, oval, deep, floral	85
Box w/cover 4.75", puff or small candy, 4.1" tall	60
Cake salver 10", footed pedestal	375

Lamp, 19.5", square acrylic base, chrome arms, electric.

Top left: Bowl 8.25", deep, dessert/sauce. **Top right:** Bowl 10", square, shallow. **Front left:** Mayonnaise 2 piece: bowl 4.75", oval, tab handled sauce; liner w/indent 6.75" oval. **Front center:** Heisey dealer glass sign ($250). **Front right:** Cigarette lighter 2", straight sided rosette w/metal insert.

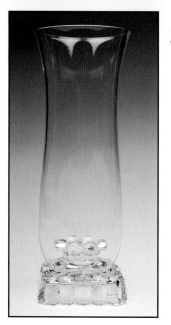

Hurricane lamp 1-lite 2.5", square candle block, w/plain 10" shade.

Candelabra 2-lite 6", vertical ribs on base, bisects w/7 plumes, bobeches/prisms, 10" spread, pair	225
Candle block 1-lite 1.8" #1503 1/4, square, rosette, pair	45
Candle block 1-lite 2", regular rosette, pair	24
Candle block 1-lite 2.1" #1503 1/2, spherical, melon shape, pair	75
Candle block 1-lite 2.2" #1502, swirl, rosette, pair	35
Candle block 1-lite 2.4" #1503 3/4, cylindrical (column type) pair	68
Candlestick 1-lite 4", footed, ribbed wings radiating upward, pair	48
Candlestick 1-lite w/vase 4", ribbed wings radiating upward & 5" plain vase, pair	145
Candlestick 2-lite 5.75", vertical ribs on base, bisects w/7 plumes, 8.75" spread, pair	98
Candlestick 3-lite 3.8", ribbed wings radiating upward, 7" spread, pair	75
Candy w/cover 6", shell shape, 3-footed	60
Candy w/cover 6.25", round, low, 3-footed, fan finial	65
Candy w/cover 6.9", round, ball finial	65
Candy w/cover 6.9", round, 3 sections, ball finial	65
Candy w/cover 6.9": round; brass plated metal lid w/glass flower finial	65
Candy w/cover 6.9": round, 3 equal sections; brass plated metal lid w/glass flower finial	70
Cheese & cracker: comport 2.75", short stem, 5.5" wide; plate w/indent 14"	50
Cherry jar w/cover, cylindrical w/round ball finial	85
Cigarette box w/cover 4", rectangle	38
Cigarette box w/cover 4.75", large, rectangle	42
Cigarette holder 3", flat, oval	30
Cigarette holder 3", flat, cylindrical	24
Cigarette holder 3.8", footed, ball stem, round	35
Cigarette lighter 2", straight sided rosette w/metal insert	60
Coaster 4", round	12
Cocktail shaker w/flat stopper, 32 oz.	350
Cologne w/stopper 5.75", cylindrical, 4 oz.	95
Cologne w/drip stopper (dauber) 5.75", cylindrical, 4 oz.	225
Comport 3.75", plain high stem, flat bowl, chocolate, 5.5" wide	40
Comport 4.8", plain high stem, flared bowl, jelly, 5.25" wide	35
Comport 5.1", plain high stem, oval 2 spout, nut, 5" wide	45
Comport 5.2", footed, deep, cupped bowl, 5" wide	32
Comport 5.75" #5003, footed, ball stem, cupped, blown, 5" wide	350
Creamer 1.9", individual, oval, 3.5 oz.	18
Creamer, oval, regular, 6 oz.	20
Creamer #1503 1/2, round w/loop handle, 6 oz.	24
Cruet w/stopper 4.75", flat, oil bottle, 2 oz.	45
Cruet w/stopper 4.75", flat, oil bottle, 3 oz.	50
Cup 2.25", flat, punch or custard, 4 oz.	10
Cup & saucer, coffee: cup 2.4", 6 oz.; saucer w/indent 6"	18
Decanter w/stopper (round ball), rye, 32 oz.	300
Goblet #5003, cordial, blown, 1 oz.	135
Goblet 3.4" #5003, oyster cocktail, blown, 3.5 oz.	18
Goblet 3.6" #5003, cocktail, blown, 3.5 oz.	26
Goblet #5003, claret, blown, 3.5 oz.	35
Goblet 3.9" #5003, sherbet/champagne, blown, 6 oz.	15
Goblet 5.75" #5003, water, blown, 10 oz.	32
Hurricane candle block 1-lite 2.5", square, no shade, each	35
Hurricane lamp 1-lite 2.5", square candle block, w/plain 10" shade, each	150
Hurricane lamp 1-lite 3", inverted flower shape w/plain 6", 9" or 12" shade, each	195
Hurricane lamp 1-lite 3", inverted flower shape w/plain 6", 9" or 12" shade electric, each	300+
Ice bucket 4.5", deep w/chrome handle	125
Jam jar w/cover 5.25", flat, apple shape	65
Lamp, 19.5", square acrylic base, chrome arms, electric	250
Mayonnaise 2 piece: bowl 4.75", oval, tab handled sauce; liner w/indent 6.75" oval	48
Mayonnaise bowl 5", crimped, Thousand Island or salad dressing	40
Mayonnaise bowl 5", flared, Thousand Island or salad dressing	30
Mayonnaise bowl 5.5", shell shape, 3-footed (also candy bottom)	25
Mayonnaise 2 piece: bowl 5.5", tab handled, oval, flared; liner w/indent 6.75", oval, tab handled	52
Mayonnaise bowl 5.5", oval, salad dressing, tab handled (total 9.5" long) Thousand Island	75
Mayonnaise 2 piece: bowl 6", tab handled, oval; liner w/indent 7.75", oval, tab handled	65
Mustard w/cover 3", flat, cylindrical	55
Mustard paddle 2.8", plain no pattern	45
Nut dish 3", shell shape, stem, handled, individual	14
Nut dish 7", shell shape, praline w/curled tab handle	38
Pitcher 8.25", flat, blown, water jug, 64 oz.	150
Pitcher 9", swan handled, w/o ice lip, water jug, 64 oz.	750
Pitcher 9", swan handled, w/ice lip, water jug, 64 oz.	795
Plate 7", shell shape, salad, turned up at edge	34
Plate 7", tea, plain center	12
Plate 7", tea, rays pattern center	15
Plate 7.3", flat w/turned up edge, coupe/salad	38
Plate 8", oval	24
Plate 8", salad, plain center	20
Plate 8", salad, rays pattern center	25

Left: Cologne w/drip stopper (dauber) 5.75", cylindrical, 4 oz. **Center:** Box w/cover 4.75", puff, 4.1" tall; handled tray, 12.25" long. **Right:** Cologne w/drip stopper (dauber) 5.75", cylindrical, 4 oz. **Note,** cologne bottles and puff box each have ornate metal filigree on them to match the tray. The bottom of the tray is marked Apollo.

Back left: Cigarette holder 3", flat, oval. **Back right:** Tray 12.75", oval, flat, turned up edge, dresser. **Front left:** Cigarette holder 3.8", footed, ball stem, round. **Front center left:** Cigarette holder 3", flat, cylindrical. **Front center right:** Cologne w/drip stopper (dauber) 5.75", cylindrical, 4 oz. (dauber shown in front of bottle). **Front right:** Box w/cover 4.75", puff or small candy, 4.1" tall.

Plate 8.5", lunch, large center	24
Plate 10.5", dinner, large plain center	125
Plate 10.5", dinner, large rays pattern center	135
Plate 11", torte	36
Plate 12", small center, sandwich	42
Plate 13", shell shape, torte	195
Plate 13", torte	95
Plate 14", small center, sandwich	48
Plate 14", torte	48
Preserve 5", shallow shell shape, stem handled, breakfast	22
Preserve 6", shallow shell shape, stem handled, breakfast	24
Preserve w/cover 6", round, tab handled	45
Preserve bowl & liner: bowl 7", oval, deep, flared; oval plate w/indent 7"	45
Punch bowl, deep, 1.8 gallon	125
Punch bowl liner 18", or buffet plate	150
Punch bowl liner 20", or buffet plate	245
Relish 6", oval, deep, pickle	28
Relish 7", oval, shallow, pickle	32
Relish 8", center handled, 2 circular sections, conserve	50
Relish 8", diamond shape, tab handled, 3 sections	45
Relish 9", clover shape, stem handle, 4 sections	40
Relish 9", oval, leaf pickle w/curled handle	28
Relish 10", round, 5 sections, 1.25" deep	55
Relish 11.9", rectangular, 2 sections, olive/celery (divided 1/3 & 2/3)	35
Relish 12", oval, tab handled, celery	38
Relish 12", oval, tab handled, 2 equal sections & celery section	38
Relish 12", rectangle, celery	32
Relish 12.8", large shell shape, 5 sections	175
Relish 13", oval, 2 equal sections & celery section	45
Shaker, spherical, w/plastic-chrome, silver plated, pair	34
Shaker, spherical, w/plastic-chrome, glass top, pair	45
Shaker #1503 1/2, straight sided, silver plated, pair	75
Shaker #1503 1/2, straight sided, glass top, pair	85
Sugar 1.75", oval, individual, 3.5 oz.	18
Sugar, oval, regular, 6 oz.	20
Sugar #1503 1/2, round w/loop handles, 6 oz.	24
Swan 1.75" tall, 2.9" long, individual, nut or ashtray	18
Swan 6.5", jelly or open candy	24
Syrup 4.5", flat, drip cut top/bakelite handle, 9 oz.	175
Tray 6.75", oval, for individual cream/sugar	25
Tray 7", round, tab handled, snack plate	22
Tray 8", oval, tab handled, cheese plate	24
Tray 12.75", oval, flat, turned up edge, dresser	80
Tumbler 4.1" #5003, flat, blown, juice, 5 oz.	54
Tumbler 4.8" #5003, footed, blown, juice, 5 oz.	38
Tumbler 4.25" #5003, flat, blown, table water, 10 oz.	48
Tumbler 3.8", flat, pressed, water, 10 oz.	45
Tumbler 6.4" #5003, footed, blown, ice tea, 12 oz.	38
Tumbler 5.75" #5003, flat, blown, ice tea, 14 oz.	54
Vase 3", short, squat (spittoon shape)	38
Vase 6", footed, flared	38
Vase 6", footed, straight	45
Vase 7", flat urn, spherical, cupped in	125
Vase 9", flat, Calendula cylindrical, straight sided	225
Vase 9", flat, lily (cylindrical) cupped	275
Vase 9", flat, aster (cylindrical) flared	250
Vase 9", footed, flared	65
Vase 10-12", footed, slightly spherical bottom & swung	250
Vase 12", flat, cylindrical, straight sided	300
Vase 12-15", footed, slightly spherical bottom & swung	250
Vase 15-18", footed, slightly spherical bottom & swung	300
Vase 18-21", footed, slightly spherical bottom & swung	375

Top left: Candlestick 2-lite 5.75", vertical ribs on base, bisects w/7 plumes, 8.75" spread. **Top center:** Candle block 1-lite 2.1" #1503 1/2, spherical, melon shape. **Top right:** Candlestick 3-lite 3.8", ribbed wings radiating upward, 7" spread. **Bottom left:** Candle block 1-lite 2.4" #1503 3/4, cylindrical (column type). **Bottom center left:** Candle block 1-lite 2", regular rosette, pair. **Bottom center right:** Hurricane candle block 1-lite 2.5", square, no shade. **Bottom right:** Candle block 1-lite 1.8" #1503 1/4, square, rosette, pair.

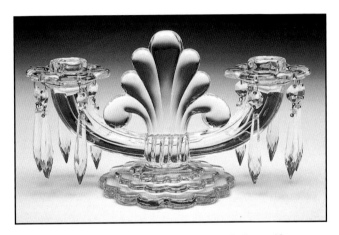

Candelabra 2-lite 6", vertical ribs on base, bisects w/7 plumes, 10 spread, bobeches/prisms.

Back row: Bottle 4.5", bitters w/chrome tube (5.75" total) 4 oz.; Syrup 4.5", flat, drip cut top/bakelite handle, 9 oz. **Front row:** Mayonnaise bowl 5.5", oval, salad dressing, tab handled Thousand Island; Swan 1.75" tall, 2.9" long, individual, nut or ashtray; Jam jar w/cover 5.25", flat, apple shape; Mustard w/cover 3", flat, cylindrical w/paddle 2.8".

Left to right: Ice bucket 4.5", deep w/chrome handle; Tumbler 4.1" #5003, flat, blown, juice, 5 oz.; Tumbler 4.25" #5003, flat, blown, table water, 10 oz.; Tumbler 5.75" #5003, flat, blown, ice tea, 14 oz.

Back left: Plate 10.5", dinner, large rays pattern center. **Front left:** Candy w/ cover 6.25", round, low, 3-footed, fan finial. **Front center:** Box w/cover 4.75", puff or small candy, 4.1" tall. **Right:** Hurricane lamp 1-lite 3", inverted flower shape w/plain 9" shade.

Left: Swan 6.5", jelly or open candy. **Right:** Cruet w/stopper 4.75", flat, oil bottle, 3 oz.

Top left: Plate 7.3", flat w/turned up edge, coupe/salad. **Top right:** Comport 5.1", plain high stem, oval 2 spout, nut, 5" wide. **Bottom left:** Cup & saucer, coffee: cup 2.4", 6 oz.; saucer w/indent 6". **Bottom center:** Tumbler 4.8" #5003, footed, blown, juice, 5 oz. **Bottom right:** Bowl 8.5", flat, floral Touraine, high, slightly cupped in.

Top left: Bonbon 7.5", shell shaped, 3-toed, slightly cupped. **Right:** Bowl 10.75", shell shape, raised curved divider, combination salad & salad dressing. **Front left:** Relish 8", center handled, 2 circular sections, conserve.

Left: Pitcher 8.25", flat, blown, water jug, 64 oz. **Right:** Pitcher 9", swan handled, w/ice lip, water jug, 64 oz.

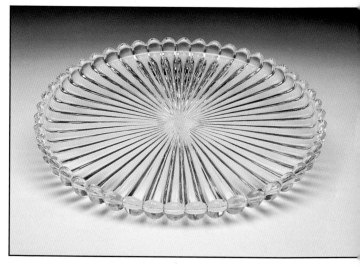

Plate 13", torte.

CUPID

Fostoria Glass Company **Etching #288** **1927-29**
Main Colors: Blue, Green, and Ebony (black)
Other Color: Amber

Fostoria made several different brocade lines, with the Cupid being the hardest to find. This etched pattern features dancing Cupid that appear to be gathering twigs for a fire. The perfume, puff box, and vanity set are considered real prizes to have in a boudoir collection.

In doing the research for this pattern, we found that amber was listed in catalogs as one of the colors produced. To date we have not seen any Cupid in amber, so it must have been done in very limited quantities. Another possibility is that it was scheduled to be made when the catalog went to print but never was. Let us know if you have a piece.

CUPID	Green	Blue	Ebony
Bowl 11" #2329, rolled edge, centerpiece	350	400	450
Bowl 12" #2297, 3-toed, shallow, flared	300	350	400
Box w/cover 5.4" #2359 1/2, flat, low, round, puff, 1.4" tall	350	400	450
Candlestick 1-lite #2298, tapered, rectangular, pair	375	425	500
Candlestick 1-lite 4" #2324, short wafer stem, pair	350	400	450
Clock #2298, domed, rectangle shape	375	425	500
Cologne w/stopper 6" #2322: footed, plain stem; stopper w/ long dauber	600	675	800
Vanity 3 piece 7.25" #2276, combination powder/cologne/ clear stopper	675	775	900

Pattern detail, Cupid - Fostoria.

Box w/cover 5.4" #2359 1/2, flat, low, round, puff, 1.4" tall, Blue.

Green grouping: **Left:** Candlestick 1-lite 4" #2324, short wafer stem. **Center:** Bowl 12" #2297, 3-toed, shallow, flared. **Right:** Candlestick 1-lite 4" #2324, short wafer stem.

Candlestick 1-lite #2298, tapered, rectangular, Ebony (black).

Cologne w/stopper 6" #2322: footed, plain stem; stopper w/ long dauber, Blue.

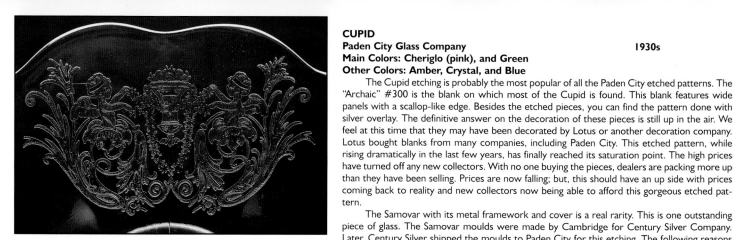

Pattern detail, Cupid – Paden City.

CUPID

Paden City Glass Company   1930s
Main Colors: Cheriglo (pink), and Green
Other Colors: Amber, Crystal, and Blue

The Cupid etching is probably the most popular of all the Paden City etched patterns. The "Archaic" #300 is the blank on which most of the Cupid is found. This blank features wide panels with a scallop-like edge. Besides the etched pieces, you can find the pattern done with silver overlay. The definitive answer on the decoration of these pieces is still up in the air. We feel at this time that they may have been decorated by Lotus or another decoration company. Lotus bought blanks from many companies, including Paden City. This etched pattern, while rising dramatically in the last few years, has finally reached its saturation point. The high prices have turned off any new collectors. With no one buying the pieces, dealers are packing more up than they have been selling. Prices are now falling; but, this should have an up side with prices coming back to reality and new collectors now being able to afford this gorgeous etched pattern.

The Samovar with its metal framework and cover is a real rarity. This is one outstanding piece of glass. The Samovar moulds were made by Cambridge for Century Silver Company. Later, Century Silver shipped the moulds to Paden City for this etching. The following reasons explain why not all collectors are looking for one however: price, where to keep it, and, last, how to use it. With this much money in one item, it makes one faint at heart to think of using it. Beaumont items and German items were also purchased by Paden City to be decorated.

Crystal and amber will be priced considerably less than the colors. Blue pieces in this etched pattern do not show up very often and would run higher than pink and green prices. For more information you can refer to the book *Paden City Glass Company* by William P. Walker, Melissa Bratkovich & Joan C. Walker.

Cheriglo (pink) grouping: **Top left:** Bowl 10.75" #300 Archaic, flared, console. **Top right:** Platter 10.75" #300 Archaic, flat, small center, oval. **Bottom left:** Bowl 9" #300 Archaic, footed, deep, oval, flared. **Bottom right:** Bowl 9" #300 Archaic, center cup handled, cupped edge.

CUPID	Green & Cheriglo (pink)
Bowl 8.5" #300 Archaic, footed, oval, melon	295
Bowl 9" #300 Archaic, footed, short stem, deep, round, flared	250
Bowl 9" #300 Archaic, footed, deep, oval, flared	275
Bowl 9" #300 Archaic, footed, deep, oval, rolled edge	250
Bowl 9" #300 Archaic, center cup handled, cupped edge	250
Bowl 10.5" #300 Archaic, flat, oyster plate (rim soup shape)	325
Bowl 10.75" #300 Archaic, flared, console	345
Bowl 11" #300 Archaic, flat w/center cup handle	275
Bowl 11" #300 Archaic, shallow or deep, rolled edge, console	275
Bowl w/cover 12", flat, oblong base w/2 handled oval 9.25" lid (casserole)	1,200+
Bowl 14" #300 Archaic, flat, flared, console	350

Cheriglo (pink) grouping: **Top left:** Cake salver 11.25" #300 Archaic, short stem w/scalloped edge, 2" high. **Top right:** Butter tub w/cover 5" #300 Archaic, flat, tab handled w/cup handle finial. **Center right:** Ice bucket 5.8" #902, flat, straight sided, w/chrome handle. **Front left:** Ice bucket 4.75" #300 Archaic, tab handled, 6" wide. **Front right:** Candy box w/cover 6.5" #300 Archaic, flat, 3 sections, cup handle finial.

Top left: Sandwich server 10.5" #300 Archaic, center cup handled, tray, Cheriglo (pink). **Top right:** Bowl 11" #300 Archaic, deep, rolled edge, console, Cheriglo (pink). **Bottom left:** Mayonnaise 2 piece #701 Triumph: bowl 6.5", octagon; liner w/indent 7.75"; ladle, Amber. **Bottom right:** Bowl 11" #300 Archaic, shallow, rolled edge, console, Green.

Bowl 14" #300 Archaic, flat, shallow, rolled, console 325
Butter tub w/cover 5" #300 Archaic, flat, tab handled w/cup handle finial 500+
Cake salver 9" #300 Archaic, tall stem 225
Cake salver 11.25" #300 Archaic, short stem w/scalloped edge, 2" high 250
Candlestick 1-lite 3" #300 Archaic, footed, rolled edge, 5" wide, pair 275
Candy jar w/cover 6" #300 Archaic, footed, short stem w/cup handle finial 450
Candy box w/cover 6.5" #300 Archaic, flat, not divided, cup handle finial 375
Candy box w/cover 6.5" #300 Archaic, flat, 3 sections, cup handle finial 345
Cheese & cracker #300 Archaic: comport 3", short stem, 5" wide; plate w/
  indent 10.5" 450
Comport 3.5" #300 Archaic, short stem, (cupped or flared w/scalloped edge)
  6" wide (2 styles) 200
Comport 6.5" #300 Archaic, tall stem, (cupped or flared w/scalloped edge)
  8" wide (2 styles) 275
Comport 6.5" #300 Archaic, tall stem, rolled edge w/scalloped edge, 8" wide 295
Creamer #300 Archaic, footed, 5 oz. 175
Creamer 4.25" #300 Archaic, footed, 7 oz. 145
Creamer 4.5" #701 Triumph, footed, octagonal w/pointed handle, 6.5 oz. 145
Cup & saucer, coffee #300 Archaic: cup 2.4", flat, 6 oz.; saucer w/indent 6" 100
Ice bucket 4.75" #300 Archaic, tab handled, 6" wide 375
Ice bucket 5.8" #902, flat, straight sided, w/chrome handle 450
Mayonnaise 2 piece #300 Archaic: bowl 3.5", short stem, rolled edge, 6" wide;
  liner w/indent 7.75" 200
Mayonnaise 2 piece #701 Triumph: bowl 6.5", octagon; liner w/indent 7.75" 265
Platter 10.75" #300 Archaic, flat, small center, oval 225
Platter 16" Keith, w/gravy tree 500
Samovar 12", low, metal frame w/handles & metal lid (made for Century Silver) 1,200+
Samovar 15.5", tall, metal frame w/handles & metal lid (made for Century Silver) 1,000+
Sandwich server 10.5" #300 Archaic, center cup handled, tray 225
Sugar #300 Archaic, footed, 5 oz. 165
Sugar 4" #300 Archaic, footed, 7 oz. 145
Sugar 4.25" #701 Triumph, footed, octagonal w/pointed handles, 6.25 oz. 145
Vase 5.1" #182-5, flat, squat, round (pillow shape) 900+
Vase 8" #182-8, flat, elliptical (pillow shape) 750
Vase 8" #184-8, flat, spherical bottom, flared 475
Vase 8" #300 Archaic, flat, sweet pea, concave sides 550
Vase 10" #184-10, flat, spherical bottom, flared 425
Vase 11.75" #180, flat, cylindrical, slightly flared (silver overlay price 275) 495
Vase 12" #184, flat, spherical bottom, flared 800+

Green grouping: **Top left:** Bowl 9" #300 Archaic, footed, short stem, deep, round, flared. **Right:** Comport 6.5" #300 Archaic, tall stem, rolled edge w/scalloped edge, 8" wide. **Bottom left:** Bowl 11" #300 Archaic, shallow or deep, rolled edge, console.

Green grouping: **Back left:** Sandwich server 10.5" #300 Archaic, center cup handled, tray. **Back right:** Vase 11.75" #180, flat, cylindrical, slightly flared. **Front left:** Creamer 4.25" #300 Archaic, footed, 7 oz.; Sugar 4" #300 Archaic, footed, 7 oz. **Front right:** Mayonnaise 2 piece #300 Archaic: bowl 3.5", short stem, rolled edge, 6" wide; liner w/indent; ladle.

Samovar 12", low, metal frame w/
handles & metal lid (made for Century
Silver), Blue.

Amber grouping: **Back:** Bowl w/cover 12", flat, oblong base w/2 handled oval 9.25" lid (casserole). **Front:** Candlestick 1-lite 3" #300 Archaic, footed, rolled edge, 5" wide, pair.

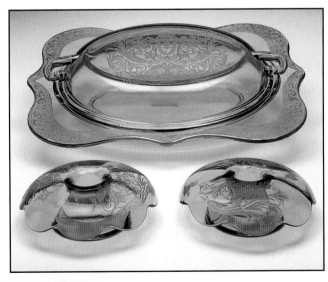

Cheriglo (pink) grouping: **Top left:** Creamer 4.5" #701 Triumph, footed, octagonal w/pointed handle, 6.5 oz. **Top center:** Candy jar w/cover 6" #300 Archaic, footed, short stem w/cup handle finial. **Right:** Vase 8" #182-8, flat, elliptical (pillow shape). **Bottom left:** Sugar 4.25" #701 Triumph, footed, octagonal w/pointed handles, 6.25 oz. **Bottom center:** Candlestick 1-lite 3" #300 Archaic, footed, rolled edge, 5" wide.

Left: Tumbler 5.25" #3080, cone footed, water, 9 oz., Green satin.
Center: Tumbler 5.25" #3080, cone footed, water, 9 oz., Crystal satin.
Right: Tumbler 5.25" #3080, cone footed, water, 9 oz., Pink satin.

DANCING NYMPH

Consolidated Glass Company   **1926-39**
Colors: Colored Stains, Crystal, Green, Pink, and Ruby Flash

The Lalique designs from the 1925 Paris Exposition had a huge influence on the making of Dancing Nymph. Reuben Haley and his son, Kenneth, both attended this exhibit and marveled at the beautiful glass creations. They came home thinking of ways to incorporate their ideas in reasonably priced glass. The Dancing Nymph was created from imitating one of those pieces. On some of the pieces a technique was utilized that had part of the piece accented with a satin finish. This was known as "French Crystal". These items are priced the same as Crystal. When you find pieces in this pattern with a metal ormolu, they always bring a premium price, around 50% higher or maybe more in some cases (some of the ormolu are more extravagant than others).

From 1926 to 1932 the outer edges of the plates were always hand ground to have a beveled edge and then were polished out. When Consolidated reopened in 1936, this extra finishing step was dropped. This was probably due to the added cost of making the plates.

Fan vases come with or without a metal ormolu, but we think that the round, crimped version is harder for collectors to locate than the fan shape. The large ceiling globe is one of the largest pieces of glass that you might find in a collection. One problem occurs with it: finding the metal parts with which to hang it. Taking into account the size, it needs to be hung from a tall ceiling and have a very strong fixture, since it is very heavy.

DANCING NYMPH	Crystal	Color Wash	Ruby Stain	Green Pink
Ashtray 6.4", bread & butter plate w/metal ormolu	100	145		195
Bowl 4.5" #3098, deep fruit	45			85
Bowl 8" #3098 1/2, deep, salad or vegetable	135	250		175
Bowl 16" #2795, hat shape, console, cupped up at edge	500	900+		
Candlestick 1-lite 3.5" #2840, triangular base, raised candle cup, pair	450	1,250+		
Cup & saucer, coffee: cup 3" #3099, flat, coffee w/slightly flared, 6 oz.; saucer 6" #3099 1/2	65		100	125
Goblet 3.75" #3094, low sherbet, 7 oz.	38			85
Lamp shade 16.75" #2795, hat shape, w/3 holes for hanging	500	900+		
Plate 6.4" #3095, bread & butter or fruit bowl liner w/indent	30			60
Plate 8.25" #3096, salad or lunch	60	95	140	110
Plate 10.1" #3097, dinner	100	185	225	195
Platter 17.75" #2795, low hat shape, flared out, flat to edge	550	1,000+		
Tumbler 3.5" #3094 1/2, cone footed, juice, 5 oz.	95			150
Tumbler 5.25" #3080, cone footed, water, 9 oz.	75			125
Vase 5.25" #3080C, round, crimped (tumbler mould)	100		225	250
Vase 5.25" #3080F, fan (tumbler mould)	90		200	225
Vase 6" #3080F, fan (tumbler mould) metal ormolu	135		295	325

Back left: Plate 10.1" #3097, dinner, Pink satin. **Back right:** Plate 8.25" #3096, salad or lunch, Crystal satin. **Front center:** Plate 6.4" #3095, bread & butter or fruit bowl liner w/indent, Crystal satin – shown as ashtray w/metal ormolu.

Ruby Flashed grouping: **Left:** Vase 5.25" #3080C, round, crimped (tumbler mould). **Right:** Vase 5.25" #3080F, fan (tumbler mould) – shown in metal ormolu.

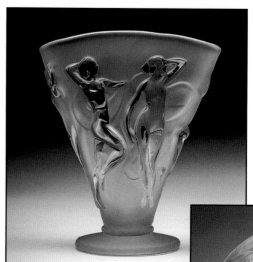

Vase 5.25" #3080F, fan (tumbler mould), Crystal w/part satin.

Lamp shade 16.75" #2795, hat shape, w/3 holes for hanging, Yellow Wash. Note, this one has an extra hole in center (probably to accept a finial type adornment).

DECAGON
Cambridge Glass Company   **1930s**
Main Colors: Amber, Crystal, Emerald Green, Peach Blo/Dianthus (pink), and Willow Blue
Other Colors: Carmen (ruby), Ebony (black), and Royal Blue (cobalt)

The name Decagon gives you an image of being with 10 sides. In this pattern, that is not always the case. Some of the pieces in this pattern have only eight sides. This pattern was ideally suited to be used for several etchings because of its plain wide panels. Cleo & Rosalie are etched on this blank. In 1934, the Peach Blo name of pink was changed to Dianthus with no difference in the actual pink color.

Many of the Cleo collectors are buying the different sizes of plates to supplement their collections. For instance, the pink dinner plate in Decagon is $40 while the Cleo plate is $175. Once covered with food, who could see the pattern? The collectors are becoming very sophisticated in their collecting and have soon found what they can do without and what really makes a difference in setting a table. They can get some of the highly prized items without spending a fortune. Availability of this blank is part of the reason and the cost is another big factor.

Very little of Carmen, Ebony, and Royal Blue pieces in this pattern show up on a regular basis. Without a constant supply, it is impossible to list a value based on the market place.

DECAGON	Amber Crystal	Pink Green	Blue
Basket 7" #760, two handles turned up	8	20	24
Basket 11.25" #977, two handles turned up	16	35	40
Bonbon 6.25" #749, handled, flared	6	14	16
Bowl 2.5" #611, footed, individual, almond	14	28	35
Bowl 3.5" #1101, flared, cranberry	12	26	28
Bowl 3.75" #1102, flat rim cranberry	10	20	30
Bowl 5.5" #758, 5.5" handled, sweetmeat	8	18	20
Bowl 5.5" #1010 or 1093, flared, fruit	7	15	18
Bowl 5.75" #1098 or #1099, flat rim or rolled edge, cereal	9	20	24
Bowl 6" #612, footed, almond	16	35	40
Bowl 6" #807, flat rim cereal	10	20	30
Bowl 6" #1011, flared, cereal	10	20	30
Bowl 8.5" #808, flat, rim soup	16	35	42
Bowl 8.5" #971, flat, deep, oval, handled	14	28	34
Bowl 8.5" #1012, flared, soup	14	28	34
Bowl 9" #1085, round, flared, vegetable	18	38	45
Bowl 9.5" #1087, oval, vegetable	20	40	48
Bowl 10" #984, flared, open handled	16	35	40
Bowl 10" #1013, flared, berry	16	35	40
Bowl 10.5" #877, footed, short stem & flared	30	54	60
Bowl 10.5" #1088, oval, vegetable	20	38	48
Bowl 11" #856, rolled edge, console	16	35	42
Bowl 11" #1086, round, flared, vegetable	16	35	42
Bowl 11" #1117, shallow, cupped up at edge	18	38	45
Bowl 11.5" #842, shallow, flared	16	35	42
Bowl 11.5" #1116, oval, shallow, cupped up at edge	20	40	48
Bowl 13" #1056, shallow w/flat wide rim	32	60	75
Bowl 15" #839, oval, rolled edge	34	62	78
Bowl 15" #840, oval, shallow, cupped up at edge	36	65	80
Bowl 15.5" #841, oval, mushroom shape	32	60	75
Candlestick 1-lite 3.5" #878, faceted ball stem, pair	34	62	78
Cheese & cracker: comport 2.8" #869, shallow, 5.6" wide; plate 10.6"	20	38	45
Comport 3.5" #608, short stem, 6.5" wide	12	26	28
Comport 7" #1090, tall stem, 7" wide	14	28	34
Cream soup & liner: bowl 2" #1075, 4.75" wide, 10 oz.; saucer w/indent 6.3"	14	28	34
Creamer #1094, individual, scalloped top, 4 oz.	5	15	16
Creamer 3.5" #1096, footed, individual, lightning handled, 4 oz.	10	30	32
Creamer 2.5" #979, flat, handled, regular, 7 oz.	4	14	15
Creamer 4" #867, footed, large (ball shape) 9.5 oz.	5	15	16
Cruet w/stopper #193, short, oil, 6 oz.	35	70	85
Cruet w/stopper #197, high, oil, 6 oz.	40	78	95
Cup & saucer, bouillon: cup 2.4" #866, handled, 9 oz.; saucer w/indent 6"	8	18	20
Cup & saucer, coffee: cup 2.5" #865, flat, 7 oz.; saucer w/indent 5.6"	7	15	16
Gravy boat & liner: #1091, sauce bowl; oval open handled plate	35	70	85
Gravy boat & liner #917/1167: bowl 5.75", handled w/2 spouts; oval tab handled, 9" plate	135	70	85
Mayonnaise 2 piece #871: bowl 5.5", footed, flared; liner w/indent 7"	18	42	45
Mayonnaise 2 piece #981: bowl 5.5", footed, flared; liner w/indent 7"	22	50	55
Mayonnaise bowl #758, flat, open handled	12	26	28
Plate 6" #809, bread & butter	4	7	8
Plate 7" #759, handled lemon server	6	12	14
Plate 7.25" #815, salad	5	9	10
Plate 8.4" #597, lunch	8	16	18
Plate 9.5" #811, small dinner	18	38	45
Plate 10" #1200, club lunch/grill	15	32	36
Plate 10.5" #812, large dinner	20	40	48
Plate 12.5" #598, service or torte	16	36	40
Platter 11" #1077, oval	18	38	45
Platter 12" #1078, oval	20	40	48
Platter 15.5" #1079/15, oval	25	50	60
Relish 8" #1167, open handled, oval pickle	8	20	24
Relish 9" #1067, oval, 2 sections	12	25	28
Relish 9" #1082, oval pickle	10	22	25
Relish 11" #1068, oval, 2 sections	14	28	34
Relish 11" #1083, oval celery	12	25	30
Salt dip 1.5" #613, footed, wide	16	32	36
Sandwich server 10.75" #870, center keyhole handle	20	42	48
Sugar #1094, individual, scalloped top, 4 oz.	5	15	16
Sugar 3.3" #1096, footed, individual, lightning handled, 4 oz.	10	30	32
Sugar 2.4" #979, flat, handled, regular, 7 oz.	8	18	20
Sugar 4" #867, footed, large (ball shape) 9.5 oz.	5	15	16
Tray 8" #1096, center lightning handle	18	38	45
Tray 10.25" #870, center keyhole handled, cupped	24	48	54
Tray 13" #1084, round, open handled	18	38	45

Green grouping: **Back row:** Sandwich server 10.75" #870, center keyhole handle. **Front left:** Cup & saucer, coffee: cup 2.5" #865, flat, 7 oz.; saucer w/indent 5.6". **Front right:** Plate 10.5" #812, large dinner.

Amethyst grouping: **Back left:** Bowl 11.5" #842, shallow, flared. **Back right:** Plate 8.4" #597, lunch; Cup & saucer, coffee: cup 2.5" #865, flat, 7 oz.; saucer w/indent 5.6". **Front left:** Bowl 8.5" #971, flat, deep, oval, handled. **Front right:** Bowl 11" #856, rolled edge, console.

Pattern detail, Deerwood.

DEERWOOD
U.S. Glass Co. (Tiffin)
1923-33

Colors: Reflex Green, and Rose (pink)
Other Colors: Crystal and Black

This etched pattern is often confused Black Forest of Paden City. Deerwood shows a forest scene with deer while Black Forest has deer but also has moose in the etched pattern. Look closely at each of the etched pattern details to see the difference. Both can also be found in Pink, Green, and Black colors. This of course adds to the confusion. Since Deerwood was manufactured first, it would appear Paden City modified the etching to include the moose to make a new pattern. Obviously, they also wanted an etched pattern that would sell well for them too. Several collectors look for both etched patterns to mix together. It is a nice accent to use both, especially with contrasting colors.

The prices we are listing are only for green and pink since they appear on the market most often. Crystal at this point doesn't have many collectors and would be about half of the price for the green and pink. Items in black are truly outstanding, especially if you are lucky enough to find any with a gold encrusting.

DEERWOOD	Black Green & Rose (pink)
Bowl #8133, breakfast	40
Bowl 10" #330/102, low, footed, flared	85
Bowl 10" #8105, salad w/straight edge	75
Bowl 11" #8098, footed, shallow	75
Bowl 12" #8177, footed, centerpiece w/straight edge	125
Cake plate 10" #336, handled	65
Cake salver 10" #330, low pedestal	125
Candy box w/cover 6" #329, flat, round, straight sided w/knob finial	145
Candy jar w/cover 7.75" #330, cone shape	165
Candlestick 1-lite 2.5" #101, straight edge on top, pair	85
Cheese & cracker: comport 3.5" #330, short stem; plate 10"	115
Comport 7" #15320, straight edge	45
Creamer 3.75" #179, flat, regular, 6 oz.	45
Cup & saucer, coffee: cup 2.5" #9395, flat, 6 oz.; saucer w/indent 6"	65
Goblet 4.75" #2809, wine, 3 oz.	60
Goblet 4" #2809, liquor cocktail, cupped, 3.5 oz.	45
Goblet 4.75" #2809, saucer champagne, 5.5 oz.	35
Goblet 6.75" #2809, water, 9 oz.	68
Plate 5.5" #8836, bread & butter	18
Plate 7.5" #8836, salad	30
Plate 10" #8836, dinner	85
Relish 10" #8177, oval w/straight edge, celery	78
Relish 12" #151, oval, celery	85
Sandwich server 10" #330, center handle, tray	85
Sugar 3.5" #179, flat, regular, 6 oz.	45
Tumbler 4.5" #2808, footed, cone, table water, 8.5 oz.	40
Tumbler 5.75" #2808, footed, cone, ice tea, 12 oz.	48
Vase 7" #151, flat, rolled edge, sweet pea	125
Vase 10" #6471, flat, straight sided, necked in w/crimped top	70
Vase 10" #15319, footed, 2-handled w/flared top	145
Whip cream 6.5" #330, short, wafer stem w/rolled edge (or mayonnaise)	75

Tumbler 4.5" #2808, footed, cone, table water, 8.5 oz., Rose (pink).

Sandwich server 10" #330, center handle, tray, Rose (pink).

DELILAH BIRD
Paden City Glass Company   1930s
Main Colors: Cheriglo (pink), Cobalt, Ebony (black), Green, Ruby, and Yellow
Other Color: Crystal

Hazel Marie Weatherman first identified the Delilah etching in her *Colored Glassware of the Depression Era 2* in 1974. Years later a new name of Peacock Reverse was given to this etched pattern by another author. With the recovery of the Paden City etching plates by the West Virginia Museum of American Glass at the L.G. Wright liquidation auction, its board of directors felt that the name of this bird etching should return to the name first given to it. Hazel was a great pioneer in the glass research field and this would honor her memory. This etching has been reestablished with the name as Delilah Bird. The bird actually is a pheasant and not a peacock, so the original name really better suits the etched pattern.

Most of the pieces are found on #412 Crow's Foot (square shape) and #411 Mrs. "B" line. Crystal prices will be less than the Pink & Green prices. For more information you can refer to the book *Paden City Glass Company* by William P. Walker, Melissa Bratkovich & Joan C. Walker.

DELILAH BIRD	Pastel Colors	Ebony	Cobalt Ruby
Bowl 5" #412 Crow's Foot (square), shallow, flared	45	52	60
Bowl 8.5" #412 Crow's Foot (square), flared	75	85	100
Bowl 8.5" #412 Crow's Foot (square), open handled, flared	125	110	150
Bowl 9" #412 Crow's Foot (square), footed, flared	85	98	115
Bowl 9.75" #412 Crow's Foot (square), footed w/flat rim edge	110	125	150
Bowl 10.5" #411 Mrs. "B", footed, rolled edge, console	100		
Bowl 11.75" #412 Crow's Foot (square), deep w/flat rim edge, console	120	135	175
Bowl 11.75" #412 Crow's Foot (square), deep flared	115	130	150
Candlestick 1-lite 5.25" #411 Mrs. "B", square dome footed, keyhole stem, pair	125		
Candlestick 1-lite 5.25" #412 Crow's Foot (square), bell footed, keyhole stem, pair	150	185	200
Candy jar w/cover 6" #701 Triumph, footed, (round bottom) square lid w/ball finial	125		
Candy jar w/cover 6.25" #503, footed, round w/flat or ball finial	250	250	295
Candy box w/cover 6.5" #411 Mrs. "B", flat, square, 2 or 3 sections	175	200	225
Candy box w/cover 7" #412 Crow's Foot (square), flat, square, 2 equal sections, w/keyhole finial	195	225	300
Candy box w/cover 7" #412 1/2 Crow's Foot (square), flat, 3-lobe sides, 3 equal sections, w/keyhole finial	195	225	300
Cheese & cracker: comport 2.25" #412 Crow's Foot (square), short stem, 5" wide; plate 10.25"	175	200	225
Comport 4.25" #412 Crow's Foot (square), short stem, oval cupped & flared, 7.5" long, sauce	150	185	200
Comport 6.5" #412 Crow's Foot (square), tall stem, cupped, 6" wide	115	130	150
Comport 6.5" #412 Crow's Foot (square), tall stem, flared, 7" wide	95	110	125
Cream soup 4.5" #412 Crow's Foot (square), flat, 2-handled, 11 oz.	45	50	70
Creamer, 3" #412 Crow's Foot (square), flat, regular, 7 oz.	75	80	85
Cup & saucer, coffee #412 Crow's Foot (square): cup 2.1", 6 oz.; saucer w/indent 5.75"	95	110	175
Goblet 4.6" #991 Penny Line, champagne, 6 oz.	55	65	75
Mayonnaise 2 piece #412 Crow's Foot (square): bowl, footed, rolled edge; liner w/indent			135
Plate 5.75" #412 Crow's Foot (square), bread & butter	30	35	40
Plate 8.5" #412 Crow's Foot (square), lunch	45	55	65
Plate 10.5" #412 Crow's Foot (square), open handled	100	125	145
Sandwich server 9.25" #701 Triumph, octagon, center handled tray	140	160	185
Sandwich server 10.25" #412 Crow's Foot (square), center handled tray	100	115	145
Sugar 2.6" #412 Crow's Foot (square), flat, regular, 6 oz.	75	80	85
Tumbler 4" #991 Penny Line, flat, water, 10 oz.	65	75	85
Vase 6.5" #210-7 Regina, flat, 3 rings on base & neck shouldered, flared	175	200	225
Vase 8" O'Kane, spherical bottom, narrow flared neck & rolled edge	195		
Vase 9" #210-9 Regina, flat, 3 rings on base & neck shouldered flared		250	
Vase 10" #184-10, flat, spherical bottom, flared	150	225	250

Pattern detail, Delilah Bird.

Crystal grouping: **Back right:** Bowl 11.75" #412 Crow's Foot (square), deep w/flat rim edge, console. **Front left:** Bowl 9" #412 Crow's Foot (square), footed, flared. **Front right:** Comport 6.5" #412 Crow's Foot (square), tall stem, flared, 7" wide.

Candy box w/cover 6.5" #411 Mrs. "B", flat, square, 2 equal sections, Cheriglo (pink).

Left: Candlestick 1-lite 5.25" #411 Mrs. "B", square dome footed, keyhole stem, Ebony (black). **Right:** Candlestick 1-lite 5.25" #411 Mrs. "B", square dome footed, keyhole stem, Cobalt.

Top left: Bowl 11.75" #412 Crow's Foot (square), deep flared, Yellow. **Top right:** Sandwich server 10.25" #412 Crow's Foot (square), center handled tray, Yellow. **Front center:** Candy jar w/cover 6.25" #503, footed, round w/flat or ball finial, Green.

DELLA ROBBIA

Westmoreland Glass Co. **Blank #1058** **1928-70s**

Colors: Crystal with dark stain or light stain

Della Robbia is a crystal pattern with embossed fruit. Color stains are then applied over the fruit. When you are looking at a piece that has the colors stained on, there will be some differences between pieces. The dark stained pieces are the favorite among collectors. However, the two stains were different not only because of being light & dark, but also due to the different colors of stains used on the fruit.

There are a very few Milk Glass items that can be found, some with gold trim. Della Robbia collectors do not seem to like them very well and they end up in Milk Glass collections. Levay, a glass designer and distributor, also had a few items produced in Ruby & Ruby Iridized for his glass line. Collectors like to have them as a novelty item. The Iridized ones have also found their way into carnival collections, by collectors who enjoy contemporary carnival glass.

New collectors sometimes confuse the Indiana Glass Company pattern of Garland with Della Robbia. Both feature embossed fruit, but remember that Della Robbia does not have a banana in its pattern. Looking at the Garland pattern, you will always find a banana and the stains are much different from those of Della Robbia. The Garland also is a much heavier weight glass for its size.

The basket, 2-lite candlesticks, oblong 13" bowl, pitcher, and oval platter are all hard to find items. Deduct 15% of the dark stain prices for the items with the light stain. Not all items were made in the light stain.

Platter 16", oval, serving tray, Crystal w/dark stain.

DELLA ROBBIA	Stain
Basket 8.5", flat, round w/applied handle	185
Basket 9", flat, flared w/applied handle	195
Basket 12", deep, flat, flared w/applied handle	295
Basket 12", flat, flared w/applied handle	250
Basket 16", deep, flat, flared w/applied handle	395
Bowl 4.5", flat, shallow, fruit or cereal	32
Bowl 6", flat, shallow	34
Bowl 6.5", shallow w/1 loop handle	38
Bowl 7.5", shallow	42
Bowl 8", rolled edge	45
Bowl 8", low, bell shape w/1 loop handle	65
Bowl 8.4", low, heart shape w/1 loop handle	130
Bowl 9", shallow	95
Bowl 11.5", footed, short stem w/rolled edge	145
Bowl 12", flat, flared, bell, salad	110
Bowl 12", footed, short stem w/rolled edge	135
Bowl 13", rolled edge, console	150
Bowl 13", oblong, 8 scalloped points on rim edge	250
Bowl 13", footed, short stem w/rolled edge	175
Bowl 14.75", footed, short stem, deep, flared, 5.75" high	195
Bowl 15", bell shape	215
Cake salver 14", footed, low	165
Candlestick 1-lite 3.25", footed, short wafer stem, pair	65
Candlestick 2-lite 5.4", footed circle in center, 6.5" spread, pair	245
Candy w/cover 6.5", flat, round, shallow, chocolate box, plain bottom	115
Candy w/cover 7", footed w/domed lid, .5 lb.	145
Comport 4", footed, shallow, flared, 6.25" wide	45
Comport 5", footed, deep, crimped, 5.25" wide	50
Comport 8", flared, sweetmeat w/tall ball stem, 8" wide	98
Creamer 3", footed, regular, 4 oz.	24
Cup & saucer, coffee: cup 2.5", footed, coffee, 4 oz.; saucer w/indent 5.1"	32
Goblet 4.9", column stem, wine, 3 oz.	35
Goblet 4.75", column stem, liquor cocktail, or claret, 3.25 oz.	32
Goblet 3.5", short column stem, sherbet, 4 oz.	24
Goblet 4.75", column stem, saucer champagne, 6 oz.	28
Goblet 6", column stem, water, 7.5 oz.	35
Mayonnaise 2 piece: bowl 5", flat, cupped; liner w/indent 6"	78
Pitcher 7", flat, water w/o ice lip, 32 oz.	295
Plate 6", bread & butter	16
Plate 7.3", salad or dessert	24
Plate 9", cupped edge	38
Plate 9", handled	58
Plate 9", lunch	38
Plate 10.5", dinner	145
Plate 13.75", flat, small center, torte	90
Plate 18", flat torte	165
Plate 18", small center, turned up edge, cabaret or punch bowl liner	170
Platter 16", oval, serving tray	195
Punch bowl 13", flat, cupped, 6" high	345
Shaker 5", footed, short stem, cylindrical w/chrome top, pair	78
Sugar 2.5", footed, regular, 4 oz.	24
Tray 9", for cream & sugar	35
Tumbler 3.75", flat, straight sided, juice or ginger ale, 4 oz.	28
Tumbler 3.8", flat, straight sided, table water, 8 oz.	32
Tumbler 5", footed, lunch water, 8 oz.	35
Tumbler 5.75", footed, low, ice tea, 11 oz.	38
Tumbler, 5.2" flat, straight sided, ice tea, 12 oz.	48

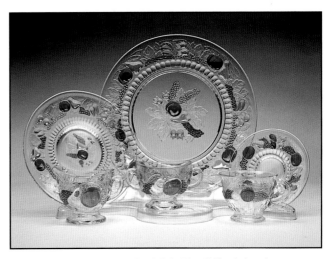

Crystal w/dark stain grouping: **Back left:** Plate 7.3", salad or dessert. **Back center:** Plate 10.5", dinner. **Front left:** Creamer 3", footed, regular, 4 oz. **Front center:** Sugar 2.5", footed, regular, 4 oz. **Front right:** Cup & saucer, coffee: cup 2.5", footed, coffee, 4 oz.; saucer w/indent 5.1".

Crystal w/dark stain grouping: Punch bowl 13", flat, cupped, 6" high; cup 2.5", footed, 4 oz.; Plate 18", small center, turned up edge, punch bowl liner.

Crystal w/dark stain grouping: **Left:** Candlestick 1-lite 3.25", footed, short wafer stem, pair. **Right:** Candlestick 2-lite 5.4", footed circle in center, 6.5" spread.

Crystal w/dark stain grouping: **Top left:** Comport 4", footed, shallow, flared, 6.25" wide. **Top right:** Comport 5", footed, deep, crimped, 5.25" wide. **Fro[nt] left:** Bowl 6", flat, shallow. **Front center:** Shaker 5", footed, short stem, cylindrical w/chrome top. **Front right:** Basket 9", flat, flared w/applied hand[le.]

Crystal w/dark stain grouping: **Left:** Candy w/cover 6.5", flat, round, shallow, chocolate box, plain bottom. **Right:** Candy w/cover 7", footed w/domed lid, .5 lb.

Crystal w/dark stain grouping: **Top left:** Tumbler 5.75", footed, low, ice tea, 11 oz. **Top right:** Goblet 6", column stem, water, 7.5 oz. **Bottom left:** Tumbler 3.8", flat, straight sided, table water, 8 oz., Goblet 3.5". **Bottom right:** short column stem, sherbet, 4 oz.

Crystal w/dark stain grouping: **Back left:** Plate 13.75", flat, small center, torte. **Back center[:]** Bowl 14.75", footed, short stem, deep, flared, 5.75" high. **Back right:** Bowl 8.4", low, heart shape w/1 loop handle. **Front:** Cake salver 14", footed, low.

DIAMOND OPTIC

Fenton Art Glass Company   **Optic #1502**   **1927-37**
Main Colors: Green, Orchid, Rose (pink), Royal Blue (cobalt), Ruby, and Tangerine
Other Colors: Aqua, Ebony (black), Jade, and Tangerine Stretch

The Diamond Optic pattern was one of Fenton's first ventures into making a tableware line. On the interior is the Diamond Optic pattern and the exterior is smooth. Several of the pieces had dolphins added to the design. The stemware has a six-sided stem with three tiered rings (getting larger as they go up) between the top of the stem and the start of the bowl. On the pieces that have a tall stem, you will find some that have just a slight twist to the stem, probably because they were removed from the mould a little to soon.

On some of the Fenton Ruby pieces, you will see that it shades to a yellow center, or in the case of stemware, the center of the stem will be yellow. Ruby is a heat sensitive color. This glass starts out a yellow color and must be reheated to turn it to a final color of red. This shading from red to yellow is just part of the reheating process. At times the red does not turn out perfect and still retains some of its original color. It is not Amberina, as some would lead you to believe.

On the opaque items, the Diamond Optic, being an interior pattern, is often hard to see. You have to look inside or feel to tell that they are really Diamond Optic. Aqua should be priced the same as Orchid. Jade & Ebony (black) will run similar to Ruby & Royal Blue (cobalt). Collectors greatly desire the cologne bottle w/dauber, dinner water goblets, high standard comport, and covered bowl. The cologne bottles usually find their way in a boudoir collection first though, and that makes it much harder for the pattern collector to locate these items.

Prices for Tangerine Stretch with the iridized carnival type finish runs somewhat higher than the plain Tangerine listed below.

DIAMOND OPTIC

	Green Rose	Orchid	Ruby Cobalt	Tangerine
Basket 4.25", flat w/metal handle, 8" wide	45	55	75	
Basket 4.75", flat w/metal handle, 7" wide	40	50	65	
Bowl 7", deep, cupped w/3 dolphins	45	55	75	
Bowl 8", rolled edge w/3 dolphins	45	55	65	
Bowl 8", deep, cupped, 3.5" high	30	40	60	
Bowl 8", flared & cupped	30	40	60	
Bowl 8.5", cupped w/3 dolphins	65	75	95	
Bowl 9", deep, crimped edge w/3 dolphins	80	90	98	
Bowl 10", shallow, flared w/3 dolphins	65	75	95	
Bowl 10", shallow, cupped	40	50		
Bowl 10", special low wide, rolled edge	50	60	75	
Bowl 11", deep, rolled edge, mushroom shape, console	50	60		85
Bowl 11", flared & cupped				85
Bowl 11", shallow, rolled edge, console				75
Bowl 12", deep, rolled edge, mushroom shape, console	60	70		
Bowl 12", shallow, cupped	60	70		
Bowl 13", shallow, flared, low, console	50	60		
Bowl 14", deep, rolled edge, mushroom shape, console	65	75	85	
Box w/cover (flat knob finial) 4", flat, round, puff #53	45	55		
Candlestick 1-lite 3", footed/candle cup w/small wafer stem, pair	45	55		65
Cheese & cracker: comport 3", plain short stem, 5" wide; plate 9.75"	70	90	100	
Cologne w/stopper; 7" tall thin bottle, footed; teardrop stopper w/long dauber	135	165		
Cologne w/flat stopper 5" #53, dome footed	95	100		
Comport 3.5", dolphin handled, flared, 6.25" wide	50	60		65
Comport 3.5", dolphin handled, flat top, 8.25" wide	65	75		
Comport 4.5", dolphin handled, 2 sides turned up, 5.5" wide	45	55		
Comport 4.5", dolphin handled, smooth top, 5.5" wide	50	60		75
Comport 4.5", dolphin handled, 4 sides turned up, 4.5" wide	60	70		
Comport 5", dolphin handled, 2 sides turned up, 7.5" wide	65	75	95	
Comport 5", dolphin handled, smooth top, 7.5" wide	70	80		
Comport 5", dolphin handled, 4 sides turned up, 7.5" wide	75	85		
Comport 7", high standard, flared, shallow, 11.75" wide				245
Comport 10", high standard, cupped, deep, 8.75" wide				225
Creamer 3.5", footed regular, 5.5 oz.	18	28	35	45
Cup & saucer, coffee: cup 2.5", footed, 6 oz.; saucer w/indent 5.9"	38	50	75	
Finger bowl & liner: bowl 5", round; plate w/indent	45	55	85	
Goblet 3.75", low sherbet, 5 oz.	20	30	38	48

Vase 6", footed, dolphin handled, fan shape, Aqua.

Top row: Vase 6", flat, flared at top, flip shape, Royal Blue (cobalt); Vase 8", footed, ball stem, cupped in for lamp base, Ruby; Plate 7.75", octagon salad, Ruby. **Bottom row:** Goblet 7", tall stem, dinner water, 9 oz., Ruby; Goblet 3.75", low sherbet, 5 oz., Ruby; Shaker 4.4", footed w/ chrome top, Royal Blue; Tumbler 4.6", footed juice, 5 oz. (Bridge Goblet), Ruby; Tumbler 5.25", footed, lunch water, 9 oz. (Bridge Goblet), Royal Blue; Tumbler 6", footed, small ice tea, 11 oz. (Bridge Goblet), Ruby.

Back top: Whip cream pail 5.5", flat, metal handle (or small ice tub), Aqua. **Center left:** Basket 4.75", flat w/metal handle, 7" wide, Ruby. **Center:** Basket 4.75", flat w/metal handle, 7" wide, Ebony (black). **Center right:** Creamer 3.5", footed regular, 5.5 oz., Green. **Front left:** Tumbler 6", footed, small ice tea, 11 oz. (Bridge Goblet), Orchid. **Front center:** Basket 4.25", flat w/metal handle, 8" wide, Jade. **Front right:** Sugar 3.5", footed, regular, 5.5 oz., Green.

Orchid grouping: **Back:** Bowl 10", shallow, flared w/3 dolphins. **Front:** Bowl 9", deep, crimped edge w/3 dolphins.

Rose (pink) grouping: **Left:** Vase 6", flat, flared at top, flip shape. **Right:** Basket 4.75", flat shown missing metal handle, 7" wide.

Goblet 7", tall stem, dinner water, 9 oz.	45	55	65	85
Guest 2 piece set 7", tumble up w/tumbler	85	125		
Ice bucket 6.5", w/chrome handle	75	100	125	
Mayonnaise bowl 5.75", footed, flared, flat top	45	55		125
Pitcher 7" #1634, tapers down w/2 bulges at base, 54 oz.	165	185	250	
Pitcher 6.5" #1635, flares out at bottom w/2 bulges, 64 oz.	175	195	300	
Pitcher 9" #1636, tapers up w/2 bulges at base, 70 oz.	195	225	350	
Plate 6", bread & butter (octagon or round)	12	18	20	
Plate 7.75", octagon salad	18	26	30	
Plate 8", octagon salad	18	26	30	40
Plate 11", octagon torte				85
Puff box w/cover 3.75", round w/pointed finial	60	70		
Puff box w/cover 4" #53, round w/flat finial	50	60		
Refrigerator set, two 4" x 5" bowls on tray 6" x 8.5"	175	195		
Sandwich server 10", dolphin center handle	85			
Sandwich server 10", loop center handle	45	55	65	85
Shaker 4.4", footed w/chrome top, pair	75	125	150	
Sugar 3.5", footed, regular, 5.5 oz.	18	28	38	45
Tray 6" x 8.5", rectangular, dresser	35	45		
Tumbler 4.6", footed juice, 5 oz. (Bridge Goblet)	20	30	40	
Tumbler 5", footed lunch water, 7 oz. (Bridge Goblet)	25	35	45	
Tumbler 4" #1634, barrel shape, 8 oz.	30	40	45	
Tumbler 5.25", footed, lunch water, 9 oz. (Bridge Goblet)	35	40	50	
Tumbler 4.5" #1635, water, 9 oz.	40	50	60	
Tumbler 5.5" #1636, ice tea, 10 oz.	40	50	60	
Tumbler 6", footed, small ice tea, 11 oz. (Bridge Goblet)	45	55	65	
Vase 5.25", dolphin handled, fan shape	45	55		85
Vase 6", flat, flared at top, flip shape	35	45	58	65
Vase 6", footed, dolphin handled, fan shape	65	70		95
Vase 7", footed, ball stem, tapered & rolled top edge	85	100		125
Vase 8", footed, ball stem, crimped	75	85	95	
Vase 8", footed, ball stem, cupped in for lamp base	100		175	
Vase 8", footed, ball stem, smooth top	65	75		
Vase 8.25", flat, flared at top, flip shape	70	80	90	125
Vase 8.5", footed, ball stem, fan shape	85	100		125
Vase 10", flat, flip shape w/flared top	75			
Vase 16-18.5", large swung w/flared top				195
Whip cream pail 5.5", flat, metal handle (or small ice tub)	40	50		

Green grouping: **Left:** Sandwich server 10", dolphin center handle. **Right top:** Creamer 3.5", footed regular, 5.5 oz. **Right bottom:** Sugar 3.5", footed, regular, 5.5 oz.

Cologne w/stopper; 7" tall thin bottle, footed; teardrop stopper w/long dauber, Rose (pink).

Tangerine grouping: **Top:** Comport 7", high standard, fla shallow, 11.75" wide. **Center left:** Mayonnaise bowl 5. footed, flared, flat top. **Center of photo:** Creamer 3.5 footed regular, 5.5 oz. **Front left:** Comport 5", dolphin handled, 2 sides turned up, 7.5" wide. **Front center:** V 7", footed, ball stem, tapered & rolled top edge. **Right:** 18.25", large swung w/flared top.

DIANE
Cambridge Glass Company **Etching #752** **1931-56**
Main Color: Crystal
Other Colors: Amber, Crown Tuscan, Crystal, Heatherbloom, and Peach Blo/Dianthus (pink)

Diane is one of several etched patterns by Cambridge to have a lady's name. The sister etched patterns of Elaine & Portia both have similar pieces made and generally run for the same price. Diane etching is characterized by a flower inside what resembles a wishbone. This is surrounded by a garland of flowers. The etched pattern was produced on the four stemware lines of #1066, #3106, #3122, and #7666. Line #3122 is the easiest to find since it was made during the entire time Diane was produced. Primarily made in Crystal, a few pieces can be found in colors, but not enough to build up a whole set. We have seen a Carmen (ruby) electric table lamp with gold encrusting. Amber prices would be about the same as Crystal. For Crown Tuscan & Peach Blo/Dianthus (pink) add 50% to the Crystal price.

The following items seem to be on most collectors' want lists: blown candy dish, cocktail churn, cocktail shakers, Doulton pitcher, French dressing bottle, hurricane lamp, nite set, and toast cover. An unusual item to find is the cigarette box on the #3011 nude stem. Pictured here in Crown Tuscan; this piece is exceedingly rare.

Very few Heatherbloom items (or the nude stem cigarette box) ever show up, making it impossible to list the fair market value of these items.

Pattern detail, Diane.

DIANE	Crystal
Ashtray 3.25" #3500/124 Gadroon, round	28
Ashtray 3.5" #3500/125 Gadroon, round	28
Ashtray 4" #3500/126 Gadroon, round	32
Ashtray 4.25" #1311, footed, round, cupped 3" tall	42
Ashtray 4.25" #3500/127 Gadroon, round	32
Ashtray 4.5" #3500/128 Gadroon, round	38
Basket 5.4" #3500/51 Gadroon, footed, applied handle	195
Basket 5.75" #3500/55 Gadroon, footed, 2-handled, crimped, 3.5" tall	38
Basket 6.25" #3500/52 Gadroon, footed, applied handle	250
Basket 6.25" #3400/1182, 2 handles turned up	34
Basket 7" #119, flared w/applied handle	400+
Bell #3575, dinner	120
Bonbon 5.6" #3400/1179, low, flared, open handled	32
Bonbon 6" #3400/201, 4-footed (fan shape) crimped	75
Bonbon 6" #3500/54 Gadroon, footed, handled	30
Bottle w/stopper 6.5" #1263, flat, French dressing, 8 oz.	245
Bottle w/stopper 7.25" #1261, footed, French dressing, 8 oz.	275
Bowl 2.75" #3400/71, 4-footed, tab handled, nut	58
Bowl 3.75" #3400/49, round, flared, plain rim, cranberry	65
Bowl 3.75" #3400/80, round, flared, scalloped rim, cranberry	68
Bowl 5" #1534 Pristine, blown, cupped, fruit	56
Bowl 5" #3500/49 Gadroon, round w/1 handle	35
Bowl 5" #3400/74, tab handled, 4-footed, mint	40
Bowl 5.25" #3400/56, shallow, fruit	48
Bowl 5.25" #3400/1180, handled, sweetmeat	35
Bowl 5.75" #3900/130, footed, tab handled, sweetmeat	28
Bowl 6" #3400/53, flared cereal	60
Bowl 6" #3400/136, 4-footed, deep, fancy crimped	85
Bowl 6" #3500/50 Gadroon, round w/1 handle	40
Bowl 7.5" #435 Pristine, deco tab handled, sweetmeat	70
Bowl 8.5" #381 Pristine, rim soup	145
Bowl 8.5" #1402/131 Tally Ho, deep, 3 equal sections	175
Bowl 9.5" #225 Pristine, blown, 2 sections	295
Bowl 9.5" #3400/34, open handled, vegetable	65
Bowl 10" #427 Pristine, sham base, deep, salad	120
Bowl 10" #3400/51, oval vegetable	58
Bowl 10" #3400/1185, handled, deep	68
Bowl 10" #3500/28 Gadroon, footed, handled, flared	68
Bowl 10" #3900/54, 4-footed, flared	58
Bowl 10.25" #3900/34, handled, flared	68
Bowl 10.5" #1359 Pristine, tab footed, smooth edge, flared	68
Bowl 10.5" #3400/168, flat, flared	65
Bowl 11" #1399, deep salad, scalloped edge	120
Bowl 11" #3400/45, footed, square crimped	75
Bowl 11" #3400/1188, handled, flared, fruit	85
Bowl 10.5" #3900/28, footed, tab handled, flared	65
Bowl 12" #1349 Pristine, tab footed, crimped edge, flared	68
Bowl 12" #3400/4, 4-toed, squared, flared edge	65
Bowl 12" #3400/160, 4-footed, oblong, crimped	65
Bowl 12" #3900/62, 4-footed, flared	70
Bowl 12" #3900/65, 4-footed, handled, oval	82
Bowl 12.5" #993, low, 4-footed, flared out	78
Bowl 12.5" #3400/32, flat, flared	72
Bowl 12.6" #3400/1240, 4-footed, oval, refractory	110
Bowl 13" #1398, shallow, fruit or salad	100
Bowl 13" #3400/1, flared, console	65
Box w/cover 4.5" #3400/95, tilt ball, puff w/keyhole finial	120

Top left: Relish 6.5" #3400/90, 2 open handles, 2 equal sections. **Top right:** Plate 8.5" #3400/62, lunch (6 sided). **Front left:** Mayonnaise bowl #3400/13 bowl 5.8", 4-toed, flared, tab handled. **Front right:** Cup & saucer, coffee #3400/54: cup 2.4", 6 oz.; saucer w/indent 5.5".

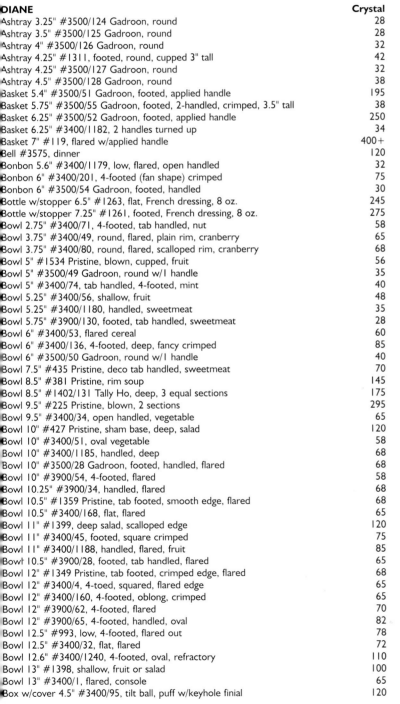

Top left: Bonbon 5.6" #3400/1179, low, flared, open handled. **Top right:** Cheese & cracker: comport 3" #3400/7, short stem cheese, flared, 5.3" wide; plate 10.5" #3400/6, tab handled, shown gold encrusted. **Bottom left:** Relish 8.75" #3400/862, center plume handled, oblong, 4 sections. **Bottom right:** Shaker 3.75" #3400/77, footed w/ glass top, pair.

Top left: Goblet 6.6" #3122, fancy stem, claret, 4 oz. **Top center:** Goblet 4.8" #3122, fancy stem, wine, 2 oz. **Top right:** Goblet 5.8" #3122, fancy stem, liquor cocktail, 4 oz. **Bottom left:** Goblet 6.25" #3122, fancy stem, saucer champagne, 7 oz. **Bottom center left:** Goblet 4.3" #3122, fancy stem, oyster cocktail, 5 oz. **Bottom center right:** Goblet 4.75" #3122, fancy stem, sherbet, 7 oz. **Bottom right:** Goblet 7.25" #3122, fancy stem, water, 10 oz.

Top left: Candlestick 2-lite 6" #3400/647, keyhole stem, 7.75" spread. **Top right:** Bowl 12" #3400/160, 4-footed, oblong, crimped. **Bottom left:** Candlestick 1-lite 5.25" #3400/646, keyhole stem. **Bottom center:** Sugar 3" #3400/68, regular, scalloped foot, 5 oz. **Bottom right:** Creamer 3.8" #3400/68, regular, scalloped foot, 4.75 oz.

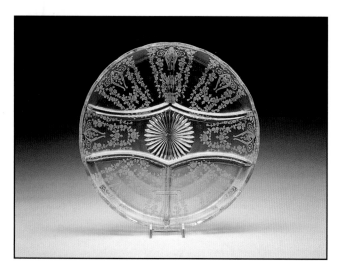

Relish 10" #394, round, 4 equal sections & celery section.

Butter w/cover 5.5" #506, round, tab handled	165
Butter w/cover 5.5" #3400/52, round, 2 open handles	185
Cake plate 11.75" #3900/35, handled	75
Cake salver 13" #170 Martha, tab footed, scalloped edge	185
Canape set #693/3000, plate/cocktail use #3000 footed cocktail, 3.5 oz. or 5 oz.	165
Candelabra 1-lite 6.25" #3400/648, keyhole stem, etched bobeches &, prisms, pair	245
Candelabra 1-lite 7.5" #3121, fancy stem w/plain bobeches & prisms, pair	245
Candelabra 2-lite 6" #3400/1268, keyhole stem, bobeches & prisms, pair	345
Candelabra 2-lite 6.5" #496 Martha, w/#19 bobeches & #1 prisms, pair	275
Candelabra 3-lite 5.5" #1545, one #19 bobeche center cup & #16 prisms, pair	275
Candlestick 1-lite 2.5" #3500/108 Gadroon, no stem	55
Candlestick 1-lite 3.5" #628 Pristine, w/wafer stem, pair	68
Candlestick 1-lite 5" #3900/67, skirted, pair	98
Candlestick 1-lite 5.25" #3400/646, keyhole stem, pair	80
Candlestick 1-lite 5.75" #3400/1192, small stem, pair	110
Candlestick 1-lite 7" #3121, fancy stem, pair	140
Candlestick 2-lite 5.75" #495 Martha, plume arms & ball center, 8.25" spread, pair	185
Candlestick 2-lite 6" #3400/647, keyhole stem, 7.75" spread, pair	75
Candlestick 2-lite 6" #3900/72, w/plume center, 8.25" spread, pair	90
Candlestick 3-lite #1307, pair	75
Candlestick 3-lite 5.5" #1545, bell footed, pair	145
Candlestick 3-lite 6" #3900/74, pair	100
Candlestick 3-lite 6.25" #3400/1338, tiered (looks like ocean waves) 7" spread, pair	125
Candlestick 3-lite 7" #3400/638, keyhole, pair	120
Candy w/cover 5.4" #1066/4, blown w/fancy ball stem, plain finial	195
Candy w/cover 5.4" #3121/4, low, blown	125
Candy w/cover 5.4" #3121/3, tall, blown	145
Candy w/cover 5.4" #3500/103 Gadroon, blown	135
Candy (open) 5.5" #3500/47 Gadroon, handled	32
Candy w/cover 6" #3500/78 Gadroon, flat, low, blown, rams head tab handles	225
Candy w/cover 6.5" #3400/9, 4-footed, tab handled, 7" wide; dome lid w/finial	120
Candy w/cover 7" #3900/165, flat, round, dome lid w/finial	110
Candy w/cover 8" #3500/57 Gadroon, 3 open handled, 3 equal sections	72
Cheese & cracker: comport 3" #3400/7, short stem cheese, flared, 5.3" wide; plate 10.5" #3400/6, tab handled	78
Cheese & cracker: comport 3" #3400/7, short stem cheese, flared, 5.3" wide; plate 11.5" #3400/8, tab handled	82
Cheese & cracker: comport 3.75" #3500/163 Gadroon, short stem, flared, 6" wide; plate 12" #3500/162, handled	95
Cheese dish w/cover 5" #980, flat, pointed finial	400+
Cigarette box w/cover 3.6" #1312, footed, rectangle w/flat lid 3.5" tall	195
Cigarette box w/cover 4" #615, oblong	175
Cigarette box w/cover 7.4" #3011, table size nude stem, rectangle w/flat lid (colors only)	Market
Cigarette holder #1066, oval, short stem w/ashtray foot	150
Cigarette holder 4" #1337, round w/cupped ashtray foot	125
Cocktail icer 4.2" #187 Pristine, footed, 2 piece w/non-etched insert	125
Cocktail icer 4.2" #3600, footed, 2 piece w/non-etched insert	65
Cocktail icer 4.6" #968, footed, 2 piece w/non-etched insert	70
Cocktail mixer #1395, w/chrome lid & spoon, 28 oz.	200
Cocktail shaker #97, small #9 chrome lid	265
Cocktail shaker #98, large #10 chrome lid	145
Cocktail shaker #99, sham base, chrome lid	150
Cocktail shaker #3400/175, w/large #10 chrome lid	140
Cologne w/keyhole stopper 2.5" #3400/97: tilt bottle, 2 oz.; stopper w/long dauber	345
Comport 5.3" #3400/28, keyhole stem, 7.25" wide	65
Comport 6.1" #3121/2 (blown), tall stem, 5.4" wide	62
Comport 7" #3500/148 Gadroon, high fancy stem, 6" wide	46
Comport 7.5" #3400/14, fancy wafer stem, flared, 7" wide	60
Comport 7.5" #3900/136, scalloped edge, 7.25" wide	52
Cream soup & liner #3400/55: bowl 4.75", 2-handled, 9 oz., saucer w/indent 6.25"	78
Creamer 2.5" #3500/15 Gadroon, footed, individual, 3 oz.	22
Creamer 2.6" #3900/40, footed, individual, 3.5 oz.	22
Creamer 3" #3900/41, footed, regular, 6 oz.	22
Creamer 3.8" #3400/68, regular, scalloped foot, 4.75 oz.	24
Cruet w/stopper #3400/96, ball shape, 2 oz.	85
Cruet w/ball stopper 4.4" #3400/99, tilt ball, 6 oz.	120
Cruet w/keyhole stopper 4.4" #3400/99, tilt, 6 oz.	130
Cruet w/stopper #3400/161, footed, handled, 6 oz.	175
Cruet w/stopper #3400/193, flat, 6 oz.	95
Cruet w/stopper 6" #3900/100, flat, spherical, 6 oz.	100
Cup & saucer, after dinner #3400/69: cup 2.25", 2 oz.; saucer w/indent 4.25", 6 sided	145
Cup & saucer, coffee #3400/54: cup 2.4", 6 oz.; saucer w/indent 5.5"	28
Cup & saucer, coffee #3900/17: cup 2.5", 7 oz.; saucer w/indent 5.5"	28
Decanter w/stopper #3400/119, tilt ball, cordial, 12 oz.	245
Decanter w/flat stopper 9" #1320, footed, cordial, 14 oz.	275
Decanter w/stopper #1380, square, 26 oz.	575
Decanter w/flat stopper 11" #1321, footed, 28 oz.	325
Decanter w/stopper 13.25" #1372, flat, slim bottle shape, 28 oz.	600+

Decanter w/stopper 6.25" #3400/92, tilt ball, 32 oz.	345
Decanter w/stopper #3400/113, ball w/long neck, 35 oz.	185
Epergne 4 piece #645, etched 3-lite candlestick w/plain arm & 2 non-etched vases	125
Epergne 5 piece #654, etched keyhole w/plain bobeche-prisms & 2 non-etched vases	100
Finger bowl & liner: bowl #3106, blown; plate w/indent	45
Finger bowl & liner: bowl #3122, fancy stem, blown; plate w/indent	54
Goblet #3106, plain stem, brandy, .75 oz.	82
Goblet 4.9" #1066, 1 ball stem, cordial, 1 oz.	100
Goblet #3106, plain stem, cordial, 1 oz.	85
Goblet #3106, pousse-cafe, 1 oz.	100
Goblet 4.8" #3122, fancy stem, cordial, 1 oz.	85
Goblet 5" #7966, flared, cone shape, cordial, 1 oz.	98
Goblet #3106, plain stem, sherry, 2 oz.	45
Goblet 5.25" #7966, flared, cone shaped, sherry, 2 oz.	80
Goblet 4.8" #3122, fancy stem, wine, 2 oz.	32
Goblet #3106, creme de menthe, 2.5 oz.	65
Goblet #3106, plain stem, wine, 2.5 oz.	35
Goblet 5.1" #1066, 1 ball stem, wine, 3 oz.	34
Goblet #3106, plain stem, cocktail, 3 oz.	26
Goblet 4.25" #1066, 1 ball stem, liquor cocktail, 3.5 oz.	28
Goblet 5.8" #3122, fancy stem, liquor cocktail, 4 oz.	24
Goblet 7.6" #1066, 1 ball stem, claret, 4.5 oz.	55
Goblet #3106, plain stem, claret, 4.5 oz.	42
Goblet 6.6" #3122, fancy stem, claret, 4 oz.	56
Goblet 4.3" #3122, fancy stem, oyster cocktail, 5 oz.	20
Goblet 4.75" #1066, 1 ball stem, sherbet, 7 oz.	22
Goblet 4.75" #3106, plain stem, sherbet, 7 oz.	18
Goblet #3106, plain stem, saucer champagne, 7 oz.	22
Goblet 4.75" #3122, fancy stem, sherbet, 7 oz.	22
Goblet 6.25" #3122, fancy stem, saucer champagne, 7 oz.	24
Goblet #3106, plain stem, dinner water, 9 oz.	30
Goblet 7.25" #3122, fancy stem, water, 10 oz.	30
Goblet #3106, plain stem, water, 10 oz.	32
Goblet 7.25" #1066, 1 ball stem, water, 11 oz.	34
Hurricane lamp 8" #1601, short stem, bobeche w/prisms & etched chimney, each	225
Hurricane lamp 9.3" #1617, skirted w/etched chimney, each	195
Hurricane lamp 11.5" #1603, keyhole stem, bobeche/prisms/chimney all etched, each	245
Ice bucket 5.75" #3400/851, flat, scalloped top w/chrome handle	110
Ice Bucket 5.75" #3900/671, chrome handle	125
Iced frappe 2 piece: #3400/41, bowl/insert no pattern	82
Icer Fruit #188, scalloped edge fits into the Pristine #427 deep salad	350
Marmalade w/cover 5.4" #147 Pristine, flat (blown) 8 oz.	130
Mayonnaise 2 piece #1532 Pristine: bowl 4.5" (blown), spherical, 3" high; liner w/indent 6.75"	48
Mayonnaise bowl 4" #3900/19, footed, ball shape, 4.1" high	45
Mayonnaise bowl 4.75" #1402/133, flared, salad dressing, 5.75" wide	45
Mayonnaise 2 piece #3900: #127 bowl 5", flared; #128 liner w/indent 6.5"	55
Mayonnaise 2 piece #3900/111: bowl 5.25", salad dressing; liner w/indent 6.75"	58
Mayonnaise 2 piece #1490 Pristine: bowl 5.5", cupped, salad dressing; use #1491 liner w/indent 6.4"	65
Mayonnaise 2 piece #1491 Pristine: bowl 5.5", flared, salad dressing; liner w/indent 6.4"	65
Mayonnaise bowl 5.75" #1402/95 Tally Ho, footed, salad dressing	48
Mayonnaise 2 piece #3400: #13 bowl 5.8", 4-toed, flared, tab handled; #11 liner w/indent 5"	65
Mayonnaise 2 piece #3500/58 Gadroon: bowl 6", footed, handled, flared; #59 liner w/indent 7.5"	58
Marmalade w/cover 5.4" #147 Pristine, blown (spherical) 8 oz.	135
Nite set #103, flat, handled jug & flat tumbler w/flared base	600+
Pitcher #1408, cocktail churn w/metal plunger, 60 oz.	1,000+
Pitcher 10" #1205, footed, cone shape, 64 oz.	995
Pitcher 8.6" #96, flat, straight side, tankard, 69 oz.	795
Pitcher #3400/100, high w/ice lip, 76 oz.	200
Pitcher 9.25" #3400/152, Doulton style w/o ice lip, 76 oz.	295
Pitcher 7.9" #3900/141, Doulton jug w/o ice lip (not optic) 80 oz.	325
Pitcher 9" #3400/38, tilt ball/ice lip, 80 oz.	245
Plate 6" #3400/60, bread & butter	10
Plate 6" #3400/1174, square, bread & butter	12
Plate 6" #3400/1181, 2 open handled lemon server	24
Plate 6.5" #3900/20, bread & butter	8
Plate 7" #131 Pristine, (blown) salad/coupe	75
Plate 7.5" #555 Pristine, dessert	14
Plate 7.5" #3400/176, square, salad or dessert	15
Plate 8" #3900/22, salad or lunch	22
Plate 8" #3900/131, handled lemon server, 9.25" counting handles	28
Plate 8.5" #3400/62, lunch (6 sided)	22
Plate 9.5" #485, crescent salad	195
Plate 9.5" #3400/63, dinner (6 sided)	70
Plate 10" #3400/22, tab handled	42

Top left: Platter 13.5" #3400/58, tab handled, oval. **Top Right:** Comport 7.5" #3400/14, fancy wafer stem, flared, 7" wide. **Center of photo:** Cruet w/ball stopper 4.4" #3400/99, tilt ball, 6 oz. **Bottom left:** Candy w/cover 8" #3500/57 Gadroon, 3 open handled, 3 equal sections. **Bottom right:** Basket 6.25" #3400/1182, 2 handles turned up.

Heatherbloom grouping: **Left:** Ashtray 4.25" #1311, footed, round, cupped 3" tall. **Right:** Cigarette box w/cover 3.6" #1312, footed, rectangle w/flat lid 3.5" tall.

Cigarette box w/cover 7.4" #3011, table size nude stem, rectangle w/ flat lid, Crown Tuscan w/ Gold encrusted.

Amber grouping: **Back left:** Plate 6" #3400/1181, 2 open handled lemon server. **Back right:** Plate 7.5" #3400/176, square, salad or dessert. **Front center:** Bowl 2.75" #3400/71, 4-footed, tab handled, nut.

Left: Ice bucket 5.75" #3400/851, flat, scalloped top w/chrome handle.
Right: Pitcher 9.25" #3400/152, Doulton style w/o ice lip, 76 oz.

Amber grouping: **Left:** Tumbler #3400/38, flat, ice tea, 12 oz. **Right:** Pitcher 9" #3400/38, tilt ball/ice lip, 80 oz.

Plate 10.5" #3400/64, large dinner	125
Plate 10.5" #3900/24, dinner	115
Plate 11" #3400/35, open handled, sandwich	48
Plate 12" #3900/26, 4-footed, service/torte	60
Plate 12.5" #3400/1186, oblong, open handled sandwich	60
Plate 13" #3900/33, rolled edge, 4-footed, torte	65
Plate 13.5" #1396 Pristine, flat torte/service	60
Plate 13.5" #1397 Pristine, small center, turned up edge, cabaret	65
Plate 14" #130 Pristine, blown, torte	175
Plate 14" #3400/65, torte or chop, large center	125
Plate 14" #3900/166, torte	68
Plate 17.5" #1402/29, Sunday nite supper	125
Plate 18" #1402/28, Sunday nite supper	125
Platter 13.5" #3400/58, tab handled, oval	145
Relish 5.5" #3500/60 Gadroon, 2 equal sections, one handle	34
Relish 5.5" #3500/68 Gadroon, no handles, 2 sections	30
Relish 6" #3400/1093, center handled, 2 sections	90
Relish 6.25" #3500/69 Gadroon, 3 equal sections, scalloped edge	32
Relish 6.5" #3400/90, 2 open handles, 2 equal sections	32
Relish 6.5" #3500/61 Gadroon, scalloped edge, 3 sections, loop handle	48
Relish 7" #3900/123, 4-toed, tab scroll handled, oblong pickle	38
Relish 7" #3900/124, 4-toed, tab scroll handled, 2 equal sections, oblong	40
Relish 7.5" #3500/62 Gadroon, handled, 4 sections, round	68
Relish 7.5" #3500/70 Gadroon, no handles, 4 sections	45
Relish 7.5" #3500/71 Gadroon, center handled, 3 equal sections	95
Relish 8" #3500/57 Gadroon, 3 equal sections, 3 handled (candy bottom)	38
Relish 8.75" #3400/862, center plume handled, oblong, 4 sections	165
Relish 8.75" #3400/86, handled, oval, pickle	48
Relish 8.75" #3400/88, 2-handled, 2 sections	52
Relish 9" #3400/59, tab handled, oval, pickle	50
Relish 9" #3900/125, handled, oblong, 3 sections	48
Relish 9.5" #464, crescent, 3 sections (kidney shape)	135
Relish 9.5" #477 Pristine, oblong w/tab feet, oval pickle or corn	65
Relish 10" #394, round, 4 equal sections & celery section	65
Relish 10" #3500/64 Gadroon, 4-toed, handled, 2 equal sections & celery section	54
Relish 11" #3400/89, handled, 2 sections, oval	68
Relish 11" #3400/200, handled, 4-toed, curved divider, 2 equal sections & celery section	58
Relish 11" #3400/652, oblong celery	48
Relish 12" #3400/67, 4 equal sections & celery section	65
Relish 12" #3500/67 Gadroon: 5 inserts & tray w/scalloped edge, round	195
Relish 12" #3900/120, oblong, 4 equal sections & celery section	60
Relish 12" #3900/126, handled, oblong, 3 sections	56
Relish 15" #3500/112 Gadroon, handled, 3 sections, oval, celery	135
Sandwich server 10.5" #3400/10, center keyhole handle	95
Shaker 2.25" #1468, egg shaped, square glass base, pair	100
Shaker 2.4" #1470, round, individual, square glass base, pair	90
Shaker #1471, round, regular, square glass base, pair	95
Shaker #3400/36, footed, chrome lid, pair	100
Shaker #3400/37, footed, chrome lid, pair	100
Shaker 4.5" #3400/18, footed, w/chrome top, pair	65
Shaker 3.25" #3400/76, footed w/glass top, pair	60
Shaker 3.75" #3400/77, footed w/glass top, pair	48
Shaker 3.5" #3900/1177, flat w/chrome top, pair	45
Sugar 3" #3400/68, regular, scalloped foot, 5 oz.	24
Sugar 2.4" #3500/15 Gadroon, footed, individual, 3 oz.	22
Sugar 2.4" #3900/40, footed, individual, 3.5 oz.	22
Sugar 2.75" #3900/41, regular footed, 6 oz.	24
Toast cover 4.5" #1533, blown w/finial	425
Tray 6" #3500/91 Gadroon, handled, square	125
Tray 8.25" #3500/161 Gadroon, footed, shallow, round, handled	30
Tumbler #3400/1341, flat, cordial, 1 oz.	58
Tumbler #3400/1344, flared, cordial, 1 oz.	48
Tumbler 2.4" #321, sham, whiskey, 2 oz.	60
Tumbler #498, straight sided, whiskey, 2 oz.	60
Tumbler #1066, whiskey, sham, 2.5 oz.	48
Tumbler 2.75" #3135, footed, straight sided, whiskey, 2.5 oz.	45
Tumbler 2.75" #3122, fancy stem, cone footed, whiskey, 2.5 oz.	40
Tumbler 2.1" #3400/92, flat, barrel, whiskey, 2.5 oz.	75
Tumbler #1066, liquor cocktail, ball stem, 3 oz.	30
Tumbler #1066, wine, ball stem, 3 oz.	30
Tumbler #3106, wine, plain stem, 3 oz.	25
Tumbler #321, sham, tapered juice, 5 oz.	42
Tumbler #498, straight sided, juice, 5 oz.	32
Tumbler #1066, juice, ball stem, 5 oz.	24
Tumbler #1066, juice, sham, 5 oz.	38
Tumbler 4" #3135, footed, juice, 5 oz.	32
Tumbler #3106, juice, plain stem, 5 oz.	22
Tumbler 5.1" #3122, fancy stem, cone footed, juice, 5 oz.	20

Tumbler #1066, footed, oyster cocktail, 5 oz.   24
Tumbler #3106, footed, oyster cocktail, 5 oz.   22
Tumbler #3400/38, flat, juice, 5 oz.   58
Tumbler #1066, sham, old fashion, 7 oz.   42
Tumbler #321, sham, old fashion, 8 oz.   54
Tumbler #498, straight sided, 8 oz.   42
Tumbler 4.75" #3135, footed water (lunch) 8 oz.   25
Tumbler 4.9" #497, sham, cut flute, straight sided, 9 oz.   45
Tumbler #1066, water, ball stem, 9 oz.   24
Tumbler #3106, water, plain stem, 9 oz.   22
Tumbler 6.75" #3122, fancy stem, cone footed, water, 9 oz.   24
Tumbler #498, straight sided, 10 oz.   35
Tumbler 4.75" #1066, sham, water, 10 oz.   38
Tumbler 5.25" #3135, footed, water (dinner) 10 oz.   24
Tumbler #497, sham, cut flute, straight sided, 11 oz.   45
Tumbler #498, straight sided, 12 oz.   40
Tumbler 7.1" #1066, ball stem, ice tea, 12 oz.   30
Tumbler #1066, sham, ice tea, 12 oz.   42
Tumbler 6" #3135, footed, ice tea, 13 oz.   34
Tumbler #3106, plain stem, ice tea, 12 oz.   28
Tumbler 7.1" #3122, fancy stem, cone footed, ice tea, 12 oz.   30
Tumbler #3400/38, flat, ice tea, 12 oz.   54
Tumbler #497, sham, cut flute, straight sided, 13 oz.   42
Tumbler #3400/100, bellied, ice tea, 13 oz.   40
Tumbler #3400/115, bellied, ice tea, 13 oz.   45
Tumbler 3.75" #3900/115, flat, barrel, 14 oz.   45
Tumbler #1066, sham, ice tea, 14 oz.   48
Vase 3.75" to 5" #1309, squat globe, necked & flared   95
Vase 5" #3400/102, globe, short neck   85
Vase 5" #6004, footed, flared, 1 ball stem, bud vase   50
Vase 6" #6004, footed, flared, 1 ball stem, bud vase   60
Vase 6.5" #3400/103, globe, short neck   90
Vase 7.8" #797, flip shape w/panel optic   150
Vase 8" #1300, footed, shouldered & flared   75
Vase 8" #1430, large, flat, flared, flip shape   175
Vase 8.4" #6004, footed, flared, 1 ball stem, bud vase   70
Vase 9" #1237, footed, keyhole stem, flared   100
Vase 9.5" #1233, footed, keyhole, shouldered   100
Vase 10" #274, footed, tapered out to top, bud vase   65
Vase 10" #1238, footed, keyhole stem, flared   125
Vase 10" #1301, footed, shouldered & flared   95
Vase 10" #1528, flat, spherical bottom, bud vase   125
Vase 10" #6004, footed, flared, 1 ball stem, bud vase, bud vase   85
Vase 10" #272, pulled in at top, bud vase   80
Vase 10.25" #3400/1242, flat, shouldered, flared   135
Vase 11" #278, footed, flared (no stem)   115
Vase 11" #3400/133, flat, opening tilted to side   595
Vase 11.5" #1299, footed, urn shape, ball stem   175
Vase 12" #1234, footed, keyhole, shouldered   135
Vase 12" #1238, footed, keyhole stem, flared   145
Vase 12" #6004, footed, 1 ball stem   100
Vase 13" #279, footed, flared (no stem)   195
Vase 13.75" #1239, footed, keyhole stem, flared   245
Vase 18" #1336, shouldered & flared   1,000+

Left: Vase 10" #6004, footed, 1 ball stem, bud vase. **Center:** Vase 13.75" #1239, footed, keyhole stem, flared. **Right:** Vase 10" #1238, footed, keyhole stem, flared.

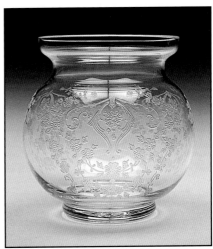

Vase 3.75" #1309, squat globe, necked & flared.

Left: Vase 11" #3400/133, flat, opening tilted to side. **Right:** Pitcher 8.6" #96, flat, straight side, tankard, 69 oz.

Tumbler 2.4" #321, sham, whiskey, 2 oz.

DIANE 105

Pattern detail, Elaine.

Left: Vase 8" #3500/44 Gadroon, footed, tab handled, urn shaped.
Back right: Plate 11.5" #3500/39 Gadroon, footed, open tab handled, round. **Front center:** Sugar 2.4" #3500/15 Gadroon, footed, individual, 3 oz. **Front right:** Creamer 2.5" #3500/15 Gadroon, footed, individual, 3 oz.

Candlestick 2-lite 6" #3900/72, w/plume center, 8.25" spread.

ELAINE
Cambridge Glass Company
Color: Crystal
1933-58

Elaine is another of several etched patterns of Cambridge to feature a lady's name. This etched pattern features an angled scroll alternating with a row of flowers. Stemware can be found on the following blanks: #3035, #1402, #3104, #3121, #3500, and #7966. This offers a variety of different types of stems. Elaine is the only etching found on the 1402/150 blank. Several Crystal pieces can be found with gold encrusting. Collectors seem to prefer the plain Crystal. Gold trimmed pieces will be priced the same as Crystal because of this preference. Like other etched patterns with gold encrusted items, those with the gold worn will bring considerably less than the crystal price. Values on this etched pattern resemble those of Diane & Portia.

The following items are hard to find: basket w/applied handle, blown candies, cheese dish decanters, Doulton pitcher, French dressing bottle, hurricane lamp, nite set, and punch bowl.

ELAINE	Crystal
Ashtray 3.25" #3500/124 Gadroon, round	28
Ashtray 3.25" #3500/129 Gadroon, square	45
Ashtray 3.5" #3500/125 Gadroon, round	28
Ashtray 4" #3500/126 Gadroon, round	32
Ashtray 4.25" #3500/127 Gadroon, round	34
Ashtray 4.5" #3500/128 Gadroon, round	40
Ashtray 4.5" #3500/131 Gadroon, oval	50
Basket 5.4" #3500/51 Gadroon, applied handle	225
Basket 5.75" #3500/55 Gadroon, footed, 2-handled, crimped, 3.5" tall	36
Basket 6.25" #3400/1182, 2 handles turned up	34
Basket 6.25" #3500/52 Gadroon, footed, applied handle	275
Basket 7" #119, flared, applied handle	400+
Bell 5.5" #3500, Gadroon stem, flared	125
Bonbon 5.6" #3400/1179, low, flared, open handled	32
Bonbon 6" #3500/54 Gadroon, footed, handled	30
Bottle w/stopper 6.5" #1263, flat, French dressing, 8 oz.	245
Bottle w/stopper 7.25" #1261, footed, French dressing, 8 oz.	275
Bowl 2.75" #3400/71, 4-footed, tab handled, nut	54
Bowl 3.5" #3400/49, round, plain rim, cranberry	65
Bowl 4.5" #1402/30 Tally Ho, footed, shallow, fruit	34
Bowl 5" #1534 Pristine, blown, cupped, fruit	58
Bowl 5" #3400/74, 4-footed, tab handled, mint	42
Bowl 5" #3500/10 Gadroon, shallow, fruit	54
Bowl 5" #3500/49 Gadroon, round w/1 handle	36
Bowl 5.25" #3400/56, shallow, fruit	50
Bowl 5.25" #3400/1180, handled, sweetmeat	34
Bowl 5.75" #3900/130, footed, tab handled, sweetmeat	28
Bowl 5.8" #3400/13, 4-toed, tab handled, flared	35
Bowl 6" #1402/89 Tally Ho, handled, sweetmeat	34
Bowl 6" #3400/53, flared cereal	60
Bowl 6" #3400/136, 4-footed, deep, fancy crimped	95
Bowl 6" #3500/11 Gadroon, cereal	65
Bowl 6" #3500/50 Gadroon, round w/1 handle	40
Bowl 6.5" #1402/32 Tally Ho, flared, rim grapefruit	50
Bowl 7.5" #435 Pristine, deco tab handled, sweetmeat	68
Bowl 8.5" #381 Pristine, rim soup	145
Bowl 8.5" #1402/131 Tally Ho, deep, 3 equal sections	165
Bowl 9" #3500/25 Gadroon, deep, footed, w/2 ram heads	345
Bowl 9.5" #225 Pristine, blown, 2 sections	295
Bowl 9.5" #3400/34, open handled, vegetable	68
Bowl 9.5" #3500/115 Gadroon, footed, handled, flared	125
Bowl 10" #427 Pristine, sham base, deep, salad	125
Bowl 10" #3400/1185, handled, deep	70
Bowl 10" #3500/28 Gadroon, footed, handled, flared	75
Bowl 10" #3900/54, 4-footed, flared	60
Bowl 10.25" #1402 Tally Ho, shallow (pan shape) open handled	75
Bowl 10.25" #3900/34, handled, flared	75
Bowl 10.4" #1402/122 Tally Ho, deep, 3 equal sections	195
Bowl 10.5" #1359 Pristine, tab footed, smooth edge, flared	70
Bowl 10.5" #1402/64 Tally Ho, footed, shallow, fruit	80
Bowl 10.5" #1402/70 Tally Ho, flat, deep, salad	72
Bowl 10.5" #1402/128 Tally Ho, fruit or salad	65
Bowl 10.5" #3400/168, flat, flared	68
Bowl 11" #1399, deep salad, scalloped edge	125
Bowl 11" #1402/88 Tally Ho, flared, shallow, salad	68
Bowl 11" #3400/45, footed, square, crimped	78
Bowl 11" #3400/1188, handled, flared, fruit	85
Bowl 11" #3500/16 Gadroon, collar footed, tab handled, flared	98
Bowl 11.5" #3900/28, footed & handled, flared	68
Bowl 12" #1349 Pristine, tab footed, crimped edge, flared	70
Bowl 12" #3400/4, 4-toed, squared, flared edge	68
Bowl 12" #3400/160, 4-footed, oblong, crimped	68
Bowl 12" #3500/17 Gadroon, footed, tab handled, shallow	98

Bowl 12" #3500/21 Gadroon, footed, handled, oval	145
Bowl 12" #3500/118 Gadroon, footed, oblong, banana	125
Bowl 12" #3900/62, 4-footed, flared	72
Bowl 12" #3900/65, 4-footed, handled, oval	85
Bowl 12.5" #993, low, 4-footed, flared out	80
Bowl 12.5" #1402/125 Tally Ho, flat, rim fruit	78
Bowl 12.5" #1402/127 Tally Ho, flared, rim fruit	70
Bowl 12.5" #3400/32, flat, flared	75
Bowl 12.6" #3400/1240, 4-footed, oval, refractory	125
Bowl 13" #1398, shallow, fruit or salad	110
Bowl 13" #3400/1, flared, console	68
Bowl 13.5" #1402/132 Tally Ho, shallow, salad	72
Box w/cover 3.5" #3400/94, puff w/keyhole finial	125
Bridge set 5 piece #3500/144 Gadroon, center handle tray & 4 straight sided, tumblers	275
Butter w/cover 5.5" #506, round, tab handled	175
Butter w/cover 5.5" #3400/52, round, 2 open handles	195
Cake plate 11.75" #3900/35, handled	80
Cake salver 13" #170 Martha, tab footed, scalloped edge	195
Canape set #693/3000, plate/cocktail use #3000 footed cocktail, 3.5" or 5 oz.	175
Candelabra 1-lite 6.25" #3400/648, keyhole stem, etched bobeches &, prisms, pair	245
Candelabra 1-lite 7.5" #3121, fancy stem, w/plain bobeches &, prisms, pair	245
Candelabra 2-lite 6" #3400/1268, keyhole stem bobeches & prisms, pair	345
Candelabra 2-lite 6.5" #496 Martha, with #19 bobeches & #1 prisms, pair	285
Candelabra 3-lite 5.5" #1545, one #19 bobeche center cup & #16 prisms, pair	275
Candlestick 1-lite 2.5" #3500/108 Gadroon, no stem, pair	58
Candlestick 1-lite 3.5" #628 Pristine, w/wafer stem, pair	70
Candlestick 1-lite 4.75" #3500/74 Gadroon, column stem, w/rams head, pair	185
Candlestick 1-lite 5" #3900/67, skirted, pair	100
Candlestick 1-lite 5.25" #3400/646, keyhole stem, pair	85
Candlestick 1-lite 5.75" #3400/1192, small stem, pair	115
Candlestick 1-lite 6" #3500/31 Gadroon, column stem, pair	195
Candlestick 1-lite 6.5" #1402/80 Tally Ho, fancy stem, pair	100
Candlestick 1-lite 7" #3121, fancy stem, pair	145
Candlestick 2-lite 5.75" #495 Martha, plume arms & ball center, 8.25" spread, pair	195
Candlestick 2-lite 6" #3400/647, keyhole stem, 7.75" spread, pair	80
Candlestick 2-lite 6" #3900/72, w/plume center, 8.25" spread, pair	95
Candlestick 3-lite #1307, pair	75
Candlestick 3-lite 5.5" #1545, bell footed, pair	145
Candlestick 3-lite 6" #3900/74, pair	100
Candlestick 3-lite 6.25" #3400/1338, tiered (looks like ocean waves) 7" spread, pair	135
Candlestick 3-lite 7" #3400/638, keyhole stem, pair	125
Candy w/cover 5.4" #1066/4, blown w/fancy ball stem, plain finial	200
Candy w/cover 5.4" #3121/4, low, blown	135
Candy w/cover 5.4" #3121/3, high, blown	145
Candy w/cover 5.4" #3500/103 Gadroon, blown	150
Candy (open) 5.5" #3500/47 Gadroon, handled	35
Candy w/cover 6" #3500/78 Gadroon, flat, low, blown, rams head tab handles	245
Candy w/cover 6.5" #3400/9, 4-footed, tab handled, 7" wide; dome lid w/finial	125
Candy w/cover 7" #3900/165, flat, round, dome lid w/finial	115
Candy w/cover 8" #3500/57 Gadroon, 3 open handled, 3 equal sections	75
Cheese & cracker: comport #1402/124 Tally Ho, short stem, cupped, 5.5" wide; Plate 11.5", handled	95
Cheese & cracker: comport 4" #1402/101 Tally Ho, short stem cheese, 9" wide; plate 13.5" #1402/129	115
Cheese & cracker: comport 3" #3400/7, short stem, flared, 5.3" wide; plate 11.5" #3400/6, cracker, tab handled	85
Cheese & cracker: comport 3.75" #3500/163 Gadroon, short stem, flared, 6" wide; plate 12" #3500/162, handled	95
Cheese dish w/cover 5" #980, flat, pointed finial	400
Cigarette box w/cover 3.6" #616, rectangle, 3.1" wide	145
Cigarette holder #1066, oval, short stem w/ashtray foot	165
Cigarette holder 4" #1337, round w/cupped ashtray foot	135
Cocktail icer 4.2" #187 Pristine, footed, 2 piece w/non-etched insert	125
Cocktail icer 4.2" #3600, footed, 2 piece w/non-etched insert	68
Cocktail icer 4.6" #968, footed, 2 piece w/non-etched insert	72
Cocktail mixer #1395, w/chrome lid & spoon, 28 oz.	225
Cocktail shaker #97, small #9 chrome lid	275
Cocktail shaker #98, large #10 chrome lid	150
Cocktail shaker #99, sham base, chrome lid	165
Cocktail shaker #3400/175, w/large #10 chrome lid	145
Cologne w/keyhole stopper 2.5" #3400/97: tilt bottle, 2 oz.; stopper w/long dauber	345
Comport 5.3" #3400/28, keyhole stem, 7.25" wide	62
Comport 6.1" #3121/2 (blown), tall stem, 5.4" wide	65
Comport 6.25" #3500/101 Gadroon, high, blown, 5.4" wide	68
Comport #1402/66 Tally Ho, fancy stem, flared, 6" wide	45
Comport #1402/67 Tally Ho, cupped, 6.5" wide	58
Comport 7" #3500/148 Gadroon, high fancy stem, 6" wide	48

Left to right: Goblet 5.25" #3121, cordial, 1 oz.; Goblet 5.25" #7966, flared, cone shaped, sherry, 2 oz.; Goblet 5.8" #3121, wine, 3.5 oz.; Goblet 6" #3121, liquor cocktail, 3 oz.; Goblet 6.5" #3500, saucer champagne, 7 oz.; Goblet 7.25" #3122, fancy stem, water, 10 oz.

Plate 8" #3900/131, handled lemon server, 9.25" counting handles.

Top left: Plate 6.5" #3400/1181, handled lemon server; Bell 5.5" #3500, Gadroon stem, flared. **Top right:** Relish 10" #3500/87 Gadroon, handled, 4 equal sections. **Bottom left:** Bowl 10.4" #1402/122 Tally Ho, deep, 3 equal sections. **Bottom right:** Relish 11.5" #3500/652 Gadroon, oblong, celery.

Mayonnaise 2 piece #1402/96/102: bowl 5.75", salad dressing; liner w/ indent 17.5".

Back left: Relish 14" #3500/97 Gadroon, handled, oval, 3 equal sections & celery section. **Back right:** Goblet 8.25" #3035, ball stem (cone bowl) water, 9 oz. **Front left:** Mayonnaise bowl 5.75" #1402/95 Tally Ho, footed, salad dressing. **Front center:** Dealer sign Ebony ($125 – we found it priced this). **Front right:** Cup & saucer, coffee #3500/1 Gadroon: cup 2.5", footed, regular, 6 oz.; saucer w/indent 6".

Shaker 3.75" #3400/77, footed w/glass top.

Comport 7.5" #3400/14, fancy wafer stem, flared, 7" wide	65
Comport 7.5" #3900/136, scalloped edge, 7.25" wide	52
Comport 7.6" #3500/37 Gadroon, tab handled, fancy stem, 7" wide	98
Cream soup & liner #3400/55: bowl 4.75", 2-handled, 9 oz., saucer w/indent 6.25"	80
Cream soup & liner #3500/2 Gadroon: bowl 5", handled, 9 oz.; saucer w/indent 6.5"	98
Creamer 2.5" #3500/15 Gadroon, footed, individual, 3 oz.	22
Creamer 2.6" #3900/40, footed, individual, 3.5 oz.	22
Creamer 3.8" #3400/68, scalloped foot, regular, 4.75 oz.	24
Creamer #1402/33 Tally Ho, footed, regular, 6 oz.	24
Creamer 2.5" #3500/14 Gadroon, footed, regular, 6 oz.	22
Creamer 3" #3900/41, footed, regular, 6 oz.	20
Cruet w/stopper #3400/96, ball shape, 2 oz.	90
Cruet w/ball stopper 4.4" #3400/99, tilt ball, 6 oz.	125
Cruet w/keyhole stopper 4.4" #3400/99, tilt, 6 oz.	135
Cruet w/stopper #3400/161, handled, footed, 6 oz.	185
Cruet w/stopper #3400/193, flat, 6 oz.	100
Cruet w/stopper 6" #3900/100, flat, spherical, 6 oz.	110
Cup & saucer, after dinner #3400/69: cup 2.25", 2 oz.; saucer w/indent 4.25", 6 sided	175
Cup 2.4" #1402/140 Tally Ho, flat, handled punch, 5 oz.	25
Cup & saucer, coffee #3400/54: cup 2.4", 6 oz.; saucer w/indent 5.5"	28
Cup & saucer, coffee #3500/1 Gadroon: cup 2.5", footed, regular, 6 oz.; saucer w/indent 6"	26
Cup & saucer, coffee #1402/19 Tally Ho: cup 2.5", footed, 7 oz.; saucer w/indent 5.9"	26
Cup & saucer, coffee #3900/17: cup 2.5", 7 oz.; saucer w/indent 5.5"	28
Decanter w/stopper #3400/119, tilt ball, cordial, 12 oz.	250
Decanter w/flat stopper 9" #1320, footed, cordial, 14 oz.	295
Decanter w/stopper #1380, square, 26 oz.	575
Decanter w/flat stopper 11" #1321, footed, 28 oz.	325
Decanter w/stopper 13.25" #1372, flat, slim bottle shape, 28 oz.	600+
Decanter w/stopper 6.25" #3400/92, tilt ball, 32 oz.	350
Decanter w/stopper #3400/113, ball w/long neck, 35 oz.	195
Epergne 4 piece #645, etched 3-lite candlestick w/plain arm & 2 non-etched vases	135
Epergne 5 piece #654, etched keyhole w/plain bobeche-prisms & 2 non-etched vases	110
Finger bowl & liner: bowl 5" #1402/14 Tally Ho, deep; plate w/indent 6.5" #1402/15	58
Goblet #3104, high stem, brandy, .75 oz.	125
Goblet 5.25" #3035, ball stem (cone bowl) cordial, 1 oz.	85
Goblet #1402/100 Tally Ho (blown) cordial, 1 oz.	110
Goblet #1402/13 Tally Ho (pressed) cordial, 1 oz.	125
Goblet #3104, high stem, cordial, 1 oz.	165
Goblet #3104, high stem, pousse-cafe, 1 oz.	175
Goblet 5.25" #3121, cordial, 1 oz.	75
Goblet 4.9" #3500, cordial, 1 oz.	70
Goblet 5" #7966, flared, cone shape cordial, 1 oz.	85
Goblet #3104, high stem, sherry, 2 oz.	100
Goblet 5.25" #7966, flared, cone shaped, sherry, 2 oz.	85
Goblet #1402/12 Tally Ho (pressed) wine, 2.5 oz.	48
Goblet 5.6" #3035, ball stem, (cone bowl) wine, 2.5 oz.	34
Goblet #3104, creme de menthe, 2.5 oz.	100
Goblet 4.75" #3500, wine, 2.5 oz.	48
Goblet #1402/100 Tally Ho (blown) wine, 2.5 oz.	40
Goblet #1402/10 Tally Ho (pressed) high, liquor cocktail, 3 oz.	38
Goblet 6" #3035, ball stem (cone bowl) liquor cocktail, 3 oz.	30
Goblet #3104, high stem, wine, 3 oz.	125
Goblet 6" #3121, liquor cocktail, 3 oz.	34
Goblet 4.6" #3500, liquor cocktail, 3 oz.	34
Goblet #3104, high stem, liquor cocktail, 3.5 oz.	95
Goblet 5.8" #3121, wine, 3.5 oz.	42
Goblet 6" #1402/100 Tally Ho, (blown) liquor cocktail, 4 oz.	35
Goblet #1402/11 Tally Ho (pressed) oyster cocktail, 4 oz.	42
Goblet 6.25" #3121, claret, 4.25 oz.	48
Goblet #1402/100 Tally Ho (blown) oyster cocktail, 4.5 oz.	24
Goblet 4.4" #3035, ball stem (cone bowl) oyster cocktail, 4.5 oz.	28
Goblet 4.4" #3121, oyster cocktail, 4.5 oz.	28
Goblet 3.6" #3500, oyster cocktail, 4.5 oz.	26
Goblet #1402/20 Tally Ho (pressed) belled sherbet, 4.5 oz.	20
Goblet #1402/100 Tally Ho (blown) claret, 4.5 oz.	45
Goblet #1402/9 Tally Ho (pressed) claret, 4.5 oz.	48
Goblet 6.25" #3035, ball stem (cone bowl) claret, 4.5 oz.	38
Goblet #3104, high stem, claret, 4.5 oz.	98
Goblet 6.1" #3500, claret, 4.5 oz.	50
Goblet #1402/8 Tally Ho (pressed) low tomato/orange juice, 5 oz.	32
Goblet #3104, high stem, roemer, 5 oz.	125
Goblet #3104, high stem, hock, 5 oz.	125

Goblet #3500, parfait, 5 oz. — 42
Goblet #1402/7 Tally Ho (pressed) tall tomato/orange juice, 6 oz. — 35
Goblet #1402/100 Tally Ho (blown) sherbet, 6 oz. — 20
Goblet 4.75" #3035, ball stem (cone bowl) sherbet, 6 oz. — 22
Goblet 4.75" #3121, sherbet, 6 oz. — 22
Goblet #1402/6 Tally Ho (pressed) sherbet, 6.5 oz. — 24
Goblet 6.25" #3121, cafe parfait, 6.5 oz. — 38
Goblet 6.4" #3035, ball stem (cone bowl) saucer champagne, 6 oz. — 25
Goblet 6.4" #3121, saucer champagne, 6 oz. — 25
Goblet #3104, high stem, saucer champagne, 7 oz. — 98
Goblet 4.75" #3500, sherbet, 7 oz. — 20
Goblet 6.5" #3500, saucer champagne, 7 oz. — 24
Goblet #1402/5 Tally Ho (pressed) saucer champagne, 7.5 oz. — 25
Goblet 6.5" #1402/100 Tally Ho (blown) saucer champagne blown, 8 oz. — 22
Goblet 8.25" #3035, ball stem (cone bowl) water, 9 oz. — 38
Goblet #3104, high stem, water, 9 oz. — 125
Goblet 6.6" #1402/100 Tally Ho, (blown) water, 10 oz. — 34
Goblet #1402/4 Tally Ho (pressed) lunch water, 10 oz. — 38
Goblet 6.3" #1402/3 Tally Ho (pressed) dinner water, 10 oz. — 40
Goblet 8.25" #3121, water, 10 oz. — 35
Goblet 7.25" #3122, fancy stem, water, 10 oz. — 40
Goblet 6.4" #3500, water, 10 oz. — 36
Goblet 7.6" #3121, ice tea, 12 oz. — 48
Goblet 6.25" #1402/2 Tally Ho (pressed) ice tea, 14 oz. — 58
Goblet 6.9" #1402/1 Tally Ho (pressed) jumbo, 18 oz. — 75
Honey dish w/cover 6" #3500/139 Gadroon, flat, square, handled — 300+
Hurricane lamp 8" #1601, short stem, bobeche w/prisms & etched chimney, each — 225
Hurricane lamp 9.3" #1617, skirted w/etched chimney, each — 195
Hurricane lamp 11.5" #1603, keyhole stem, bobeche/prisms & etched chimney, each — 245
Ice bucket 5.8" #1402/52 Tally Ho, chrome handle — 145
Ice bucket 5.75" #3400/851, flat, scalloped top w/chrome handle — 115
Ice Bucket 5.75" #3900/671, chrome handle — 135
Iced frappe 2 piece: #3400/41, bowl/insert non-etched — 85
Icer fruit #188, scalloped edge fits into the Pristine #427 deep salad — 350
Marmalade w/cover 5.4" #147 Pristine, flat (blown) 8 oz. — 135
Mayonnaise 2 piece #1532 Pristine: bowl 4.5" (blown), spherical, 3" high; liner w/indent 6.75" — 48
Mayonnaise bowl 4" #3900/19, footed, ball shape, 4.1" high — 55
Mayonnaise 2 piece #1402 Tally Ho: #16 bowl 4.5", 2 spouted, #17 liner w/indent 7" — 65
Mayonnaise bowl 4.75" #1402/133 Tally Ho, flared, salad dressing, 5.75" wide — 48
Mayonnaise 2 piece #3900: #127 bowl 5", flared; #128 liner w/indent 6.5" — 55
Mayonnaise 2 piece #3900/111: bowl 5.25", salad dressing; liner w/indent 6.75" — 58
Mayonnaise 2 piece #1490 Pristine: bowl 5.5", cupped, salad dressing; use #1491 liner w/indent 6.4" — 60
Mayonnaise bowl 5.75" #1402/95 Tally Ho, footed, salad dressing — 48
Mayonnaise 2 piece #1402/96/102: bowl 5.75", salad dressing; liner 17.5" w/indent — 175
Mayonnaise 2 piece #3400: #13 bowl 5.8", 4-toed, flared, tab handled; #11 liner w/indent 5" — 68
Mayonnaise 2 piece #3500/58 Gadroon: bowl 6", footed, handled, flared; #59 liner w/indent 7.5" — 60
Mug #1402/78 Tally Ho, flat, punch or Tom & Jerry, 6 oz. — 45
Marmalade w/cover 5.4" #147 Pristine, blown (spherical) 8 oz. — 135
Nite set #103, flat, handled jug & flat tumbler w/flared base — 600+
Pitcher #1408, cocktail churn w/metal plunger, 60 oz. — 1,000+
Pitcher #3400/100, high w/ice lip, 76 oz. — 200
Pitcher 9.25" #3400/152, Doulton style w/o ice lip, 76 oz. — 325
Pitcher 7.9" #3900/141, Doulton jug w/o ice lip (not optic) 80 oz. — 295
Pitcher 9" #3400/38, tilt ball w/ice lip, 80 oz. — 245
Pitcher #119, flat, high w/ice lip, 83 oz. — 475
Pitcher #1561, flat ball w/ice lip, 86 oz. — 295
Plate 6" #1402/21 Tally Ho, bread & butter — 8
Plate 6" #3400/60, bread & butter — 10
Plate 6" #3500/3 Gadroon, bread & butter — 12
Plate 6.5" #3400/1181, handled lemon server — 24
Plate 6.5" #3900/20, bread & butter — 8
Plate 7" #1402/99 Tally Ho, handled, lemon server — 28
Plate 7" #1402/138 Tally Ho, dessert or salad — 14
Plate 7.5" #555 Pristine, dessert — 14
Plate 7.5" #3400/176, dessert or salad — 15
Plate 8" #1402/23 Tally Ho, salad — 20
Plate 8" #3900/22, salad — 22
Plate 8" #3900/131, handled lemon server, 9.25" counting handles — 28
Plate 8.5" #3400/62, salad or lunch — 22
Plate 8.5" #3500/5 Gadroon, salad or lunch — 22
Plate 9.5" #1402/24 Tally Ho, lunch or small dinner — 48
Plate 9.5" #485, crescent salad — 195

Left: Vase 10" #274, footed, tapered, bud vase. **Center:** Ice bucket 5.75" #3400/851, flat, scalloped top w/chrome handle. **Right:** #3400/38 tilt ball pitcher 80 oz.

Top left: Vase 5" #3400/102, flat, globe, short neck. **Top right:** Bowl 10.25" #1402 Tally Ho, shallow (pan shape) open handled. **Bottom left:** Relish 7.5" #3500/71 Gadroon, 1 fancy center handle, 3 equal sections. **Bottom center:** Vase 6" #6004, footed, flared, 1 ball stem, bud vase. **Bottom right:** Cheese comport 3.75" #3500/163 Gadroon, short stem, flared, 6" wide.

Plate 9.5" #3400/63, small dinner	72
Plate 10" #3400/22, tab handled	42
Plate 10.5" #1402/25 Tally Ho, large dinner	98
Plate 10.5" #3400/64, large dinner	125
Plate 10.5" #3900/24, dinner	115
Plate 11" #3400/8, tab handled	48
Plate 11" #3400/35, open handled, sandwich	50
Plate 11.5" #1402/34 Tally Ho, handled, sandwich	62
Plate 11.5" #3500/39 Gadroon, footed, open tab handled, round	95
Plate 12" #3900/26, 4-footed, service or torte	60
Plate 12.5" #3400/1186, oblong, open handled sandwich	60
Plate 13" #1402/126 Tally Ho, small center, turned up edge, cabaret	65
Plate 13" #3500/110 Gadroon, footed, tab handled, torte	85
Plate 13" #3900/33, 4-footed, service or torte	68
Plate 13.5" #1396 Pristine, flat, torte/service	60
Plate 13.5" #1397 Pristine, small center, turned up edge, cabaret	60
Plate 14" #130 Pristine, flat, blown, torte	175
Plate 14" #1402/26 Tally Ho, chop plate	60
Plate 14" #1402/104 Tally Ho, w/4" indent in center	58
Plate 14" #3400/65, torte or chop, large center	125
Plate 14" #3900/166, torte	65
Plate 18" #1402/28 Tally Ho, flat, Sunday nite supper	125
Plate 18" #1402/119 Tally Ho, footed, week end supper	175
Punch bowl 13" #1402/77 Tally Ho, large, footed, deep	800+
Punch bowl liner 17.5" #1402/29 Tally Ho, or Sunday nite supper	195
Punch bowl 13" #3500/119 Gadroon, footed, w/2 rams heads, 1.5 gallon	1,500+
Relish 5.5" #3500/60 Gadroon, 2 sections, one handle	35
Relish 5.5" #3500/68 Gadroon, no handles, 2 sections	30
Relish 6" #1402/90 Tally Ho, handled, 2 sections	35
Relish 6" #3400/1093, center handled, 2 sections	85
Relish 6.25" #3500/69 Gadroon, 3 equal sections, scalloped edge	34
Relish 6.5" #3400/90, 2 open handles, 2 equal sections	32
Relish 6.5" #3500/61 Gadroon, scalloped edge, 3 sections, loop handle	48
Relish 7" #3900/123, 4-toed, tab scroll handled, oblong pickle	35
Relish 7" #3900/124, 4-toed, tab scroll handled, 2 equal sections, oblong	38
Relish 7.5" #3500/69 Gadroon, handled, 4 sections, round	68
Relish 7.5" #3500/70 Gadroon, no handles, 4 sections	45
Relish 7.5" #3500/71 Gadroon, 1 fancy center handle, 3 equal sections	98
Relish 8" #1402/91 Tally Ho, 2-handled, 3 sections	48
Relish 8" #3500/57 Gadroon, 3 equal sections, 3 handled (candy bottom)	38
Relish 8.5" #3400/86, handled, oval pickle	48
Relish 8.75" #3400/88, handled, 2 sections	52
Relish 8.75" #3400/862, center plume handled, oblong, 4 sections	165
Relish 9" #3400/59, tab handled, oval pickle	54
Relish 9" #3900/125, handled, 3 sections, oblong	50
Relish 9.5" #464, crescent, 3 sections (kidney shape)	135
Relish 9.5" #477 Pristine, oblong w/tab feet, oval pickle or corn	68
Relish 10" #394, round, 4 equal sections & celery section	65
Relish 10" #1402/92 Tally Ho, handled, shallow, 4 sections	58
Relish 10" #3500/64 Gadroon, 4-toed, handled, 2 equal sections & celery section	54
Relish 10" #3500/87 Gadroon, handled, 4 equal sections	68
Relish 11" #3400/89, handled, 2 sections, oval	68
Relish 11" #3400/200, handled, 4-toed, curved divider, 2 equal sections & celery section	58
Relish 11" #3400/652, oblong, celery	48
Relish 11" #3500/152 Gadroon, handled, rectangular, 3 equal sections & celery section	98
Relish 11.5" #3500/652 Gadroon, oblong, celery	48
Relish 12" #1402/94 Tally Ho, oval, scalloped, celery	70
Relish 12" #3400/67, 4 equal sections & celery section	65
Relish 12" #3500/67 Gadroon: 5 inserts & tray w/scalloped edge, round	195
Relish 12" #3900/126, handled, 3 sections, oblong	56
Relish 12" #3900/120, oblong, 4 equal sections & celery section	60
Relish 14" #3500/97 Gadroon, handled, oval, 3 equal sections & celery section	120
Relish 15" #3500/112 Gadroon, handled, oval, 2 equal sections & celery section	130
Relish 15" #3500/113 Gadroon, handled, narrow, 4 sections	175
Sandwich server 10.5" #3400/10, center keyhole handle	95
Shaker 2.25" #1468, egg shaped, square glass base, pair	100
Shaker 3.25" #1402/116 Tally Ho, flat, w/clear glass top, pair	95
Shaker #1470, round, individual all glass, pair	90
Shaker #1471, round, regular all glass, pair	95
Shaker #3400/36, footed, chrome lid, pair	100
Shaker 3.75" #3400/37, footed, chrome lid, pair	100
Shaker 4.5" #3400/18, footed, w/chrome top, pair	65
Shaker 3.25" #3400/76, footed w/glass top, pair	58
Shaker 3.5" #3900/1177, flat w/chrome top, pair	45

Shaker 3.75" #3400/77, footed w/glass top, pair	48
Sugar 2.4" #3500/15 Gadroon, footed, individual, 3 oz.	22
Sugar 2.4" #3900/40, footed, individual, 3.5 oz.	22
Sugar, 3" #3400/68, scalloped foot, regular, 5 oz.	24
Sugar #1402/33 Tally Ho, footed, regular, 6 oz.	24
Sugar 2.4" #3500/14 Gadroon, footed, regular, 6 oz.	22
Sugar 2.75" #3900/41, regular footed, 6 oz.	20
Toast cover 4.5" #1533, blown w/finial	400+
Tray 6" #3500/91 Gadroon, handled, square	125
Tray 8.25" #3500/161 Gadroon, footed, shallow, round, handled	28
Tray 13" #3500/72 Gadroon, handled, flat, round, server	145
Tumbler #1402/150 Tally Ho, (blown) footed, cordial, 1 oz.	45
Tumbler #3400/1341, flat, cordial, 1 oz.	65
Tumbler #3400/1344, flared, cordial, 1 oz.	48
Tumbler 2.4" #321, sham, whiskey, 2 oz.	65
Tumbler #498, flat, cut flute, straight sided, whiskey, 2 oz.	68
Tumbler 3" #3035, footed (cone bowl) whiskey, 2.5 oz.	65
Tumbler 2.1" #3400/92, flat, barrel, whiskey, 2.5 oz.	75
Tumbler #1402/150 Tally Ho (blown) footed, wine, 3 oz.	26
Tumbler #1402/150 Tally Ho (blown) footed, cocktail, 3.5 oz.	24
Tumbler 5.75" #3035, footed (cone bowl) juice, 5 oz.	30
Tumbler #321, sham, tapered juice, 5 oz.	40
Tumbler #498, flat, cut flute, straight sided, juice, 5 oz.	38
Tumbler #1402/150 Tally Ho (blown) footed, claret, 5 oz.	40
Tumbler 5.75" #3121, footed, juice, 5 oz.	28
Tumbler #3400/38, flat, juice, 5 oz.	38
Tumbler 5.25" #3500, juice, 5 oz.	28
Tumbler #7801, footed, juice, 5 oz.	30
Tumbler #1402/150 Tally Ho (blown) footed, low sherbet, 6 oz.	22
Tumbler #1402/150 Tally Ho (blown) footed, champagne, 6 oz.	24
Tumbler 6.5" #3035, footed, (cone bowl) 8 oz.	38
Tumbler #321, sham, old fashion, 8 oz.	60
Tumbler #498, flat, cut flute, straight sided, 8 oz.	35
Tumbler 4.9" #497, sham, cut flute, straight sided, 9 oz.	38
Tumbler 4.5" #1402/150 Tally Ho (blown) footed, water, 9 oz.	28
Tumbler 7" #3035, footed (cone bowl) water, 10 oz.	38
Tumbler #498, flat, cut flute, straight sided, 10 oz.	38
Tumbler 7" #3121, water, 10 oz.	40
Tumbler 6.4" #3500, water, 10 oz.	36
Tumbler #497, sham, cut flute, straight sided, 11 oz.	40
Tumbler 7.5" #3035, footed (cone bowl) ice tea, 12 oz.	42
Tumbler #498, flat, cut flute, straight sided, 12 oz.	40
Tumbler #1402/150 Tally Ho (blown) footed, ice tea (low bowl) 12 oz.	32
Tumbler #1402/150 Tally Ho (blown) footed, ice tea (tall bowl) 12 oz.	38
Tumbler 7.5" #3121, footed, ice tea, 12 oz.	42
Tumbler #3400/38, flat, ice tea, 12 oz.	54
Tumbler 7.5" #3500, ice tea, 12 oz.	40
Tumbler #7801, footed, ice tea, 12 oz.	50
Tumbler #497, sham, cut flute, straight sided, 13 oz.	45
Tumbler #3400/100, bellied, ice tea, 13 oz.	40
Tumbler #3400/115, bellied, ice tea, 13 oz.	45
Tumbler 4.1" #3900/115, flat, barrel, 13 oz.	48
Urn w/cover 10" #3500/41 Gadroon, footed, tab handled	450+
Urn w/cover 12" #3500/42 Gadroon, footed, tab handled	550+
Vase 4.5" to 5" #1309, squat globe, necked & flared	95
Vase 5" #3400/102, flat, globe, short neck	85
Vase 5" #6004, footed, flared, 1 ball stem, bud vase	50
Vase 6" #6004, footed, flared, 1 ball stem, bud vase	60
Vase 6.5" #3400/103, globe, short neck	90
Vase 7.8" #797, flip shape w/panel optic	145
Vase 8" #1300, footed, shouldered & flared	85
Vase 8" #1430, large, flat, flared, flip	175
Vase 8" #3500/44 Gadroon, footed, tab handled, urn shaped	125
Vase 8.4" #6004, footed, flared, 1 ball stem, bud vase	70
Vase 9" #1234, footed, keyhole, shouldered	100
Vase 9" #1237, footed, keyhole stem, flared	115
Vase 10" #272, footed, pulled in at top, bud vase	80
Vase 10" #274, footed, tapered, bud vase	75
Vase 10" #1301, footed, shouldered & flared	95
Vase 10" #6004, footed, flared, 1 ball stem	85
Vase 10.25" #1528, flat, spherical bottom, w/concave neck, bud vase	125
Vase 10.25" #3400/1242, flat, shouldered, flared	135
Vase 11" #278, footed, flared (no stem)	125
Vase 11.5" #1299, footed, urn shape, ball stem	175
Vase 12" #1234, footed, keyhole, shouldered	135
Vase 12" #1238, footed, keyhole stem, flared	145
Vase 12" #6004, footed, flared, 1 ball stem	100
Vase 13.25" #279, footed (no stem) wide w/flared top	200
Vase 18" #1336, shouldered & flared	1,250+

EMPRESS / QUEEN ANN

Heisey Glass Company **Blank #1401 / #1509 1930-38, 1938-57**
Main Colors: Crystal, Flamingo (pink), Moongleam (green), and Sahara (yellow)
Other Colors: Alexandrite, Cobalt, and Tangerine

Many Heisey collectors requested that Empress/Queen Ann be added to this next edition. The Empress pattern #1401 was introduced in 1930 and stayed in the Heisey line for eight years. It was discontinued in 1938. This pattern is characterized by alternating fans around the edge. Heisey collectors call this design "fleur-de-lis". Thomas Clarence Heisey designed this pattern, with the first patent being applied for on March 29, 1930. Most of the items in this pattern are marked with the trademark capital H in a diamond. Note, the capital H in a diamond mark on the dolphin footed items is usually found on the back side of the foot. After 1938 the mould was reworked with an added internal optic. The optic has extra glass added to the piece and causes what feels like a bulge. The pattern was given the new name of Queen Ann and was only made in crystal. For years there has been so much discussion about these being two different patterns. With adding this pattern to our book, we felt there should be an explanation about these patterns. Since Empress was designed first and then was reworked to create Queen Ann, they need to be under one heading so collectors could fully understand the background between the two. There is no price difference between crystal Empress & Queen Ann.

The pattern also had some pieces made in Alexandrite, Cobalt, and Tangerine. All of these prices would run quite a bit higher. Not enough of them are on the market at any given time and thus prevent any consistent prices from being established. Several of the pieces were reissued later by Imperial in Sunshine Yellow.

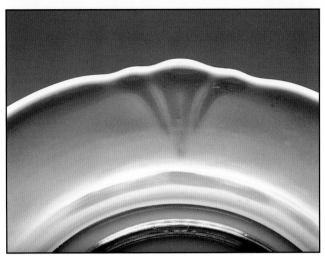

Pattern detail, Empress.

EMPRESS

	Crystal	Sahara	Flamingo Moongleam
Ashtray, 7" long, diamond shape with fans on end, indents in center, 3" wide	45	95	145
Bonbon 6", flared	8	20	30
Bowl 3", dolphin footed, individual nut	15	30	45
Bowl 4.5", flat, flared, fruit	12	24	35
Bowl 5", tab footed, 2-handled preserve	8	20	30
Bowl 6", square, rim grapefruit	12	24	32
Bowl 6", tab footed, 2-handled, flared, jelly	8	20	30
Bowl 6", 3 dolphin footed, flared, mint	18	39	50
Bowl 7.5", dolphin footed, nappy	30	60	75
Bowl 7.5", dolphin footed, deep, nasturtium	50	125	170
Bowl 8", flat, flared, vegetable	20	40	55
Bowl 8.5", tab footed, flared w/loop handles, floral	25	50	70
Bowl 9", rolled edge, floral	20	40	55
Bowl 9", flared, plumes on side, floral	29	59	79
Bowl 10", oval, 2-handled, V shaped edge, deep, dessert	25	50	70
Bowl 10", oval, (round or square) 2-handled, salad	30	60	75
Bowl 10", oval, vegetable	27	55	75
Bowl 10" claw footed, lion's heads on sides, shallow, floral	225	450	600
Bowl 11", dolphin footed, flared, floral	50	70	95
Candlestick 1-lite 1.5", tab footed handled, pair	60	120	165
Candlestick 1-lite 6", dolphin footed, tall stem, 2 stacked wafers, pair	85	150	195
Candy w/cover 6": dolphin footed; lid w/fan finial on, 6.25" wide	75	150	195
Compotier 6" dolphin footed	95	195	265
Comport 6", plain stem	35	75	95
Comport 6", ribbed wafer stem, square top	40	90	125
Comport 7", tall stem, oval w/rolled ends	39	79	95
Cream soup & saucer: bowl 5", flat, handled, 10 oz.; saucer w/indent, round or square	25	50	70
Creamer 3", collar footed, individual, 3.5 oz.	19	40	55
Creamer 3.25", dolphin footed, regular, 6 oz.	30	50	70
Cruet w/wafer shape stopper, 6.25", footed oil bottle, 4 oz.	65	125	165
Cup 2.2", handled, punch or custard, 4 oz.	15	30	45
Cup & saucer, after dinner: cup 2.5", flat, 4 oz.; saucer w/indent 4.75"	25	50	70
Cup & saucer, bouillon: cup 2.6", 7 oz., 2-handled; saucer w/indent 6.5"	25	50	70
Cup & saucer, coffee: cup 2.6", flat, 6 oz, wide band around top; saucer w/indent 6.5"	20	40	55
Cup & saucer, coffee: cup 2.6", flat, 6 oz.; saucer w/indent 6.5"	16	32	45
Frappe bowl & center piece 2.5" inside, 3" outside, deep	25	50	70
Goblet 2.5", oyster cocktail, 2.5 oz.	10	20	29
Goblet sherbet, 4 oz.	12	24	32
Goblet saucer champagne 4 oz.	19	39	45
Goblet 7", water, 9 oz.	30	60	79
Ice Bucket 6.75", 4 dolphin feet, deep, 5" wide, w/ chrome handle	75	125	165
Lemon w/cover 6.5", oval, tab handled, w/dolphin finial	50	95	145
Marmalade 4.9", dolphin footed, covered	75	150	195
Mayonnaise 3.25", dolphin footed, deep, flared top, 5.4" wide	40	75	125
Mustard w/cover 3.5", collar footed, deep w/paneled finial	50	95	145
Pitcher flat, water, 48, oz.	75	150	195

Sahara (yellow) grouping: **Back:** Plate 12", oval, handled, sandwich. **Front left:** Ashtray, 7" long, diamond shape w/fans on end, indents in center, 3" wide. **Front center:** Goblet 7", water, 9 oz. **Front right:** Bowl 6", 3 dolphin footed, mint.

Candy w/cover 6": dolphin footed; lid w/fan finial, 6.25" wide, Flamingo (pink).

Left: Cup & saucer, coffee: cup 2.6", flat, 6 oz.; saucer w/indent 6.5", Alexandrite. **Right:** Cup & saucer, after dinner: cup 2.5", flat, 4 oz.; saucer w/indent 4.75", Flamingo (pink).

Left: Plate 8", square, salad, Moongleam (green). **Center:** Mustard w/ cover 3.5", footed w/o stem, Crystal. **Right:** Mayonnaise 3.25" tall, 5.4" wide, dolphin footed, Flamingo (pink).

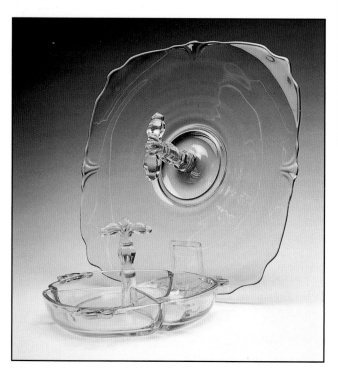

Pitcher 6.75", dolphin footed, water jug w/o ice lip, 48 oz.	100	195	265
Plate 4.4", round, butter	4	9	12
Plate 6", round or square, bread & butter	5	10	14
Plate 7", round or square, dessert (round or square) also grapefruit liner	6	12	16
Plate 8", round or square, salad	7	15	24
Plate 9", round, large lunch	10	20	29
Plate 10", round, small dinner	45	95	125
Plate 10.5", round or square, large dinner	90	125	150
Plate 12", round, torte	25	50	70
Plate 12", round, 2-handled, sandwich	30	60	79
Plate 13", handled, hors d'oeuvre	30	60	79
Platter 14", oval	24	49	69
Punch bowl 15", dolphin footed	395	795	1,000
Relish 7", round, 3-tab handled, 3 sections	20	40	55
Relish 7", 3 sections, center handled	38	50	69
Relish 10", rectangular, tab handles on 2 corners, celery	15	30	40
Relish 10", 3 sections, curlicue shape	24	50	69
Relish 10", 7 sections, handled, hors d'oeuvre	50	100	135
Relish 10", 3 sections	24	50	69
Relish 13", rectangular, tab handles on 2 corners, celery	19	39	52
Relish 13", rectangular, tab handle on 2 corners, 2 sections, olive/celery (divided 1/3 & 2/3)	19	39	52
Relish 16", 4 sections, handled, diamond shape, buffet	30	60	79
Sandwich server 12", center handle (round or square)	55	98	125
Shaker, footed, chrome top, pair	48	95	120
Sugar 3", collar footed, individual 3.5 oz.	19	40	55
Sugar 3.25", dolphin footed regular, 3 handled, 6 oz.	30	50	70
Tray 7", handled, individual creamer & sugar	20	45	60
Tray 12", 2 handles turned up (round or square) muffin	45	85	110
Tumbler 5", soda, 5 oz.	15	40	55
Tumbler 4", water, 8 oz.	20	45	60
Tumbler 4.5", dolphin footed, water, 8 oz.	65	135	175
Tumbler 5.25", ice tea, 12 oz.	24	49	65
Vase 8", footed, flared	50	125	175
Vase 9", dolphin footed, straight sided, cylindrical	95	195	265

Top: Bowl 10" claw footed, lion's heads on sides, shallow, floral, 3.75" tall, Crystal. **Bottom:** Bowl 10" claw footed, lion's heads on sides, shallow, floral, 3.75" tall, Sahara (yellow).

Sahara (yellow) grouping: **Back:** Sandwich server 12", square, center handle. **Front:** Relish 7", center handled, 3 sections.

FAIRFAX

Fostoria Glass Company **Blank #2375** **1933-60**

Main Colors: Amber, Azure (blue), Crystal, Green, Orchid, Rose (pink), and Topaz (yellow)

Other Colors: Burgundy (amethyst) and Ebony (black)

Fairfax has wide panels that are all the same width. Several of Fostoria's etched patterns, such as June, Trojan, and Versailles, can be found on this pattern. While this pattern doesn't have any stemware, we have found that collectors seem to like using Fostoria #5098 stemware. When you look at the ice dish, liners, and plate, you will notice that they have a different line number than the rest of the Fairfax pieces. These are not really part of the original Fairfax line, but most collectors that have Fairfax include it with their pattern. We have decided to include it in our listing, since it resembles Fairfax.

Collectors are now adding some of these plain Fostoria blank patterns with their etched pieces. Variety can be added to their collection without paying a high price for the same piece that was etched. Some of the items collectors are actively seeking are: the butter dish, sauce boat with liner, large platter, lemon insert, salad dressing bottle, and shakers.

There are very few Burgundy & Ebony pieces showing up in this pattern. With this in mind, it is impossible to list the fair market value of these colors.

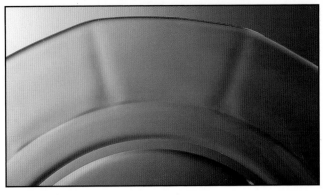

Pattern detail, Fairfax.

Topaz (yellow) grouping: **Left:** Plate 7.35", salad or dessert. **Back right:** Plate 10.25", large dinner. **Front right:** Cup & saucer, coffee: cup 2.5" footed, 6 oz.; saucer w/indent 5.75".

FAIRFAX	Crystal Amber	Topaz	Green Rose	Azure	Orchid
Almond 3", footed, individual nut, 1.6" tall	18	20	24	28	32
Ashtray 2.5", individual	14		18	18	24
Ashtray 3.75", round, rim edge	16	20	22	22	
Bonbon 6.75", 2 style of handles, both turned up	18	18	22	22	25
Bottle w/rounded top stopper 7" #2375 Fairfax, flat, salad dressing, 4.75 oz.	150	165	185	225	
Bowl 5.1", flared, fruit	18	18	20	22	24
Bowl 5.4", 2 style of handles, sweetmeat	12	14	22	24	34
Bowl 6", flared, cereal	26	28	32	34	35
Bowl 6.25", master nut, 3.25" high	28	25	32	35	38
Bowl 7", flared soup	55	58	60	68	68
Bowl 8", round (can flare over 9")	58	62	65	72	75
Bowl 8.5", handled, dessert	52	55	65	85	85
Bowl 9", oval, vegetable	52	55	65	85	85
Bowl 10.5", oval, vegetable	55	58	75	85	95
Bowl 12", mushroom-shaped	40	58	62	65	85
Bowl 12", 3-footed, flared, console	42	58	64	62	65
Bowl 13" #2375 1/2, oval, mushroom-shaped	60		90	95	95
Bowl 15", mushroom-shaped	50		80	85	
Butter w/cover 6.25", low, round w/ domed lid	110	120	145	180	180
Cake plate 10", open handled	38	52	60	60	
Candlestick 1-lite 3" #2375 1/2, mushroom-shaped pair	40	48	48	65	68
Candlestick 1-lite 3.25", pair	42	42	42	60	68
Cheese & cracker: comport 2.4" #2375, short stem, 5.25" wide; plate 9.75", 2 style handles	58	72	75	80	88
Comport 6", lady leg stem, flared, 6.75" wide	42	48	52	58	65
Cream soup & liner: 5", footed, handled, flared, 10 oz.; saucer w/indent 7.4"	38	40	42	48	58
Creamer 3" #2375 1/2, footed, individual, 3.25 oz.	12	12	12	16	
Creamer 3.75" #2375 1/2, footed, regular, 6.75 oz.	14	14	14	21	24
Creamer 3.5", flat, regular, 9 oz.	16	15	16	24	28
Cruet w/stopper 9.25", footed, oil w/handle, 5 oz.	165	195	225	225	
Cup & saucer, after dinner: cup 2.75", footed, 2.5 oz.; saucer w/indent 4.75"	15	18	22	26	30
Cup & saucer, bouillon: cup 2.5", footed, handled, 5 oz., 4" wide; saucer w/indent 5.75"	14	16	20	24	28
Cup & saucer, coffee: cup 2.3" flat, 7 oz.; saucer w/indent 5.75"	10	12	16	18	22
Cup & saucer, coffee: cup 2.5" footed, 6 oz.; saucer w/indent 5.75"	10	12	16	18	22
Ice bucket 6", chrome handle, 5.15" wide	85	95	110	95	125
Ice dish 2.75" #2451, bowl w/3-tabs hold liners, 4.8" wide	20	22	24	25	
Ice dish liner 2.75" #2451, crab meat, 4 oz.	24	30	35	40	
Ice dish liner 1.9" #2451, fruit cocktail, 5 oz.	28	35	40	45	
Ice dish liner 3.5" #2451, tomato juice, 5 oz.	18	24	28	34	
Ice dish plate 7" #2451, plain w/indent	12	12	14	16	
Mayonnaise 2 piece: bowl 5.6", footed, flared; plate w/indent 7.4"	48	65	68	75	85

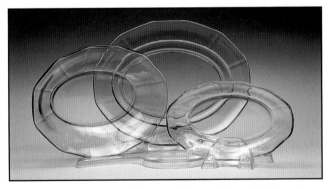

Left: Bowl 10.5", oval, vegetable, Green. **Center:** Platter 12.25", oval, Amber. **Right:** Relish 8.5", oval, pickle, Azure (blue).

Butter w/cover 6.25", low, round w/domed lid, Amber.

Item					
Plate 6.25", bread & butter	5	6	6	7	8
Plate 6.25", canape w/offset indent	22	22	24	25	24
Plate 6.8", 2 style of handles, lemon server	18	20	20	22	24
Plate 7.35", salad or dessert	8	8	9	12	12
Plate 8.6", lunch	12	12	14	16	20
Plate 9.25", small dinner	25	30	30	30	28
Plate 10.25", grill, 3 sections	30	34	40	45	42
Plate 10.25", large dinner	58	68	68	68	75
Plate 13.75", large center, chop or torte	65	75	110	110	110
Platter 10.5", oval	52	65	70	78	78
Platter 12.25", oval	58	85	90	95	95
Platter 15", oval	125	165	175	175	295
Relish 8.5", oval, pickle	18	24	28	38	38
Relish 8.5", oval, 2 equal sections	18	24	28	38	38
Relish 11.5", oval, celery	30	28	34	48	48
Relish 11.5", oval, 3 sections	30	28	34	48	48
Sandwich server 11", center "fleur-de-lis" handle	45	45	48	58	65
Sauce & liner: bowl 6.75", oval 2 spouted, 3.5" wide; oval liner w/indent 8"	98	120	145	165	175
Shaker 3.1", footed w/chrome or glass top, pair	62	75	90	95	110
Sugar bowl 2.75" #2375 1/2, footed, individual, 3 oz.	12	12	12	16	
Sugar bowl 3.1" #2375 1/2, footed, regular, 6.75 oz.	14	14	14	21	24
Sugar bowl cover #2375 1/2, lid	28	30	35	45	60
Sugar bowl 2.75", flat regular, 9 oz.	16	15	16	24	28
Sugar pail 3", w/o optic, chrome handle	78	95	95	95	110
Tray 12" #2429, oblong service or cordial tray, 7" wide	54	70	90	90	
Tray 12" #2429, oblong service, 2 piece w/lemon insert (plain not etched)	135	175	225	225	
Vase 5" #4128, flared, flip shape w/ regular optic	72	85	85	110	110
Whip cream pail 3.5", w/o optic, chrome handle	68	75	95	110	110
Whip cream bowl 5.5", 2 style of handles	20	20	25	28	32

Orchid grouping: **Back:** Plate 8.6", lunch. **Front:** Relish 8.5", oval, 2 equal sections.

Shaker 3.1", footed w/chrome or glass top, pair, Ebony (black).

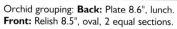

Top to Bottom:

Green grouping: **Back row:** Platter 12.25", oval. **Front left:** Plate 6.8", 2 style of handles, lemon server. **Front right:** Cup & saucer, after dinner: cup 2.75", footed, 2.5 oz.; saucer w/ indent 4.75".

Top: Sauce & liner: bowl 6.75", oval 2 spouted, 3.5" wide; oval liner w/indent 8", Amber. **Bottom left:** Sugar bowl 2.75", flat regular, 9 oz., Green. **Bottom right:** Creamer 3.5", flat, regular, 9 oz., Green.

Back row: Plate 13.75", large center, chop or torte, Azure (blue). **Center left:** Plate 6.8", 2 style of handles, lemon server, Green. **Center:** Bowl 5.4", 2 style of handles, sweetmeat, Amber. **Center right:** Bonbon 6.75", 2 style of handles, both turned up, Green. **Front center:** Bowl 5.1", flared, fruit, Amber.

Back row: handled cake plate 10", green. Azure (blue) grouping: **Front left:** Cup, bouillon 2.5", footed, handled, 5 oz., 4" wide. **Front center:** Creamer 3.75" #2375 1/2, footed, regular, 6.75 oz. **Front right:** Sugar bowl 3.1" #2375 1/2, footed, regular, 6.75 oz.

FIRST LOVE

Duncan & Miller Glass Company Late 1930s & 1940s

Color: Crystal

First Love is the top selling etched pattern from Duncan & Miller. This etched pattern was designed to go with the 1847 Rogers silver plate pattern, also called First Love. The design faithfully imitates the silver plate. Both were sold in fine jewelry and department stores. They were a nice complement to each other. First Love can be found etched on both Canterbury & Terrace blanks. Most popular with collectors are the Terrace items. When pricing items with a sterling silver foot, add 10% to the price listed.

The following items would make great additions to anyone's collection: basket, breakfast set, square crimped 10" bowl, cocktail shaker, deviled egg plate, hurricane lamp, and pitcher. First Love is steadily attracting new collectors.

Pattern detail, First Love.

FIRST LOVE	Crystal
Ashtray, 3.5" #30/96 Pall Mall, rectangle 2.5" wide	18
Ashtray 4" #12, club (heavy) round, deep, 3-footed	24
Ashtray 5" #12, club (heavy) round, deep, 3-footed	26
Ashtray 5" #30/97 Pall Mall, rectangle 3.25" wide	28
Ashtray 6.5" #30/98 Pall Mall, rectangle 4.25" wide	30
Basket 6" #111 Terrace, bowl w/2-tab handles pulled up	45
Basket 10" #115/92 Canterbury, flat, low, oval w/applied tall handle	195
Breakfast 3 piece set 3.5" high #28, (nesting) sugar, creamer & butter plate	125
Bowl 5" #115/84 Canterbury, flat fruit	24
Bowl 5.5" #115/85 Canterbury, flat, heart shape, 1-tab handle	30
Bowl 5.5" #111 Terrace, shallow, square	38
Bowl 6" #111 Terrace, 2-tab handles	30
Bowl 6" #115/86 Canterbury, flat, round, 2-tab handles	24
Bowl 7" #111 Terrace, shallow, square	48
Bowl 8.5" #111 Terrace, shallow, square crimped	52
Bowl 9" #111 Terrace, deep salad	75
Bowl 10" #111 Terrace, tab handled, round, fruit	80
Bowl 10" #126, footed w/wafer stem, square crimped	125
Bowl 10.5" #115/108 Canterbury, flat, shallow, crimped, fruit	50
Bowl 11" #30 Pall Mall, round, shallow, cupped up edge, gardenia	60
Bowl 11" #111 Terrace, flat, shallow, cupped, salad	68
Bowl 11.25" #111 Terrace, flat, flared, flower	85
Bowl 11.5" #115 Canterbury, flat, oval, shallow w/2 sides pulled up	95
Bowl 12" #6, scalloped collar foot & flared flower	125
Bowl 12" #111 Terrace, collar footed, shallow, cupped, console	100
Bowl 12" #115 Canterbury, flat, oval, flared	70
Bowl 12" #117 Three Feathers, oval, 2 feather tab handles, flower	135
Bowl 13" #115/110 Canterbury, flat, deep, oval, flared, center piece	100
Bowl 14" #126, flat, oval, 7.5" high, 2 sides pulled out, 2 sides flared up, 8" wide	195
Bowl 14.25" long, 3.25" tall, curled handles, boat shape	250
Candelabra 2-lite 5.5" #41, footed, w/plume bobeches & prisms, 9.5" spread, pair	225
Candelabra 2-lite 6.5" #30 Pall Mall, footed, large plain circle in center, 7.5" spread, pair	225
Candelabra 3-lite 5.5" #41, footed, with bobeches & prisms, 9.5" spread, pair	295
Candlestick 1-lite 3" #115/121 Canterbury, low, footed wafer stem, pair	50
Candlestick 1-lite 4" #111 Terrace, footed, terrace stem, pair	68
Candlestick 1-lite 4" #117 Three Feathers, footed, cornucopia w/curled tail, pair	96
Candlestick 2-lite 5" #41, footed, w/plume center, 8.5" spread, pair	110
Candlestick 2-lite 6" #30 Pall Mall, footed, large plain circle in center, 7" spread, pair	125
Candlestick 3-lite 5" #41, footed, 8.5" spread, pair	145
Candy w/cover 5" #25, footed, short wafer stem, 7.25" high	125
Candy w/cover 6" #106, flat, 3 sections w/scalloped sides, 3 open loop finial	95
Candy w/cover 8" #115/89 Canterbury, flat, 3-tab handled, 3 sections, cylindrical, paneled finial	85
Cheese & cracker #111 Terrace: comport 3", short stem, 5.25" wide; plate w/indent, tab handled 10.75"	75
Cigarette box w/cover 4.5" x 3.75" x 2.5" tall #30/100 Pall Mall, rectangle	95
Cigarette urn 3.25" #2, footed flared top edge	75
Cocktail shaker 6.5" #5200, flat, sham bottom w/chrome top, 14 oz.	135
Cocktail shaker 7.25" #5200, flat, sham bottom w/chrome top, 18 oz.	145
Cocktail shaker 9" #5200, flat, sham bottom w/chrome top, 32 oz.	175
Comport 3.5" #115/82 Canterbury, short stem, 5.75" wide	30
Comport 4.75" #115 Canterbury, crimped, 6" wide	38
Comport 5.5" #115/87 Canterbury, flared, 6" wide	45
Creamer 2.6" #115/62 Canterbury, flat, individual, open handle, 3 oz.	20
Creamer 1.75" #28, flat, nesting breakfast size, 3 oz.	40
Creamer 3.75" #115/66 Canterbury, flat, regular, open handle, 7 oz.	24
Creamer 3" #111 Terrace, collar footed, regular, wing handle, 10 oz.	28
Cup & saucer, coffee or tea #115/32 Canterbury: cup 2.6", flat, 6 oz.; saucer w/indent 6"	32
Decanter w/ball stopper #5200, sham bottom, 16 oz.	145
Decanter w/ball stopper 9.25" #5200, sham bottom, 32 oz.	175
Deviled egg plate 12" #30 Pall Mall, smooth rim	175
Finger bowl 4.25" #5111 1/2, flat, deep (blown)	32
Goblet 3.75" #5111 1/2, 1 ball stem, cordial, 1 oz.	68

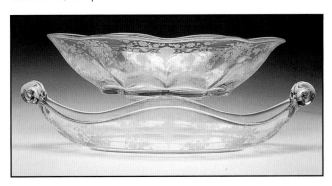

Bowl 12" #6, scalloped collar foot & flared flower.

Left: Bowl 13" #115/110 Canterbury, flat, deep, oval, flared, center piece. **Bottom:** Bowl 14.25" long, 3.25" tall, curled handles, boat shape.

Top left: Creamer 3" #111 Terrace, collar footed, regular, wing handle, 10 oz. **Top right:** Tray 8", oval, scrolled handles for cream/sugar. **Bottom left:** Sugar 2.8" #111 Terrace, collar footed, regular, wing handles, 10 oz. **Bottom center:** Sugar 2.5" #115/61 Canterbury, flat, individual, open handles, 3 oz. **Bottom right:** Creamer 2.6" #115/62 Canterbury, flat, individual, open handle, 3 oz.

Top left: Candlestick 2-lite 6" #30 Pall Mall, footed, large plain circle in center, 7" spread. **Top right:** Cheese & cracker #111 Terrace: comport 3", short stem, 5.25" wide; plate w/indent, tab handled 10.75". **Bottom left:** Candy w/cover 8" #115/89 Canterbury, flat, 3-tab handled, 3 sections cylindrical, paneled finial. **Bottom right:** Candlestick 1-lite 4" #111 Terrace, footed, terrace stem.

Left to right: Goblet 3.75" #5111 1/2, 1 ball stem, oyster cocktail; Goblet 4" #5111 1/2, 1 ball stem, sherbet or ice cream, 5 oz.; Goblet 5" #5111 1/2, 3 ball stem, saucer champagne, 5 oz.; Tumbler 5.75" #5111 1/2, footed, 1 ball stem, lunch water, 10 oz.; Goblet 6.75" #5111 1/2, 3 ball stem, water, 10 oz.

Left: Plate 7.5" #115/26 Canterbury, salad or dessert. **Right:** Plate 8.5" #111 Terrace, round, lunch.

Goblet 5.25" #5111 1/2, 3 ball stem, wine, 3 oz.	58
Goblet 4.5" #5111 1/2, 3 ball stem, liquor cocktail, 3.5 oz.	35
Goblet 3.75" #5111 1/2, 1 ball stem, oyster cocktail, 4.5 oz.	20
Goblet 6" #5111 1/2, 3 ball stem, claret, 4.5 oz.	54
Goblet 4" #5111 1/2, 1 ball stem, sherbet or ice cream, 5 oz.	18
Goblet 5" #5111 1/2, 3 ball stem, saucer champagne, 5 oz.	22
Goblet 6.75" #5111 1/2, 3 ball stem, water, 10 oz.	36
Hurricane lamp 15" #1-41, swirled foot, fancy stem w/prisms & #505 etched chimney each	275
Ice bucket 6" #30 Pall Mall, scalloped edge with chrome handle, 5.5" wide	145
Mayonnaise 2 piece #111 Terrace: bowl 5.5", collar footed, wing handled; liner, tab handled 7.5"	54
Mayonnaise 2 piece #115/50 Canterbury: bowl 5.5", flat, crimped; liner w/indent, tab handled 7.5"	54
Mayonnaise 2 piece #30 Pall Mall: bowl 5.5", footed, wafer stem, salad dressing; liner w/indent 7.5"	80
Mayonnaise bowl 6" #111 Terrace, collar footed, flared, salad dressing	55
Mayonnaise 2 piece #115 Canterbury: bowl 6", flat; liner w/indent 8.5"	50
Mayonnaise 2 piece #115 Canterbury: bowl 6", flat, salad dressing; liner w/indent 8.5"	65
Pitcher 9.25" #115 Canterbury, flat, martini mixer w/ice lip, 32 oz.	225
Pitcher 9.25" #115 Canterbury, flat, handled, martini mixer w/ice lip, 32 oz.	245
Pitcher 8.6" #5202, flat, ball jug w/ice lip, 80 oz.	265
Plate 3" #28, round, flat, butter pat	30
Plate 6" #111 Terrace, round, bread & butter	16
Plate 6" #111 Terrace, square, bread & butter	24
Plate 6" #115/25 Canterbury, bread & butter	12
Plate 6" #111 Terrace, round, tab handled, lemon server	24
Plate 7" #111 Terrace, round, dessert or salad	20
Plate 7.5" #111 Terrace, square, salad	30
Plate 7.5" #115/26 Canterbury, salad or dessert	18
Plate 7.5" #115/30 Canterbury, tab handled, lemon server	30
Plate 8.5" #111 Terrace, round, lunch	26
Plate 8.5" #115/27 Canterbury, lunch	22
Plate 10.75" #111 Terrace, round, tab handled, sandwich, small center	38
Plate 11" #115/28 Canterbury, large dinner or service	65
Plate 11.5" #115/31 Canterbury, tab handled, sandwich	45
Plate 13" #111 Terrace, flat, round, torte	58
Plate 13" #111 Terrace, round, small center, turned up edge, cabaret	68
Plate 14", round, torte, small center	60
Relish 6" #111 Terrace, tab handled, 2 sections, 3 styles (diamond, round, & square)	40
Relish 6" #115 Canterbury, flat, oval, tab handled, olive	30
Relish 6" #115/52 Canterbury, round, flat, tab handled, 2 sections	38
Relish 7" #117 Three Feathers, 3-tab handles, 3 equal sections	56
Relish 8" #111 Terrace, tab handled, oblong, celery	35
Relish 9" #111 Terrace, tab handled, 4 sections, round	58
Relish 9" #115/53 Canterbury, flat, tab handled, oblong, 2 sections	45
Relish 9" #115/54 Canterbury, flat, 3-tab handled, 3 sections, flared	48
Relish 10" #31 1/2, round, 4 equal sections & celery section	65
Relish 10.5" #111 Terrace, 2-tab handled, round, 4 equal sections & round center	68
Relish 10.5" #115/55 Canterbury, flat, 2-tab handled, 2 equal sections & celery section	60
Relish 11" #91, oval celery	45
Relish 12" #30 Pall Mall, graduated bead handles, oblong, 2 equal sections & celery section	65
Shaker, 3" #30 Pall Mall, flat, tapered, pair	65
Sugar 2.5" #115/61 Canterbury, flat, individual, open handles, 3 oz.	20
Sugar 1.75" #28, flat, nesting breakfast 5 oz. (use butter plate for lid)	40
Sugar 3.25" #115/65 Canterbury, flat, regular, open handles, 7 oz.	24
Sugar 2.8" #111 Terrace, collar footed, regular, wing handles, 10 oz.	28
Sugar bowl lid #111 Terrace, finial	25
Tray 8", oval, scrolled handles for cream/sugar	28
Tumbler 2" #5200, flat, sham bottom, straight sided, whiskey, 1.5 oz.	58
Tumbler 3" #5200, flat, sham bottom, straight sided, cocktail, 3.5 oz.	35
Tumbler 5.25" #5111 1/2, footed, 1 ball stem, juice, 5 oz.	26
Tumbler 3.25" #5200, flat, sham bottom, straight sided, juice, 5 oz.	35
Tumbler 2.25" #5200, flat, sham bottom, straight sided, hi ball, 7 oz.	40
Tumbler 5.75" #5111 1/2, footed, 1 ball stem, lunch water, 10 oz.	32
Tumbler 3.75" #5200, flat, sham bottom, straight sided, water, 10 oz.	38
Tumbler 6.5" #5111 1/2, footed, 1 ball stem, ice tea, 12 oz.	36
Tumbler 4.5" #5200, flat, sham bottom, straight sided, ice tea, 12 oz.	40
Tumbler 6.75" #5111 1/2, footed, 1 ball stem, beverage, 14 oz.	42
Tumbler 4.75" #5200, flat, sham bottom, straight sided, beverage, 14 oz.	48
Tumbler 5" #5200, flat, sham bottom, straight sided, beverage, 16 oz.	54
Tumbler 5.25" #5200, flat, sham bottom, straight sided, beverage, 18 oz.	60
Vase 4" #117 Three Feathers, footed, flared, cornucopia w/curled tail	55
Vase 5" #115/111 Canterbury, straight sided, flared, crimped top	50
Vase 5" #525, round foot, Grecian urn shape, no stem, flared	72
Vase 6" #507, footed w/no stem, flared, trumpet shape	78
Vase 7" #529, square footed, Grecian urn shape, wafer stem	98
Vase 7" #5200, flat, sham bottom, straight sided, cylindrical	125

Vase 8" #117 Three Feathers, footed, flared, cornucopia w/curled tail	110
Vase 8" #505, footed w/no stem, convex sides	125
Vase 8" #506, footed w/no stem, straight sided, cylindrical	98
Vase 8" #507, footed w/no stem, flared trumpet shape	110
Vase 8" #5200, flat, sham bottom, straight sided	145
Vase 9" #506, footed w/no stem, straight sided, slender bud vase	95
Vase 9" #509, footed, faceted ball stem, straight sided	85
Vase 9" #510, footed, faceted ball stem, flared	85
Vase 10" #111 Terrace, footed, large w/terrace stem, flared	175
Vase 10" #505, footed w/no stem, convex sides	160
Vase 10" #506, footed w/no stem, straight sided, cylindrical	125
Vase 10" #507, footed w/no stem, flared, trumpet shape	135
Vase 10" #5200, flat, sham bottom, straight sided, cylindrical	175
Vase 11" #126, round foot w/short stem, flared & squared	145
Vase 12" #115 Canterbury, straight sided, slightly flared	135
Vase 12" #505, footed w/no stem, convex sides	175
Vase 12" #506, footed w/no stem, straight sided, cylindrical	150
Vase 12" #507, footed w/no stem, flared, trumpet shape	160

Back: Bowl 12" #111 Terrace, collar footed, shallow, cupped, console.
Front: Relish 7" #117 Three Feathers, 3-tab handles, 3 equal sections – shown w/sterling silver base.

Left: Vase 9" #506, footed w/no stem, straight sided, slender bud vase. **Center:** Pitcher 8.6" #5202, flat, ball jug w/ice lip, 80 oz. **Right:** Pitcher 9.25" #115 Canterbury, flat, handled, martini mixer w/ice lip, 32 oz.

Deviled egg plate 12" #30 Pall Mall, smooth rim.

Left: Vase 8" #506, footed w/no stem, straight sided, cylindrical. **Center:** Vase 6" #507, footed w/no stem, flared, trumpet shape. **Right:** Vase 8" #117 Three Feathers, footed, flared, cornucopia w/curled tail.

Pattern detail, Flanders.

Rose (pink) grouping: **Left:** Sugar #6, flat, regular, tapered, 9 oz. **Center:** Creamer #6, flat, regular, tapered, 6.5 oz. **Right:** Cup & saucer, coffee #8869: cup 2.4", flat, w/optic, 6 oz.; saucer w/indent 6".

FLANDERS

Tiffin Glass Company   **1927-35**
Main Colors: Crystal, and Rose (pink)
Other Color: Mandarin (yellow)

Flanders is Tiffin's version of an etched poppy flower. This etched pattern can easily be confused with Cambridge's poppy etch Gloria. Besides Rose (pink) and Crystal, Flanders can also be found in a delicate yellow color called Mandarin. The price for this color usually runs about 2/3 of the price of pink. The color of choice by collectors is pink, as the prices would indicate.

There seems to be an abundance of Crystal stems. The hard to find items are: candy dishes, decanter, hurricane lamp, pitcher, and vase.

FLANDERS	Crystal	Pink
Bonbon #5831, 2 handles turned up	28	70
Bowl 4" #194, footed, deep	35	75
Bowl 6.25" #5831, 2-handled	38	85
Bowl 8" #194, footed, deep	58	145
Bowl 10" #8105, salad w/straight edge	68	175
Bowl 11" #179, centerpiece	90	225
Bowl 11.25" #5831, footed, flared, centerpiece	98	250
Bowl 13" #8153, rolled edge, centerpiece	100	275
Cake plate 10.5" #320, handled	58	145
Candlestick 1-lite 5" #5831, wafer stem, pair	58	145
Candy w/cover #9557, footed, egg shape .5 lb. w/teardrop finial	195	495
Candy w/cover 6" #329, flat, round, straight sided, knob finial	160	395
Candy Jar w/cover 7.75" #179, footed, cone w/bell shape lid	110	295
Cheese & cracker: comport #151, short stem, cupped; plate	58	
Cheese & cracker: comport #337, short stem, octagonal; plate	50	135
Comport #4, blown, wide optic, high wafer stem, 6" wide	68	175
Comport 3.5" #5831, short stem, cupped, 6.5" wide	45	125
Comport #319, high, 7.5" wide	72	195
Creamer 4.5" #5831, footed regular, 6 oz.	40	95
Creamer #6, flat, regular, tapered, 6.5 oz.	58	145
Cup & saucer, coffee #5831: cup 2.25", footed, 6 oz.; saucer w/indent 6.25"	40	95
Cup & saucer, coffee #8869: cup 2.4", flat, w/optic, 6 oz.; saucer w/indent 6"	42	98
Decanter w/cut stopper #14179, handled, bell shape, 32 oz.	160	395
Decanter w/stopper 11.8" #13624, bottle shape, optic, 32 oz.; paneled stopper w/flat top	145	350
Finger bowl 4.5" #185, footed, 8 oz.	40	95
Goblet 5.4" #15024, cordial, 1.5 oz.	68	175
Goblet 6" #15024, wine, 3 oz.	36	85
Goblet 5" #15024, liquor cocktail, 3.5 oz.	28	65
Goblet 3.5" #630, oyster cocktail, 4 oz.	22	60
Goblet 6.75" #15024, cafe parfait, 4.5 oz.	50	165
Goblet 6.75" #15024, handled, cafe parfait, 4.5 oz.		175
Goblet 6.5" #15024, claret, 5 oz.	45	125
Goblet 4" #15047, sherbet or sundae, 5 oz.	18	45
Goblet 4.5" #15024, sherbet, 6 oz.	20	48
Goblet 6.2" #15024, saucer champagne, 6 oz.	16	40
Goblet 7.9" #15047, water, 8 oz.	28	65
Goblet 8.25" #17660, water, 9 oz.	30	70
Goblet 8" #15071, water, 9 oz.	30	70
Goblet 8.25" #15024, water, 9 oz.	32	75
Grapefruit 4.24" #251, 2 piece (plain 6 oz. insert) 20 oz.	72	195
Hurricane lamp 12", Chinese, 2 piece, footed candlestick & chimney	300	700+
Pitcher 8" #14194, footed jug w/o ice lip, 64 oz.	175	350
Pitcher w/cover 9.4" #14194, footed w/o ice lip, 64 oz.	225	500+
Plate 6.2" #8814, bread & butter, w/o optic	7	18
Plate 7.5" #5831, salad or dessert	9	22
Plate 8.2" #8833, salad or lunch, w/o optic	12	26
Plate 10.5" #8818, dinner, w/o optic	45	125
Relish 10.5" #5831, oval celery	42	98
Relish 12.25" #8897, 5 sections	40	95
Sugar 3.4" #5831, footed regular, 6 oz.	40	95
Sugar #6, flat, regular, curved sides, 9 oz.	58	145
Tray #337, center handled server, octagon shape	68	175
Tumbler #020, footed whiskey, 2 oz.	42	98
Tumbler #020, footed seltzer, 4 oz.	24	56
Tumbler 4" #020, footed, 4.25 oz.	24	56
Tumbler 3.75" #020, footed seltzer, 5 oz.	25	58
Tumbler 4.75" #020, footed water, 10 oz.	32	72
Tumbler 5.8" #020, footed, ice tea, 12 oz.	42	98
Vase 8" #2, footed, shouldered, flared	90	225
Vase 8" #151, footed, cupped, Dahlia	110	295
Whip cream bowl 6.5" #151, footed, flared	45	125

Rose (pink) grouping: **Left:** Plate 8.2" #8833, salad or lunch, w/o optic. **Right:** Plate 10.5" #8818, dinner, w/o optic. **Center:** Candlestick 1-lite 5" #5831, wafer stem.

Left: Goblet 4" #15047, sherbet or sundae, 5 oz. **Center:** Goblet 7.9" #15047, water, 8 oz. **Right:** Tumbler #020, footed seltzer, 4 oz.

Rose (pink) grouping: **Left:** Tumbler #020, footed whiskey, 2 oz. **Center:** Goblet 3.5" #630, oyster cocktail, 4 oz. **Right:** Goblet 4.5" #15024, sherbet, 6 oz.

Decanter w/stopper 11.8" #13624, bottle shape, optic, 32 oz.; paneled stopper w/flat top, Rose (pink).

Left: Tumbler 3.75" #020, footed seltzer, 5 oz. **Center:** Tumbler 4" #020, footed, 4.25 oz. **Right:** Tumbler 5.8" #020, footed, ice tea, 12 oz.

Rose (pink) grouping: **Left:** Tumbler 4.75" #020, footed water, 10 oz. **Center:** Goblet 6" #15024, wine, 3 oz. **Right:** Goblet 8.25" #15024, water, 9 oz.

Pattern detail, Florentine.

Topaz (yellow) grouping: **Left:** Sugar 3.6" #2440 Lafayette, footed, scroll handled, regular, 6.75 oz. **Right:** Creamer 4.25" #2440 Lafayette, footed, scroll handle, regular, 6.75 oz.

Back: Cake plate 10" #2470, handled. **Front:** Cup & saucer, coffee #2440 Lafayette: cup 2.75", footed, 6 oz.; saucer w/indent 5.8".

Left: Goblet 4.9" #6005, lady leg stem, liquor cocktail, 4 oz. **Center:** Goblet 5.4" #6005, lady leg stem, saucer champagne, 5.5 oz. **Right:** Goblet 7.4" #6005, lady leg stem, water, 9 oz.

FLORENTINE

Fostoria Glass Company Etching #311 1931-44
Colors: Crystal and Topaz (yellow)

The Florentine etching is a handled urn filled with a bouquet of flowers. There is a garland trailing in either direction to a scroll-like design. This etched pattern is sometimes mixed up with another Fostoria stemware pattern called Sheraton #317. However, the Sheraton blank #6010 and the urn looks more like a Samovar server. There is a flower with leaves under the urn that looks like a snowflake.

The Lafayette #2440 blank is most often used on the pieces in Florentine. The stemware will be found on the #6005 blank, that has a "lady leg stem". The tumblers are found on the #4005 and #6005 blanks. Stemware, as well as some of the footed items, can be found in all Crystal or with a Topaz base and clear bowl or top. The delicate flowers in a vase make this an attractive etched pattern. It takes some looking to assemble a place setting.

Being another hard to find Fostoria etched pattern, some of the serving pieces can be used with Lafayette on a table. Some of the items in Topaz were only made for a few years, making them much more difficult to find than the same items in Crystal.

FLORENTINE	Crystal	Topaz
Bonbon 7" #2470, handles turned up	22	30
Bowl 6" #2470, handled, sweetmeat	22	30
Bowl 10.5" #2470 1/2, 4-footed, flared	72	110
Bowl 12" #2470, fancy base, w/no stem	90	135
Cake plate 10" #2470, handled	38	58
Candlestick 1-lite 5.5" #2470, fancy base w/tall stem, pair	110	135
Candlestick 1-lite 5.5" #2470 1/2, pair	95	125
Comport 3.5" #2470, fancy base w/no stem, 6" wide	32	48
Comport 6" #2470, fancy base w/tall stem, 6" wide	95	140
Creamer 3.75" #2470, footed regular, 6 oz.	20	28
Creamer 4.25" #2440 Lafayette, footed, scroll handle, regular, 6.75 oz.	24	32
Cup & saucer, coffee #2440 Lafayette: cup 2.75", footed, 6 oz.; saucer w/indent 5.8"	24	35
Finger bowl & liner: bowl 4.6" #869, blown, 8 oz.; plate w/indent 6"	35	
Goblet 3.75" #6005, lady leg stem, cordial, 1 oz.	50	75
Goblet 5" #6005, lady leg stem, wine, 3 oz.	30	45
Goblet 4.9" #6005, lady leg stem, liquor cocktail, 4 oz.	24	36
Goblet 5.9" #6005, lady leg stem, claret, 5 oz.	32	45
Goblet 5.4" #6005, lady leg stem, saucer champagne, 5.5 oz.	25	32
Goblet 3.5" #6005, oyster cocktail, 6 oz.	12	22
Goblet 6" #6005, lady leg stem, parfait, 6 oz.	30	38
Goblet 4.25" #6005, lady leg stem, sherbet, 7 oz.	14	24
Goblet 7.4" #6005, lady leg stem, water, 9 oz.	35	52
Pitcher 9.75" #5000, footed, applied handle, water w/o ice lip, 48 oz.	395	
Plate 5.25" #2440 Lafayette, flat, tab plume handled, lemon server	20	30
Plate 6.25" #2440 Lafayette, bread & butter	10	15
Plate 7.25" #2440 Lafayette, salad or dessert	18	24
Plate 8.5" #2440 Lafayette, lunch	22	32
Plate 9.5" #2440 Lafayette, dinner	45	68
Plate 13" #2440 Lafayette, small center, torte or salad bowl liner	72	110
Relish 9.25" #2470, tab handled, 3 sections	42	65
Sugar 3.5 #2470, footed regular, 6 oz.	20	28
Sugar 3.6" #2440 Lafayette, footed, scroll handled, regular, 6.75 oz.	24	32
Tray 8.75" #2470, oval for creamer/sugar	26	38
Tumbler 2.5" #4005, flat whiskey, 2.5 oz.	24	
Tumbler 3.1" #6005, footed whiskey, 2.5 oz.	38	58
Tumbler 3.25" #4005, flat juice, 5 oz.	24	
Tumbler 4.1" #6005, footed juice, 5 oz.	28	42
Tumbler 3.9" #4005, flat water, 9 oz.	26	
Tumbler 5.1" #6005, footed water, 9 oz.	35	52
Tumbler 4.9" #4005, flat ice tea, 12 oz.	32	
Tumbler 5.5" #6005, footed, ice tea, 12 oz.	45	68

FUCHSIA

Fostoria Glass Company　　　　**Etching #310**　　　**1931-44**

Colors: Crystal and Wisteria (lilac)

This Fuchsia etched pattern features a very delicate looking flower with tendrils flowing from the branch. New collectors will sometimes confuse this etched pattern with Tiffin's Fuchsia or even Cambridge's Marjorie, which also is a Fuchsia etching.

The Lafayette #2440 is the blank on most of the pieces in this etched pattern. The stemware will be found on the #6004 blank. Stemware as well as some of the footed items can be found in all Crystal or with a Wisteria base with a clear bowl or top. The two tone pieces are exceptional pieces to have in this etched pattern. All of the two tone items were only made for a few short years thus making all that much harder to find. Candlesticks with the Wisteria base are a true prize to find in this etched pattern.

Pattern detail, Fuchsia – Fostoria.

FUCHSIA	Crystal	Wisteria
Bonbon 7" #2470, handles turned up	32	
Bowl 6" #2470, handled, sweetmeat	36	
Bowl 10" #2395, oval, large scroll handles, console	95	
Bowl 10.5" #2440 Lafayette, flat, flared	85	
Bowl 10.5" #2470 1/2, 4-footed, flared	80	
Bowl 12" #2470, fancy base, w/no stem	100	250
Cake plate 10" #2470, handled	70	
Candlestick 1-lite 3.25" #2375 Fairfax, pair	65	
Candlestick 1-lite 5" #2395 1/2, 2 high scroll handles, pair	98	
Candlestick 1-lite 5.5" #2470, fancy base w/tall stem, pair	160	450
Candlestick 1-lite 5.5" #2470 1/2, pair	145	
Comport 3.5" #2470, fancy base w/no stem, 6" wide	48	125
Comport 6" #2470, fancy base w/tall stem, 6" wide	95	195
Creamer 4.25" #2440 Lafayette, footed, scroll handle, regular, 6.75 oz.	28	
Cup & saucer, coffee #2440 Lafayette: cup 2.75", footed, 6 oz.; saucer w/indent 5.8"	22	
Finger bowl & liner: bowl 4.6" #869, blown, 8 oz.; plate w/indent 6"	28	
Goblet 3.6" #6004, lady leg stem, cordial, .75 oz.	50	145
Goblet 5" #6004, lady leg stem, wine, 2.5 oz.	38	70
Goblet 4.75" #6004, lady leg stem, liquor cocktail, 3 oz.	28	65
Goblet 5.6" #6004, lady leg stem, claret, 4 oz.	45	95
Goblet 3.5" #6004, oyster cocktail, 4.5 oz.	18	50
Goblet 4.1" #6004, lady leg stem, sherbet, 5.5 oz.	22	55
Goblet 5.4" #6004, saucer champagne, 5.5 oz.	24	60
Goblet 6" #6004, lady leg stem, parfait, 5.5 oz.	40	75
Goblet 7.4" #6004, lady leg stem, water, 9 oz.	48	75
Plate 5.25" #2440 Lafayette, flat, tab plume handled, lemon server	24	
Plate 6.25" #2440 Lafayette, bread & butter	8	
Plate 6.75" #2470, 2-tab handles (4 pleats), lemon server	24	
Plate 7.25" #2440 Lafayette, salad or dessert	12	
Plate 8.5" #2440 Lafayette, lunch	16	
Plate 9.5" #2440 Lafayette, dinner	45	
Shaker, 3.25" #2375 Fairfax, footed, w/glass top, pair	195	
Sugar 3.6" #2440 Lafayette, footed, scroll handled, regular, 6.75 oz.	28	
Tumbler 2" #833, flat whiskey, 2 oz.	28	
Tumbler 2.75" #6004, footed whiskey, 2.5 oz.	30	62
Tumbler 3.75" #833, flat juice, 5 oz.	25	
Tumbler 4.25" #6004, footed juice, 5 oz.	25	48
Tumbler 4.4" #833, flat water, 8 oz.	28	
Tumbler 5.25" #6004, footed water, 9 oz.	28	60
Tumbler 5.25" #833, flat ice tea, 12 oz.	30	
Tumbler 6" #6004, footed, ice tea, 12 oz.	32	65

Left: Cup & saucer, coffee #2440 Lafayette: cup 2.75", footed, 6 oz.; saucer w/indent 5.8". **Back right:** Plate 7.25" #2440 Lafayette, salad or dessert. **Front right:** Candlestick 1-lite 5" #2395 1/2, 2 high scroll handles.

Crystal bowl w/Wisteria stem/foot grouping: **Left to right:** Goblet 4.1" #6004, lady leg stem, sherbet, 5.5 oz.; Goblet 3.6" #6004, lady leg stem, cordial, .75 oz.; Goblet 5.4" #6004, saucer champagne, 5.5 oz.; Goblet 4.75" #6004, lady leg stem, liquor cocktail, 3 oz.; Goblet 7.4" #6004, lady leg stem, water, 9 oz.

Back left: Plate 6.75" #2470, 2-tab handles (4 pleats), lemon server. **Back right:** Plate 9.5" #2440 Lafayette, dinner. **Front left:** Tumbler 5.25" #6004, footed water, 9 oz., Crystal bowl w/Wisteria foot. **Front left:** Comport 6" #2470, fancy base w/tall stem, 6" wide.

Pattern detail, Fuchsia, Tiffin.

Goblet 7.25" #17457, "S"-stem, water 9 oz.

Vase 10.5" #14185, footed, tapered, bud vase.

Lamp 28" total, electric (glass part is the trophy handled vase), Ruby Flashed also came w/ White Flashed background.

FUCHSIA

Tiffin Glass Company   **1936-40**
Color: Crystal

    Fuchsia is a favorite among collectors of flower items. Tiffin's Fuchsia is much easier to find than Fostoria's Fuchsia etched pattern. The real plus to this etched pattern is that it has much more extensive listing than Fostoria. Many of the people that raise Fuchsia collect this etched pattern. Several types of stemware were made, with the "S" stems being much harder to find and very ornate. These stems run much higher in price. There is an abundance of different types of serving pieces, enabling a person to choose the styles they like best.

    Having a nice table lamp in your dinnerware pattern to light up your living room is a nice plus that is not offered by most of the companies. The lamp and almond bowl are probably the hardest to find, followed closely by the bar bottle, cruet, decanter, pitcher, and urn shaped vase.

FUCHSIA	Crystal
Ashtray 2.25", individual w/cigarette rest	32
Basket 8.2", 2 sides turned up, 3 raised alternating points	60
Bell 5" #15083, dinner (made from champagne)	72
Bell 5.75" #9743, dinner, 7 graduated beads on handle	85
Bell 5.9" #17378, dinner (made from wine)	78
Bell 6.25" #17687, dinner (made from wine)	78
Bell 6.25" #9742, dinner, 7 graduated beads on handle	85
Bell 6.6" #17441, dinner (made from wine)	78
Bonbon 5" #5831, 2 handles turned up	40
Bottle w/chrome top 4.75" #9739, bitters, 5 oz.	175
Bottle w/cut stopper 11.5" #99, bar, 24 oz.	225
Bowl 2.5", flat, individual, almond	45
Bowl 4.9" #310, 3-footed, nut	48
Bowl 5.2" #5831, 2-handled	32
Bowl 6.25" #1502, nut	35
Bowl 7.25" #5902, shallow, flared, soup or salad	38
Bowl 8.4" #5831, 2-handled, salad	48
Bowl 9.5" #5831, 2-handled (novella)	56
Bowl 9.75", deep, salad, smooth edge	68
Bowl 10" #310, flared, salad	60
Bowl 10", rolled & crimped edge, salad	65
Bowl 10.5" #319, fan shape, 2 sides turned up	78
Bowl 10.5" #5831, 2-handled (morso tray)	70
Bowl 10.75" #5902, straight sided, salad	68
Bowl 11" #310, 3-footed, flared, salad	72
Bowl 11.6" #5831, flanged, centerpiece	78
Bowl 11.9", flared, smooth edge, console	75
Bowl 12.6" #5902, flared, centerpiece	85
Bowl 12.6", flared, smooth edge, console	75
Bowl 13" #5902, cone shape, centerpiece	74
Bowl 13" #5902, crimped, centerpiece	74
Cake plate 10.5" #5831, 2-handled	85
Candelabra 2-lite 6" #5831, pointed center, 7.1" spread, bobeches & prisms, pair	195
Candlestick 1-lite 3.5" #348, pair	65
Candlestick 1-lite 5" #5831, wafer stem, pair	78
Candlestick 2-lite 5" #17350, ball center, 9.1" spread, pair	98
Candlestick 2-lite 5.4" #15360, tapered center, 7" spread, pair	95
Candlestick 2-lite 5.6" #5902, plume center, 7.5" spread, pair	98
Cigarette box w/cover 4" #9305, rectangle	85
Cocktail shaker 11" #9798, flat, cylindrical, chrome top, 32 oz.	245
Comport 3.5" #5831, short stem, cupped, 6.5" wide	45
Comport 6.25" #5831, high stem, flared, 6.5" wide	40
Comport 6.25" #15082, 6 beads on stem, cupped, 6.5" wide	45
Cream soup & liner #5831: bowl 6.25", footed, handled, 9 oz.; saucer w/indent 7.1"	54
Creamer 3.25" #5831, footed, individual, 3.5 oz.	28
Creamer 3.4" #5902, flat, regular w/beaded handle, 6 oz.	24
Creamer 4.5" #5831, footed, regular, 6 oz.	24
Creamer 4.75" #185, footed, regular, 6 oz.	24
Cruet w/cut stopper #194, footed	145
Cup & saucer, coffee #5831: cup 2.25", footed, 6 oz.; saucer w/indent 6.25"	42
Decanter w/cut stopper 11.6" #9737, footed, 30 oz.	295
Decanter w/cut stopper 10.9" #14185, footed, 32 oz.	265
Finger bowl 4.25" #041, footed, 2.4" tall	40
Finger bowl & liner: bowl 4.6" #14196 (blown), flat, 12 oz.; #8814 plate w/ indent 6.25"	48
Goblet 4.1" #15083, cordial, 1 oz.	45
Goblet 4.9" #15083, #17453 stem, cordial, 1 oz.	48
Goblet 5.4" #17457, "S"-stem, cordial, 1.5 oz.	98
Goblet 5.4" #15083, sherry, 2 oz.	38
Goblet 5.1" #15083, wine, 3 oz.	32
Goblet 5.6" #17576, wine, 3 oz.	32
Goblet 4.25" #15083, liquor cocktail, 3.5 oz.	24
Goblet 4.6" #17453, cocktail, 3.5 oz.	24
Goblet 5.4" #17457, "S"-stem, cocktail, 3.5 oz.	48
Goblet 3.25" #14196, oyster cocktail, 4 oz.	18
Goblet 5.9" #15083, cafe parfait, 4.5 oz.	40
Goblet 5.25" #15083, #17453 stem, claret, 5 oz.	36
Goblet 5.25" #15083, claret, 5 oz.	36

Goblet 4.1" #15083, sundae or sherbet, 5.5 oz.	18
Goblet 3.9" #17457, "S"-stem, sherbet, 6 oz.	34
Goblet 5.4" #15083, champagne, 6 oz.	28
Goblet 5.75" #15083, #17453 stem, champagne, 6 oz.	28
Goblet 5.9" #17457, "S"-stem, champagne, 6 oz.	48
Goblet 5.75" #17453, saucer champagne, 6 oz.	28
Goblet 4.9" #13773, hollow stem champagne, 7 oz.	78
Goblet 6.25" #15083, lunch water, 9 oz.	26
Goblet 7.25" #17457, "S"-stem, water 9 oz.	58
Goblet 7.5" #15083, dinner water, 10 oz.	34
Goblet 7.9" #15083, #17453 stem, water, 10 oz.	34
Goblet 7.4" #17453, water, 10 oz.	34
Goblet 7.2" #17457, "S"-stem, ice tea, 11 oz.	68
Grapefruit 2 piece: bowl #215; use w/#881 insert (non-etched)	85
Hurricane lamp 12", 2 piece, 4" wide	245
Hurricane lamp 15", 2 piece, 3" wide	225
Ice dish 5.25" #5250, w/insert (plain)	75
Lamp 28" total, electric (glass part is the trophy handled vase)	475
Marmalade 7" #310 1/2, 3-footed	68
Mayonnaise 2 piece #5902: bowl 4.4", cupped; liner w/indent 6.25"	54
Mayonnaise bowl 4.5" #5909, salad dressing	58
Mayonnaise 2 piece #5831, bowl 5.4", footed; liner w/indent 7.1"	58
Pitcher 8" #5859, flat jug w/o ice lip, 64 oz.	325
Pitcher 8" #14194, footed w/o ice lip, 64 oz.	375
Pitcher w/cover 9.4" #14194, footed w/o ice lip, 64 oz.	475
Pitcher 8.4" #128, footed, wide optic, 66 oz.	300
Plate 6.25" #5831, sherbet	10
Plate 6.25" #5902, sherbet, 2.25" base	8
Plate 6.25" #8814, sherbet, 3.25" base	10
Plate 6.4" #5831, handled	14
Plate 7.5" #8814, dessert or salad	15
Plate 8" #8814, salad	16
Plate 8.1" #8833, salad or lunch (w/o optic)	20
Plate 8.25" #5902, salad or lunch	24
Plate 9.5", dinner	75
Plate 12.1" #310, crimped edge	58
Plate 13", rolled & crimped edge	65
Plate 13.5" #5902, small center, turned up edge, cabaret	68
Plate 14.25" #8833, sandwich or torte	58
Plate 14.6" #5902, small center, sandwich (no handles)	65
Platter 12.9" #5831, oval	145
Relish 6.4" #5902, round, 3 sections	35
Relish 7.4" #5831, oval pickle	28
Relish 9.25" #5902, square, 2 equal sections & celery section	40
Relish 10.5" #5831, oval celery	40
Relish 10.5" #5902, rectangle celery	48
Relish 12.5" #5902, tab handled, oblong, 2 equal sections & celery section	58
Relish 12.5" #5902, tab handled, 4 equal sections & celery section	65
Shaker 3.1" #2, chrome top, pair	98
Sugar 2.9" #5831, footed, individual, 3.5 oz.	28
Sugar 3.4" #5831, footed, regular, 6 oz.	24
Sugar 3.25" #5902, flat, regular w/beaded handle, 8 oz.	24
Sugar 4.6" #185, footed, regular, 6 oz.	24
Tray 7" #310 1/2, 3-footed, mint	32
Tray 9.25" #5831	42
Tray 9.5", tab handled for cream/sugar	35
Tray 10.5" #5909, 2 handles, turned up sides, muffin	75
Tray 12.5" #5902, center beaded handle	65
Tumbler 2.4" #15083, footed, bar whiskey, 2 oz.	42
Tumbler 2.5" #450, flat, sham, whiskey, 2.5 oz.	65
Tumbler 4.3" #15083, footed, seltzer/juice, 5 oz.	24
Tumbler 4.9" #517, flat, sham, seltzer/juice, 5 oz.	35
Tumbler 3.4" #663, flat, sham, old fashion, 7 oz.	48
Tumbler #9872, flat sham, hi ball, 7 oz.	48
Tumbler 7.4" #17454, footed, pilsner, 8 oz.	58
Tumbler 5.3" #15083, table water, 10 oz.	28
Tumbler 5.2" #517, flat, sham, table water, 10 oz.	45
Tumbler 6.5" #15083, footed, ice tea, 12 oz.	38
Tumbler 6.9" #15083, footed, #17453 stem, ice tea, 12 oz.	38
Tumbler 6" #517, flat, sham, ice tea, 12 oz.	50
Vase 4.5" #526, rose bowl	98
Vase 6.5" #14185, footed, tapered, bud vase	34
Vase 7.25" #17350, sweet pea	95
Vase 8.2", flared & crimped	85
Vase 8.25" #14185, footed, tapered, bud vase	38
Vase 8.5" #5856, footed, tear drop	135
Vase 9.25" #17350, footed, 1 ball stem, large tub shape	195
Vase 10.5" #14185, footed, tapered, bud vase	42
Vase 10.5" #319, large, handled, urn shape	275
Vase 10.75" #5872, spherical bottom	145
Vase 10.9" #15082, footed w/6 bead stem, flared, bud vase	78
Vase 11.25" #15144 1/2, footed, square base, handled	145
Vase 12" #5855, footed, short stem, flared	175

Left: Goblet 3.25" #14196, oyster cocktail, 4 oz. **Right:** Tumbler 6.5" #15083, footed, ice tea, 12 oz.

Back: Plate 14.6" #5902, sandwich (small center). **Front:** Bowl 10.75" #5902, straight sided, salad.

Back left to right: Vase 10.5" #14185, footed, tapered, bud vase; Vase 8.25" #14185, footed, tapered, bud vase; Plate 8" #8814, salad; Cocktail shaker 11" #9798, flat, cylindrical, chrome top, 32 oz. **Front row:** Sugar 3.25" #5902, flat, regular w/beaded handle, 8 oz.

Pattern detail, Gloria.

Top left: Cup & saucer, after dinner: cup 2.25" #69, 2 oz.; saucer 4.25" #69, 6 sided, Crystal. **Bottom left:** Creamer 3.8" #68, regular scalloped foot, 4.75 oz., Ebony (black). **Bottom center:** Bottle w/tube 3.5" #1217, flat, spherical bottom, bitters, 4 oz., Crystal. **Right:** Comport 7.5" #3400/14, fancy wafer stem, flared, 7" wide, Moonlight Blue.

Back left: Bowl 11" #3400/3, footed, flared, console, Peach Blo/ Dianthus (pink). **Back right:** Vase 9" #1228, oval, flared, melon shape, Ebony (black). **Front left & center:** Candlestick 1-lite 5.25" #3400/646, keyhole stem, pair, Peach Blo/Dianthus (pink). **Front center left:** Tumbler 2.5" #1070, flat, pinch, whiskey, 2 oz., Ruby w/silver encrusted. **Front right:** Bowl 2.4" #3400/71, tab handled, 4-footed, nut, Crystal; Bowl 3.25" #3400/70, tab handled, 4-footed, cranberry, Amber.

GLORIA
Cambridge Glass Company **Etching #746** **1931-58**
Main Colors: Crystal, Emerald Green, Green, Gold Krystol (yellow), and Peach Bl
Dianthus (pink)
Other Colors: Amber, Cobalt, Crown Tuscan, Ebony (black), Moonlight Blue, and Rub

With the poppy being a popular flower of the time period, Gloria was Cambridge's po trayal of this flower. This etched pattern is most often found in Crystal & Gold Krystol, a pa yellow color. Peach Blo came a close second and then followed by a multitude of colors. 1934, the Peach Blo name was changed to Dianthus but with no change in the color formula Most of the Gloria items are found on the #3400 blank. The boudoir collector highly prizes th perfume & puff boxes and will usually snatch them up ahead of the Gloria collector. Five differ ent nudes can be found etched in Gloria. These make a super addition to a nude collection. Th is an exciting etched pattern for those collectors that like unusual items, because of all th different items and treatments that can be found.

Many collectors will at times seem overwhelmed with all of the unusual pieces that coul be collected in Gloria. However, it still takes endless hours of looking to turn up even one. Th colors, treatments, and many blanks make this a fun etched pattern, since you never kno what will turn up. If you love glass, inevitably you seem to own at least one example of th elegant etched pattern.

There are many items that are hard for collectors to find. The following are just an ex ample: butter dish, cruet, nude stem, perfume bottle, pitcher, puff box, sugar sifter, and vase

Very few Amber, Black, Cobalt, Crown Tuscan, and Ruby pieces in this etched patter have shown up, thus making it hard to establish a consistent price.

GLORIA

	Crystal	Yellow	Green Pink
Basket 6.25" #3400/1182, 2 handles turned up	40	54	68
Bonbon 5.6" #3400/1179, low, flared, open handled	24	34	38
Bottle w/stopper (dauber) 2.5" #97, tilt ball, perfume, 2 oz.	295	375	400
Bottle w/tube 3.5" #1217, flat, spherical bottom, bitters, 4 oz.	125	165	185
Bowl 2.4" #3400/71, tab handled, 4-footed, nut	42	64	68
Bowl 3.25" #3400/70, tab handled, 4-footed, cranberry	60	78	86
Bowl 5" #25, footed/no stem, ruffled, nut	28	38	42
Bowl 5.25" #3400/56, shallow, fruit	24	32	36
Bowl 5.25" #3400/74, tab handled, 4-toed, mint	30	38	42
Bowl 5" #81, shallow, square, fruit	20	28	34
Bowl 5.25" #1180, handled, sweetmeat	24	32	36
Bowl 5.5" #26, footed/no stem, mint	26	34	38
Bowl 6" #13, tab handled, 4-footed, flared	28	36	42
Bowl 6" #3400/53, flared, cereal	32	42	48
Bowl 6" #82, square cereal	38	50	56
Bowl 9" #21, tab handled, salad	48	68	80
Bowl, 9.5" #3400/30, open handled, footed, keyhole stem	325	395	425
Bowl 9.5" #3400/34, open handled, vegetable	72	100	110
Bowl 10" #3400/51, oval, vegetable	64	92	100
Bowl 10" #3400/1185, deep, open handled	52	75	85
Bowl 11" #3400/3, footed, flared, console	64	92	100
Bowl 11" #3400/1188, handled, flared, fruit	64	92	100
Bowl 12" #3400/4, 4-footed, square, flared, edge	58	82	90
Bowl 12" #3400/5, footed, rolled edge, console	58	82	90
Bowl 12" #1240, 4-footed, oval, refectory	100	145	175
Bowl 13" #3400/1, flared, console	60	80	90
Box w/cover 4.5" #3400/95, tilt ball, puff w/keyhole finial	125	195	250
Butter w/cover 5.5" #3400/52, round, 2 open handles	210	295	350
Cake plate 10" #22, tab handled	60	82	90
Cake salver 11" #707, low, footed	115	175	200
Candlestick 1-lite 4" #627, round foot, faceted ball stem, pair	60	80	90
Candlestick 1-lite 5.25" #3400/646, keyhole stem, pair	80	110	125
Candlestick 1-lite 5.75" #3400/1192, small stem, pair	85	115	135
Candlestick 3-lite 7" #3400/638, keyhole stem, pair	115	175	200
Candy w/cover 6.5" #3400/9, 4-footed, tab handled, 7" wide; dome lid w/finial	150	195	225
Cheese & cracker: comport 3" #3400/7, short stem, flared, 5.3" wide, plate 11.5" #8, tab handled	70	90	100
Cigarette box w/cover 3.5" #1312, footed	100	135	150
Cigarette holder 4.6" #1066, oval, short stem, w/ashtray foot	70	95	110
Cocktail icer 4.6" #968, footed, 2 piece w/non-etched insert	70	90	98
Cocktail shaker #78, handled w/spout	165	225	250
Comport #15, no stem, 4" wide	20	28	34
Comport 5.3" #3400/28, keyhole stem, 7.25" wide	68	85	92
Comport 7" #1090 Decagon, tall stem, 7" wide	45	60	68
Comport 7.25" #3400/29, high, keyhole stem, 7" wide	70	90	100
Comport 7.5" #3400/14, fancy wafer stem, flared, 7" wide	60	82	86
Comport 7.75" #3011, banquet size nude stem, 6.6" wide	750	1,000+	
Cream soup & liner #3400/55: bowl 4.75", 2-handled, 9 oz., saucer w/indent 6.25"	85	115	130
Creamer 3.8" #68, regular scalloped foot, 4.75 oz.	24	32	36
Creamer #16, cone footed, regular, 6 oz.	28	38	42
Cruet w/stopper #3400/79, spherical, 6 oz.	135	195	225

Item			
Cup & saucer, after dinner #3400/69: cup 2.25", 2 oz.; saucer w/indent 4.25", 6 sided	80	110	125
Cup & saucer, after dinner: cup 2.25" #3400/83, 2 oz.; saucer w/indent 4", square	80	110	125
Cup & saucer, coffee #3400/50: cup 2.6", square footed, 6 oz.; saucer w/indent 5.8"	26	35	40
Cup & saucer, coffee #3400/54: cup 2.4", 6 oz.; saucer w/indent 5.5"	24	32	36
Decanter w/stopper 11" #1321, footed, 28 oz.	275	365	395
Decanter w/stopper 12" #1323, footed, 28 oz.	295	395	425
Finger bowl #3025, footed, bellied	38	52	58
Finger bowl & liner: bowl #3120, blown, tapered; plate w/indent	40	55	62
Finger bowl & liner: bowl #3134, blown; plate w/indent	40	55	62
Goblet 5.25" #3035, ball stem (cone bowl) cordial, 1 oz.	90	130	145
Goblet 5.25" #3120, wafer stem cordial, 1 oz.	70	100	120
Goblet 4.25" #3130, cordial, 1 oz.	65	95	115
Goblet 5.6" #3035, ball stem (cone bowl) wine, 2.5 oz.	30	42	50
Goblet 4.9" #3130, wine, 2.5 oz.	32	45	54
Goblet 6" #3035, ball stem (cone bowl) liquor cocktail, 3 oz.	24	32	36
Goblet 6" #3120, wafer stem cocktail, 3 oz.	24	32	36
Goblet 5.25" #3130, liquor cocktail, 3 oz.	50	65	75
Goblet 7.6" #3011, table size nude stem, cocktail, 3.5 oz.	450	600	
Goblet 4.4" #3035, ball stem (cone bowl) oyster cocktail, 4.5 oz.	20	28	32
Goblet 6.25" #3035, ball stem (cone bowl) claret, 4.5 oz.	48	72	80
Goblet 6.25" #3120, wafer stem claret, 4.5 oz.	45	70	78
Goblet 4.25" #3135, oyster cocktail, 4.5 oz.	20	26	30
Goblet 3.5" #1066, ball stem, oyster cocktail, 5 oz.	22	30	34
Goblet 4.75" #3035, ball stem (cone bowl) sherbet, 6 oz.	18	26	28
Goblet 6.4" #3035, ball stem (cone bowl) saucer champagne, 6 oz.	22	30	34
Goblet 4.75" #3120, wafer stem sherbet, 6 oz.	18	26	30
Goblet 6.4" #3120, wafer stem saucer champagne, 6 oz.	20	28	32
Goblet 4.25" #3130, sherbet, 6 oz.	18	24	28
Goblet 5.6" #3130, saucer champagne, 6 oz.	22	28	32
Goblet 4.25" #3135, sherbet, 6 oz.	18	26	28
Goblet 5.6" #3135, saucer champagne, 6 oz.	20	28	32
Goblet #3011, table size nude stem, saucer champagne, 7 oz.	375	500	
Goblet 7.25" #3130, water, 8 oz.	32	45	54
Goblet 7.25" #3135, water, 8 oz.	30	42	50
Goblet 8.25" #3035, ball stem (cone bowl) water, 9 oz.	30	42	56
Goblet 8.1" #3120, wafer stem water, 9 oz.	32	45	54
Goblet #3011, table size nude stem, water (table) 11 oz.	500	675	
Goblet 8.9" #3011, banquet size nude stem, water, 11 oz.	750	1,000	
Ice bucket 5.75" #3400/851, flat, scalloped top w/chrome handle	100	145	165
Mayonnaise 2 piece #3400: #13 bowl 5.8", 4-toed, flared, tab handled; #11 liner w/indent 5"	62	90	110
Pitcher 9.5" #3400/122, flat, tomato juice, 38 oz.	195	395	345
Pitcher w/cover #1205, footed, water, 64 oz.	295	450	500
Pitcher #3400/27, flat w/ice lip, 67 oz.	225	345	395
Pitcher 9" #3400/38, tilt ball w/ice lip, 80 oz.	295	450	500
Plate 6" #3400/60, bread & butter (6 sided)	10	14	16
Plate 6" #3400/1174, square, bread & butter	12	16	18
Plate 6" #3400/1181, 2 open handled, lemon server	18	24	28
Plate 7" #3400/61, tea or salad (6 sided)	14	18	20
Plate 8.5" #3400/62, lunch (6 sided)	18	24	28
Plate 8.5" #3400/1176, square, salad	15	19	22
Plate 9.5" #3400/63, dinner (6 sided)	65	86	95
Plate 9.5" #3400/1177, square, dinner	68	92	100
Plate 10.5" #3400/1178, square, service	36	48	54
Plate 11" #3400/35, open handled, sandwich	48	64	72
Plate 12.5" #3400/1186, oblong, open handled sandwich	50	68	76
Plate 14" #3400/65, chop w/large center	68	90	100
Platter 13.25" #3400/57, tab handled, oval	80	125	140
Relish 6" #3400/1093, center handled, oval, 2 sections	65	88	98
Relish 6.5" #3400/90, 2 open handles, 2 equal sections	34	45	50
Relish 8" #3500/57 Gadroon, 3 equal sections, 3 handled (candy bottom)	38	50	58
Relish 8.75" #3400/86, handled, oval, pickle	28	38	42
Relish 8.75" #3400/88, oblong, 2-handled, 2 sections	35	48	54
Relish 9" #3400/59, tab handled, oval, pickle	48	64	72
Relish 9" #862, center plume handled, 4 sections, oval	80	110	125
Relish 12" #3400/67, 4 equal sections & celery section	60	80	90
Sandwich server 11" #3400/10, center keyhole handle, tray	45	65	78
Shaker 3.25" #3400/76, footed, w/glass top, pair	58	80	90
Shaker 3.75" #3400/77, footed, w/glass top, pair	48	68	75
Shaker 4.5" #3400/18, footed, w/chrome top, pair	65	86	95

Top left: Bowl 5.25" #3400/56, shallow, fruit, Gold Krystol (yellow). **Top right:** Plate 7" #3400/61, tea or salad (6 sided), Gold Krystol (yellow). **Top right front:** Tumbler 2.5" #3130, footed, fruit salad, 8 oz., Gold Krystol (yellow). **Front left:** Cocktail icer 4.6" #968, footed, 2 piece w/non-etched insert, Crystal. **Front center:** Creamer & sugar #68, regular scalloped foot, Gold Krystol (yellow).

Back row: Plate 8.5" #3400/62, lunch (6 sided), Peach Blo/Dianthus (pink); Platter 13.25" #3400/57, tab handled, oval, Peach Blo/Dianthus (pink). **Front row:** Ice bucket 5.75" #3400/851, flat, scalloped top w/chrome handle, Peach Blo/Dianthus (pink); Cup & saucer, coffee #3400/54: cup 2.4", 6 oz.; saucer w/indent 5.5", Peach Blo/Dianthus (pink); Shaker 5" #3400/37, footed, chrome lid, Crystal; Tumbler 2.1" #3400/92, flat, whiskey, 2.5 oz., Crystal; Tumbler 2.5" #1070, flat, pinch, whiskey, 2 oz., Mocha (light amber); Vase 7.75" #1283, footed, convex sided, bud vase, Crystal.

Left: Goblet 4.25" #3130, cordial, 1 oz., Peach Blo/Dianthus (pink). **Center:** Goblet 5.25" #3130, liquor cocktail, 3 oz., Green). **Right:** Goblet 7.25" #3130, water, 8 oz., Gold Krystol (yellow).

Comport 7.75" #3011, banquet size nude stem, 6.6" wide, Emerald Green w/Crystal stem/foot

Back row: Tray 11.25" #660, flat, rectangular, dresser, Amber. **Front left & right:** Cologne w/keyhole stopper 2.5" #3400/97: tilt bottle, 2 oz.; stopper w/long dauber, Crystal. **Front center:** Box w/cover 4.5" #3400/95, tilt ball, puff w/keyhole finial, Crystal.

Plate 12.5" #3400/1186, oblong, open handled sandwich, Cobalt w/Platinum encrusted.

Shaker 5" #3400/37, footed, chrome lid, pair	100	145	175
Sugar 3" #3400/68 regular, scalloped foot, 5 oz.	24	32	36
Sugar #3400/16, cone footed, regular, 6 oz.	28	38	42
Sugar sifter 6.75" #3400/40, cone footed, shaker	195	295	345
Syrup or creamer 6.25" #3400/39, goes with sugar sifter	95	145	160
Tray 9" #1071, handled, round, service	38	50	58
Tray 11.25" #660, flat, rectangular, dresser	125	195	225
Tumbler 2.5" #1070, flat, pinch, whiskey, 2 oz.	48	64	72
Tumbler 2.1" #3400/92, flat, barrel, whiskey, 2.5 oz.	54	72	80
Tumbler 3.75" #3120, wafer stem, whiskey, 2.5 oz.	34	45	52
Tumbler 2.75" #3130, footed whiskey, 2.5 oz.	60	80	90
Tumbler 3.8" #3025, footed juice, 4 oz.	24	32	36
Tumbler 4" #3130, footed juice, 4.5 oz.	24	32	36
Tumbler 5.75" #3035, footed (cone bowl) juice, 5 oz.	22	30	34
Tumbler 5.75" #3120, wafer stem juice, 5 oz.	22	30	34
Tumbler 4" #3135, footed juice, 5 oz.	24	32	36
Tumbler 2.5" #3035, footed, fruit salad, 6 oz.	18	26	28
Tumbler 2.5" #3135, footed, fruit salad, 6 oz.	18	26	28
Tumbler #497, sham, cut flute, hi ball, 8 oz.	35	48	52
Tumbler 2.5" #3130, footed, fruit salad, 8 oz.	20	28	30
Tumbler 4.9" #497, sham, cut flute, straight sided, 9 oz.	38	52	58
Tumbler 4.8" #3130, footed, water (dinner) 9.5 oz.	34	45	52
Tumbler 7" #3035, footed (cone bowl) water, 10 oz.	26	36	40
Tumbler 7" #3120, wafer stem, water, 10 oz.	28	38	42
Tumbler 5.25" #3135, footed, water (dinner) 10 oz.	28	40	45
Tumbler 5.25" #3130, footed beverage, 11 oz.	30	42	50
Tumbler #3400/27, flat, ice tea, 12 oz.	32	48	54
Tumbler #3400/38, flat, ice tea, 12 oz.	30	45	52
Tumbler 7.5" #3035, footed (cone bowl) ice tea, 12 oz.	32	48	54
Tumbler 7.5" #3120, wafer stem, ice tea, 12 oz.	30	45	52
Tumbler 5.5" #1630, flat, straight sided, flared, 13 oz.	36	52	58
Tumbler 6" #3135, footed, ice tea, 13 oz.	32	48	54
Tumbler #3400/100, flat, beverage, 14 oz.	40	58	65
Tumbler #497, sham, cut flute, straight sided, 21 oz.	80	110	125
Vase 7" #1303, footed, spherical, necked, flared	100	135	150
Vase 7.75" #1283, footed, convex sided, bud vase	65	85	95
Vase 9" #1228, oval, flared, melon shape	120	175	195
Vase 10" #23, rectangular shape	145	225	250
Vase 10" #274, footed, flower holder, bud vase	75	98	120
Vase 10" #1284, footed, bud vase	70	95	115
Vase 10" #1305, keyhole stem, spherical shape	100	135	150
Vase 10.5" #3400/1242, flat, shouldered, flared	145	195	225
Vase 11" #1297, ribbed w/foot	120	165	190
Vase 11.5" #1299, footed, urn shape, ball stem	175	260	295
Vase 11.5" #3400/17, flat, rectangular shape	175	260	295
Vase 12" #402, spherical base, tapered sides, flared	145	195	225
Vase 12" #1238, keyhole stem, flared	145	195	225
Vase 14" #779, shouldered, flared	185	250	295
Vase 14" #1239, keyhole stem, flared	165	225	250

Back left: Vase 7" #1303, footed, spherical, necked, flared, Emerald Green w/Crystal foot. **Back center:** Relish 12" #3400/67, 4 equal sections & celery section, Moonlight Blue. **Front left:** Cigarette box w/cover 3.5" #1312, footed, Crown Tuscan w/Gold encrusted. **Center of photo:** Shaker 3.25" #3400/76, footed, w/glass top, Crystal w/Green foot. **Front center:** Butter w/cover 5.5" #3400/52, round, 2 open handles, Gold Krystol (yellow). **Right:** Vase 12" #402, spherical base, tapered sides, flared, Peach Blo/Dianthus (pink).

Left to right: Tumbler 3.8" #3025, footed juice, 4 oz., Crystal w/Green foot; Tumbler 3.75" #3120, wafer stem, whiskey, 2.5 oz., Crystal; Tumbler 2.75" #3130, footed whiskey, 2.5 oz., Gold Krystol (yellow); Tumbler 4" #3130, footed juice, 4.5 oz., Gold Krystol (yellow); Tumbler 4.8" #3130, footed, water (dinner) 9.5 oz., Gold Krystol (yellow).

Vase 9" #1228, oval, flared, melon shape, Ebony (black) w/Gold encrusted.

GOLF BALL

Morgantown Glass Works   **1931-39**

Main Colors: Crystal, Ritz Blue (cobalt), and Ruby

Other Colors: Anna Rose (pink), Milk Glass, Stiegel Green, Smoke, Topaz (yellow), and Venetian Green

The Golf Ball pattern actually resembles the texture of a real golf ball. There are many of the Morgantown blanks that use the Golf Ball pattern. They are: #78, #79, #1212, #7643, and #7678. Collectors will find stemware items fairly easy to find, while candlesticks and especially covered items are especially difficult. The price on the later items will preclude some collectors from adding them to their collections. The colored stems can be used with many of the plain crystal patterns of Morgantown. Cobalt & Ruby items are the most desirable of all of the colors.

All covered pieces are considered scarce. Collectors of stems are always vying for pieces of Golf Ball. There are other colors besides the Crystal, Cobalt, and Ruby that show up, but only sparingly, making it impossible to establish a normal value.

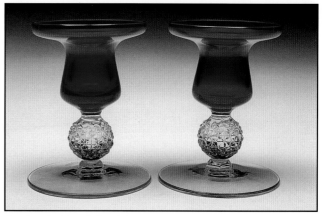

Candlesticks 1-lite 4" #7643 (Jacobi), cupped candle bowl & flared out top rim, Ruby.

GOLF BALL	Crystal	Cobalt	Ruby
Bell #7643 (Golf Ball), dinner	60	125	145
Candlestick 1-lite 4" #7643 (Jacobi), cupped candle bowl & flared out top rim, pair	150	325	350
Candlestick 1-lite 4.6" #7643 (Dupont), straight sided & tapered out top half, pair	90	365	395
Candlestick 1-lite 6" #7643 (Golf Ball), straight sided bowl & flared top rim, pair	125	350	450
Candy w/cover 5.25" #2938 (Helga), low footed	165	485	545
Candy w/cover 5.25" #7643-1 (Alexandra), flat, round, cone lid, 6" wide	185	545	600+
Candy w/cover 5.25" #9074 (Belton), footed, cone shaped lid & base, 4.5" wide	150	395	425
Candy w/cover 5.5" #1212 (Michael), flat w/golf ball finial, round, 7" wide	125	325	350
Candy w/cover 6" #7858 (Leora), footed, cone lid w/ golf ball finial, 5" wide	150	395	425
Candy w/cover 8" #14 1/2 (Fairway), footed, cone shape, 22 oz.	165	425	475
Cookie jar w/cover 6" #64 (Ravena), footed, ball shape	125	325	350
Comport 6" #7678 (Old English), footed, wide	30	80	95
Comport w/cover 9" #7643 (Celeste), footed, clear golf ball finial & stem, 6" wide	150	395	495
Creamer 5.25" #7643 (Golf Ball), footed, applied handle	36	95	115
Goblet 3.5" #7643 (Golf Ball), cordial, 1.5 oz.	32	50	60
Goblet #7678 (Old English), cordial, 1.5 oz.	35	65	75
Goblet 4.6" #7643 (Golf Ball), wine, 3 oz.	20	52	65
Goblet 4.6" #7678 (Old English), wine, 3 oz.	22	55	68
Goblet 4.2" #7643 (Golf Ball), liquor cocktail, 3.5 oz.	15	40	45
Goblet 5.25" #7643 (Golf Ball), claret, 4.5 oz.	15	40	45
Goblet 6.25" #7678 (Old English), claret, 5 oz.	22	55	68
Goblet #7678 (Old English), high, cafe parfait, 5 oz.	28	72	82
Goblet 3.9" #7643 (Golf Ball), sherbet or sundae, 5.5 oz.	14	35	40
Goblet 4.9" #7643 (Golf Ball), saucer champagne, 5.5 oz.	15	40	45
Goblet 5.25" #7643 (Golf Ball), handled, Irish coffee, 6 oz.	65	145	175
Goblet #7678 (Old English), saucer champagne, 6.5 oz.	15	40	45
Goblet 6.75" #7643 (Golf Ball), water, 9 oz.	20	52	65
Goblet #7678 (Old English), water, 10 oz.	22	55	68
Goblet 9.1" #7643 (Golf Ball), pilsner, 11 oz.	40	100	120
Goblet 6.5" #7643 (Golf Ball), brandy snifter, 21 oz.	45	125	140
Goblet 8.5" #7643 (Golf Ball), schooner, 32 oz.	65	180	195
Sugar 4" #7643 (Golf Ball), cone footed, applied handle	36	90	110
Tumbler 4.3" #7643 (Golf Ball), footed wine, 2.5 oz.	18	52	60
Tumbler 4.6" #7643 (Golf Ball), footed sherry, 2.5 oz.	22	55	68
Tumbler #7678 (Old English), footed wine, 2.5 oz.	16	48	54
Tumbler 4.25" #7643 (Golf Ball), footed, flared, oyster cocktail, 4 oz.	15	40	45
Tumbler 4.3" #7643 (Golf Ball), footed, cupped, oyster cocktail, 4.5 oz.	16	48	54
Tumbler 5" #7643 (Golf Ball), footed juice, 5 oz.	15	40	45
Tumbler 6.25" #7643 (Golf Ball), footed cafe parfait, 5 oz.	26	72	82
Tumbler #7678 (Old English), footed juice, 5 oz.	15	40	45
Tumbler 6.1" #7643 (Golf Ball), footed water, 9 oz.	18	52	60
Tumbler #7678 (Old English), footed lunch, 10 oz.	16	48	54
Tumbler 6.75" #7643 (Golf Ball), footed, ice tea, 12 oz.	16	48	54
Tumbler #7678 (Old English), footed, ice tea, 13 oz.	18	52	60
Vase 6.75" #7643 (Kennon), footed, ivy ball, plain top	24	68	75
Vase 6.75" #7643 (Kimball), footed, ivy ball, short flared neck	28	78	85
Vase 6.75" #7643, footed, urn shape, flared	50	135	145
Vase 8" #7643 (Charlotte), footed, flared	75	245	275
Vase 8" #7643 (Charlotte), footed, flared & crimped top	80	235	265
Vase 10.5" #78 (Lancaster), footed, symmetrical	110	345	375
Vase 11" #79 (Montague), footed, shouldered, flared	145	375	400

Ritz Blue (cobalt) grouping: **Left to right:** Goblet 3.5" #7643 (Golf Ball), cordial, 1.5 oz.; Goblet 4.6" #7643 (Golf Ball), wine, 3 oz.; Goblet 4.2" #7643 (Golf Ball), liquor cocktail, 3.5 oz.; Goblet 3.9" #7643 (Golf Ball), sherbet or sundae, 5.5 oz.; Goblet 4.9" #7643 (Golf Ball), saucer champagne, 5.5 oz.; Goblet 6.75" #7643 (Golf Ball), water, 9 oz.

Ritz Blue (cobalt) grouping: **Left:** Goblet #7678 (Old English), saucer champagne, 6.5 oz. **Right:** Goblet #7678 (Old English), water, 10 oz.

Left: Vase 6.75" #7643, footed, urn shape, flared, Ruby w/Crystal stem/foot. **Center left:** Candlestick 1-lite 6" #7643 (Golf Ball), straight sided bowl & flared top rim, Ruby w/Crystal stem/foot. **Center right:** Vase 6.75" #7643 (Kimball), footed, ivy ball, short flared neck, Stiegel Green w/Crystal stem/foot. **Right:** Vase 6.75" #7643 (Kimball), footed, ivy ball, short flared neck, Ruby w/Crystal stem/foot.

Pattern detail, Gothic Garden.

Crystal w/Gold encrusted grouping: **Back row:** Plate 11.25" #211 Spire, 2 handled, sandwich. **Front left:** Bowl 9.25" #211 Spire, flat, round, flared w/tab handles. **Front right:** Cake salver 12" #211 Spire, footed, round, 3.75" high.

Ebony (black) grouping: **Left:** Vase 8" #182-8, flat, elliptical (pillow shape). **Right:** Vase 10" #184-10, flat, spherical bottom, flared.

GOTHIC GARDEN
Paden City Glass Company   1930s-40s
Main Colors: Cheriglo (pink), Ebony (black), Green, and Yellow
Other Colors: Amber and Crystal

A large number of collectors for Gothic Garden enthusiastically asked to have this etched pattern included with the many elegant listings. Gothic Garden is another Paden City etched pattern we had in our first edition. Like other Paden City etched patterns, we are not always sure what pattern we will find etched with Gothic Garden. Line #411, also known as Mrs. "B", seems to be the blank most often etched with Gothic Garden.

Everyone is looking for the elusive stemware. Yellow is the most predominant color in this etched pattern. A complete place setting can be found, but it will take extensive looking. The goblets are found on a Tiffin blank number 15041 lady leg stem and seem to be less prevalent on the West Coast.

Crystal & Amber should be priced at 50% the price of Black & Yellow. Amber seems to be hard to find and only has a very limited collector interest. We would think that Cobalt or Ruby could be possibly found, but several knowledgeable people have reported that they have never found any pieces so far. On eBay, a ruby #412 flared vase was reported to us in 2003. For more information you can refer to the book *Paden City Glass Company* by William P. Walker, Melissa Bratkovich & Joan C. Walker.

GOTHIC GARDEN	Black Yellow	Green Cheriglo (pink)
Bowl 4.5", handled, deep	35	45
Bowl 4.75", handled, flared	38	48
Bowl 6.25" #411 Mrs. "B", flat	35	45
Bowl 6.75" (decagon shape), handles turned up	45	58
Bowl 9" #411 Mrs. "B", cupped center handled server	125	160
Bowl 9" #411 Mrs. "B", deep, handled	75	95
Bowl 9" #411 Mrs. "B", footed, flared	95	120
Bowl 9" #411 Mrs. "B", shallow, flared	75	95
Bowl 9.25" #211 Spire, flat, round, flared w/tab handles	125	160
Bowl 9.75" #411 Mrs. "B", 2 open handled	100	125
Bowl 10" #300 Archaic, deep, flared	225	285
Bowl 10" #411 Mrs. "B", flared	125	160
Bowl 10.5" #411 Mrs. "B", handled, oval	150	185
Bowl 10.5" #411 Mrs. "B", rolled edge	125	160
Bowl 10.75" #411 Mrs. "B", oval, handled	125	160
Bowl 11.25" #411 Mrs. "B", flat top	100	125
Bowl 13" #411 Mrs. "B", rolled edge	150	185
Cake salver 9.25" #411 Mrs. "B", low, footed, 1.9" high	95	120
Cake salver 9.5" #412 Crow's Foot (square), low, footed, 2" high	85	110
Cake salver 12" #211 Spire, footed, round, 3.75" high	125	160
Candlestick 1-lite 5.25" #411 Mrs. "B", square dome footed, keyhole stem, pair	165	185
Candy jar w/cover 6" #701 Triumph, footed, (round bottom) square lid w/ball finial	145	185
Candy box w/cover 6.5" #411 Mrs. "B", flat, square, 2 or 3 sections	125	165
Candy w/cover 7" #211 Spire, round	150	185
Candy w/cover 7.5" #411 Mrs. "B", flat, (round bottom) square lid, 3 equal sections	150	185
Cheese & cracker: comport 2.25" #411 Mrs. "B", low stem, 4.75" wide; plate 9.75"	100	145
Comport 3.1" #411 Mrs. "B", low, flared, 6.4" wide	65	80
Comport 3.75" #411 Mrs. "B", low, flared, 6.25" wide	65	80
Comport 4" #411 Mrs. "B", low, deep, 6" wide	75	90
Comport 4" #411 Mrs. "B", low, flat, 9.5" wide	85	110
Comport 4.25" #411 Mrs. "B", low, flared oval, 7.5" wide	95	120
Comport 4.5" #411 Mrs. "B", cupped & flared, oval, 7.5" wide	125	160
Comport 4.5" #411 Mrs. "B", low, flared, 9" wide	95	120
Comport 6" #411 Mrs. "B", high, deep, 6.8" wide	95	120
Comport 6.6" #411 Mrs. "B", high, flared, 7" wide	95	120
Creamer 3.5" #411 Mrs. "B", flat, deco handle, 6 oz.	45	58
Cup & saucer, coffee #411 Mrs. "B": cup 2.4", 6 oz.; saucer w/indent 5.75"	75	92
Goblet 3.4" #15047 Tiffin Blank, lady leg stem, sherbet (paneled optic) 5 oz.	75	125
Goblet 5.75" #15047 Tiffin Blank, lady leg stem, saucer champagne (paneled optic) 7 oz.	85	160
Goblet 7.5" #15047 Tiffin Blank, lady leg stem, water (paneled optic) 10 oz.	95	185
Mayonnaise 2 piece #411 Mrs. "B": footed bowl 5.75", rolled edge; liner w/indent 7.25"	95	145
Pitcher w/cover 8" #3, flat, rectangular batter w/knob finial, 30 oz.	150	185
Plate 7.25" #411 Mrs. "B", footed, 1.6" high	40	50
Plate 8.5" #411 Mrs. "B", lunch	60	75
Plate 9.75" #411 Mrs. "B", dinner	95	120
Plate 10" #411 Mrs. "B", handled	85	110
Plate 10.5" #211 Spire, service	75	90
Plate 11.25" #211 Spire, 2-handled, sandwich	85	110
Plate 11.5" #211 Spire, handled	85	110

...ate 14" #211 Spire, 4-footed	125	160
...andwich server 10" #411 Mrs. "B", center handled tray	75	120
...andwich server 10.5" #300 Archaic, center cup handled tray	175	225
...andwich server 11" #211 Spire, center handled tray	85	110
...ugar 3.5" #411 Mrs. "B", flat, deco handled, 6 oz.	45	58
...ray 12" #411 Mrs. "B", handled, oval	125	160
...ase 4" #411-4 Mrs. "B", footed, ivy ball, cupped top	145	175
...ase 4.75" #191 1/2 party Line, flat, 1 ring on base, shouldered, flared	150	185
...ase 4.75" #411-5 Mrs. "B", footed, rose bowl, flared top	115	150
...ase 6.5" #210-7 Regina, flat, 3 rings on base & neck shouldered, flared	125	160
...ase 8" O'Kane, spherical bottom, narrow flared neck	200	250
...ase 8" #182-8, flat, elliptical (pillow shape)	200	250
...ase 8" #184-8, flat, spherical bottom, flared	145	175
...ase 9.25" #411-9 Mrs. "B", flat, rectangular	175	225
...ase 10" #184-10, flat, spherical bottom, flared	200	250
...ase 10.25", flat, necked in at top & flared	250	300
...ase 10.25" #412-10 Crow's Foot (square), flat, concave sided w/slightly flared	350	425

Yellow grouping: **Left:** Goblet 3.4" #15047 Tiffin Blank, lady leg stem, sherbet (paneled optic) 5 oz. **Center:** Goblet 5.75" #15047 Tiffin Blank, lady leg stem, saucer champagne (paneled optic). **Right:** Goblet 7.5" #15047 Tiffin Blank, lady leg stem, water (paneled optic) 10 oz.

Top left: Vase 4.75" #191 1/2 Party Line, flat, 1 ring on base, shouldered, flared, Ebony (black). **Top center:** Sugar 3.5" #411 Mrs. "B", flat, deco handled, 6 oz., Green. **Top right:** Vase 4" #411-4 Mrs. "B", footed, ivy ball, cupped top, yellow. **Bottom left:** Bowl 9" #411 Mrs. "B", deep, handled, Amber. **Bottom center:** Creamer 3.5" #411 Mrs. "B", flat, deco handle, 6 oz., Green. **Bottom right:** Candlestick 1-lite 5.25" #411 Mrs. "B", square dome footed, keyhole stem, Cheriglo (pink).

Yellow grouping: **Top left:** Bowl 9" #411 Mrs. "B", shallow, flared. **Top right:** Bowl 9" #411 Mrs. "B", deep, handled. **Center of photo:** Bowl 6.25" #411 Mrs. "B", flat. **Bottom left:** Bowl 4.5", handled, deep. **Bottom right:** Bowl 4.75", handled, flared.

Yellow grouping: **Left:** Candy box w/cover 6.5" #411 Mrs. "B", flat, square, 3 equal sections. **Right:** Candy box w/cover 6.5" #411 Mrs. "B", flat, square, 2 equal sections.

Left: Bowl 9" #411 Mrs. "B", cupped center handled server, Yellow. **Top right:** Bowl 10.5" #411 Mrs. "B", handled, oval, Green. **Bottom left:** Sandwich server 10.5" #300 Archaic, center cup handled tray, Yellow.

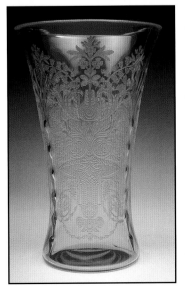

Vase 10.25" #412-10 Crow's Foot (square), flat, concave sided w/slightly flared, Green.

HEATHER
Fostoria Glass Company **Etching #343** **1949-82**
Color: Crystal

Fostoria was the only glass company to have an etched pattern based on the Heather flower. This etching utilizes the #2630 Century blank. For many years collectors seemed to prefer the Century over the etched Heather. This caused Heather items to remain below the prices of Century pieces. In 2003, new collectors were finding this etched pattern and prices are gradually starting to climb. The stemware and tumblers are on the Silver Flutes #6037 blank.

Dealers are reporting that this is one of the up and coming etched patterns among young collectors. Finally, more people are asking for it at shows. All of the vases were only produced in the 1950s, thus making them harder to find today. The pitcher with the ice lip was only made for two years. All of the other pieces were made for the whole length of the etched pattern, which gives the collector an easier time finding these items.

Pattern detail, Heather.

HEATHER	Crystal
Basket 10.25" #2630 Century, oval w/reed handle	95
Bonbon 7.1" #2630 Century, 3-toed, tri-corn, cupped	24
Bonbon 7.25" #2630 Century, 3-toed, round, flared	24
Bowl 3.5" #2630 Century, footed, deep, snack	38
Bowl 4.5" #2630 Century, one handled	20
Bowl 5" #2630 Century, fruit or berry	20
Bowl 6" #2630 Century, flared cereal	35
Bowl 8", #2630 Century, deep, cupped or w/slightly flared	45
Bowl 8.5" #2630 Century, deep salad	50
Bowl 9" #2630 Century, flat, shallow lily pond, cupped edge	42
Bowl 9.5" #2630 Century, flat, oval vegetable, 6.5" wide	55
Bowl 10" #2630 Century, handled, oval, utility	45
Bowl 10.5" #2630 Century, deep, cupped, salad	65
Bowl 10.5" #2630 Century, handled, oval	48
Bowl 10.75" #2630 Century, footed, flared, fruit (sherbet shape)	48
Bowl 11" #2630 Century, footed, rolled edge, console	60
Bowl 11.25" #2630 Century, flat, shallow lily pond, cupped edge	58
Bowl 12" #2630 Century, flared, shallow, fruit	50
Butter w/cover 7.5" #2630 Century, handled, oblong, .25 lb.	58
Cake plate 9.5" #2630 Century, handled	36
Cake salver 12.25" #2630 Century, low pedestal	85
Candlestick 1-lite 4.5" #2630 Century, curled stem, pair	45
Candlestick 2-lite 7" #2630 Century, w/curled "C" stems, 6.6" spread, pair	76
Candlestick 3-lite 7.75" #2630 Century, w/1 curled "C" arm over a leaning "S" arm, 7.5" spread, pair	92
Candy jar w/cover 6.75" #2630 Century: footed, short stem; curlicue finial	58
Cheese & cracker #2630 Century: comport 2.5", short stem, 5.4" wide; plate w/indent 10.75"	48
Comport 4.3" #2630 Century, flared, 4.75" wide	20
Creamer 3.5" #2630 Century, footed individual, 3.5 oz.	16
Creamer 4.25" #2630 Century, footed regular, 7 oz.	18
Cruet w/stopper 6" #2630 Century, oil bottle, 5 oz.	65
Cup & saucer, coffee #2630 Century: cup 2.5", footed, 6 oz.; saucer w/indent 6"16	16
Goblet 4" #6037 Silver Flutes, cordial, 1 oz.	48
Goblet 5" #6037 Silver Flutes, cocktail, 4 oz.	24
Goblet 6" #6037 Silver Flutes, claret/wine, 4 oz.	30
Goblet 4" #6037 Silver Flutes, oyster cocktail, 4.5 oz.	16
Goblet 6.1" #6037 Silver Flutes, parfait, 6 oz.	30

	Crystal
Goblet 4.75" #6037 Silver Flutes, sherbet, 7 oz.	1
Goblet 6" #6037 Silver Flutes, saucer champagne, 7 oz.	1
Goblet 6.4" #6037 Silver Flutes, lunch water, 9 oz.	2
Goblet 7.9" #6037 Silver Flutes, dinner water, 9 oz.	2
Ice bucket 4.8" #2630 Century, chrome handle, 7.3 wide	85
Mayonnaise 2 piece #2630 Century: bowl 3.25", footed, flared; liner w/indent 7"	48
Mayonnaise 2 piece #2630 Century: bowl 3.25", footed, salad dressing; liner w/indent 7"	58
Mustard 3 piece #2630 Century 4"; footed jar, cover, & spoon	85
Pitcher 6.1" #2630 Century, cereal w/o ice lip, 16 oz.	90
Pitcher 7.1" #2630 Century, water w/o ice lip, 48 oz.	145
Pitcher 9.5" #2630 Century, water w/large ice lip, 48 oz.	185
Plate 6" #2630 Century, bread & butter	8
Plate 7.25" #2630 Century, salad or dessert	10
Plate 7.5" #2630 Century, crescent salad (kidney shape)	65
Plate 8.25" #2630 Century, party round w/off center indent	35
Plate 8.1" #2630 Century, 3-toed, round, tidbit	18
Plate 8.5" #2630 Century, lunch	18
Plate 9.5" #2630 Century, small dinner	30
Plate 10.25" #2630 Century, large dinner	45
Plate 14" #2630 Century, torte (small center)	48
Plate 16" #2630 Century, torte (small center)	58
Platter 12" #2630 Century, oval	75
Preserve w/cover 6" #2630 Century, footed	58
Relish 7.4" #2630 Century, handled, oval, 2 sections	28
Relish 8.75" #2630 Century, oval pickle	24
Relish 11.1" #2630 Century, handled, oval, 2 equal sections & celery section	35
Sandwich server 11.25" #2630 Century, center "S" shaped handle	40
Shakers 3.25" #2630 Century, regular w/chrome top, pair	45
Sugar 3.4" #2630 Century, footed, individual, 3.5 oz.	16
Sugar 4" #2630 Century, footed regular, 7 oz.	18
Tray 7.1" #2630 Century, for cream/sugar or oil/vinegar	28
Tray 9.1" #2630 Century, handled, utility, cupped	38
Tray 9.75" #2630 Century, handles turned up, muffin	45
Tray 2 tier 10.25" #2630 Century, plates w/chrome center handle	75
Tray 10.5" #2630 Century, small center, turned up edge, cabaret	34
Tumbler 4.9" #6037 Silver Flutes, footed juice, 5 oz.	28
Tumbler 6.1" #6037 Silver Flutes, footed, ice tea, 12 oz.	38
Vase 5" #4121, flat, symmetrical, melon shape, necked & flared	48
Vase 6" #2630 Century, footed, short stem, bud vase	38
Vase 6" #4143, footed, large flared top	75
Vase 6" #6021, footed, necked flared, bud vase	45
Vase 7.5" #2630 Century, flat, flared, 2-handled	85
Vase 8" #2660, flat, flip w/o optic	98
Vase 8" #5092, footed, spherical base, flared, bud vase	50
Vase 8.5" #2630 Century, flat, oval shape	95
Vase 9.5" #2470, footed w/3 scroll stem & flared	125

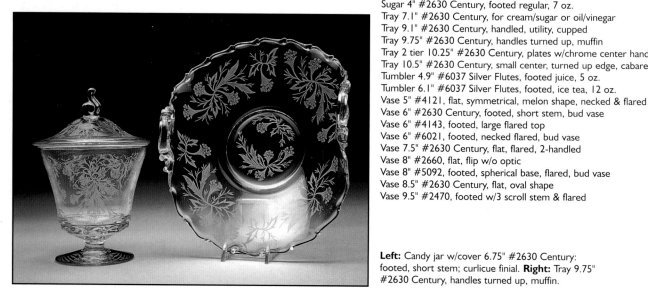

Left: Candy jar w/cover 6.75" #2630 Century: footed, short stem; curlicue finial. **Right:** Tray 9.75" #2630 Century, handles turned up, muffin.

HEIRLOOM
Fostoria Glass Company
1959-70

Colors: Bittersweet (orange), Blue Opalescent, Green Opalescent, Pink Opalescent, Ruby, White Opalescent, and Yellow Opalescent

Heirloom was one of Fostoria's first attempts at making a pattern exclusively for decorating homes and not for serving on the table. This marked a revolutionary change to how people viewed Fostoria. Now people could associate Fostoria with glass to decorate their homes. The glass starts in a mould and then is hand formed into dramatic statements. Heirloom was given the name since it looks modern but was made the same way as antique glass. You would almost think this was two completely different patterns since this has both wide and narrow panels. All the pastel colors have an opalescent fire look to them. Ruby & Bittersweet (orange) were also available but not in every shape.

Many people look only for particular items that will blend in with the decor in their home and don't necessarily collect this pattern. Note: any star-crimped item is hard to find. The Bittersweet orange color is gradually attracting collectors. These pieces are a real delight to have during the fall season and when decorating for Halloween. The large orange epergne is hard to find and looks great for a centerpiece on a table with black flowers.

Green Opalescent grouping: **Top left:** Bowl 11" #2727/231, shallow, flared round. **Top right:** Candle bowl 1-lite 7.5" to 9" #2183/311, flared flora, one point pulled up. **Front left:** Bonbon 6" #2729/135, hand grip plate. **Front center left:** Vase 11" #1515/827, medium swung. **Front center right:** Vase 6" #1229/757, small swung, bud vase. **Front right:** Bowl 6" #2727/152, handkerchief shape.

HEIRLOOM

	Orange	White opal	Ruby	Green opal	Blue Pink opal	Yellow opal
Basket 12" #2720/126, 4 pointed bowl, w/2 points curled over (does not touch)	30	32		40	45	50
Bonbon 6" #2729/135, hand grip plate	14	20	28	28	35	38
Bowl 5.5" #2727/3, star shape, 5 points	24	33	35	45	50	55
Bowl 6" #2727/152, handkerchief shape	15	22	24	35	40	45
Bowl 6" #2727/155, square crimped	14	20		26	30	35
Bowl 6.5" #2720/168, crinkle, pulled up	12	20		26	30	35
Bowl 7" #2183/168, straight sided	14	20	24	30	35	38
Bowl 7" #2720/170, square florette, 4 pointed, w/4 points curled over (does not touch)	14	20		30	35	38
Bowl 8.5" #2720/191, star shape, 4 points pulled out at 90° angles	24	32		38	40	45
Bowl 9" #2727/202, flat, square crimped	24	32		35	45	58
Bowl 10" #1515/208, deep, handkerchief shape	24	42		60	75	85
Bowl 10" #2183/415, shallow, flower float	18	22		38	42	48
Bowl 10" #2729/540, narrow, flared oval	18	22	32	35	40	45
Bowl 11" #2727/231, shallow, flared round	20	34		40	45	52
Bowl 11" #2727/239, low, round, crimped	22	35	40	45	50	55
Bowl 12" #2730/255, narrow oval, flared centerpiece	18	30		34	45	60
Bowl 15" #1515/270, flat, oblong, low flared, console	28	45		65	75	85
Bowl 16" #1515/279, flat, oval, irregular edge, centerpiece, flared & crimped	30	55	60	75	85	95
Candle bowl 1-lite 7.5" to 9" #2183/311, flared flora, one point pulled up (one side only) pair	40	45		60	65	75
Candle vase 1-lite 10" #1515/311, pulled up on 1 side, pair	40	50		65	75	85
Candlestick 1-lite 3" to 3.5" #2726/311, looks like a sheaf of wheat, pair	30	35	45	50	60	68
Candlestick 1-lite 6" #2730/319, bell footed, pair	40	45		75	85	95
Epergne 12" #2730/364, small, 2 piece, oval	75	75		100	125	145
Epergne 16" #1515/364, large, 2 piece, oblong, Note use vase #312 for center horn	125	125		195	225	245
Plate 8" #2727/550, flat, round, small	14	20		24	28	32
Plate 11" #2727/557, flat, round, large	18	30		38	48	55
Plate 17" #2470/575, flat, large pulled out service	24	40		52	68	75
Table charms 10" #2722/364, consisting of: 3-lite candle arm (clear), 1 peg vase, 3 flora candle bowls		100		145	165	185
Table charms 10" #2722/364, consisting of: 3-lite candle arm (clear), 3 peg vases, 1 flora candle bowl		100		145	165	185

Blue Opalescent grouping: **Top:** Bowl 5.5" #2727/3, star shape, 5 points. **Front left:** Bowl 6" #2727/152, handkerchief shape. **Front right:** Bowl 6.5" #2720/168, crinkle, pulled up.

Bowl 16" #1515/279, flat, oval, irregular edge, centerpiece, flared & crimped, Blue Opalescent.

Grouping of Candle bowls 1-lite 7.5" to 9" #2183/311, flared flora, one point pulled up. **Top left:** Blue Opalescent. **Top Right:** Pink Opalescent. **Bottom left:** Bittersweet (orange). **Bottom right:** Yellow Opalescent.

Vase 9" #2728/807, ewer or pitcher vase, 1 curled handle w/long pulled spout (will not pour liquid), Blue Opalescent.

Epergne 12" #2730/364, small, 2 piece, oval, Pink Opalescent.

Table charms 10" #2722/364, consisting of: 3-lite candle arm (clear), 3 flora candle bowls		85		115	125	145
Table charms 10" #2722/364, consisting of: 3-lite candle arm (clear), 3 peg vases		85		115	125	145
Vase 4.5" #2728/751, 2 curled handles	30	40		50	60	85
Vase 6" #1229/757, small swung, bud vase	20	20	24	24	28	28
Vase 9" #2728/807, ewer or pitcher vase 1 curled handle w/long pulled spout (will not pour liquid)	24	32	45	60	85	110
Vase 11" #1515/827, medium swung	30	35	40	40	45	60
Vase 11" #2728/827, winged 2 pulled sides form wings (1960 only)	100	125		150	160	175
Vase 18" #1002/833, large swung flared (1959 only)	95	195		195	200	225
Vase 20" #1002/834, large swung flared	95	150		160	175	195
Vase 24" #1002/834, large swung flared	95	195		195	200	225

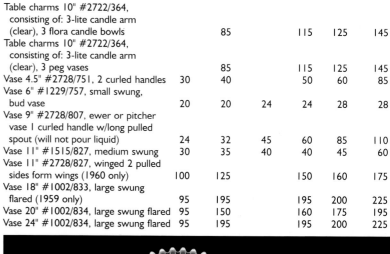

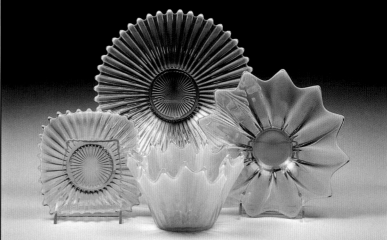

Pink Opalescent grouping: **Back top:** Bowl 11" #2727/231, shallow, flared round. **Left:** Bowl 6" #2727/155, square crimped. **Center:** Bowl 6" #2727/152, handkerchief shape. **Right:** Bowl 10" #2183/415, shallow, flower float.

Candlestick 1-lite 6" #2730/319, pulled to fan shape, bud vase, whimsey, 4.75" wide, Yellow Opalescent.

Grouping of Candlesticks 1-lite 3" to 3.5" #2726/311, looks like a sheaf of wheat. **Top left:** Ruby. **Top Center:** Pink Opalescent. **Top right:** Green Opalescent. **Bottom left:** Yellow Opalescent. **Bottom center left:** White Opalescent. **Bottom center right:** Bittersweet (orange). **Bottom right:** Blue Opalescent.

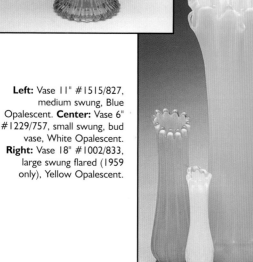

Left: Vase 11" #1515/827, medium swung, Blue Opalescent. **Center:** Vase 6" #1229/757, small swung, bud vase, White Opalescent. **Right:** Vase 18" #1002/833, large swung flared (1959 only), Yellow Opalescent.

Left: Table charms 10" #2722/364, consisting of: 3-lite candle arm (clear), 1 peg vase, 3 flora candle bowls, Pink Opalescent. **Right:** Table charms 10" #2722/364, consisting of: 3-lite candle arm (clear), 3 peg vases, 1 flora candle bowl, Yellow Opalescent.

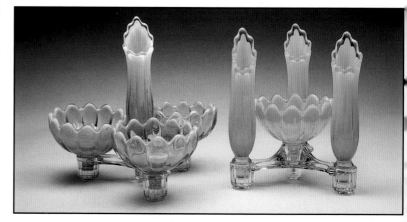

Wisteria grouping: **Left:** Goblet 3", sherbet, 7 oz. **Center:** Tumbler 3.25", flat old fashion, 6 oz. **Right:** Goblet 5.25", water, 9 oz.

HERMITAGE
Fostoria Glass Company   **Blank #2449**   **1932-45**
Main Colors: Amber, Azure (blue), Crystal, Green, Topaz (yellow), and Wisteria (lilac)
Other Color: Ebony (black)

  With the repeal of Prohibition, Fostoria was ready to offer the public a complete barware line. Hermitage became popular and, as sales grew, the line was expanded to offer a full dinnerware line. In early advertisements, Fostoria suggested mixing of the colors to create a rainbow effect on your table. What was once popular, eventually is again. More customers now seem to be buying several colors to mix together.

  The bar bottle seems to have been made in two versions. One had a plain glass topper while another had a chrome shield that came down over the top of the bottle and over the shoulder. The ice dish with the matching colored insert is extremely hard to find. The ice dishes are most often found without any #2451 insert, or if an insert is there, it is the tomato. We find the #2451 crab meat and fruit cocktail inserts much harder to find. One added problem is that these #2451 inserts are also used in other patterns. When you have several collectors vying for the same item, the availability quickly fades.

  For some reason the 2" and 4" ashtrays were only produced in Ebony. Maybe cigarette ashes only looked good on black.

HERMITAGE

	Crystal	Amber	Green Topaz	Azure	Wisteria
Ashtray 2", individual size	5	6	9	12	
Ashtray set, 4 individual, stacking w/holder	25	30	45	60	
Bar bottle w/stopper 12.5", high, 27 oz. (2 styles of top)	70	85	85	85	
Bowl 4.5", finger	10	12	18	24	28
Bowl 5", fruit	8	10	14	18	20
Bowl 6", cereal	10	12	18	24	28
Bowl 7", soup	12	14	20	26	
Bowl 8", footed, deep salad	20	25	30	38	45
Bowl 10", footed, flared	22	28	34		
Cake salver 11.25", pedestal footed, 1.25" tall	30	45	60	85	95
Candlestick 1-lite 6", pair	28	32	48	75	95
Coaster 5.6", raised ring & raised 4 rays	12	15	15	15	20
Comport 3.5", shallow, 6" wide	12	16	24	30	35
Creamer 4", footed, regular, 6.5 oz.	8	10	14	18	20
Cruet w/stopper 4.25", oil bottle, 3 oz.	35	45	68		
Cup & saucer, coffee: cup 2.75", footed, 6 oz.; saucer w/indent 5.75"	10	12	18	24	28
Decanter w/stopper 10.25", carafe, 32 oz.	30	45	68	95	110
Goblet 3", oyster cocktail, 4 oz.	8	10	15	20	25
Goblet 4.6", claret, 4 oz.	10	12	18		
Goblet 2.4", fruit cocktail, 5 oz.	5	6	9	12	15
Goblet 3.25", high sherbet, 5.5 oz.	8	10	14	18	20
Goblet 3", sherbet, 7 oz.	6	8	12	16	20
Goblet 5.25", water, 9 oz.	10	15	20	26	30
Grapefruit bowl	10	14	25		
Grapefruit liner plate	10				
Ice bucket 4.5", tab handled, 6" wide	28	35	50	60	75
Ice dish 2.75", bowl w/3-tabs hold liners, 5" wide	15	20	30	33	45
Ice dish liner 2.75" #2451, crab meat, 4 oz.	24	28	30	40	45
Ice dish liner 1.9" #2451, fruit cocktail, 5 oz.	28	32	35	45	50
Ice dish liner 3.5" #2451, tomato juice, 5 oz.	18	22	24	34	38
Ice dish plate 7", under plate w/indent	10	12	18	24	28
Ice bucket 4.5", tab handled, 6" wide	28	35	50	60	75
Mayonnaise 2 piece: bowl 5.9", flared; plate w/indent 7"	18	25	38		
Mug 4.25", footed beer w/applied handle, 9 oz.	12	18	22	34	45
Mug 5.25", footed beer w/applied handle, 12 oz.	24	28	40	50	55
Mustard w/cover 3.5", footed, jar	24	28	40		
Pitcher 5", footed milk or cereal w/o ice lip, 16 oz.	65	75	85	110	145
Pitcher 7.5", flat, water w/o ice lip, 36 oz.	85	130	140	150	225
Pitcher 7.5", footed, water w/o ice lip, 48 oz.	125	145	150	175	525
Plate 6", bread & butter	6	8	12	16	18
Plate 6.5", coupe, turned up edge	12	15	22	28	30
Plate 7", salad	6	8	12	16	18
Plate 7.4", crescent salad	24	28	40	50	55
Plate 7.5", coupe, turned up edge	14	18	24	34	40
Plate 8", lunch	8	10	14	18	20
Plate 9", dinner	16	20	28	36	40
Plate 12", sandwich	12	15	25		
Relish 6", round, 2 sections	10	12	18		28
Relish 7.25", round, 3 sections	10	14	25		35

Wisteria grouping: **Left:** Tumbler 5.25", footed, ice tea, 12 oz. **Center:** Tumbler 4.1", footed, 6.5 oz. **Right:** Pitcher 7.5", footed, water w/o ice lip, 48 oz.

Green grouping: **Back:** Plate 7.4", crescent salad. **Front left:** Tumbler 4", footed juice, 5 oz. **Front center left:** Goblet 3", oyster cocktail, 4 oz. **Front center right:** Tumbler 2.5", flat whiskey, 2 oz. **Front right:** Goblet 5.25", water, 9 oz.

Azure (blue) grouping: **Left:** Goblet 3.25", high sherbet, 5.5 oz. **Center:** Tumbler 4.75", flat water, 9 oz. **Right:** Tumbler 5.25", footed, ice tea, 12 oz.

Relish 8", oval pickle	10	12	18	24	28
Relish 11", oval celery	12	15	24	30	38
Salt dip 1.6", individual	5	6	9	12	15
Shaker 3.75", flat, salt & pepper, pair	20	24	35	48	75
Sugar 3", footed, regular, 6.5 oz.	8	10	14	18	20
Tray 6.5", oval, condiment	18	20	30	38	42
Tumbler 2.5", flat whiskey, 2 oz.	8	10	15	20	25
Tumbler 2.5", footed whiskey, 2 oz.	8	10	15		
Tumbler 3.9", flat juice, 5 oz.	8	10	15	20	25
Tumbler 4", footed juice, 5 oz.	10	12	18	24	28
Tumbler 3.25", flat old fashion, 6 oz.	8	10	15	20	25
Tumbler 4.1", footed, 6.5 oz.	12	14	20	28	32
Tumbler 4.2", footed table, 9 oz.	12	14	20	28	32
Tumbler 4.75", flat water, 9 oz.	10	12	18	24	28
Tumbler 5.25", footed, ice tea, 12 oz.	12	15	22	28	30
Tumbler 5.9", flat beverage, 13 oz.	13	16	24	30	35
Vase 6", footed, large flared	26	30	45	60	70

Amber grouping: **Left:** Cup & saucer, coffee: cup 2.75", footed, 6 oz.; saucer w/indent 5.75". **Right:** Bowl 8", footed, deep salad.

Wisteria grouping: **Left:** Ice dish liner 3.5" #2451, tomato juice, 5 oz. **Right:** Ice dish 2.75", bowl w/3-tabs to hold liners, 5" wide.

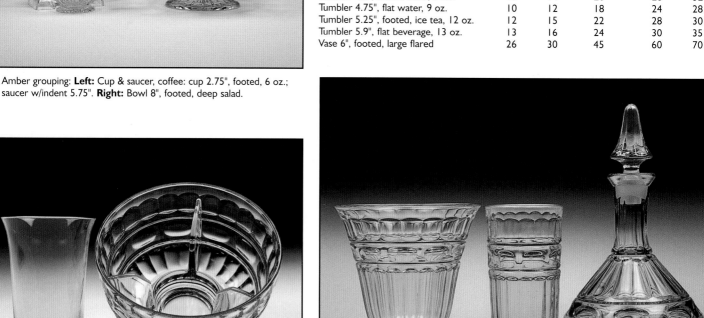

Amber grouping: **Left:** Vase 6", footed, large flared. **Center:** Tumbler 5.9", flat beverage, 13 oz. **Right:** Decanter w/stopper 10.25", carafe, 32 oz.

Left: Mustard w/cover 3.5", footed, jar, Crystal. **Right:** Ice bucket 4.5", tab handled, 6" wide, Green.

Wisteria grouping: **Left:** Shaker 3.75", flat, salt & pepper, pair. **Right:** Goblet 3", oyster cocktail, 4 oz.

HOBNAIL, OPALESCENT
Fenton Art Glass Company
1939-90s
Main Colors: French (clear), Blue, Cranberry, and Topaz (yellow)
Other Colors: Green, Lime, Pink, and Plum

Opalescent Hobnail is probably more closely associated with Fenton than any of their other patterns. It was introduced in 1939 and remained in Fenton's line almost every year in some color through the 1990s. Cranberry opalescent seems to be the favorite among collectors. Topaz pieces now run a very close second. Fenton has been very creative in their use of different types of crimps on pieces from the same mould. Also, you will find that they made several different pieces for other companies.

On July 1, 1952, Fenton changed the way they numbered. Items with three digit numbers were changed to four digit numbers if they were still going to be produced. This is the reason some items will have both numbers.

Between all of the items produced, different crimping, satin finish, and unusual pieces, collectors of Hobnail could obtain a vast collection. As if this were not enough, Fenton has produced many colors of Hobnail over the years. More recently, Hobnail with an optic has been made in a heat sensitive glass like Burmese. At almost every show we go to there will be Hobnail in some color. Collectors would love to find the following items to add to their collections: barber bottle, large basket , cookie jar with a lid, hanging bowl, lamp, and water pitcher. As for square Hobnail items, we would consider any item to be a delight for any collector to find. Remember that all square Hobnail plates are measured diagonally.

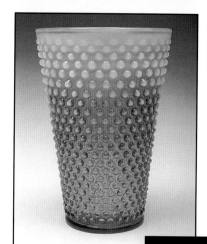

Vase 8.5" #3859 (389), flat, flip shape, smooth top, Cranberry Opalescent.

Shakers 4.5" #389, footed w/ chrome or glass top, Topaz Opalescent (Note, 2 styles).

HOBNAIL OPALESCENT	French	Blue	Topaz	Cranberry
Ashtray 2.75" #389, oval, individual w/cigarette rest	35	35	45	
[2] Ashtray 3.5" #3972, round		20		
Ashtray 4" #3873 (389), oval, 1 cigarette indent	18	28	30	
Ashtray 4" #3876, flat, octagon, nesting #1 of set	24			
[2] Ashtray 5" #3973, round		24		
Ashtray 5.25" #3877, flat, octagon, nesting #2 of set	26			
Ashtray 5.5" #3872 (389), open, fan shape	16	24	30	
[2] Ashtray 6.5" #3976, round		26		
Ashtray 6.5" #3878, flat, octagon, nesting #3 of set	30		50	
[1] Banana stand 12" #3720, footed, 2 sides turned up		175	245	
Barber bottle w/metal tube 7.25", made for L.G. Wright	145	195	275	295
[1] Basket 4.5" #3834 (389), footed, deep w/ applied handle	35	45	98	75
Basket 5.5" #3835 (389), low w/applied handle	75	85		150
Basket 6.25" #389, cone w/applied handle	95	125	190	
[2] Basket 7" #3337, double crimped			75	
Basket 7" #3637, deep crimped w/applied handle				445
[1] Basket 7" #3837 (389), flat, flared, crimped w/ applied handle	55	65	120	110
Basket 8" #389, footed cone, fan shape w/ applied handle	95	185	225	
[2] Basket 8" #3335, deep, straight sided, double crimped			85	
[2] Basket 8.5" #1158, double crimped (1997 iridized)			85	
[2] Basket 8.5" #3346, double crimped (open ends pulled down)				85
[1] Basket 10" #3830 (389), flat, flared, crimped w/applied clear handle	125	145	195	215
[2] Basket 10.5" #3348, double crimped (pleated in right angles)				145
Basket 12" #3734, applied handle			395	
Basket 13.5" #389, deep, hat, crimped w/applied clear handle	325	495	595	695
[2] Bell 6" #3667, dinner		35	45	
Bonbon 4" #389, handled, oval	18	28	25	
Bonbon 4" #389, handled, squared	20	30	30	
Bonbon 5" #3935 (389), footed, handled, oval	20	30	30	
Bonbon 5" #3935 (389), footed, handled, squared	24	40	45	
Bonbon 6" #3926 (389), flat plate, crimped	18	28	35	40
Bonbon 6" #3926 (389), oval, crimped w/2 sides turned up	14	22	28	36
Bonbon 6" #3926 (389), deep, flared, crimped	16	24	30	38
Bonbon 6" #3926 (389), low, ruffled, double crimped	18	28	30	40
Bonbon 6" #3926 (389), low, squared, double crimped	16	24	30	38
Bonbon 6" #3926, low, triangle, double crimped	18	28	30	40
Bonbon 6.5" #389, handled, squared	20	28	32	
Bonbon 6.5" #389, handled, oval	24	32	38	
Bonbon 7" #3926 (389), flat, shallow, crimped	20	30	45	42
Bonbon 7" #3926 (389), oval, crimped w/2 sides turned up	16	24	45	38
Bonbon 7" #3926 (389), deep, flared, crimped	18	26	45	40
Bonbon 7" #3926 (389), low, ruffled, double crimped	20	30	45	42
Bonbon 7" #3926 (389), low, squared, double crimped	18	26	45	40
Bonbon 7" #3926, low, triangle, double crimped	20	30	45	42
Bonbon 7" #3937, handled, squared	20	30		

Candy jar w/cover 8.5" #3887, footed, (Hobbs style) w/hobs on domed foot, Blue Opalescent.

Topaz Opalescent grouping: **Top left:** Basket 8" #389, footed cone, fan shape w/applied Crystal handle. **Top right:** Basket 10" #3830 (389), flat, flared, crimped w/applied Crystal handle. **Center of photo:** Basket 13.5" #389, deep, hat, crimped w/applied Crystal handle. **Front left:** Basket 7" #3637, deep crimped w/applied Topaz handle. **Front right:** Basket 4.5" #3834 (389), footed, deep w/applied Crystal handle.

Topaz Opalescent grouping: **Left:** Candlestick 1-lite 3" #3974 (389), footed, no stem, crimped. **Center:** Candlestick 1-lite 3.5" #3971 (389), footed, miniature cornucopia. **Right:** Candlestick 1-lite 6.5" #3874 (389), footed, crimped cornucopia.

Candlestick 1-lite 3.25" #3870, round, squat w/applied loop handle, Cranberry Opalescent.

Top: Bowl 7" #3927 (389), oval, crimped, sides turned up, Cranberry Opalescent. **Bottom left:** Vase 5.5" #3656 (389), flared, smooth edge, Blue Opalescent. **Bottom right:** Vase 4.5" #3854 (389), spherical, flared, crimped, Blue Opalescent.

Item				
Bonbon 8" #389, handled, oval	50	75		
Bonbon 8.5" #3733, heart shape w/1 handle		95	85	
Boot 4" #3992, high top style 1980s			20	
Bowl 5" #3719, cereal			95	
Bowl 5" #3921, star crimped	35	48		125
Bowl 6.75" #3730, footed, candy ribbon edge w/ ribbed stem			75	
Bowl 7" #3927 (389), flat, flared, double crimped	18	28	48	45
Bowl 7" #3927 (389), flat, flared, triangle crimped		28	48	
Bowl 7" #3927 (389), oval, crimped, sides turned up	20	32	50	48
Bowl 7.5" #389, footed, flared, melon	60	75	85	
Bowl 8" #3706, handled		60		
Bowl 8" #3727, footed, double crimped (comport shape) 3.75" high		64	90	
Bowl 8.5" #3724, 3-footed w/scallops between feet			175	
[2] Bowl 9" #3324 (389), deep, flared, pie crimped edge			85	
Bowl 9" #3735, cupped, ribbon crimped			165	
Bowl 9" #3924, deep, single crimped	45	70	100	110
Bowl 9" #3924 (389), deep, flared	65	80	120	130
[1] Bowl 9" #3924 (389), deep, double crimped	45	70	100	110
[1] Bowl 9" #3924, deep, triangle, double crimped			110	
Bowl 10" #3731, footed w/ribbed stem, double crimped		95	145	
Bowl 11" #3824 (389), shallow, flared, crimped	65	85	110	145
Bowl 11" #3824 (389), shallow, double crimped	65	85	110	145
Bowl 11" #3824 (389), shallow, oval, crimped	75	110	145	175
Bowl 11" #3824 (389), shallow, triangle, double crimped	90	125	175	225
[1] Bowl 11" #3325, footed, tall plain stem, double crimped			115	
Bowl 11" #3923 (389), high (comport shape) double crimped	95	125	185	
Bowl 11" #3705, hanging w/3 holes for metal chain			295	
Bowl 12" #3723 (389), high footed, pie crimped, shallow	95	125	195	
Bowl 12" #3723 (389), high footed, pie crimped, deep	95	125	195	
Butter w/cover 6.75" #3977, oblong, .25 lb.	195	395		
[2] Butter w/cover 8.25" #3677, round scalloped edge w/domed top		225	275	
Cake stand 12" #3913 389), footed, flat top, plain smooth edge	125	175	225	
Cake stand 12" #3913 (389), footed, flat top, pie crust crimped	100	145	215	
[2] Candle bowl 1-lite 5" #3971, dome footed, short stem, scalloped edge, pair		95		
Candle bowl 1-lite 6" #3770, footed, ribbon crimped, pair			295	
Candle bowl 1-lite 7.75" #3770, footed, low (flattened) ribbon crimped, pair			265	
Candle bowl 1-lite 8" #3771, footed, double crimped, pair		145	195	
[1] Candlestick 1-lite 3" #3974 (389), footed, no stem, crimped, pair	48	60	95	
Candlestick 1-lite 3.25" #3870, round, squat w/applied loop handle, pair	160			150
Candlestick 1-lite 3.5" #3971 (389), footed, miniature cornucopia, pair	40	58	60	
[1] Candlestick 1-lite 6.5" #3874 (389), footed, crimped cornucopia, pair	85	90	95	
Candy jar w/cover 3.5" #3880, flat, chocolate box shape, 6.5" wide	95	165		
Candy jar w/cover 5" #3883, flat, round (Hobbs style) hobnail finial	95	135	195	265
[2] Candy w/cover 5.25" #3802, flat, round, squat w/ribbed knob finial		60		
Candy jar w/cover 6.5" #3980 (389), footed, squat domed lid w/pointed ribbed finial (or ribbed & wafer finial)	55	80	95	
Candy w/cover 8" #389, footed (plain foot) squat, scalloped	95	125	195	
Candy jar w/cover 8.5" #3887, footed, (Hobbs style) w/hobs on domed foot		85	155	
Comport 1.75" #389, flat plate top, 8" wide	50	98	115	
Comport 4" #389, deep flared top, 6" wide	45	85	125	
Comport 4" #389, shallow triangle top, 6" wide	55	85	125	
[2] Comport 6" #3628, paneled stem, double crimped		45		
Comport 6" #3920, flared, double crimped			95	

Item			
Comport 5.5" #3728, double crimped		42	72	
Cookie jar w/cover 6" #389, w/wicker handle	650	950	1,100	
Creamer 2.1" #3900 (389), flat, individual, short, handled, 3 oz.	12	20	25	
[1] Creamer 3.5" #3901 (389), flat, individual, tall, handled, 3.4 oz.	20	28	28	85
[1] Creamer 3" #3906 (389), flat, regular, handled, crimped, 5 oz.	24	38		125
[2] Creamer 4" #3606, flat, scalloped top w/ beaded handle, 6 oz.			38	
[1] Cruet w/stopper 4.75" #3869 (389), flat, oil bottle, handled	30	48	78	85
Cruet w/clear stopper 6" #3863 (389), spherical, necked, handled	60	95	195	175
[1] Cup 2.25" #3847 (389), flat, round punch, 4.5 oz.	18	28		
Decanter w/clear stopper 12" #3761 (389), handled, 47 oz.	345	395	495	450
Epergne 2 piece petite 4.5" #3902 (389), single horn	125	175		
Epergne w/block 2 piece 8.25" #389, single horn	245	395	600	
[1] Epergne 4 piece 8" #3801, miniature D.C. 6.5" high apartment, 3 horns	98	145	295	
[2] Epergne 4 piece 10" #3701, double crimped, 3 horns			345	
[2] Fairy light 2 piece 4.5" #3608, footed base (paneled) w/dome top		45	65	
[2] Fairy light 3 piece 6.5" #3380, base crimped & rolled over, clear candle insert, revised shape squat dome top (large top opening)				125
Goblet 3.75" #3843 (389), footed wine, 4 oz.	30	48	72	
Goblet 4" #3825 (389), footed sherbet, 6 oz.	18	28	38	
Goblet 5.5" #3845 (389), footed water, 8 oz.	25	35	60	
Hat 2.75" #3991 (389), small #1, two sides turned down	35	55	60	
Hat 2.75" #3992 (389), large #2, two sides turned down	18	28	35	
Jar w/cover (smooth plain) 4.5" #389, small, ginger jar shape	45			
Jar w/cover 5" #389, squat, large, rose bowl shape w/domed lid	295	345	550	595
Jam 4 piece 4.75" #3903 (389), jar-cover-liner crimped w/clear ladle	60	95		155
Lamp (bottle) 6.75" #389, flat, spherical bottom w/neck, made for William F.B. Johnson 1949-50		80	95	
Lamp (bottle) 7" #9210, cylindrical w/2 rings & short neck, made for Edward P. Paul & Co.		85	100	
[2] Lamp (student) 15" #3307, brass bottom, 7" shade w/pie crimped edge				175
Lamp (student) 19" #3707, pear font, 7" shade w/pie crimped edge		295	500	375
[2] Lamp (student) 22" #1174, pear font, 10" shade D.C. w/prisms				395
[2] Lamp (G.W.W.) 25" #3308, 10" ball base, ball shade double crimped				450
[2] Lamp (pillar) 26" #3907, pear font, double crimped 10" ball shade			395	400
Mayonnaise 3 piece #3803 (389): bowl 4.5", crimped; liner w/indent 6"; clear ladle	48	85		125
Mustard w/cover 3.5" #3889 (389), w/clear paddle 3.1" long	28	42	60	
Pitcher 4.5 #3964 (389), flat, squat jug, applied handle, 12 oz.	36	58	98	65
Pitcher 5.5" #389, syrup jug w/clear ribbed handle, 12 oz.	40	64	85	95
[2] Pitcher 5.5" #3366, syrup jug, smooth top w/opal ribbed handle, 12 oz.				55
Pitcher 5.75" #3762, syrup jug crimped w/colored handle, 12 oz.		95	95	145
Pitcher 5.25" #3965 (389), flat, squat jug, 32 oz.	99	110	225	175
[2] Pitcher 11" #3360, spherical base, long neck, rolled crimped top, 46 oz.			295	
Pitcher 8.25" #389, high tankard, jug, 48 oz.	295	345	495	550
Pitcher 9.5" #3664, spherical ball w/ice lip & ribbed handle, 70 oz.	165			345
Pitcher 7.5" #3967 (389), spherical, water jug, 80 oz.	195	295	525	350
Plate 6.75" #389, crescent salad	36	56	75	
Plate 8" #3816 (389), salad, pie crust crimped	34	48	65	
Plate 8" #3918, salad, plain edge	24	35	65	
Plate 13.5" #3714, pie crust crimped			75	

Cranberry Opalescent grouping: **Top:** Bowl 9" #3924 (389), deep, double crimped. **Bottom left:** Cruet w/stopper 4.75" #3869 (389), flat, oil bottle, handled. **Center:** Cruet w/clear stopper 6" #3863 (389), spherical, necked, handled. **Right:** Pitcher 7.5" #3967 (389), spherical, water jug, 80 oz.

Blue Opalescent grouping: **Left:** Hat 1.75" #3991 (389), small #1, two sides turned down. **Right:** Hat 2.75" #3992 (389), large #2, two sides turned down.

Topaz Opalescent grouping: **Left & right:** Candle bowls 1-lite 7.75" #3770, footed, low (flattened) ribbon crimped, Topaz Opalescent (one is turned on its side).

Topaz Opalescent grouping: **Left:** Vase 6" #389, hand shape – flared, smooth top. **Right:** Vase 6" #389, hand shape – flared, crimped.

Topaz Opalescent grouping: **Left:** Candy jar w/cover 6.5" #3980 (389), footed, squat domed lid w/ribbed & wafer finial. **Right:** Candy jar w/cover 6.5" #3980 (389), footed, squat domed lid w/pointed ribbed finial.

Topaz Opalescent grouping: **Left:** Goblet 5.5" #3845 (389), footed water, 8 oz. **Center:** Goblet 4" #3825 (389), footed sherbet, 6 oz. **Right:** Tumbler 5.75" #3842 (389), footed, ice tea, 12 oz.

Topaz Opalescent grouping: **Left:** Tumbler 3.5" #3945 (389), flat, straight sided, juice, 5 oz. **Center:** Tumbler 4.25" #3949 (389), flat, straight sided, water, 9 oz. **Right:** Tumbler 4.75" #3947, flat, convex sides, 12 oz.

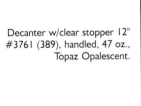

Decanter w/clear stopper 12" #3761 (389), handled, 47 oz., Topaz Opalescent.

Item				
Plate 13.5" #3791, w/metal handle, pie crust crimped			115	
Punch bowl 10.5" #3827 (389), deep, round, crimped, 1 gallon	295	395		
Punch bowl 10.5" #3827 (389), deep, round, flared, 1 gallon	295	395		
Punch bowl 10.5" #3827 (389), deep, round, w/handle (cup shape) 1 gallon	395	650		
² Punch bowl 15" #3722, flared, pie crimped edge, 1.75 gallon			295	395
Punch bowl liner 16" #3817, torte plate	95	145		
² Punch bowl base 8" #3778, scalloped		75	100	
Relish 7.5" #3822, clover leaf, 3 sections	175	245		
Relish 12" #3739, oval, celery w/flat tab handles			135	
Relish 12" #3740, oval, 3 sections w/flat tab handles			145	
¹ Shaker 3.25" #3806, flat, straight sided w/metal top, pair	40	60	125	100
² Shaker 3.75" #3609, scalloped foot, straight sided, pair			58	
Shaker 4.5" #389, footed w/chrome top, pair	55	68	95	
¹ Slipper 5" #3995 (389), cat head style	20	28	28	
Sugar 2.1" #3900 (389), flat, individual, short, handled, 3 oz.	12	20	25	
¹ Sugar 3.5" #3901 (389), flat, individual, tall, handled, 3.4 oz.	20	28	28	85
¹ Sugar 3" #3906 (389), flat, regular, handled, crimped, 5 oz.	24	28		125
² Sugar w/cover 5.75" #3606, flat, scalloped top (no handles) 7 oz.			60	
² Toothpick holder 3" #3795, scalloped top/bottom w/3-tab feet			18	
² Toothpick holder 3.25" #3392, scalloped foot, straight sided			24	
Tray 7.75" #3879 (389), round, divided condiment, center chrome handle	95	115		
Tray 10.5" #389, open fan shape w/tab handle	35	48	48	
Tray 13.5" #3794, 2 tiered w/handle 8" & 13.5", pie crimped edge, tidbit			195	
Tumbler 3.5" #3945 (389), flat, straight sided, juice, 5 oz.	12	20	25	
¹ Tumbler 4.25" #3949 (389), flat, straight sided, water, 9 oz.	18	28	30	
Tumbler 4.75" #3947, flat, convex sides, 12 oz.	30	45	75	85
Tumbler 5" #3942 (389), flat, straight sided, ice tea, 12 oz.	40	58		
Tumbler 5.75" #3842 (389), footed, ice tea, 12 oz.	38	48	85	
Tumbler 6" #3946, flat, high straight sided, beverage, 16 oz.	45	65	115	
Vanity bottle w/(clear on cranberry) flat stopper 4.5" #3865 (389), 4 oz.	40	58	110	98
Vanity bottle w/clear pointed stopper 5.25" #3865 (389), cologne, 4 oz.	48	55		110
Vanity "Boxtle" 3 piece 7.1" #3986, cologne & powder lid 1 piece w/clear beaded teardrop stopper/dauber, no logo	295	450		
Vanity "Boxtle" 3 piece 7.1" #3986, cologne & powder lid 1 piece w/clear beaded teardrop stopper/dauber, with logo	250	175		
Vanity puff w/(clear on cranberry) domed cover 4.5" #3885 (389), round box	45	68	120	110
Vanity puff w/(clear on cranberry) pointed finial cover 4.5" #3885 (389), round box	48	68		110
Vase 3" #389, miniature, oval				60
Vase 3" #3853 (389), cupped, crimped, rose bowl	65	95		195
¹ Vase 3" #3853 (389), squat, double crimped	30	38	95	80
Vase 4" #3855 (389), miniature, crimped	15	25	30	40
Vase 4" #3855 (389), miniature, cup flared	16	28	38	42
Vase 4" #3855 (389), miniature, fan/cigarette holder	28	45	55	75
Vase 4" #3855 (389), miniature, flared flat	16	28	35	42
Vase 4" #3855 (389), miniature, triangle crimped	20	36	35	54
Vase 4" #3855 (389), miniature, 2 sides rolled over	24	40	45	65
¹ Vase 4" #3953, footed cone, crimped fan	20	36		
¹ Vase 4" #3952, footed, symmetrical, double crimped	18	30		
² Vase 4.25" #3861, rose bowl, crimped in			38	48
Vase 4.5" #389, spherical ball, necked, bud vase	48	95	125	
² Vase 4.5" #3323, cupped, rose bowl				35
¹ Vase 4.5" #3854 (389), spherical, rose bowl, crimped	32	50	48	185
Vase 4.5" #3854 (389), spherical, flared, crimped	32	50	48	78
¹ Vase 4.5" #3854 (389), spherical, ruffled, double crimped	32	50	48	78

...ase 4.5" #3854 (389), spherical, squared, double crimped	38	60	55	95
...ase 4.5" #3854 (389), spherical, triangle, double crimped		60	55	
...ase 4.75" #3726, crimped in, ivy ball w/ribbed stem			50	
...ase 5" #3850 (389), squat, rose bowl, crimped	38	65	98	98
...ase 5" #3850 (389), squat, flared, crimped	32	55	60	88
...ase 5" #3850 (389), squat, double crimped	34	58	55	95
...ase 5" #3850 (389), squat, squared, double crimped	36	60	58	100
...ase 5" #3850 (389), squat, triangle, double crimped	38	64	68	110
...ase 5.5" #3656 (389), flared, smooth edge	34	58	85	95
...ase 5.5" #3656 (389), flared, crimped	30	52	76	84
...ase 5.5" #3656 (389), squared, crimped	34	58	85	95
...ase 5.5" #3656 (389), triangle, crimped	36	60	88	100
...ase 5.5" #3656, tulip (J.I.P.) smooth edge	38	64	98	110
...ase 6" #3750, handkerchief - swung			98	
...ase 6" #3856 (389), symmetrical, flared, smooth	36	60	98	125
...ase 6" #3856 (389), symmetrical, flared, crimped	36	60	98	125
...ase 6" #3856 (389), symmetrical, flared, double crimped	32	55	80	88
...ase 6" #3856 (389), symmetrical, squared, double crimped	38	64	98	110
...ase 6" #3856 (389), symmetrical, triangle, double crimped	40	68	110	115
...ase 6" #389, hand shape - flared, smooth top	125	195	225	
...ase 6" #389, hand shape - flared, crimped	125	195	225	
...ase 6.25" #389, footed cone, fan w/pointed edge	30	52	60	
...ase 6.25" #3956 (389), footed cone, cupped in top	38	64	96	
...ase 6.25" #3956 (389), footed cone, double crimped	32	55	80	
...ase 6.25" #3956 (389), footed cone, flared, crimped		60	80	
...ase 6.25" #3956 (389), footed cone, necked cup	40	68	90	
...ase 6.25" #3956 (389), footed cone, squared, double crimped	36	60	80	
...ase 6.25" #3956 (389), footed cone, triangle, double crimped	36	60	80	
...ase 6.5" #389, footed, flared, scalloped, swung	40	68	100	
...ase 6.5" #389, footed, fan, scalloped, swung	48	80	120	
...ase 6.75" #389, sample lamp base (William F.B. Johnson) spherical	85	100	125	
...ase 7" #9210, sample lamp base (Edward P. Paul & Co.) cylindrical		120	145	
...ase 7" #389, rose bowl	48	68	125	125
Vase 7.5" #1155, flat, crimped top				75
Vase 7.5" #3356, flat, spherical, crimped, tulip top				85
...ase 8" #3756, dome footed, swung, bud vase	16	28	40	42
...ase 8" #389, footed, fan, scalloped	48	75	120	
...ase 8" #3858 (389), flat, symmetrical, flared, smooth	65	110	125	295
...ase 8" #3858 (389), flat, symmetrical, flared, crimped	65	110	125	195
...ase 8" #3858 (389), flat, symmetrical, double crimped	50	70	100	110
...ase 8" #3858 (389), flat, symmetrical, squared, double crimped	48	80	120	135
...ase 8" #3858 (389), flat, symmetrical, triangle, double crimped	50	85	125	140
...ase 8" #3958 (389), footed cone, squared, double crimped	42	60	78	
...ase 8" #3958 (389), footed cone, triangle, double crimped	36	55	68	
...ase 8.5" #3859 (389), flat, flip shape, smooth top	195	295	350	350
...ase 8.5" #3859 (389), flat, flared, flip shape, double crimped	125	165	195	195
...ase 8.5" #3859 (389), flat, flared, squared, double crimped	120	165	195	195
...ase 8.5" #3859 (389), flat, flared, triangle, double crimped	125	175	225	245
Vase 8.5" #3859, flat, tapered out, ruffled top				195
Vase 8.5" #3959 (389), footed cone, fan crimped	42	60	110	
Vase 9" #389, footed, Melon, flared, crimped, swung	95	145	165	
Vase 10" #389, flared, bottle shape	195	215	295	315
Vase 10" #3950, dome footed, swung (paneled) bud vase		45		
Vase 11" #3752, spherical base, high neck, double crimped				150
Vase 12" #3753, rib footed, swung			115	
Vase 14.5" #3758, footed, no stem, medium swung		95	135	
Vase 18" #3759, footed, no stem, large swung		135	175	

French Opalescent grouping: **Back row:** Vanity puff w/wood lid when sold by Wrisley 4.5" #389, round box. **Front left:** Vase 4.5" #3854 (389), spherical, rose bowl, crimped. **Front center:** Bonbon 4" #389, handled, squared. **Front right:** Vase 6.25" #389, footed cone, fan w/ pointed edge.

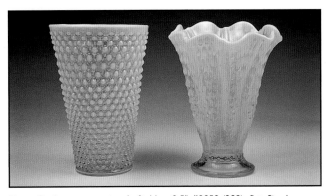

Topaz Opalescent grouping: **Left:** Vase 8.5" #3859 (389), flat, flip shape, smooth top. **Right:** Vase 9" #389, footed, melon, flared, crimped, swung.

Topaz Opalescent grouping: **Left:** Bowl 7.5" #389, footed, flared, melon. **Right:** Comport 4" #389, deep flared top, 6" wide.

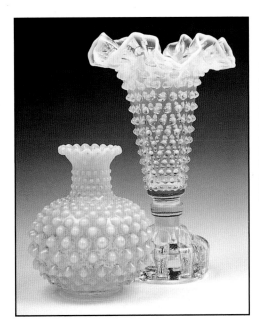

Left: Vase 4.5" #389, spherical ball, necked, bud vase, Topaz Opalescent. **Right:** Epergne w/flower frog block 2 piece 8.25" #389, single horn, French Opalescent.

Grouping of Vanity "Boxtle" 3 piece 7.1" #3986, cologne & powder lid 1 piece w/clear beaded teardrop stopper/dauber: **Left:** French Opalescent. **Right:** Blue Opalescent (shown together & in sections).

[1] Note: were also remade with logo after 1978 price 75% of old (listed)
[2] Note: were only made with logo after 1978

SQUARE HOBNAIL	French	Blue
Bowl 3.5" #3828 (389), square, dessert	45	6
Cup & saucer, coffee #3808 (389): cup 4", square, 2.1" high, 6 oz.; saucer w/indent 7"	85	12
Goblet 3.75" #3844 (389), footed, square wine, 3 oz.	45	7
Goblet 4" #3826 (389), footed, square sherbet, 5 oz.	42	6
Goblet 5.5" #3846 (389), footed, square water, 8 oz.	55	7
Plate 7" #3919 (389), square, salad	50	6
Plate 11" #3910 (389), square, dinner	85	12
Tray 11" #389, 2 tiered w/handle 7" & 11" square plates, tidbit	155	215

Left: Vanity bottle w/flat stopper 4.5" #3865 (389), 4 oz., Topaz Opalescent (extra stopper shown for comparison of top). **Center left:** Vanity bottle w/flat stopper 4.5" #3865 (389), 4 oz., French Opalescent. **Center:** Vanity puff w/domed cover 4.5" #3885 (389), round box, Blue Opalescent. **Center right:** Vanity bottle w/(clear on cranberry) flat stopper 4.5" #3865 (389), 4 oz., Cranberry Opalescent. **Right:** Vanity bottle w/flat stopper 4.5" #3865 (389), 4 oz., Blue Opalescent.

Cranberry Opalescent grouping: **Top left:** Cruet w/stopper 4.75" #3869 (389), flat, oil bottle, handled. **Top right:** Pitcher 4.5" #3964 (389), flat, squat jug, applied handle, 12 oz. **Front left:** Basket 7" #3837 (389), flat, flared, crimped w/applied handle. **Front center left:** Candlestick 1-lite 3.25" #3870, round, squat w/applied loop handle. **Front center right:** Shaker 3.25" #3806, flat, straight sided w/metal top. **Front right:** Vase 4.5" #3854 (389), spherical, rose bowl, crimped.

Blue Opalescent grouping: **Left:** Mayonnaise 2 piece #3803 (389): bowl 4.5", crimped; liner w/indent 6". **Center:** Punch bowl 15" #3722, flared, pie crimped edge, 1.75 gallon. **Right:** Cup 2.25" #3847 (389), flat, round punch, 4.5 oz.

Topaz Opalescent grouping: **Back left:** Pitcher 5.75" #3762, syrup jug crimped w/colored handle, 12 oz. **Back center:** Pitcher 4.5" #3964 (389), flat, squat jug, applied handle, 12 oz. **Back right:** Pitcher 8.25" #389, high tankard, jug, 48 oz. **Front left:** Pitcher 5.25" #3965 (389), flat, squat jug, 32 oz. **Front right:** Pitcher 5.5" #3366, syrup jug, smooth top w/opal ribbed handle, 12 oz.

Cranberry Opalescent grouping: **Top center:** Fairy light 3 piece 6.5" #3380, base crimped & rolled over, clear candle insert, revised shape squat dome top (large top opening). **Left:** Vase 7.5" #3356, flat, spherical, crimped, tulip top. **Right:** Basket 10.5" #3348, double crimped (pleated in right angles).

Topaz Opalescent grouping: **Top left:** Vase 8" #3858 (389), flat, symmetrical, flared, crimped. **Top right:** Vase 6" #3856 (389), symmetrical, squared, double crimped. **Bottom left:** Vase 4.5" #3854 (389), spherical, ruffled, double crimped. **Bottom right:** Vase 5" #3850 (389), squat, rose bowl, crimped.

Topaz Opalescent grouping: **Top left:** Vase 4" #3855 (389), miniature, flared flat. **Top center:** Vase 4" #3855 (389), miniature, cup flared. **Top right:** Vase 4" #3855 (389), miniature, fan/cigarette holder. **Bottom left:** Vase 4" #3855 (389), miniature, crimped. **Bottom center:** Vase 4" #3855 (389), miniature, triangle crimped. **Bottom right:** Vase 4" #3855 (389), miniature, 2 sides rolled over.

Blue Opalescent grouping: **Left:** Plate 7" #3919 (389), square, salad. **Center:** Cup & saucer, coffee #3808 (389): cup 4", square, 2.1" high, 6 oz.; saucer w/indent 7". **Right:** Plate 11" #3910 (389), square, dinner.

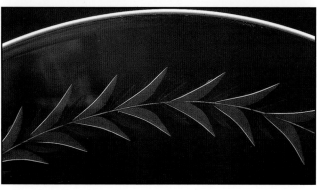

Pattern detail, Holly.

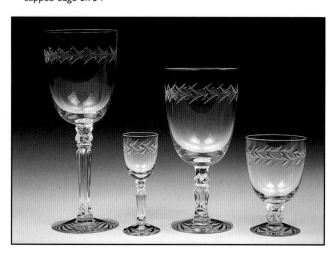

Mayonnaise 2 piece #2364 Sonata: bowl 5", deep; liner w/indent, cupped edge 6.75".

Left: Goblet 7.9" #6030 Astrid, dinner water, 10 oz. **Center left:** Goblet 3.9" #6030 Astrid, cordial, 1 oz. **Center right:** Goblet 6.4" #6030 Astrid, lunch water, 10 oz. **Right:** Goblet 3.75" #6030 Astrid, oyster cocktail, 4 oz.

Left: Goblet 5.25" #6030 Astrid, liquor cocktail, 3.5 oz. **Center left:** Goblet 4.4" #6030 Astrid, sherbet, 6 oz. **Center right:** Goblet 6" #6030 Astrid, claret/wine, 3.5 oz. **Right:** Goblet 5.6" #6030 Astrid, saucer champagne, 6 oz.

HOLLY
Fostoria Glass Company   **Cutting #815**   **1941-82**
Color: Crystal

Holly is a simple pattern with a band of leaves cut on crystal. The Sonata #2364 is th[e] blank on which most of the Holly pieces are found. Stemware will be found on the Astri[d] #6030 blank. The pattern itself was only made until 1980. After that date, any stemware coul[d] be ordered until 1982. This is another pattern where stemware seems to be in an abundan[t] supply with any other items requiring some patience to locate. Fostoria offered a special pr[o] motional package, called the Nostalgia line, to reintroduce formally discontinued patterns t[o] new brides. Since this pattern was produced so late, it was also included in the Nostalgia line[.]

HOLLY	Crystal
Ashtray 2.6" #2364 Sonata, (blown) flat, round, shallow	20
Bowl 5" #2364 Sonata, flat, rim fruit	16
Bowl 6" #2364 Sonata, flat, rim baked apple	20
Bowl 8" #2364 Sonata, flat, rim soup	32
Bowl 9" #2364 Sonata, shallow, salad	45
Bowl 9" #6023, footed, short stem, blown	60
Bowl 10.5" #2364 Sonata, deep, salad	55
Bowl 12" #2364 Sonata, flat, flared	38
Bowl 12.5" #2364 Sonata, flat, shallow lily pond, cupped edge	48
Bowl 13" #2364 Sonata, shallow, fruit	45
Candlestick 1-lite 4" #2324, short wafer stem, pair	38
Candlestick 2-lite 5.5" #6023, plain "U" shape stem, 6" spread, pair	65
Cigarette holder 2" #2364 Sonata, flat, round (toothpick holder shape)	32
Cheese & cracker #2364 Sonata: comport 2.9", short stem, 5.75" wide; plate w/indent 11.25"	58
Comport 5.25" #6030 Astrid, cupped, plain stem, 5" wide	35
Comport 8" #2364 Sonata, lady leg stem, flared, 7.5" wide	38
Creamer, 3" #2666 Contour, individual, applied handle, 3.5 oz.	16
Creamer 3.25" #2350 1/2, footed, regular, 7 oz.	14
Cup & saucer, coffee #2350 1/2: cup 2.6", footed, coffee, 6 oz.; saucer w/indent 5.75"	13
Finger bowl 4.1" #1769, flat, blown	30
Goblet 3.9" #6030 Astrid, cordial, 1 oz.	38
Goblet 5.25" #6030 Astrid, liquor cocktail, 3.5 oz.	14
Goblet 6" #6030 Astrid, claret/wine, 3.5 oz.	25
Goblet 3.75" #6030 Astrid, oyster cocktail, 4 oz.	12
Goblet 4.4" #6030 Astrid, sherbet, 6 oz.	10
Goblet 5.6" #6030 Astrid, saucer champagne, 6 oz.	12
Goblet 6.4" #6030 Astrid, lunch water, 10 oz.	18
Goblet 7.9" #6030 Astrid, dinner water, 10 oz.	24
Mayonnaise 2 piece #2364 Sonata: bowl 5", deep; liner w/indent, cupped edge 6.75"	50
Pitcher 8.5" #6011, footed, water w/o ice lip, 53 oz.	185
Plate 6" #2337, bread & butter	5
Plate 7.25" #2337, salad	10
Plate 8.5" #2337, lunch	12
Plate 9.4" #2337, dinner	28
Plate 11" #2364 Sonata, small center, sandwich or 9" salad bowl liner	24
Plate 14" #2364 Sonata, small center, turned up edge, cabaret or 10.5" salad bowl liner	38
Plate 16" #2364 Sonata, small center, turned up edge, cabaret	50
Relish 6.5" #2364 Sonata, tab handled, oblong (tear drop shape) 2 sections	24
Relish 8" #2364 Sonata, oval, rim pickle	20
Relish 10" #2364 Sonata, tab handled, oblong (tear drop shape) 3 sections	38
Relish 11" #2364 Sonata, oval, rim celery	28
Sandwich server 11.25" #2364 Sonata, center plume handle	35
Shaker 2.4" #2364 Sonata, flat, individual, chrome or glass top, pair	36
Shaker 3.25" #2364 Sonata, flat, regular chrome top, pair	42
Sugar 2.8" #2666 Contour, individual, applied handles, 3.5 oz.	16
Sugar 3.1" #2350 1/2, footed, regular, 7 oz.	14
Tray 6.8" #2666 Contour, for individual cream/sugar no cutting (plain)	14
Tumbler 4.6" #6030 Astrid, footed, juice, 5 oz.	19
Tumbler 6" #6030 Astrid, footed, ice tea, 12 oz.	24
Vase 6" #2619 1/2, flat, straight sided	70
Vase 7.5" #2619 1/2, flat, straight sided	80
Vase 9.5" #2619 1/2, flat, straight sided	98

Sandwich server 11.25" #2364 Sonata, center plume handle.

IMPERIAL HUNT

Cambridge Glass Company   **Etching #718**   **1927 - mid-1930s**

Colors: Amber, Crystal, Ebony (black), Emerald Green, Green, Peach Blo (pink), and Willow Blue

A classic English activity, Imperial Hunt portrays a fox hunt where men are on horseback running through the woods with dogs in search of the elusive fox. It is assumed, since this is a favorite pastime of the royal family, that the name was given to this etched pattern to recognize their participation in this sport. Not every item is found in all of the colors. This etching was the only one found to be used on the blanks #3075 and #3085.

You would think that you could easily find more of this attractive etching, since there were so many items produced. This is definitely not the case. There is scarcely a piece at most of the shows and sometimes none. Collectors of Imperial Hunt need to have lots of patience. The word "hunt" in the name is also an indicator of how hard it is to obtain this etched pattern.

Pattern detail, Imperial Hunt.

Humidor w/cover 6" #1025, cylindrical, straight sided (flat top), Ebony (black) w/Gold encrusted – shown missing cover.

IMPERIAL HUNT	Crystal	Colors
Candlestick 1-lite, 3.5" #628 Pristine, w/wafer stem, pair	60	115
Candlestick 2-lite 6" #3400/647, keyhole stem, 7.75" spread, pair	75	145
Candlestick 3-lite 7" #3400/638, keyhole, pair	85	165
Cheese & cracker: comport, 3" #1496 Pristine, short stem, flared, 5" wide; plate 11.5"	70	135
Comport #3075 or #3085, stem, 5.5" wide	32	65
Cracker jar w/cover, cylindrical, straight sided (ice bucket shape) chrome handle	245	485
Cup & saucer, coffee #1402/19 Tally Ho: cup 2.5", footed, 7 oz.; saucer w/indent 5.9"	28	60
Decanter w/blown stopper 12.25" #3077, flat, bar bottle shape w/long neck, 30 oz.	150	295
Finger bowl #3077, sherbet (blown)	22	45
Finger bowl & liner: bowl #3085 (blown), flat; plate w/indent	42	85
Finger bowl & liner: bowl #1402/14 Tally Ho, deep; plate w/ indent #1402/15	65	
Goblet #1402/13 Tally Ho (pressed) cordial, 1 oz.	85	
Goblet 4.6" #3075 or #3085, knob stem, cordial, 1 oz.	95	195
Goblet 4.6" #3077, plain stem, cordial, 1 oz.	110	225
Goblet #1402/12 Tally Ho (pressed) wine, 2.5 oz.	45	
Goblet 4.9" #3075 or #3085, knob stem, liquor cocktail, 2.5 oz.	24	48
Goblet 4.9" #3077, plain stem, liquor cocktail, 2.5 oz.	28	58
Goblet #3075 or #3085, knob stem, wine, 2.5 oz.	24	48
Goblet #3077, plain stem, wine, 2.5 oz.	28	58
Goblet #1402/10 Tally Ho (pressed) high, liquor cocktail, 3 oz.	40	
Goblet #3075 or #3085, knob stem, oyster cocktail, 4 oz.	20	40
Goblet #1402/11 Tally Ho (pressed) oyster cocktail, 4 oz.	32	
Goblet #1402/9 Tally Ho (pressed) claret, 4.5 oz.	42	
Goblet 5.6" #3075 or #3085, knob stem, claret, 4.5 oz.	28	58
Goblet 5.6" #3077, plain stem, claret, 4.5 oz.	30	65
Goblet #1402/20 Tally Ho (pressed) belled sherbet, 4.5 oz.	25	
Goblet #1402/8 Tally Ho (pressed) low tomato/orange juice, 5 oz.	32	
Goblet #3075 or #3085, knob stem, cafe parfait, 5.5 oz.	38	78
Goblet #3077, plain stem, cafe parfait, 5.5 oz.	42	85
Goblet 2.5" #3075, footed w/o stem, fruit salad, 6 oz.	16	34
Goblet 2.5" #3077, w/o stem, fruit salad, 6 oz.	20	40
Goblet #1402/7 Tally Ho (pressed) tall tomato/orange juice, 6 oz.	36	
Goblet 4.25" #3075 or #3085, short plain knob stem, sherbet, 6 oz.	17	34
Goblet 4.25" #3077, plain stem, sherbet, 6 oz.	20	40
Goblet #1402/6 Tally Ho (pressed) sherbet, 6.5 oz.	28	
Goblet #1402/5 Tally Ho (pressed) saucer champagne, 7.5 oz.	30	
Goblet 5.5" #3075 #3085, tall plain knob stem, saucer champagne, 6 oz.	18	36
Goblet 5.5" #3077, plain stem, saucer champagne, 6 oz.	19	38
Goblet 6.5" #3077, plain stem, lunch water, 9 oz.	19	38
Goblet 7.1" #3075 or #3085, short plain knob stem, water, 9 oz.	28	56
Goblet 7.1" #3077, plain stem, dinner water, 9 oz.	30	60
Goblet #1402/4 Tally Ho (pressed) lunch water, 10 oz.	38	
Goblet 6.3" #1402/3 Tally Ho (pressed) dinner water, 10 oz.	42	
Goblet 6.25" #1402/2 Tally Ho (pressed) ice tea, 14 oz.	48	
Goblet 6.9" #1402/1 Tally Ho (pressed) jumbo, 18 oz.	60	
Humidor w/cover 6" #1025, cylindrical, straight sided (flat top)	295	550
Ice bucket 5.75" #3400/851, flat, scalloped top w/chrome handle	90	175
Pitcher w/cover 6.5" #3075, squat, ringed bottom, circle finial, 23 oz.	195	395
Pitcher w/cover #3077/10, footed, tall cone shaped, 63 oz.	295	550
Pitcher 8.25" #935, flat, oval shape, w/o ice lip, 64 oz.	345	495
Pitcher #3135/712, footed, squat cone shape, 76 oz.	175	350
Pitcher w/cover #3135/711, footed, squat cone shape, 76 oz.	225	450
Plate 6.5" #3077, bread & butter	6	12
Plate 8" #556, salad	8	16
Plate 12" #487, oval, service	34	65
Plate, 13.5" #242, serving	40	75
Sandwich server 11" #173, oval, center handle	48	95
Shaker #395, footed, cone shape	125	250
Tray #880/881, center handled (bridge set w/4 tumblers)	42	85

Decanter w/blown stopper 12.25" #3077, flat, bar bottle shape w/long neck, 30 oz., Peach Blo (pink).

Peach Blo (pink) w/Gold encrusted grouping: **Left:** Goblet 7.1" #3077, plain stem, dinner water, 9 oz. **Center:** Goblet 5.6" #3077, plain stem, claret, 4.5 oz. **Right:** Tumbler 6" #3077, cone footed, ice tea, 12 oz.

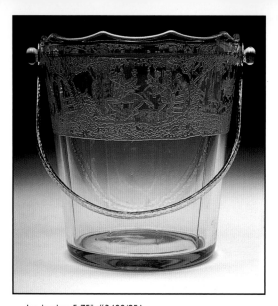

Ice bucket 5.75" #3400/851, flat, scalloped top w/chrome handle, Peach Blo (pink).

Tumbler 5" #880/881, flat, ringed 6 oz. (bridge set 4 tumblers w/tray)	24	48
Tumbler 2.25" #3085, flat, whiskey, 2 oz.	30	60
Tumbler 2.75" #3075 or #3085, footed, whiskey, 2.5 oz.	32	65
Tumbler 2.75" #3077, cone footed, whiskey, 3 oz.	35	68
Tumbler #3075 or #3085, footed, juice, 5 oz.	20	40
Tumbler #3077, cone footed, juice, 5 oz.	20	40
Tumbler #3085, flat, juice, 5 oz.	22	45
Tumbler #3075 or #3085, footed, lunch water, 8 oz.	26	55
Tumbler #3077, cone footed, lunch water, 8 oz.	30	60
Tumbler 4.75" #3085, flat, water, 10 oz.	35	65
Tumbler 5.25" #3075 or #3085, footed, dinner water, 10 oz.	28	55
Tumbler 5.25" #3077, cone footed, dinner water, 10 oz.	30	60
Tumbler #3085, flat, ice tea, 12 oz.	32	65
Tumbler 6" #3075 or #3085, footed, ice tea, 12 oz.	32	65
Tumbler 6" #3077, cone footed, ice tea, 12 oz.	32	65
Vase 6.5" #1005, footed, squat, urn shape w/flared top	95	195
Vase 7.8" #797, flat, flip shape w/panel optic	110	225
Whipping pail 3.3" #847, or ice tub, chrome handle, 5.4" wide	38	80

Tumbler 5" #880/881, flat, ringed, 6 oz., Peach Blo (pink).

Vase 7.8" #797, flat, flip shape w/ panel optic, Green.

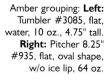

Amber grouping: **Left:** Tumbler #3085, flat, water, 10 oz., 4.75" tall. **Right:** Pitcher 8.25" #935, flat, oval shape, w/o ice lip, 64 oz.

Peach Blo (pink) grouping: **Left:** Tumbler #3077, cone footed, juice, 5 oz. **Right:** Pitcher w/cover 6.5" #3075, squat, ringed bottom, circle finial, 23 oz.

Plate, 13.5" #242, serving, Amber w/Gold encrusted edge.

. H. Heisey & Company   **Blank #1405**   **1931-46**

ain Colors: Crystal, Flamingo (pink), Moongleam (green), and Sahara (yellow)
ther Colors: Alexandrite and Cobalt

Ipswich resembles an old pressed glass pattern, Comet, from the Sandwich Glass Company. This was a very early pattern produced in the 1840-1850s. The pattern differs from omet in several ways. Comet has a round foot, pattern over most of the area, and a six-sided em with a bulge at the top. Ipswich has the following: square foot, the pattern forms a wide and, and the stem has a half skirted wafer.

A candle vase is listed that some people may not recognize. It is actually two pieces of ass. The footed bottom is 7.5" and has prisms hanging around the top, flat edge. This piece as referred to as a centerpiece, but would make a nice vase. The insert is a footed candle cup at was referred to as a vase. To us it looks more like a toothpick. Note, on this pattern the sert has no holes in the foot, so it can't be used as a vase and candlestick at the same time.

The cocktail shaker, cologne bottle, and pitcher are highly sought-after items. Perfume ollectors would just love to have an Ipswich cologne in their collections. There are two footed andies, one is .25 lb. while the other is a .5 lb. size. On the smaller one, the bottom is a 12 oz. ooted goblet with a lid. One would not want to pass up the small lid (note, 3.5" diameter).

The color of Alexandrite is a favorite among collectors but not much shows up in this attern. Whenever it does, the price is much higher than the Cobalt.

Back left: Plate 8.1", square lunch, Moongleam (green). **Front top left:** Creamer 3.1", flat, loop handle, 7.5 oz., Crystal. **Front bottom left:** Sugar 2.6", flat, loop handle, 7.5 oz., Crystal. **Front right:** Pitcher 8.25", flat, squat, flat top w/o ice lip, 64 oz., Sahara (yellow).

PSWICH	Crystal	Sahara	Flamingo	Moongleam	Cobalt
owl 11.4", footed w/short fat stem, flared	80	300	800	900	450
andle vase 1-lite 9.5", footed base w/ prisms & candle insert	175	400	550	750	700
andlestick 1-lite 6", footed, paneled column stem, pair	150	250	375	500	
andy w/cover 8.4", footed 1/4 lb. size, 3.5" wide	175			500	
andy w/cover, footed .5 lb. size, 4.1" wide	175	450	550	700	
ocktail shaker, flat, shouldered w/ strainer & stopper	350	700	800	1,000	
ologne w/octagon stopper, footed w/long dauber	350	550	700	750	
reamer 3.1", flat, loop handle, 7.5 oz.	35	90	125	150	
ruet w/stopper 6.4", footed, 2 oz.	125	275	285	300	
inger bowl & liner: bowl 4.4", flat, flared; plate w/indent 5.6"	56	85	95	145	
oblet 3.3", oyster cocktail w/o stem, 4 oz.	15	50	60	70	
oblet 3.2", sherbet w/skirted wafer stem 4 oz.	15	45	55	65	
oblet 4.75", skirted wafer stem, saucer champagne, 4 oz.	20	35	60	75	
oblet 5.25", skirted wafer stem, water, 10 oz.	25	70	85	90	
oblet 5.6", skirted wafer stem, water, 12 oz.	35	55	90	95	
itcher 8.25", flat, squat, flat top w/o ice lip, 64 oz.	350	750	1,000	1,250	
late 7", square salad	30	50	60	70	
late 8.1", square lunch	35	45	65	75	
ugar 2.6", flat, loop handle, 7.5 oz.	35	90	125	150	
umbler 4.7", footed, juice/soda w/o stem, 5 oz.	30	40	80	105	
umbler, footed, soda w/o stem, 8 oz.	30	40	80	105	
umbler 4", flat, straight or cupped, water, 10 oz.	70	100	110	140	
umbler 5.5", footed, soda w/o stem, 10 oz.	40	70	85	110	
umbler 5.75", footed, soda w/o stem, 12 oz.	40	70	85	110	
umbler, flat, schoppen, 12 oz.	100				

Top left: Tumbler 4", flat, cupped, water, 10 oz., Crystal. **Top center:** Goblet 3.2", sherbet w/skirted wafer stem 4 oz., Sahara (yellow). **Top right:** Goblet 3.3", oyster cocktail w/o stem, 4 oz., Flamingo (pink). **Bottom left:** Tumbler 4.7", footed, juice/soda w/o stem, 5 oz., Moongleam (green). **Bottom center left:** Goblet 4.75", skirted wafer stem, saucer champagne, 4 oz., Moongleam (green). **Bottom center:** Goblet 5.25", skirted wafer stem, water, 10 oz., Sahara (yellow). **Bottom center right:** Tumbler 5.5", footed, soda w/o stem, 10 oz., Moongleam (green). **Bottom right:** Tumbler 5.75", footed, soda w/o stem, 12 oz., Flamingo (pink).

Cobalt grouping: Left: Bowl 11.4", footed w/short fat stem, flared. **Center:** Dealer glass sign 3.8" ($125 – we found it priced this). **Right:** Candle vase 1-lite 9.5", footed base w/prisms & candle insert.

Left: Finger bowl & liner: bowl 4.4", flat, flared; plate w/indent 5.6", Crystal. **Center left:** Cruet w/stopper 6.4", footed, 2 oz., Sahara (yellow). **Center right:** Goblet 5.6", skirted wafer stem, water, 12 oz., Crystal. **Right:** Candy w/cover 8.4", footed 1/4 lb. size, 3.5" wide, Moongleam (green).

Left: Jelly w/cover 6.1" #447, footed, tall stem; knob finial, Green.
Center: Tumbler 4.25" #73, flat, water, 9 oz., Blue. **Right:** Tumbler 5.1" #64, flat, beverage, 12 oz., Blue.

Blue grouping: **Left:** Tumbler 4.75" #88, footed, juice, 5 oz. **Center:** Goblet 4.25" #7, sherbet, 6.5 oz. **Right:** Goblet 5.75" #2, water, 9.5 oz.

Left: Goblet 5.75" #2, water, 9.5 oz., Ruby. **Right:** Pitcher 7.5" #456, collar footed, water, straight sided w/ice lip, 48 oz., Amber.

Left: Tumbler 6" #63, footed, short stem, ice tea, 11 oz., Pink. **Center:** Goblet 5.75" #2, water, 9.5 oz., Amethyst. **Right:** Tumbler 6" #63, footed, short stem, ice tea, 11 oz., Amethyst.

JAMESTOWN

Fostoria Glass Company   **Blank #2719**   **1958-82**
Colors: Amber, Amethyst, Blue, Crystal, Green, Pink, Ruby, and Smoke

The religious suppression in England forced many hard working men and women to come to America to establish a new life. The Jamestown settlement was settled in 1607. A year later the first glass-making facility was set up to provide items for the colonists. As the 350th anniversary approached in 1958, it was felt these ambitious colonists should be honored for their efforts of establishing glass-making in America. A replica of the original glass house was reconstructed according to historical records. For this celebration, Fostoria created a pattern to honor the town. The swirled panels were reminiscent of early American designs. The pattern was meant to be used during everyday meals.

Jamestown seems to be another pattern where stemware is in abundant supply and any other items will take some patience to locate. Hardest to find are the cake salver and salad set. The handled 11" sandwich has a large center and seems to have been used most often for a decorating company. We see the tray in crystal with the Happy Anniversary silver overlay decoration on a regular basis.

JAMESTOWN	Amber Crystal Smoke	Green	Blue Amethyst	Pink Ruby
Bowl 4.5" #421, fruit or dessert	8	14	18	25
Bowl 9" #648, handled, vegetable	22	35	45	65
Bowl 10" #211, flat, deep, salad	22	48	70	75
Butter w/cover 7.9" #300, oblong, .25 lb.	28	48	65	80
Cake plate 9.5" #306, handled, 12" counting handles, small center	20	32	40	54
Cake salver 10" #630, pedestal foot	40	110	95	135
Creamer 4" #681, footed, regular, 6 oz.	8	12	16	24
Goblet 4.3" #26, wine, 4 oz.	8	12	20	26
Goblet 4.25" #7, sherbet, 6.5 oz.	6	10	16	20
Goblet 5.75" #2, water, 9.5 oz.	10	18	24	30
Jelly w/cover 6.1" #447, footed, tall stem; knob finial	28	45	54	72
Pitcher 7.5" #456, collar footed, water, straight sided w/ice lip, 48 oz.	45	80	125	175
Plate 8" #550, lunch	8	12	16	22
Plate 14" #567, small center, turned up edge, cabaret or salad bowl liner	16	24	40	54
Relish 8.4" #540, oval pickle	10	18	24	28
Relish 9.25" #360, oval celery	12	20	26	30
Relish 9.25" #620, oval, 2 sections	14	22	28	32
Sauce w/cover 4.5" #635, or small candy	20	35	45	58
Shaker 3.5" #653, chrome top, pair	24	35	45	60
Sugar 3.5" #679, footed, regular, 6 oz.	8	12	16	24
Tray 9.4" #726, handles turned up, muffin	22	35	45	60
Tray 11", flat, 2 open handled, 13.5" counting handles, sandwich, large center	20	32	42	56
Tumbler 4.75" #88, footed, juice, 5 oz.	8	14	23	28
Tumbler 4.25" #73, flat, water, 9 oz.	10	16	25	30
Tumbler 6" #63, footed, short stem, ice tea, 11 oz.	12	20	28	32
Tumbler 5.1" #64, flat, beverage, 12 oz.	14	22	30	34

Blue grouping: **Back:** Plate 8" #550, lunch.
Front: Bowl 4.5" #421, fruit or dessert.

Back: Tray 11", flat, 2 open handled, 13.5" counting handles, sandwich, large center, Crystal – shown w/silver overlay decoration.
Right: Shaker 3.5" #653, chrome top, pair, Pink.

JENNY LIND

Fostoria Glass Company 1955-65

Main Colors: Aqua Milk Glass, Milk Glass, and Peach Milk Glass
Other Colors: Amethyst and Olive Green

Jenny Lind was a Swedish singer who toured America in the early 1850s. She was famous all over the world for her great singing ability. The same year that Fostoria was established, the world lost this famous singer. In its early years, Fostoria first made this pattern with a lady's face in opal glass. These were hand painted with the dark colors of the time. It wasn't too attractive. At this time the pattern was called Actress and only a few items were made.

In 1954, Fostoria decided to reintroduce this pattern. This time it was called Jenny Lind. The new colors were milk glass along with an opaque aqua and pink. The opaque pink was called Peach Milk Glass. A complete line of items was made to accommodate the needs of the lady.

The cologne bottle in this pattern will throw off new collectors, because it is so large it will make you think that it is a decanter. In fact, it would be more accurate to refer to it as a toilet water bottle rather than a cologne. It seems that the white Milk Glass cologne bottle is in abundant supply, but the Blue & Pink are much harder to find. The small pomade is elusive to collectors in any of the colors.

Later in the mid-1960s, Jenny Lind was again reissued as part of the Garden line Fostoria developed to attract new customers. Not all of the items were made in the new colors of amber, amethyst, olive green, and pink. Many of the items were only sampled and not put in actual production. The former cologne flask was now made as a vase with its top polished off to fit with the garden assortment. We will work on developing a list of these items as we run across them.

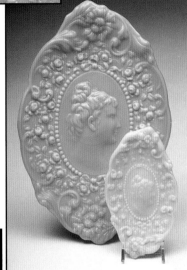

Pattern detail, Jenny Lind.

JENNY LIND	White	Pink	Blue
Cologne w/blown stopper 11", flask shape w/neck	70	135	160
Glove box w/cover 10.5", oval w/4-tab feet	125	165	195
Handkerchief box w/cover 5.5", square w/4-tab feet	65	110	125
Jewel box w/cover 6", oval w/4-tab feet	48	75	85
Pin box w/cover 5", oval w/4-tab feet	40	65	75
Pitcher 8.5", handled, water w/o ice lip, 36 oz.	85	150	175
Pomade w/cover 2.25", round w/4-tab feet, 2.1" tall	95	135	160
Jewel box w/cover 6", oval w/4-tab feet	50	80	90
Tray 6", flat, oval, pin	28	48	55
Tray 11.5", flat, oval, comb & brush	48	85	95
Tumbler 4.5", flat, straight sided (blown) 13 oz.	32	48	60

Back left: Tray 11.5", flat, oval, comb & brush, Aqua Milk Glass. **Front right:** Tray 6", flat, oval, pin, Peach Milk Glass.

Top: Glove box w/cover 10.5", oval w/4-tab feet, Aqua Milk Glass. **Bottom left:** Pin box w/cover 5", oval w/4-tab feet, Peach Milk Glass. **Bottom right:** Jewel box w/cover 6", oval w/4-tab feet, Aqua Milk Glass.

Vase made from cologne w/o stopper, 7.75", flask shape w/neck, Pink Lady (sample color $85 – we found it priced this).

Left: Jewel box w/cover 6", oval w/4-tab feet, Milk Glass. **Center:** Handkerchief box w/cover 5.5", square w/4-tab feet, Peach Milk Glass. **Right:** Pomade w/cover 2.25", round w/4-tab feet, 2.1" tall, Aqua Milk Glass.

Left: Cologne w/blown stopper 11", flask shape w/neck, Milk Glass. **Center:** Tumbler 4.5", flat, straight sided (blown) 13 oz., Milk Glass. **Right:** Pitcher 8.5", handled, water w/o ice lip, 36 oz., Peach Milk Glass.

Pattern detail, Jubilee.

Candy Jar w/cover 5.25", 3-footed, 7.4" wide, Yellow.

JUBILEE
Lancaster Glass Company **Cutting #1200** **1930s**
Colors: Crystal, Pink, and Yellow

Jubilee is being added to this edition by request of many collectors. For years this pattern has been relegated to the Depression glass books. We feel it definitely belongs in with the elegant patterns since the floral pattern on it was all cut by hand. This extra intricate step was done by skilled workers in a special location within the glass factory.

The floral design consists of a 12 petal flower with an open center. A single stem of leaves trails between the flowers. The Jubilee pattern is found on blanks with scalloped edges. There are a few variations of the flower having only 11 petals. That probably occurred with the space allowed for the placement of the flower on that particular item. The workers were only concerned at the time with making a product and not with the later questions from collectors. Standard Glass also made a pattern similar to Jubilee they called Martha Washington. These pieces are found on round items with a paneled optic. Many collectors mix these two patterns to get a large variety.

Yellow & pink are the colors of choice among collectors. Crystal hasn't yet caught on but I am sure it will eventually because of its cheaper cost.

JUBILEE	Yellow	Pink
Bowl 8", 3-footed	245	295
Bowl 9" #835, open handles	135	
Bowl 11.5", 3-footed	260	265
Bowl 13", 3-footed	250	265
Candlestick 1-lite 2", scalloped edge, each	98	125
Candy Jar w/cover 5.25", 3-footed, 7.4" wide	385	425
Cheese & cracker: comport #822; plate #879, open handled	225	265
Creamer 3.25" tall, #879, footed	24	30
Cup & saucer, coffee: cup 2.25" tall, flat, 6 oz.; saucer w/indent 6"	16	48
Goblet 7.5", water, 11 ounces	160	
Goblet 3", sherbet, 8 ounces	85	
Goblet 5.5", champagne, 7 ounces	110	
Goblet 4.75", oyster cocktail, 4 ounces	85	
Goblet 4.8", cocktail, 3 ounces	150	
Goblet 4", cordial, 1 ounce	245	
Mayonnaise 2 piece: #889 bowl 4.75" tall, 3 ball feet; #890 liner w/indent	225	275
Plate 7", salad	12	20
Plate 8.75" lunch	14	28
Plate 11" #895 sandwich, open 2-handled or cake tray	45	62
Plate 13.5" sandwich, 3-footed	225	245
Sandwich server 11" #885, center handle	175	195
Sugar 3.25" #879, footed	22	34
Tumbler 5", footed, juice, 6 ounces	98	
Tumbler 6", footed, water, 10 ounces	38	75
Tumbler 6.1", footed, ice tea, 12.5 ounces	175	
Vase 12", footed, bud vase	375	425

Back right: Plate 8.75" lunch. **Front left:** Goblet 7.5", water, 11 ounces. **Front center left:** Cup & saucer, coffee: cup 2.25" tall, flat, 6 oz.; saucer w/indent 6". **Front center right:** Creamer 3.25" tall, #879, footed. **Front right:** Sugar 3.25" #879, footed.

Fostoria Glass Company **Etching #279** **1928-52**

Colors: Azure (blue), Crystal, Rose (pink), and Topaz (yellow)

June is often confused with Romance by new collectors. This is one of the reasons we have included detail shots of the etched patterns to eliminate any confusion and to aid the collectors in properly identifying an etched pattern. If you are a new collector, it takes a lot of studying to realize all the differences. Take time to look at each of the close-up shots of each of these etched patterns. The June ribbon is formed by two parallel lines, as opposed to Romance, which has a wide solid line for the ribbon.

The Fairfax 2375 is the blank on which most of this etched pattern is found. Stemware was produced on the #5098 (5298) blank. Note, stemware has a Crystal foot & stem but with a colored bowl. Some of the items most collectors seem to want include: candy, cruet, decanter, sauce boat with liner, salad dressing bottle, shakers, sugar pail, and vase. In past times the blue was the hot color. Now the new collectors are attracted to the Topaz color since it is cheaper in price and still a very pretty color for their table.

Pattern detail, June.

JUNE	Crystal	Topaz	Rose	Azure
Ashtray 3.75" #2350, individual	20	45	50	55
Ashtray 5" #2350, large, round, flared edge	25	50	55	60
Bonbon 6.75" #2375 Fairfax, 2 style of handles, both turned up	15	38	45	48
Bottle w/rounded top stopper 7" #2375 Fairfax, flat, salad dressing, 4.75 oz.	350	600+	800+	900+
Bottle w/flat stopper 6.5" #2083, flat, salad dressing, 7 oz.	400	750+	900+	1,000+
Bowl 5.1" #2375 Fairfax, flared, fruit	24	32	35	38
Bowl 5.4" #2375 Fairfax, 2 style of handles, sweetmeat	22	30	35	40
Bowl 6" #2375 Fairfax, flared, cereal	25	55	65	85
Bowl 6" #5098 (5298), footed	40	65	70	80
Bowl 7" #2375 Fairfax, flared, soup	65	125	145	160
Bowl 8" #2375 Fairfax, (can flare out to 9") round	48	78	90	100
Bowl 8.5" #2375 Fairfax, handled, dessert	60	100	125	145
Bowl 9.25" #2375 Fairfax, oval, vegetable	50	85	120	160
Bowl 10" #2395, oval, console w/large scroll handles	85	150	175	200
Bowl 10.5" #2375 Fairfax, oval, vegetable	55	95	135	175
Bowl 11" #2375 Fairfax, centerpiece			150	175
Bowl 12" #2375 Fairfax, 3-footed, flared, console	50	85	90	110
Bowl 12" #2375 1/2 Fairfax, mushroom-shaped, console	65	90	120	145
Bowl 12" #2394, flared, 3-footed, console	60	80	85	90
Bowl 13" #2375 1/2 Fairfax, oval, mushroom-shaped, centerpiece w/frog	145		275	295
Cake plate 9.75" #2375 Fairfax, small center, open handled	40	60	75	85
Candle bowl 1-lite 2" #2394, 3-footed, flared, pair	35	48	65	75
Candlestick 1-lite, 2.75" #2375 1/2 Fairfax, mushroom-shaped, pair	60	85	100	120
Candlestick 1-lite 3.25" #2375 Fairfax, pair	32	60	65	70
Candlestick 1-lite 4" #2324, plain short stem, pair	40	65	70	75
Candlestick 1-lite 5" #2395 1/2, 2 high scroll handles, pair	75	110	135	160
Candy w/cover 7" #2331, 3 sections, "fleur-de-lis" finial		225	250	295
Candy jar w/cover 6" #2394, 3-footed w/ dome lid, .5 lb.	135	175	195	225
Cheese & cracker #2375 Fairfax: comport 2.4", short stem, 5.25" wide; liner w/indent, 2 style handles 9.75"	65	95	125	145
Cheese & cracker: comport 2.9" #2368, short stem, cupped w/o optic, 5" wide; plate 11", handled (w/o optic)	58	90	115	135
Comport 4.5" #2400, low lady leg stem, flared, 6" wide	48	68	88	98
Comport 4.75" #5098 (5298) flared, 5" wide	38	65	85	90
Comport 6" #2375 Fairfax, lady leg stem, flared, 6.75" wide		80	90	98
Comport 7.5" #2400, high, lady leg stem, flared, 8" wide		115	125	145
Cream soup & liner #2375 Fairfax: bowl 6", footed, handled & flared, 10 oz.; saucer w/indent 7.4"	45	75	85	95
Creamer, 3" #2375 1/2 Fairfax, footed, individual, 3.25 oz.	20	40	45	50
Creamer 3.3" #2375 1/2 Fairfax, footed, regular, 6.75 oz.	15	25	30	35
Cruet w/stopper 9.25" #2375 Fairfax, footed, 5 oz.	350	650+	795+	895+
Cup & saucer, after dinner #2375 Fairfax: cup 2.75", footed, 2.5 oz.; saucer w/indent 4.75"	40	80	90	100
Cup & saucer, bouillon #2375 Fairfax: cup 2.5", footed, handled, 5 oz., 4" wide; saucer w/indent 5.75"	26	34	40	46
Cup & saucer, coffee #2375 Fairfax: cup 2.5" footed, 6 oz.; saucer w/indent 5.75"	20	28	34	40
Decanter w/stopper 10.75" #2439, flat, reverse cone shape, 30 oz.	400	600	1,600+	1,800+
Finger bowl & liner: bowl 4.6" #869, blown, 8 oz.; plate w/indent 6"	45	75	95	125+
Goblet 3.9" #5098 (5298), cordial, .75 oz.	45	85	110	125
Goblet 5.4" #5098 (5298), wine, 2.5 oz.	24	50	75	85
Goblet 5.1" #5098 (5298), liquor cocktail, 3 oz.	22	36	45	50

Azure (blue) grouping: **Top left:** Finger bowl & liner: bowl 4.6" #869, blown, 8 oz.; plate w/indent 6". **Bottom left:** Bowl 5.4" #2375 Fairfax, 2 style of handles, sweetmeat. **Bottom right:** Cup & saucer, coffee #2375 Fairfax: cup 2.5" footed, 6 oz.; saucer w/indent 5.75".

Topaz (yellow) grouping: **Back:** Plate 8.6" #2375 Fairfax, lunch. **Front left:** Candle bowl 1-lite 2" #2394, 3-footed, flared, pair (one turned on side). **Front center:** Candlestick 1-lite 4" #2324, plain short stem. **Front right:** Tumbler 6" #5098 (5298), footed, ice tea, 12 oz.

Rose (pink) grouping: **Left:** Plate 7.35" #2375 Fairfax, salad or dessert. **Right:** Cup & saucer, coffee #2375 Fairfax: cup 2.5" footed, 6 oz.; saucer w/indent 5.75".

Pitcher 9.75" #5000, footed, applied handle, water w/o ice lip, 48 oz., Azure (blue).

Left: Vase 8" #4100, straight sided, flip shape, Rose (pink). **Right:** Vase 8" #4100, straight sided, flip shape, Azure (blue).

Crystal grouping: **Left:** Goblet 5.1" #5098 (5298), liquor cocktail, 3 oz. **Center left:** Goblet 6" #5098 (5298), claret, 4 oz. **Center right:** Goblet 6" #5098 (5298), saucer champagne, 6 oz. **Right:** Goblet 8.25" #5098 (5298), water, 9 oz.

Topaz (yellow) grouping: **Top:** Bowl 9.25" #2375 Fairfax, oval, vegetable. **Bottom left:** Creamer, 3" #2375 1/2 Fairfax, footed, individual, 3.25 oz. **Bottom center:** Sugar 2.75" #2375 1/2 Fairfax, footed, individual, 3 oz. **Bottom right:** Cup & saucer, after dinner #2375 Fairfax: cup 2.75", footed, 2.5 oz.; saucer w/indent 4.75".

Topaz (yellow) grouping: **Back:** Platter 12.25" #2375 Fairfax, oval. **Front left:** Candlestick 1-lite 5" #2395 1/2, 2 high scroll handles. **Front right:** Comport 4.75" #5098 (5298) flared, 5" wide.

Goblet 6" #5098 (5298), claret, 4 oz.	36	65	110	125
Goblet 3.75" #5098 (5298), footed oyster cocktail, 5 oz.	14	24	30	40
Goblet 4.1" #5098 (5298), sherbet, 6 oz.	15	24	28	32
Goblet 6" #5098 (5298), saucer champagne, 6 oz.	16	28	38	45
Goblet 8.25" #5098 (5298), water, 9 oz.	32	55	85	95
Grapefruit bowl #5082 1/2, large sherbet shape	45	75	110	125
Grapefruit insert #945 1/2, small version of grapefruit	34	55	75	85
Ice bucket 6" #2375 Fairfax, chrome handle, 5.15" wide	85	100	165	175
Ice bucket 6" #2378, flat, cylindrical chrome handle	85	100	165	175
Ice dish 2.75" #2451, bowl w/3-tabs hold liners, 4.8" wide	40	60	75	85
Ice dish liner 2.75" #2451, crab meat, 4 oz.	24	30	35	40
Ice dish liner 1.9" #2451, fruit cocktail, 5 oz.	28	35	40	45
Ice dish liner 3.5" #2451, tomato juice, 5 oz.	18	24	28	34
Ice dish plate 7" #2451, plain w/indent	12	18	20	22
Mayonnaise 2 piece #2375 Fairfax: bowl 5.6", footed, flared; plate w/indent 7.4"	58	95	110	125
Pitcher 9.75" #5000, footed, applied handle, water w/o ice lip, 48 oz.	295	345	695	595
Plate 6.25" #2375 Fairfax, bread & butter	8	12	14	16
Plate 6.25" #2375 Fairfax, canape w/offset indent	25	35	45	50
Plate 6.8" #2375 Fairfax, 2 style of handles, lemon server	15	25	30	35
Plate 7.35" #2375 Fairfax, salad or dessert or dessert	10	14	16	18
Plate 8.6" #2375 Fairfax, lunch	16	18	22	28
Plate 9.25" #2375 Fairfax, small dinner	20	30	45	48
Plate 10.25" #2375 Fairfax, grill, 3 sections	40	65	75	85
Plate 10.25" #2375 Fairfax, large dinner	55	100	145	175
Plate 13.75" #2375 Fairfax, large center, chop or torte	50	90	125	145
Platter 12.25" #2375 Fairfax, oval	60	135	150	160
Platter 15" #2375 Fairfax, oval	95	175	250	260
Relish 8.5" #2375 Fairfax, oval pickle	18	35	42	48
Relish 8.5" #2375 Fairfax, oval, 2 equal sections	24	40	45	55
Relish 11.5" #2375 Fairfax, oval, celery	40	80	100	115
Relish 11.5" #2375 Fairfax, oval, 3 sections	50	85	110	125
Sandwich server 11" #2375 Fairfax, center "fleur-de-lis" handle	60	100	125	145
Sauce & liner #2375 Fairfax: bowl 6.75", oval 2 spouted, 3.5" wide; oval liner w/indent 8"	165	350	395	450
Shaker, 3.25" #2375 Fairfax, footed, w/ chrome or glass top, pair	125	195	225	245
Sugar 2.75" #2375 1/2 Fairfax, footed, individual, 3 oz.	20	40	45	50
Sugar 3.1" #2375 1/2 Fairfax, footed, regular 6.75 oz.	15	25	30	35
Sugar bowl cover #2375 1/2 Fairfax, lid	60	110	150	175
Sugar pail 3.75" #2378, chrome handle	95	245	275	295
Tray 6" #2394, 3-footed, mint		38	45	48
Tray 12" #2429 Fairfax, oblong service or cordial tray, 7" wide	68	120	140	150
Tray 12" #2429 Fairfax, oblong service, 2 piece w/lemon insert (plain not etched)	165	300	350	375
Tumbler 2.9" #5098 (5298), footed, whiskey, 2.5 oz.	30	65	85	95
Tumbler 4.4" #5098 (5298), footed, juice, 5 oz.	18	32	45	65
Tumbler 5.25" #5098 (5298), parfait, 6 oz.	40	70	90	125
Tumbler 5.25" #5098 (5298), footed, water, 9 oz.	20	35	45	60
Tumbler 6" #5098 (5298), footed, ice tea, 12 oz.	26	40	75	85
Vase 5.5" #2385, footed, wafer & ball stem, fan shape		125	135	145
Vase 8" #4100, straight sided, flip shape	125	275	300	395
Vase 8.5" #2385, footed, fan shape		250	275	295
Whip cream bowl 5.5" #2375 Fairfax, handled	18	38	48	55
Whip cream pail 4.5" #2378, chrome handle, 2.5" tall	135	250	275	300

Crystal grouping: **Left:** Bottle w/flat stopper 6.5" #2083, flat, salad dressing, 7 oz. **Right:** Bottle w/ rounded top stopper 7" #2375 Fairfax, flat, salad dressing, 4.75 oz

JUNE NIGHT
Tiffin Glass Company
Color: Crystal

1941-58

June Night features flowers in a scalloped oval medallion. Stems were produced on line #17392. When Tiffin applied a plain gold band at the top of the stems, they were given a different name of Cherry Laurel. When pricing items with a gold band, add 10% to the price listed. Since many of the serving pieces are on the same blank #5902, new collectors tend to confuse this etched pattern with Cherokee Rose, another Tiffin etched pattern. Be sure to check the pattern detail of each to distinguish the difference between the two etched patterns.

Oddly, this was one of the few dinnerware patterns for which no cups & saucers were made. For most collectors, this doesn't matter since cups and saucers are not that desirable. It isn't an item that is used extensively anymore.

Pattern detail, June Night.

JUNE NIGHT	Crystal
Bell 5.75" #9743, dinner, 7 graduated beads on handle	75
Bell 6.25" #9742, dinner, 7 graduated beads on handle	85
Bowl 6" #5902, flat, cupped, nut	30
Bowl 7.25" #5902, shallow, flared, soup or salad	34
Bowl 10" #5902, cupped, salad	74
Bowl 12" #5902, crimped, centerpiece	85
Bowl 12.6" #5902, flared, centerpiece	75
Bowl 13" #5902, flared, cone, centerpiece	70
Candlestick 2-lite 5.75" #5902, plume center, 7.6" spread, pair	95
Comport 6.25" #15082, 6 beads on stem, cupped, 6.5" wide	45
Creamer 3.4" #5902, flat, regular w/beaded handle, 6 oz.	18
Finger bowl 4.6" #14196 (blown), flat, 12 oz.	24
Goblet 5.4" #17392, cordial, 1.5 oz.	42
Goblet 5.4" #17392, sherry, 2 oz.	35
Goblet 5.1" #17392, liquor cocktail, round bowl bottom 3.5 oz.	20
Goblet 5.35" #17392, liquor cocktail, bulging sides bowl 3.5 oz.	28
Goblet 5.8" #17392, wine, 3.5 oz.	28
Goblet 3.25" #17392, footed oyster cocktail, 4.5 oz.	18
Goblet 6.25" #17392, claret, 4.5 oz.	38
Goblet #17392, parfait, 5.5 oz.	40
Goblet 4.1" #17392, sherbet or sundae, round bowl bottom 6.5 oz.	14
Goblet 4.35" #17392, sherbet or sundae, bulging sides bowl 6.5 oz.	20
Goblet 6.2" #17392, saucer champagne, round bowl bottom 6.5 oz.	16
Goblet 6.5" #17392, saucer champagne, sherbet or sundae, bulging sides bowl 6.5 oz.	22
Goblet #17392, water, 10 oz.	28
Mayonnaise 2 piece #5902: bowl 4.4", cupped; liner w/indent 6.25"	45
Pitcher 8" #5859, flat, jug w/o ice lip, 64 oz.	275
Pitcher 8.5" #14194, footed w/o ice lip, 64 oz.	300
Pitcher w/cover 9.4" #14194, footed w/o ice lip, 64 oz.	425
Plate 6" #5902, bread & butter	8
Plate 8.25" #5902, salad or lunch	10
Plate 13.5" #5902, small center, turned up edge, cabaret	48
Plate 14.6" #5902, sandwich (small center)	48
Relish 6.4" #5902, round, 3 sections	38
Relish 10.5" #5902, rectangle, celery	40
Relish 10.75" #5902, tab handled, oblong, 2 equal sections & celery section	60
Sugar 3.25" #5902, flat, regular w/beaded handle, 8 oz.	18
Tray 12.5" #5902, center beaded handle	48
Tumbler 5.25" #17392, footed, juice, 5 oz.	18
Tumbler 5.9" #17392, footed, water, 9 oz.	20
Tumbler 6.6" #17392, footed, ice tea, 12 oz.	24
Vase 6.5" #14185, footed, tapered, bud vase	24
Vase 8.25", flat (bottle shaped) bud vase	48
Vase 8.25" #14185, footed, tapered, bud vase	35
Vase 8.5" #5856, footed, tear drop	78
Vase 9.25" #17350, footed w/1 ball stem, large tub shape	85
Vase 10.5" #14185, footed, tapered, bud vase	42
Vase 10.9" #15082, footed w/6 bead stem, flared, bud vase	48
Vase 11" #5943, footed urn w/1 large ball stem	98
Vase 12" #5855, footed, short stem, flared	85

Bowl 13" #5902, flared, cone, centerpiece.

Left: Candlestick 2-lite 5.75" #5902, plume center, 7.6" spread. **Right:** Relish 10.75" #5902, tab handled, oblong, 2 equal sections & celery section.

Left: Goblet 5.8" #17392, wine, 3.5 oz. **Right:** Goblet 5.4" #17392, sherry, 2 oz.

Vase 8.25", flat (bottle-shaped) bud vase.

Left: Goblet 3.25" #17392, footed oyster cocktail, 4.5 oz. **Center:** Goblet 5.35" #17392, liquor cocktail, bulging sides bowl 3.5 oz. **Right:** Tumbler 6.6" #17392, footed, ice tea, 12 oz.

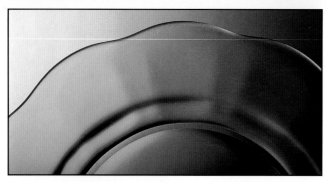

Pattern detail, Lafayette.

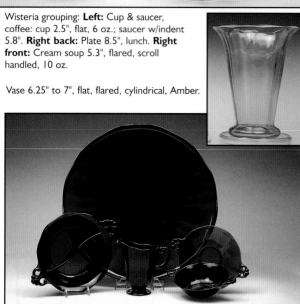

Wisteria grouping: **Left:** Cup & saucer, coffee: cup 2.5", flat, 6 oz.; saucer w/indent 5.8". **Right back:** Plate 8.5", lunch. **Right front:** Cream soup 5.3", flared, scroll handled, 10 oz.

Vase 6.25" to 7", flat, flared, cylindrical, Amber.

Burgundy (amethyst) grouping: **Back row:** Plate 13.9", small center, turned up edge, cabaret. **Front left:** Relish 6.25", tab plume handled, round, 2 equal sections. **Front center:** Creamer 4.25", footed, scroll handle, regular, 6.75 oz. **Front right:** Plate 5.25", flat, tab plume handled, lemon server; Bowl 4.5", tab plume handled, oval, sweetmeat.

LAFAYETTE

Fostoria Glass Company   #2440   1931-60

Main Colors: Amber, Crystal, Green, Rose (pink), Topaz (yellow), and Wisteria (lilac)
Other Colors: Burgundy (amethyst), Empire Green, Regal Blue (cobalt), and Ruby

At first glance, this pattern can be confused with Fairfax, since both have optic patterns in their design. Lafayette features an optic that has a wide panel alternating with a very narrow panel. Fairfax optic, on the other hand, has panels with all the same width.

This is probably one of the fastest rising of all the Fostoria patterns. It is starting to get lots more attention for its simplicity. This blank was used on the Fuchsia, Midnight Rose, and Navarre etchings. Collectors can buy items from this pattern to supplement their etched patterns and not be out much money.

A complete set can be assembled in Topaz & Crystal, but limited items can be found in Wisteria, which is very attractive. Crystal, when satinized, is called Silver Mist. Collectors of Fostoria's dark colors can add several pieces in this pattern to their specific color collections.

Wisteria pieces of Lafayette tend to elude collectors. So many collectors of this color are vying for a very limited supply. A good example would be the after dinner cup & saucer set.

At the request of several collectors, we are adding values for Burgundy, Empire Green, Regal Blue, and Ruby. Not every item was made in all the colors within the color groupings. We have combined colors that sell for similar prices for ease in making our price columns.

LAFAYETTE	Amber Crystal	Green Rose Topaz	Ruby Wisteria	Burgundy Empire Green Regal Blue
Almond, 3", flat flared, individual, nut, 1.6" tall	10	18	36	
Bonbon 5", tab plume handles turned up	14	20	38	32
Bowl 4.5", tab plume handled, oval, sweetmeat	16	22	48	32
Bowl 5", flat flared, fruit	12	22	30	
Bowl 6", flat flared, cereal	16	24	38	
Bowl 7", flat deep, "D" shape, cupped in	18	38	85	
Bowl 10", flat, "B" shape, slightly cupped up edge	16	35	95	
Bowl 10", flat, oval, slightly flared, vegetable (baker)	20	40	95	
Bowl 10.5", flat, flared	22	42	95	
Bowl 12", deep, slightly cupped up edge, salad	24	45	125	
Cake plate 10.5", tab plume handled	30	45		65
Creamer 4.25", footed, scroll handle, regular, 6.75 oz.	14	24	45	42
Cream soup 5.3", flared, scroll handled, 10 oz.	18	35	68	
Cup & saucer, after dinner: cup 2.6", footed, 2.5 oz.; saucer w/indent 4.75"	20	32	85	
Cup & saucer, coffee: cup 2.5", flat, 6 oz.; saucer w/indent 5.8"	18	24	48	45
Cup & saucer, coffee: cup 2.75", footed, 6 oz.; saucer w/indent 5.8"	18	24	48	
Mayonnaise 6.5", tab plume handled, salad dressing	24	35	85	55
Plate 5.25", flat, tab plume handled, lemon server	18	22	45	28
Plate 6.25", bread & butter	8	12	18	
Plate 7.25", salad or dessert	10	14	28	
Plate 8.5", lunch	12	16	35	
Plate 9.5", small dinner	16	28	58	
Plate 10.25", large dinner	28	40	95	
Plate 13", small center, torte or salad bowl liner	28	48	98	110
Plate 13.9", small center, turned up edge, cabaret	30	50	98	110
Platter 12", oval	35	48	110	
Relish 6.25", tab plume handled, round, 2 equal sections	18	32	60	45
Relish 6.5", flat flared, oval olive	16	24	45	
Relish 7.25", 3-tab plume handles, 3 equal sections	24	38	68	52
Relish 9.25", flat, flared, oval pickle	16	26	45	
Relish 11.5", flat, flared, oval celery	24	34	65	
Sauce 2 piece: bowl 6.75" tab plume handled, oval; oval liner w/indent 8.5"	38	60	125	100
Sugar 3.6", footed, scroll handled, regular, 6.75 oz.	14	24	45	42
Vase 6.25" to 7", flat, flared, cylindrical	35	58		

Empire Green grouping: **Back row:** Sugar 3.6", footed, scroll handled, regular, 6.75 oz. **Front left:** Cup & saucer, coffee: cup 2.5", flat, 6 oz.; saucer w/indent 5.8". **Front right:** Relish 6.5", flat flared, oval olive.

Relish 6.25", tab plume handled, round, 2 equal sections, Ruby.

Regal Blue (cobalt) grouping: **Back row:** Cake plate 10.5", tab plume handled. **Front left:** Relish 7.25", 3-plume handles, 3 equal sections. **Front center:** Bonbon 5", tab plume handles turned up. **Front right:** Relish 6.25", tab plume handled, round, 2 equal sections.

LARIAT
A. H. Heisey & Company   **Blank #1540**   **1941-57**
Color: Crystal

Heisey was looking to develop a pattern similar to Imperial's Candlewick. It had been selling at a very fast rate for the five years before Heisey brought out Lariat. Heisey needed to find a pattern that would compete with Candlewick and get customers back buying their glass. With the Heisey family having their own stable of horses, it seemed a natural to develop a pattern with this type of theme. A rope with a loop in it was the basis for this pattern. This equestrian influenced type of glassware became an instant success. The #5040 line is the blown stemware for this pattern. Two of the more common cuttings that are found on the stemware are #980 Moonglo and #1003 Ivy. Most customers prefer the plain Lariat.

An interesting fact is that the indents in the deviled egg plates, one round and the other oval, are not really deep enough to hold your eggs in place. It still makes a nice, unusual collector's item. This is a case of adapting one mould to become another item. Both of the deviled egg servers are very hard to find and on most want lists. Other items desired in this pattern: basket, horse head candy, hurricane lamp, 3-lite candle block, and shakers.

Probably the most unusual thing in this pattern is the blackout light. This special candlestick was developed during World War II. The idea behind it was to develop a small light that could still be used in the house during an air raid, but didn't throw out much light. The correct chimney is cylindrical-shaped with a slight flare at the top. This would be an excellent piece to have in your collection.

Close up of Heisey diamond "H" mark on Lariat stem.

Left: Basket 8.5", footed, loop stem, turned up sides. **Center:** Basket 8.25", flat, handled, oval w/2 turned up sides. **Right:** Basket 10", footed 1 ball stem, turned up sides, graduated loops on sides.

LARIAT	Crystal
Ashtray 4", round or individual, nut	20
Ashtray 4.1", round w/1 indent for cigarette	12
Basket 7.25", flat, handled, round, shallow, sweetmeat (loops point up)	125
Basket 7.5", flat, handled, rolled edge, confection (loops lay flat)	145
Basket 8.25", flat, handled, oval w/2 turned up sides	115
Basket 8.5", footed, loop stem, turned up sides	145
Basket 10", footed 1 ball stem, turned up sides, graduated loops on sides	225
Bowl 5", cupped, apple sauce	20
Bowl 6", fruit or sauce	48
Bowl 7", cupped, baked apple or cereal	25
Bowl 7", round, jelly w/1 loop handle	32
Bowl 8", cupped, dessert	28
Bowl 9", flat, small floral	38
Bowl 9.5", shallow, cupped, Camellia	32
Bowl 10", flared, fruit or floral	36
Bowl 10", small center, flared, floating flower	30
Bowl 10.5", deep, salad	48
Bowl 10.5", deep, 2-handled, party or salad	78
Bowl 11.5", flared, fruit or floral, 3.25" high	28
Bowl 13", shallow, cupped, floral float	50
Bowl 13", oval, shallow, cupped floral	48
Bowl 13", low, cupped, shallow, gardenia	38
Bowl 13", flared, crimped	55
Bowl 13", shallow, flared (heavy Lariat)	90
Bowl 14", flared (heavy Lariat)	95
Bowl 15", cupped, shallow, gardenia (heavy Lariat)	125
Bowl 17", deep, punch, 1.8 gallon	95
Candle block 1-lite 1.5", bowl shape, pair	45
Candle block 3-lite 4.5", loops along edge, 8" spread, pair	650
Candlestick 2-lite 5.25", twisted loop center, 6.5" spread, pair	110
Candlestick 3-lite 7", 3 intersecting loops, 6.5" spread, pair	135
Candy w/cover 6", spherical, loop & leaf finial, .75 lb. size	75
Candy 7", open, small center, flared	28
Candy 7", open, sides turned up handles	28
Candy w/cover 6", squat, loop & leaf finial, 1 lb.	50
Candy w/cover 7", bulbous w/loop & leaf finial, 1.5 lb.	100
Candy w/cover 7", bulbous, 2 sections w/loop & leaf finial, 1.5 lb.	115
Candy w/cover 7", flat w/horse head finial	2,500+
Candy w/cover 8", flat w/horse head finial	1,500+
Candy w/cover 8", flat w/plume finial	450
Candy w/cover 10", footed, graduated loops lid	145
Cheese & cracker: comport 2.75" short, loop stem, 5.75" wide; plate 14"	85
Cheese w/cover 5.75", footed, short stem, 5" wide	65
Cigarette box w/cover 4", rectangle	60
Coaster 4.1", round, raised rays	10
Cologne w/loop stopper 5.75", flat, round, bottle, 6 oz.	125
Comport 3.25" short, loop stem, shallow, 5.9" wide	48
Cream soup & liner: bowl 4.9", flared or cupped, 9 oz.; saucer w/indent 7"	75
Creamer 3.25", regular, 5 oz.	12
Cruet w/loop stopper, flat, oil bottle w/loop handle, 4 oz.	165
Cup 2.75", flat, handled punch, 4 oz.	8
Cup & saucer, coffee: cup 2.75", footed, 7 oz.; saucer w/indent 6.25"	24
Deviled egg server 14" (shallow indents for eggs) round plate	200
Deviled egg server 14" (shallow indents for eggs) oval plate	375
Goblet 3.2" #5040, cordial (blown) low 1 loop stem, 1 oz.	150
Goblet 4.8" #5040, cordial (blown) tall 2 loop stem, 1 oz.	250

Back left: Plate 10.5", service, small center. **Back right:** Plate 10.75", dinner plate. **Front left:** Basket 8.25", flat, handled, oval w/2 turned up sides. **Front right:** Sugar 3", regular, 6 oz.; Creamer 3.25", regular, 5 oz.; Tray 8.25", for cream/sugar.

Top left: Comport 3.25" short, loop stem, shallow, 5.9" wide. **Top right:** Bowl 11.5", flared, fruit or floral, 3.25" high. **Bottom left:** Cup & saucer, coffee: cup 2.75", footed, 7 oz.; saucer w/indent 6.25". **Bottom center:** Candy w/cover 6", spherical, loop & leaf finial, .75 lb. size. **Bottom right:** Candlestick 2-lite 5.25", twisted loop center, 6.5" spread.

Deviled egg server 14" (shallow indents for eggs) round plate. **Front:** Cologne w/loop stopper 5.75", round, bottle, 6 oz.

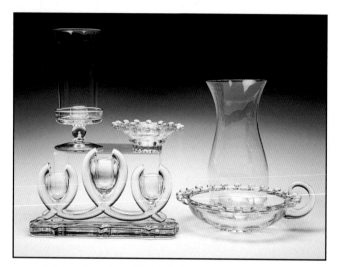

Top left: Hurricane lamp 2.25", high, footed & w/5" cylindrical shade (black out light). **Top center:** Candle block 1-lite 1.5", bowl shape. **Bottom left:** Candle block 3-lite 4.5", loops along edge, 8" spread. **Right:** Hurricane lamp 7" wide, 1 loop handle; w/plain no pattern 7" shade.

Relish 8.5", 4-tab handled, round, 4 sections.

Goblet 4.1" #5040, wine (blown) 2.5 oz.	24
Goblet 3.6" #5040, liquor cocktail (blown) 3.5 oz.	24
Goblet 5.25" #1540 Lariat, wine (pressed) 3.5 oz.	20
Goblet 5" #1540 Lariat, liquor cocktail (pressed) 3.5 oz.	24
Goblet 3.75" #5040, oyster cocktail (blown) 4 oz.	16
Goblet 4.5" #5040, claret (blown) 4 oz.	28
Goblet 3.9" #1540 Lariat, oyster cocktail (pressed) 4.5 oz.	14
Goblet 5.25" #1540 Lariat, shrimp cocktail (pressed) 4.5 oz.	58
Goblet 4.75" #5040, saucer champagne (blown) 5.5 oz.	16
Goblet 4.25" #1540 Lariat, sherbet (pressed) 6 oz.	10
Goblet 4.75" #1540 Lariat, saucer champagne (pressed) 6 oz.	12
Goblet 5.9" #1540 Lariat, water (pressed) 9 oz.	16
Goblet 5.8" #5040, water (blown) 10 oz.	20
Hurricane lamp 2.25", high, footed & with 5" cylindrical shade (black out light), each	400
Hurricane lamp 7" wide, plain no pattern 7" shade, each	250
Hurricane lamp 7" wide, 1 loop handle; w/plain no pattern 7" shade, each	275
Ice bucket 7", medium bowl (no handles)	75
Mayonnaise 2 piece: bowl 5", sauce; liner w/indent 6" or 7" (2 plate sizes)	45
Mayonnaise bowl 5", footed, loop stem w/rolled edge (comport shape)	75
Mayonnaise 2 piece: bowl 7", salad dressing; liner w/indent 8"	68
Plate 6", bread & butter	10
Plate 7", tea or dessert	15
Plate 8", baked apple liner or salad	24
Plate 8", small center, turned up edge, cabaret or marshmallow	30
Plate 8.25", flat, nougat, small center	12
Plate 10", demitasse, small center, turned up edge, cabaret	45
Plate 10.5", service, small center	50
Plate 10.75", dinner plate	150
Plate 11", cookie tray	28
Plate 13", small center, turned up edge, cabaret	52
Plate 14", cookie or cocktail tray	35
Plate 14", tab handled, sandwich	75
Plate 16", small center, torte (heavy Lariat)	98
Plate 21", buffet or punch bowl liner	75
Platter 14", oval serving	110
Relish 7", round, 2 equal sections, jelly	40
Relish 8.5", 4-tab handled, round, 4 sections	80
Relish 10", round, 2 equal sections & celery section	48
Relish 10", handled heart, celery	65
Relish 11", 2-handled, oblong, 2 equal sections & celery section	28
Relish 13", 2-handled, oblong, celery	42
Relish 13", 2-handled, oblong, 2 sections, olive/celery (divided 1/3 & 2/3)	45
Sandwich server 14", center (loop & ball) handle	175
Shaker, footed, loop stem w/plain spherical top, pair	1,500+
Sugar 3", regular, 6 oz.	12
Toast or cheese dome w/plate 4.5", plain tall dome (no pattern) 8" wide	95
Tray 8.25", for cream/sugar	26
Tumbler 5.25" #1540 Lariat, footed, juice/soda (pressed) 5 oz.	24
Tumbler 5.3" #5040, footed, juice/soda (blown) 5 oz.	28
Tumbler 6.6" #1540 Lariat, footed, ice tea/soda (pressed) 12 oz.	30
Tumbler 6.5" #5040, footed, ice tea/soda (blown) 12 oz.	32
Urn w/cover 12", footed, graduated loops, lid inverted graduated loop handles	250
Vase #5 shape 5.5", footed, loop stem, round, crimped top	65
Vase #6 shape 6.5", footed, loop stem, fan shape, crimped top	75
Vase #1 shape 7", footed, ball stem, round, flared top w/graduated loop handles	65
Vase #2 shape 7", footed, ball stem, flared, fan shape w/graduated loop handles	65
Vase #3 shape 7", footed, ball stem, round, crimped top w/graduated loop handles	65
Vase #4 shape 7", footed, ball stem, round, square crimped top w/graduated loop handles	95
Vase #7 shape 10-12", footed, loop stem, swung	250
Vase #8 shape 12-15", footed, loop, stem swung	300

Left: Goblet 3.6" #5040, liquor cocktail (blown) 3.5 oz., w/Moonglo #980 cutting. **Center left:** Goblet 4.75" #5040, saucer champagne (blown) 5.5 oz., w/Moonglo #980 cutting. **Center:** Goblet 4.5" #5040, claret (blown) 4 oz. **Center right:** Goblet 5.8" #5040, water (blown) 10 oz., w/Moonglo #980 cutting. **Right:** Tumbler 6.6" #1540 Lariat, footed, ice tea/soda (pressed) 12 oz., w/Moonglo #980 cutting.

LIDO
Fostoria Glass Company   **Etching #329**   **1937-55**
Colors: Azure (blue) and Crystal

This floral etched pattern, when first looked at, reminds you of fireworks. To us, it looks like the plant called Squirrel Tail Grass (Hordeum Jubatum). This is a perennial plant that is mainly grown as a decorative annual in most gardens. It is easy to recognize due to its fluffy seed-heads.

Crystal is the main color but pieces were also made in Azure. An outstanding set can be obtained if you have the patience to wait through long periods of time in between finding pieces. The Baroque #2496 is the blank on which most of this etched pattern is found. Stemware is found on Sceptra #6017 blank, while the tumblers are found on Sceptra #6017 and #4132 blanks.

The candelabras are especially fancy and are usually bought to make a statement on the center of a table. Most of the collectors want several good size bowls for serving when having company during the holidays.

Pattern detail, Lido.

LIDO	Crystal	Azure
Bonbon 7.4" #2496 Baroque, 3-toed, flared or crimped	38	65
Bowl 4" #2496 Baroque, 3-toed, square w/1 handle, mint	26	55
Bowl 4.25" #2496 Baroque, 3-toed, round w/1 handle, mint	22	45
Bowl 4.6" #2496 Baroque, 3-toed, tri-corn w/1 handle	24	48
Bowl 5" #2496 Baroque, round w/1 handle, flared	24	48
Bowl 6" #2496 Baroque, 4-toed, tab flame handled, square, sweetmeat	26	55
Bowl 6.9" #2496 Baroque, 3-toed, crimped, nut	38	58
Bowl 8.5" #2496 Baroque, 2-tab flame handled, flared, vegetable	48	98
Bowl 10.75" #2496 Baroque, 4-toed, oval, flame handled	75	145
Bowl 12" #2496 Baroque, flat, round, flared	75	110
Bowl 12.5" #2545 Flame, flat, oval, flared	65	125
Cake plate 10.25" #2496 Baroque, 2-tab flame handled	48	95
Candlestick 1-lite 4" #2496 Baroque, cornucopia flame shape, pair	48	95
Candlestick 1-lite 5.5" #2496 Baroque, fancy flame stem, pair	60	125
Candlestick 2-lite 5.25" #2496 Baroque, flame arms, 8" spread, pair	85	145
Candlestick 2-lite 6.75" #2545 Flame, ball & flame center, 10.25" spread, pair	95	185
Candy w/cover 6.25" #2496 Baroque, triangular, 3 sections, lid w/flame finial	110	185
Cheese & cracker #2496 Baroque: comport 3.25", short stem, 5.25" wide; plate w/indent 10.75"	75	135
Comport 4.75" #2496 Baroque, fancy flame stem, flared, 5.5" wide	32	65
Comport 5.75" #2496 Baroque, fancy flame stem, 6.5" wide	45	95
Creamer 3.1" #2496 Baroque, footed, individual, 4 oz.	20	42
Creamer 3.75" #2496 Baroque, collar footed, regular, 7.5 oz.	18	38
Cruet w/stopper 5.75" #2496 Baroque, oil bottle, 3.5 oz.	135	275
Cup & saucer, coffee #2496 Baroque: cup 2.4", footed, 6 oz.; saucer w/indent 5.6"	20	40
Finger bowl 4.5" #766, (blown) flared	35	55
Goblet 3.9" #6017 Sceptra, cordial, .75 oz.	48	80
Goblet 5.5" #6017 Sceptra, wine, 3 oz.	24	65
Goblet 4.9" #6017 Sceptra, liquor cocktail, 3.5 oz.	18	35
Goblet 3.5" #6017 Sceptra, oyster cocktail, 4 oz.	14	30
Goblet 5.9" #6017 Sceptra, claret, 4 oz.	24	50
Goblet 4.5" #6017 Sceptra, sherbet, 6 oz.	14	30
Goblet 5.4" #6017 Sceptra, saucer champagne, 6 oz.	18	34
Goblet 7.5" #6017 Sceptra, water, 9 oz.	24	55
Ice bucket 4.5" #2496 Baroque, flat, squat, chrome handle, 6.5" wide	85	165
Jelly 5" #2496 Baroque, fancy flame stem, cupped w/scalloped edge	32	65
Jelly w/cover 7.5" #2496 Baroque, fancy flame stem & finial	65	135
Mayonnaise 2 piece #2496 Baroque: bowl 5", flared, crimped, 3.5" high; liner w/indent 6.5"	48	95
Pitcher 8.5" #6011, footed, water w/o ice lip, 53 oz.	275	550
Plate 6" #2496 Baroque, bread & butter	9	20
Plate 7.25" #2496 Baroque, salad	18	32
Plate 8.5" #2496 Baroque, lunch	22	45
Plate 9.5" #2496 Baroque, dinner	50	110
Plate 14" #2496 Baroque, small center, turned up edge, cabaret	45	85
Relish 6" #2496 Baroque, tab flame handled, 2 equal sections, square	26	55
Relish 8" #2496 Baroque, oval, pickle	22	58
Relish 10" #2496 Baroque, 4-tab feet, tab flame handled, oblong, 2 equal sections & celery section	48	85
Relish 10.75", oval celery	38	72
Relish 13.25" #2419 Mayfair, irregular shape, 4 equal sections & celery section	70	
Sauce 2 piece #2496 Baroque: bowl 6.5", oblong, tab flame handled; liner 6.75"	48	90
Shakers 2.75" #2496 Baroque, regular, straight sided w/glass top, pair	95	175
Sugar 2.9" #2496 Baroque, footed, individual, 4 oz.	20	42
Sugar 3.6" #2496 Baroque, collar footed, regular, 7.5 oz.	18	38
Tray 6.5" #2496 Baroque, rectangle, tab flame handled, for individual cream/sugar	24	48
Tray 8" #2496 Baroque, tab flame handled, oblong	35	72

Back center: Plate 9.5" #2496 Baroque, dinner. **Back right:** Plate 7.25" #2496 Baroque, salad. **Front left:** Cup & saucer, coffee #2496 Baroque: cup 2.4", footed, 6 oz.; saucer w/indent 5.6". **Front center:** Sugar 3.6" #2496 Baroque, collar footed, regular, 7.5 oz. **Front right:** Creamer 3.75" #2496 Baroque, collar footed, regular, 7.5 oz.

Top left: Relish 10" #2496 Baroque, 4-tab feet, tab flame handled, oblong, 2 equal & celery section. **Top right back:** Tray 8" #2496 Baroque, tab flame handled, oblong. **Top right front:** Candlestick 1-lite 4" #2496 Baroque, cornucopia flame shape. **Bottom left:** Bowl 6.9" #2496 Baroque, 3-toed, crimped, nut. **Bottom right:** Bowl 12" #2496 Baroque, flat, round, flared.

Top: Bowl 10.75" #2496 Baroque, 4-toed, oval, flame handled, Crystal. **Front left:** Relish 8" #2496 Baroque, oval, pickle, Azure (blue). **Front right:** Sauce bowl #2496 Baroque, 6.5", oblong, handled, Azure (blue).

Tray 8.25" #2496 Baroque, flat, 3-toed, turned up edge, tidbit	22	42
Tumbler 2.1" #4132, sham base, whiskey, 1.5 oz.	24	45
Tumbler 3.5" #4132, sham base, juice, 4 oz.	14	24
Tumbler 3.75" #4132, sham base, juice, 5 oz.	16	32
Tumbler 4.75" #6017 Sceptra, juice, 5 oz.	14	28
Tumbler 4.1" #4132, sham base, high soda, 7 oz.	20	40
Tumbler 3.1" #4132, sham base, old fashion, 7.5 oz.	18	38
Tumbler 3.75" #4132,sham base, table water, 9 oz.	22	42
Tumbler 5.5" #6017 Sceptra, table water, 9 oz.	22	42
Tumbler 4.9" #4132, sham base, ice tea, 12 oz.	24	45
Tumbler 6" #6017 Sceptra, ice tea, 12 oz.	24	45
Tumbler 5.4" #4132, sham base, beverage, 14 oz.	28	50
Tumbler 6.5" #6017 Sceptra, beverage, 14 oz.	28	50
Vase 5" #4128, flat, flared flip shape w/regular optic	95	165
Vase 8" #2496 Baroque, large, flared w/flame handles	125	195
Vase 9.5" #2470, footed, w/fancy 3 scroll stem, flared	225	395

Top: Tray 6.5" #2496 Baroque, rectangle, tab flame handled, for individual cream/sugar. **Front left:** Sugar 2.9" #2496 Baroque, footed, individual, 4 oz. **Front right:** Creamer 3.1" #2496 Baroque, footed, individual, 4 oz.

Pitcher 8.5" #6011, footed, water w/o ice lip, 53 oz.

Ice bucket 4.5" #2496 Baroque, flat, squat, chrome handle, 6.5" wide, Azure (blue).

Left: Ice bucket 4.5" #2496 Baroque, flat, squat, chrome handle, 6.5" wide. **Center left:** Goblet 3.5" #6017 Sceptra, oyster cocktail, 4 oz. **Center right:** Goblet 5.4" #6017 Sceptra, saucer champagne, 6 oz. **Right:** Goblet 7.5" #6017 Sceptra, water, 9 oz.

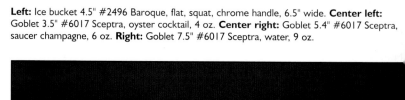

Left: Vase 9.5" #2470, footed, w/fancy 3 scroll stem, flared. **Center top:** Vase 5" #4128, flat, flared flip shape w/regular optic. **Center bottom:** Candlestick 2-lite 5.25" #2496 Baroque, flame arms, 8" spread. **Right:** Plate 9.5" #2496 Baroque, dinner.

LINCOLN INN

Fenton Art Glass Company   **Blank #1700**   **1928-37**

Colors: Aqua, Ebony (black), Crystal, Green, Jade, Rose (pink), Royal Blue (cobalt), and Ruby

Lincoln Inn was another of Fenton's attempts to move into the dinnerware market. Heisey later came out with a pattern with fine ribs called Ridgeleigh that resembles this pattern. Everyone was always looking to copy what was popular with another company.

Versatility is the key when developing moulds that were expensive to make. When researching this pattern, we discovered how Fenton adapted a particular shape to make new pieces. The oval nut & mint comports were all made from the sherbet mould. The shallow and plate comports both came from the water goblet moulds. In the old inventory records a mayonnaise jar and a 2-piece snack were listed. In talking to Frank Fenton about this pattern, we learned he has the mayonnaise bottom but not the lid, so we are not sure of the shape of the top. We do not know the shapes of the 2-piece snack set, either. We can only assume it is a small plate with an indent for a tumbler. These are pieces to keep a sharp eye out for, since they would be an incredible treasure to locate.

In 1940, Fenton adapted the Lincoln Inn moulds to accommodate an intaglio pattern of fruit in the center. This was a special contract done for Blackwell Wielandy. A crystal 15 piece luncheon offering featured four 8" plates, four cups & saucers, 11" cake plate, creamer, and sugar.

For their 90th anniversary in 1995, Fenton reintroduced several of their old moulds in the antique color of Celeste Blue. For that year only, a Lincoln Inn 4-1/2" tumbler and the pitcher were made again. Both of these pieces bear the Fenton logo.

The availability of stemware gives collectors a chance to mix this pattern with other pieces by color. On many occasions, items are snapped up by color collectors looking for items in that color, rather than by pattern. Cobalt, Jade, and Ruby colors are prime examples of this fact.

Ruby grouping: **Top left:** Goblet 7", dinner water, flared, 9 oz. **Top center:** Goblet 4", liquor cocktail or wine, flared, 4 oz. **Top right:** Plate 8", salad or dessert. **Bottom left:** Tumbler 5.25", low, footed, juice, flared, 5 oz. **Bottom center:** Finger bowl & liner: bowl 5", or flat mayonnaise; plate w/indent 6.6"; **Bottom right:** Goblet 4.25", sherbet, flared, 4 oz.

LINCOLN INN	Crystal	Green Pink	Aqua	Black Jade	Cobalt Ruby
Ashtray	10				
Bonbon 4", handled, square crimped		16	18	22	24
Bonbon 4", oval w/2 handles turned up		16	18	22	24
Bowl 4", nappy	15				
Bowl 5", shallow, flared, fruit	12	16	18	22	24
Bowl 6", shallow, wide cone, flared cereal/oatmeal		17	19	35	40
Bowl 6", shallow, flared, crimped (ruffled)		18	20		28
Bowl 7", cupped	22				
Bowl 7", flared	24				
Bowl 8", serving	28				
Bowl 9.25", flared, vegetable	45				
Bowl 10.5", footed, flared, fruit	42	58	68	85	95
Bowl 12", cupped	45				
Cigarette holder, 2.8", flat, cylindrical, straight sided	24	32	35	45	50
Comport 3.75", flared, flat, mint, 4.5" wide	14	22	28	36	40
Comport 4", shallow, cupped, nut, 3.25" wide	18	30	35	45	50
Comport 4", flared, flat, plate, 6.5" wide	14	22	24	30	34
Comport 4.25", shallow, cupped, 5.25" wide	16	22	28	36	40
Comport 4.5", oval, turned up 2 sides, 4.25" wide	15	28	32	40	45
Creamer, footed, regular, 7 oz.	14	18	20	25	28
Cup & saucer, coffee: cup 2.5", footed, 6 oz.; saucer w/indent 4"	15	20	22	26	30
Finger bowl & liner: bowl 5", or flat mayonnaise; plate w/indent 6.6"	20	28	35	42	48
Goblet 4", liquor cocktail or wine, flared, 4 oz.	15	20	26	32	36
Goblet 4.25", sherbet, flared, 4 oz.	14	18	22	27	30
Goblet 4.6", champagne, flared, 6 oz.	14	18	24	30	34
Goblet 7", dinner water, flared, 9 oz.	20	27	30	36	40
Mayonnaise jar, w/cover	45				
Pitcher 7.5", straight sided w/o ice lip	400	550	600	750	850
Plate 6", bread & butter	6	8	9	11	12
Plate 8", salad or dessert	11	15	18	22	25
Plate 9.25", dinner	22	30	36	45	65
Plate 10", torte	30	40	45		
Plate 12", service	25	34	38	48	
Plate 13", torte				50	
Plate 14", torte					65
Relish, turned up 1 side w/handle, olive	14	18	20	25	28
Relish, 4 sections	35				
Sandwich server 12", center handle		85		145	165
Shaker 4.4", footed, symmetrical, with chrome top, pair	200	275	300	375	425
Sugar, footed, regular, 7 oz.	13	18	20	25	28
Tray 5.5", center handled, for s & p, 6" tall		54	60	72	80
Tumbler 4.5", flat, straight sided, juice, 5 oz.	15	20	26	32	36
Tumbler 5.25", low, footed, juice, flared, 5 oz.	15	20	26	32	36
Tumbler 5.25", footed, claret, flared, 7 oz.	15	20	26	32	36
Tumbler, flat, straight sided, table water, 9 oz.	16	22	28	35	38
Tumbler, flat, straight sided, ice tea or high ball, 12 oz.	16	27	30	36	40
Tumbler 6", footed, ice tea, flared, 12 oz.	22	30	36	45	50
Vase 10", footed, round or square top					250

Shaker 4.4", footed, symmetrical, w/chrome top, pair, Jade; Tray 5.5", center handled, for s & p, 6" tall, Ebony (black).

Grouping of 4.4", footed, shakers: **Left to right:** Shakers, Jade on 5.5", center handled tray Ebony (black); Shaker, Crystal; Shaker, Ruby; Shaker, Cobalt.

Rose (pink) grouping: **Back center:** Plate 9", square, dinner. **Front left:** Cup & saucer, after dinner 2.3": round cup, footed, 3 oz.; saucer w/ indent 4.25". **Front center:** Cream soup 4.6", footed, round, 2.3" high, 10 oz. **Front right:** Cup & saucer, coffee 2.6": round footed, 6 oz.; saucer w/indent 5.1".

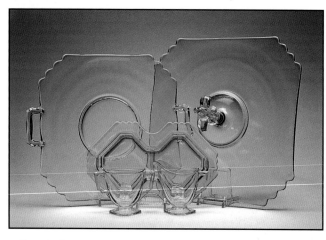

Topaz (yellow) grouping: **Back left:** Cake plate 9.5", square, open handled. **Back right:** Sandwich server 10.75", square, center "fleur-de-lis" handle, tray. **Center:** Tray 8.75", oblong, divided condiment w/flat rim. **Front left:** Sugar bowl 2.75", square footed, individual, 3.25 oz. **Front right:** Creamer 3.2", individual w/square foot, 3.25 oz.

Green grouping: **Back left:** Relish 8.5", square, 2 open handled, 4 equal sections. **Back right:** Plate 6.5", square, open handled, lemon server. **Front left:** Sauce boat 5.5", 2 spouted gravy w/attached square liner. **Front right:** Syrup jug w/cover 4.25", flat, straight sided w/handle; Syrup liner 5", square, plate w/indent.

MAYFAIR

Fostoria Glass Company   Blank #2419   1930-44

Main Colors: Amber, Crystal, Ebony (black), Green, Rose (pink), Topaz (yellow), and Wisteria (lilac)

Other Colors: Azure (blue), Burgundy (amethyst), Empire Green, and Regal Blue (cobalt)

Mayfair has straight sides with each corner consisting of 3 rounded bumps. This pattern was designed in 1930 by George Sakier. It has an Art Deco style. Mayfair can be assembled in several colors with relative ease. However, the real challenge is building a set in Ebony. Though not all pieces were made in Ebony, a small luncheon set can be assembled.

Catalogs list a 15" platter, but to get this measurement you have to measure diagonally, so we listed it under the actual length of 13.6". The almond individual nut is not really part of Fostoria's Mayfair line, but many dealers and collectors put it with this pattern. You will note that it is in our listing since it makes a nice go-along-with item. Collectors find it a little hard to locate a complete syrup pitcher set (jug, cover, & plate). Some dealers will list the pitcher as a large creamer, when they don't have the cover and plate. Many of the etched patterns like Lido, Meadow Rose, Midnight Rose, and Navarre all utilize the five section relish.

The availability of items in Mayfair make it a realistic pattern to collect and some people find it very attractive to mix and match it with etched pieces. Prices on the plain, as opposed to the etched, make this a viable option. Very few Azure, Amethyst, Empire Green, and Regal Blue pieces in this pattern have surfaced, making it impossible to list the fair market value.

MAYFAIR	Crystal	Amber	Topaz	Green	Black	Rose	Wisteria
Almond, 3" #2440 Lafayette, flat flared, individual, nut, 1.6" tall	8	18	20	22	25	25	45
Ashtray 4", square, individual, 2 cigarette rests	8	12	14	15	16	16	45
Bonbon 6.5", square, turned up handles	12	20	24	24		26	48
Bowl 5", flared, fruit	10	16	16	16		20	
Bowl 5.8", flared, cereal	18	30	32	38		38	
Bowl 7", flared, soup	20	35	36	45		42	
Bowl 9.75", oblong, rim vegetable	30	54	68	72	75	78	125
Cake plate 9.5", square, open handled	20	36	38	40	42	45	85
Comport 5.25", plain stem, flared, 5.5" wide	20	32	35	38	40	45	
Cream soup 4.6", footed, round, 2.3" high, 10 oz.	15	24	28	30		30	
Creamer 3.2", individual square footed, 3.25 oz.	12	20	22	24		26	45
Creamer 3.75", round footed, squat, 6 oz.	14	24	26	28		30	
Creamer 4", square footed, high, 6 oz.	15	26	28	30		32	
Cruet w/clear stopper 7.4", flat, oil bottle, 6 oz.	70	125	135	145		145	
Cup & saucer, after dinner 2.3": round cup, footed, 3 oz.; saucer w/indent 4.25"	12	20	24	26		28	
Cup & saucer, coffee 2.6": round footed, 6 oz.; saucer w/indent 5.1"	10	14	16	16		20	
Jelly 6", low, handled, flared	15	22	26	28	30	30	
Mayonnaise 2 piece: bowl 5.75", handled, flared; liner w/indent 6.25", handled	26	44	48	48		58	
Plate 6", square, bread & butter	4	6	7	7	8	8	16
Plate 6.5", square, open handled, lemon server	12	20	22	24		26	45
Plate 7", square, salad or dessert	5	8	9	10	12	12	20
Plate 8.2", square, lunch	8	16	18	18	20	20	38
Plate 9", square, dinner	18	32	36	38	60	42	78
Platter 11.25", oblong w/flat rim	30	54	65	68		78	
Platter 13.6" (15" diagonally), oblong w/flat rim	42	70	85	95		100	
Relish 8.5", oblong, deep, rim pickle	14	20	22	24		28	
Relish 8.5", oblong, 2 sections w/flat rim	15	22	24	26	28	30	56
Relish 8.5", square, 2 open handled, 4 sections	18	34	40	38	40	42	95
Relish 10.8", oblong, deep, rim celery	18	26	30	34		38	
Relish 13.25", irregular shape, 4 equal sections & celery section	30	58	65	70	72	75	
Sandwich server 10.75", square, center "fleur-de-lis" handle, tray	24	35	40	45	46	48	

Sauce boat 5.5", 2 spouted gravy w/attached square liner	20	38	38	45		45	
Shaker 2.9", flat, tapered, pair	40	68	85	75	85	95	
Sugar bowl 2.75", square footed, individual, 3.25 oz.	12	20	24	24		26	45
Sugar bowl 3.2", round footed, squat, regular, 6 oz.	14	24	26	28		30	
Sugar bowl 4", square footed, high regular, 6 oz.	15	26	28	30		32	
Syrup jug 4.25", flat, straight sided w/handle	32	50	58	65		75	
Syrup cover 3" wide, pointed to cover spout	22	35	40	45		50	
Syrup liner 5", square, plate w/indent	16	30	32	35		35	
Tray 8.75", oblong, divided condiment w/flat rim	14	22	24	26	28	28	58

Amber grouping: **Back:** Relish 13.25", irregular shape, 4 equal sections & celery section. **Front left:** Ashtray 4", square, individual, 2 cigarette rests. **Front center left:** Comport 5.25", plain stem, flared, 5.5" wide. **Front center right:** Cruet w/clear stopper 7.4", flat, oil bottle, 6 oz. **Front right:** Almond, 3" #2440 Lafayette, flat flared, individual, nut, 1.6" tall.

Top left: Sugar bowl 2.75", square footed, individual, 3.25 oz., Burgundy (amethyst). **Top center:** Ashtray 4", square, individual, 2 cigarette rests, Regal Blue (cobalt). **Top right:** Sugar bowl 2.75", square footed, individual, 3.25 oz., Empire Green. **Bottom left:** Creamer 3.2", individual square footed, 3.25 oz., Burgundy (amethyst). **Bottom right:** Creamer 3.2", individual square footed, 3.25 oz., Empire Green.

Ebony (black) grouping: **Top left:** Comport 5.25", plain stem, flared, 5.5" wide. **Top center:** Cup & saucer, after dinner 2.3": round cup, footed, 3 oz.; saucer w/indent 4.25". **Top right:** Cake plate 9.5", square, open handled. **Bottom left:** Sandwich server 10.75", square, center "fleur-de-lis" handle, tray. **Bottom right:** Dealer plastic sign ($48 – we found it priced this).

Back left: Cruet w/clear stopper 7.4", flat, oil bottle, 6 oz., Amber. **Back right:** Platter 13.6" (15" diagonally), oblong w/flat rim, Green. **Front left:** Bonbon 6.5", square, turned up handles, Wisteria. **Center of photo:** Creamer 3.75", round footed, squat, 6 oz., Amber. **Front center left:** Shaker 2.9", flat, tapered, Amber. **Front center right:** Sugar bowl 3.2", round footed, squat, regular, 6 oz., Amber. **Front right:** Relish 8.5", square, 2 open handled, 4 equal sections, Ruby.

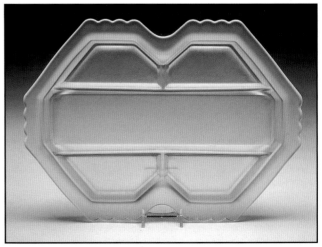

Relish 13.25", irregular shape, 4 equal sections & celery section, Silver Mist (crystal w/satin finish).

MAYFLOWER
Fostoria Glass Company   **Etching #332**   **1938-55**
Color: Crystal

Spring is in the air, it seems, when looking at this etched pattern. The etching has a cornucopia vase filled with an over flowing bouquet of flowers surrounded by garlands of petite flowers. The Coronet #2560 is the blank on which most of this etched pattern is found. You can find an interesting mix of serving bowls on the #2430 Diadem, #2560, and #2496 blanks. While most of the etched patterns used the #5000 blank for the pitcher, Mayflower also is found on the #4140 pitcher. This pitcher was only made from 1938 to 1943, which is why it is so hard to find. Stemware was produced on the Melody #6020 blank, which has a twist stem.

The candelabras always seem to go to decorators and the vanity finds a home with the boudoir collector. Items that collectors want when they set their table are 2-lite candlesticks, ice bucket, five section celery, and pitcher.

Pattern detail, Mayflower.

MAYFLOWER	Crystal
Bonbon 6.25" #2560 Coronet, flat, tab plume handles turned up	22
Bonbon 7.25" #2560 Coronet, 3-toed, flared	24
Bowl 5" #2560 Coronet, rim fruit	22
Bowl 5.5" #2560 Coronet, flat, tab plume handled, sweetmeat	28
Bowl 5.9" #2560 Coronet, cupped, 3-toed, nut	26
Bowl 6" #2560 Coronet, rim cereal, flared	30
Bowl 7" #2430 Diadem, jelly	20
Bowl 8.5" #2560 Coronet, flat, tab plume handled, vegetable	46
Bowl 10" #2560 Coronet, deep, salad	55
Bowl 10.75" #2496 Baroque, 4-toed, oval, flame handled	72
Bowl 11" #2430 Diadem, shallow, flared, fruit	40
Bowl 11" #2560 Coronet, plume handled, flared	68
Bowl 11.5" #2560 Coronet, deep, crimped, fruit	55
Bowl 12" #2560 Coronet, round, flared	55
Bowl 12.5" #2545 Flame, oblong w/smooth rim	58
Bowl 13" #2560 Coronet, shallow, fruit	48
Cake plate 10.5" #2560 Coronet, tab plume handled	48
Candelabra 1-lite 4.5" #2545 Flame, lustre w/bobeche & U drop prisms, pair	110
Candelabra 2-lite 6.75" #2545 Flame, bobeches & "B" prisms, 10.5" spread, pair	195
Candlestick 1-lite 2" #2430 Diadem, pair	48
Candlestick 1-lite 4" #2560 1/2, column stem/drip ring on candle cup, pair	98
Candlestick 1-lite 4.25" #2560 Coronet, graduated plume handled, pair	85
Candlestick 1-lite 4.5" #2545 Flame, pair	70
Candlestick 2-lite 5.1" #2560 Coronet, w/plume center, 9" spread, pair	85
Candlestick 2-lite 5.25" #2496 Baroque, 8" spread, pair	95
Candlestick 2-lite 6.75" #2545 Flame, ball & flame center, 10.25" spread, pair	98
Candy w/cover 5.5" #2430 Diadem, flat, squat, .5 lb., 5.2" wide	75
Cheese & cracker #2560 Coronet: comport 2.8", short stem, 5.25" wide; plate w/indent 11"	65
Comport 4.6" #2560 Coronet, flared w/plain stem, 6" wide	38
Creamer 3.25" #2560 Coronet, footed, individual, 4 oz.	18
Creamer 4.1" #2560 Coronet, footed, regular, 7 oz.	16
Cruet w/stopper 4.5" #2560 Coronet, footed, oil bottle, 3 oz.	115
Cup & saucer, coffee #2560 Coronet: cup 2.75", footed, 5.5 oz.; saucer w/indent 5.75"	20
Finger bowl #869, 4.6" (blown) 8 oz.	28
Goblet 3.75" #6020 Melody, cordial, 1 oz.	48
Goblet 5.4" #6020 Melody, wine, 3.5 oz.	26
Goblet 4.9" #6020 Melody, liquor cocktail, 3.5 oz.	22
Goblet 3.75" #6020 Melody, oyster cocktail, 4 oz.	18
Goblet 5.75" #6020 Melody, claret, 4.5 oz.	32
Goblet 6.1" #6020 Melody, parfait, 5.5 oz.	34
Goblet 4.6" #6020 Melody, sherbet, 6 oz.	18
Goblet 5.5" #6020 Melody, saucer champagne, 6 oz.	20
Goblet 7.25" #6020 Melody, water, 9 oz.	30
Ice bucket 4.9" #2560 Coronet, footed w/chrome handle	98
Mayonnaise 3 piece #2560 Coronet: bowl 5.5", footed, 3.25" high; liner w/indent 7.1"; ladle 5.75"	48
Mayonnaise 4 piece #2560 Coronet: bowl 6.75", footed, salad dressing, 3.5" high; liner w/indent 7.1"; 2 ladles 5.75"	
Pitcher 9.75" #5000, footed, applied handle, water w/o ice lip, 48 oz.	
Pitcher 7.5" #4140, flat, water jug w/o ice lip, 60 oz.	
Plate 6" #2560 Coronet, bread & butter	
Plate 6.25" #2560 Coronet, flat, handled, lemon server	
Plate 7.5" #2560 Coronet, salad or dessert	
Plate 8.5" #2560 Coronet, lunch	
Plate 9.5" #2560 Coronet, dinner	
Plate 14" #2560 Coronet, torte or salad bowl liner	
Relish 6.5" #2560 Coronet, flat, tab plume handled, 2 sections	
Relish 6.75" #2560 Coronet, oval, olive	
Relish 8.75" #2560 Coronet, oval, pickle	
Relish 10" #2560 Coronet, tab plume handled, 2 equal sections & celery section	
Relish 10" #2560 Coronet, tab plume handled, 3 equal sections & celery section	
Relish 11" #2560 Coronet, oval, celery	
Relish 13.25" #2560 Coronet, oval, 4 equal sections & celery section	
Sandwich server 12" #2545 Flame, center handle	
Shaker 2.9" #2560 Coronet, footed w/glass or chrome top, pair	
Sugar 3" #2560 Coronet, footed, individual, 4 oz.	
Sugar 3.5" #2560 Coronet, footed, regular, 7 oz.	
Tray 5.5" #2430 Diadem, mint	
Tray 7.5" #2560 Coronet, rectangular, for individual cream/sugar	
Tray 8.25" #2560 Coronet, flat 3-toed, tidbit	
Tray 10" #2560 Coronet, tab plume handles turned up, muffin	
Tumbler 4.9" #6020 Melody, footed, juice, 5 oz.	
Tumbler 5.75" #6020 Melody, footed, water, 9 oz.	
Tumbler 6.4" #6020 Melody, footed, ice tea, 12 oz.	
Vanity 3 piece 7.5" #2276, combination powder/cologne/stopper	
Vase 3.75" #2430 Diadem, small, tapered	
Vase 6" #2560 Coronet, handled	
Vase 8" #2430 Diadem, tapered with diamond point pat. on foot	
Vase 10" #2545 Flame, footed, tapered	
Vase 10" #5100, footed, large, flared	
Whip cream bowl 5" #2560 Coronet, flat, tab plume handled	

Top left: Sugar 3.5" #2560 Coronet, footed, regular, 7 oz. **Bottom left:** Creamer 4.1" #2560 Coronet, footed, regular, 7 oz. **Right:** Cheese & cracker #2560 Coronet: comport 2.8", short stem, 5.25" wide; plate w/indent 11".

Vase 8" #2430 Diadem, tapered w/diamond point pattern on foot.

MEADOW ROSE

Fostoria Glass Company   **Etching #328**   **1937-82**

Colors: Azure (blue) and Crystal

Meadow Rose etching is another of Fostoria's floral patterns. It looks like a blanket of small flowers in a meadow. The Baroque #2496 is the blank on which most of this etched pattern was found. Stemware was produced on the Wilma #6016 blank.

This is another etched patterns that is most often found in Crystal even though Azure was also made. Since Azure was made only during the war years of 1937 - 1944, this explains why it is so hard to find. There were probably not a lot of pieces sold, since people's attention was not focused on hosting a formal party. When pricing Azure, add 50% to the listed Crystal prices.

The etched pattern was made in crystal through 1975, but stemware was on a special order basis until 1982. In the early 1980s, Fostoria came up with an idea to revive some of their former lines by including them in what they called the Nostalgia Line. The thought was to give brides more ideas when trying to decide on a pattern for their new homes.

Most collectors seem to want the hard to find items that were just made during the war years like the salad dressing bottle, Sani-cut syrup, shakers, and vases. There were several styles of bowls made to suit anyone's taste. The 2-lite candelabra is quite elegant with its oval medallion between the arms.

Pattern detail, Meadow Rose.

MEADOW ROSE	Crystal
Bonbon 7.4" #2496 Baroque, 3-toed, flared or crimped	38
Bottle w/flat stopper 6.5" #2083, flat, salad dressing, 7 oz.	475
Bowl 4.6" #2496 Baroque, 3-toed, tri-corn, w/1 handle	28
Bowl 5" #2496 Baroque, round, w/1 handle, flared	34
Bowl 6" #2496 Baroque, 4-toed, tab flame handled, square, sweetmeat	40
Bowl 8.5" #2496 Baroque, 2-tab flame handled, flared, vegetable	95
Bowl 10" #2496 Baroque, 4-tab feet, rectangle, tab flame handled, shallow, floating garden	125
Bowl 10.75" #2496 Baroque, 4-toed, oval, flame handled	95
Bowl 12" #2496 Baroque, flat, round, flared	80
Bowl 12.5" #2545 Flame, oblong, smooth rim	110
Cake plate 10.25" #2496 Baroque, 2-tab flame handled	65
Candelabra 2-lite 6.5" #2510 Sunray, center circle w/bobeches & prisms, 8" spread, pair	375
Candelabra 2-lite 7.5" #2545 Flame, bobeches & "B" prisms 10.5" spread, pair	245
Candlestick 1-lite 4" #2496 Baroque, cornucopia flame shape, pair	75
Candlestick 1-lite 5.5" #2496 Baroque, fancy flame stem, pair	95
Candlestick 2-lite 5.25" #2496 Baroque, flame arms, 8" spread, pair	125
Candlestick 2-lite 6.5" #2510 Sunray, center circle, rays on arms, 7" spread, pair	195
Candlestick 2-lite 6.75" #2545 Flame, ball & flame center, 10.25" spread, pair	125
Candlestick 3-lite 6" #2496 Baroque, flame arms, 8.25" spread, pair	150
Candy w/cover 6.25" #2496 Baroque, triangular, 3 equal sections, flame finial	135
Cheese & cracker #2496 Baroque: comport 3.25", short stem, 5.25" wide; plate w/indent 10.75"	95
Comport 4.75" #2496 Baroque, fancy flame stem, flared 5.5" wide	48
Creamer 3.1" #2496 Baroque, footed, individual, 4 oz.	24
Creamer 3.75" #2496 Baroque, collar footed, regular, 7.5 oz.	20
Cup & saucer, coffee #2496 Baroque: cup 2.4", footed, 6 oz.; saucer w/indent 5.6"	25
Finger bowl 4.6" #869, blown, 8 oz.	38
Goblet 3.9" #6016 Wilma, cordial, .75 oz.	60
Goblet 5.25" #6016 Wilma, wine, 3.25 oz.	45
Goblet 5.25" #6016 Wilma, liquor cocktail, 3.5 oz.	32
Goblet 3.9" #6016 Wilma, oyster cocktail, 4 oz.	26
Goblet 6" #6016 Wilma, claret, 4.5 oz.	58
Goblet 4.4" #6016 Wilma, sherbet, 6 oz.	18
Goblet 5.6" #6016 Wilma, saucer champagne, 6 oz.	20
Goblet 7.6" #6016 Wilma, water, 10 oz.	45
Ice bucket 4.5" #2496 Baroque, flat, squat, chrome handle, 6.5" wide	145
Jelly 5" #2496 Baroque, fancy flame stem, cupped w/scalloped edge	48
Jelly w/cover 7.5" #2496 Baroque, fancy flame stem & finial	115
Mayonnaise 3 piece #2496 Baroque: bowl 5", flared, crimped, 3.5" high; liner w/indent 6.5"; ladle 5.75"	85
Mayonnaise 2 piece #2496 Baroque: bowl 6.5", salad dressing, oblong, handled; liner 6.75"	110
Mayonnaise 3 piece #2375 Fairfax: bowl 5.6", footed, flared; plate w/indent 7.4"; ladle 5.75"	110
Pitcher 9.75" #5000, footed, applied handle, water w/o ice lip, 48 oz.	495
Plate 6" #2496 Baroque, bread & butter	12
Plate 7.25" #2496 Baroque, salad or dessert	16
Plate 8.5" #2496 Baroque, lunch	24
Plate 9.5" #2496 Baroque, dinner	75
Plate 14" #2496 Baroque, small center, turned up edge, cabaret	75
Plate 16" #2364 Sonata, small center, turned up edge, cabaret	98
Relish 6" (or sweetmeat) #2496 Baroque, 4-tab feet, tab flame handled, 2 sections, square	40
Relish 7.25" #2440 Lafayette, 3-tab plume handled, 3 equal sections	48
Relish 8" #2496 Baroque, oval, pickle	32
Relish 10" #2496 Baroque, 4-tab feet, tab flame handled, oblong, 2 equal sections & celery section	55

Top left: Candlestick 3-lite 6" #2496 Baroque, flame arms, 8.25" spread. **Top right:** Candlestick 2-lite 6.75" #2545 Flame, ball & flame center, 10.25" spread. **Bottom left:** Candlestick 2-lite 5.25" #2496 Baroque, flame arms, 8" spread. **Bottom center:** Candlestick 1-lite 4" #2496 Baroque, cornucopia flame shape. **Bottom right:** Candlestick 1-lite 5.5" #2496 Baroque, fancy flame stem.

Left: Plate 7.25" #2496 Baroque, salad or dessert. **Back center:** Plate 9.5" #2496 Baroque, dinner. **Front center:** Bowl 4.6" #2496 Baroque, 3-toed, tri-corn, w/1 handle. **Right:** Cup & saucer, coffee #2496 Baroque: cup 2.4", footed, 6 oz.; saucer w/indent 5.6".

Pitcher 9.75" #5000, footed, applied handle, water w/o ice lip, 48 oz.

Vase 5" #4128, flat, flared flip shape w/regular optic, Azure (blue).

Relish 10.75", oval celery   4
Relish 13.25" #2419 Mayfair, irregular shape, 4 equal sections & celery section   9
Sandwich server 11" #2375 Fairfax, center "fleur-de-lis" handle   7
Sauce 2 piece #2496 Baroque: bowl 6.5", oblong, tab flame handled; liner 6.75"   12
Shaker 3.5" #2375 Fairfax, footed w/chrome or glass top, pair   14
Sugar 2.9" #2496 Baroque, footed, individual, 4 oz.   2
Sugar 3.6" #2496 Baroque, collar footed, regular, 7.5 oz.   2
Syrup 5.5" #2586, flat, chrome Sani-cut top, 9 oz.   500
Tray 6.5" #2496 Baroque, for individual cream/sugar   3
Tray 8.25" #2496 Baroque, flat, 3-toed, turned up edge, tidbit   3
Tumbler 4.6" #6016 Wilma, footed, juice, 5 oz.   2
Tumbler 5.4" #6016 Wilma, footed, water, 10 oz.   3
Tumbler 5.9" #6016 Wilma, footed, ice tea, 13 oz.   3
Vase 5" #4128, flat, flared flip shape w/regular optic   14
Vase 9.5" #2470, footed, w/fancy 3 scroll stem, flared   29

Left: Goblet 3.9" #6016 Wilma, oyster cocktail, 4 oz. **Center:** Goblet 4.4" #6016 Wilma, sherbet, 6 oz.
Right: Goblet 7.6" #6016 Wilma, water, 10 oz.

Back left: Relish 10" #2496 Baroque, 4-tab feet, tab flame handled, oblong, 2 equal sections & celery section. **Back right:** Bowl 8.5" #2496 Baroque, 2-tab flame handled, flared, vegetable. **Front left:** Comport 4.75" #2496 Baroque, fancy flame stem, flared 5.5" wide. **Front center:** Dealer sign, oval 5.5" ($50 – we found it priced this). **Front right:** Creamer 3.1" #2496 Baroque, footed, individual, 4 oz.; Sugar 2.9" #2496 Baroque, footed, individual, 4 oz.

MIDNIGHT ROSE

Fostoria Glass Company   **Etching #316**   **1933-57**

Color: Crystal

Fostoria offered several etchings with roses. Midnight Rose is another of these etched patterns. This one features two large prominent roses alternating with scroll work. It is an absolutely stunning etched pattern that is bound to attract collectors that like roses. The Lafayette #2440 is the blank on which most of the pieces in this etched pattern are found, except for the stemware, which will be found on the #6009 blank. There are several pieces that are unique to this pattern like the #2464 squat pitcher, #2485 crescent shape vase, and #2486 square shape vase.

When out looking, collectors would love to find the squat lemonade pitcher or any vase as an addition to their pattern. Items in this etched pattern turn up infrequently, so a lot of patience is need to collect this pattern.

Pattern detail, Midnight Rose.

MIDNIGHT ROSE	Crystal
Bonbon 5" #2440 Lafayette, tab plume handles turned up	24
Bowl 4.5" #2440 Lafayette, tab plume handled, oval, sweetmeat	26
Bowl 7" #2470 1/2, 4-footed	42
Bowl 10.5" #2470 1/2, 4-footed	85
Bowl 11" #2481, rectangle	85
Cake plate 9.75" #2375 Fairfax, small center, open handled	68
Cake plate 10.5" #2440 Lafayette, tab plume handled	68
Candlestick 1-lite 5" #2481, pair	78
Candlestick 1-lite 5.5" #2470 1/2, pair	85
Candlestick 2-lite 4.75" #2472, curlicue arms w/pointed center, 8.25" spread, pair	98
Candlestick 3-lite 6.75" #2482, pair	125
Candy box w/cover #4099	125
Creamer 4.25" #2440 Lafayette, footed, scroll handle, regular, 6.75 oz.	20
Cup & saucer, coffee #2440 Lafayette: cup 2.75", footed, 6 oz.; saucer w/indent 5.8"	24
Finger bowl 4.6" #869 (blown), flat, 8 oz.	30
Goblet 3.75" #6009, cordial, 1 oz.	60
Goblet 4.6" #846, sherry, 2 oz.	38
Goblet 4.75" #6009, cocktail, 3.75 oz.	22
Goblet 5.4" #6009, claret/wine, 3.75 oz.	30
Goblet 3.75" #6009, oyster cocktail, 4.75 oz.	18
Goblet 5.1" #795, hollow stem, champagne, 5 oz.	50
Goblet 4.4" #6009, sherbet, 5.5 oz.	18
Goblet 5.6" #6009, saucer champagne, 5.5 oz.	22
Goblet 4.75" #906, brandy inhaler, 8 oz.	55
Goblet 7.6" #6009, water, 9 oz.	38
Mayonnaise 6.5" #2440 Lafayette, tab plume handled, salad dressing	48
Pitcher 6.75" #2464, squat, lemonade, ice jug, .5 gallon (rum pot style)	295+
Plate 5.25" #2440 Lafayette, flat, tab plume handled, lemon server	28
Plate 6.25" #2440 Lafayette, bread & butter	6
Plate 7.25" #2440 Lafayette, salad or dessert	10
Plate 8.5" #2440 Lafayette, lunch	18
Plate 9.5" #2440 Lafayette, dinner	48
Plate 13" #2440 Lafayette, small center, torte or salad bowl liner	65
Relish 6.5" #2440 Lafayette, flat flared, oval olive	30
Relish 7.25" #2440 Lafayette, 3-tab plume handled, 3 equal sections	38
Relish 8.5" #2419 Mayfair, 2-handled, 4 equal sections	54
Relish 9.25" #2440 Lafayette, flat, flared, oval pickle	35
Relish #2470, 4 sections	45
Relish 11" #2462, flower shaped, 5 sections	60
Relish 11" #2462, flower shape, 5 sections w/metal center handle	70
Relish 11.5" #2440 Lafayette, flat, flared, oval celery	42
Relish 13.25" #2419 Mayfair, irregular shape, 4 equal sections & celery section	75
Sauce 2 piece #2440 Lafayette: bowl 6.75" tab plume handled, oval; oval liner w/indent 8.5"	85
Sugar 3.6" #2440 Lafayette, footed, scroll handled, regular, 6.75 oz.	20
Tray 8.75" #2470, oval, for cream/sugar	28
Tumbler #887, whiskey, 1.75 oz.	30
Tumbler 4.4" #6009, footed, juice, 5 oz.	18
Tumbler #1184, old fashion, 7 oz.	28
Tumbler 5.25" #6009, footed, water, 9 oz.	28
Tumbler #2464, squat, lemonade, 11 oz.	30
Tumbler 5.9" #6009, footed, ice tea, 12 oz.	34
Vase 5" #2485, crescent shape	125
Vase 6.5" #4111, footed	145
Vase 7" #2485, crescent shape	165
Vase 7" #2486, square shape	175
Vase 7.5" #2467, footed w/handles	95
Vase 7.5" #4110, collar footed, flared	125
Vase 8.5" #4112, footed	165
Vase 9" #2486, square shape	185
Vase 9.5" #2470, footed, w/fancy 3 scroll stem, flared	195

Left: Plate 7.25" #2440 Lafayette, salad or dessert. **Center:** Plate 9.5" #2440 Lafayette, dinner. **Right:** Plate 6.25" #2440 Lafayette, bread & butter.

Left: Goblet 4.4" #6009, sherbet, 5.5 oz. **Right:** Goblet 5.4" #6009, claret/wine, 3.75 oz.

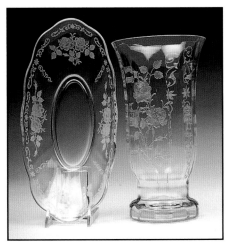

Left: Relish 9.25" #2440 Lafayette, flat, flared, oval pickle. **Right:** Vase 7.5" #4110, collar footed, flared.

MINUET
A. H. Heisey & Company   **Etching #503**   **1939-56**
Color: Crystal

The Minuet etching imitates the extravagant setting for an elegant old fashioned ball given by only the wealthy. There are four different scenes that make up this etching: a lady holding a fan, a man offering a bouquet of flowers, a lady holding a dance card, and a man playing the cello. Each of these scenes are featured inside an oval medallion that is surrounded by lots of scroll work. Just looking at this etching lets you imagine the opulence of the time period with fancy ball gowns and orchestras playing at a party given by royalty. The stemware is found on the #5010 Symphone blank. Finding accessory items will require some time to locate them.

Like other Heisey etched patterns, the collector of Minuet almost always has the complete candle vase on the want list. Stemware is very abundant and easy to find. All of the accessory pieces will take some time to gather up.

Pattern detail, Minuet.

MINUET

	Crystal
Bell #3408 Jamestown, dinner	110
Bowl 6" #1509 Queen Ann, 4-toed, 2 loop handled, flared, jelly	40
Bowl 6" #1509 Queen Ann, 3 dolphin, footed, mint	45
Bowl 7.5" #1509 Queen Ann, 3-footed, sauce	68
Bowl 10" #1511 Toujours, deep, salad	110
Bowl 11" #1509 Queen Ann, footed, floral	95
Bowl 12" #1511 Toujours, footed, oval, floral	95
Bowl 12" #1514, oval	85
Bowl 13" #1509 Queen Ann, shallow, salad	85
Bowl 13" #1511 Toujours, floral	85
Bowl 13" #1511 Toujours, floral, plateau	95
Candle vase 1-lite 2 piece 9.5" centerpiece #1511 Toujours, w/mini footed vase (becomes candle cup) & prisms, pair	495+
Candelabra 1-lite 7.5" #1509 Queen Ann, rosette on ribbed column w/prisms, pair	295
Candelabra 8" #1511 Toujours, 2-lite, ribbed fan, concave panel arms taper to curlicue, bobeches/prisms, 6.5" spread, pair	275
Candlestick 1-lite, 3.5" #112 Mercury, striated ball center, pair	85
Candlestick 2-lite 5" #134 Trident, curvilinear arms, 5.5" spread, pair	135
Candlestick 8" #1511 Toujours, 2-lite, ribbed fan, concave panel arms taper to curlicue, pair	195
Candlestick 3-lite 7.5" #142 Cascade, curling arms w/tendril, pair	165
Cocktail icer w/liner #3304, footed	145
Comport 5.5" #5010 Symphone, short stem	42
Comport 7.5" #1511 Toujours, high stem	65
Creamer #1509 Queen Ann, dolphin footed, individual, 3.5 oz.	32
Creamer #1511 Toujours, footed, individual, 6 oz.	45
Creamer #1509 Queen Ann, dolphin footed, 6 oz.	40
Creamer #1511 Toujours, footed, 6 oz.	80
Cup & saucer, coffee #1509 Queen Ann: cup 2.6", 6 oz.; saucer w/indent 6.5"	42
Finger bowl #5010 Symphone Symphone, (blown)	48
Goblet #5010 Symphone, cordial, 1 oz.	145
Goblet 5.8" #5010 Symphone, high wine, 2.5 oz.	60
Goblet #5010 Symphone, liquor cocktail, 3.5 oz.	40
Goblet 6.5" #5010 Symphone, claret, 4 oz.	50
Goblet #5010 Symphone, oyster cocktail, 4.5 oz.	20
Goblet 3.4" #5010 Symphone, sherbet, 6 oz.	22
Goblet 6.2" #5010 Symphone, saucer champagne, 6 oz.	24
Goblet #5010 Symphone, lunch water, 9 oz.	42
Goblet 8.1" #5010 Symphone, dinner water, 9 oz.	45
Ice bucket #1509 Queen Ann, 4 dolphin feet w/chrome handle	195
Marmalade w/cover #1511 Toujours, apple shape	175
Mayonnaise bowl 5.5" #1509 Queen Ann, 3 dolphin footed, flared	65
Mayonnaise 2 piece #1509 Queen Ann: bowl 6.5", tab handled, salad dressing; liner w/indent 7"	72
Mayonnaise bowl #1511 Toujours, footed	65
Pitcher #4164, squat, ice jug, 73 oz.	475
Plate 7" #1509 Queen Ann, dessert or salad	18
Plate 7" #1511 Toujours, dessert or salad	16
Plate 8" #1509 Queen Ann, salad or small lunch	28
Plate 8" #1511 Toujours, salad or small lunch	26
Plate 10.5" #1509 Queen Ann, dinner	175
Plate 12" #1509 Queen Ann, 2-handled, large center, sandwich	145
Plate 14" #1511 Toujours, torte	68
Plate 15" #1511 Toujours, sandwich	68
Relish 7" #1509 Queen Ann, round, 3-tab handles, 3 sections	65
Relish 9.5" #1509 Queen Ann, oblong, 2 equal sections & celery section	75
Relish 11" #1509 Queen Ann, oblong, 2 equal sections & celery section	80

	Crystal
Relish 12" #1511 Toujours, oval, celery	55
Relish 12" #1514, 3 sections	75
Relish 13" #1509 Queen Ann, oval, pickle & olive	70
Shaker #10, flat, chrome top, pair	85
Sugar #1509 Queen Ann, dolphin footed, individual, 3.5 oz.	32
Sugar #1511 Toujours, footed, individual, 3.5 oz.	45
Sugar #1509 Queen Ann, dolphin footed, 6 oz.	40
Sugar #1511 Toujours, footed, 6 oz.	50
Tray #1509 Queen Ann, for individual cream/sugar	38
Tray 15" #1509 Queen Ann, social hour	95
Tray 16" #1509 Queen Ann, snack plate	100
Tumbler #5010 Symphone, footed, juice, 5 oz.	35
Tumbler #5010 Symphone, footed, ice tea, 12 oz.	65
Tumbler #2351, flat, high straight sided, soda/ice tea, 12 oz.	85
Vase 5.5" #1511 Toujours, footed, ivy ball w/optic	98
Vase 6" #5012, square sham foot, 1 ball stem, urn	125
Vase 7.5" #5012, square sham foot, 1 ball stem, urn	145
Vase 8" #4196	125
Vase 9" #5012, square sham foot, 1 ball stem, urn	175
Vase 10" #4191, footed, wafer stem, slim bud vase	175
Vase 10" #4192, footed, w/o stem, flared	195

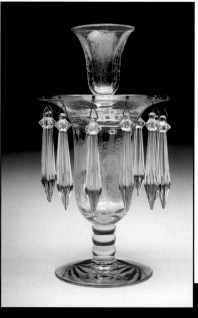

Candle vase 1-lite 2 piece 9.5" centerpiece #1511 Toujours, w/mini footed vase (becomes candle cup) & prisms.

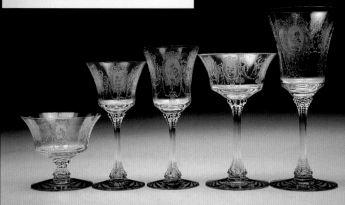

Left: Goblet 3.4" #5010 Symphone, sherbet, 6 oz. **Center left:** Goblet 5.8" #5010 Symphone, high wine, 2.5 oz. **Center:** Goblet 6.5" #5010 Symphone, claret, 4 oz. **Center right:** Goblet 6.2" #5010 Symphone, saucer champagne, 6 oz. **Right:** Goblet 8.1" #5010 Symphone, dinner water, 9 oz.

MOONDROPS

New Martinsville Glass Co.   **Blank #37**   **1932-40s**

Colors: Amber, Amethyst, Sky Blue, Crystal, Evergreen, Jade, Ritz Blue (cobalt), Rose pink), and Ruby

The combination of rings and oval embossed disks make Moondrops a very unique pattern. New collectors will sometimes have a hard time spotting plates and oval bowls. They have rings on the underside, but not the raised oval pattern that you expect to find.

The rocket design, in the time period it came out, was really an inventive idea. It could be the early science fiction movies might have played an influential role for the designer. Rocket shaped items are all hard to find and greatly coveted by the collectors. The covered vegetable and butter dishes are all hard to locate and the prices reflect their scarcity.

Most of the collectors look for the Cobalt & Ruby items. The Evergreen pieces look absolutely gorgeous when mixed with the Ruby during Christmas time. A very few items were made in a the Sky Blue color and should be priced the same as the Rose prices.

Top left: Candlestick 3-lite 5.5", 2 winged, 7" spread, Amber. **Top right:** Candle bowl 1-lite 5", footed, crimped, 2" high, Ruby. **Bottom left:** Candle bowl 1-lite 5", footed, crimped, 2" high, Ruby. **Bottom right:** Candle bowl 1-lite 4.75", footed, flared, 2" high, Amber.

MOONDROPS	Amber Crystal	Jade Ever-green Rose	Amethyst Ruby Cobalt
Ashtray 4", round, 3-toed	10	16	28
Bonbon 3.9", deep, 5.75" high	15	32	45
Bowl 5.4", round, 3-toed w/1-tab handle	12	28	48
Bowl 4.25", soup	35	75	85
Bowl w/cover 8", collar footed, oval, vegetable, lid w/ beehive finial	95	195	295
Bowl 9.5", crimped edge	25	60	90
Bowl 9.75", flat, oval, rim vegetable	20	48	95
Bowl 10", 3-tab feet (flared or crimped) w/pie crimped edge	30	78	125
Bowl 10", footed, wing handled, oval	38	85	130
Bowl 11.5", footed, round, flared, console	20	48	95
Box w/cover 3.75", rocket shape, puff w/plume finial	95	195	250
Butter w/glass cover 6", round, plume finial	145	345	475
Butter w/chrome cover 6", round	35	85	95
Candle bowl 1-lite 3.75", footed, cupped, 2.6" high, pair	30	56	68
Candle bowl 1-lite 4.75", footed, flared, 2" high, pair	28	54	65
Candle bowl 1-lite 5", footed, crimped, 2" high, pair	32	62	75
Candlestick 1-lite 4", 2-winged, pair	48	72	110
Candlestick 3-lite 5.5", 2-winged, 7" spread, pair	75	125	175
Candy w/metal cover 4.5", 3-footed	24	50	60
Cocktail shaker 10", martini w/chrome lid, 21 oz.	40	85	95
Cocktail shaker 10", footed, handled, martini w/chrome top, 21 oz.	50	98	125
Cologne w/plume stopper 4.75", rocket shape, 3 open stems	125	250	295
Comport 4", short stem, flared, 5.75" wide	18	38	48
Cream soup 4.25", collar footed, 2-handled	40	85	95
Creamer 3", footed, individual, 3 oz.	8	16	18
Creamer 4", footed, regular, 7 oz.	10	18	20
Cup & saucer, coffee: cup 2.5", footed, 6 oz.; saucer w/ indent 5.6"	12	24	28
Decanter beehive/plume stopper 8.5", footed, 16 oz.	48	85	95
Decanter beehive/plume stopper 12", rocket shape, 3 open stems, 16 oz.	185	375	495+
Decanter beehive/plume stopper 11", footed, 28 oz.	60	115	125
Goblet 4", chrome stem & foot, cordial, .5 oz.	12	25	35
Goblet 3", cordial, .75 oz.	16	38	48
Goblet 3.25", short stem, oyster cocktail, 3 oz.	12	18	24
Goblet 4", wine, 3 oz.	14	24	32
Goblet 5.1", chrome stem & foot, wine, 3 oz.	8	15	20
Goblet 4.5", saucer champagne, 5 oz.	12	24	28
Goblet 6.4", water, 9 oz.	16	38	48
Jelly 5", footed (looks like short sherbet)	12	24	28
Mayonnaise bowl 5.25", 3 short feet, flared	24	50	60
Pitcher 6.9", footed, w/o ice lip, 21 oz.	70	145	185
Pitcher 8.25", footed, w/o ice lip, 50 oz.	80	165	195
Plate 6" plain (no pattern) oval party w/off center indent, for sundae	6	12	14
Plate 6.25", bread & butter or sherbet liner	5	10	12
Plate 7.5", dessert or salad	6	14	16
Plate 8.5", lunch	8	16	20
Plate 9.5", dinner	12	24	35
Platter 12", oval	18	38	45
Relish 7.5", flat, oval, pickle	14	32	36
Relish 8.25", 3-tab feet, round, 3 sections, flared w/pie crimped edge	16	38	48
Relish 10", rectangular, 3 sections, handled	24	46	54
Relish 11.3", flat, oval, celery	15	35	45
Sugar 2.75", footed, individual, 3 oz.	8	16	18
Sugar 3.75", footed, regular, 7 oz.	10	18	20
Tray 7.5", used for individual cream & sugar	14	30	35

Ruby grouping: **Back left:** Plate 6.25", bread & butter or sherbet liner. **Back center:** Plate 9.5", dinner. **Front left:** Ashtray 4", round, 3-toed. **Front center:** Comport 4", short stem, flared, 5.75" wide. **Front right:** Cup & saucer, coffee: cup 2.5", footed, 6 oz.; saucer w/indent 5.6".

Ruby grouping: **Top left:** Goblet 4.5", saucer champagne, 5 oz. **Top center:** Goblet 3.25", short stem, oyster cocktail, 3 oz. **Bottom left:** Goblet 4", wine, 3 oz. **Bottom center:** Tumbler 2.6", footed, sundae or sherbet, 5.5 oz. **Bottom right:** Goblet 6.4", water, 9 oz.

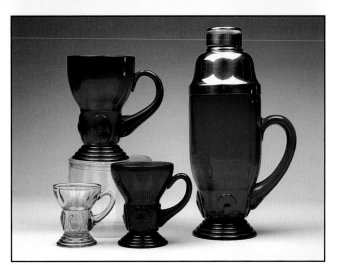

Top left: Tumbler 5", footed, handled, ice tea, 11 oz., Ruby. **Right:** Cocktail shaker 10", footed, handled, martini w/chrome top, 21 oz., Ruby. **Bottom left:** Tumbler 2.75", footed, handled, shot or whiskey, 2 oz., Amber. **Bottom center:** Tumbler 3.6", footed, handled, juice, 5 oz., Ritz Blue (cobalt).

Left to right: Tumbler 4.75", footed, table water, 8 oz., Ritz Blue (cobalt); Tumbler 2.75", footed, shot or whiskey, 2 oz., Amber; Tumbler 5", footed, ice tea, 11 oz., Ruby; Tumbler 3.6", footed, juice, 5 oz., Ritz Blue (cobalt); Pitcher 8.25", footed, w/o ice lip, 50 oz., Amber.

Top left: Relish 8.25", 3-tab feet, round, 3 sections, flared w/pie crimped edge, Ruby. **Top right:** Vase 7.5", footed, flared, tri-crimped, Crystal. **Center row left:** Creamer 3", footed, individual, 3 oz., Ruby. **Center of photo:** Relish 11.3", flat, oval, celery, Ruby. **Center row right:** Creamer 4", footed, regular, 7 oz., Ruby. **Bottom left:** Sugar 2.75", footed, individual, 3 oz., Ruby. **Bottom center:** Relish 7.5", flat, oval, pickle, Ruby. **Bottom right:** Sugar 3.75", footed, regular, 7 oz., Ruby.

Tray 15", rectangle, handled sandwich, scalloped corners	25	65	75
Tumbler 2", footed, shot or whiskey, 1 oz.	10	20	24
Tumbler 2.75", footed, shot or whiskey, 2 oz.	9	18	20
Tumbler 2.75", footed, handled, shot or whiskey, 2 oz.	10	20	24
Tumbler 3.5", rocket shape, 3 open stems, whiskey, 3 oz.	20	40	48
Tumbler 2.6", footed, sundae or sherbet, 5.5 oz.	8	18	20
Tumbler 3.6", footed, juice, 5 oz.	9	20	22
Tumbler 3.6, footed, handled, juice, 5 oz.	12	24	26
Tumbler 4.75", footed, table water, 8 oz.	12	24	28
Tumbler 4.75", footed, handled, table water, 8 oz.	16	34	36
Tumbler 5", footed, ice tea, 11 oz.	12	26	30
Tumbler 5", footed, handled, ice tea, 11 oz.	16	36	38
Vase 7.5", footed, flared, tri-crimped	40	75	85
Vase 8.75", rocket shape, 3 stems, tri-crimped	95	245	295

Back: Bowl 10", 3-tab feet, crimped, Sky Blue. **Front:** Bowl w/cover 8", collar footed, oval, vegetable, lid w/beehive finial, Evergreen.

Left: Goblet 4", chrome stem & foot, cordial, .5 oz., Ruby. **Center left:** Decanter beehive stopper 8.5", footed, 16 oz., Ruby. **Center:** Goblet 3", cordial, .75 oz., Ruby. **Center right:** Decanter plume stopper 11", footed, 28 oz., Ritz Blue (cobalt). **Right:** Goblet 4", wine, 3 oz., Ruby.

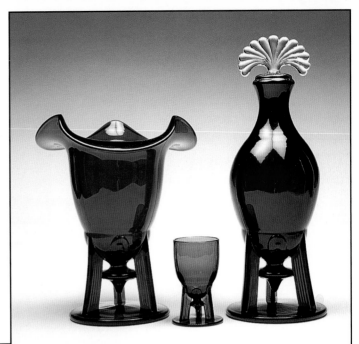

Left: Vase 8.75", rocket shape, 3 stems, tri-crimped, Ritz Blue (cobalt). **Center:** Tumbler 3.5", rocket shape, 3 open stems, whiskey, 3 oz., Amethyst. **Right:** Decanter beehive/plume stopper 12", rocket shape, 3 open stems, 16 oz., Ritz Blue (cobalt).

Evergreen grouping: **Left:** Vase 7.5", footed, flared, tri-crimped. **Center:** Bowl 10", 3-tab feet (flared or crimped) w/pie crimped edge. **Right:** Pitcher 6.9", footed, w/o ice lip, 21 oz.

Left: Tumbler 4.75", footed, table water, 8 oz., Jade. **Center left:** Candle bowl 1-lite 3.75", footed, cupped, 2.6" high, Amethyst, shown on its side. **Center right:** Candle bowl 1-lite 3.75", footed, cupped, 2.6" high, Ritz Blue (cobalt), shown w/white candle. **Right:** Vase 7.5", footed, flared, tri-crimped, Evergreen (so dark it almost looks black).

Pattern detail, Morgan.

MORGAN
Central Glass Works   1922-30s
Main Colors: Green and Pink
Other Colors: Black, Blue, Crystal, and Lilac

A fairy sitting in an ornate circle is a wonderfully delicate description of the Morgan etched pattern that was made by Central Glass . She reminds you of Tinkerbell® from the Disney movie, *Peter Pan*. Joseph Balda, a Heisey employee, designed this etching, but the patent was assigned to Central Glass. Obviously, he was doing some free lance work for Central. The name Morgan was given to honor the governor of the great state of West Virginia at the time, Ephraim Morgan. Given this special name, I am sure a whole table service was purchased for use in the governor's mansion for special, elegant parties. It is obvious though, by the pieces that have been found, that several different blanks were used. The plates come plain and with an optic. We are sure more people would like to find this etched pattern to add it to their collections. Several colors were made but it is not known if sets can be built in every color. We are looking for more pieces to surface and to be reported, so a more accurate list can be developed. Please contact us for a list of pieces that you have. Pink seems to be the most common color that is found.

The candy dish, cruet, and pitcher seem to be some of the items for which collectors are looking. In a pattern where all items are difficult to find, it becomes hard to say what item is sought after most.

In pricing, Crystal should be 75% less than Pink & Green prices. However, all other colors should be priced 25% more than the Pink & Green.

Left: Cup & saucer, coffee: cup 2.25", flat, angle handle, 6 oz.; saucer 5.3", square w/scalloped corners. **Right:** Plate 9.6", round, dinner (w/o optic).

Back left: Cake plate 10.5", 4-toed, round, Crystal. **Back right:** Bowl 12.25", shallow mushroom shape, console, Pink. **Front left top:** Comport 5.3", shallow bell shape, mint, 6.6" wide, Crystal. **Front left bottom:** Bowl 10.5", rolled edge, console, Blue. **Front right:** Comport 5.8", ribbed & wafer stem, flared 7.3" wide, Pink.

MORGAN	Green Pink
Bowl 4", footed	55
Bowl 6", 2 handles turned up	60
Bowl 10.5", rolled edge, console	95
Bowl 10.5", 2-handled	85
Bowl 12", octagon shape, rolled edge, console	100
Bowl 12.25", shallow mushroom shape, console	125
Bowl 13", rolled edge, console	100
Cake plate 10.5", 4-toed, round	95
Cake plate 10.5", octagon, open handled	85
Candlestick 1-lite 3", wafer stem, pair	145
Candy w/cover, footed, blown	495+
Candy w/cover, 4-tab feet, diamond shape	395
Cheese & cracker: comport 2.75", short stem, 4.75" wide; plate 10.25"	165
Comport 5.3", shallow bell shape, mint, 6.6" wide	60
Comport 5.8", ribbed & wafer stem, flared 7.3" wide	85
Comport 6.5", tall, 5" wide	70
Comport 6.5", tall, 6" wide	80
Creamer, footed, regular, 6 oz.	68
Cruet w/stopper, footed, 4 oz.	295
Cup & saucer, coffee: cup 2.25", flat, angle handle, 6 oz.; saucer 5.3", square w/scalloped corners	165
Decanter w/stopper, flat	395+
Goblet 5.1", liquor cocktail, 3 oz.	40
Goblet 5.25", beaded stem, wine, 4 oz.	58
Goblet 6", tall plain stem w/wafer at top, wine, 4 oz.	60
Goblet, oyster cocktail, 4 oz.	28
Goblet 4.5", beaded stem, sherbet, 6 oz.	38
Goblet 5.4", saucer champagne, 6 oz.	48
Goblet 7.25", water, 10 oz.	70
Ice tub 7.5", tab handled	550+
Mayonnaise 2 piece: bowl 5.25", footed, ball stem, flared, 3.6" high; liner w/recessed center 6.25"	85
Pitcher, footed, water	450+
Plate 6.25", round, bread & butter (w/o optic)	16
Plate 7", octagon, salad (w/o optic)	20
Plate 7.25", round, salad (w/o optic)	20
Plate 7.5", round, salad (diamond optic)	20
Plate 8.5", lunch	35
Plate 9.6", round, dinner (w/o optic)	98
Sandwich server 9.5", or tidbit tray, octagon, center handle	98
Sandwich server 11", round or octagon (2 styles), center handle	95
Shaker 4.25", footed, w/chrome top, pair	95
Sugar, footed, regular, 6 oz.	68
Tumbler 2.1", flat, whiskey, 2 oz.	75
Tumbler 4.4", footed, juice, 5 oz. (paneled optic)	38
Tumbler 5.4", footed wafer stem, soda, 7.5 oz. (paneled optic)	38
Tumbler 5.4", flat, water, 10 oz.	40
Tumbler 5.4", footed, cone shape, ice tea, 12 oz. (loop optic)	58
Tumbler 5.6", footed, ice tea, 12 oz. (paneled optic)	60
Vase 8"	175
Vase 10", bud vase	185
Vase 10", cylindrical, ruffled or smooth top	495+

Left: Goblet 4.5", beaded stem, sherbet, 6 oz., Pink. **Center:** Goblet 5.25", beaded stem, wine, 4 oz., Pink. **Right:** Goblet 6", tall plain stem w/wafer at top, wine, 4 oz., Crystal bowl w/Green stem/foot.

Back: Plate 7.25", round, salad (w/o optic). **Front:** Shaker 4.25", footed, w/chrome top.

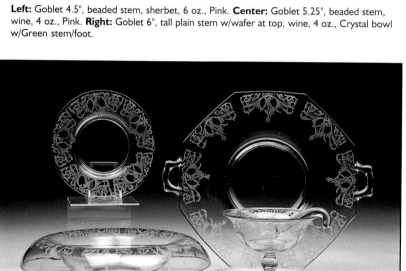

Pink grouping: **Top left:** Plate 6.25", round, bread & butter (w/o optic). **Top right:** Cake plate 10.5", octagon, open handled. **Bottom left:** Bowl 10.5", rolled edge, console. **Bottom right:** Mayonnaise 2 piece: bowl 5.25", footed, ball stem, flared, 3.6" high; liner w/recessed center 6.25"; shown w/ladle.

Cheese & cracker: comport 2.75", short stem, 4.75" wide; plate 10.25", Blue.

Left: Tumbler 4.4", footed, juice, 5 oz. (paneled optic), Pink. **Center left:** Tumbler 5.4", footed wafer stem, soda, 7.5 oz. (paneled optic), Crystal. **Center right:** Tumbler 5.6", footed, ice tea, 12 oz. (paneled optic), Crystal bowl w/Green foot. **Right:** Tumbler 5.4", footed, cone shape, ice tea, 12 oz. (loop optic), Green.

Vase 10", cylindrical, smooth top, Lilac.

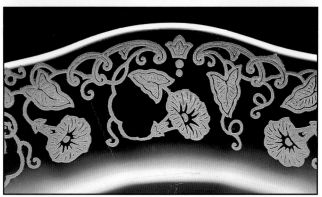

Pattern detail, Morning Glory.

Back left: Plate 7.25" #2440 Lafayette, salad or dessert. **Front left:** Goblet 4.75" #6007, liquor cocktail, 3.5 oz. **Front right:** Goblet 5.4" #6007, saucer champagne, 5.5 oz.

Candlestick 1-lite 5.5" #2470, fancy base w/tall stem, pair.

Relish 11.5" #2440 Lafayette, flat, flared, oval celery.

MORNING GLORY
Fostoria Glass Company   Etching #313   1931-44
Color: Crystal

Morning glory is a beautiful trailing flower that is found in most older gardens. This pattern is unique in that it is the only pattern that Fostoria etched and then produced a later sand carved version. Sand carved pieces that were done with the same name would certainly make a nice addition to this pattern.

This pattern is on the #2440 Lafayette blank and a pitcher is found on the #2270 blank. The stemware can be found on the #6007 blank that has a paneled optic. Some pieces are found in all Crystal or with an Amber base & clear bowl. Alvin Sterling made a sterling tableware pattern with the same name that resembles Fostoria's pattern. Combining the sterling set with the glass pieces would really make your formal table setting stand out from others.

MORNING GLORY	Crystal
Bonbon 7" #2470, handles turned up	18
Bowl 5" #2440 Lafayette, flat flared, fruit	18
Bowl 6" #2440 Lafayette, flat flared, cereal	22
Bowl 6" #2470, handled, sweetmeat	20
Bowl 10" #2440 Lafayette, flat, oval, slightly flared, vegetable (baker)	54
Bowl 10.5" #2470 1/2, 4-footed	50
Bowl 12" #2470, fancy base w/o stem	60
Cake plate 10" #2470, handled	45
Candlestick 1-lite 5.5" #2470, fancy base w/tall stem, pair	65
Candlestick 1-lite 5.5" #2470 1/2, pair	54
Comport, 3.5" #2470, fancy base w/o stem, 6" wide	34
Creamer 4.25" #2440 Lafayette, footed, scroll handle, regular, 6.75 oz.	18
Creamer 3.75" #2470, footed, regular, 6 oz.	18
Cup & saucer, after dinner #2440 Lafayette: cup 2.6", footed, 2.5 oz.; saucer w/indent 4.75"	38
Cup & saucer, coffee #2440 Lafayette: cup 2.75", footed, 6 oz.; saucer w/indent 5.8"	20
Finger bowl #869, 4.6" blown, 8 oz.	24
Goblet 3.6" #6007, cordial, 1 oz.	45
Goblet 5" #6007, wine, 3 oz.	28
Goblet 4.75" #6007, liquor cocktail, 3.5 oz.	26
Goblet 5.6" #6007, claret, 4 oz.	28
Goblet 3.5" #6007, oyster cocktail, 4.5 oz.	12
Goblet 4.1" #6007, sherbet, 5.5 oz.	14
Goblet 5.4" #6007, saucer champagne, 5.5 oz.	16
Goblet 7.4" #6007, water, 10 oz.	24
Ice dish 2.75" #2451, bowl w/3-tabs hold liners, 4.8" wide	38
Ice dish liner 2.75" #2451, crab meat, 4 oz.	24
Ice dish liner 1.9" #2451, fruit cocktail, 5 oz.	28
Ice dish liner 3.5" #2451, tomato juice, 5 oz.	18
Ice dish plate 7" #2451, plain w/indent	18
Pitcher #2270, w/o ice lip	145+
Plate 5.25" #2440 Lafayette, flat, tab plume handled, lemon server	18
Plate 6.25" #2440 Lafayette, bread & butter	6
Plate 7.25" #2440 Lafayette, salad or dessert	10
Plate 8.5" #2440 Lafayette, lunch	12
Plate 9.5" #2440 Lafayette, small dinner	28
Plate 10.25" #2440 Lafayette, large dinner	54
Plate 13" #2440 Lafayette, small center, torte or salad bowl liner	58
Platter 12" #2440 Lafayette, oval	68
Relish 6.5" #2440 Lafayette, flat flared, oval olive	22
Relish 9.25" #2470, tab handled, 3 sections	35
Relish 9.25" #2440 Lafayette, flat, flared, oval pickle	28
Relish 8.5" #2419 Mayfair, 2-handled, 4 equal sections	40
Relish 11.5" #2440 Lafayette, flat, flared, oval celery	35
Sandwich server 11.5" #2470, center plume handle	48
Sugar 3.6" #2440 Lafayette, footed, scroll handled, regular, 6.75 oz.	18
Sugar 3.5" #2470, footed, regular, 6 oz.	18
Tray 8.75" #2470, oval, for creamer/sugar	24
Tumbler 2.75" #6007, footed, whiskey, 2 oz.	24
Tumbler 4.25" #6007, footed, juice, 5 oz.	16
Tumbler 5.25" #6007, footed, water, 9 oz.	20
Tumbler 6" #6007, footed, ice tea, 12 oz.	24
Vase 6.25" to 7" #2440 Lafayette, flat, flared, cylindrical	60
Vase 7.75" #2470, footed, w/fancy 3 scroll stem, flared	75
Vase 7.5" #2467, footed w/handles	95

MOUNT VERNON
Cambridge Glass Company   1931-57
Main Colors: Amber, Carmen (ruby), Crystal, Emerald Green, and Royal Blue (cobalt)
Other Colors: Ebony (black), Heatherbloom, and Violet

    The heavily quilted diamond pattern of Mount Vernon has two different styles of edges: saw tooth edge & scalloped. Since this was a fairly heavy glass pattern, we believe it was more commonly used as an everyday dish set. All pieces were made in Crystal but not in all of the colors. Collectors seem to use a color theme with their serving pieces. The Westmoreland Glass Company designed a quilted pattern of their own called English Hobnail in the 1920s. This may have been a pattern that influenced the creation of Mount Vernon at Cambridge.

    A few pieces of Ebony, Heatherbloom, and Violet pieces were made but not enough to develop a whole place setting.

Back left: Plate 8.5" #5, salad, scalloped edge. **Back right:** Plate 11.5" #37, tab handled, scalloped edge. **Front left:** Bowl 4.5" #31, shallow, scalloped edge, fruit. **Front center left:** Cup & saucer, coffee: cup 2.25" #7, coffee, 6 oz.; saucer w/indent 5.5". **Front center right:** Decanter w/stopper #47, flat, spherical, 11 oz. **Front right:** Goblet 4" #42, ball stem, sherbet, 5.5 oz.

MOUNT VERNON

	Amber Crystal	Royal Blue Emerald Carmen
Ashtray 3.5" #63, round, saw tooth or smooth edge	6	18
Bonbon 5.5" #114, footed, square crimped	12	38
Bonbon 7.5" #115, footed, handles turned up	12	36
Bottle w/chrome tube #62, bitters, 5 oz.	35	85
Bottle w/faceted stopper 6.25" #18, square, toilet, 9 oz.	40	95
Bowl 4.5" #31, shallow, scalloped edge, fruit	5	15
Bowl 5.25" #6, shallow, scalloped edge, fruit	6	18
Bowl 6" #32, flared, scalloped edge, cereal	12	36
Bowl 6" #76, cupped, scalloped edge, jelly/preserve	10	30
Bowl 6", #119 deep, ruffled (vase like) pattern to edge	20	65
Bowl 9", #100 footed, handled, saw tooth or scalloped edge, trophy	28	85
Bowl 10", #39 flared, saw tooth or scalloped edge	20	65
Bowl 10", #126 shallow, cupped, saw tooth or scalloped edge	20	65
Bowl 10" #128, bell shape, smooth edge	28	75
Bowl 10" #148, bell footed, cupped, scalloped edge	15	48
Bowl 10.5" #43, cupped	30	85
Bowl 10.5" #120, deep, salad, scalloped edge	24	75
Bowl 11" #48, footed, Tom & Jerry or fruit	65	195
Bowl 11" #126, shallow, scalloped edge	20	60
Bowl 11" #135, oval, scalloped edge	18	48
Bowl 11" #136, oval, 4-footed, scalloped edge	20	60
Bowl 11.5", #61 low, cupped, saw tooth or scalloped edge	20	65
Bowl 11.5" #128, flared, wide flat rim, saw tooth or scalloped edge	18	55
Bowl 12" #117, shallow, rolled scalloped edge, crimped	20	65
Bowl 12" #118, oblong, deep, crimped	24	70
Bowl 12" #129, mushroom shape	30	90
Bowl 12.5" #44, flared	28	75
Bowl 12.5" #45, mushroom shape	30	90
Bowl 12.5" #121, wide, flared	28	75
Bowl 13" #116, shallow, ruffled, fruit	30	85
Box w/cover 3" #16, round, flat top, vanity	20	65
Box w/cover 4" #17, square, flat top, powder	24	75
Box w/cover 4.5" #15, round, puff or toilet, fancy finial	30	95
Butter tub w/cover 5" #73, tab handled (lid notched for tab handles)	48	125
Cake salver 10.5" #150, ball stem, scalloped edge	45	135
Cake salver 12" #49, bell footed, cupped up edge	45	135
Candelabra 1-lite 4.5" #131, ball stem w/bobeche & prisms, pair	75	
Candelabra 1-lite 8.5" #36, fancy stem w/bobeche & prisms, pair	125	375
Candelabra 1-lite 9.5" #1612, dolphin stem w/bobeche & prisms, pair	195	
Candelabra 2-lite 5.5" #111, ball center w/bobeches & prisms, pair	185	
Candelabra 2-lite 13.5" #38, keyhole w/bobeches & prisms, pair	250	750
Candlestick 1-lite 4" #130, ball stem, pair	35	85
Candlestick 1-lite 8" #35, fancy stem, pair	65	195
Candlestick 2-lite 5" #110, ball center, pair	45	
Candy jar w/cover 8" #9, footed, ball stem, urn or candy, 1 lb.	75	150
Cigarette holder 4.6" #66, footed, ball stem, round	30	85
Cigarette box w/cover 4" #67, square	35	95
Coaster 3" #60, round, plain rim	5	15
Coaster 3.5" #70, round, 6 raised rays	6	18
Cocktail icer 4.6" #85, footed, tab handled, 2 piece w/non-etched insert	20	60
Cologne w/faceted stopper #1340, 2.5 oz.	45	100
Comport #33, tall stem, scalloped edge, 4.5" wide	18	65
Comport #77, handled, ball stem, saw tooth or scalloped edge, 5.5" wide	20	70
Comport 4" #96, handled, saw tooth or scalloped edge, 6.25" wide	22	75
Comport 3.5" #97, cupped, scalloped edge, 6.25" wide	18	65
Comport #10, cupped, ball stem, 7" wide	18	65
Comport #11, footed, ball stem, flared, 7.5" wide	24	70
Comport #81, cupped, fancy stem, 8" wide	24	70
Comport #100, footed, handled, trophy shape, 9" wide	35	95
Comport #99, footed, ball stem, flared, 9.5" wide	28	85
Creamer #4, footed, open handle, individual, 3.5 oz.	8	24
Creamer 4.25" #8, footed, open handle, regular, 6 oz.	6	20
Cup & saucer, coffee: cup 2.25" #7, coffee, 6 oz.; saucer w/indent 5.5"	8	24

Top left: Salt dip 2" #24, round, smooth top, Amber. **Bottom left:** Dealer sign 4.4" ($125). **Bottom right:** Bottle w/faceted stopper 6.25" #18, square, toilet, 9 oz., Carmen (ruby).

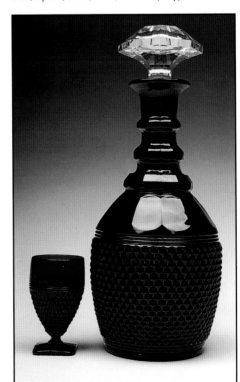

Left: Tumbler 3.3" #22, footed, wine, 3 oz. **Right:** Decanter w/ stopper 11.5" #52, flat, spherical, 40 oz., Royal Blue (cobalt).

Back left: Plate 10.5" #40, dinner, scalloped edge, Emerald Green.
Back right: Plate 11.5" #37, tab handled, scalloped edge, Crystal.
Front right top: Creamer 4.25" #8, footed, open handle, regular, 6 oz., Emerald Green. **Front right bottom:** Sugar 3.3" #8, footed, tab handled, regular, 6 oz., Emerald Green.

Left: Comport 4" #96, tab handled, saw tooth or scalloped edge, 6.25" wide. **Right:** Comport 3.5" #97, cupped, scalloped edge, 6.25" wide.

Left: Cigarette holder 4.6" #66, footed, ball stem, round, Crystal.
Right: Vase 5.5" #12, footed, fancy ball stem, rose bowl or ivy ball, Violet.

Item		
Decanter w/stopper #47, flat, spherical, 11 oz.	55	115
Decanter w/stopper 11.5" #52, flat, spherical, 40 oz.	65	150
Finger bowl & liner: bowl 5" #23, (use b & b plate for liner)	14	40
Goblet 4.5" #27, ball stem, wine, 3 oz.	16	48
Goblet 3.9" #26, ball stem, cocktail, 3.5 oz.	16	48
Goblet #41, ball stem, oyster cocktail, 4 oz.	6	20
Goblet 4" #42, ball stem, sherbet, 5.5 oz.	10	24
Goblet 5" #25, ball stem, claret, 4.5 oz.	15	48
Goblet #2, ball stem, saucer champagne, 6.5 oz.	8	24
Goblet #1, ball stem, water, 10 oz.	16	48
Honey jar/cover #74, notched lid, 7 oz.	38	125
Hurricane lamp 9" #1607, footed, ball stem w/bobeche prisms & chimney, each	95	195
Ice bucket #92, chrome handle	40	100
Mayonnaise #30, footed, handled, sauce boat, 2 spouted	24	75
Mayonnaise 2 piece: bowl 6" #112, footed, handled, deep; liner w/ indent 8.5", scalloped edge	28	85
Mug #84, stein w/applied handle, 14 oz.	24	75
Mustard jar w/cover #29, straight sided w/notched lid, 2.5 oz.	35	85
Pitcher #13, juice jug, 24 oz.	45	95
Pitcher #13, jug, 48 oz.	60	125
Pitcher #90, upright jug w/o ice lip, 50 oz.	75	145
Pitcher #95, tilt ball, jug w/ice lip, 80 oz.	90	180
Pitcher #91, squat water jug, 86 oz.	90	185
Plate 6.4" #19, bread & butter or finger bowl liner	4	12
Plate 7.5" #72, coupe/salad or water jug liner	10	30
Plate 8" #124, footed, handled, lemon server	10	30
Plate 8.5" #5, salad, scalloped edge	8	28
Plate 10.5" #40, dinner, scalloped edge	20	60
Plate 11.5" #37, tab handled, scalloped edge	20	58
Plate 13.5" #122, small center, turned up scalloped edge, cabaret	22	65
Plate 14.5" #123, chop, scalloped edge	22	65
Relish 6" #78, handled, round, pickle, scalloped edge	10	32
Relish 6" #106, handled, 2 sections	12	36
Relish 8" #65, round, pickle, saw tooth edge	12	36
Relish 8" #101, center handled, 2 sections	16	45
Relish 8" #103, 3 open handles, 3 sections	18	46
Relish 8.5" #105, handled, 4 sections, saw tooth or scalloped edge, sweetmeat	20	48
Relish 10.5" #79, oval, saw tooth edge, celery	20	65
Relish 11" #98, oblong, shallow, scalloped edge, celery	18	48
Relish 11" #200, 4-footed, handled, oblong, scalloped edge, celery	24	75
Relish 12" #80, oblong, 2 sections, divided diagonally	24	75
Relish 12" #104, oblong, scalloped edge, 4 equal sections & celery section	28	85
Salt dip 2" #24, round, smooth top	8	24
Salt dip #102, oval footed, handled, saw tooth or scalloped edge	12	36
Shaker #28, straight side, glass top, pair	24	75
Shaker #88, short tapered, glass top, pair	25	78
Shaker #89, high tapered, glass top, pair	28	85
Sugar #4, footed, tab handled, individual, 3.5 oz.	8	24
Sugar 3.3" #8, footed, tab handled, regular, 6 oz.	6	20
Tray #4, oblong, cupped, for individual cream/sugar	12	36
Tray 7" #113, footed, handled, flared, mint	12	36
Tumbler #55, flat, straight sided, whiskey, 2 oz.	12	
Tumbler 3.3" #22, footed, wine, 3 oz.	12	36
Tumbler #56, flat, straight sided, juice, 5 oz.	10	
Tumbler #21, footed, juice, 5 oz.	15	45
Tumbler #57, flat, straight sided, old fashion, 7 oz.	10	
Tumbler #51, flat, straight sided, lunch water, 10 oz.	12	
Tumbler #3, footed, water, 10 oz.	16	48
Tumbler #58, flat, straight sided, dinner water, 10 oz.	12	
Tumbler #13, barrel shaped, ice tea, 12 oz.	18	48
Tumbler #20, footed, ice tea, 12 oz.	18	50
Tumbler #14, barrel shaped, beverage, 14 oz.	22	65
Tumbler #59, flat, straight sided, beverage, 14 oz.	20	
Vase 5", footed, flared, saw tooth edge	18	50
Vase 5.5" #12, footed, fancy ball stem, rose bowl or ivy ball	20	60
Vase 6" #50, footed, squat, saw tooth or scalloped edge	20	60
Vase 6.5" #106, rose bowl	20	60
Vase 6.5" #107, squat	22	65
Vase 7" #58, footed, cone shape, flared, saw tooth or scalloped edge	30	90
Vase 10" #46, footed, flared, saw tooth or scalloped edge	34	98

Candy jar w/cover 8" #9, footed, ball stem, urn or candy, 1 lb., Amber.

NAVARRE
Fostoria Glass Company   **Etching #327**   **1936-82**
Colors: Blue, Crystal, and Pink

     Navarre features an upside down bouquet of flowers inside a scrolled horseshoe. Initially, Navarre was only made in Crystal. This was the longest running of all the Fostoria etched patterns. The pieces can be found on the blanks of #2496 Baroque, #2666 Contour, #2375 Fairfax, #2440 Lafayette, and #2364 Sonata. The stemware can be found on the #6016 Wilma blank.

     In the 1970s, Navarre was reintroduced with Crystal stemware and a limited number of serving pieces. New this time was a larger assortment of stemware that was also offered in Pink & Blue. At this time all these pieces were stamped with the acid Fostoria mark. In 1983 Lenox purchased this and other moulds. Lenox kept making colored stemware for several more years and put their Lenox acid stamp on the pieces replacing the Fostoria name. Lenox now has made a new stemware piece that incorporates much of the old Navarre etched pattern and is called Wedding Promises. It has three bunches of hanging flowers with one of them incorporating wedding bells. This new item is the 9.9" fluted champagne and holds 8.5 oz. The value of this item would be $25.

     A bell also was produced for the Avon Company as a gift to their representatives. It is easy to tell because of a different pattern on the handle and its height.

     Community Silver made a silver plate pattern called Coronation that matches the Navarre etching.

Pattern detail, Navarre.

Left: Bell 6.6" #6016 Wilma, dinner, Crystal. **Center left:** Bell 6.6" #6016 Wilma, dinner, Pink. **Center right:** Bell 6.6" #6016 Wilma, dinner, Blue. **Right:** Bell 7.5", dinner, made for Avon, Crystal.

Left: Tumbler 4.9" #NA01/064, flat, hi ball, 12 oz. **Center:** Tumbler 3.6" #NA01/023, flat, double old fashion, 13 oz. **Right:** Pitcher 6.9" #2666 Contour, flat, applied handle, ice lip, 32 oz.

NAVARRE

	Crystal	Blue Pink
Bell 6.6" #6016 Wilma, dinner	95	145
Bell 7.5", dinner, made for Avon	75	
Bonbon 7.4" #2496 Baroque, 3-toed, flared or crimped	48	
Bottle w/flat stopper 6.5" #2083, flat, salad dressing, 7 oz.	495	
Bowl 4" #2496 Baroque, 3-toed, square, w/1 handle, mint	26	
Bowl 4.3" #2496 Baroque, 3-toed, round, w/1 handle	20	
Bowl 4.6" #2496 Baroque, 3-toed, tri-corn, w/1 handle	28	
Bowl 5" #2496 Baroque, flared, fruit	20	
Bowl 6" #2496 Baroque, 4-toed, tab flame handled, square, sweetmeat	40	
Bowl 6.9" #2496 Baroque, 3-toed, crimped, nut	28	
Bowl 10" #2496 Baroque, 4-tab feet, rectangle, tab flame handled, shallow, floating garden	98	
Bowl 10.5" #2470 1/2, 4-footed, flared	75	
Bowl 10.75" #2496 Baroque, 4-toed, oval, flame handled	110	
Bowl 12" #2496 Baroque, flat, round, flared	85	
Bowl 12.5" #2545 Flame, oblong w/smooth rim	115	
Cake plate 10.25" #2496 Baroque, 2-tab flame handled	65	
Cake plate 10.5" #2440 Lafayette, tab plume handled	70	
Candelabra 2-lite 7.5" #2545 Flame, 10.25" spread w/bobeches & prisms, pair	395	
Candlestick 1-lite 4" #2496 Baroque, cornucopia flame shape, pair	65	
Candlestick 1-lite 5.5" #2496 Baroque, fancy flame stem, pair	75	
Candlestick 2-lite 4.75" #2472, curlicue arms w/pointed center, 8.25" spread, pair	135	
Candlestick 2-lite 5.25" #2496 Baroque, flame arms, 8" spread, pair	95	
Candlestick 2-lite 6.75" #2545 Flame, ball & flame center, 10.25" spread, pair	175	
Candlestick 3-lite 6" #2496 Baroque, flame arms, 8.25" spread, pair	145	
Candlestick 3-lite 6.75" #2482, pair	165	
Candy w/cover 6.25" #2496 Baroque, triangular, 3 sections, lid w/flame finial	145	
Carafe, 6" #NA01/750, rib optic, only 24 made, 10 oz.	3,000+	
Carafe, 9", #NA01/790, rib optic, only 24 made, 65 oz.	3,000+	
Cheese & cracker: comport 3.25" #2496 Baroque, short stem, 5.25" wide; plate 11"	98	
Comport 4.5" #2400, low lady leg stem, flared, 6" wide	38	
Comport 4.75" #2496 Baroque, fancy flame stem, flared, 5.5" wide	40	
Creamer 3.1" #2496 Baroque, footed, individual, 4 oz.	24	
Creamer 4.25" #2440 Lafayette, footed, scroll handle, regular, 6.75 oz.	20	
Cup & saucer, coffee #2440 Lafayette: cup 2.75", footed, 6 oz.; saucer w/indent 5.8"	26	
Finger bowl & liner: bowl 4.6" #869, blown, 8 oz.; plate w/indent 6"	65	
Goblet 3.9" #6016 Wilma, cordial, .75 oz.	95	
Goblet 5.25" #6016 Wilma, wine, 3.25 oz.	45	
Goblet 5.25" #6016 Wilma, liquor cocktail, 3.5 oz.	32	
Goblet 3.9" #6016 Wilma, oyster cocktail, 4 oz.	26	
Goblet 6" #6016 Wilma, claret, 4.5 oz.	65	135
Goblet 8.1" #6016 Wilma, continental champagne, 5 oz.	145	195
Goblet 4.4" #6016 Wilma, sherbet, 5.5 oz.	22	
Goblet 5.6" #6016 Wilma, saucer champagne, 5.5 oz.	24	58
Goblet 6.1" #6016 Wilma, sherry, 6 oz.	80	
Goblet 6.5" #6016 Wilma, large claret, 6.5 oz.	60	115
Goblet 7.6" #6016 Wilma, water, 10 oz.	45	85
Goblet 6.5" #6016 Wilma, brandy inhaler, 15 oz.	145	

Back: Cake plate 10.25" #2496 Baroque, 2-tab flame handled. **Front:** Bowl 12" #2496 Baroque, flat, round, flared.

Top: Bowl 12.5" #2545 Flame, oblong w/smooth rim. **Bottom:** Bowl 10.75" #2496 Baroque, 4-toed, oval, flame handled.

Goblet 7.25" #6016 Wilma, magnum, 16 oz.	135	175
Ice bucket 6" #2375, chrome handle	175	
Ice bucket 4.5" #2496 Baroque, flat, squat, chrome handle, 6.5" wide	135	
Ice dish 2.75" #2451, bowl w/3-tabs hold liners, 4.8" wide	150	
Ice dish liner 3.5" #2451, tomato juice, 5 oz.	18	
Jelly 5" #2496 Baroque, cupped, scalloped edge	38	
Mayonnaise 2 piece #2496 1/2 Baroque: bowl 5", flat, flared, 3.5" high; liner w/indent 6.75"	95	
Mayonnaise 2 piece #2375 Fairfax: bowl 5.6", footed, flared; plate w/indent 7.4"	85	
Pitcher 6.9" #2666 Contour, flat, applied handle, ice lip, 32 oz.	295	
Pitcher 8" #2666 Contour, flat, applied handle, ice lip, 48 oz.	400+	
Pitcher 9.75" #5000, footed, applied handle, water w/o ice lip, 48 oz.	395	
Plate 6.25" #2440 Lafayette, bread & butter	12	
Plate 7.25" #2440 Lafayette, salad or dessert	16	
Plate 8.5" #2440 Lafayette, lunch	24	
Plate 9.5" #2440 Lafayette, dinner	65	
Plate 14" #2496 Baroque, small center, turned up edge, cabaret	75	
Plate 16" #2364 Sonata, small center, turned up edge, cabaret	95	
Relish 6" #2496 Baroque, tab flame handled, 2 equal sections, square	34	
Relish 8" #2496 Baroque, oval, pickle	36	
Relish 9.25" #2440 Lafayette, flat, flared, oval pickle	35	
Relish 10" #2496 Baroque, 4-tab feet, tab flame handled, oblong, 2 equal sections & celery section	65	
Relish 10" #2496 Baroque, 4-tab feet, tab flame handled, oblong, 4 equal sections	95	
Relish 10.75", oval celery	60	
Relish 13.25" #2419 Mayfair, irregular shape, 4 equal sections & celery section	125	
Sauce 2 piece #2496 Baroque: bowl 6.5", oblong, tab flame handled; liner 6.75"	110	
Shaker 2.6" #2363, chrome top, pair	95	
Shaker, 3.25" #2375 Fairfax, footed, w/chrome or glass top, pair	145	
Sugar 2.9" #2496 Baroque, footed, individual, 4 oz.	24	
Sugar 3.6" #2440 Lafayette, footed, scroll handled, regular, 6.75 oz.	20	
Syrup 5.5" #2586, Sani-cut, bakelite handle, 9 oz.	500+	
Tray 6.5" #2496 Baroque, rectangle, tab flame handled for individual creamer & sugar	38	
Tray 8.25" #2496 Baroque, flat, 3-toed, turned up edge, tidbit	38	
Tumbler 4.6" #6016 Wilma, footed, juice, 5 oz.	28	
Tumbler 5.4" #6016 Wilma, footed, water, 10 oz.	35	
Tumbler 4.9" #NA01/064, flat, hi ball, 12 oz.	95	
Tumbler 3.6" #NA01/023, flat, double old fashion, 13 oz.	85	
Tumbler 5.9" #6016 Wilma, footed, ice tea, 13 oz.	38	75
Vase 5" #4121, flat, symmetrical, melon shape, necked & flared	125	
Vase 5" #4128, flat, flared, flip shape w/regular optic	135	
Vase 6" #4143, footed, large, flared top	225	
Vase 8" #2660, flat, flip shape w/o optic	195	
Vase 9.5" #2470, footed, w/fancy 3 scroll stem, flared	245	

Azure (blue) w/Crystal stem/foot grouping: **Left:** Goblet 7.25" #6016 Wilma, magnum, 16 oz. **Center:** Goblet 6" #6016 Wilma, claret, 4.5 oz. **Right:** Goblet 7.6" #6016 Wilma, water, 10 oz.

Back left: Relish 10" #2496 Baroque, 4-tab feet, tab flame handled, oblong, 2 equal sections & celery section. **Back right:** Tray 8.25" #2496 Baroque, flat, 3-toed, turned up edge, tidbit. **Front left:** Candlestick 1-lite 5.5" #2496 Baroque, fancy flame stem. **Front right:** Candlestick 2-lite 4.75" #2472, curlicue arms w/pointed center, 8.25" spread.

Back left: Cake plate 10.25" #2496 Baroque, 2-tab flame handled. **Back right:** Plate 9.5" #2440 Lafayette, dinner. **Front left:** Sauce bowl 6.5" #2496 Baroque, oblong, handled. **Front center:** Sugar 2.9" #2496 Baroque, footed, individual, 4 oz. **Front right:** Creamer 3.1" #2496 Baroque, footed, individual, 4 oz.

Pitcher 9.75" #5000, footed, applied handle, water w/o ice lip, 48 oz.

Left: Carafe, 6" #NA01/750, rib optic, only 24 made, 10 oz. **Right:** Carafe, 9", #NA01/790, rib optic, only 24 made, 65 oz.

Vase 5" #4128, flat, flared, flip shape w/regular optic.

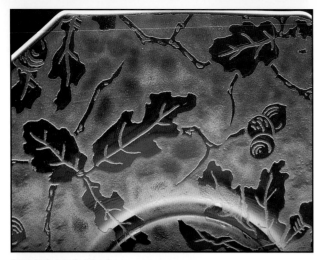

Pattern detail, Oak Leaf.

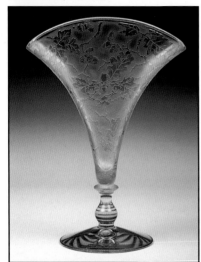

Vase 5.5" #2385, footed, wafer & ball stem, fan shape, Azure (blue).

Bowl 11" #2398, footed, nasturtium shape, Green.

Left: Candlestick 1-lite 3" #2395, short, scroll handled, Ebony (black).
Center: Ice bucket 6" #2378, flat, cylindrical chrome handle, Crystal.
Right: Candlestick 1-lite, 2.75" #2375 1/2 Fairfax, mushroom shaped, Green.

OAK LEAF & OAK WOOD
Fostoria Glass Company   **Etching #290**   **1928-31**
Main Colors: Azure (blue), Crystal, Green, Orchid, and Rose (pink)
Other Color: Ebony (black)

Oak Leaf & Oak Wood are among the most popular of the brocades that Fostoria designed. They have the same etched pattern design, which incorporate the use of oak leaves. The difference is in the colors that were produced and the finish. Oak Leaf was made in the plain colors of Crystal, Black, Green, and Rose. Oak Wood was produced with an Iridized finish and trimmed with gold in Azure (blue) and Orchid. These etched patterns were part of the Brocade line that also included Cupid, Grape, Paradise, and Palm Leaf.

When pricing one of the few items made in Ebony, add 25% to the listed Rose price. Sometimes you may find an iridized piece of Oak Wood that does not have any gold trim on it. If yours has no gold, then it is because it has worn off and should be priced accordingly.

OAK LEAF & OAK WOOD	Crystal	Green	Rose	Azure	Orchid
Bonbon 6.75" #2375 Fairfax, 2 style of handles, both turned up	28	38	45	50	60
Bowl 4.5" #2394, 3-footed, flared, mint	26	36	40	55	65
Bowl 5.4" #2375 Fairfax, 2 style of handles, sweetmeat	34	42	48	55	65
Bowl 8.5" #2375 Fairfax, handled, dessert	85	100	115	165	195
Bowl 10" #2395, oval, large scroll handles	95	125	145	175	225
Bowl 11" #2398, footed, nasturtium shape	110	135	150	165	195
Bowl 12" #2342, footed, octagon shape	110	125	145	175	225
Bowl 12" #2375 Fairfax, 3-toed, flared, console	80	100	110	165	185
Bowl 12" #2394, flared, 3-footed, "A" shape, console	85	110	135	175	195
Bowl 13" #2375 1/2 Fairfax, oval, mushroom-shaped, centerpiece w/frog	110	125	200	275	335
Cake plate 9.75" #2375 Fairfax, small center, open handled	70	80	90	115	135
Candlestick 1-lite 2" #2394, flared, 3-footed, pair	75	85	100	125	145
Candlestick 1-lite, 2.75" #2375 1/2 Fairfax, mushroom-shaped, pair	80	100	125	145	175
Candlestick 1-lite 3" #2395, short, scroll handled, pair	85	110	145	165	195
Candlestick 1-lite 3.25" #2375 Fairfax, pair	75	85	100	125	145
Candy w/cover 7" #2331, 3 equal sections, "fleur-de-lis" finial	110	140	165	300	350
Candy w/cover #2380, confection box	98	110	145	225	250
Candy w/cover #2395, oval, confection		135	165	250	275
Cheese & cracker #2368: comport 2.9", short stem, cupped w/o optic, 5" wide; handled plate w/o optic, 11"	90	115	150	175	210
Cigarette w/cover 3.5" #2391 small, oblong	85	110	145	165	195
Cigarette w/cover 4.75" #2391 large, oblong	95	125	160	185	225
Comport #2350, shallow, short stem, 8" wide	48	58	78	110	135
Comport 7.5" #2400, high, lady leg stem, flared, 8" wide	65	85	95	145	175
Flower block 3.75" #2309, use in #2394 console bowl, non-etched	25	35	50	60	70
Goblet 3.5" #877, oyster cocktail w/optic, 4.5 oz.	18	22	26	32	40
Goblet 4" #877, sherbet w/optic, 6 oz.	20	24	30	36	45
Goblet 6.1" #877, saucer champagne w/optic, 6 oz.	24	28	34	45	54
Goblet 7.9" #877, water/optic, 10 oz.	45	52	58	85	95
Ice bucket 6" #2378, flat, cylindrical chrome handle	95	110	145	195	245
Mayonnaise 2 piece: bowl #2315; #2332 liner w/indent 7.25"	65	85	95	165	195
Pitcher 9.75" #5000, footed, applied handle, water w/o ice lip, 48 oz.	450	600	745	1,000	1,200
Plate 6.8" #2375 Fairfax, 2 style of handles, lemon server	30	40	48	60	75
Plate 7" #2283, dessert	20	25	30	35	40
Plate 8" #2283, salad	25	30	35	40	48
Plate 12" #2315, salver	95	115	135	160	175
Plate 13" #2315, lettuce	65	85	100	150	165
Sandwich server 12" #2342, center "fleur-de-lis" handle	75	85	125	160	195
Sugar pail 3.75" #2378, chrome handle	95	140	160	250	275
Tumbler 4.25" #877, footed, juice w/ optic, 5 oz.	24	28	34	45	54

...mbler 5.25" #877, footed, water w/ optic, 9 oz.	38	48	56	68	85
...mbler 6" #877, footed, ice tea w/ optic, 12 oz.	40	52	62	75	95
...rn w/cover #2413		185	200	375	425
...se 3" #4103, short, shouldered w/optic	50	65	75	125	160
...se 6" #4105, flat, shouldered w/optic	60	80	95	145	180
...se 7" #2369, footed, shouldered w/optic	80	110	125	165	185
...se 8" #2292,	75	100	115	145	175
...se 8" #2387, flat, 6 pleated sides	100	125	145	275	335
...se 8" #4105, flat, shouldered w/optic	70	85	100	225	245
...se 5.5" #2385, footed, wafer & ball stem, fan shape	140	185	200	450	495
...se 9" #2369, footed, shouldered w/optic	100	125	145	175	195
...se 2 piece window box #2373: 3.5" tall, 7.25" long, 2 bar feet, oblong; flower block 7.25" long, frog non-etched	165	200	325	475	525
...se 2 piece window box #2373: 4.25" tall, 8.25" long, 2 bar feet, oblong; flower block 8.25" long, frog non-etched	185	225	365	525	575
...hip cream bowl 5.5" #2375 Fairfax, handled	35	45	50	60	70
...hip cream pail 4.5" #2378, chrome handle, 2.5" tall	120	175	195	225	245

Vase 8" #4105, flat, shouldered w/optic, Azure (blue).

...owl 5.4" #2375 Fairfax, 2 style of handles, sweetmeat, Azure ...lue).

Cheese & cracker #2368: comport 2.9", short stem, cupped w/o optic, 5" wide; handled plate w/o optic, 11", Azure (blue).

Pitcher 9.75" #5000, footed, applied handle, water w/o ice lip, 48 oz., Azure (blue).

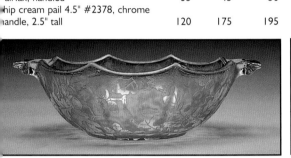

...zure (blue) grouping: **Left:** Goblet 6.1" #877, saucer champagne w/ ...tic, 6 oz. **Right:** Tumbler 6" #877, footed, ice tea w/optic, 12 oz.

Sandwich server 12" #2342, center "fleur-de-lis" handle, Green.

Candlestick 1-lite 2" #2394, flared, 3-footed, Azure (blue).

Vase 2 piece window box #2373: 3.5" tall, 7.25" long, 2 bar feet, oblong; flower block 7.25" long, frog non-etched, Rose (pink).

Pattern detail, Old Colony.

Sahara (yellow) grouping: **Back:** Tray 13" #1401 Empress, square, 2 handled, sandwich. **Front:** Cup & saucer, bouillon #1401 Empress: cup 2.6", footed, 2 handled, 7 oz.; saucer 6.5" w/indent.

Bowl 8.1" #1401 Empress, deep, flared, Sahara (yellow).

OLD COLONY

A. H. Heisey & Company   **Etching #448**   **1930-39**
Main Colors: Crystal, Flamingo (pink), Moongleam (green), and Sahara (yellow)
Other Color: Alexandrite

Old Colony features a 15 petal flower on a triangle that is surrounded by ornate scro work. All the accessory pieces are found on blank #1401 Empress, unless otherwise note Items were also done on #1509 Queen Ann (this pattern is the same as #1401 Empre except that an interior wide optic was added). Note, #1401 Empress round items have s plumes and square items only four. The stemware is found on #3380 Old Dominion, #338 Duquesne, #3390 Carcassonne, and #3397 Gascony. The colors on #3380 stemware a combination of Moongleam bowl with clear foot and stem or Crystal bowl with Moonglea foot and stem. Old Colony stemware seems to be the easiest to locate. When you are lookir for other pieces, it takes a lot of searching.

Some of the items were made in Alexandrite but few pieces have shown up.

OLD COLONY

	Crystal	Sahara	Flamingo Moongleam
Bowl 3" #1509 Queen Ann, dolphin footed, individual nut	15	35	42
Bowl 4.5" #1509 Queen Ann, deep, fruit	10	18	22
Bowl 5" #1401 Empress, tab footed, 2-handled preserve	15	30	36
Bowl 6" #1401 Empress, square, rim grapefruit	22	45	55
Bowl 6" #1509 Queen Ann, tab footed, 2-handled, flared jelly	22	45	55
Bowl 6" #1509 Queen Ann, 3 dolphin footed, flared, mint	20	40	48
Bowl 7.5" #1509 Queen Ann, dolphin footed, nappy	30	65	78
Bowl 8.1" #1401 Empress, deep, flared	26	55	65
Bowl 8.5" #1401 Empress, tab footed, flared w/loop handles, floral	30	65	80
Bowl 9" #1401 Empress, 3 handled	42	85	110
Bowl #1183 Revere, oval, vegetable	75		
Bowl 10" #1401 Empress, oval, vegetable	42	80	115
Bowl 10" #1401 Empress, (round or square) 2-handled, salad	35	75	95
Bowl 10" #1401 Empress, oval, 2-handled, deep, dessert	35	75	95
Bowl 10" #3397 Gascony, low foot, floral	40	85	
Bowl 11" #1509 Queen Ann, dolphin footed, flared, floral	48	95	115
Bowl 13" #1401 Empress, footed, flared	42	85	105
Candlestick 1-lite 6" #135 Empress, dolphin footed, tall stem, 2 stacked wafers, pair	145	295	325
Candlestick 2-lite 5" #134 Trident, plume/pointed center 6.5" spread, pair	100	250	275
Cigarette holder #3390 Carcassonne, footed, wafer stem, straight sided	48	95	115
Cocktail shaker #4225 Cobel, low foot, straight sided, 3 piece, 32 oz.	95	195	235
Cocktail shaker #4225 Cobel, low foot, straight sided, 3 piece, 64 oz.	125		
Comport 7" #3368 Old Dominion	45	85	110
Comport 7" #1509 Queen Ann, tall stem, oval w/rolled ends	48	95	110
Cream soup & liner #1401 Empress: bowl 5", flat, handled, 10 oz.; saucer w/indent, round or square	48	95	115
Creamer 3" #1401 Empress, collar footed, individual, 3.5 oz.	18	38	45
Creamer 3.25" #1401 Empress, dolphin footed, regular, 6 oz.	25	50	60
Cruet w/wafer shape stopper 6.25" #1401 Empress, footed, oil bottle, 4 oz.	85	145	175
Cup & saucer, after dinner #1401 Empress: cup 2.5", flat, 4 oz.; saucer 4.75" w/indent	65	125	155
Cup & saucer, coffee #1183 Revere: cup, 6 oz.; saucer w/indent	35		
Cup & saucer, coffee #1401 Empress: cup 2.6", 6 oz.; saucer 6.5" w/indent	32	65	80
Cup & saucer, coffee #1401 1/2 Empress: cup 2.6", wide band around top, 6 oz.; saucer 6.5" w/indent	32	65	80
Cup & saucer, bouillon #1401 Empress: cup 2.6", footed, 2-handled, 7 oz.; saucer 6.5" w/indent	38	75	90
Decanter w/stopper #3390 Carcassonne, 16 oz.	165	345	395
Decanter w/stopper #3397 Gascony, low foot, 16 oz.	175	375	
Finger bowl #3390 Carcassonne, footed	32	65	80
Finger bowl #4071 Duquesne, flat	22	45	
Finger bowl #4075 Old Dominion, flat	20	45	55
Grapefruit #3368 Old Dominion, footed	20	45	60
Grapefruit #3389 Duquesne, flat	20	45	
Goblet #3380 Old Dominion, cordial, 1 oz.	75	145	175
Goblet #3389 Duquesne, cordial, 1 oz.	75	145	

Sahara (yellow) grouping: **Left:** Goblet 2.4" #3390 Carcassonne, cocktail, 3 oz. **Center:** Goblet 3.4" #3390 Carcassonne, sherbet, 6 oz. **Right:** Goblet 5.2" #3390 Carcassonne, lunch water, 11 oz.

Item			
Goblet #3390 Carcassonne, cordial, 1 oz.	75	145	175
Goblet #3380 Old Dominion, wine, 2.5 oz.	25	45	60
Goblet #3389 Duquesne, wine, 2.5 oz.	22	40	
Goblet #3390 Carcassonne, wine, 2.5 oz.	25	45	60
Goblet #3397 Gascony, wine, 2.5 oz.	45	25	
Goblet #3380 Old Dominion, cocktail, 3 oz.	18	35	42
Goblet #3389 Duquesne, cocktail, 3 oz.	18	35	
Goblet 2.4" #3390 Carcassonne, cocktail, 3 oz.	18	35	42
Goblet #3397 Gascony, cocktail, 3 oz.	18	35	
Goblet #4002 Aqua Caliente, wafer stem, straight tapered cocktail	15	20	25
Goblet #3390 Carcassonne, oyster cocktail, 3 oz.	10	20	24
Goblet #3380 Old Dominion, oyster cocktail, 4 oz.	9	18	22
Goblet #3389 Duquesne, oyster cocktail, 4 oz.	9	20	
Goblet #3397 Gascony, oyster cocktail, 4 oz.	9	18	
Goblet #3380 Old Dominion, claret, 4 oz.	22	45	55
Goblet #3389 Duquesne, claret, 4 oz.	18	25	
Goblet #3390 Carcassonne, claret, 4 oz.	22	45	55
Goblet #3380 Old Dominion, parfait, 5 oz.	18	35	42
Goblet #3389 Duquesne, parfait, 5 oz.	18	35	
Goblet #3389 Duquesne, sherbet, 5 oz.	12	25	
Goblet #3389 Duquesne, saucer champagne, 5 oz.	22	45	
Goblet #3380 Old Dominion, sherbet, 6 oz.	10	25	30
Goblet 3.4" #3390 Carcassonne, sherbet, 6 oz.	10	20	25
Goblet #3397 Gascony, sherbet/finger bowl, 6 oz.	10	20	
Goblet #3380 Old Dominion, saucer champagne, 6 oz.	18	35	42
Goblet #3390 Carcassonne, saucer champagne, 6 oz.	18	35	42
Goblet #3397 Gascony, saucer champagne, 6 oz.	32	65	
Goblet #3389 Duquesne, water, 9 oz.	30	65	
Goblet #3380 Old Dominion, lunch water, 10 oz.	32	65	80
Goblet #3380 Old Dominion, dinner water, 10 oz.	32	65	80
Goblet 5.2" #3390 Carcassonne, lunch water, 11 oz.	32	65	80
Goblet #3390 Carcassonne, dinner water, 11 oz.	45	95	100
Goblet #3397 Gascony, low foot, water, 12 oz.	48	95	
Ice bucket #500 Octagon, oval w/chrome handle (held on w/nut)	80	125	
Ice bucket #1401 Empress, 4 dolphin feet, deep, 5" wide w/chrome handle	85	165	195
Mayonnaise bowl 5.4" #1509 Queen Ann, dolphin footed, deep, flared top, 3.25" tall	38	75	90
Mug #4163 Whaley, flat, sham, 16 oz. (clear bowl colored handle)	95		
Mustard w/cover 3.5" #1401 Empress, collar footed, deep w/paneled finial	145	175	
Pitcher 6.75" #1509 Queen Ann, dolphin footed, water jug w/o ice lip, 48 oz.	145	295	355
Pitcher #3390 Carcassonne fancy wafer stem, tall water jug w/o ice lip, 48 oz.	125	245	295
Pitcher #3397 Gascony, footed, straight sided, tomato j juice	75	145	
Pitcher #4164 Gallagher, flat, squat water jug w/o ice lip, 73 oz.	195	225	475
Plate 4.4" #1401 Empress, round, butter	7	15	18
Plate 6" #1509 Queen Ann, round or square bread & butter	15	30	36
Plate 6" #3350 Wabash, round pressed (plain small center)	10	20	24
Plate 7" #1183 Revere, salad	10		
Plate 7" #1509 Queen Ann, dessert (round or square) also grapefruit liner	15	30	36
Plate 8" #1509 Queen Ann, round or square, salad	18	35	42
Plate 9" #1401 Empress, round, large lunch	22	45	55
Plate 10" #1183 Revere, dinner	100		
Plate 10" #1401 Empress, round small dinner	75	150	180
Plate 10.5" #1509 Queen Ann, round or square, large dinner	95	195	240
Plate 12" #1401 Empress, round, torte	45	85	105
Plate 12" #1509 Queen Ann, round, 2-handled, sandwich	45	95	115
Platter 14" #1401 Empress, oval	45	85	105
Relish 7" #1509 Queen Ann, round, 3-tab handled, 3 sections	22	45	55
Relish 10" #1401 Empress, rectangular, tab handles on 2 corners, celery	22	45	55
Relish 13" #1401 Empress, rectangular, tab handles on 2 corners, celery	30	60	72
Relish 13" #1401 Empress, flat, oblong hors d'oeuvre, 2-handled	75	145	180
Relish 13" #1401 Empress, rectangular, tab handle on 2 corners, 2 sections, olive/celery (divided 1/3 & 2/3)	22	65	80
Sandwich server 12" #1401 Empress, center handle (round or square)	85	175	210
Shaker #1509 Queen Ann, footed, chrome top, pair	42	145	175
Sugar 3" #1401 Empress, collar footed, individual 3.5 oz.	18	38	45
Sugar 3.25" #1401 Empress, dolphin footed, regular, 3 handled, 6 oz.	25	50	60
Tray 12" #1401 Empress, 2 handles turned up (round or square) muffin	48	95	135
Tray 13" #1401 Empress, square, 2-handled, sandwich	32	65	78
Tumbler #3380 Old Dominion, footed, bar, 1 oz.	22	45	55
Tumbler #3380 Old Dominion, footed, bar, 2 oz.	12	25	30
Tumbler #3390 Carcassonne, footed, bar, 2 oz.	18	35	42
Tumbler #2401 Oakwood, flat, sham, straight tapered sides, soda, 5 oz.	10		
Tumbler #3380 Old Dominion, footed, soda, 5 oz.	9	18	22
Tumbler #3389 Duquesne, footed, soda, 5 oz.	9	18	
Tumbler #3390 Carcassonne, footed, soda, 5 oz.	9	18	22
Tumbler #3397 Gascony, footed, juice/soda, 5 oz.	22	45	
Tumbler 4.5" #1401 Empress, dolphin footed, water, 8 oz.	26	55	65
Tumbler #2351 Newton, flat, sham, straight sided, soda, 8 oz.	18	35	42
Tumbler #3380 Old Dominion, footed, soda, 8 oz.	18	35	42
Tumbler #3389 Duquesne, footed, soda, 8 oz.	18	35	
Tumbler #3390 Carcassonne, footed, soda, 8 oz.	18	35	50
Tumbler #2930 Plain & Fancy, flat, straight sided soda, 10 oz.	14	28	34
Tumbler #3380 Old Dominion, footed, water, 10 oz.	18	35	42
Tumbler #3389 Duquesne, footed, water, 10 oz.	18	35	
Tumbler #3397 Gascony, footed, soda (2 styles) 10 oz.	35	42	
Tumbler #2351 Newton, flat, sham, straight sided, soda, 12 oz.	20	40	48
Tumbler #3380 Old Dominion, footed, ice tea, 12 oz.	20	38	45
Tumbler #3389 Duquesne, footed, ice tea, 12 oz.	18	35	
Tumbler #3390 Carcassonne, footed, ice tea, 12 oz.	18	35	42
Tumbler #3390 Carcassonne, flagon, 12 oz.	35	45	95
Tumbler #3397 Gascony, footed, ice tea, 12 oz.	38	75	
Tumbler #3397 Gascony, footed, soda, 14 oz.	40	80	
Tumbler #3397 Gascony, footed, soda, 18 oz.	45	95	
Vase 8" #3390 Carcassonne, footed, wafer stem, flared to top, bud vase	45	95	115
Vase 8" #4205 Valli, footed, wafer stem, convex sides, necked, flared top, bud vase	60	125	145
Vase 9.5" #1401, dolphin footed, straight sided, cylindrical	115	225	275

Vase 9.5" #1401, dolphin footed, straight sided, cylindrical, Sahara (yellow).

Tumbler #3390 Carcassonne, flagon, 12 oz., Sahara (yellow).

Left: Pitcher 8.25", very short square foot, rectangular w/ice lip, 64 oz., Sahara (yellow). **Right:** Ashtray 2", square, individual, Cobalt.

OLD SANDWICH

A. H. Heisey & Company　　　　**Blank #1404**　　　**1931-56**

Main Colors: Crystal, Flamingo (pink), Marigold, Moongleam (green), and Sahara (yellow)

Other Colors: Amber and Cobalt

Old Sandwich was based on the pattern of Pillar that was produced by the Sandwich Glass Company. Heisey gave it the name Old Sandwich to honor this company. The pattern is composed of a series of vertical circles in a panel alternating with a blank panel. This design makes it an easy pattern to identify. After Heisey closed, Imperial purchased the moulds and continued to make the goblets & tumblers in Crystal. They were still marked with the Heisey logo.

A special large bowl called popcorn is hard to find. We assume it was made to hold a big batch of popcorn. This bowl, along with most items (other than goblets & tumblers), seems to take longer to find. On the cruets, there was a special version made for churches and these have a Maltese Cross stopper instead of the usual faceted one.

Even though Amber & Cobalt pieces were made, they show up so infrequently to add to any collection.

Left: Bowl 12", very short oval foot, deep oval, floral, Moongleam (green). **Right:** Candlestick 1-lite 6", dome footed, tall stem, Cobalt.

Top center: Creamer 3.25", footed (flared base) oval, 6 oz., Flamingo (pink). **Bottom left:** Cigarette holder 2.5", square skirt footed, square straight sided, Crystal. **Bottom center:** Sugar 2.75", footed (flared base) oval, 6 oz., Flamingo (pink). **Bottom right:** Pitcher 4.9", flat, convex sided, cream w/o ice lip, 12 oz., Crystal.

Left: Basket 7.25", footed w/applied handle, 6.8" wide, Crystal. **Right:** Pitcher 4.9", flat, convex sided, cream w/o ice lip, 12 oz., Flamingo (pink).

OLD SANDWICH

	Crystal	Sahara	Moongleam Flamingo
Ashtray 2", square, individual	15	30	45
Basket 7.25", footed w/applied handle, 6.8" wide	450+		
Bottle w/paneled stopper, flat, tall, 2 spouted, catsup	60	145	195
Bowl 4.25", flat, fruit	35	75	80
Bowl footed, 1 large wafer stem, deep, cupped, popcorn	115	195	295
Bowl 11", footed, 1 large wafer stem, flared, floral	45	95	145
Bowl 12", very short oval foot, deep oval, floral	40	80	100
Candlestick 1-lite 6", dome footed, tall stem, pair	85	195	295
Cigarette holder 2.5", square skirt footed, square straight sided	60	85	125
Comport 6", footed 1 wafer (tall) stem, cupped top	35	75	80
Creamer, flat, round w/angular handle, 6 oz.	35	55	75
Creamer 3.25", footed (flared base) oval, 6 oz.	12	26	30
Cruet w/ball stopper, flat, bell shaped, 2 oz.	60	95	140
Cup & saucer, coffee: cup, footed (flared base), 6 oz.; saucer 6", square	28	55	65
Decanter w/stopper, footed, spherical shaped, sherry, 16 oz.	100	145	225
Finger bowl, flat, deep, flared top edge	18	35	38
Goblet, footed, 1 wafer (tall) stem, wine, 2.5 oz.	20	45	50
Goblet, footed, 1 wafer (tall) stem, cocktail, 3 oz.	18	40	45
Goblet, footed, 1 wafer (tall) stem, claret, 4 oz.	14	26	32
Goblet, footed, 1 wafer (short) stem, sherbet, 4 oz.	12	28	32
Goblet, footed, 1 wafer (short) stem, parfait, 4.5 oz.	24	50	56
Goblet 4.5", footed, 1 wafer (tall) stem, saucer champagne, 5 oz.	14	32	38
Goblet, 5", footed, 1 wafer (short) stem, water, 10 oz.	24	50	56
Mug, flat, convex sided, handled, 10 oz.	35	125	195
Mug 4.4", flat, convex sided, handled, 12 oz.	45	165	295
Mug, flat, convex sided, handled, 14 oz.	60	195	395
Mug, flat, convex sided, handled, 18 oz.	75	265	450
Pitcher 4.9", flat, convex sided, cream w/o ice lip, 12 oz.	45	145	195
Pitcher, flat, convex sided, cream w/o ice lip, 14 oz.	60	165	185
Pitcher, flat, convex sided, cream w/o ice lip, 18 oz.	65	175	195
Pitcher 7", very short square foot, rectangular w/o ice lip, 64 oz.	85	165	195
Pitcher 8.25", very short square foot, rectangular w/ ice lip, 64 oz.	95	185	250
Plate 6", square, bread & butter w/scalloped edge	10	24	24
Plate 7", square, salad w/scalloped edge	12	30	30
Plate 8.25", square, lunch w/scalloped edge	15	30	35
Shaker, footed (flared base) convex sided, chrome top, pair	35	75	85
Sugar, flat, round w/angular handles, 6 oz.	35	55	75
Sugar 2.75", footed (flared base) oval, 6 oz.	12	26	30
Tumbler 2.1", flat, straight sided, bar or whiskey, 1.5 oz.	35	125	140
Tumbler, footed (flared base) convex sided, oyster cocktail, 4 oz.	12	24	28
Tumbler, flat, straight sided, soda, 5 oz.	18	40	45
Tumbler, flat, straight sided, cupped in at top, soda, 5 oz.	14	26	32
Tumbler, footed (flared base) sundae, 6 oz.	18	40	45
Tumbler, flat, straight sided (squat) toddy, 6.5 oz.	18	40	45
Tumbler, flat, straight sided, short high ball, 8 oz.	20	45	50
Tumbler, flat, straight sided, cupped in at top, short high ball, 8 oz.	18	40	45
Tumbler 5.1", flat, straight sided (slim) soda, 8 oz.	20	45	50
Tumbler, flat, straight sided, cupped in at top, soda, 8 oz.	20	45	50
Tumbler 7.6", footed (flared base) cone shape, pilsner, 8 oz.	24	45	60
Tumbler, flat, straight sided, water, 10 oz.	18	38	42
Tumbler, flat, straight sided, cupped in at top, water, 10 oz.	20	45	50
Tumbler, footed (flared base) pilsner, 10 oz.	20	45	50
Tumbler, footed (flared base) convex sided, water, 10 oz.	20	45	50
Tumbler, flat, straight sided, ice tea, 12 oz.	24	50	56
Tumbler, flat, straight sided, cupped in at top, ice tea, 12 oz.	24	50	56
Tumbler, footed (flared base) convex sided, soda, 12 oz.	24	50	56

ORCHID

A. H. Heisey & Company **Etching #507** **1940-57**

Color: Crystal

Orchid is one of the most recognized etchings that was ever put on glass. It is certainly one of the top collected etched patterns, especially among people raising orchid flowers. There are three different stemware blanks that were used on Orchid: #5022 Graceful, #5025 Tyrolean, and #5089 Princess. Stemware, along with creamers & sugars, are the easiest items to find.

After Heisey closed, Imperial continued making a few Orchid pieces, especially water goblets. This explains just why there are so many water goblets on the market. The blown candlestick is exceptionally hard to find. Because of all the different blanks, not everyone will recognize a rare item that is a common shape but on a hard to find blank.

So many elegant shapes and items can be found in this etched pattern that collectors seem to only be limited in their collecting by the depth of their pockets. Any new collector starting with this etched pattern will have some wonderful choices of pieces to buy. Most people now don't have the room to buy every piece in the collection. They just buy the shapes they like and limit their stemware to just one blank.

Pattern detail, Orchid – Heisey.

Top left: Mayonnaise bowl 5.5" #1519 Waverly, footed, flared. **Top right:** Plate 12.25" #1509 Queen Ann, 2 handled, large center, sandwich. **Bottom left:** Cup & saucer, coffee #1509 Queen Ann: cup 2.6", 6 oz.; saucer w/indent 6.5". **Bottom center left:** Creamer 4" #1519 Waverly, footed, regular, 5 oz. **Bottom center right:** Shaker 4" #1519 Waverly, footed, chrome top. **Bottom right:** Sugar 3.75" #1519 Waverly, footed, regular, 5 oz.

ORCHID	Crystal
Ashtray 3" #1435, square	42
Basket 8.5" #1540 Lariat, footed, loop stem, turned up sides	1,500+
Bell #5022 Graceful, or #5025 Tyrolean, dinner (modified claret)	175
Bottle w/stopper 6.5" #5031, flat, French dressing, 8 oz.	195
Bottle w/stopper #4037, oval, sherry, 16 oz.	295
Bowl 4.5" #1509 Queen Ann, flat, flared, fruit	48
Bowl 5.5" #1519 Waverly, 3-footed, mint	48
Bowl 6" #1509 Queen Ann, 3 dolphin, footed, mint	60
Bowl 6" #1509 Queen Ann, 4-toed, 2 loop handled, flared, jelly	55
Bowl 7" #1509 Queen Ann, flat, deep, lily pond, cupped edge	145
Bowl 7" #1519 Waverly, deep, salad	68
Bowl 7.5" #1509 Queen Ann, 3-footed, sauce	60
Bowl 8" #1509 Queen Ann, flared, vegetable	85
Bowl 8" #1509 Queen Ann, 4-footed, sauce or floral	70
Bowl 8.5" #1509 Queen Ann, flared, floral	70
Bowl 8.5" #1509 Queen Ann, 4-footed, handled, floral	70
Bowl 9" #485, deep, salad	175
Bowl 9" #1509 Queen Ann, crimped, sunburst	85
Bowl 9" #1509 Queen Ann, shallow, gardenia	70
Bowl 9" #1519 Waverly, footed, fruit or salad	85
Bowl 9" #1519 Waverly, deep, salad	195
Bowl 9.5" #1519 Waverly, crimped, floral	95
Bowl 10" #1509 Queen Ann, crimped, sunburst	100
Bowl 10" #1519 Waverly, crimped, floral or fruit	95
Bowl 10" #1519 Waverly, shallow, gardenia	78
Bowl 10.5" #1519 Waverly, footed, floral	95
Bowl 11" #1495 Fern, footed, oval	750
Bowl 11" #1519 Waverly, flared, floral	135
Bowl 11" #1519 Waverly, footed, shallow, rolled edge	195
Bowl 11" #1519 Waverly, 3 seahorse footed, floral or fruit	195
Bowl 11" #1519 Waverly, 4-footed, oval, floral	165
Bowl 11.4" #1519 Waverly, footed, flared, floral (comport shape)	245
Bowl 12" #1519 Waverly, crimped, floral or fruit	90
Bowl 13" #485, shallow, gardenia	350
Bowl 13" #1519 Waverly, crimped or flared, floral	100
Bowl 13" #1519 Waverly, shallow, gardenia	80
Bowl 13" #1519 Waverly, shallow, gardenia centerpiece w/candle cup (used w/any non-etched items below)	250
Bowl 13", #1519 Waverly, centerpiece, 2 piece, w/epergnette 6" & 6.5"	295
Bowl 13", #1519 Waverly, centerpiece, 2 piece, w/#5013 vase 5"	285
Bowl 13", #1519 Waverly, centerpiece, 2 piece, w/#4233 vase 6"	295
Butter w/cover 6" #1951 Cabochon, oblong, .25 lb.	350
Butter w/cover 5.5" #1519 Waverly, square	165
Cake salver 12" #1519 Waverly, low pedestal	225
Cake salver 13.5" #1519 Waverly, low pedestal	295
Candelabra 1-lite 7.5" #1509 Queen Ann, rosette on ribbed column w/prisms, pair	295
Candelabra 2-lite #1495 Fern, fern motif center, curlicue at tip of arm, w/bobeches & prisms, pair	325
Candlestick 1-lite, 3.5" #112 Mercury, striated ball center, pair	95
Candlestick 1-lite 7.5" #5026 Heirloom, bell footed, spherical center large candle cup (blown) pair	600+
Candlestick 2-lite 5" #134 Trident, curvilinear arms, 5.5" spread, pair	135
Candlestick 2-lite #1495 Fern, fern motif center, curlicue at tip of arm, pair	225
Candlestick 2-lite 6.5" #1519 Waverly, beaded sea foam arms, 7" spread, pair	150
Candlestick 2-lite 10" #1615 Flame, plume center w/fingers, 9" spread, pair	395
Candlestick 3-lite 7.5" #142 Cascade, curling arms w/tendril, pair	165
Candlestick 3-lite 7.5" #1519 Waverly, beaded broken waves, 8"spread, pair	225
Candy w/cover 5" #1519 Waverly, flat, squat, tab handled, chocolate box w/crescent finial	245
Candy w/cover 5" #1519 Waverly, high footed, seahorse handled w/plume finial	325

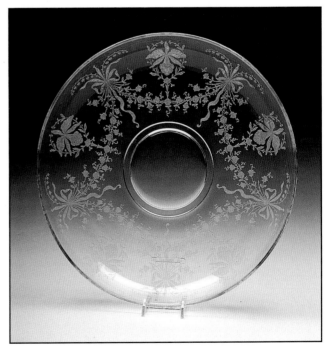

Bowl 13" #485, shallow, gardenia.

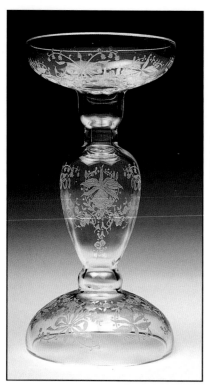

Candlestick 1-lite 7.5"
#5026 Heirloom, bell
footed, spherical center
large candle cup (blown).

Back left: Relish 8.75" #1495 Fern, round, 2-tab wave handles, 4 equal sections. **Back right:** Bowl 10" #1519 Waverly, shallow, gardenia. **Front left:** Candlestick 3-lite 7.5" #1519 Waverly, beaded broken waves, 8" spread. **Center of photo:** Ashtray 3" #1435, square. **Front right top:** Butter w/cover 5.5" #1519 Waverly, square. **Front right bottom:** Bowl 5.5" #1519 Waverly, 3-footed, mint.

Left: Candy w/cover 5" #1519 Waverly, flat, squat, tab handled, chocolate box w/crescent finial. **Right:** Comport 7" #1519 Waverly, deep, oval, flared, jelly.

Candy w/cover 6.2" #1519 Waverly, squat, round w/bow finial	225
Candy w/cover 6" #5022 Graceful, blown, low footed w/fancy stem/finial	295
Cheese & cracker: comport 2.4" #1509 Queen Ann, short stem, 5.4" wide; plate 12"	135
Cheese & cracker: comport 6.5" #1519 Waverly, short stem; plate 11"	125
Cheese & cracker: comport 6.5" #1519 Waverly, short stem; plate 14"	145
Cigarette box w/cover 4" #1489 Puritan, rectangle	145
Cigarette holder #4035, round, footed, ball stem	95
Cigarette jar/cover #1519 Waverly, sea horse handled	195
Cocktail icer w/liner #3304, footed	195
Cocktail shaker 3 piece #4225, bottle/strainer/plain stopper straight sided, 16 oz.	225
Cocktail shaker 3 piece #4225, bottle/strainer/rooster head stopper straight sided, 16 oz.	325
Cocktail shaker 3 piece #4036, bottle/strainer/plain stopper curved sides, 32 oz.	225
Cocktail shaker 3 piece #4036, bottle/strainer/horse head stopper curved sides, 32 oz.	365
Cocktail shaker 3 piece #4036, bottle/strainer/rooster head stopper curved sides, 32 oz.	325
Cocktail shaker 3 piece #4225, bottle/strainer/plain stopper straight sided, 32 oz.	245
Cocktail shaker 3 piece #4225, bottle/strainer/horse head stopper straight sided, 32 oz.	395
Cocktail shaker 3 piece #4225, bottle/strainer/rooster head stopper straight sided, 32 oz.	345
Comport 5.5" #5027, high, cupped, blown	125
Comport 6" #1519 Waverly, round, flared, short stem	65
Comport 6.5" #1519 Waverly, short stem honey	65
Comport 6.5" #1519 Waverly, deep, flared, jelly	68
Comport 7" #1519 Waverly, deep, oval, flared, jelly	72
Comport 7" #1519 Waverly, oval bowl, nut	125
Comport 7" #1519 Waverly, crescent stem w/oval bowl	195
Creamer #1519 Waverly, footed, individual, 3.5 oz.	28
Creamer 4" #1519 Waverly, footed, regular, 5 oz.	30
Cruet w/stopper #1519 Waverly, footed, oil bottle, 3 oz.	185
Cup & saucer, coffee #1509 Queen Ann: cup 2.6", 6 oz.; saucer w/indent 6.5"	45
Cup & saucer, coffee #1519 Waverly: cup 2.5", 6 oz.; saucer w/indent 6"	45
Decanter w/stopper #4036 1/2, spherical, 16 oz.	350
Decanter w/stopper #4036, footed, 16 oz.	495
Epergne bowl 9.5" #1187, footed (w/either 5", 6" or 7" vase)	795
Epergnette bowl 6" #1519 Waverly, etched pattern	300
Finger bowl & liner: bowl 4.5" #5022 Graceful or #5025 Tyrolean, flat; #3350 plate 6"	145
Goblet #4090 Coventry, cordial, 1 oz.	195
Goblet #5022 Graceful, cordial, 1 oz.	135
Goblet 4.6" #5025 Tyrolean, cordial, 1 oz.	125
Goblet #5089 Princess, plain stem, cordial, 1 oz.	145
Goblet #4090 Coventry, sherry, 2 oz.	125
Goblet #5022 Graceful, sherry, 2 oz.	110
Goblet #3311 Velvedere, sherry, 2.5 oz.	165
Goblet #5089 Princess, plain stem, wine, 2.5 oz.	95
Goblet #5022 Graceful, wine, 3 oz.	70
Goblet 5.1" #5025 Tyrolean, wine, 3 oz.	65
Goblet #5089 Princess, short stem, oyster cocktail, 2.5 oz.	48
Goblet 3.8" #5022 Graceful, oyster cocktail, 4 oz.	42
Goblet 3.6" #5025 Tyrolean, oyster cocktail, 4 oz.	40
Goblet #5089 Princess, plain stem, liquor cocktail, 3.5 oz.	58
Goblet #4002, short stem, liquor cocktail, 4 oz.	54
Goblet #5022 Graceful, liquor cocktail, 4 oz.	48
Goblet 5.4" #5025 Tyrolean, liquor cocktail, 4 oz.	45
Goblet #5089 Princess, plain stem, claret, 4 oz.	165
Goblet #5022 Graceful, claret, 4.5 oz.	135
Goblet #5025 Tyrolean, claret, 4.5 oz.	125
Goblet #5089 Princess, plain stem, sherbet, 5.5 oz.	40
Goblet #5022 Graceful, sherbet, 6 oz.	26
Goblet 3.9" #5025 Tyrolean, sherbet, 6 oz.	24
Goblet #5022 Graceful, saucer champagne, 6 oz.	32
Goblet 6" #5025 Tyrolean, saucer champagne, 6 oz.	30
Goblet #5022 Graceful, lunch water, 10 oz.	40
Goblet #5025 Tyrolean, lunch water, 10 oz.	42
Goblet #5022 Graceful, dinner water, 10 oz.	42
Goblet 8.25" #5025 Tyrolean, dinner water, 10 oz.	45
Goblet #5089 Princess, plain stem, water, 10 oz.	75
Hurricane lamp 2.5", square (Crystolite) candle block, w/etched 10" shade, each	2,500+
Ice bucket #1509 Queen Ann, 4 dolphin feet w/chrome handle	275
Ice bucket #1519 Waverly, 2 crescent shaped handles	495
Lemon w/cover 6.5" #1509 Queen Ann, oval, tab handled, dolphin finial	245
Lemon w/cover 6" #1519 Waverly, oval, tab handled, wave finial	650
Marmalade w/cover #4121, straight sided	375
Mayonnaise bowl 5.5" #1519 Waverly, footed, flared	65
Mayonnaise 2 piece #1495 Fern: bowl 6", tab handle (also called whip cream bucket; liner w/indent 8", tab handle	165

Mayonnaise 2 piece #1495 Fern: bowl 6", tab handle, salad dressing; liner w/indent 8", tab handle	195
Mayonnaise 2 piece #1509 Queen Ann: bowl 6.5", tab handled, salad dressing; liner w/indent 7"	95
Mayonnaise 2 piece #1519 Waverly: bowl 6.5", tab handled; liner w/indent 7"	85
Mayonnaise 2 piece #1519 Waverly: bowl 6.5", tab handled, salad dressing; liner w/indent 7"	98
Mayonnaise bowl #1540 Lariat, footed, loop stem, rolled edge (comport shape)	175
Mayonnaise bowl 8" #1519 Waverly, tab handled, oval, salad dressing	85
Mustard w/cover #1509 Queen Ann, footed, w/o stem	165
Mustard paddle #10, plain no etching	45
Pitcher #3484, spherical base, tapered water jug w/ice lip, 64 oz.	450
Pitcher #5032, high, straight sided, water tankard w/ice lip, 64 oz.	950
Pitcher #5034, ice jug, 64 oz.	450
Pitcher #4164, squat, ice jug, 73 oz.	550
Plate 6" #4182, bread & butter	12
Plate 7" #4182, tea or dessert	20
Plate 7.25" #1519 Waverly, tea or dessert	20
Plate 8" #1519 Waverly, salad	25
Plate 8" #4182, salad	25
Plate 10.5" #1509 Queen Ann, dinner	165
Plate 10.5" #1519 Waverly, dinner	185
Plate 11" #1509 Queen Ann, rolled edge, torte	68
Plate 11" #1519 Waverly, demitasse small center, turned up edge, cabaret	75
Plate 11" #1519 Waverly, small center, sandwich	70
Plate 12.25" #1509 Queen Ann, 2-handled, large center, sandwich	80
Plate 14" #485 (plain), small center, turned up edge, cabaret or torte	78
Plate 14" #1519 Waverly, small center, turned up edge, cabaret or torte	90
Plate 16" #1509 Queen Ann, flat, snack, sandwich	125
Relish 7" #1509 Queen Ann, round, 3-tab handles, 3 sections	54
Relish 7" #1519 Waverly, round, 3-tab handles, 3 sections	56
Relish 8" #1519 Waverly, round, 2-tab handles, 4 sections	62
Relish 8.75" #1495 Fern, round, 2-tab wave handles, 4 equal sections	85
Relish 9" #1519 Waverly, round, 2-tab handles, 4 sections	65
Relish 11" #1495, footed, oval, handled, 2 equal sections & celery section	78
Relish 11" #1509 Queen Ann, oblong, 2 equal sections & celery section	68
Relish 11" #1519 Waverly, oblong, 2 equal sections & celery section	72
Relish 12" #1519 Waverly, oval, celery	58
Relish 13" #1519 Waverly, oval, celery	60
Sandwich server 12" #1509 Queen Ann, center handle	195
Sandwich server 14" #1519 Waverly, center handle	225
Shaker #42, footed, high slim, glass or plastic top, pair	125
Shaker #57, chrome top, pair	85
Shaker 4" #1519 Waverly, footed, chrome top, pair	100
Sugar #1519 Waverly, footed, individual, 3.5 oz.	28
Sugar 3.75" #1519 Waverly, footed, regular, 5 oz.	30
Toast or cheese dome 4.5" #1519 Waverly, with 8" plate (cover non-etched)	175
Tray #1509 Queen Ann, for individual cream/sugar	75
Trinket box/cover #1519 Waverly, oval, lion finial	3500+
Tumbler #2052, flat, sham, tapered bar/whiskey, 2.5 oz.	250
Tumbler 5.3" #5022 Graceful, footed, juice, 5 oz.	75
Tumbler #5025 Tyrolean, footed, juice, 5 oz.	75
Tumbler #5089 Princess, footed, plain stem, juice, 5 oz.	72
Tumbler #2351, flat, high, straight sided, soda/juice, 6 oz.	145
Tumbler #2401, flat, sham, tapered, soda/juice, 6 oz.	115
Tumbler #2351, flat, high, straight sided, soda/juice, 7 oz.	135
Tumbler #2401, flat, sham, tapered soda/juice, 7 oz.	115
Tumbler #3389, cone footed, lunch, 10 oz.	115
Tumbler 5" #2351, flat, high, straight sided, soda/ice tea, 12 oz.	145
Tumbler #2401, flat, sham, tapered soda/ice tea, 12 oz.	125
Tumbler #5022 Graceful, footed, ice tea, 12 oz.	70
Tumbler 6.6" #5025 Tyrolean, footed, ice tea, 12 oz.	70
Tumbler #5089 Princess, footed, plain stem, ice tea, 12 oz.	78
Tumbler 5" #3484, flat, spherical base w/curved sides, ice tea, 13 oz.	125
Vase 3.5" to 4" #1519 Waverly, footed, round, violet	175
Vase 6" #1540 Lariat, loop stem, round, crimped top	175
Vase 6" #4191, footed, wafer stem, slim bud vase	225
Vase 6.5" #1540 loop stem, fan shape, crimped top	95
Vase 7" #1519 Waverly, footed, round, flared top	175
Vase 7" #1519 Waverly, footed, fan shape, 2 crescent handles	150
Vase 7" #1540 Lariat, footed, loop stem, flared top w/graduated loop handles	175
Vase 7" #1540 Lariat, footed, loop stem, flared fan shape w/graduated loop handles	100
Vase 7" #1540 Lariat, footed, loop stem, square crimped w/graduated loop handles	225
Vase 7" #4045, round, ivy ball	450
Vase 7.25" 1540, footed, loop stem, crimped top w/graduated loop handles	175
Vase 8" #4191, footed, wafer stem, slim bud vase	350
Vase 8" #4198, flat, concave sided	400+
Vase 8" #4205, footed, necked in & flared	275
Vase 8" #5012, sham square footed w/1 large ball stem, spherical & flared	275

Left to right: Tumbler 5" #2351, flat, high, straight sided, soda/ice tea, 12 oz.; Goblet 3.8" #5022 Graceful, oyster cocktail, 4 oz.; Goblet 4.6" #5025 Tyrolean, cordial, 1 oz.; Goblet 5.1" #5025 Tyrolean, wine, 3 oz.; Tumbler #5025 Tyrolean, footed, juice, 5 oz.; Goblet 6" #5025 Tyrolean, saucer champagne, 6 oz.; Goblet #5025 Tyrolean, lunch water, 10 oz.

Top left: Cheese & cracker: comport 2.4" #1509 Queen Ann, short stem, 5.4" wide; plate 12" (Cheese comport in center front of photo). **Top right:** Candy w/cover 6.2" #1519 Waverly, squat, round w/bow finial. **Front left:** Vase 7.25" 1540, footed, loop stem, crimped top w/ graduated loop handles. **Front right:** Bowl 11.4" #1519 Waverly, footed, flared, floral (comport shape).

Left: Relish 11" #1519 Waverly, oblong, 2 equal & celery section. **Back right:** Bowl 9.5" #1519 Waverly, crimped, floral. **Front right:** Cruet w/ stopper #1519 Waverly, footed, oil bottle, 3 oz.

Left: Vase 6" #1540 Lariat, loop stem, round, crimped top. **Center:** Vase 10.5" #4057, flat, flip shape w/o optic. **Right:** Vase 7" #1519 Waverly, footed, fan shape, 2 crescent handles.

Vase 8" #5012, square footed, high, slim bud vase   225
Vase 9" #4192 1/2, footed, w/o stem, flared   265
Vase 9" #5012, footed   295
Vase 10"-12" #1540 Lariat, footed, loop stem, swung   295
Vase 10" #4198, flat, concave sided   550+
Vase 10" #5012, square footed, high, slim bud vase   225
Vase 10.5" #4057, flat, flip shape w/o optic   450
Vase 12" #4191, footed, wafer stem, slim bud vase   395
Vase 12" #4198, flat, concave sided   800+
Vase 12" #5012, square footed, high, slim bud vase   295
Vase, 12"-15" #1540 Lariat, footed, loop stem, swung   350
Vase 14" #4198, flat, concave sided   950+

Cigarette jar/cove
5.1" #1519 Wave
sea horse handled
3.75" wide.

Pitcher 11" #5032, high, straight sided, water tankard w/ice lip, 64 oz.

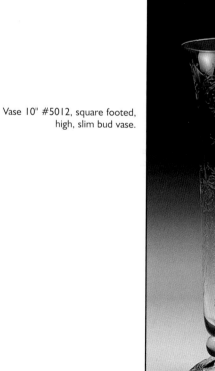

Vase 10" #5012, square footed, high, slim bud vase.

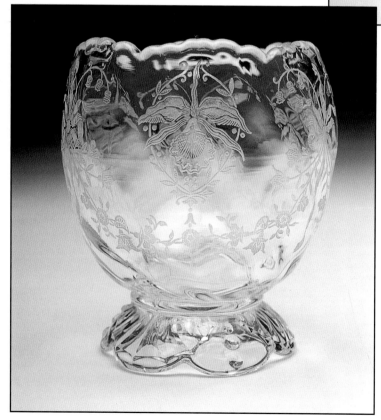

Vase 4" #1519 Waverly, footed, round, violet.

ORCHID

Paden City Glass Company　　　　**1930s**

Colors: Cobalt, Crystal, Cheriglo (pink), Ebony (black), Green, Ruby, and Yellow

This was Paden City's version of an orchid. The etching is quite heavy as compared to the Heisey Orchid. More collectors are being drawn to this etched pattern all the time. Most of this etched pattern is found on #412 Crow's Foot (square) shape. Gardeners raising this plant are attracted to this etched pattern. According to Barnett's book *Paden City*, there are three versions of the Orchid etch. Collectors seem to buy them all and mix them together. No stemware or tumblers have yet surfaced.

After so many years of increasing prices for Orchid, they have now declined as the supply of customers has also decreased. Hopefully, this will cause some new collectors to be attracted to the lower prices. Crystal should be priced 50% less than pastel colors. For more information you can refer to the book *Paden City Glass Company* by William P. Walker, Melissa Bratkovich & Joan C. Walker.

Pattern detail, Orchid – Paden City.

ORCHID	Green Cheriglo (pink) Yellow	Ebony	Cobalt Ruby
Bowl 8.5" #412 Crow's Foot (square), flared	95	125	150
Bowl 9" #412 Crow's Foot (square), footed, flared	115	150	175
Bowl 9.25" #411 Mrs. "B", footed, rolled edge, console	115	150	175
Bowl 9.75" #412 Crow's Foot (square), footed, w/flat rim edge	125	175	195
Bowl 10.25" #412 Crow's Foot (square), handled, flared	160	175	200
Bowl 11" #412 Crow's Foot (square), deep, flared	135	185	225
Bowl 11.75" #412 Crow's Foot (square), deep, w/flat rim edge, console	135	185	225
Bowl 14" #300 Archaic, shallow, rolled & scalloped edge, console	195	225	245
Cake salver 9.5" #412 Crow's Foot (square), low footed, 2" high	175	185	225
Candlestick 1-lite 2.5" #412 Crow's Foot (square), dome footed, mushroom-shaped, 4" wide, pair	225	295	350
Candlestick 1-lite 5.25" #412 Crow's Foot (square), bell footed, keyhole stem, pair	195	225	245
Candy w/cover 6.5" #411 Mrs. "B" (lid) on #503, footed bottom	250	275	300
Candy box w/cover 7" #412 Crow's Foot (square), flat, square, 2 equal sections, lid w/keyhole finial	250	285	325
Candy box w/cover 7" #412 1/2 Crow's Foot (square), flat, 3-lobe sides, 3 equal sections, lid w/keyhole finial	300	345	375
Comport 3.75" #412 Crow's Foot (square), short stem, flared, 6.5" wide	85	90	95
Comport 3.75" #412 Crow's Foot (square), short stem, crimped, 6.5" wide	85	90	95
Comport 6.5" #412 Crow's Foot (square), tall stem, flared, 7" wide	95	115	125
Comport 6.5" #881, high foot, flared, 6.75" wide	95	115	125
Cream soup 4.5" #412 Crow's Foot (square), flat, 2-handled, 11 oz.	60	68	75
Creamer 3" #412 Crow's Foot (square), flat, regular, 7 oz.	75	80	85
Cup & saucer, coffee #412 Crow's Foot (square): cup 2.1", 6 oz.; saucer w/indent 5.75"	145	165	175
Mayonnaise 2 piece #412 Crow's Foot (square): bowl, footed, rolled edge; liner w/indent	145	170	185
Pitcher #154 Rena	150	175	195
Plate 8.5" #412 Crow's Foot (square), lunch	60	68	75
Plate 10.5" #412 Crow's Foot (square), open handled	120	130	135
Plate 11.75" #412 Crow's Foot (square), open handled, sandwich	125	160	185
Sandwich server 10.25" #412 Crow's Foot (square), center handled tray	125	135	145
Sandwich server 10.75" #881 Gadroon, center handled tray	125	135	145
Sugar 2.6" #412 Crow's Foot (square), flat, regular, 6 oz.	75	80	85
Vase 4.75" #191 1/2 party Line, flat, 1 ring on base, shouldered, flared	145	160	175
Vase 4.6" #412-5 Crow's Foot (square), footed, flared, rose bowl	145	160	175
Vase 5.1" #182-5, flat, squat (pillow shape)	300	300	300
Vase 7.75" #61-8, flat (hourglass shape) flared	275	300	325
Vase 8" #182-8, flat, elliptical (pillow shape)	250	250	250
Vase 8" #184-8, flat, spherical bottom, flared	225	250	275
Vase 8" O'Kane, spherical bottom, narrow flared neck	250	275	300
Vase 8" O'Kane, spherical bottom, narrow flared neck & rolled edge	275	300	325
Vase 9" #411-9 Mrs. "B", flat, rectangular	200	225	225
Vase 9" #888-9, cupped low sides scalloped	300	400	500+
Vase 10" #184-10, flat spherical, bottom flared	275	300	325
Vase 10" #210-10 Regina, flat, 3 rings on base & neck shouldered flared	300	300	300
Vase 10" #412-10 Crow's Foot (square), flat, concave sided, cupped top	250	265	275
Vase 10.25" #412-10 Crow's Foot (square), flat, concave sided w/slightly flared top	300	325	350
Vase 11.75" #412-12 Crow's Foot (square), flat, concave sided, cupped top	300	300	300
Vase 11.75" #412-12 Crow's Foot (square), flat, concave sided, flared	250	250	250

Ruby grouping: **Top left:** Comport 3.75" #412 Crow's Foot (square), short stem, flared, 6.5" wide. **Top right:** Plate 10.5" #412 Crow's Foot (square), open handled. **Bottom left:** Bowl 10.25" #412 Crow's Foot (square), handled, flared. **Bottom right:** Cake salver 9.5" #412 Crow's Foot (square), low footed, 2" high.

Back left: Plate 10.5" #412 Crow's Foot (square), open handled, Cobalt. **Back right:** Sandwich server 10.25" #412 Crow's Foot (square), center handled tray, Crystal. **Front center:** Bowl 10.25" #412 Crow's Foot (square), handled, flared, Ruby.

Vase 8" #182-8, flat, elliptical (pillow shape), Ebony (black).

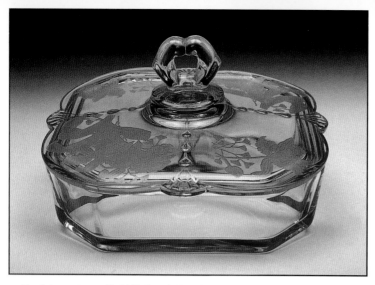

Candy box w/cover 7" #412 Crow's Foot (square), flat, square, 2 equal sections, w/keyhole finial, Cheriglo (pink).

Green grouping: **Top left:** Bowl 9.25" #411 Mrs. "B", footed, rolled edge, console **Right:** Vase 10" #184-10, flat spherical, bottom flared. **Front left:** Bowl 14" #300 Archaic, shallow, rolled & scalloped edge, console.

Cobalt grouping: **Left:** Bowl 11.75" #412 Crow's Foot (square), deep, w/flat rim edge, console. **Top center:** Candlestick 1-lite 5.25" #412 Crow's Foot (square), bell footed, keyhole stem. **Bottom center:** Bowl 9" #412 Crow's Foot (square), footed, flared. **Right:** Vase 10.25" #412-10 Crow's Foot (square), flat, concave sided w/slightly flared top.

Crystal grouping: **Top center:** Plate 11.75" #412 Crow's Foot (square), open handled, sandwich. **Left:** Comport 6.5" #412 Crow's Foot (square), tall stem, flared, 7" wide. **Bottom center:** Candy box w/cover 7" #412 Crow's Foot (square), flat, square, 2 equal sections, w/keyhole finial. **Right:** Bowl 9" #412 Crow's Foot (square), footed, flared.

Yellow grouping: **Back left:** Bowl 9.75" #412 Crow's Foot (square), footed, w/flat rim edge. **Back right:** Comport 6.5" #412 Crow's Foot (square), tall stem, flared, 7" wide. **Front left:** Sandwich server 10.25" #412 Crow's Foot (square), center handled tray.

Ruby grouping: **Left:** Vase 7.75" #61-8, flat (hourglass shape) flared. **Top center:** Creamer 3" #412 Crow's Foot (square), flat, regular, 7 oz. **Top right:** Sugar 2.6" #412 Crow's Foot (square), flat, regular, 6 oz. **Bottom center:** Candy box w/cover 7" #412 1/2 Crow's Foot (square), flat, 3-lobe sides, 3 equal sections, lid w/keyhole finial. **Bottom right:** Vase 4.6" #412-5 Crow's Foot (square), footed, flared, rose bowl.

PEACOCK & ROSE
Paden City Glass Company   **1928-30s**
Main Colors: Cheriglo (pink), Cobalt, Green, and Ruby
Other Colors: Amber, Blue, Crystal, and Ebony (black)

Hazel Marie Weatherman first identified and named Peacock & Rose in her *Colored Glass-ware of the Depression Era 2*. Years later all the collectors began to call it Peacock & Wild Rose since an author gave it that name. Bill Walker brought it to our attention that it should be left with its original name to honor Hazel because of all the early research work she did. We totally agree.

Like Cupid, most of the pieces are on the "Archaic" #300 blank. This blank features wide panels with a scallop-like edge. There are also some items on the "Triumph" #701 blank. This very pretty etched pattern continues to attract collectors. Predominately found in Cheriglo & Green, you can also find some Ruby with a lot of effort. When it comes to Ebony, there is not much around, mostly vases, and they would be priced just above Cheriglo (pink) & Green. A Pink set is the easiest to assemble.

Crystal & Amber should be priced less than Pink & Green. Blue pieces in this etched pattern are very rare and will probably bring more than Cobalt & Ruby. One scarce piece that almost all collectors are looking for is the #180-12 vase. For more information, you can refer to the book *Paden City Glass Company* by William P. Walker, Melissa Bratkovich & Joan C. Walker.

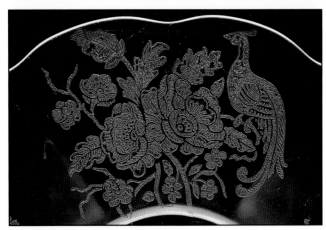

Pattern detail, Peacock & Rose.

PEACOCK & ROSE	Green Cheriglo (pink)	Black Red
Bowl 8.5" #300 Archaic, flat	145	175
Bowl 8.5" #300 Archaic, footed, oval melon	175	210
Bowl 9" #300 Archaic, footed, deep, oval, flared	165	250
Bowl 9" #300 Archaic, footed, deep, oval, rolled edge	185	225
Bowl 9" #300 Archaic, center cup handled, cupped edge	135	175
Bowl 10.5" #300 Archaic, oyster plate (rim soup shape)	215	260
Bowl 10.5" #300 Archaic, deep, rolled edge, console	150	225
Bowl 11" #300 Archaic, shallow, rolled edge, console	125	210
Bowl 11" #300 Archaic, center cup handle	140	175
Bowl 11.25" #701 Triumph, footed, rolled edge, console	150	175
Bowl 14" #300 Archaic, shallow, rolled & scalloped edge, console	180	310
Butter tub w/cover 5" #300 Archaic, flat, tab handled w/cup handle finial	400	500
Cake salver 9" #300 Archaic, tall stem	145	165
Cake salver 11.25" #300 Archaic, short stem w/scalloped edge, 2" high	145	210
Candlestick 1-lite 3" #300 Archaic, footed, rolled edge (no bird shows in etch) 5" wide, pair	125	250
Candy jar w/cover 6" #300 Archaic, footed, short stem, cup handle finial	245	295
Candy box w/cover 6.5" #300 Archaic, flat, shallow, cup handle finial (also 2 or 3 section)	295	350
Cheese & cracker #300 Archaic: comport 3", short stem, 5" wide; plate w/indent 10.5"	175	300+
Comport 3.5" #300 Archaic, short stem, (cupped or flared w/scalloped edge) 6" wide (2 styles)	90	110
Comport 3.5" #300 Archaic, short stem, rolled edge, 6" wide	98	125
Comport 6.5" #300 Archaic, tall stem, (cupped or flared w/scalloped edge) 8" wide (2 styles)	145	175
Comport 6.5" #300 Archaic, tall stem, rolled edge, 8" wide	125	195
Creamer 4.5" #701, footed, octagonal, pointed handle, 6.5 oz.	50	65
Creamer #300 Archaic, footed, 5 oz.	85	100
Creamer 4" #300 Archaic, footed, 7 oz.	75	90
Cup & saucer, coffee #300 Archaic: cup 2.4", flat, 6 oz.; saucer w/indent 6"	95	120
Goblet #300 Archaic, low cone footed, sherbet, 5 oz.	125	150
Ice bucket 4.75" #300 Archaic, tab handled, 6" wide	245	295
Ice bucket 5.8" #902, flat, straight sided, w/chrome handle	195	225
Ice bucket 6.25" #191, flat, straight sided, chrome handle	195	225
Ice tub, 4" #210 Regina, flat, tab handled, 6" wide	225	275
Mayonnaise 2 piece #300 Archaic: bowl 3.5", short stem, rolled edge, 6" wide; liner w/indent 7.75"	95	125
Pitcher 7" #3, flat, rectangular w/o ice lip, 30 oz.	200	350+
Pitcher 8.5", flat, straight sided w/o ice lip, 60 oz.	200	350+
Plate 8.5" #300 Archaic, lunch	50	65
Plate 10" #701, octagonal dinner	75	90
Plate 10.5" #300 Archaic, round, small center, service	65	80
Platter 10.5" #300 Archaic, oval	120	145
Relish 7" #300 Archaic, oval, pickle	125	150
Relish 11" #300 Archaic, oval, celery	150	165
Sandwich server 10.5" #300 Archaic, center cup handled tray	135	175
Sugar 4.25" #701, footed, octagonal, pointed handles, 6.25 oz.	50	65
Sugar #300 Archaic, footed, 5 oz.	85	100
Sugar 4" #300 Archaic, footed, 7 oz.	75	90
Tray 10.5" #300 Archaic, center cup handled	125	160
Vase 5" #300 Archaic, flat, sweet pea, concave sides	250	300
Vase 5.1" #182-5, flat, squat (pillow shape)	225	350

Cheriglo (pink) grouping: **Back left:** Platter 10.5" #300 Archaic, oval. **Back right:** Bowl 9" #300 Archaic, footed, deep, oval, flared. **Front center:** Tray 10.5" #300 Archaic, center cup handled.

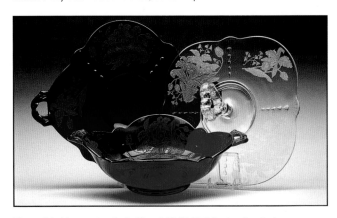

Ebony (black) grouping: **Left:** Vase 6.5" #210-7 Regina, flat, 3 rings on base & neck shouldered, flared. **Center:** Vase 10" #184-10, flat, spherical bottom, flared. **Right:** Vase 8" #182-8, flat, elliptical (pillow shape).

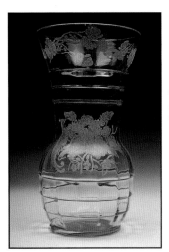

Vase 10" #210-10 Regina, flat, 3 rings on base & neck shouldered flared, Cheriglo (pink).

Vase 6.5" #210-7 Regina, flat, 3 rings on base & neck shouldered, flared	200	275
Vase 8" #182-8, flat, elliptical (pillow shape)	300	350
Vase 10" #184-10, flat, spherical bottom, flared	175	275
Vase 10" #210-10 Regina, flat, 3 rings on base & neck shouldered flared	250	300
Vase 11.75" #180-12, flat, cylindrical, slightly flared	400+	500+
Vase 12" #184-12, flat, spherical bottom, flared	245	350

Vase 5.1" #182-5, flat, squat (pillow shape), Ebony (black).

Left: Bowl 11.25" #701 Triumph, footed, rolled edge, console, Amber. **Front center:** Comport 6.5" #300 Archaic, tall stem, rolled edge, 8" wide, Green. **Back center:** Vase 12" #184-12, flat, spherical bottom, flared, Ebony (black). **Right:** Ice bucket 6.25" #191, flat, straight sided, chrome handle, Amber.

Crystal grouping: **Left:** Bowl 10.5" #300 Archaic, deep, rolled edge, console. **Back right:** Tray 10.5" #300 Archaic, center cup handled. **Front right:** Bowl 11" #300 Archaic, shallow, rolled edge, console.

Back left: Tray 10.5" #300 Archaic, center cup handled, Blue. **Front left:** Ice tub, 4" #210 Regina, flat, tab handled, 6" wide, Ebony (black). **Right:** Vase 8" #182-8, flat, elliptical (pillow shape), Blue.

Cheriglo (pink) grouping: **Left:** Bowl 8.5" #300 Archaic, footed, oval melon. **Right:** Pitcher 8.5", flat, straight sided w/o ice lip, 60 oz.

PLANTATION

A. H. Heisey & Company   Blank #1567   1948-57

Color: Crystal

Embossed pineapples are the design on the Plantation pattern. The #5067 blank features blown items for this pattern. Some of the pieces can be found with an ivy decoration. This is not necessarily the best of news. Most collectors don't like any adornment on this pattern. The ivy etching seems to distract from the beauty of the pineapple. Why in the world would an etched ivy be put on with pineapples? It was actually a play on words when it reminds you of the ivy which would have grown all over the sides of old Southern plantation mansions. One would almost see a vision of "Tara" (the name of Scarlet O'Hara's plantation) from *Gone With The Wind* when looking at the Ivy decoration. With all of this said, collectors still do not seem to love it the way I am sure that Heisey thought the public would envision it. We guess collectors don't like the way the ivy interacts with the pineapple part of the pattern.

Some pieces of glass are impressive. The Plantation punch bowl would be one of those items. When sitting on the under plate, the tall stately bowl certainly sets itself apart from other punch bowls. The 7.5" coupe plate is impressive with the embossed design of a lady with fruit on her head surrounded by a mountain and pineapple plant. One small but very fine addition to this pattern is the special shaped mayonnaise ladle. The embossed ladle has repeating sets of leaves spaced along the handle. This is easily overlooked and one must be paying attention in order to find it.

Back left: Tray 8", round, 2 sections, indent for cup, bridge. **Back right:** Relish 13.4", large oval, 4 equal sections & celery section. **Front left top:** Creamer & sugar, footed, short patterned stem, 5 oz. on oval tray 8.5". **Front left bottom:** Butter w/cover 7", tab handled, oblong, .25 lb. **Front center:** Shaker 3.25", flat, chrome top. **Front right:** Pair marmalades w/covers 5.75", flat, squat, pineapple shape on oval tray 8.5".

PLANTATION	Crystal
Ashtray 3.5", round, 4-tab seats for cigarettes	35
Bowl 5", low, dessert/sauce	75
Bowl 5.5", low, dessert/sauce	50
Bowl 6.5", handled, jelly	25
Bowl 7.5", deep, salad	95
Bowl 9.5", deep, salad	145
Bowl 9.5", cupped, shallow, gardenia	68
Bowl 9.5", flared, crimped, flower or fruit	78
Bowl 12", footed, large, cupped, shallow, gardenia	135
Bowl 12", footed, large, floral	145
Bowl 12", flared, centerpiece or floral	85
Bowl 12", flared, crimped, flower or fruit	80
Bowl 13", cupped, shallow, gardenia	85
Butter w/cover 7", tab handled, oblong, .25 lb.	100
Butter 5", flat, round, tab handled, pineapple finial (or low candy)	125
Cake salver 13.75", pedestal, 4.75" high	225
Candle block 1-lite 3.2", pineapple shape, pair	195
Candle epergne bowl 5", pineapple stem, 5" wide, pair	250
Candle epergne bowl 7", pineapple stem, 5" wide, pair	295
Candelabra 3-lite 7.25", pineapple center w/flames, 2 bobeches & prisms, 10.5" spread, pair	450
Candlestick 1-lite 4.25", footed, pineapple stem, pair	125
Candlestick 2-lite 5.8", small pineapple center w/7 fronds, 8.75" spread, pair	175
Candlestick 3-lite 7", small pineapple center w/7 fronds, 10" spread, pair	245
Candy 5", footed, deep bowl w/pineapple stem, 5" wide	95
Candy 7,25", flat, 4 leaf clover shape (open), pineapple finial	195
Candy w/cover 7.25", flat, 4 leaf clover shape w/pineapple finial	500+
Candy w/cover 8", footed, deep bowl w/pineapple stem & finial, 5" wide	165
Cheese & cracker: comport 3.2", short pineapple stem, 5" wide; plate 11"	125
Cigarette box w/cover 6.25", rectangle w/pineapple finial	195
Coaster 4", round, raised rays	50
Comport 3.6", low w/pineapple stem, cupped, honey, 6.5" wide	54
Comport 4", shallow w/pineapple stem, jelly, 6.75" wide	48
Comport w/cover 6", cheese, short pineapple stem & finial, 5" wide	85
Comport 7", pineapple stem plain rim, 6.5" wide	40
Creamer 5", footed, short patterned stem, 5 oz.	34
Cruet w/stopper 6.25", flat, oil bottle, pineapple finial, 3 oz.	150
Cup 2.3", footed punch, 6 oz.	15
Cup & saucer, coffee: cup 2.7", footed, 6 oz.; saucer w/indent 6.2"	38
Goblet 3.25" #5067 (blown), cordial, 1 oz.	145
Goblet 4.8" #5067 (blown), wine, 3 oz.	38
Goblet 3.8" #1567 (pressed), oyster cocktail, 3.5 oz.	30
Goblet 4.25" #5067 (blown), liquor cocktail, 3.5 oz.	32
Goblet 4.4" #1567 (pressed), liquor cocktail, 3.5 oz.	42
Goblet 2.5" #1567 (pressed), ice cream (sherbet shape) 4 oz.	50
Goblet 4.1" #5067 (blown), oyster cocktail, 4 oz.	22
Goblet 5.1" #1567 (pressed), claret, 4 oz.	50
Goblet 5.3" #5067 (blown), claret, 4.5 oz.	42
Goblet 4.25" #1567 (pressed), sherbet, 5 oz.	28
Goblet 4.6" #1567 (pressed), saucer champagne, 5 oz.	30
Goblet 4.5" #5067 (blown), sherbet, 6.5 oz.	20
Goblet 4.25" #5067 (blown), saucer champagne, 6.5 oz.	24
Goblet 5.9" #5067 (blown), water, 10 oz.	35
Goblet 6.3" #1567 (pressed), water, 10 oz.	48
Hostess helper set 11", ice bowl/one piece mayonnaise/3 toothpick holders w/clips	295
Hurricane lamp 13.5", pineapple shape w/9" plain chimney, each	350
Hurricane lamp 16.5", pineapple shape w/12" plain chimney (2 styles) each	450+

Top left: Cigarette box w/cover 6.25", rectangle w/pineapple finial. **Top center:** Candy w/cover 8", footed, deep bowl w/pineapple stem & finial, 5" wide. **Top right:** Urn w/cover 10.25", tall, footed w/pineapple stem & finial. **Bottom left:** Candy 7.25", flat, 4 leaf clover shape (open), pineapple finial. **Bottom center:** Butter 5", flat, round, tab handled, pineapple finial (or low candy). **Bottom right:** Comport w/cover 6", cheese, short pineapple stem & finial, 5" wide.

Top left: Candlestick 1-lite 4.25", footed, pineapple stem, pair. **Top center:** Candle epergne bowl 5", pineapple stem, 5" wide. **Top right:** Candle block 1-lite 3.2", pineapple shape. **Bottom left:** Candlestick 2-lite 5.8", small pineapple center w/7 fronds, 8.75" spread. **Bottom right:** Candlestick 3-lite 7", small pineapple center w/7 fronds, 10" spread.

Top row: Goblet 3.25" #5067 (blown), cordial, 1 oz.; Goblet 4.1" #5067 (blown), oyster cocktail, 4 oz.; Goblet 4.25" #5067 (blown), liquor cocktail, 3.5 oz. **Bottom row:** Goblet 4.5" #5067 (blown), sherbet, 6.5 oz.; Goblet 4.8" #5067 (blown), wine, 3 oz.; Tumbler 5.25" #5067 (blown), footed, soda/juice, 5 oz.; Goblet 5.3" #5067 (blown), claret, 4.5 oz.; Goblet 5.9" #5067 (blown), water, 10 oz.; Tumbler 7" #5067 (blown), footed, soda/ice tea, 12 oz.

Marmalade w/cover 5.75", flat, squat, pineapple shape	150
Mayonnaise 4.5", footed, very short pineapple stem, 1 piece w/rolled foot	85
Mayonnaise 2 piece: bowl 5.4", flat, deep, flared; liner w/indent 7.6"	50
Mayonnaise 2 piece: bowl 5.4", flat, deep, flared, salad dressing; liner w/indent 7.6"	60
Mayonnaise 8.5", oval, tab handled, salad dressing	75
Mayonnaise ladle 5.7", handle has 4 repeating sets of leaves & dots (marked at end)	85
Pitcher 8", flat, applied handle w/ice lip, 64 oz.	450
Plate 7", salad, large center	26
Plate 7.25", coupe, (lady w/fruit on her head, mountain & pineapple plant)	500+
Plate 8", lunch, large center	36
Plate 10.5", small party or demitasse torte	68
Plate 14", sandwich or torte, small center	80
Plate 14", party or torte, turned up edge	90
Plate 18", buffet w/indent for 1 piece mayonnaise	135
Punch bowl, Dr. Johnson - deep, 2.25 gallon	500+
Punch bowl liner 18", plate w/indent	185
Relish 8", round, 4 sections	95
Relish 11", oblong, tab handled, 2 equal sections & celery section	55
Relish 13", oval, celery	60
Relish 13", oval, 2 sections, olive/celery (divided 1/3 & 2/3)	68
Relish 13.4", large oval, 4 equal sections & celery section	90
Shaker 3.25", flat, plastic or chrome top, pair	85
Sugar 4.4", footed, short patterned stem, 5 oz.	34
Syrup 4.75", flat, drip cut top/bakelite handle, 10 oz.	175
Tray 8", round, 2 sections, indent for cup, bridge	150
Tray 8.5", oval for (2 marmalades, 2 cruets s & p) or (sugar/cream – s & p, syrup/marmalade)	60
Tumbler #5067 (blown), footed, no stem, grapefruit	40
Tumbler 5.25" #5067 (blown), footed, soda/juice, 5 oz.	50
Tumbler 5.6" #1567 (pressed), footed, juice, 5 oz.	70
Tumbler 3.75", flat, straight sided, juice/soda, 5 oz.	95
Tumbler 6.25" #5067 (blown), footed, water, 10 oz.	40
Tumbler 5", flat, straight sided, water, 10 oz.	115
Tumbler 6.6" #1567 (pressed), footed, ice tea, 12 oz.	75
Tumbler 7" #5067 (blown), footed, soda/ice tea, 12 oz.	65
Tumbler 5.25", flat, straight sided or flared (2 styles), ice tea, 12 oz.	185
Urn w/cover 10.25", tall, footed w/pineapple stem & finial	250
Vase 5.25", footed, flared cone shape w/o stem, bud vase	95
Vase 9.5", footed, ball stem, flared cone shape	150

Top left: Plate 8", lunch, large center. **Top center:** Bowl 7.5", deep, salad. **Top right:** Comport 3.6", low w/pineapple stem, cupped, honey, 6.5" wide. **Bottom left:** Cup & saucer, coffee: cup 2.7", footed, 6 oz.; saucer w/indent 6.2". **Bottom center:** Mayonnaise 3 piece: bowl 5.4", flat, deep, flared; liner w/indent 7.6" & ladle. **Bottom right:** Mayonnaise 4.5", footed, very short pineapple stem, 1 piece w/rolled foot.

Top row: Tumbler 5.25", flat, flared, ice tea, 12 oz.; Tumbler 3.75", flat, straight sided, juice/soda, 5 oz. **Bottom row:** Goblet 2.5" #1567 (pressed), ice cream (sherbet shape) 4 oz.; Goblet 3.8" #1567 (pressed), oyster cocktail, 3.5 oz.; Goblet 4.25" #1567 (pressed), sherbet, 5 oz.; Goblet 5.1" #1567 (pressed), claret, 4 oz.; Tumbler 5.6" #1567 (pressed), footed, juice, 5 oz.; Goblet 6.3" #1567 (pressed), water, 10 oz.; Tumbler 6.6" #1567 (pressed), footed, ice tea, 12 oz.

Left: Hurricane lamp 16.5", pineapple shape w/12" plain chimney. **Right:** Hurricane lamp 16.5", pineapple shape w/12" plain chimney w/cutting on chimney. Note, the 2 styles of chimneys.

Back top: Plate 7.25", coupe, (lady w/fruit on her head, mountain & pineapple plant). **Left:** Vase 9.5", footed, ball stem, flared cone shape. **Center left:** Vase 5.25", footed, flared cone shape w/o stem, bud vase. **Center:** Cruet w/stopper 6.25", flat, oil bottle, pineapple finial, 3 oz. **Center right:** Syrup 4.75", flat, drip cut top/bakelite handle, 10 oz. **Right:** Pitcher 8", flat, applied handle w/ice lip, 64 oz.

Comport 4", shallow w/pineapple stem, jelly, 6.75" wide.

PLEAT & PANEL

A. H. Heisey & Company **Blank #1170** **1924-37**

Colors: Flamingo (pink), Moongleam (green), and Sahara (yellow)

An alternating design of plain and ribbed blocks gives this pattern an attractive, yet simple appearance. It definitely has an Art Deco look to this pattern. This was the first time Heisey included a luncheon service in any of their lines. The flat hat shaped vase is sought after by Heisey collectors and collectors of glass hats. The small flat bowl with a ground bottom, which Heisey listed as a "Chow Chow", is what most dealers would call a fruit bowl. There are still many pieces out there with reasonable prices that continue to attract collectors to this pattern.

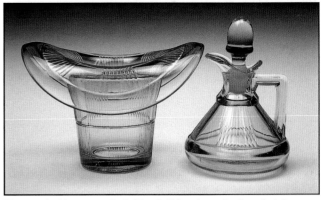

Flamingo (pink) grouping: **Left:** Vase 3.6", hat shape, 2 sides rolled down (not a regular in line item). **Right:** Cruet w/stopper 4.75", w/L shaped handle, 4 oz.

PLEAT & PANEL	Colors
Bowl 4.4", flat, shallow, "Chow Chow"	18
Bowl 4.5", deep, cupped	24
Bowl 5", shallow, 2-handled, jelly	20
Bowl 6.5", rim cereal or grapefruit	24
Bowl 8", deep, cupped	40
Bowl 9", oval, rim vegetable	50
Candy w/cover 6.2" tall, footed, short stem (listed as comport) 6" wide	85
Candy w/cover 8.5" tall, footed, tall stem (listed as comport or compotier) 5" wide	145
Cheese & cracker: comport 3", short stem, handled 4.75" wide; plate 10.5" or 14"	78
Comport 5", footed, tall stem, 4.75" wide	45
Creamer 2.6", footed, regular, 6 oz.	32
Creamer, footed, cone shape, Hotel	50
Cruet w/stopper 4.75", w/L shaped handle, 4 oz.	110
Cup & saucer, bouillon: cup 5" handled, 9 oz.; saucer w/indent 6.75"	40
Cup & saucer, coffee: cup 2.6", 6 oz.; saucer w/indent 6"	45
Goblet, short stem, sherbet, 5 oz.	15
Goblet, tall stem, saucer champagne, 5 oz.	28
Goblet 5.25", short stem, lunch water, 7.5 oz.	48
Goblet, tall stem, dinner water, 8 oz.	52
Lemon w/cover 5", flat, tab handled (cover notched for tab handles)	65
Marmalade 3" tall x 4.75" wide, short stem (comport shape)	35
Pitcher 7.1", flat, straight sided, w/o ice lip water, 48 oz.	150
Pitcher 7.25", flat, straight sided, w/ice lip water, 48 oz.	195
Plate 6", bread & butter	8
Plate 7", salad or dessert	12
Plate 8.1", lunch	15
Plate 10.6", dinner	58
Plate 14", chop or torte	40
Platter 12", oval	48
Relish 10.5", round, 5 sections, spice tray	68
Sugar 2.5", footed, regular, 6 oz.	32
Sugar w/cover, footed, cone shape, Hotel	65
Tumbler, flat, straight sided, water, 8 oz.	35
Tumbler, flat, straight sided, ice tea, 12 oz.	38
Vase 3.6", hat shape, 2 sides rolled down (not a regular in line item)	125
Vase 8", flat, tall, cylindrical & flared top	95

Candy w/cover 6.2" tall, footed, short stem (listed as comport) 6" wide, Flamingo (pink).

Relish 10.5", round, 5 sections, spice tray, Moongleam (green).

Flamingo (pink) grouping: **Top left:** Plate 8.1", lunch. **Top center:** Plate 10.6", dinner. **Bottom left:** Bowl 4.4", flat, shallow, "Chow Chow". **Bottom center:** Creamer 2.6", footed, regular, 6 oz. **Bottom right:** Cup & saucer, coffee: cup 2.6", 6 oz.; saucer w/indent 6".

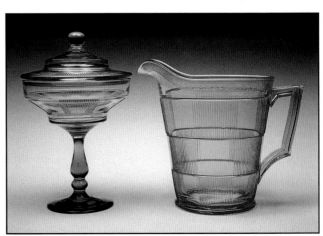

Left: Candy w/cover 8.5" tall, footed, tall stem (listed as comport or compotier) 5" wide, Moongleam (green). **Right:** Pitcher 7.1", flat, straight sided, w/o ice lip water, 48 oz., Flamingo (pink).

Ice bucket 6", straight sided w/chrome handle, 5.2" wide, Ruby.

PLYMOUTH

Fenton Art Glass Company **Blank #1620** **1933-37**

Main Colors: Crystal, Royal Blue, and Ruby

Other Colors: Amber, French Opalescent, and Stiegel Green

After Prohibition ended, glass companies were scrambling to design a new line of item for the home bar. Fenton was among them, looking for something to entice the public to bu their glassware. Plymouth was Fenton's entry into making glassware for the home bar. Th Repeal set was how this set was first advertised. Examples of hard to find pieces are the baske and jigger.

The ruby & cobalt collectors love this pattern because of the intensity of the colors. In th early years, Fenton had some trouble maintaining a good, dark ruby color. In this patter though, every piece we have seen had a dense, rich ruby color with no hint of any yello Fenton collectors also will add the accessory pieces to their collections. Because of this, mor interest is shown in the Royal Blue & Ruby. Not all items were made in Royal Blue. For som reason, the French Opalescent pieces have a faint bluish cast when you see them. These piece have a very limited collector base. Amber does not hold much interest for collectors. Very fe French Opalescent & Stiegel Green pieces in this pattern have shown up.

PLYMOUTH

	Crystal	Ruby	Royal Blue
Basket 6", ice bucket pulled up & flared w/metal bail	35	95	125
Bottle w/stopper, flat, straight sided, bar shape, 32 oz.	125	250	295
Cocktail shaker, flat, straight sided, chrome top, 32 oz.	90	225	295
Goblet 4", wine, 4 oz.	9	18	28
Goblet 4.1", low sherbet, 6 oz.	6	18	28
Goblet 5.75", water, 10 oz.	10	20	30
Ice bucket 6", straight sided w/chrome handle, 5.2" wide	45	125	165
Jigger 3.75", reversible, 1 oz. at one end & 2 oz. on other	48	135	175
Mug 4.5", flat, handled, 10 oz.	24		
Plate 6", bread & butter	4	8	14
Plate 8", salad or lunch	10	20	36
Tumbler, flat, whiskey, 2.5 oz.	12	24	40
Tumbler 3.9", flat, orange juice, 5 oz.	10	20	30
Tumbler 3.5", flat, old fashion, 7 oz.	12	24	32
Tumbler 4", flat, high ball, 8 oz. (also listed as 9 oz.)	12	24	32
Tumbler, footed, high, cone pilsner, 8 oz.	16	32	48
Tumbler 4", flat, water tumbler, 9 oz.	12	24	32
Tumbler, footed, high, cone pilsner, 10 oz.	17	34	50
Tumbler 6", flat, ice tea, 12 oz.	14	26	35

Ruby grouping: **Left:** Tumbler 3.9", flat, orange juice, 5 oz. **Center:** Tumbler 3.5", flat, old fashion, 7 oz. **Right:** Tumbler 4", flat, high ball, 8 oz.

Stiegel Green grouping: **Left:** Tumbler 4", flat, high ball, 8 oz. **Right:** Goblet 4.1", low sherbet, 6 oz.

PORTIA

Cambridge Glass Company   **1932-53**

Color: Crystal

Other Colors: Amber, Carmen (ruby), Crown Tuscan, Gold Krystol (yellow), Green, and Heatherbloom

Portia is another of the etched patterns with a lady's name. A basket of flowers is featured, surrounded by scroll work. All pieces were made in Crystal. A few items were made in the other colors but not enough to build a collection in that color. Collectors of specific colors are delighted to find them to add to their collections. Pieces are found on a variety of blanks: #1402 Tally Ho, #1534 Pristine, #3400, and #3500 Gadroon. The stemware can be found on #3035, 3130, and 7966. You can choose the style that best suits your preference. Some of the lines are complete, while others are just partial sets.

All the pitchers are hard to find, along with the elusive toast cover. Desirable pieces are three section bowls, French salad dressing, cocktail shakers, decanters, and a nite set.

Pattern detail, Portia.

PORTIA	Crystal
Ashtray 3.25" #3500/124 Gadroon, round	26
Ashtray 3.5" #3500/125 Gadroon, round	26
Ashtray 4" #3500/126 Gadroon, round	30
Ashtray 4.25" #3500/127 Gadroon, round	30
Ashtray 4.5" #3500/128 Gadroon, round	34
Basket 5.4" #3500/51 Gadroon, footed, applied handle	165
Basket 5.75" #3500/55 Gadroon, footed, 2-handled, crimped, 3.5" tall	35
Basket 6.25" #3400/1182, 2 handles turned up	32
Basket 6.25" #3500/52 Gadroon, footed, applied handle	225
Basket 7" #119, flared, applied handle	295
Bell #3130, dinner	100
Bonbon 5.6" #3400/1179, low, flared, open handled	32
Bonbon 6" #3500/54 Gadroon, footed, handled	30
Bottle w/stopper 6.5" #1263, flat, French dressing, 8 oz.	225
Bottle w/stopper 7.25" #1261, footed, French dressing, 8 oz.	245
Bowl 2.5" #3400/71, tab handled, 4-footed, nut	50
Bowl 3.5" #3400/49, round, cranberry w/plain edge	54
Bowl 3.75" #3400/80, square, cranberry w/scalloped edge	60
Bowl 5" #1534 Pristine, blown, cupped, fruit	50
Bowl 5" #3500/49 Gadroon, round w/1 handle	32
Bowl 5" #3400/74, tab handled, 4-footed, mint	38
Bowl 5.25" #3400/56, shallow, fruit	45
Bowl 5.25" #3400/1180, handled, sweetmeat	32
Bowl 5.75" #3900/130, footed, tab handled, sweetmeat	25
Bowl 5.8" #3400/13, 4-toed, tab handled, flared	32
Bowl 6" #3400/53, flared, cereal	54
Bowl 6" #3400/136, 4-footed, deep, fancy crimped	72
Bowl 6" #3500/50 Gadroon, round w/1 handle	40
Bowl 7.5" #435 Pristine, deco tab handle	64
Bowl 8.5" #381, rim soup	120
Bowl 8.5" #1402/131 Tally Ho, round, 3 equal sections	150
Bowl 9.5" #225 Pristine, blown, 2 sections	250
Bowl, 9.5" #3400/30, open handled, footed, keyhole stem	295
Bowl 9.5" #3400/34, open handled, vegetable	60
Bowl 10" #427 Pristine, sham base, salad	100
Bowl 10" #3400/1185, handled	60
Bowl 10" #3500/28 Gadroon, footed, handled, flared	60
Bowl 10" #3900/54, 4-footed, flared	52
Bowl 10.25" #3900/34, handled, flared	62
Bowl 10.4" #1402/122 Tally Ho, deep, 3 equal sections	175
Bowl 10.5" #1359, footed, flared	62
Bowl 10.5" #3400/168, flat, flared	60
Bowl 11" #1399, deep salad, scalloped edge	100
Bowl 11" #3400/45, footed, square crimped	68
Bowl 11" #3400/1188, handled, fruit	75
Bowl 11.5" #3900/28, handled, footed, flared	62
Bowl 12" #1349 Pristine, tab footed, crimped edge, flared	64
Bowl 12" #3400/4, 4-toed, squared, flared edge	65
Bowl 12" #3400/160, 4-footed, oblong, crimped	68
Bowl 12" #3900/62, 4-footed, flared	64
Bowl 12" #3900/65, 4-footed, handled, oval	75
Bowl 12.5" #993, 4-footed, low	72
Bowl 12.5" #3400/32, flat, flared	65
Bowl 12.6" #3400/1240, 4-footed, oval, refractory	100
Bowl 13" #1398, shallow, fruit or salad	90
Bowl 13" #3400/1, flared, console	60
Box w/cover 3.5" #3400/94, puff w/keyhole finial	110
Butter w/cover 5.5" #506, round, tab handled	145
Butter w/cover 5.5" #3400/52, handled	165
Cake plate 11.75" #3900/35, handled	68
Cake salver 13" #170 Martha, tab footed, scalloped edge	165
Canape set #693/3000, plate, use w/#3000 footed cocktail (3.5 oz. or 5 oz.)	145
Candelabra 1-lite 6.25" #3400/648, keyhole stem, etched bobeches &, prisms, pair	225

Top left: Plate 8.5" #3400/62, salad or lunch. **Bottom left:** Candy w/ cover 6" #3500/78 Gadroon, flat, low, blown, rams head tab handles. **Right:** Ice bucket 5.75" #3400/851, scalloped top, chrome handle.

Cocktail shaker 9.8" #101 Pristine, sham spouted w/glass top ball finial 32 oz.

Left: Plate 6.75" #3400/1181, 2-tab handled, lemon server. **Right:** Goblet 7.5" #3130, water, 10 oz.

Bowl, 9.5" #3400/30, open handled, footed, keyhole stem.

Comport 5.3" #3400/28, keyhole stem, flared, 7.25" wide.

Candelabra 1-lite 7.5" #3121, fancy stem w/plain bobeches & prisms, pair	225
Candelabra 2-lite 6" #3400/1268, keyhole stem bobeches & prisms, pair	325
Candelabra 2-lite 6.5" #496 Martha, w/#19 bobeches & prisms, pair	250
Candelabra 3-lite 5.5" #1545, w/1 #19 bobeche on center cup & prisms, pair	250
Candlestick 1-lite 2.5" #3500/108 Gadroon, no stem, pair	50
Candlestick 1-lite 3.5" #628 Pristine, w/wafer stem, pair	62
Candlestick 1-lite 5" #3900/67, skirted, pair	95
Candlestick 1-lite 5.25" #3400/646, keyhole stem, pair	72
Candlestick 1-lite 5.75" #3400/1192, small stem, pair	100
Candlestick 1-lite 7" #3121, single fancy stem, pair	125
Candlestick 2-lite 5.75" #495 Martha, plume arms & ball center, 8.25" spread, pair	165
Candlestick 2-lite 6" #3400/647, keyhole stem, 7.75" spread, pair	68
Candlestick 2-lite 6" #3900/72, w/plume center, 8.25" spread, pair	85
Candlestick 3-lite #1307, pair	65
Candlestick 3-lite 5.5" #1545, bell footed, pair	125
Candlestick 3-lite 6" #3900/74, pair	95
Candlestick 3-lite 6.25" #3400/1338, tiered (looks like ocean waves) 7" spread, pair	115
Candlestick 3-lite 7" #3400/638, keyhole stem, pair	100
Candy w/cover 5.4" #1066/4, blown w/fancy ball stem, plain finial	175
Candy w/cover 5.4" #3121/4 (blown), low	110
Candy w/cover 5.4" #3121/3 (blown), high	125
Candy w/cover 5.4" #3500/103 Gadroon, blown	125
Candy (open) 5.5" #3500/47 Gadroon, handled	30
Candy w/cover 6" #3500/78 Gadroon, flat, low, blown, rams head tab handles	200
Candy w/cover 6.5" #3400/9, 4-footed, tab handled, 7" wide; dome lid w/finial	110
Candy w/cover 7" #3900/165, flat, round, dome lid w/finial	100
Candy w/cover 8" #3500/57 Gadroon, 3 open handled, 3 equal sections	70
Cheese & cracker: comport 3" #3400/7, short stem, flared, 5.3" wide; plate 10.5" #3400/6, tab handled or 11.5" #3400/8, tab handled	68
Cheese & cracker: comport 3.75" #3500/163 Gadroon, short stem, flared, 6" wide; plate 12" #3500/162, handled	85
Cheese dish w/cover 5" #980, flat, pointed finial	375
Cigarette box w/cover 3.6" #616, rectangle, 3.1" wide	125
Cigarette holder #1066, oval w/ashtray foot	125
Cigarette holder 4" #1337, round w/cupped ashtray foot	115
Cocktail icer 4.2" #187 Pristine, footed, 2 piece w/non-etched insert	100
Cocktail icer 4.2" #3600, footed 2 piece, w/non-etched insert	60
Cocktail icer 4.6" #968, footed 2 piece, w/non-etched insert	64
Cocktail mixer #1395, w/chrome lid & spoon, 28 oz.	185
Cocktail shaker #97, small #9 chrome lid	245
Cocktail shaker #98, large #10 chrome lid	135
Cocktail shaker #99, sham base, chrome lid	145
Cocktail shaker w/cover #3400/108, tilt w/chrome top, 80 oz.	195
Cocktail shaker #3400/175, w/large #10 chrome lid	135
Cocktail shaker 9.8" #101 Pristine, sham spouted w/glass top ball finial 32 oz.	195
Cologne w/keyhole stopper 2.5" #3400/97: tilt bottle, 2 oz.; stopper w/long dauber	295
Comport 5.3" #3400/28, keyhole stem, flared, 7.25" wide	58
Comport 6.1" #3121/2 (blown), tall stem, 5.4" wide	62
Comport 7" #3500/148 Gadroon, high fancy stem, 6" wide	45
Comport 7.5" #3400/14, fancy wafer stem, flared, 7" wide	54
Comport 7.5" #3900/136, scalloped edge, 7.25" wide	48
Cream soup & liner #3400/55: bowl 4.75", 2-handled, 9 oz., saucer w/indent 6.25"	72
Creamer 2.5" #3500/15 Gadroon, footed, individual, 3 oz.	20
Creamer 2.6" #3900/40, footed, individual, 3.5 oz.	20
Creamer 3.8" #3400/68, regular, scalloped foot, 4.75 oz.	24
Creamer 3" #3900/41, footed, regular, 6 oz.	22
Creamer #3400/98, tilt ball w/1 handle, 8 oz.	35
Cruet w/stopper #3400/96, ball shape, 2 oz.	85
Cruet w/ball stopper 4.4" #3400/99, tilt ball, 6 oz.	110
Cruet w/stopper #3400/161, footed, handled, 6 oz.	160
Cruet w/stopper #3400/193, flat, 6 oz.	90
Cruet w/stopper 6" #3900/100, flat, spherical, 6 oz.	95
Cup & saucer, after dinner #3400/69: cup 2.25", 2 oz.; saucer w/indent 4.25", 6-sided	125
Cup & saucer, coffee #3400/54: cup 2.4", 6 oz.; saucer w/indent 5.5"	26
Cup & saucer, coffee #3400/50: cup 2.6", square footed, 6 oz.; saucer w/indent 5.8"	24
Cup & saucer, coffee #3900/17: cup 2.5", 7 oz.; saucer w/indent 5.5"	26
Decanter w/stopper #3400/119, tilt ball, cordial, 12 oz.	225
Decanter w/flat stopper 9" #1320, footed, cordial, 14 oz.	250
Decanter w/stopper #1380, square, 26 oz.	495
Decanter w/flat stopper 11" #1321, footed, 28 oz.	275
Decanter w/stopper 13.25" #1372, flat, slim bottle shape, 28 oz.	500+
Decanter w/stopper 6.25" #3400/92, tilt ball, 32 oz.	295
Decanter w/stopper #3400/113, ball w/long neck, 35 oz.	165
Epergne 4 piece #645, etched 3-lite candlestick w/plain arm & 2 non-etched vases	125
Epergne 5 piece #654, etched keyhole w/plain bobeche-prisms & 2 non-etched vases	100
Finger bowl & liner: bowl #3121; plate w/indent	50
Finger bowl & liner: bowl #3124, blown, bowl; plate w/indent	50
Finger bowl & liner: bowl #3126, blown; plate w/indent	50
Goblet 5.25" #3121, cordial, 1 oz.	75

oblet #3126, cordial, 1 oz.	64
oblet 4.25" #3130, cordial, 1 oz.	72
oblet 5.25" #3035, ball stem (cone bowl) cordial, 1 oz.	75
oblet 5" #7966, flared, cone shape, cordial, 1 oz.	78
oblet 5.25" #7966, flared, cone shaped, sherry, 2 oz.	65
oblet 5.6" #3035, ball stem (cone bowl) wine, 2.5 oz.	32
oblet #3126, wine, 2.5 oz.	38
oblet 4.9" #3130, wine, 2.5 oz.	38
oblet 6" #3035, ball stem (cone bowl) liquor cocktail, 3 oz.	28
oblet 6" #3121, liquor cocktail, 3 oz.	30
oblet #3124, liquor cocktail, 3 oz.	24
oblet 5.25" #3130, liquor cocktail, 3 oz.	24
oblet #3126, cocktail, 3 oz.	24
oblet #3124, wine, 3 oz.	32
oblet 5.8" #3121, wine, 3.5 oz.	38
oblet #7801 Pristine, plain stem, liquor cocktail, 4 oz.	30
oblet 6.25" #3121, claret, 4.25 oz.	48
oblet 4.4" #3035, ball stem (cone bowl) oyster cocktail, 4.5 oz.	26
oblet 4.4" #3121, oyster cocktail, 4.5 oz.	22
oblet 4.25" #3130, oyster cocktail, 4.5 oz.	22
oblet 6.25" #3035, ball stem (cone bowl) claret, 4.5 oz.	36
oblet #3124, claret, 4.5 oz.	50
oblet #3126, claret, 4.5 oz.	48
oblet 6.1" #3130, claret, 4.5 oz.	48
oblet 4.75" #3035, ball stem (cone bowl) sherbet, 6 oz.	22
oblet 6.4" #3035, ball stem (cone bowl) saucer champagne, 6 oz.	24
oblet 4.75" #3121, sherbet, 6 oz.	22
oblet 6.4" #3121, saucer champagne, 6.75 oz.	24
oblet #3124, sherbet, 7 oz.	18
oblet #3126, sherbet, 7 oz.	18
oblet 4.25" #3130, sherbet, 6 oz.	18
oblet #3124, saucer champagne, 7 oz.	20
oblet #3126, saucer champagne, 7 oz.	20
oblet 5.6" #3130, saucer champagne, 5 oz.	20
oblet 7.25" #3130, water, 8 oz.	30
oblet 8.25" #3035, ball stem (cone bowl) water, 9 oz.	36
oblet #3126, water, 9 oz.	32
oblet 7.5" #3130, water, 10 oz.	32
oblet 8.25" #3121, water, 10 oz.	32
oblet 8.25" #3124, water, 10 oz.	30
oblet 7.6" #3121, ice tea, 12 oz.	45
rricane lamp 8" #1601, short stem, bobeche w/prisms & etched chimney, each	225
rricane lamp 9.3" #1617, skirted w/etched chimney, each	185
rricane lamp 11.5" #1603, keyhole stem, bobeche/chimney (etched) & prisms, each	245
bucket 5.75" #3400/851, flat, scalloped top w/chrome handle	100
Bucket 5.75" #3900/671, chrome handle	125
d frappe #3400/41, bowl/insert non-etched	75
r Fruit #188, scalloped edge fits Pristine #427 deep salad	300
rmalade w/cover 5.4" #147 Pristine, flat (blown) 8 oz.	125
yonnaise 2 piece #1402/137 Tally Ho: salad dressing, 2-spouted; liner w/indent	85
yonnaise bowl 4" #3900/19, footed, ball shape, 4.1" high	45
yonnaise 2 piece #1532 Pristine: bowl 4.5" (blown), spherical, 3" high; ner w/indent 6.75"	42
yonnaise bowl 4.75" #1402/133 Tally Ho, footed, salad dressing, 5.75" wide	48
yonnaise 2 piece #3900: #127 bowl 5", flared; #128 liner w/indent 6.5"	45
yonnaise 2 piece #3900/111: bowl 5.25", salad dressing; liner w/indent 6.75"	55
yonnaise 2 piece #1490 Pristine: bowl 5.5", cupped, salad dressing; se #1491 liner w/indent 6.4"	65
yonnaise 2 piece #1491 Pristine: bowl 5.5", flared, salad dressing; ner w/indent 6.4"	65
yonnaise bowl 5.75" #1402/95 Tally Ho, footed, salad dressing	48
yonnaise 2 piece #3400: #13 bowl 5.8", 4-toed, flared, tab handled; 11 liner w/indent 5"	65
yonnaise 2 piece #3500/58 Gadroon: bowl 6", footed, handled, flared; 59 liner w/indent 7.5"	68
ustard w/cover 3" #151 Pristine, blown, spherical, 3 oz.	135
te set #103, flat, handled jug & flat tumbler w/flared base	500+
cher #1408, cocktail churn/plunger, 60 oz.	900+
cher #3400/100, high w/ice lip, 76 oz.	200
cher 9.25" #3400/152, Doulton style w/o ice lip, 76 oz.	325
cher 9" #3400/38, tilt ball w/ice lip, 80 oz.	245
cher 8.1" #3400/141, water jug w/o ice lip, 80 oz.	275
te 6" #3400/60, bread & butter	8
te 6.5" #3900/20, bread & butter	8
te 6.75" #3400/1181, 2-tab handled, lemon server	24
te 7" #131 Pristine, blown, salad/coupe	68
te 7.5" #555, dessert	14
te 7.5" #3400/176, square, salad or dessert	15
te 8" #3900/22, salad	20
te 8" #3900/131, handled, lemon server	26

Top left: Goblet 5.25" #3035, ball stem (cone bowl) cordial, 1 oz., Crystal. **Top center:** Bowl 2.5" #3400/71, tab handled, 4-footed, nut, Crystal. **Top right:** Plate 8.5" #3400/62, salad or lunch, Heatherbloom. **Bottom left:** Tumbler 4" #3400/112, flat, water, 8 oz., Amber. **Bottom center left:** Bowl 3.75" #3400/80, square, cranberry w/scalloped edge, Gold Krystol (yellow). **Bottom center right:** Cigarette holder 4" #1337, round w/cupped ashtray foot, Crystal. **Bottom right:** Tumbler 2.1" #3400/92, flat, barrel, whiskey, 2.5 oz., Green.

Left: Vase 10" #274, footed, tapered out at top, bud vase, Crown Tuscan w/Gold encrusted. **Center:** Plate 6" #3400/60, bread & butter, Ruby w/Gold encrusted. **Right:** Goblet 6.4" #3035, ball stem (cone bowl) saucer champagne, 6 oz., Crystal stem/foot & Ruby bowl w/Gold encrusted.

Plate 8.5" #3400/62, salad or lunch
Plate 8.5" #3400/1176, square, salad plate
Plate 9.5" #485, crescent salad
Plate 9.5" #3400/63, small dinner
Plate 10" #3400/22, tab handled
Plate 10.5" #3400/64, large dinner
Plate 10.5" #3900/24, dinner
Plate 11" #3400/35, open handled, sandwich
Plate 12" #3900/26, 4-footed, service
Plate 12.5" #3400/1186, oblong, open handled sandwich
Plate 13" #3500/110 Gadroon, footed, tab handled, torte
Plate 13" #3900/33, 4-footed, service
Plate 13.5" #1396, torte or service
Plate 13.5" #1397, small center, turned up edge, cabaret
Plate 14" #130 Pristine, flat, blown, torte
Plate 14" #3400/65, torte or chop, large center
Plate 14" #3900/166, torte
Plate 17.5" #1402/29, flat, Sunday nite Supper
Plate 18" #1402/28, flat, Sunday nite Supper
Relish 5.5" #3500/60 Gadroon, 2 sections, one handle
Relish 5.5" #3500/68 Gadroon, no handles, 2 sections
Relish 6" #3400/1093, 2 sections, center handled
Relish 6.25" #3500/69 Gadroon, 3 equal sections, scalloped edge
Relish 6.5" #3400/90, 2 open handles, 2 equal sections
Relish 6.5" #3500/61 Gadroon, scalloped edge, 3 sections, loop handle
Relish 7" #3900/123, 4-toed, tab scroll handled, oblong pickle
Relish 7" #3900/124, 4-toed, tab scroll handled, 2 equal sections, oblong
Relish 7.5" #3500/62 Gadroon, handled, 4 sections, round
Relish 7.5" #3500/70 Gadroon, no handles, 4 sections
Relish 7.5" #3500/71 Gadroon, center handled, 3 equal sections
Relish 8" #3500/57 Gadroon, 3 equal sections, 3 handled (candy bottom)
Relish 8.75" #3400/86, handled, oval, pickle
Relish 8.75" #3400/88, 2 sections, 2-handled
Relish 8.75" #3400/862, center plume handled, oblong, 4 sections
Relish 9" #3400/59, oval, pickle
Relish 9" #3900/125, handled, 3 sections, oval
Relish 9.5" #464 Pristine, crescent salad shape, 3 sections
Relish 9.5" #477, oblong w/tab feet, oval pickle or corn
Relish 10" #394, round, 4 equal sections & celery section
Relish 10" #3500/64 Gadroon, 4-toed, handled, 2 equal sections & celery section
Relish 11" #652, oval, celery
Relish 11" #3400/89, handled, 2 sections, oval
Relish 11" #3400/200, handled, 4-toed, curved divider, 2 equal sections & celery section
Relish 11.5" #3500/652 Gadroon, oblong, celery
Relish 12" #3400/67, 4 equal sections & celery section
Relish 12" #3500/67 Gadroon: 5 inserts & tray w/scalloped edge, round
Relish 12" #3900/120, oblong, 4 equal sections & celery section
Relish 12" #3900/126, handled, 3 sections, oblong
Sandwich server 10.5" #3400/10, center keyhole handle
Shaker 2.25" #1468, egg shaped, square glass base, pair
Shaker #1470, ball shaped, individual, square glass base, pair
Shaker #1471, ball shaped, regular, square glass base, pair
Shaker 4.5" #3400/18, footed w/chrome top, pair
Shaker #3400/36, footed, chrome lid, pair
Shaker #3400/37, footed, chrome lid, pair
Shaker 3.25" #3400/76, footed w/glass top, pair
Shaker 3.75" #3400/77, footed w/glass top, pair
Shaker 3.5" #3900/1177, flat w/chrome top, pair
Sugar 2.4" #3500/15 Gadroon, footed, individual, 3 oz.
Sugar 2.4" #3900/40, footed, individual, 3.5 oz.
Sugar 3" #3400/68, scalloped foot, regular, 5 oz.
Sugar #3400/98, tilt ball w/1 handle, 8 oz.
Sugar 2.75" #3900/41, regular footed, 6 oz.
Toast cover 4.5" #1533, blown w/finial
Tray 6" #3500/91 Gadroon, handled, square
Tray 8.25" #3500/161 Gadroon, footed, shallow, round, handled
Tumbler #3121, brandy, 1 oz.

20 Tumbler #3126, footed, brandy, 1 oz.
22 Tumbler #3400/1344, flared, cordial, 1 oz.
195 Tumbler #321, sham base, whiskey, 2 oz.
70 Tumbler #498, flat, cut flute, straight sided, whiskey, 2 oz.
40 Tumbler 2.8" #1341, sham base, whiskey, 2.5 oz.
110 Tumbler 2.75" #3121, footed, stem whiskey, 2.5 oz.
95 Tumbler #3126, footed, whiskey, 2.5 oz.
50 Tumbler 2.1" #3400/92, flat, barrel, whiskey, 2.5 oz.
58 Tumbler #3124, footed, whiskey, 3 oz.
60 Tumbler #3124, footed, oyster cocktail, 4.5 oz.
80 Tumbler #3126, footed, oyster cocktail, 4.5 oz.
65 Tumbler 4" #3130, footed, juice, 4.5 oz.
58 Tumbler #321, sham base, tapered juice, 5 oz.
58 Tumbler #498, flat, cut flute, straight sided, juice, 5 oz.
145 Tumbler #3121, footed, parfait, 5 oz.
115 Tumbler 5.75" #3121, footed, juice, 5 oz.
70 Tumbler #3124, footed, juice, 5 oz.
125 Tumbler #3126, footed, juice, 5 oz.
125 Tumbler #3400/38, flat, juice, 5 oz.
34 Tumbler 5.75" #3035, footed (cone bowl) juice, 5 oz.
30 Tumbler #321, sham base, old fashion, 8 oz.
80 Tumbler #498, flat, cut flute, straight sided, 8 oz.
32 Tumbler 4" #3400/112, flat, water, 8 oz.
30 Tumbler 4.9" #497, sham, cut flute, straight sided, 9 oz.
45 Tumbler 4.8" #3130, footed, water (dinner) 9.5 oz.
34 Tumbler #498, flat, cut flute, straight sided, 10 oz.
38 Tumbler 7" #3035, footed (cone bowl) water, 10 oz.
62 Tumbler 7" #3121, footed, water, 10 oz.
45 Tumbler #3124, footed, water, 10 oz.
90 Tumbler #3126, footed, water, 10 oz.
38 Tumbler #497, sham, cut flute, straight sided, 11 oz.
45 Tumbler 5.25" #3130, footed, beverage, 11 oz.
50 Tumbler #498, flat, cut flute, straight sided, 12 oz.
145 Tumbler 7.5" #3035, footed (cone bowl) ice tea, 12 oz.
50 Tumbler 7.5" #3121, footed, ice tea, 12 oz.
48 Tumbler #3124, footed, ice tea, 12 oz.
125 Tumbler #3400/38, flat, ice tea, 12 oz.
62 Tumbler #497, sham, cut flute, straight sided, 13 oz.
60 Tumbler #3126, footed, ice tea, 13 oz.
   Tumbler #3400/100, bellied, ice tea, 13 oz.
52 Tumbler #3400/115, bellied, ice tea, 13 oz.
45 Tumbler 4.1" #3900/115, flat, barrel, 13 oz.
60 Vase 4.5" to 5" #1309, squat globe, necked & flared
   Vase 5" #3400/102, globe, short neck
54 Vase 5" #6004, footed, flared, 1 ball stem, bud vase
45 Vase 5.25" #3400/93, tilt, ivy ball
60 Vase 6.5" #3400/103, globe, short neck
165 Vase 6" #6004, footed, flared, 1 ball stem, bud vase
58 Vase 7.8" #797, flip shape w/panel optic
54 Vase 8" #1300, footed, shouldered & flared
90 Vase 8" #1430, large, flat, flared, flip shape
95 Vase 8.4" #6004, footed, flared, 1 ball stem, bud vase
85 Vase 9" #1228, oval, melon shape
90 Vase 9" #1237, footed, keyhole stem, flared
60 Vase 9.5" #1233, footed, keyhole, shouldered
95 Vase 10" #272, footed, pulled in at top, bud vase
95 Vase 10" #274, footed, tapered out at top, bud vase
54 Vase 10" #1301, footed, shouldered & flared
45 Vase 10" #6004, footed, flared, 1 ball stem, bud vase
42 Vase 10.25" #3400/1242, flat, shouldered, flared
20 Vase 11" #278, large, footed, flared
20 Vase 11.5" #1299, footed, ball stem, urn shape
24 Vase 12" #83, straight sided, slightly flared
22 Vase 12" #1234, footed, keyhole shouldered
35 Vase 12" #1238, footed keyhole stem, flared
395 Vase 12" #6004, footed, 1 ball stem
125 Vase 13.25" #279, footed (no stem) wide w/flared top
28 Vase 18" #1336, shouldered & flared
55

900

PRELUDE

Viking Glass Company   **1948-82**

Color: Crystal

This is definitely a Viking only etched pattern. New Martinsville underwent some huge financial problems and closed in 1944. The stockholders met later that year and restructured the whole company. The company was given the new name of Viking to enable it to start fresh, without the problems that were associated with New Martinsville.

The Prelude etching consisted of a V-shaped wreath with a small sprig in the center and surrounded by a circular design of flowers on a branch. This etched pattern is found on the following blanks: Princess, Radiance, and Janice. Note: in a 1980-81 catalog, a switch was made from an etched to a painted decoration. All of these items have a "D" prefix on the ware number. The white enamel paint is not as noticeable as one would think. From a slight distance, it looks much like an etching. However, this must have been unacceptable to customers because Viking changed back to making it an etched pattern in 1982.

In a catalog from 1948, there was a line of four stems on the #4900 line. Later, in the early 1950s catalog, two new lines of stemware were offered. The #4901 had a lady leg stem and the #4902 featured a single ball stem. It would appear from this style of stem that they were not made by Viking. These blown stems had more of the appearance of Morgantown. In going through company records, it was discovered that the price lists show FOB (freight on board) from Morgantown, West Virginia. It has also been discovered that there were some Prelude etching plates found at Morgantown after they closed. From all of this, we can assume that Morgantown did do the stemware for Viking.

With gaining more catalogs since the last edition, we were able to add 50 more listings to this etched pattern. This goes to show you the importance of having original catalogs to refer to when doing research. Please let us know if you have any original catalogs or copies that we could purchase for our records.

One very important part of collecting is to always be on the look out for a different shape of your pattern. Until recently, we had not seen the Viking swan open candy with any etching. At a show, the swan was seen with a Prelude etching. This was a great discovery.

The style of the two 20 oz. wine goblets was designed to allow the red wine to breathe and is not meant to be filled to capacity.

Pattern detail, Prelude.

Candlestick 2-lite 5" #4457, twisted arms w/pointed finial, 7.5" spread.

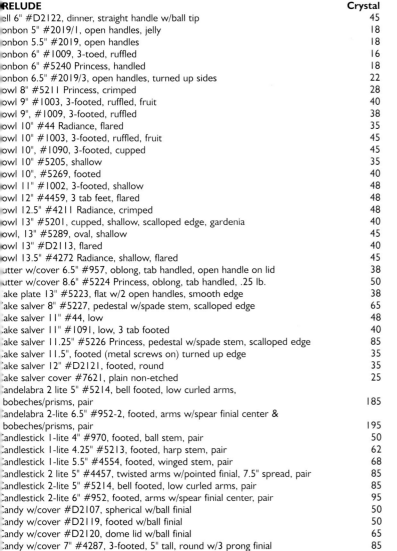

Candy w/cover 7" #4287, 3-footed, round w/3 prong finial, 5" tall.

PRELUDE	Crystal
Bell 6" #D2122, dinner, straight handle w/ball tip	45
Bonbon 5" #2019/1, open handles, jelly	18
Bonbon 5.5" #2019, open handles	18
Bonbon 6" #1009, 3-toed, ruffled	16
Bonbon 6" #5240 Princess, handled	18
Bonbon 6.5" #2019/3, open handles, turned up sides	22
Bowl 8" #5211 Princess, crimped	28
Bowl 9" #1003, 3-footed, ruffled, fruit	40
Bowl 9", #1009, 3-footed, ruffled	38
Bowl 10" #44 Radiance, flared	35
Bowl 10" #1003, 3-footed, ruffled, fruit	45
Bowl 10", #1090, 3-footed, cupped	45
Bowl 10" #5205, shallow	35
Bowl 10", #5269, footed	40
Bowl 11" #1002, 3-footed, shallow	48
Bowl 12" #4459, 3 tab feet, flared	48
Bowl 12.5" #4211 Radiance, crimped	48
Bowl 13" #5201, cupped, shallow, scalloped edge, gardenia	40
Bowl, 13" #5289, oval, shallow	45
Bowl 13" #D2113, flared	40
Bowl 13.5" #4272 Radiance, shallow, flared	45
Butter w/cover 6.5" #957, oblong, tab handled, open handle on lid	38
Butter w/cover 8.6" #5224 Princess, oblong, tab handled, .25 lb.	50
Cake plate 13" #5223, flat w/2 open handles, smooth edge	38
Cake salver 8" #5227, pedestal w/spade stem, scalloped edge	65
Cake salver 11" #44, low	48
Cake salver 11" #1091, low, 3 tab footed	40
Cake salver 11.25" #5226 Princess, pedestal w/spade stem, scalloped edge	85
Cake salver 11.5", footed (metal screws on) turned up edge	35
Cake salver 12" #D2121, footed, round	35
Cake salver cover #7621, plain non-etched	25
Candelabra 2 lite 5" #5214, bell footed, low curled arms, bobeches/prisms, pair	185
Candelabra 2-lite 6.5" #952-2, footed, arms w/spear finial center & bobeches/prisms, pair	195
Candlestick 1-lite 4" #970, footed, ball stem, pair	50
Candlestick 1-lite 4.25" #5213, footed, harp stem, pair	62
Candlestick 1-lite 5.5" #4554, footed, winged stem, pair	68
Candlestick 2 lite 5" #4457, twisted arms w/pointed finial, 7.5" spread, pair	85
Candlestick 2-lite 5" #5214, bell footed, low curled arms, pair	85
Candlestick 2-lite 6" #952, footed, arms w/spear finial center, pair	95
Candy w/cover #D2107, spherical w/ball finial	50
Candy w/cover #D2119, footed w/ball finial	50
Candy w/cover #D2120, dome lid w/ball finial	65
Candy w/cover 7" #4287, 3-footed, 5" tall, round w/3 prong finial	85
Candy w/cover 7.5" #44, 3-footed, round, flame finial, 3 sections	65

Top left: Plate 6.5" #2019/5, decagon shape, open handled, lemon server.
Top right: Cake salver 11.5", footed (metal screws on) turned up edge.
Bottom left: Tray 10.25", Radiance, deco fin tab handled, oval, for regular cream/sugar; Sugar 3.25", footed w/smooth top, plain loop handles, 6 oz.; Creamer 3.75", footed w/smooth top, plain loop handle, 6 oz.

Left: Goblet #4902, ball stem, cocktail, 4 oz. **Center left:** Goblet 6" #4901, lady leg stem, saucer champagne, 6 oz. **Center:** Goblet 7.75" #4901, lady leg stem, water, 9 oz. **Center right:** Tumbler 5.6" #4901, footed, ice tea, 12 oz. **Right:** Goblet 6.5" #4902, ball stem, ice tea, 12 oz.

Relish 12.5", footed, open handled, pie crust edge, 2 equal sections & celery section.

Candy w/cover 6.5" #5229 Princess, footed, round	70
Carafe #7540, shouldered & flared, wine	50
Cheese & cracker: comport 3" #5232, short stem, 5" wide; plate 11"	45
Cheese & cracker: compote #794, short stem, 6" wide; plate 11"	48
Comport 5", harp stem, scalloped & rolled edge, 5" wide	45
Compote #5234, harp stem, scalloped edge, flared, 6" wide	45
Compote #795, 5.5" wide	38
Compote #5270, flared, 7" wide	40
Comport #5228 Princess, cupped edge, 7.5" wide	45
Creamer, #959, footed w/smooth top, individual	10
Creamer 3.75", footed w/smooth top, plain loop handle, 6 oz.	12
Creamer 3.75" #42, 3-footed, smooth top, fancy handle, 6 oz.	14
Creamer #5247 Princess, footed, scalloped top, 6 oz.	18
Cruet w/ball stopper #980, flat, spherical, 5 oz.	75
Cup & saucer #797, cup footed, round saucer	24
Goblet #4901, lady leg stem, cordial, 1 oz.	38
Goblet #4902, ball stem, cordial, 1 oz.	40
Goblet #4902, ball stem, wine, 3 oz.	24
Goblet #4900, lady leg stem, cocktail, 3.5 oz.	18
Goblet #4901, lady leg stem, cocktail, 3.5 oz.	18
Goblet #4902, ball stem, cocktail, 4 oz.	20
Goblet 3.6" #4902, ball stem, sherbet, 5 oz.	12
Goblet #7548, straight sided, cylindrical bowl w/plain stem, sherbet, 6 oz.	14
Goblet, #4900, lady leg stem, sherbet, 6 oz.	12
Goblet #4901, lady leg stem, sherbet, 6 oz.	12
Goblet 6" #4901, lady leg stem, saucer champagne, 6 oz.	14
Goblet #7547, straight sided, cylindrical bowl w/plain stem, high wine, 8 oz.	26
Goblet #4900, water, lady leg stem, 9 oz.	25
Goblet 7.75" #4901, lady leg stem, water, 9 oz.	25
Goblet 5.75" #4902, ball stem, water, 10 oz.	24
Goblet #7549, straight sided, cylindrical w/plain stem, water, 11 oz.	22
Goblet 6.5" #4902, ball stem, ice tea, 12 oz.	28
Goblet #7542, high, elliptical, slim, wine, 20 oz.	32
Goblet #7541, short, spherical, wine, 20 oz.	35
Hurricane 10" #D2111, 2 pc., ftd. ball stem, candlestick w/hour glass shade, each	85
Lazy Susan 16" #4273, 3 pc, plate, 4 section relish, center small cup	145
Mayonnaise 2 piece #1009/789: bowl, 3-footed; ladle	24
Mayonnaise 3 piece #44: bowl, flared; liner w/indent; ladle	40
Mayonnaise 3 piece #D2115: bowl, flared; liner w/indent; ladle	42
Mayonnaise 3 piece #5236: bowl, flared; liner w/indent; ladle	48
Pitcher, martini mixer, 32 oz.	75
Pitcher 8.8" #1012, flat, spherical w/o ice lip, 78 oz.	175
Plate 6" #791, bread & butter	5
Plate 6.5" #2019/5, decagon shape, open handled, lemon server	18
Plate 6.6" #5241 Princess, open handled, lemon server	18
Plate 7" #976, dessert	8
Plate 7" #1010, 3-toed, lemon server	18
Plate 8" #790, salad	12
Plate 9" #5221, rolled edge	16
Plate 10.5" #796, dinner	35
Plate 11" #44 Janice	38
Plate 11" #5219	28
Plate 11" #5220, rolled edge	20
Plate 12" #D2103, torte	20
Plate 14" #42 Radiance	28
Plate 14" #44 Janice	28
Plate 14" #4271 Radiance, small center, turned up scalloped edge, cabaret	28
Plate 14" #5217 Princess, rolled edge	24
Platter 14.5" #5288, oval	55
Plate 16" #D2105, torte	24
Relish 5" #2019/6, handled, 2 sections	18
Relish 5" #2019/6, open handled, 2 sections	24
Relish 6" #5239 Princess, handled, 2 sections	24
Relish 7" #5237, open handled, rectangular, 2 equal sections & celery section	24
Relish 7" #5265 Princess, open handled, 2 sections	24
Relish 10" #42 oval, celery	28
Relish 10" #971, tab handle, oval, 2 equal sections & celery section	28
Relish 10" #3715, open handled, scalloped edge, 2 equal sections & celery section	28
Relish 10" #5238, open handled, rectangular, 2 equal sections & celery section	30
Relish 10.5" #5249 Princess, oval, scalloped edge, celery	24
Relish 12" #D2104, 3 sections	24
Relish 12.5", footed, open handled, pie crust edge, 2 equal sections & celery section	35
Relish 13" #5287 Princess , footed, oval, 4 equal sections & celery section	40
Relish 14" #D2102, 2 sections, 8" wide	30
Sandwich server 10.5" #5294, harp center handle, cupped up, nut server	38
Sandwich server 11" #44 Princess, double curlicue center handle	35
Sandwich server 11" #5246 Princess, plume center handle	35
Shaker 3" #D2117, flat, cylindrical, straight sided, pair	35
Shaker 3.5" #13, flat (skirted) flared out at bottom, pair	40

Shaker 3.5" #986, flat tapered w/chrome top, pair	45
Shrimp Server #100 Princess, round, 4 sections, small bowl sits in center	45
Sugar, #959, footed w/smooth top, individual	10
Sugar 3.25", footed w/smooth top, plain loop handles, 6 oz.	12
Sugar 3.25" #42, 3-footed, smooth top, fancy handles, 6 oz.	14
Sugar bowl #5247 Princess, footed, scalloped top, 6 oz.	18
Swan dish 5.5", open candy w/applied swan neck	95
Tidbit 2 Tier 8" & 12" #D2114, center chrome handle, tidbit	35
Tidbit 3 Tier, 16 plate, compote stacked on another compote	75
Tray 8" #D2106, center chrome handle	14
Tray 10.25", Radiance, deco fin tab handled, oval, for regular cream/sugar	24
Tray 12" #5223 two handles	35
Tray 12" #D2101, flat, rectangle, 5" wide	30
Tray 13" #4462, round, scrolled handles	38
Tumbler #4901, footed, juice, 5 oz.	15
Tumbler #7543, flat, straight, concave sided, juice, 6 oz.	16
Tumbler #7544, flat, straight, concave sided, old fashion, 10 oz.	18
Tumbler #D2118, flat, straight sided, beverage, 12 oz.	28
Tumbler #4900, footed, ice tea, 12 oz	28.
Tumbler 5.6" #4901, footed, ice tea, 12 oz.	25
Tumbler #7545, flat, straight, concave sided, ice tea, 13 oz.	24
Tumbler #7546, flat, straight, concave sided, jumbo beverage, 17 oz.	38
Vase 8" #D2109, flat, hour, glass shape	24
Vase 8" #7539, footed w/plain stem, spherical, flared	30
Vase 8.5" #D2112, flat, flared out base, necked & flared out top	28
Vase 10" #42 Radiance, flat, spherical base, flared	38
Vase 10" #D2108, footed, flared top	28
Vase 10" #D2110, footed, large spherical base, necked & flared out top	30
Vase 10" #4232 Radiance, flat, spherical base, crimped	48
Vase 10" #7538, footed w/plain stem, spherical, flared	40
Vase 10.25" #1154, footed w/plain stem, flared, bud	28
Vase 11" #1106, footed, straight sided, flared at top	50
Vase 12" #4230 Radiance, flat, spherical base, crimped	60

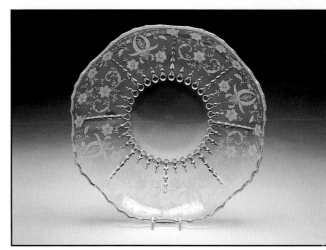

Bowl 13.5" #4272 Radiance, flared, shallow.

Sandwich server 11" #44 Princess, double curlicue center handle.

Pitcher 8.8" #1012, flat, spherical w/o ice lip, 78 oz.

Sandwich server 11" #5246 Princess, plume center handle.

Vase 10.25" #1154, footed w/plain stem, flared, bud (painted on pattern).

Sky Blue grouping: **Back left:** Relish 8.75", round, flared, 3 equal sections, flared & crimped. **Back right:** Plate 8.5", salad, large center. **Front left:** Butter w/cover 5.8", flat, round, low; domed lid w/plume finial. **Front center:** Cup & saucer, coffee: cup 2.4", footed, wing handle, 6 oz.; saucer w/indent 6". **Front right:** Shaker 3", footed, spherical w/chrome top.

Sky Blue grouping: **Top center:** Candle bowl 1-lite 2.5", flat, flared & crimped, 6" wide. **Bottom left:** Candy box w/cover 7.75", flat, shallow, 3 equal sections; lid w/radiating fan finial. **Bottom right:** Candlestick 2-lite 6", footed, no stem, circular fan center, 7.5" spread.

Bowl 12", shallow, flared & crimped, Ruby.

RADIANCE
New Martinsville Glass Co.   Blank #42   1936-44
Main Colors: Amber, Crystal, Cobalt, Sky Blue, and Ruby
Other Color: Amethyst

Radiance gives the appearance of having raindrops lined up in a row. New Martinsville was looking to create a new pattern to help them through their financial troubles in the late 1930s. They announced this new pattern to the trade in 1936, by placing an ad in the *Crocker, & Glass Journal*. The most unusual thing about this was the ad had no pictures of the Radiance pattern that they were trying to promote. New Martinsville hyped the pattern so much in the ad and encouraged everyone to come to the trade show to see their display. They were so sure this new pattern would sell, once the salesmen saw the actual glass. Were they ever right! Salesmen poured in because of the enticing advertising and placed huge orders. Sales of Radiance, along with Moondrops, kept New Martinsville afloat during difficult times.

Amethyst pieces should be priced the same as Sky Blue items. The butter dish, candy dish, candelabra, honey jar, pitcher, and punch bowl are actively sought by collectors.

RADIANCE	Crystal Amber	Sky Blue	Cobalt Ruby
Bonbon 5", footed, flared, wing handles turned up	16	34	42
Bonbon 5", footed, wing handles	12	28	38
Bowl 6", flared	10	25	35
Bowl 6", shallow, flared & crimped	14	30	40
Bowl 6", flared, square crimped	10	25	35
Bowl 6", collar foot, deep, cupped	16	34	42
Bowl 6", collar foot, deep, slightly flared & crimped	16	34	42
Bowl 6", collar foot, shallow, cupped	18	36	45
Bowl 10", deep, slightly flared & crimped, fruit	22	50	60
Bowl 10", flared, vegetable	20	40	50
Bowl 10", shallow, flared & crimped, fruit	22	50	60
Bowl 10", footed, short stem, flared, (comport shape)	22	58	68
Bowl 10", footed, short stem, shallow, flared & crimped (comport shape)	24	64	75
Bowl 11", 3-footed, flared, fruit	30	65	78
Bowl 11", 3-footed, shallow, flared & crimped, centerpiece	32	70	85
Bowl 12", deep, slightly flared, fruit	24	54	65
Bowl 12", deep, slightly flared & crimped, fruit	30	65	75
Bowl 12", shallow, flared, fruit	22	50	60
Bowl 12", shallow, flared & crimped	24	60	70
Butter w/cover 5.8", flat, round, low; domed lid w/plume finial	185	450	495
Cake salver (small) 8", footed	26	60	75
Cake salver 11.25", footed	30	65	85
Candy w/cover 4.75", 3-footed, spherical, dome cover w/ 3 scroll finial 60	165	195	
Candy w/cover 6", flat, deep, radiating fan finial (covered bonbon shape)	45	135	165
Candy box w/cover 7.75", flat, shallow, 3 equal sections; lid w/radiating fan finial	50	145	185
Candle bowl 1-lite 2.5", flat, flared & crimped, 6" wide, pair	64	145	185
Candelabra 1-lite 8", footed, bobeche w/prisms, pair	150	250	300
Candelabra 2-lite, footed, 2 feather arms & bobeches w/ prisms, pair	195	350	395
Candlestick 2-lite 6", footed, no stem, circular fan center, 7.5" spread, pair	85	165	195
Cheese & cracker: comport 2.5", short stem, shallow, 6" wide; plate, small center 11"	32	75	95
Compote, 3.1", short stem, shallow, crimped, 5" wide	18	36	45
Creamer 3.1", footed, regular, wing handle, 6 oz.	12	24	28
Cruet w/radiating fan stopper 4.75", spherical, applied handle, 4 oz.	45	85	95
Comport 5.25", short stem, shallow, crimped, 5" wide	18	35	45
Cup 2.5", flat, wing handled punch, 4 oz.	5	12	20
Cup & saucer, coffee: cup 2.4", footed, wing handle, 6 oz.; saucer w/indent 6"	14	26	30
Decanter w/ball stopper 8.75", flat, spherical, long neck, 16 oz.	95	200	250
Honey jar w/cover, fan finial (lid fits over top edge of jar)	75	165	195
Goblet 2.75", cordial, 1 oz.	14	28	35
Mayonnaise 2 piece: bowl, flat, flared; liner w/indent	45	85	98
Pitcher 10", flat, spherical base (rings in center) flared w/o ice lip, 64 oz.	145	300	350
Plate 8.5", salad, large center	8	18	20
Plate 14", torte or punch bowl liner, small center	35	85	98
Punch bowl 9", flat, spherical, round ball shape (used as vase) 1.25 gallon	85	225	250
Punch ladle 11.5", applied long plain handle w/pattern on ladle bowl	65	145	165
Relish 7", oval, pickle	12	26	36
Relish 7", round, cupped or flared, 2 sections	14	28	40
Relish 7", round, flared, 2 sections, crimped	16	35	45
Relish 8.5", oval, pickle	16	35	45

Relish 8.75", round, flared, 3 equal sections	18	45	55
Relish 8.75", round, flared, 3 equal sections, flared & crimped or tri-crimped	20	50	60
Relish 10", oval, celery	16	38	48
Shaker 3", footed, spherical w/chrome top, pair	35	85	98
Sugar 2.75", footed, regular, wing handles, 6 oz.	12	24	28
Tray 10.25", deco fin tab handled, oval, for regular cream/sugar	14	30	40
Tumbler, flat, cylindrical, belled top, 9 oz.	16	38	48
Vase 10", flat, spherical base (rings in center) tall, flared, smooth top	30	75	100
Vase 10", flat, spherical base (rings in center) tall, flared, crimped top	35	85	120
Vase 12", flat, spherical base (rings in center) tall, flared, smooth top	40	95	125
Vase 12", flat, spherical base (rings in center) tall, flared, crimped top	45	115	145

Left: Vase 10", flat, spherical base (rings in center) tall, flared, crimped top, Pink. **Right:** Vase 10", flat, spherical base (rings in center) tall, flared, crimped top, Amethyst.

Amber grouping: Back: Tray 10.25", deco fin tab handled, oval, for regular cream/sugar. **Front left:** Sugar 2.75", footed, regular, wing handles, 6 oz. **Front right:** Creamer 3.1", footed, regular, wing handle, 6 oz.

Sky Blue grouping: **Back center:** Punch bowl 9", flat, spherical, round ball shape 1.25 gallon w/liner plate 14", small center. **Front left:** Cup 2.5", flat, wing handled punch, 4 oz. **Front right:** Punch ladle 11.5", applied long plain handle w/pattern on ladle bowl.

Top row left: Creamer 3.75", flat, Hotel w/square handle, 8 oz. **Top row center:** Marmalade w/cover 4.75", square, flat rim, slotted lid. **Top row right:** Comport w/cover 6", footed w/ringed finial lid, 6.25" wide. **Center row left:** Sugar 3.6", flat, Hotel w/square handle, 8 oz. **Center row center:** Lemon dish w/cover 5", 2-tab raised handle; lid w/ringed finial. **Center row right:** Shaker 3", flat, double cone, chrome top. **Bottom row left to right:** Ashtray 3.4", heart w/cigarette rest; Ashtray 3.25", club w/cigarette rest; Ashtray 3.75", diamond w/cigarette rest; Ashtray 3.25", spade w/cigarette rest, all bridge ashtrays.

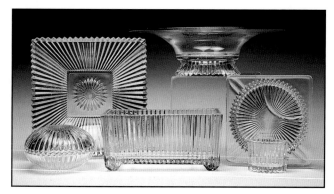

Top left: Bowl 8.75", square, small center, flared. **Top right:** Plate 11.75", footed, pattern on foot w/plain top surface. **Bottom left:** Box w/cover 5", round, domed, puff. **Bottom center:** Vase 8", rectangle, 4-toed, window box. **Bottom right:** Ashtray 6", square, offset oval indent (fits oval cigarette holder) shown in front of it.

Top center: Candelabra 2-lite 10.5", sheaf center column, 2 arms, 2 bobeches, 2 candle cups & prisms, 12.25" spread. **Front left:** Candelabra 1-lite 10", footed, ball & ribbed stem, bobeche candle cup & prisms. **Front center left:** Candlestick 1-lite 2", footed square base, round top; Candle block 1-lite 3", flat, straight sided, cylindrical. **Front center right:** Candelabra 2-lite 6.5", ridged center column, 2 short plain arms, 1 bobeche & prisms. **Front right:** Candelabra 1-lite 10.5", bell shaped base, bobeche, candle cup & prisms, pair.

RIDGELEIGH

A. H. Heisey & Company   **Blank #1469**   **1935-44**
Main Color: Crystal
Other Colors: Sahara (yellow) and Zircon (greenish)

Ridgeleigh was the first pattern to utilize both pressed & blown stemware. The fine ray provide a depth of brilliance to this glassware. This is a great Art Deco pattern with fine, sharr ridges that make it quite striking. The glass sparkles under the light and gives one almost the feeling of looking at cut glass. The blown stemware and tumblers only have a pattern on th stem. Ridgeleigh was another of Heisey's extremely large patterns. Fenton made a patter called Sheffield that sometimes is confused with Ridgeleigh by new collectors.

The covered marmalade does not come with a liner, but it would have been nice to hav a place to rest your spoon. Because of this, collectors favor using Imperial Glass Co. "Empire #7798 square 6.25" plate with an indent (Heisey's marmalade fits so perfectly in it you will b amazed). The reason this plate has an indent is that it is really the liner for Imperial's mayon naise set.

Art Deco collectors are vying for some of the accessory items in this pattern, because c the simple but elegant design. This demand makes it hard to find some of the following: swa handled bowl, cake plate, candelabra, cocktail shaker, decanter, and the straight sided 10" vase

This primarily Crystal pattern does have some colored items, like Sahara & Zircon, tha show up very occasionally.

RIDGELEIGH	Crystal
Almond 3.1", tab handled, individual, nut	20
Almond 3.1", tab handled, individual, 2 sections, nut	30
Ashtray 2.6", square w/cigarette rest	10
Ashtray 3", round (coaster shape)	12
Ashtray 5", round, deep w/cigarette rest (heavy)	18
Ashtray 3.25", spade w/cigarette rest	18
Ashtray 3.25", club w/cigarette rest	18
Ashtray 3.4", heart w/cigarette rest	18
Ashtray 3.75", diamond w/cigarette rest	25
Ashtray 4", round w/cigarette rest	24
Ashtray 5", round, deep w/cigarette rest (heavy)	18
Ashtray 5", oval, deep indent for oval cigarette holder, w/2 cigarette rests	40
Ashtray 6", under plate	125
Ashtray 6", square w/cigarette rest	38
Ashtray 6", square, offset oval indent (fits oval cigarette holder)	30
Bonbon 6.75", turned up tab handles	22
Bottle w/#105 stopper 5.75" square, straight sided, cologne, 4 oz.	125
Bottle perfume w/#1469 stopper exact width of bottle, no neck, square, 5 oz.	300
Bottle w/chrome tube, square, bitters, 5 oz.	65
Bottle w/#100 stopper 7", flat, 2 spout, French dressing, 8 oz.	90
Bowl 3.1", oval, individual, jelly	18
Bowl 4.5", cupped	20
Bowl 4.5", bell shape, flared	22
Bowl 4.5", scalloped shape, dessert	25
Bowl 5", straight sided	24
Bowl 5", square, flared	20
Bowl 5.25", shallow	20
Bowl 6", tab handled, jelly	20
Bowl 6", tab handled, 2 equal sections, jelly	25
Bowl 6", triangular shape, 3 open handled, jelly or candy	35
Bowl 8", bell shape, flared	65
Bowl 8", straight sided, round centerpiece	65
Bowl 8", square, flared	55
Bowl 8.5", cupped, berry	45
Bowl 8.75", square, small center, flared	65
Bowl 9", cupped	45
Bowl 9", deep, salad	65
Bowl 10", flared, fruit	50
Bowl 10", handled, dessert	45
Bowl 10", shallow, floral	45
Bowl 11", deep, salad (plain band at top)	125
Bowl 11", straight sided, round centerpiece	85
Bowl 11.5", shallow, flared, floral	65
Plate 11.75", footed, pattern on foot w/plain top surface	125
Bowl 12", flared, fruit	60
Bowl 12", oval, flared	50
Bowl 14", swan handled, oblong, centerpiece	350
Bowl 14", swan handled, oblong	450
Bowl 14", oblong, centerpiece (no handles)	95
Bowl 13", cone floral (lamp shade shape)	90
Box w/cover 5", round, domed, puff	110
Cake plate 12", round, 2 fin shaped tab handles	300
Candle block 1-lite 3", flat, straight sided, cylindrical, pair	60
Candle vase 1-lite 4.5", footed, ringed ball stem, flared, pair	35
Candelabra 1-lite 10", footed, ball & ribbed stem, bobeche candle cup & prisms, pair	295
Candelabra 1-lite 10.5", bell shaped base, bobeche, candle cup & prisms, pair	275
Candelabra 2-lite 6.5", ridged center column, 2 short plain arms, 1 bobeche & prisms, pair	295

Candelabra 2-lite 10.5", sheaf center column, 2 arms, 2 bobeches, 2 candle cups & A prisms, 12.25" spread, pair	450
Candlestick 1-lite 2", footed square base, round top, pair	50
Candlestick 2-lite 6.5", ridged center column, 2 short plain arms, 6" spread, pair	175
Cigarette holder 2", oval (fits indent in 5" & 6" ashtray)	25
Cigarette holder 3", square, straight sided	20
Cigarette holder 3", cylindrical, straight sided	20
Cigarette w/cover 4.5", cylindrical (laying down)	85
Cigarette box 3.75" x 2.6", rectangle shape, flat lid	45
Cigarette box 5.75", rectangle shape, chrome lid w/dolphin finial	35
Cigarette box 5.75", rectangle shape	45
Cigarette jar w/cover 3.75", cylindrical	65
Coaster 3.5", round	12
Coaster 4", round	12
Cocktail rest/coaster 3.25", round w/plain roly poly (used reversible) 2 piece set	65
Cocktail shaker 12", 3 piece, round bottle/plain strainer/plain stopper	325
Comport 2.75", footed, flared plain stem, 7.75" wide	30
Comport w/cover 6", footed w/ringed finial lid, 6.25" wide	60
Creamer 2.25", flat, individual w/ridged handle, 2 oz.	20
Creamer 2.75", flat, regular w/ridged handle, 5 oz.	30
Creamer 3.75", flat, Hotel w/square handle, 8 oz.	45
Cruet w/stopper 4.25", flat oil bottle (teepee shape) 3 oz.	75
Cup 2.5", flat, (beverage cup) straight sided 3.5 oz.	18
Cup 2.25", flat, handled punch, bellied, 4 oz.	14
Cup & saucer, coffee: cup 2.75", footed, 5.5 oz.; saucer w/indent 5.5"	25
Decanter w/stopper 11.5", bullet shape, 16 oz.	210
Decanter w/stopper, square, "Rock & Rye"	195
Goblet, cone cordial #4069 (blown) 1 oz.	175
Goblet, cone sherry #4069 (blown) 2 oz.	75
Goblet, cone wine #4069 (blown) 2.5 oz.	65
Goblet 4.5", wine (plain top band) 2.5 oz.	65
Goblet, cone cocktail #4069 (blown) 3.5 oz.	45
Goblet 3.75" cocktail (plain top band) 3.5 oz.	42
Goblet, cone claret #4069 (blown) 4 oz.	50
Goblet, claret (plain top band) 4 oz.	48
Goblet, cone oyster cocktail #4069 (blown) 4 oz.	35
Goblet 3.75", oyster cocktail (plain top band) 4 oz.	25
Goblet 2.6", ice cream, sherbet shape (plain top band) 4 oz.	45
Goblet 4.1", sherbet (plain top band) 5 oz.	25
Goblet, cone sherbet #4069 (blown) 5 oz.	30
Goblet, cone saucer champagne #4069 (blown) 5 oz.	35
Goblet 5", saucer champagne (plain top band) 6 oz.	30
Goblet, cone water #4069 (blown) 8 oz.	75
Goblet 5.6", water (plain top band) 8 oz.	45
Ice tub & liner: tub 4.6", 2-tab raised handles; liner w/indent, 2-tab handles	125
Lamp 6", footed, ringed ball stem, slightly flared, glass part electrified w/metal parts	100
Lamp 10", flat, straight side, cylindrical, glass part electrified w/metal parts	125
Lemon dish w/cover 5", 2-tab raised handle; lid w/ringed finial	60
Marmalade w/cover 4.75", square, flat rim, slotted lid	95
Mayonnaise bowl 5", deep, slightly flared	22
Mustard w/cover 3", straight sided	85
Pitcher 7.6", flat, round, straight sided w/ice lip, 64 oz.	400
Pitcher 8.5", spherical ball w/ice lip 64 oz.	325
Pitcher 8.1", spherical ball, flat top w/o ice lip 64 oz.	300
Plate 6", round, bread & butter	12
Plate 6", slightly six sided, dessert bowl liner	20
Plate 6", square edge, round center, bread & butter	25
Plate 6", tab handled, lemon server or cheese	20
Plate 7", square edge, round center, dessert	22
Plate 8", round	24
Plate 8", square edge, round center, salad	45
Plate 8.4", round, salad or dessert	20
Plate 10", square edge, round center, dinner	175
Plate 11", torte, small center	45
Plate 11", sandwich, small center	40
Plate 13", torte, small center	50
Plate 13.5" #1469 1/2, footed, pattern on foot w/plain top surface, torte (cabaret shape)	95
Plate 13.5", sandwich, small center	40
Plate 14" #1469 1/2, footed, pattern on foot w/plain top surface, salver	150
Plate 14", round, large center	45
Plate 18", torte, small center	65
Plate 20", service, large center, torte	110
Punch bowl 11", flared, (cone beverage shape) 1 gallon	150
Punch bowl 11", spherical, 1 gallon	200
Relish 7", flat, oval, 2 sections, straight sided	35
Relish 9.5", star shape, 4 small sections w/1 large sections, party server	55
Relish 10.5", oblong, celery tray	35
Relish 10.5", oblong, 2 equal sections & celery section	40

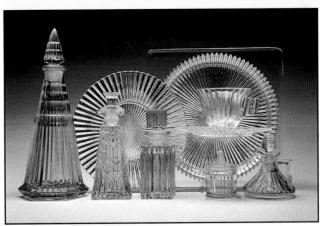

Back center: Plate 8.4", round, salad or dessert. **Back right:** Plate 10", square edge, round center, dinner. **Front left:** Decanter w/stopper 11.5", bullet shape, 16 oz. **Front center left:** Bottle w/#100 stopper 7", flat, 2 spout, French dressing, 8 oz. **Front center:** Bottle w/#105 stopper 5.75" square, straight sided, cologne, 4 oz. **Front center right:** Cup & saucer, coffee: cup 2.75", footed, 5.5 oz.; saucer w/indent 5.5"; Mustard w/cover 3", straight sided. **Front right:** Cruet w/stopper 4.25", flat oil bottle (teepee shape).

Left: Cocktail shaker 12", 3 piece, round bottle/plain strainer/plain stopper. **Center:** Pitcher 7.6", flat, round, straight sided w/ice lip, 64 oz. **Right:** Pitcher 8.1", spherical ball, flat top w/o ice lip 64 oz.

Left to right: Goblet 2.6", ice cream, sherbet shape (plain top band) 4 oz.; Goblet 3.75", oyster cocktail (plain top band) 4 oz.; Goblet 4.1", sherbet (plain top band) 5 oz.; Goblet 4.5", wine (plain top band) 2.5 oz.; Goblet 5", saucer champagne (plain top band) 6 oz.; Goblet 5.6", water (plain top band) 8 oz.

Relish 10.6", round, 3 sections (irregular divided) celery	40
Relish 11", straight sided, 4 sections (or centerpiece)	72
Relish 12", footed, oblong, half circle, celery	35
Relish 12", footed, oblong, half circle, 2 sections	40
Relish, large, oval, hors d'oeuvre tray	500+
Salt dip 1.75", square, individual	12
Shaker 3", flat, double cone, glass or chrome top, pair	45
Shaker, flat, spherical, glass or chrome top, pair	45
Sugar 2", flat, individual, 2 ridged handles, 2 oz.	20
Sugar 2.75", flat, regular, 2 ridged handles, 5 oz.	30
Sugar 3.6", flat, Hotel w/square handle, 8 oz.	45
Tray 7", oval, 2-tab handled, for individual cream/sugar	25
Tumbler 2.2", sham base, whiskey or shot (plain top band) 2.5 oz.	35
Tumbler 4.1" #1469 3/4, flat, soda, 5 oz.	32
Tumbler, cone footed, juice #4069 (blown) 5 oz.	65
Tumbler 4.9", footed, juice (plain top band) 5 oz.	36
Tumbler, cone footed, water #4069 (blown) 8 oz.	60
Tumbler #1469 3/4, flat, soda (plain top band) 8 oz.	45
Tumbler, soda, 8 oz.	40
Tumbler 3.6", sham base, old fashion (plain top band) 8 oz.	32
Tumbler, soda, 10 oz.	38
Tumbler, water (plain top band) 10 oz.	42
Tumbler, flat, soda, 12 oz.	42
Tumbler 5.6", flat, flared (pattern to top edge) 12 oz.	75
Tumbler 5.75", flat, cupped (pattern to top edge) 12 oz.	75
Tumbler 5.9", #1469 3/4, flat soda (plain top band) 12 oz.	48
Tumbler 6.25", footed, ice tea (plain top band) 12 oz.	45
Tumbler #4069, cone footed, ice tea (blown) 13 oz.	75
Vase #4 shape 2.5", very shallow & flared, turned up 2 sides (basket shape) 6.8" wide	40
Vase 3.5", short squat, flared, crimped top edge (ruffled bowl shape)	30
Vase #5 shape 3.75", short squat, flared (plain band at top)	45
Vase #3 shape 4", short, flared out wide (console bowl shape)	30
Vase #1 shape 4.5", short squat, flared (spittoon shape)	45
Vase #2 shape 4.75", short squat, cupped (rose bowl shape)	45
Vase 5.25", footed, ringed ball stem, flared out top (candle vase)	40
Vase 6", footed, ringed ball stem, slightly flared	45
Vase 6.3", spherical, rose bowl	95
Vase 7.5", rose bowl, plain flared top	125
Vase 8", cylindrical, large	75
Vase 8", rectangle, 4-toed, window box	85
Vase 8", alternating horizontal & diagonal pattern, scalloped top	60
Vase 8.2", alternating horizontal & diagonal pattern, flat top	75
Vase 8.5", footed, ringed ball stem, flared out top	65
Vase 8.8", footed, ringed ball stem, slightly flared	75
Vase 9.8", straight sided, cylindrical	110

Top center: Bowl 14", swan handled, oblong. **Center left:** Cigarette box 3.75" x 2.6", rectangle shape, flat lid. **Center of photo:** Cigarette box 5.75", rectangle shape, chrome lid w/dolphin finial. **Center right:** Ice tub 4.6", 2-tab raised handles. **Bottom left:** Cigarette jar w/cover 3.75", cylindrical. **Bottom center left:** Cocktail rest/coaster 3.25", round w/plain roly poly (used reversible) 2 piece set. **Bottom center right:** Bowl 4.5", scalloped shape, dessert w/liner 6", slightly six sided. **Bottom right:** Ashtray 5", oval, deep indent for oval cigarette holder, w/ 2 cigarette rests – shown w/Cigarette holder 2", oval, in it.

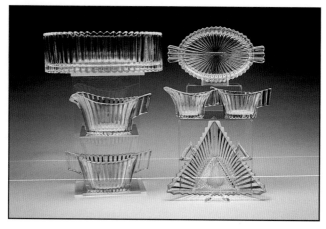

Top left: Bowl 8", straight sided, round centerpiece. **Top right:** Tray 7", oval, 2-tab handled, for individual cream/sugar. **Center left:** Creamer 2.75", flat, regular w/ridged handle, 5 oz. **Center right:** Creamer & sugar, flat, individual w/ridged handle, 2 oz. **Bottom left:** Sugar 2.75", flat, regular, 2 ridged handles, 5 oz. **Bottom right:** Bowl 6", triangular shape, 3 open handled, jelly or candy.

Back row: Tumbler 2.2", sham base, whiskey or shot (plain top band) 2.5 oz.; Tumbler 4.1" #1469 3/4, flat, soda, 5 oz. **Front row:** Tumbler 5.9", #1469 3/4, flat soda (plain top band) 12 oz.; Tumbler 5.75", flat, cupped (pattern to top edge) 12 oz.; Tumbler 5.6", flat, flared (pattern to top edge) 12 oz.; Tumbler 3.6", sham base, old fashion (plain top band) 8 oz.; Tumbler 4.9", footed, juice (plain top band) 5 oz.; Tumbler 6.25", footed, ice tea (plain top band) 12 oz.

Top left: Vase 5.25", footed, ringed ball stem, flared out top (candle vase), Zircon (greenish). **Top right:** Vase 6.3", spherical, rose bowl, Sahara (yellow). **Bottom left:** Vase 8.8", footed, ringed ball stem, slightly flared, Crystal. **Bottom center left:** Vase 8", alternating horizontal & diagonal pattern, scalloped top, Zircon (greenish). **Bottom center right:** Vase 8.2", alternating horizontal & diagonal pattern, flat top, Crystal. **Bottom right:** Vase 9.8", straight sided, cylindrical, Crystal.

ROMANCE

Fostoria Glass Company **Etching #341** **1942-82**

Color: Crystal

Romance can be confused with June, especially since both were made in crystal. Take time to look at each of the close-up shots of these etched patterns. The Romance ribbon is formed by one solid wide line, as opposed to June, which has two parallel lines that form the ribbon. This was the last etched pattern being designed at Fostoria before the start of World War II. Stems & tumblers are only found on the #6017 Sceptre blank. Most of the other pieces are found on the #6030 Astrid, #2350 Pioneer, #2364 Sonata, and #2337 blanks. Production of this etched pattern ceased in 1971.

In 1980, Fostoria revived some of their top selling patterns as part of a Nostalgia Line. Romance was one of these to encourage brides to more choices on their selection of stemware for their home. This promotion lasted about two years.

When looking for items to add to a collection, some of the harder to find would be the following: candlesticks, tall comport, ice bowl, pitcher, and rim soup.

Pattern detail, Romance.

ROMANCE	Crystal
Ashtray 2.6" #2364 Sonata, round, blown	25
Bowl 6" #2364 Sonata, rim baked apple	32
Bowl 8" #2364 Sonata, rim soup	95
Bowl 9" #2364 Sonata, deep, salad	45
Bowl 9.25" #6023 (blown), footed, short stem	145
Bowl 10" #2594, plume handled, oval, console (13.5" overall)	85
Bowl 10.5" #2364 Sonata, deep, salad	65
Bowl 11" #2596, shallow, rectangle, concave corners	95
Bowl 12" #2364 Sonata, deep, flared, fruit	55
Bowl 12" #2364 Sonata, flat, shallow lily pond, cupped edge	55
Bowl 12.75" #2364 Sonata, shallow, fruit	48
Candlestick 1-lite 3.25" #2324, plain stem, pair	45
Candlestick 1-lite 5" #2596, column stem, pair	75
Candlestick 1-lite 5.5" #2594, plume stem, pair	68
Candlestick 2-lite 5.5" #6023, tiered "U" shape stem, 6" spread, pair	85
Candlestick 3-lite 8" #2594, tiered 3 plume stem, 6.5" spread, pair	135
Candy w/cover 4" #2364 Sonata, blown, low w/bullet finial, 3.75" wide	195+
Cheese & cracker #2364 Sonata: comport 2.9", short stem, 5.75" wide; plate w/indent 11.25"	58
Cigarette holder (toothpick shape) 2" #2364 Sonata, blown	60
Comport 5.25" #6030 Astrid, plain stem, cupped, 5" wide	45
Comport 7.5" #2364 Sonata, lady leg stem, flared, 8" wide	65
Creamer 3.5" #2350 1/2, footed, regular, 7 oz.	18
Cup & saucer, coffee #2350: cup 2.5", footed, 6 oz.; saucer w/indent 5.75"	22
Goblet 3.9" #6017 Sceptra, cordial, .75 oz.	45
Goblet 5.5" #6017 Sceptra, wine, 3 oz.	32
Goblet 4.9" #6017 Sceptra, liquor cocktail, 3.5 oz.	22
Goblet 3.5" #6017 Sceptra, oyster cocktail, 4 oz.	16
Goblet 5.9" #6017 Sceptra, claret, 4 oz.	32
Goblet 4.4" #6017 Sceptra, sherbet, 6 oz.	14
Goblet 5.4" #6017 Sceptra, saucer champagne, 6 oz.	18
Goblet 7.5" #6017 Sceptra, water, 9 oz.	26
Ice bowl 4.75" #4132, deep, no handles, 6" wide	135
Mayonnaise 2 piece #2364 Sonata: bowl 5", deep; liner w/indent, cupped edge 6.75"	48
Pitcher 8.5" #6011, footed, water w/o ice lip, 53 oz.	345
Plate 6" #2337, bread & butter	6
Plate 7" #2337, dessert or salad	10
Plate 7.25" #2364 Sonata, crescent salad (kidney)	58
Plate 8" #2337, salad or small lunch	15
Plate 9" #2337, dinner	50
Plate 11" #2364 Sonata, small center, sandwich or 9" salad bowl liner	38
Plate 14" #2364 Sonata, torte or 10.5" salad bowl liner	60
Plate 16" #2364 Sonata, torte, small center	75
Relish 8" #2364 Sonata, oval, rim pickle	28
Relish 10" #2364 Sonata, tab handled, 3 sections w/curved dividers, oval	48
Relish 11" #2364 Sonata, oval, rim celery	40
Sandwich server 11.25" #2364 Sonata, center plume handle	48
Shaker 2.6" #2364 Sonata, flat, egg shape, glass or chrome top, pair	65
Sugar 3.1" #2350 1/2, footed, regular, 8 oz.	18
Tumbler 4.75" #6017 Sceptra, juice, 5 oz.	20
Tumbler 5.5" #6017 Sceptra, table water, 9 oz.	18
Tumbler 5.9" #6017 Sceptra, ice tea, 12 oz.	28
Vase 5" #4121, shouldered, flared	75
Vase 6" #2619 1/2, cylindrical, straight sided	75
Vase 6" #4143, footed, large, flared	65
Vase 6" #6021, footed, shouldered, bud vase	80
Vase 7.5" #2619 1/2, cylindrical, straight sided	85
Vase 7.5" #4143, footed, large, flared	75
Vase 9.5" #2619 1/2, cylindrical, straight sided	145
Vase 9.5" #2470, footed, w/fancy 3 scroll stem, flared	160
Vase 10" #2614, bulging ring near bottom, flared top	195

Back left: Cheese & cracker #2364 Sonata: comport 2.9", 5.75" wide; plate w/indent 11.25". **Back right:** Sandwich server 11.25" #2364 Sonata, center plume handle. **Front left:** Creamer 3.5" #2350 1/2, footed, regular, 7 oz. **Front center:** Sugar 3.1" #2350 1/2, footed, regular, 8 oz.

Back left: Cup & saucer, coffee #2350: cup 2.5", footed, 6 oz.; saucer w/indent 5.75". **Back right:** Bowl 12.75" #2364 Sonata, shallow, fruit. **Center right:** Candlestick 1-lite 3.25" #2324, plain stem. **Front:** Bowl 10" #2594, plume handled, oval, console (13.5" overall).

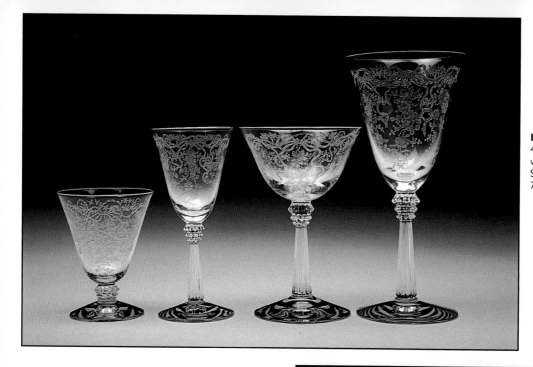

Left: Goblet 3.5" #6017 Sceptra, oyster cocktail, 4 oz. **Center left:** Goblet 5.5" #6017 Sceptra, wine, 3 oz. **Center right:** Goblet 5.4" #6017 Sceptra, saucer champagne, 6 oz. **Right:** Goblet 7.5" #6017 Sceptra, water, 9 oz.

Relish 10" #2364 Sonata, tab handled, 3 sections w/curved dividers, oval.

Left: Tumbler 4.75" #6017 Sceptra, juice, 5 oz. **Center:** Tumbler 5.5" #6017 Sceptra, table water, 9 oz. **Right:** Tumbler 5.9" #6017 Sceptra, ice tea, 12 oz.

ROSALIE

Cambridge Glass Company　　　**Etching #731**　　　**1928-38**

Main Colors: Emerald Green (light), Peach Blo/Dianthus (pink), and Willow Blue

Other Colors: Amber, Carmen, Crystal, Ebony (black), Gold Krystol (yellow), Royal Blue, and Topaz (yellow)

Rosalie is found mostly on the Decagon blank like the Cleo etched pattern. When you look at just the etched pattern, it has a somewhat oriental theme with flowers trailing down. Rosalie can be assembled easily in light Emerald Green, Peach Blo, and Willow Blue but the other colors are more difficult to find a complete set. Amber is mainly found in bowls and doesn't have too much interest among collectors. Two tone stems show up and prices for these should be the same as the color prices given. Since a set cannot be built, the only ones interested seem to be the goblet collectors. Gold Krystol runs about the same as Peach Blo. The salad dressing bottles can be found both flat & footed. Collectors are using several items from Decagon to mix with their Rosalie to make it a more affordable pattern. One of the commonly substituted items is the gravy & liner. The Rosalie gravy is $150 while the Decagon runs for $85, a substantial difference in price.

Tougher items to find are: cordial, cruets, gravy boat with liner, oval vegetable #910, pitcher, sugar sifter, syrup, toast cover, and vase.

Subtract 50% for Amber & Crystal. Very little of the other colors in this etched pattern have shown up, thus no prices have yet been established.

Pattern detail, Rosalie.

ROSALIE	Blue Green & Pink
Basket 11.25" #977 Decagon, 2 handles turned up	72
Bonbon 6.25" #749, handled, flared	24
Bottle w/stopper 6.5" #1263, flat, French dressing, 8 oz.	195
Bottle w/stopper 7.25" #1261, footed, French dressing, 8 oz.	225
Bowl 3.5" #1101 Decagon, flared, cranberry	48
Bowl 5.5" #1098, fruit	20
Bowl 8" #7, flat, rolled edge, small console	48
Bowl 8.5" #971 Decagon, flat, deep, oval, handled	40
Bowl 8.5" #1012 Decagon, flared, soup	58
Bowl 9" #1085 Decagon, round, flared, vegetable	68
Bowl 9.5" #1087 Decagon, oval, vegetable	72
Bowl 10" #863, cupped	70
Bowl 10" #984 Decagon, flared, open handled	75
Bowl 10.5" #1088 Decagon, oval, vegetable	72
Bowl 11" #1086 Decagon, round, flared, vegetable	72
Bowl 11" #1117 Decagon, shallow, cupped up at edge	68
Bowl 11.5" #842 Decagon, shallow, flared	86
Bowl 11.5" #1116 Decagon, oval, shallow, cupped up at edge	80
Bowl 13" #1056 Decagon, shallow w/flat wide rim	115
Bowl 15" #837, round console, mushroom shape	125
Bowl 15" #839 Decagon, oval, rolled edge	125
Bowl 15" #840 Decagon, oval, shallow, cupped up at edge	125
Bowl 15.5" #841 Decagon, oval, mushroom shape	135
Cake plate 11" #972 Decagon, small center, open handled	42
Cake salver 11" #707	45
Candlestick 1-lite 3.5" #637, wafer stem, pair	68
Candlestick 1-lite 4.4", plain cylindrical stem, pair	75
Candlestick 1-lite 5.25" #3400/646, keyhole stem, pair	85
Candlestick 3-lite 7" #3400/638, keyhole, pair	150
Candy w/cover 6" #864, 3-footed, egg shape	165
Candy w/cover 6.75" #733, footed, cone shape, w/ball stem, .5 lb.	175
Cheese & cracker: comport 2.8" #869 Decagon, shallow, 5.6" wide; plate 10.6"	85
Cheese w/cover 5" #980, flat, w/pointed finial	225
Cigarette jar w/cover 5" #617, flat, cylindrical; lid w/ball finial	85
Coaster 5.25" #602, round, raised rays	38
Cocktail shaker 12" #1020, flat, 4 flat sides, chrome top, 34 oz.	195
Comport, 3.5" #608 Decagon, short stem, 6.5" wide	40
Comport 6.5" #532 Pristine, footed, plain stem, flared, 6" wide	45
Comport 7" #3011, banquet size nude stem (price for crystal)	750+
Creamer, 3.5" #1096 Decagon, footed, individual, lightning handle, 4 oz.	45
Creamer 2.5" #979 Decagon, flat, handled, regular, 7 oz.	28
Creamer 4" #867 Decagon, footed, large (ball shape) 9.5 oz.	32
Cup & saucer, coffee: cup 2.5" #865 Decagon, flat, 7 oz.; saucer w/indent 5.6"	32
Decanter w/stopper 9.5" #315, flat, cylindrical, long neck, 28 oz.	245
Finger bowl & liner: bowl #3115, blown; plate w/indent	65
Goblet 4" #3051, plain stem, cordial, 1 oz.	65
Goblet 4.6" #3077, cordial, 1 oz.	95
Goblet 4.9" #3077, liquor cocktail, 2.5 oz.	20
Goblet 5.25" #3130, liquor cocktail, 1 oz.	24
Goblet 7.6" #3011, table size nude stem, cocktail 3.5 oz. (price for crystal)	350+
Goblet 6.1" #3115, paneled stem, liquor cocktail, 3.5 oz.	24
Goblet 4.25" #3077, sherbet, 6 oz.	18
Goblet 4.75" #3115, paneled stem, sherbet, 6 oz.	18
Goblet 5.5" #3077, saucer champagne, 6 oz.	20
Goblet 5.6" #3060, saucer champagne, 6 oz.	22
Goblet 6.5" #3115, paneled stem, saucer champagne, 6 oz.	20

Back left: Platter 15.5" #1079/15 Decagon, oval, Green. **Front left:** Tray 10.25" #870 Decagon, center keyhole handled, cupped, Peach Blo/Dianthus (pink). **Right:** Sandwich server 10.75" #870 Decagon, center keyhole handled, Peach Blo/Dianthus (pink).

Peach Blo/Dianthus (pink) grouping: **Front left:** Cocktail shaker 12" #1020, flat, 4 flat sides, chrome top, 34 oz. **Back left:** Tumbler 3.6" #1021, cone footed, 4 flat sides, 2 oz.; Decanter w/stopper 9.5" #315, flat, cylindrical, long neck, 28 oz.; Tumbler 2.8" #1341, sham footed, whiskey, 2.5 oz. **Back right:** Pitcher w/cover 11" #124, flat, lemonade, 68 oz. **Front center:** Dealer sign ($300). **Front right:** Tumbler 5.5" #1630, flat, straight sided, flared, 13 oz.

Left: Goblet 4" #3051, plain stem, cordial, 1 oz., Crystal. **Center left:** Goblet 6.1" #3115, paneled stem, liquor cocktail, 3.5 oz., Crystal/Ebony. **Center:** Goblet 6.5" #3115, paneled stem, saucer champagne, 6 oz., Gold Krystol/Willow Blue. **Center right:** Goblet 7.1" #3077, water, 9 oz., Royal Blue ($125 – we found it priced this). **Right:** Goblet 8.3" #3115, paneled stem, water, 9 oz., Willow Blue.

Back left: Tray 9" #1019, flat, oblong wafer, 3.5" wide, Amber. **Back center:** Creamer 4" #867 Decagon, footed, large (ball shape) 9.5 oz., Amber. **Back right:** Syrup w/chrome top 4.5" #170, flat, squat shape, 9 oz., Willow Blue; Creamer 2.5" #979 Decagon, flat, handled, regular, 7 oz., Peach Blo/Dianthus (pink). **Front left:** Bowl 8" #7, flat, rolled edge, small console, Amber. **Front center:** Candlestick 1-lite 4.4", plain cylindrical stem, Amber. **Front right:** Sugar & creamer, #1096 Decagon, footed, individual, lightning handle, 4 oz., shown on Tray 8" #1096 Decagon, center lightning handle, Willow Blue.

Peach Blo/Dianthus (pink) grouping: **Left:** Bottle w/stopper 6.5" #1263, flat, French dressing, 8 oz. **Right:** Bottle w/stopper 7.25" #1261, footed, French dressing, 8 oz.

Ice tub w/cover 6.5" tall, #876, straight sided, 5.5" wide, Amber.

Green grouping: **Left:** Vase 8" #1243, flat, spiral optic. **Center:** Cigarette jar w/cover 5" #617, flat, cylindrical; lid w/ball finial. **Back right:** Cracker plate #869 Decagon, 10.6". **Front right:** Bottle w/stopper 6.5" #1263, flat, French dressing, 8 oz.

Goblet #3011, table size nude stem, saucer champagne, 7 oz. (price for crystal)	400+
Goblet 8.3" #3115, paneled stem, water, 9 oz.	28
Goblet 7.1" #3077, water, 9 oz. (Royal Blue $125)	30
Goblet #3011, table size nude figured stem, water (table) 11 oz. (price for crystal)	450+
Goblet 8.9" #3011, banquet size nude figured stem, water 11 oz. (price for crystal)	675+
Gravy boat & liner #917/1167 Decagon: bowl 5.75", handled w/2 spouts; oval tab handled, 9" plate	150
Ice tub 3.25" #1147, low w/open handles	98
Ice tub 6" tall, #846, straight sided, 5.5" wide	200
Ice tub w/cover 6.5" tall, #876, straight sided, 5.5" wide	450
Mayonnaise bowl 5.5" #758 Decagon, flat, open handled	65
Mayonnaise 2 piece #981 Decagon: bowl 5.5", footed, flared; liner w/indent 7"	85
Mug 5.25" #731, flat, 9 oz.	95
Mustard #838, flat	80
Pitcher #955, squat, water jug, 62 oz.	275
Pitcher w/cover 11" #124, flat, lemonade, 68 oz.	295
Plate 7" #759 Decagon, handled, lemon server	20
Plate 8.4" #597 (Decagon), lunch	24
Plate 9.5" #3400/1177, square, dinner	68
Plate 10.5" #3400/1178, square, service	58
Platter 11" #1077 Decagon, oval	85
Platter 12" #1078 Decagon, oval	100
Platter 15.5" #1079/15 Decagon, oval	145
Relish 9" #1082 Decagon, oval pickle	42
Relish 9" #1067 Decagon, oval, 2 sections	48
Relish 10.5" #962, tab handled, 2 sections	50
Relish 10.5" #963, tab handled, 4 sections	68
Relish 11" #1068 Decagon, oval, 2 sections	48
Relish 11" #1083 Decagon, oval, celery	38
Sandwich server 10.75" #870 Decagon, center keyhole handled	48
Sugar 3.3" #1096 Decagon, footed, individual, lightning handled, 4 oz.	45
Sugar 2.4" #979 Decagon, flat, handled, regular, 7 oz.	28
Sugar 4" #867 Decagon, footed, large (ball shape) 9.5 oz.	32
Syrup w/chrome top 4.5" #170, flat, squat shape, 9 oz.	245
Toast w/cover 9" #951; dome lid w/open finial, plate w/tab handles	350
Tray 8" #1096 Decagon, center lightning handle	38
Tray 9" #1019, flat, oblong wafer, 3.5" wide	125
Tray 10.25" #870 Decagon, center keyhole handled, cupped	50
Tray 13" #1031, round, service	60
Tray 13" #1084 Decagon, round, open handled, sandwich	68
Tumbler 3.6" #1021, cone footed, 4 flat sides, 2 oz.	45
Tumbler 2.8" #1341, sham footed, whiskey, 2.5 oz.	55
Tumbler 2.75" #3115, cone footed, whiskey, 2.5 oz.	42
Tumbler 2.75" #3077, cone footed, whiskey, 3 oz.	40
Tumbler 4" #3130, footed, juice, 4.5 oz.	32
Tumbler #3077, cone footed, juice, 5 oz.	32
Tumbler 5.75" #3115, cone footed, juice, 5 oz.	30
Tumbler #3077, cone footed, lunch water, 8 oz.	22
Tumbler 6" #3115, cone footed, lunch, 8 oz.	24
Tumbler 5.25" #3077, cone footed, dinner water, 10 oz.	30
Tumbler 6.5" #3115, cone footed, dinner water, 10 oz.	35
Tumbler 6" #3077, cone footed, ice tea, 12 oz.	40
Tumbler 7.1" #3115, cone footed, ice tea, 12 oz.	42
Tumbler 5.5" #1630, flat, straight sided, flared, 13 oz.	48
Vase 6" #1308, straight sided (rippled)	85
Vase 6.5" #1005, footed, squat, necked & flared (optic)	120
Vase 8" #1243, flat, spiral optic	110
Vase 9.5" #1033, flat, square, straight sided, round necked top	225
Whipping pail 3.3" #847, or ice tub, chrome handle 5.4" wide	85

ROSE

R. H. Heisey & Company   Etching #515   1949-57

Color: Crystal

Rose is a close second to Orchid as one of the most recognized etchings that was ever put into the Heisey line. It is a favorite among collectors that like rose items. The roses prominently displayed are very elegant. A rose bud was actually used as part of the stem on the goblet in this etched pattern. This makes a very striking contrast. No other etched pattern incorporated part of the design on the stem. After Heisey closed, Imperial still continued to make items in Rose, especially the water goblets. It is this reason why there are so many goblets on the market.

With all the elegant shapes and number of items that can be found in this etched pattern, collectors can pick and choose exactly which ones fit in with their decor.

Pattern detail, Rose.

ROSE	Crystal
Ashtray 3" #1435, square	36
Bell #5072, dinner (modified claret)	175
Bottle w/stopper 6.5" #5031, flat, French dressing, 8 oz.	245
Bowl 6" #1509 Queen Ann, 4-toed, 2 loop handled, flared, jelly	48
Bowl 6" #1509 Queen Ann, 3 dolphin, footed, mint	55
Bowl 6.25" #1519 Waverly, scalloped skirt footed, flared, jelly	50
Bowl 6.5" #1509 Queen Ann, flat, deep, cupped	60
Bowl 7" #1509 Queen Ann, flat, shallow lily pond, cupped edge	145
Bowl 7" #1519 Waverly, deep, salad	95
Bowl 9" #485, deep, salad	145
Bowl 9" #1519 Waverly, footed, deep, fruit or salad	195
Bowl 9.5" #1519 Waverly, crimped, floral	98
Bowl 10" #1519 Waverly, crimped, floral or fruit	110
Bowl 10" #1519 Waverly, shallow, gardenia	85
Bowl 11" #1519 Waverly, 3 seahorse footed, floral or fruit	195
Bowl 11" #1519 Waverly, flat, flared, floral	135
Bowl 11" #1519 (from #1495 fern), 4-footed, tab handled, oval	175
Bowl 12" #1519 Waverly, crimped, floral or fruit	95
Bowl 13" #1519 Waverly, flat, crimped or flared (2 styles), floral	135
Bowl 13" #1519 Waverly, shallow, gardenia	95
Bowl 13" #1519 Waverly, shallow, gardenia centerpiece w/candle cup (used w/any non-etched items below)	250
Bowl 13", #1519 Waverly, Centerpiece, 2 piece, w/epergnette 6" & 6.5"	295
Bowl 13", #1519 Waverly, Centerpiece, 2 piece, w/#5013 vase 5"	285
Bowl 13", #1519 Waverly, Centerpiece, 2 piece, w/#4233 vase 6"	295
Butter w/cover 7" #1951 Cabochon, oblong, .25 lb.	395
Butter w/cover 6" #1519 Waverly, square, seahorse finial	195
Cake salver 12" #1519 Waverly, low pedestal (listed in catalog as bowl)	275
Cake salver 13.5" #1519 Waverly, low pedestal	350
Candlestick 1-lite, 3.5" #112 Mercury, striated ball center, pair	95
Candlestick 2-lite 5" #134 Trident, curvilinear arms, 5.5" spread, pair	125
Candlestick 2-lite 10" #1615 Flame, plume center w/fingers, 9" spread, pair	595
Candlestick 3-lite 7.5" #142 Cascade, curling arms w/tendril, pair	245
Candlestick 3-lite 7.5" #1519 Waverly, beaded broken waves, 8"spread, pair	200
Candy w/cover 5" #1519 Waverly, high, footed, seahorse handled, plume finial	345
Candy w/cover 5.25" #1519 Waverly, squat, tab handled, crescent finial, chocolate box	185
Candy w/cover 6" #1519 Waverly, squat, round, bow finial	225
Candy w/cover 6.25" #1951 Cabochon	650
Cheese & cracker #1509 Queen Ann: comport, short stem, 5.5" wide; plate 12"	145
Cheese & cracker #1519 Waverly: comport 3.75", short stem, 6.5" wide; plate 11"	135
Cigarette holder 3.6" #4035, round, footed, ball stem	145
Cocktail icer w/liner #3304, footed	345
Cocktail shaker 3 piece #4036, bottle/strainer/plain stopper, 32 oz.	225
Cocktail shaker 3 piece #4036, bottle/strainer/horse head stopper, 32 oz.	365
Cocktail shaker 3 piece #4036, bottle/strainer/rooster head stopper, 32 oz.	325
Cocktail shaker 3 piece #4225, bottle/strainer/plain stopper, 32 oz.	245
Cocktail shaker 3 piece #4225, bottle/strainer/horse head stopper, 32 oz.	395
Cocktail shaker 3 piece #4225, bottle/strainer/rooster head stopper, 32 oz.	345
Comport 4.25" #1951 Cabochon, cupped, mint, 5.75" wide	110
Comport 3.75" #1519 Waverly, round, short stem, flared, 6" wide	60
Comport 6.25" #1519 Waverly, deep, flared, jelly, 3.6" wide	62
Comport 6.5" #1519 Waverly, short stem, flat top, honey	60
Comport 7" #1519 Waverly, deep, flared, jelly	65
Comport 7" #1519 Waverly, oval bowl, crescent stem	165
Creamer #1509 Queen Ann, footed, individual, 2.5 oz.	32
Creamer #1519 Waverly, footed, individual, 3.5 oz.	30
Creamer 4" #1519 Waverly, footed, regular, 5 oz.	38
Cruet w/stopper #1519 Waverly, oil bottle, 3 oz.	195
Cup & saucer, coffee #1519 Waverly: cup 2.5", 6 oz.; saucer w/indent 6"	48
Decanter w/stopper #4036 1/2, spherical, 16 oz.	450
Epergnette bowl 6" #1519 Waverly, etched pattern	275
Finger bowl 4.5" #5072, flat	95
Goblet #5072, rose stemmed, cordial, 1 oz.	145
Goblet #5072, rose stemmed, wine, 3 oz.	95
Goblet #5072, rose stemmed, oyster cocktail, 3.5 oz.	42

Back top: Butter w/cover 6" #1519 Waverly, square, seahorse finial. **Front left:** Sugar 3.75" #1519 Waverly, footed, regular, 5 oz. **Front right:** Creamer 4" #1519 Waverly, footed, regular, 5 oz.

Left: Relish 11.25" #1519 Waverly, oblong, 2 equal sections & celery section. **Top right:** Cup & saucer, coffee #1519 Waverly: cup 2.5", 6 oz.; saucer w/indent 6". **Bottom right:** Bowl 6" #1509 Queen Ann, 4-toed, 2 loop handled, flared, jelly.

Back left: Plate 10.4" #1519 Waverly, small center, turned up edge, cabaret. **Back right:** Relish 8.75" #1495 Fern, round, 2-tab handles, 4 equal sections. **Center of photo:** Comport 4.25" #1951 Cabochon, cupped, mint, 5.75" wide. **Front left:** Bowl 6.5" #1509 Queen Ann, flat, deep, cupped. **Front center:** Butter w/cover 7" #1951 Cabochon, oblong, .25 lb. **Front right:** Candy w/cover 5.25" #1519 Waverly, squat, tab handled, crescent finial, chocolate box.

Goblet 5" #5072, rose stemmed, liquor cocktail, 4 oz.	40
Goblet #5072, rose stemmed, claret, 4 oz.	185
Goblet 3.75" #5072, rose stemmed, sherbet, 6 oz.	24
Goblet 4.75" #5072, rose stemmed, saucer champagne, 6 oz.	28
Goblet 6.75" #5072, rose stemmed, water, 9 oz.	55
Hurricane lamp 16" #1567, pineapple base, #5080 high 12" shade, each	600+
Hurricane lamp 17" #301, paneled base, #5080 high 12" shade, each	500+
Ice bucket #1509 Queen Ann, 4 dolphin feet w/chrome handle	325
Ice bucket #1519 Waverly, 2 crescent handles	575
Lemon w/cover 6" #1519 Waverly, oval, tab handled, wave finial	375
Lemon w/cover 6.5" #1509 Queen Ann, oval, tab handled, dolphin finial	295
Mayonnaise 2 piece #1495 Fern: bowl 6", tab handle (also called whip cream bucket); liner w/indent 8", tab handle	115
Mayonnaise 2 piece #1495 Fern: bowl 6", tab handle, salad dressing; liner w/indent 8", tab handle	125
Mayonnaise bowl 5.5" #1519 Waverly, footed, flared	75
Mayonnaise 2 piece #1519 Waverly: bowl 6.5", tab handled; liner w/indent 7"	125
Mayonnaise 2 piece #1519 Waverly: bowl 6.5", tab handled, salad dressing; liner w/indent 7"	135
Mayonnaise 2 piece #1509 Queen Ann: bowl 6.5", tab handled, salad dressing; liner w/indent 7"	85
Pitcher #4164, squat, ice jug, 73 oz.	575
Plate 7" #1519 Waverly, tea or dessert	24
Plate 8" #1519 Waverly, salad	30
Plate 10.4" #1519 Waverly, small center, turned up edge, cabaret	78
Plate 10.5" #1519 Waverly, dinner	300+
Plate 11" #1519 Waverly, sandwich, small center	85
Plate #1951 Cabochon, square, torte	300
Plate 14" #1519 Waverly, sandwich, small center	95
Plate 14" #1519 Waverly, small center, turned up edge, cabaret/torte	110
Relish 7" #1519 Waverly, round, 3-tab handles, 3 sections	65
Relish 8.75" #1495 Fern, round, 2-tab handles, 4 equal sections	125
Relish 9" #1519 Waverly, round, 2-tab handles, 4 sections	95
Relish 11.25" #1519 Waverly, oblong, 2 equal sections & celery section	98
Relish 12" #1519 Waverly, oval, celery	68
Relish 13" #1519 Waverly, oval, celery	75
Sandwich server 14.5" #1519 Waverly, center crescent handle	195
Shaker 4" #1519 Waverly, footed, chrome top, pair	95
Sugar #1509 Queen Ann, footed, individual, 2.5 oz.	32
Sugar #1519 Waverly, footed, individual, 3.5 oz.	30
Sugar 3.75" #1519 Waverly, footed, regular, 5 oz.	38
Tray #1509 Queen Ann, for individual cream/sugar	75
Tray #1519 Waverly, for individual cream/sugar	85
Tumbler #5072, rose stemmed, footed, juice, 5 oz.	60
Tumbler #5072, rose stemmed, footed, ice tea, 12 oz.	68
Vase 4" #1519 Waverly, collar footed, round, violet	150
Vase 7" #1519 Waverly, footed, round, flared top	195
Vase 7" #1519 Waverly, footed, fan shape, 2 crescent handles	175
Vase 8" #4198, flat, concave sided	350+
Vase 8" #5012, square footed, high slim bud vase	275
Vase 10" #4198, flat, concave sided	850+
Vase 10" #5012, square footed, high slim bud vase	295
Vase 12" #5012, square footed, high slim bud vase	325

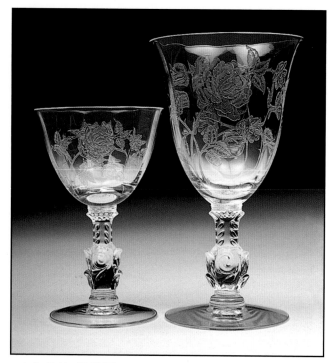

Left: Goblet 5" #5072, rose stemmed, liquor cocktail, 4 oz. **Right:** Goblet 6.75" #5072, rose stemmed, water, 9 oz.

Top left: Vase 4" #1519 Waverly, collar footed, round, violet. **Top right:** "Cabochon" dealer sign ($400 – we found it priced this). **Center row:** Bowl 6" #1509 Queen Ann, 3 dolphin, footed, mint. **Right:** Sandwich server 14.5" #1519 Waverly, center crescent handle. **Bottom left:** Comport 3.75" #1519 Waverly, round, short stem, flared, 6" wide. **Bottom center:** Bowl 6.25" #1519 Waverly, scalloped skirt footed, flared, jelly.

Cambridge Glass Company   Etching #1041   1935-54
Main Color: Crystal
Other Colors: Amber, Carmen (ruby), Crown Tuscan, and Ebony (black)

Rose Point is the most famous of all the Cambridge etchings. The beauty of the delicate roses surrounding a medallion with more roses was very popular with brides and it became known as the Wedding Crystal. This etched pattern was designed to harmonize with Wallace "Rose Point" sterling silver (flatware & serving pieces) and the Pope-Gosser China. The department stores capitalized on these combinations and built elaborate display for brides to make their selections. Ladies were showed how to coordinate all these items on a table. This was another extremely large etched pattern for Cambridge that allowed for many choices in entertaining. There are a few pieces around that were produced with the Wallace sterling Rose Point border attached to Cambridge clear glass etched with Rose Point. When pricing pressed Rose Point goblets that also have an etched bowl, add at least 75% to the clear pressed price.

New collectors sometimes confuse this etched pattern with Cherokee Rose. Take time to compare the close-up shots of each etched pattern. Rose Point has made so many items that in one lifetime to even see everything would be impossible. Pieces just keep showing up that one never knew existed. One would almost think that if Cambridge, during late 1930s to early 1950s, produced an item, it would be possible that Rose Point was etched on it. Lamp companies would take glass from any glass house and make lamps from these parts. We have found additional items to add to the list from our last edition.

Many of the collectors are now only buying the water to set a table. They don't have room for all the different sizes. The water works far better today to serve wine rather than the original wine, which is much too small. A few colored pieces show up occasionally, but not on any regular basis, which makes it difficult to establish any regular prices.

Pattern detail, Rose Point.

ROSE POINT	Crystal
Ashtray 2.5" #721, square, individual	38
Ashtray 3.25" #3500/124 Gadroon, round	40
Ashtray 3.25" #3500/129 Gadroon, square	65
Ashtray 3.5" #3500/125 Gadroon, round	40
Ashtray 4" #3500/126 Gadroon, round	45
Ashtray 4.5" #3500/130 Gadroon, oval	110
Ashtray 4.25" #3500/127 Gadroon, round	48
Ashtray 4.5" #3500/128 Gadroon, round	60
Ashtray 4.5" #3500/131 Gadroon, oval	75
Ashtray caddy #728, plain (non-etched)	30
Ashtray "Stack-a-way" set #1715, 4 piece (bowl shape w/center rest)	150
Basket 3" #3500/79 Gadroon, footed, applied handle	375
Basket 5.4" #3500/51 Gadroon, footed, applied handle	325
Basket 5.75" #3500/55 Gadroon, footed, 2-handled, crimped, 3.5" tall	50
Basket 6.25" #3500/52 Gadroon, footed, applied handle	395
Basket 6.25" #3400/1182, 2 handles turned up	45
Basket 7" #119, flared, applied handle	595
Basket 7" #3500/56 Gadroon, footed bowl, 2 handles	70
Bell 5.8" #3121, dinner, from cocktail size stem	175
Bobeche #19 w/prisms (bobeche etched with pattern)	75
Bonbon 3.5" tall #3400/204, 4-footed, deep, crimped	95
Bonbon 5.6" #3400/1179, low, flared, open handled	45
Bonbon 6" #3400/201, 4-footed (fan shape) crimped	95
Bonbon 6" #3400/205, shallow, 4-footed, cupped	98
Bonbon 6.5" #3400/202, 4-footed, shallow, oblong, crimped	98
Bonbon 6" #3500/54 Gadroon, footed, handled	40
Bottle w/stopper 6.5" #1263, flat, French dressing, 8 oz.	350
Bottle w/stopper 7.25" #1261, footed, French dressing, 8 oz.	375
Bowl 2.75" #3400/71, tab handled, 4-footed, nut	75
Bowl 3" #3400/70, tab handled, 4-footed, cranberry	98
Bowl 5" #1534 Pristine, blown, cupped, fruit	95
Bowl 5" #3500/10 Gadroon, shallow, fruit	85
Bowl 5" #3500/49 Gadroon, round w/1 handle	48
Bowl 5.25" #3400/74, tab handled, 4-toed, mint	60
Bowl 5.25" #3400/56, shallow, fruit	75
Bowl 5.25" #3400/1180, handled, sweetmeat	45
Bowl 5.75" #3900/130, footed, tab handled, sweetmeat	38
Bowl 5.8" #3400/13, 4-toed, tab handled, flared	45
Bowl 6" #1402/89, handled, sweetmeat	48
Bowl 6" #3400/53, flared, cereal	100
Bowl 6" #3400/136, 4-toed, deep, fancy crimped	150
Bowl 6" #3500/11 Gadroon, cereal	110
Bowl 6" #3500/50 Gadroon, round w/1 handle	48
Bowl 7.5" #435 Pristine, deco tab handled, sweetmeat	120
Bowl 8" #3500/27 Gadroon, square, w/2 ram heads	550+
Bowl 8.5" #221 Pristine, round, 3 equal sections	200
Bowl 8.5" #381, rim soup	250
Bowl 8.5" #1402/131 Tally Ho, deep, 3 equal sections	225
Bowl 9" #3400/135, 4-footed, cupped	275
Bowl 9" #3500/25 Gadroon, deep, footed, w/2 ram heads	500+
Bowl 9.5" #3500/115 Gadroon, footed, handled, flared	175
Bowl 9.5" #225 Pristine, blown, 2 sections	500+

Back left: Plate 8.5" #3400/62, salad or lunch (6 sided). **Back center:** Plate 10.25" #3900/24, dinner. **Center of photo:** Creamer 3.8" #3400/68, scalloped foot, regular, 4.75 oz. **Front left:** Sugar 3" #3400/68 scalloped foot, regular, 5 oz. **Front center:** Shaker 3.5" #3900/1177, flat, chrome top, pair. **Front right:** Cup & saucer, coffee #3400/54: cup 2.4", 6 oz.; saucer w/indent 5.5".

Candlestick 2-lite 6" #3400/647, keyhole stem, 7.75" spread, Ebony (black) w/Gold encrusted.

Back left: Candelabra 1-lite 6.25" #3400/648, keyhole stem, etched bobeches & prisms. **Back center:** Hurricane lamp 10" #1604, low 7" wide base, bowl shaped, etched chimney. **Back right:** Candlestick 2-lite 5.75" #495 Martha, plume arms & ball center, 8.25" spread. **Front left:** Candlestick 3-lite 6.25" #3400/1338, tiered (looks like ocean waves) 7" spread. **Front center:** Candlestick 1-lite 4.75" #3500/74 Gadroon, column stem, w/ram's head. **Front right:** Candlestick 2-lite 6" #3900/72, plume center, 8.25" spread.

Back left: Syrup 4.6" #1670, flat, straight sided, drip cut top, 9.5 oz. **Back center left:** Goblet 6.25" #3121, cafe parfait, 6.5 oz. **Back center right:** Cruet w/stopper 6" #3900/100, flat, spherical, 6 oz. **Back right:** Ice bucket 5.75" #3400/851, scalloped top, chrome handle. **Front left:** Candy w/cover 6" #306, sham base, low; cut cylinder knob finial, 5.1" tall. **Front center:** Marmalade w/metal cover 5.25" #157, footed cone shape (blown) 7 oz. – shown w/Wallace "Rose Point" marmalade spoon in front of it. **Front right:** Candy w/cover 8" #3500/57 Gadroon, 3 open handled, 3 equal sections.

Left: Decanter w/stopper 6.25" #3400/92, tilt ball; ball stopper, 32 oz. **Center left:** Decanter w/flat stopper 9" #1320, footed, cordial, 14 oz. **Center right:** Cocktail shaker 9.8" #101 Pristine, sham spouted w/glass top ball finial, 32 oz. **Right:** Cocktail shaker 11.5" #3400/157, flat, straight sided, #5 chrome lid.

Bowl 9.5" #3400/34, open handled, vegetable	98
Bowl 10" #427 Pristine, sham base, deep, salad	175
Bowl 10" #3400/1185, deep, open handled	100
Bowl 10" #3500/28 Gadroon, footed, handled, flared	100
Bowl 10" #3900/54, 4-footed, flared	85
Bowl 10.25" #3900/34, flat, handled, flared	100
Bowl 10.4" #1402/122 Tally Ho, deep, 3 equal sections	300
Bowl 10.5" #222 Pristine, round, deep, 3 sections	375
Bowl 10.5" #1359 Pristine, tab footed, smooth edge, flared	100
Bowl 10.5" #1351 Pristine, crimped, flared	100
Bowl 10.5" #3400/168, flat, flared	98
Bowl 11" #384 Pristine, oval, curled handles	125
Bowl 11" #1399, deep salad, scalloped edge	175
Bowl 11" #3400/3, dome footed, flared	145
Bowl 11" #3400/45, 4-footed, square crimped	110
Bowl 11" #3400/48, 4-footed, shallow, ruffled edge	115
Bowl 11" #3400/1188, open handled, fruit	125
Bowl 11" #3500/16 Gadroon, collar footed, tab handled, flared	145
Bowl 11" #3500/19 Gadroon, footed, handled, ruffled	225
Bowl 11" #3500/109 Gadroon, 4-toed, oval	575
Bowl 10.5" #3900/28, footed, tab handled, flared	98
Bowl 11.5" #3900/62, 4-footed, flared	98
Bowl 12" #3400/4, 4-footed, square, flared, edge	95
Bowl 12" #136 Pristine, crimped, pan shape	350
Bowl 12" #430 Pristine, sham base, belled & flared	95
Bowl 12" #1349 Pristine, tab footed, crimped edge, flared	100
Bowl 12" #3400/4, 4-toed, squared, flared edge	95
Bowl 12" #3400/5, 4-footed, rolled edge, console	175
Bowl 12" #3400/160, 4-footed, oblong, crimped	98
Bowl 12" #3500/17 Gadroon, footed, tab handled, shallow	145
Bowl 12" #3500/21 Gadroon, footed, handled, oval	250
Bowl 12" #3500/118 Gadroon, footed, oblong, banana	195
Bowl 12" #3500/26 Gadroon, footed,w/2 ram heads, fruit	595
Bowl 12" #3900/65, 4-footed, handled, oval	125
Bowl 12.5" #993, low 4-tab feet, flared out	115
Bowl 12.5" #3400/2, footed, mushroom shape	175
Bowl 12.6" #3400/1240, 4-footed, oval, refractory	150
Bowl 13" #1398, shallow, fruit or salad	145
Bowl 13" #3400/1, flared, console	95
Bowl 13" #3400/47, narrow (fan shape) crimped	145
Bowl 14" #1247, 4-footed, shallow, oblong, crimped	165
Bridge set 5 piece #3500/144 Gadroon, center handle tray & 4 straight sided, tumblers	400+
Butter w/cover 5.5" #506, round, tab handled	195
Butter w/cover 5.5" #3400/52, round, 2 open handles	200
Butter w/cover 7.5" #3900/52 Corinth, rectangle, 2.75" tall, 3.25" wide, .25 lb.	400
Cake plate 11.75" #3900/35, handled	100
Cake salver 13" #170 Martha, tab footed, scalloped edge	275
Canape set #693/3000, plate/cocktail, use #3000 footed cocktail, 3.5 oz. or 5 oz.	200
Candle block 1-lite 3.75" #495 Pristine, square, pair	300
Candelabra 1-lite 6.25" #3400/648, keyhole stem, etched bobeches &, prisms, pair	295
Candelabra 1-lite 6.5" #3500/32 Gadroon, bobeche & prisms, pair	375
Candelabra 1-lite 7.5" #497 Martha, curved stem, one prism, pair	295
Candelabra 1-lite 7.5" #3121, fancy stem w/etched bobeches & prisms, pair	325
Candelabra 1-lite 9" #3011, figured nude stem, with bobeche/prisms, pair	3,200
Candelabra 2-lite #1700/501, center flower, pair	475
Candelabra 2-lite 6" #3400/1268, keyhole stem bobeches & prisms, pair	450
Candelabra 2-lite 6.5" #496 Martha, #19 bobeches & #1 prisms, pair	375
Candelabra 2-lite #3500/95 Gadroon, "Horn of Plenty" pattern bobeches/prisms, pair	395
Candelabra 3-lite 5.5" #1545, one #19 bobeche on center cup & prisms, pair	375
Candlestick 1-lite 2.5" #3500/108 Gadroon, no stem, pair	75
Candlestick 1-lite 3.5" #628 Pristine, wafer stem, pair	95
Candlestick 1-lite 4" #494 Martha, dome footed, skirted, pair	125
Candlestick 1-lite 4" #627, round foot, faceted ball stem, pair	145
Candlestick 1-lite 4.4" #3900/68, bell footed, skirted, pair (also is a comport)	125
Candlestick 1-lite 4.75" #3500/74 Gadroon, column stem, w/rams head, pair	245
Candlestick 1-lite 5" #3900/67, skirted, pair	145
Candlestick 1-lite 5.25" #3400/646, keyhole stem, pair	100
Candlestick 1-lite 5.75" #3400/1192, small stem, pair	165
Candlestick 1-lite 6" #3500/31 Gadroon, column stem, pair	295
Candlestick 1-lite 6.5" #499, footed, Cala Lily, pair	250
Candlestick 1-lite 6.5" #500 Pristine, winged, pair	325
Candlestick 1-lite 7" #3121, fancy stem, pair	200
Candlestick 1-lite 9" #3011, figured nude stem, pair	3,000
Candlestick 2-lite 5.75" #495 Martha, plume arms & ball center, 8.25" spread, pair	295
Candlestick 2-lite 6" #3400/647, keyhole stem, 7.75" spread, pair	110
Candlestick 2-lite 6" #3900/72, plume center, 8.25" spread, pair	135
Candelabra 2-lite #3500/95 Gadroon, "Horn of Plenty" pattern bobeches/prisms, pair	250

Candlestick 3-lite 5.5" #1545, bell footed, pair	200
Candlestick 3-lite #1307, pair	100
Candlestick 3-lite 6" #3900/74, pair	145
Candlestick 3-lite 6.25" #3400/1338, tiered (looks like ocean waves) 7" spread, pair	175
Candlestick 3-lite 7" #3400/638, keyhole stem, pair	165
Candy w/cover #316 Pristine, apple shape	1,200+
Candy w/cover 4.5" #3500/77 Gadroon, footed, handled	395
Candy w/cover 5.4" #1066/4, blown w/fancy ball stem, plain finial	275
Candy w/cover 5.4" #3121/4, low, blown	175
Candy w/cover 5.4" #3121/3, tall, blown	185
Candy w/cover 5.4" #3500/103 Gadroon, blown	195
Candy (open) 5.5" #3500/47 Gadroon, handled	45
Candy w/cover 5.5" #313, flat, wafer finial	295
Candy w/cover 5.5" #300 Pristine, 3-footed, rose finial	395
Candy w/cover 6" #300 Pristine, 3-footed, knob finial	295
Candy w/cover 6" #306, sham base, low; cut cylinder knob finial, 5.1" tall	145
Candy w/cover 6" #307 Pristine, 3 sections, ball shape	295
Candy w/cover 6" #3500/78 Gadroon, flat, low, blown, rams head tab handles	325
Candy w/cover 6.5" #3400/9, 4-footed, tab handled, 7" wide; dome lid w/finial	165
Candy w/cover 7" #500 Pristine, 3-footed, knob finial	295
Candy w/cover 7" #500 Pristine, 3-footed, rose finial	395
Candy w/cover 7" #3900/165, flat, round, dome lid w/finial	150
Candy w/cover 8" #3500/57 Gadroon, 3 open handled, 3 equal sections	100
Candy w/cover 8" #3900/138, footed, wafer stem, dome lid w/finial (optic)	145
Cheese & cracker: comport 3" #1496 Pristine, short stem, flared, 5" wide; plate 11.5"	165
Cheese & cracker: comport 3" #3400/7, short stem, flared, 5.3" wide; plate 10.5" #3400/6, tab handled	125
Cheese & cracker: comport 3.75" #3500/163 Gadroon, short stem, flared, 6" wide; plate 12" #3500/162, handled	165
Cheese & cracker: comport 3.5" #3900/135, short stem, 5" wide; plate 13.5"	145
Cheese dish w/cover 5" #980, flat, pointed finial	575
Cigarette box w/cover 4.25" #615, oblong	175
Cigarette box w/cover 4.5" #747 Pristine, rectangle	195
Cigarette holder #1066, oval w/ashtray foot	225
Cigarette holder 4" #1337, round w/cupped ashtray foot	175
Cigarette holder #3400/144, ball shape w/ball stem	195
Cigarette holder 7" #3500/88 Gadroon, (also called a torchere) flat foot	250
Cigarette holder 7" #3500/90 Gadroon, (also called a torchere) ashtray foot	275
Coaster 3" #1628, made to stack	60
Cocktail icer 4.2" #187 Pristine, footed, 2 piece w/on-etched insert	175
Cocktail icer 4.2" #3600, footed, 2 piece w/on-etched insert	85
Cocktail icer 4.6" #968, footed, 2 piece w/on-etched insert	90
Cocktail mixer #1395, chrome lid & spoon, 28 oz.	295
Cocktail shaker #97, small #9 chrome lid	395
Cocktail shaker #98, large #10 chrome lid	200
Cocktail shaker #99, sham base, chrome lid	200
Cocktail shaker 9.8" #101 Pristine, sham spouted w/glass top ball finial, 32 oz.	245
Cocktail shaker #102 Pristine, sham spouted w/glass top ball finial, 48 oz.	225
Cocktail shaker 11.5" #3400/157, flat, straight sided, #5 chrome lid	200
Cocktail shaker #3400/175, w/large #10 chrome lid	195
Cologne w/keyhole stopper 2.5" #3400/97: tilt bottle, 2 oz.; stopper w/ long dauber	475
Comport 5" #1066, blown, 1 ball stem, 5.4" wide	85
Comport 5.25" #3111, low, blown, cupped, 5.5" wide	125
Comport 5.25" #3114/2, low, blown, cupped, 5.4" wide	145
Comport #643, footed, flared, 6" wide	45
Comport 5.3" #3400/28, keyhole stem, flared, 7.25" wide	98
Comport 6.1" #3121/2 (blown) tall stem, 5.4" wide	95
Comport 6.25" #3500/101 Gadroon, high, blown, 5.4" wide	85
Comport 6.5" #532 Pristine, footed, plain stem, flared, 6" wide	58
Comport 7" #3114, high, blown, cupped, 6" wide	195
Comport 7" #3500/148 Gadroon, high fancy stem, 6" wide	60
Comport 7.25" #3400/29, high, keyhole stem, 7" wide	145
Comport 7.5" #3400/14, fancy wafer stem, flared, 7" wide	95
Comport 7.5" #3900/136, scalloped edge, 5.75" wide	75
Comport #3500/36 Gadroon, cupped, 6" wide	150
Comport #3500/111 Gadroon, bellied, tab handled, 6" wide	195
Comport 7.6" #3500/37 Gadroon, tab handled, fancy stem, 7" wide	145
Cream soup & liner: bowl #922 Pristine, handled, 9 oz.; saucer w/indent 6.5"	245
Cream soup & liner #3500/2 Gadroon: bowl 5", handled, 9 oz.; saucer w/ indent 6.5"	145
Creamer #136, flat, barrel shape, handled	200
Creamer 2.5" #3500/15 Gadroon, footed, individual, 3 oz.	28
Creamer #3900/38, footed, individual, 3 oz.	28
Creamer 2.25" #252 Pristine, flat, individual, handle, 3.5 oz.	38
Creamer 2.6" #3900/40, footed, individual, 3.5 oz.	28
Creamer 3.8" #3400/68, scalloped foot, regular, 4.75 oz.	24

Back: Relish 12" #3400/67, 4 equal sections & celery section. **Center of photo:** Creamer 2.25" #252 Pristine, flat, individual, handle, 3.5 oz. **Front left:** Sugar 2" #252 Pristine, flat, individual, handled, 4 oz. **Front center:** Creamer 2.5" #3500/15 Gadroon, footed, individual, 3 oz. **Front right:** Sugar 2.4" #3500/15 Gadroon, footed, individual, 3 oz.

Back: Shaker 2.25" #1468, egg shaped, square glass base. **Front left:** Shaker 3.75" #3400/77, footed, glass top. **Front center:** Shaker 3.5" #3900/1177, flat, glass top. **Front right:** Bottle w/stopper 6.5" #1263, flat, French dressing, 8 oz.

Left: Goblet 4.75" #3500, sherbet, 7 oz. **Center left:** Goblet 5.8" #3121, wine, 3.5 oz. **Center:** Goblet 6.1" #3500, liquor cocktail, 3 oz. **Center right:** Goblet 6.4" #3121, saucer champagne, 6.75 oz. **Right:** Goblet 8.25" #3121, dinner water, 11 oz.

Basket 5.75" #3500/55 Gadroon, footed, 2 handled, crimped, 3.5" tall, w/gold trim edge.

Left: Goblet 3.6", pressed cordial, 1 oz., Crystal foot & Royal Blue (cobalt) bowl. **Center left:** Goblet 4", pressed, oyster cocktail, 4.5 oz., Crystal foot & Carmen (ruby) bowl. **Center right:** Goblet 4.6", pressed, sherbet, 7 oz., Crystal w/etched bowl. **Right:** Goblet 6.3", pressed, water 10 oz., Crystal foot & Amber bowl, (all shown have pressed Rose Point foot).

Top left: Bowl 10.25" #3900/34, flat, handled, flared. **Top right:** Bowl 12" #3400/4, 4-toed, squared, flared edge, Gold encrusted. **Center row left:** Relish 6.25" #3500/69 Gadroon, 3 equal sections, scalloped edge. **Bottom left:** Relish 7" #3900/123, 4-toed, tab scroll handled, oblong pickle. **Bottom right:** Relish 9.5" #477 Pristine, oblong w/tab feet, oval pickle or corn.

Back center: Mayonnaise 2 piece #1532 Pristine: bowl 4.5" (blown), spherical, 3" high; liner w/indent 6.75". **Front left:** Marmalade w/cover 5.4" #147 Pristine, blown (spherical) 8 oz. **Front center:** Mustard w/cover, 3" #151 Pristine, blown, spherical, 3 oz. **Front right:** Mayonnaise bowl 4" #3900/19, footed, ball shape, 4.1" high.

Candy w/cover 8" #3500/57 Gadroon, 3 open handled, 3 equal sections, Crystal w/Gold encrusted.

Creamer #137, flat squat, regular, handled, 6 oz.	125
Creamer #138 Pristine, flat, regular, 6 oz.	45
Creamer #944, flat, handled, regular, 6 oz.	125
Creamer #3400/16, cone footed, regular, 6 oz.	85
Creamer 2.5" #3500/14 Gadroon, footed, regular, 6 oz.	28
Creamer #3900/39, footed, regular, 6 oz.	28
Creamer 3" #3900/41, footed, regular, 6 oz.	24
Cruet w/stopper #3400/96, ball shape, 2 oz.	125
Cruet w/flat stopper 5.75" #293 Pristine, 6 oz.	145
Cruet w/flat stopper #293 Pristine, 6 oz.	145
Cruet w/stopper #3400/79, spherical, 6 oz.	275
Cruet w/ball stopper 4.4" #3400/99, tilt ball, 6 oz.	175
Cruet w/stopper #3400/193, flat, 6 oz.	125
Cruet w/stopper #3400/161, footed, handled, 6 oz.	275
Cruet w/stopper 6" #3900/100, flat, spherical, 6 oz.	145
Cup & saucer, after dinner #3400/69: cup 2.25", 2 oz.; saucer w/indent 4.25", 6-sided	295
Cup 2.5" #488 Martha, punch w/fancy handle, 5 oz.	45
Cup & saucer, coffee #3400/54: cup 2.4", 6 oz.; saucer w/indent 5.5"	38
Cup & saucer, coffee #3500/1 Gadroon: cup 2.5", footed, regular, 6 oz.; saucer w/indent 6"	42
Cup & saucer, coffee #3900/17: cup 2.5", 7 oz.; saucer w/indent 5.5"	42
Decanter w/stopper #3400/119, tilt ball, cordial, 12 oz.	345
Decanter w/flat stopper 9" #1320, footed, cordial, 14 oz.	495
Decanter w/stopper #1380, square, 26 oz.	900+
Decanter w/flat stopper 11" #1321, footed, 28 oz.	450
Decanter w/stopper 13.25" #1372, flat, slim bottle shape, 28 oz.	900+
Decanter w/stopper 6.25" #3400/92, tilt ball; ball stopper, 32 oz.	450
Epergne 4 piece #645, etched 3-lite candlestick w/plain arm & 2 non-etched vases	175
Epergne 4 piece #663, etched 3-lite candlestick w/plain arm & 2 vases	165
Epergne 4 piece #3900/75, etched 3-lite candlestick w/plain arm & 2 vases	175
Epergne 5 piece #654, etched keyhole w/plain bobeche-prisms & 2 non-etched vases	145
Epergne 7 piece #667, etched candlestick w/plain arms & 4 vases	200
Finger bowl & liner: bowl #3106, flat, blown; plate w/indent	65
Finger bowl & liner: bowl #3121, flat, blown; plate w/indent	75
Finger bowl #3500, footed, blown	65
Finger bowl & liner: bowl #3500, flat, blown; plate w/indent	75
Goblet #3106, plain stem, brandy, .75 oz.	125
Goblet #3121, plain stem, brandy, 1 oz.	195
Goblet 3.6", pressed cordial (colored bowl) 1 oz.	245
Goblet #16 Pristine, 3 wafer stem, cordial, 1 oz.	145
Goblet #3106, plain stem, cordial, 1 oz.	125
Goblet 5.25" #3121, cordial, 1 oz.	75
Goblet 4.9" #3500, cordial, 1 oz.	75
Goblet 5" #7966, flared, cone shape, cordial, 1 oz.	145
Goblet #3106, plain stem, pousse cafe, 1 oz.	135
Goblet #3106, plain stem, sherry, 2 oz.	65
Goblet 5.25" #7966, flared, cone shaped, sherry, 2 oz.	125
Goblet #3106, plain stem, wine, 2.5 oz.	50
Goblet 4.75" #3500, wine, 2.5 oz.	75
Goblet #3106, plain stem, creme de menthe, 2.5 oz.	98
Goblet 5.2", pressed, wine, 3 oz. (colored bowl)	145
Goblet #12 Pristine, 3 wafer stem, wine, 3 oz.	45
Goblet #3106, plain stem, liquor cocktail, 3 oz.	38
Goblet 6" #3121, liquor cocktail, 3 oz.	35
Goblet 6.1" #3500, liquor cocktail, 3 oz.	38
Goblet #8 Pristine, 3 wafer stem, liquor cocktail, 3.5 oz.	35
Goblet 5.8" #3121, wine, 3.5 oz.	65
Goblet #7801 Pristine, plain stem, liquor cocktail, 4 oz.	65
Goblet 6.25" #3121, claret, 4.25 oz.	95
Goblet 4", pressed, oyster cocktail, 4.5 oz. (colored bowl)	125
Goblet 3.6" #3500, oyster cocktail, 4.5 oz.	38
Goblet #10 Pristine, 3 wafer stem, claret, 4.5 oz.	48
Goblet #3106, plain stem, claret, 4.5 oz.	60
Goblet 6.1" #3500, claret, 4.5 oz.	115
Goblet 4.4" #3121, oyster cocktail, 4.75 oz.	35
Goblet #7 Pristine, wafer stem, oyster cocktail, 5 oz.	28
Goblet #3106, oyster cocktail, 5 oz.	35
Goblet #3500, cafe parfait, 5 oz.	125
Goblet #6 Pristine, 2 wafer stem, sherbet, 6 oz.	24
Goblet #4 Pristine, 3 wafer stem, saucer champagne, 6 oz.	28
Goblet 6.25" #3121, cafe parfait, 6.5 oz.	100
Goblet 4.75" #3121, sherbet, 6.75 oz.	22
Goblet 6.4" #3121, saucer champagne, 6.75 oz.	24
Goblet 4.6", pressed, sherbet (colored bowl) 7 oz.	95
Goblet 4.75" #3106, plain stem, sherbet, 7 oz.	25
Goblet 4.75" #3500, sherbet, 7 oz.	24
Goblet #3106, saucer champagne, 7 oz.	32

Item	Price
Goblet 6.5" #3500, saucer champagne, 7 oz.	30
Goblet 6.3", pressed, water (colored bowl) 10 oz.	125
Goblet #3106, plain stem, water, 10 oz.	40
Goblet 6.4" #3500, lunch water, 10 oz.	42
Goblet 8.25" #3500, dinner water, 10 oz.	48
Goblet #1 Pristine, 3 wafer stem, water, 11 oz.	40
Goblet 8.25" #3121, dinner water, 11 oz.	40
Hat 5" #1701, brim turned down on 2 sides	475
Hat 6" #1701, brim turned down on 2 sides	500
Hat 8" #1701, brim turned down on 2 sides	600
Hat 9" #1701, brim turned down on 2 sides	750
Honey dish w/cover 6" #3500/139 Gadroon, flat, square, handled	395
Hurricane lamp 8" #1601, short stem, bobeche w/prisms & etched chimney, each	295
Hurricane lamp 9.3" #1617, skirted w/etched chimney, each	295
Hurricane twin lamp 10" #1590, 2 arms, bobeches w/prisms & only chimneys etched, each	400
Hurricane lamp 10" #1604, low 7" wide base, bowl shaped, etched chimney, each	400
Hurricane lamp 10.25" #1603, keyhole stem, bobeche w/prisms & etched chimney, each	295
Hurricane lamp 16" #1612/1614, dolphin stem, bobeche & prisms large w/etched chimney, each	525
Hurricane lamp 16" #1613/1614, bobeche & prisms large w/etched chimney, each	450
Hurricane lamp 18" #1612/1615, dolphin stem, bobeche & prisms large w/etched chimney, each	550
Hurricane lamp 18" #1613/1615, bobeche & prisms large w/etched chimney, each	475
Ice bucket 4.75" #671 # Pristine, sham base, graduated deco tab handled	245
Ice bucket #672 Pristine, sham base, chrome handle	245
Ice bucket 5.75" #3900/671, chrome handle	195
Ice bucket 5.75" #1705 Pristine, footed, chrome handle	275
Ice bucket 5.75" #3400/851, scalloped top, chrome handle	165
Ice bucket 5.8" #1402/52 Tally Ho, chrome handle	200
Icer fruit #188, scalloped edge fits in pristine #427 deep salad	500
Lamp 9.25" (glass only), electric produced from a vase	600
Liquor set 7 piece #3500/114 Gadroon, center handle tray & 6 whiskey tumblers	600
Marmalade w/metal cover 5.25" #157, footed cone shape (blown) 7 oz.	195
Marmalade w/cover 5.4" #147 Pristine, flat (blown) 8 oz.	175
Mayonnaise 2 piece #1402/96 Tally Ho; footed, salad dressing; liner w/indent 17.5"	275
Mayonnaise 2 piece #1402/137 Tally Ho: salad dressing, 2 spouted; liner w/indent	175
Mayonnaise 2 piece #3500/166 Gadroon: salad dressing; liner w/indent	95
Mayonnaise bowl 4" #3900/19, footed, ball shape, 4.1" high	70
Mayonnaise 2 piece #1532 Pristine: bowl 4.5" (blown), spherical, 3" high; liner w/indent 6.75"	95
Mayonnaise 2 piece bowl #1402/133 Tally Ho: 4.75" tall x 5.75" wide, flat, salad dressing; liner w/indent	115
Mayonnaise 2 piece #3900: #127 bowl 5", flared; #128 liner w/indent 6.5"	75
Mayonnaise 2 piece #3900/111: bowl 5.25", salad dressing; liner w/indent 6.75"	65
Mayonnaise 2 piece #1490 Pristine: bowl 5.5", cupped, salad dressing; use #1491 liner w/indent 6.4"	95
Mayonnaise 2 piece #1491 Pristine: bowl 5.5", flared, salad dressing; liner w/indent 6.4"	95
Mayonnaise 2 piece #287 Pristine: bowl 5.5", sham, tab handled, salad dressing; liner w/indent 6.5"	110
Mayonnaise 2 piece #533 Pristine: bowl 5.75", footed sauce; liner w/indent 6.4"	150
Mayonnaise 2 piece #1402/95 Tally Ho: bowl 5.75", salad dressing; liner w/indent	100
Mayonnaise 2 piece #3400: #13 bowl 5.8", 4-toed, flared, tab handled; #11 liner w/indent 5"	70
Mayonnaise 2 piece #3500/58 Gadroon: bowl 6", footed, handled, flared; #59 liner w/indent 7.5"	68
Mayonnaise comport 6" #3900/137, footed, wafer stem, flared w/optic	70
Marmalade w/cover 5.4" #147 Pristine, blown (spherical) 8 oz.	175
Mustard w/cover 3" #151 Pristine, blown, spherical, 3 oz.	165
Mustard w/cover 4.25" #1329, ball stem, 4.5 oz.	375
Nite set #103, flat, handled, jug & flat tumbler w/flared base	900+
Pitcher #70 Pristine, handled jug w/ice lip, 20 oz.	375
Pitcher 9.25" #100 Pristine, handled, martini mixer, 32 oz.	395
Pitcher #3900/117, milk jug w/ice lip, 20 oz.	375
Pitcher #3900/114, martini jug w/ice lip, 32 oz.	450
Pitcher #3900/118, jug/ice lip, 32 oz.	400
Pitcher #1408, cocktail churn/plunger, 60 oz.	2,000+
Pitcher #3400/100, high w/ice lip, 76 oz.	245
Pitcher 9.25" #3400/152, Doulton style w/o ice lip, 76 oz.	395
Pitcher #3900/115, water jug w/ice lip (optic), 76 oz.	295
Pitcher 9" #3400/38, tilt ball w/ice lip, 80 oz.	295
Pitcher 8.1" #3400/141, water jug w/o ice lip, 80 oz.	395
Pitcher 9" #3900/116, ball w/ice lip, 80 oz.	295
Pitcher 7.9" #3900/141, Doulton jug w/o ice lip (not optic) 80 oz.	395
Pitcher #119, high w/ice lip, 83 oz.	750
Pitcher #1561, ball w/ice lip, 86 oz.	395
Plate 6" #3400/60, bread & butter (6 sided)	18

Back row: Plate 14" #3400/65, chop, large center. **Left:** Comport low cupped 5.25". **Center:** Tray 8.25" #3500/161 Gadroon, footed, shallow, round, open handled; Bonbon 6" #3500/54 Gadroon, footed, handled. **Right:** Comport 7.6" #3500/37 Gadroon, tab handled, fancy stem, 7" wide.

Left: Tumbler 5.75" #3121, footed, juice, 5 oz. **Center:** Tumbler 7" #3121, footed, water, 10 oz. **Right:** Tumbler 7.5" #3121, footed, ice tea, 12 oz.

Trivet 5", flat, round, (all over etching), w/original label, set in metal holder, 6.25" wide overall, Crystal set in gold colored metal frame.

Pitcher 9" #3900/116, ball w/ice lip, 80 oz.

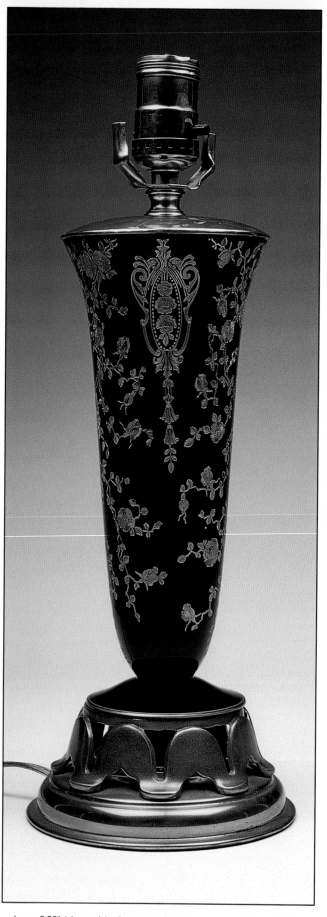

Lamp 9.25" (glass only), electric produced from a vase, Ebony (black) w/ Gold encrusted.

Plate 6" #3400/1181, handled, lemon server	28
Plate 6" #3500/3 Gadroon, bread & butter	18
Plate 7" #131 Pristine, (blown) salad/coupe	110
Plate 7" #1402/99, handled, lemon server	32
Plate 7.5" #555, dessert	24
Plate 7.5" #556, dessert	24
Plate 7.5" #3400/176, square, salad or dessert	20
Plate 7.5" #3500/4 Gadroon, dessert	20
Plate 8" #163 Pristine, side salad	225
Plate 8" #3900/22, salad or lunch	22
Plate 8" #3900/131, handled, lemon server	40
Plate 8.5" #3400/62, salad or lunch (6 sided)	24
Plate 8.5" #3500/5 Gadroon, salad or lunch	24
Plate 9.5" #485, crescent salad	275
Plate 9.5" #3400/63, small dinner	95
Plate 10.25" #3900/24, dinner	160
Plate 10.5" #244, service	135
Plate 10.5" #3400/64, large dinner	160
Plate 11" #3400/35, open handled, sandwich	68
Plate 11.5" #3500/39 Gadroon, footed, open tab handled, round	98
Plate 12" #3900/26, 4-footed, service	85
Plate 12.5" #3400/1186, oblong, open handled sandwich	75
Plate 13" #3500/110 Gadroon, footed, tab handled, torte	125
Plate 13" #3900/33, 4-footed, rolled edge, torte	85
Plate 13.5" #242, torte	165
Plate 13.5" #1396 Pristine, flat, torte/service	85
Plate 13.5" #1397 Pristine, small center, turned up edge, cabaret	95
Plate 14" #130 Pristine, flat, blown, torte	350
Plate 14" #3400/65, chop, large center	175
Plate 14" #3900/166, torte	85
Plate 14" #3900/167, service/torte	95
Plate 17.5" #1402/29, Sunday nite supper	175
Plate 17.5" #1402/102, large mayo liner/indent in center	150
Plate 18" #1402/28, Sunday nite supper	185
Plate 18" #1402/101, liner w/indent in center	160
Plate 18" #170 Pristine, torte	195
Punch bowl 15" #478 Martha, 2.5 gallon	4.500+
Punch bowl liner 18" #129 Martha, scalloped edge	500
Punch bowl 13" #3500/119 Gadroon, footed, w/2 rams heads, 1.5 gallon	2,500+
Relish 5.5" #3500/60 Gadroon, 2 sections, one handle	40
Relish 5.5" #3500/68 Gadroon, no handles, 2 sections	35
Relish 6" #1402/90, handled, 2 sections	45
Relish 6" #1497 Pristine, tab handled, oval, 2 sections	48
Relish 6" #3400/1093, center handled, oval, 2 sections	125
Relish 6.25" #3500/69 Gadroon, 3 equal sections, scalloped edge	42
Relish 6.5" #3400/90, 2 open handles, 2 equal sections	38
Relish 6.5" #3500/61 Gadroon, scalloped edge, 3 sections, loop handle	70
Relish 7" #3900/123, 4-toed, tab scroll handled, oblong pickle	45
Relish 7" #3900/124, 4-toed, tab scroll handled, 2 equal sections, oblong	48
Relish 7.5" #3500/62 Gadroon, handled, 4 sections, round	90
Relish 7.5" #3500/70 Gadroon, no handles, 4 sections	65
Relish 7.5" #3500/71 Gadroon, center handled, 3 equal sections	150
Relish 8" #1498 Pristine, tab handled, 3 sections	115
Relish 8" #3500/57 Gadroon, 3 equal sections, 3 handled (candy bottom)	45
Relish 8.75" #3400/88, 2-handled, 2 sections, oblong	95
Relish 8.75" #3400/862, center plume handled, oblong, 4 sections	275
Relish 9" #3400/59, tab handled, oval, pickle	85
Relish 9" #3900/125, handled, oval, 2 equal sections & celery section	65
Relish 9.5" #464 Pristine, crescent salad shape, 3 sections	200
Relish 9.5" #477 Pristine, oblong w/tab feet, oval pickle or corn	95
Relish 10" #393, oval, 4 equal sections & celery section	85
Relish 10" #394, round, 4 equal sections & celery section	85
Relish 10" #3500/63 Gadroon, 4-toed, handled, not divided	120
Relish 10" #3500/64 Gadroon, 4-toed, handled, 2 equal sections & celery section	75
Relish 10" #3500/65 Gadroon, 4-toed, handled, 4 sections	95
Relish 10" #3500/85 Gadroon, handled, not divided	115
Relish 10" #3500/86 Gadroon, handled, 3 sections	75
Relish 10" #3500/87 Gadroon, handled, 4 equal sections	98
Relish 11" #248 Pristine, narrow oblong, celery	70
Relish 11" #3400/200, handled, 4-toed, curved divider, 2 equal sections & celery section	75
Relish 11" #3400/89, handled, 2 sections	100
Relish 11" #3400/652, oblong, celery	65
Relish 11" #3500/152 Gadroon, handled, rectangular, 3 equal sections & celery section	145
Relish 12" two piece 12" #419 Pristine, round, 6 sections w/center cup	245
Relish 12" #3500/67 Gadroon: 5 inserts & tray w/scalloped edge, round	300
Relish 11.5" #3500/652 Gadroon, oblong, celery	65
Relish 12" #3900/120, oblong, 4 equal sections & celery section	90

Relish 12" #3900/126, handled, oval, 2 equal sections & celery section	80
Relish 12" #3400/67, 4 equal sections & celery section	90
Relish 14" #3500/97 Gadroon, handled, oval, 3 equal sections & celery section	175
Relish w/cover 14" #3500/142 Gadroon, handled, 4 sections, oval	1,000+
Relish 15" #3500/112 Gadroon, handled, oval, 2 equal sections & celery section	195
Relish 15" #3500/113 Gadroon, handled, narrow, 4 sections	245
Sandwich server 10.5" #3400/10, center keyhole handle	145
Shade hurricane #1614, trumpet shape	275
Shade hurricane #1615, trumpet shape	345
Shaker #360 Pristine, flat, spherical, metal top, pair	90
Shaker 2.25" #1468, egg shaped, square glass base, pair	145
Shaker #1470, ball shaped, individual, square glass base, pair	125
Shaker #1471, ball shaped, regular, square glass base, pair	135
Shaker 3.25" #3400/76, footed, glass top, pair	75
Shaker 3.5" #3900/1177, flat, chrome or glass top, pair	58
Shaker 3.75" #3400/77, footed, glass top, pair	58
Shaker 5" #3400/37, footed, chrome top, pair	145
Sugar #136, flat, barrel shape, handled	200
Sugar 2.4" #3500/15 Gadroon, footed, individual, 3 oz.	28
Sugar #3900/38, footed, individual, 3 oz.	28
Sugar 2.4" #3900/40, footed, individual, 3.5 oz.	28
Sugar 2" #252 Pristine, flat, individual, handled, 4 oz.	38
Sugar 3" #3400/68 scalloped foot, regular, 5 oz.	24
Sugar #137, flat, squat, handled, regular, 6 oz.	125
Sugar #138 Pristine, flat, regular, 6 oz.	45
Sugar #944, flat, handled, regular, 6 oz.	125
Sugar #3400/16, footed, cone shape, 6 oz.	85
Sugar 2.4" #3500/14 Gadroon, footed, regular, 6 oz.	28
Sugar #3900/39, footed, regular, 6 oz.	28
Sugar 2.75" #3900/41, regular footed, 6 oz.	24
Sugar pail #3500/13 Gadroon, chrome handle	295
Syrup 4.6" #1670, flat, straight sided, drip cut top, 9.5 oz.	450
Toast or cheese cover 4.5" #1533, blown, ball finial	600+
Tray 6" #3500/91 Gadroon, handled, square	195
Tray 6.5" #3900/38, individual cream/sugar	40
Tray 8.25" #3500/161 Gadroon, footed, shallow, round, open handled	38
Tray 8.5" #3900/37, regular cream/sugar	35
Tray 12" #3500/99 Gadroon, handled, oval, service	300
Tray 13" #3500/38 Gadroon, flat, round, torte	225
Tray 13" #3500/72 Gadroon, handled, flat, round, server	225
Tray 14" #3500/100 Gadroon, flat, handled, round, server	200
Trivet 5", flat, round, (all over etching)	200
Tumbler 2.4" #321, sham, whiskey, 2 oz.	100
Tumbler #498, flat, cut flute, straight sided, whiskey, 2 oz.	100
Tumbler 2.75" #3121, footed, stem, whiskey, 2.5 oz.	75
Tumbler 2.1" #3400/92, flat, barrel, whiskey, 2.5 oz.	115
Tumbler 2.1" #3400/127, flat, handled, whiskey, 2.5 oz.	195
Tumbler 2.75" #3500, footed, whiskey, 2.5 oz.	75
Tumbler #3106, footed, wine, 3 oz.	38
Tumbler, pressed, footed, juice, 5 oz. (colored bowl)	115
Tumbler #321, sham, tapered juice, 5 oz.	68
Tumbler #498, flat, cut flute, straight sided, juice, 5 oz.	50
Tumbler #3106, footed, juice, 5 oz.	36
Tumbler 5.75" #3121, footed, juice, 5 oz.	40
Tumbler #3400/38, flat, juice, 5 oz.	95
Tumbler 5.25" #3500, juice, 5 oz.	42
Tumbler #3900/117, flat, juice, 5 oz.	75
Tumbler #7801, footed, juice, 5 oz.	65
Tumbler #321, sham, old fashion, 8 oz.	125
Tumbler #498, flat, cut flute, straight sided, 8 oz.	50
Tumbler 4.9" #497, sham, straight sided, water, 9 oz.	60
Tumbler #3106, footed, water, 9 oz.	40
Tumbler #498, flat, cut flute, straight sided, 10 oz.	50
Tumbler 7" #3121, footed, water, 10 oz.	35
Tumbler 6.4" #3500, water, 10 oz.	35
Tumbler #497, sham, straight sided, 11 oz.	65
Tumbler, pressed, footed, ice tea, 12 oz. (colored bowl)	195
Tumbler #498, flat, cut flute, straight sided, 12 oz.	65
Tumbler #3106, footed, ice tea, 12 oz.	45
Tumbler 7.5" #3121, footed, ice tea, 12 oz.	42
Tumbler #3400/38, flat, ice tea, 12 oz.	65
Tumbler 7.5" #3500, ice tea, 12 oz.	48
Tumbler #7801, footed, ice tea, 12 oz.	85
Tumbler #497, sham, straight sided, 13 oz.	80
Tumbler #3400/115, bellied, ice tea, 13 oz.	60
Tumbler #3500, ice tea, 13 oz.	45
Tumbler 4.1" #3900/115, flat, barrel, 13 oz.	58
Urn w/cover 10" #3500/41 Gadroon, footed, tab handled	695
Urn w/cover 12" #3500/42 Gadroon, footed, tab handled	795

Left: Vase 13.25" #279, footed (no stem) wide w/flared top. **Center:** Vase 12" #1238, footed, keyhole stem, flared. **Right:** Pitcher 8.1" #3400/141, water jug w/o ice lip, 80 oz.

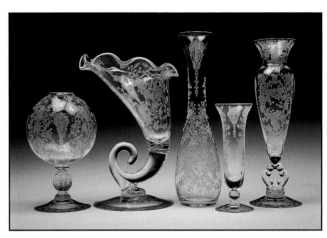

Left: Vase 7" #1066, footed, fancy ball stem, ivy ball. **Center left:** Vase 9" #576 Pristine, footed, crimped or smooth top, cornucopia. **Center:** Vase 10.25" #1528, flat, spherical bottom, bud vase. **Center right:** Vase 6" #6004, footed, flared, 1 ball stem, bud vase, flared. **Right:** Vase 9.75" #1233, footed, keyhole stem, shouldered.

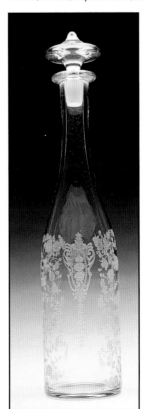

Decanter w/stopper 13.25" #1372, flat, slim bottle shape, 28 oz.

Left: Vase 10" #274, footed, tapered out top, bud vase, Ebony (black).
Right: Vase 10.25" #3400/1242, flat, shouldered, flared, Carmen (ruby).

Vase #629 Pristine, spherical, flared	295
Vase 3.5" #3400/203, 4-footed, cupped in sphere shape, violet	100
Vase 4.5" to 5" #1309, squat globe, necked & flared	125
Vase 5" #596 Pristine, footed, bell shape	250
Vase 5" #3400/102, globe, short neck	125
Vase 5" #6004, footed, flared, 1 ball stem, bud vase, flared	65
Vase 6" #572 Pristine, flared	175
Vase 6" #6004, footed, flared, 1 ball stem, bud vase, flared	75
Vase 6.5" #3400/103, globe, short neck	135
Vase 7" #597 Pristine, footed, cone shape	395
Vase 7" #1066, footed, fancy ball stem, ivy ball	345
Vase 7" #3500/122 Gadroon, footed, tab handled, squared, urn shape	400
Vase 7.8" #797, flip shape w/panel optic	225
Vase 8" #417 Pristine, cylinder shape, floating flower	450
Vase 8" #580 Pristine, straight sided	275
Vase 8" #1300, footed, shouldered & flared	100
Vase 8" #1430, large, flat, flared, flip shape	295
Vase 8" #1630, "Horn of Plenty" centerpiece	500
Vase 8" #3500/44 Gadroon, footed, tab handled, urn shaped	195
Vase 8" #3500/123 Gadroon, footed, tab handled, squared, urn shape	395
Vase 8.4" #6004, footed, flared, 1 ball stem, bud vase	85
Vase 9" #277, footed, flared	145
Vase 9" #576 Pristine, footed, crimped or smooth top, cornucopia	275
Vase 9" #1620, footed, ball stem, flared	175
Vase 9" #1623, footed, ball stem, cornucopia	295
Vase 9.75" #1233, footed, keyhole stem, shouldered	145
Vase 10" #274, footed, tapered out top, bud vase	175
Vase 10" #400, flat, ball sham bottom	275
Vase 10" #1237, footed, keyhole stem, flared	150
Vase 10" #1301, footed, shouldered & flared	125
Vase 10" #1621, footed, tab handled, urn shape	195
Vase 10" #3500/45 Gadroon, footed, tab handled, urn shape	225
Vase 10" #575 Pristine, footed, smooth top, cornucopia	195
Vase 10" #6004, footed, flared, 1 ball stem, bud vase, flared	125
Vase 10.2" #272, footed, cupped in at top, bud vase	100
Vase 10.25" #1528, flat, spherical bottom, w/concave neck, bud vase	175
Vase 10.25" #3400/1242, flat, shouldered, flared	195
Vase 11" #278, large footed (no stem) flared top	150
Vase 11.5" #1299, footed, ball stem, urn shape	245
Vase 12" #1234, footed, keyhole stem, crimped	185
Vase 12" #1238, footed, keyhole stem, flared	175
Vase 12" #6004, footed, 1 ball stem, flared	150
Vase 13.25" #279, footed (no stem) wide w/flared top	295
Vase 18" #1336, shouldered, flared	3,000+
Water bottle #1544, flat (large tumble up shape) 26 oz	1,500+

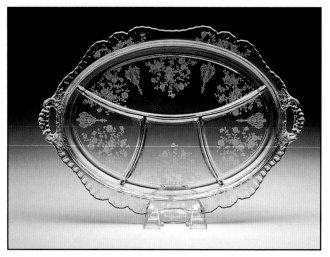

Relish 14" #3500/97 Gadroon, handled, oval, 3 equal sections & celery section, 9.5" wide.

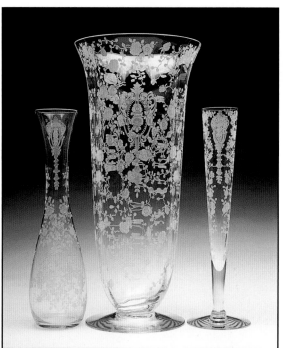

Left: Vase 10.25" #1528, flat, spherical bottom, w/concave neck, bud vase. **Center:** Vase 13.25" #279, footed (no stem) wide w/flared top. **Right:** Vase 10" #274, footed, tapered out top, bud vase.

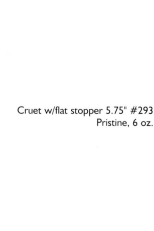

Cruet w/flat stopper 5.75" #293 Pristine, 6 oz.

RUBA ROMBIC

Consolidated Glass Company   **1928-32**

Colors: Jade, Jungle Green, Lilac, Sepia, Smoky Topaz, and Sunshine (yellow)

Ruba Rombic was an inspiration taken from the Art Moderne exhibit at the Paris Exposition. Reuben Haley created this most unusual pattern. The name was developed as a combination of names. Ruba came from *rubaiy*, which means a poem. Rombic came from the word rhomboid, which means an irregularly shaped object that has no parallel lines. Advertising in trade journals listed it as an epic in modern art. The pattern reminds you of randomly placed shapes of ice blocks. An outstanding modernistic and attractive pattern, it could be described as a work of art in glass. Due to this fact, the prices of these items amaze us. It would be hard to start collecting this pattern unless you had plenty of money. Even then it would take a lot of patience to search out these pieces. Many collectors would love to own even one piece of Ruba Rombic. If you have a piece in your collection, consider yourself very fortunate.

We were extremely lucky to find a collection to photograph for this edition. Enjoy the several pieces pictured here and think about how long it might take to find these pieces.

Jade, Lilac, and Sunshine are the cased colors. Jungle Green and Smoky Topaz are the transparent colors.

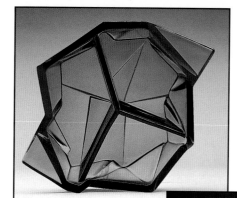

Relish 8" #832, flat, 2-tab handled, 3 sections, irregular round, Smokey Topaz.

RUBA ROMBIC

	Transparent Colors	Cased Colors
Ashtray 3.5" #829, flat	595	695
Bottle w/stopper, cologne 4.75", small round (umbrella shape stopper hangs down over sides)	1,400	1,600
Bottle w/stopper, toilet 7.8" #826, tall upright flask shape, (fan shape stopper hangs down slightly) 14 oz.	1,200	1,450
Bottle w/stopper, liquor 9" #824, large round decanter (fan shape stopper hangs down slightly)	1,500	1,800
Bowl 3" #831, flat, tab handled, almond or nut	295	395
Bowl 8" #803, flat, cupped in top (rose bowl shape)	1,000	1,200
Bowl 9" #811, flat, flared	1,000	1,200
Bowl 12" #804, flat, oblong	1,500	1,800
Bouillon #819, footed, no stem (looks like fat sherbet)	150	195
Candlestick 1-lite 2.6" #805, large foot, no stem w/candle cup, pair	600	725
Cigarette box w/cover #828, rectangular	850	1,100
Comport 7", small foot, no stem w/large (compared to foot) bowl top	745	895
Creamer, flat, upright (mug shaped) 1 angular handle, 7 oz.	200	250
Finger bowl #810, flat, deep	100	125
Pitcher #812, flat water jug w/angular handle	2,250	2,750
Plate 6" #806, bread & butter	75	100
Plate 8" #807, salad	100	125
Plate 10" #808, dinner or service	225	275
Plate 15" #809, torte or round platter	1,400	1,700
Powder box w/cover 5", flat	850	1,100
Relish 8" #832, flat, 2-tab handled, 3 sections, irregular round	200	250
Relish #833, flat, tab handled, 2 sections, rectangular	295	395
Relish 12" #834, flat, tab handled, 3 sections, oblong	300	350
Sugar, flat, shallow, squat, 2 angular handles, 7 oz.	200	250
Sundae 2.5" #818, footed, sherbet, no stem 5 oz.	145	195
Tumbler 2.65" #823, flat, whiskey, 2.5 oz.	95	125
Tumbler, footed, juice, 5 oz.	110	135
Tumbler #813, flat, water, 9 oz.	125	165
Tumbler #815, footed, water, 10 oz.	195	295
Tumbler 5.5" #814, ice tea, 12 oz.	185	225
Tray #825, serving (for liquor bottle & 6 whiskeys)	1,600	1,950
Vase 6.5", flat, upright (squat in shape)	750	950
Vase 9.5", flat, upright (standard shape)	1,350	1,850
Vase 16.5", flat, upright (very tall shape)	7,500	9,500

Bottle w/stopper, toilet 7.8" #826, tall upright flask shape, (fan-shaped stopper hangs down slightly) 14 oz., Jungle Green.

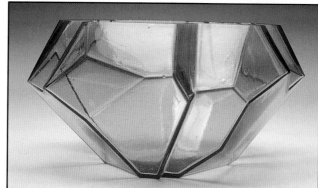

Bowl 9" #811, flat, flared, Emerald Green.

Top Left: Sundae 2.5" #818, footed, sherbet, no stem 5 oz., Jade. **Bottom Left:** Sugar 2.5" flat, shallow, squat, 2 angular handles, 7 oz., Sunshine (yellow). **Bottom Right:** Vase 6.5", flat, upright (squat in shape), Sepia (cased).

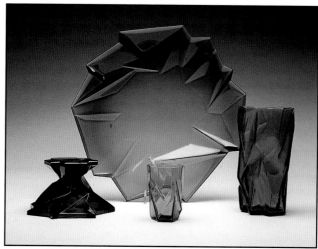

Jungle Green grouping: **Back:** Plate 10" #808, dinner or service. **Front Left:** Candlestick 1-lite 2.6" #805, large foot, no stem w/candle cup. **Center:** Tumbler 2.65" #823, flat, whiskey, 2.5 oz. **Right:** Tumbler 5.5" #814, ice tea, 12 oz.

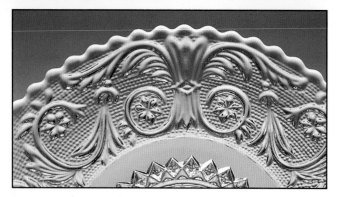

Pattern detail, Sandwich.

Left: Sugar 2.75" #61, footed, individual (no handles), saw tooth edge, 5 oz. **Right:** Creamer 3" #62, footed w/handle, saw tooth edge, individual, 5 oz. **Bottom:** Tray 8" #64, handled, for individual cream/sugar, saw tooth edge.

Left: Candy w/cover 8.75" #102, footed, wafer stem. **Center:** Butter w/cover 8" #85, round bottom w/saw tooth edge, fancy finial (or cheese dish) 5" high. **Right:** Basket 11.5", upright, 2 sides pulled out, pressed handle.

SANDWICH
Duncan & Miller Glass Co.   **Blank #41**   **1924-55**
Color: Crystal
Other Colors: Amber, Chartreuse (yellow-green), Cobalt, Green, Milk, and Ruby

    Sandwich was originally called Lace and later was changed to honor the early glass-making community. This pattern was based on an early pressed pattern produced by Sandwich. A few other companies also made their versions of Sandwich. Duncan's pattern has a six-pointed star in the scroll design. On the bottom of plates, most bowls, and relishes is a ten-pointed star surrounded by a quilted effect. Produced primarily in Crystal, some items can be found in colors.

    The Flower Arranger and Garden epergne have a shallow bowl & center horn. The Flower Arranger also has a pedestal base. This is the same one that is used on the candelabra.

    After Duncan closed, the moulds went to Tiffin, where the pattern was produced for several years in colors. Upon Tiffin's closure, the moulds became property of Lancaster Colony. The Sandwich moulds were used with the Indiana Sandwich moulds to be part of the Tiara Sandwich line in Amber, Pink, Green, and Black.

    A small set of Green can be accumulated. Collectors are on the lookout for the following items to include with their collection: basket, round butter, candelabra, epergne, hurricane, and covered urn.

SANDWICH	**Crystal**
Almond 2.5", individual, nut, saw tooth edge	12
Ashtray 2.75" #92, small, rectangular, saw tooth edge	8
Basket 5.5", flat, shallow w/applied handle, saw tooth edge, candy	68
Basket 6", upright, pressed handle	145
Basket 6.5", w/applied handle, saw tooth edge, candy	85
Basket 11.5", oval, applied handle, saw tooth edge	225
Basket 11.5", upright, 2 sides pulled out, pressed handle	185
Basket 12", star crimped, applied handle, saw tooth edge	275
Bowl 3.5" #94, small, saw tooth edge, fruit or nut	12
Bowl 5" #95, cupped, saw tooth edge, fruit	16
Bowl 5", heart, applied circular handle, saw tooth edge	20
Bowl 5", round, applied circular handle, saw tooth edge	16
Bowl 5.5" #97, round, handle (cup type), saw tooth edge	20
Bowl 5.5" #98, heart, handle (cup type), saw tooth edge	28
Bowl 6" #96, shallow, saw tooth edge, dessert	16
Bowl 6", cupped saw tooth edge, rim grapefruit	20
Bowl 6", heart, applied circular handle, saw tooth edge	24
Bowl 6", round, applied circular handle, saw tooth edge	20
Bowl 6.5", cupped, saw tooth edge, fruit salad	18
Bowl 10", flat, cupped edge, saw tooth edge, shallow lily pond	65
Bowl 10" #41, deep, saw tooth edge, salad	75
Bowl 10", deep, 3 equal sections, saw tooth edge, fruit	125
Bowl 10.5", oblong, shallow, saw tooth edge, Camellia	65
Bowl 11", deep, cupped, saw tooth edge, nut	60
Bowl 11.5" #109, shallow 2.35" high, saw tooth edge, gardenia	58
Bowl 11.5", footed, (large comport shape) ruffled, saw tooth edge, fruit	85
Bowl 11.75" #111, ruffled, saw tooth edge, fruit	60
Bowl 12" #110, flared out, bell shape, saw tooth edge	60
Bowl 12", shallow, slightly cupped, saw tooth edge, ice cream tray, 1.25" high	50
Bowl 12" #42, shallow, cupped, saw tooth edge, salad	48
Bowl 12", oblong 6.75" wide, 3.75" high, saw tooth edge, window box	100
Butter w/cover 7" #84, rectangle, .25 lb.	65
Butter w/cover 8" #85, round bottom w/saw tooth edge, fancy finial (or cheese dish) 5" high	130
Cake salver 11.5" #80, large fancy pedestal, saw tooth edge	145
Cake salver 13" #79, plain pedestal, flat or turned up edge (2 styles)	100
Candelabra 1-lite 10" #124, footed base w/bobeche prisms & candle cup, pair	195
Candelabra 2-lite 5", wafer stem, cornucopia arms bobeches & prisms, pair	195
Candelabra 2-lite 5.5" #123, fancy arms w/plume center, bobeches & prisms, pair	195
Candelabra 3-lite 7", wafer stem, cornucopia arms bobeches & prisms, pair	275
Candelabra 3-lite 10", footed tall stem, 2 candle cups, bobeches & prisms, pair	400
Candelabra 3-lite 16", footed tall stem, 2 candle cups, bobeches & prisms, pair	500
Candlestick 1-lite 4" #121, bell footed, pair	45
Candlestick 2-lite 5" #122, fancy arms, plume center, pair	85
Candlestick 2-lite 5", wafer stem, cornucopia arms, pair	95
Candlestick 3-lite 7", wafer stem, cornucopia arms, pair	125
Candy w/cover 5" #102, flat, squat, round	65
Candy w/cover 7" #100, flat, square, 3 sections	375
Candy w/cover 7.5", low, footed	115
Candy w/cover 8.75" #102, footed, wafer stem	80
Cheese & cracker: comport 3" #81, short stem, 5.5" wide; plate, saw tooth edge, 13"	48
Cigarette box w/cover #92, 3.5" x 2.75" wide, rectangular	45
Cigarette holder 3", footed, cylindrical	32
Coaster 5" #37, or individual plate	10
Comport 2.5" #101, footed, no stem, crimped (looks like a ruffled sundae) 5.5" wide	18
Comport 3", footed, no stem (flared or crimped) candy, 7" wide (2 styles)	30
Comport 4.25", flared bell shape, 5.5" wide, smooth rim	28
Comport 4.5", cone shape or flared, 6" wide (2 styles)	28

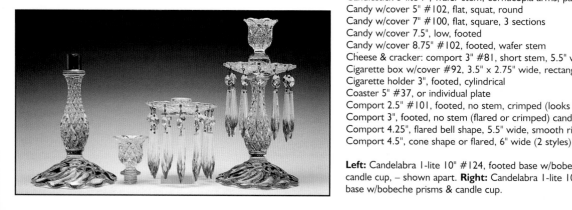

Left: Candelabra 1-lite 10" #124, footed base w/bobeche prisms & candle cup, – shown apart. **Right:** Candelabra 1-lite 10" #124, footed base w/bobeche prisms & candle cup.

Creamer 3" #62, footed w/handle, saw tooth edge, individual, 5 oz.	10
Creamer 4" #66, footed, regular, saw tooth edge, 9 oz.	12
Cruet w/stopper 5.75" #72, flat, oil, 3 oz.	38
Cup & saucer, coffee: cup 2.25" #34, 6 oz.; saucer w/indent 6"	14
Deviled Egg plate 12" #83, round, indents for eggs, saw tooth edge	95
Epergne 9" #106, flat, one horn, garden	145
Epergne 14" #107, pedestal base, one horn, fruit or flower arranger	250
Finger bowl & liner: bowl 4", straight sided; plate 6.5" w/indent, smooth edge	18
Frozen fruit server 5.5" goblet shape, large (used with 5.75" rim liner), smooth edge	45
Goblet 4.25" #3, wafer stem, cocktail, 3 oz.	12
Goblet 4.5" #4, wafer stem, wine, 3 oz.	16
Goblet 5.25" #8, wafer stem, parfait, 4 oz.	32
Goblet 4.25" #10, wafer stem, ice cream or sherbet, 5 oz.	12
Goblet 5.25" #2, wafer stem, saucer champagne, 5 oz.	16
Goblet 6" #1, wafer stem, water, 9 oz.	18
Grapefruit 5.5", footed (use 6 oz. fruit cup as insert) bowl shape, smooth edge	25
Hurricane lamp 15" #124, footed, candle cup/bobeche/prisms/plain chimney, each	175
Mayonnaise 3 piece: bowl 5" #45, footed; liner, saw tooth edge, w/indent 7"; ladle 5.75"	48
Mayonnaise 3 piece: bowl 6", footed; liner, saw tooth edge, w/indent 8"; ladle 5.75"	50
Mayonnaise 4 piece: bowl 6", footed, salad dressing; liner, saw tooth edge, w/indent 8"; 2 ladles 5.75"	68
Pitcher 8" #88, water w/ice lip, 64 oz.	145
Plate 3", individual, jelly or butter, saw tooth edge	8
Plate 6" #25, bread & butter, saw tooth edge	8
Plate 7" #26, dessert, saw tooth edge	10
Plate 8" #27, salad, saw tooth edge	12
Plate 9.5" #28, dinner, saw tooth edge	50
Plate 11.5" #33, handled, saw tooth edge	40
Plate 12.5" #29, torte/service, saw tooth edge	48
Plate 13" #30, torte/service, saw tooth edge	48
Plate 13" #31, small center, turned up edge, cabaret	50
Plate 16" #32, hostess/torte, saw tooth edge	95
Relish 5.5" #46, 2 sections, applied circular handle (2 styles)	20
Relish 6", round, 2 sections, applied circular handle (2 styles)	24
Relish 7" #47, oblong, saw tooth edge, pickle	18
Relish 7" #48, oblong, 2 equal sections, saw tooth edge	24
Relish 10" #49, oblong, saw tooth edge, celery	28
Relish 10" #50, oblong, saw tooth edge, 2 equal sections & celery section	34
Relish 10" #51, round, handled, saw tooth edge, 3 equal sections & celery section	38
Relish 12.5" #52, round, 3 sections, wide patterned border w/saw tooth edge, celery	45
Salt dip 2.5" #93, or individual nut, saw tooth edge	12
Shaker 2.5" #67/68, flat, bullet shape, individual, glass or chrome top, pair	24
Shaker 3.75" #69/70, flat, tear drop shape, glass or chrome top, pair	28
Shaker 4.25" #87, sugar or grated cheese, 13 oz.	75
Sugar 2.75" #61, footed, individual (no handles), saw tooth edge, 5 oz.	10
Sugar 3.25" #65, footed, regular (no handles), saw tooth edge, 9 oz.	12
Syrup 4.5" #86, metal drip cut top, 13 oz.	95
Tray 6" #64, 2-tab handles, for individual shakers, saw tooth edge	12
Tray 8" #64, handled, for individual cream/sugar, saw tooth edge	14
Tray 8" #73, tab handled, for 2 cruets, saw tooth edge	20
Tray 8" #74, tab handled, for shakers/2 cruets, saw tooth edge	24
Tumbler 2.75" #7, footed, sea food/oyster cocktail, 5 oz.	10
Tumbler 3.25" #6, footed, juice, 5 oz.	12
Tumbler 3.4" #13, flat, straight sided, juice, 5 oz.	14
Tumbler 2.5", footed, flared, fruit cup/jello or grapefruit insert, 6 oz.	12
Tumbler 3.25" #14, flat, straight sided, old fashion, 7 oz.	14
Tumbler 4.5" #12, flat, straight sided, water, 9 oz.	16
Tumbler 4.75" #9, footed, water, 9 oz.	18
Tumbler 5.5" #5, footed, ice tea, 12 oz.	20
Tumbler 5.25" #11, flat, straight sided, ice tea, 13 oz.	24
Urn w/cover 12", footed, wafer stem	195
Vase 3", footed, flared & crimped edge	20
Vase 4.5", flat, flared & crimped edge	32
Vase 5", footed, ivy ball, flared & crimped edge	42
Vase 10" #108, footed, straight sided, wafer stem	80

Back row: Deviled Egg plate 12" #83, round, indents for eggs, saw tooth edge. **Front left:** Basket 5.5", flat, shallow w/applied handle, saw tooth edge, candy. **Front right:** Plate 9.5" #28, dinner, saw tooth edge.

Left: Goblet 4.25" #10, wafer stem, ice cream or sherbet, 5 oz. **Center left:** Tumbler 2.75" #7, footed, sea food/oyster cocktail, 5 oz. **Center right:** Goblet 6" #1, wafer stem, water, 9 oz. **Right:** Goblet 4.5" #4, wafer stem, wine, 3 oz.

Green grouping: **Back left:** Plate 8" #27, salad, saw tooth edge. **Back center:** Plate 12.5" #29, torte/service, saw tooth edge. **Front center:** Bowl 6", cupped saw tooth edge, rim grapefruit. **Front center right:** Goblet 4.25" #10, wafer stem, ice cream or sherbet, 5 oz. **Front right:** Goblet 6" #1, wafer stem, water, 9 oz.

Cake salver 11.5" #80, large fancy pedestal, saw tooth edge.

Pattern detail, Shirley.

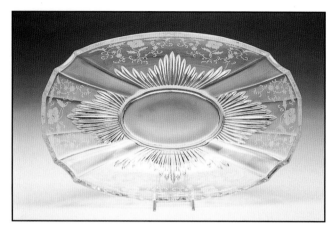

Bowl 12.5" #2545 Flame, oblong w/smooth rim.

Candlestick 1-lite 4" #2496 Baroque, cornucopia flame shape.

Left: Goblet 7.4" #6017 Sceptra, water, 9 oz. **Center:** Goblet 3.6" #6017 Sceptra, oyster cocktail, 4 oz. **Right:** Goblet 4.5" #6017 Sceptra, sherbet, 6 oz.

SHIRLEY
Fostoria Glass Company   Etching #331   1939-69
Main Color: Crystal

Shirley is a new listing to this elegant edition. This was one of several Fostoria etched patterns suggested by collectors. This etched pattern was introduced in 1939 and discontinued in 1957. The etching, #331, features a four petal flower surrounded by a petite garland of leaves. The etched pattern is on the #2496 Baroque, #2350 Pioneer, and #2337. The stemware is found on the #6017 Sceptre.

It is said this etching was named to honor Shirley Temple. We don't know if this is really true or not though. Like several of the other Fostoria patterns, even after they were discontinued, special orders for stems and plates were available for customers until 1969.

SHIRLEY	Crystal
Bonbon 7.4" #2496 Baroque, 3-toed, flared or crimped	48
Bowl 4.6" #2496 Baroque, 3-toed, tri-corn w/1 handle	24
Bowl 5" #2496 Baroque, flared, fruit	28
Bowl 6" #2496 Baroque, 4-toed, tab flame handled, square, sweetmeat	48
Bowl 6.25" #2496 Baroque, 3-toed, flared	28
Bowl 9.5" #2496 Baroque, oval, vegetable	50
Bowl 10" #2496 Baroque, 4-tab feet, rectangle, tab flame handled, shallow, floating garden	75
Bowl 10.75" #2496 Baroque, 4-tab footed, oval, flame handled	85
Bowl 12" #2496 Baroque, flat, round, flared	80
Bowl 12.5" #2545 Flame, oblong w/smooth rim	85
Cake plate 10.25" #2496 Baroque, 2-tab flame handled	68
Candle lustre 1-lite 7.5" #2545 Flame, bobeche & 8 U drop prisms, pair	150
Candelabra 2-lite 6.75" #2545 Flame, ball & flame center, bobeches & 12 "B" prisms, 10.5" spread, pair	295
Candlestick 1-lite 4" #2496 Baroque, cornucopia flame shape, pair	65
Candlestick 1-lite 4.5" #2545 Flame, pair	75
Candlestick 1-lite 5.5" #2496 Baroque, fancy flame stem, pair	75
Candlestick 2-lite 5.25" #2496 Baroque, flame arms, 8" spread, pair	95
Candlestick 2-lite 6.75" #2545 Flame, ball & flame center, 10.25" spread, pair	195
Candy w/cover 6.25" #2496 Baroque, triangular, 3 sections, lid w/flame finial	125
Cheese & cracker #2496 Baroque: comport 3.25", short stem, 5.25" wide; plate w/indent 10.75"	98
Comport 4.75" #2496 Baroque, fancy flame stem, flared 5.5" wide	45
Cream soup & liner #2496 Baroque: bowl 4.75", footed w/2 handles, 9 oz.; saucer w/indent 7.5"	60
Creamer 3.1" #2496 Baroque, footed, individual, 4 oz.	25
Creamer 3.75" #2496 Baroque, collar footed, regular, 7.5 oz.	28
Cup & saucer, coffee #2350 1/2: cup 2.6", footed, coffee, 6 oz.; saucer w/indent 5.75"	38
Finger bowl 4.5" #766, (blown) flared	38
Goblet 3.9" #6017 Sceptra, cordial, .75 oz.	36
Goblet 5.5" #6017 Sceptra, wine, 3 oz.	30
Goblet 4.9" #6017 Sceptra, cocktail, 3.5 oz.	24
Goblet 5.9" #6017 Sceptra, claret, 4 oz.	30
Goblet 3.6" #6017 Sceptra, oyster cocktail, 4 oz.	12
Goblet 4.5" #6017 Sceptra, sherbet, 6 oz.	14
Goblet 5.5" #6017 Sceptra, champagne, 6 oz.	22
Goblet 7.4" #6017 Sceptra, water, 9 oz.	28
Ice bucket 4.5" #2496 Baroque, flat, squat, chrome handle, 6.5" wide	125
Mayonnaise 2 piece #2496 Baroque: bowl 5", flared, crimped, 3.5" high; liner w/indent 6.5"	75
Pitcher 8.9" #6011, footed with no ice lips, 53 oz.	295
Plate 6" #2337, bread & butter	8
Plate 7" #2337, salad	10
Plate 8" #2337, lunch	18
Plate 9" #2337, dinner	45
Plate 14" #2496 Baroque, small center, turned up edge, cabaret	85
Platter 12.5" #2496 Baroque, oval	135
Relish 6" (or sweetmeat) #2496 Baroque, 4-tab feet, tab flame handled, 2 sections, square	48
Relish 8" #2496 Baroque, oval pickle	38
Relish 10" #2496 Baroque, 4-tab feet, tab flame handled, oblong, 2 equal sections & celery section	60
Relish 10.75", oval celery	48
Sauce 2 piece #2496 Baroque: bowl 6.5", oblong, tab flame handled; liner 6.75"	98
Shakers 2.75" #2496 Baroque, regular straight sided, clear glass top, pair	150
Sugar 2.9" #2496 Baroque, footed, individual, 4 oz.	25
Sugar 3.6" #2496 Baroque, collar footed, regular, 7.5 oz.	28
Tray 6.5" #2496 Baroque, rectangle tab flame handled for individual creamer & sugar	28
Tray 8.25" #2496 Baroque, flat, 3-toed, turned up edge, tidbit	58
Tumbler 4.75" #6017 Sceptra, footed juice, 5 oz.	18
Tumbler 5.5" #6017 Sceptra, footed water, 9 oz.	24
Tumbler 6" #6017 Sceptra, footed, ice tea, 12 oz.	36
Tumbler 6.5" #6017 Sceptra, footed soda, 14 oz.	45
Vase 10" #2545, footed, flared	245

SPIRAL FLUTES

Duncan & Miller **Blank #40** **1924-30s**

Main Colors: Green, and Pink

Other Colors: Amber, Crystal, and Crystal w/stain

Spiral Flutes is another pattern that was requested to add to this edition. It was introduced in 1924. Originally called Colonial Flutes, Line #40 was later renamed Spiral Flutes. A complete collection could be gathered in crystal, pink, green or amber. Both pink & green are the collectors' favorite colors. Neither crystal nor amber draw much attention from collectors and are left languishing on shelves.

SPIRAL FLUTES	Green Pink
Almond 2.25", footed, wafer stem	12
Bowl 3.75", bouillon, soup, footed	16
Bowl 4.25", finger	6
Bowl 4.75", cream soup, footed	14
Bowl 5", nappy, plain center	6
Bowl 6", plain loop handle	24
Bowl 6", plain loop handles, covered	48
Bowl 6.5", grapefruit, plain center	10
Bowl 6.75", rim soup	16
Bowl 7", serving	14
Bowl 8", serving	18
Bowl 9", serving	28
Bowl 10", flared, small center	42
Bowl 10.25", oval, vegetable	40
Bowl 11.5", flared, collar footed	95
Bowl 12", flared, plain center	36
Bowl 12", console, cupped up	42
Candlestick 1-lite 3.5", dome foot, wafer stem, pair	59
Candlestick 1-lite 7.5", pair	125
Candlestick 1-lite 9.25", dome foot, pair	145
Candlestick 1-lite 11.5", pair	195
Candy w/cover 7.75", footed, wafer knob finial	135
Cigarette Holder 4", wafer stem	45
Comport 4.5", wafer stem	18
Compote 6.5", wafer stem	24
Creamer 3", flat, 24 point star in bottom	8
Cruet oil bottle, 6 oz.	225
Cup & saucer, after dinner: cup 2.75"; saucer 5" w/indent	24
Cup & saucer, coffee: cup 2.5"; saucer 6.25" w/indent	12
Goblet 3.75", wine, 3.5 oz.	18
Goblet 5.45", parfait, 4. 5 oz., wafer stem, plain rim	18
Goblet 3.8", sherbet, 5 oz., wafer stem, plain rim	8
Goblet 4.75", champagne, 6 oz., wafer stem, plain rim	12
Goblet 6.25", water, 7 oz., wafer stem, plain rim	20
Ice bucket 6" tall, metal handle	65
Mayonnaise 4.5", footed, plain rim, wafer stem	20
Pitcher 10.5" tall, tankard style	165
Plate 6.25", bread & butter	2
Plate 7.5", salad	4
Plate 9.35", lunch	5
Plate 10.5", dinner	18
Plate 14", sandwich	20
Platter 11", oval	30
Platter 12.75", oval	45
Relish 11", celery, oval	18
Sugar 3", flat, 24 point star in the bottom	8
Tumbler 3.2", footed, cocktail, 2.5 oz.	8
Tumbler 4.4", footed, juice, 5.5 oz.	12
Tumbler 4.75", flat, soda, 7 oz.	30
Tumbler 5", footed, water, 7 oz.	10
Tumbler 4.25", flat, water, 8 oz.	28
Tumbler 5.25", footed, 9 oz.	22
Tumbler 5.6", flat, ice tea, 11 oz.	65
Vase 6.25", flared, footed	24
Vase 8.5", flared, footed	32
Vase 10.25", flared, footed	38
Window Box 10" long, 5.5" wide, 4-footed	350

Green grouping: **Back left**: Bowl 6.75", rim soup. **Back right:** Platter 12.75", oval. **Front left**: Bowl 4.25", finger. **Front right:** Relish 11", celery, oval.

Green grouping: **Back**: Plate 10.5", dinner. **Front left**: Cup & saucer, coffee: cup 2.5", saucer 6.25" w/indent. **Front center:** Tumbler 4.75", flat, soda, 7 oz. **Front right:** Tumbler 5.6", flat, ice tea, 11 oz.

Green grouping: **Left:** Candlestick 1-lite 9.25", dome foot. **Right:** Ice bucket 6" tall, metal handle.

Green grouping: **Back:** Bowl 6.5", grapefruit, plain center. **Front left:** Goblet 3.8", sherbet, 5 oz., wafer stem, plain rim. **Center:** Tumbler 5.25", footed, 9 oz.; **Right:** Pitcher 8.5" tall, flat.

Left: Coaster 4", six raised rays. Right: Plate 8.5", lunch.

Left: Mustard 3 piece: 3.75" collar footed jar; cover w/finial. Right: Mayonnaise 2 piece: bowl 5.5", round; liner w/indent 7.1", Golden Glow color was made from 1935-37.

Left: Creamer 3.4", footed, trophy shaped handle, individual, 4.5 oz. Center: Jelly w/cover 7.25", footed, fancy concave stem; lid w/finial. Right: Sugar 2.75", trophy shaped handles, individual, 4.5 oz.

Bowl 11" wide, 13.5" long counting handles, large plume handled, oval, console.

SUNRAY
Fostoria Glass Company Blank #2510 1935-44
Main Color: Crystal
Other Colors: Amber, Azure (blue), Crystal, Empire Green, Golden Glow, Topaz (yellow), and Ruby

This clean, sleek pattern features 4 ribs alternating with a wide panel. Sunray is primaril a crystal pattern. Only a very few pieces were produced in any of the colors and a set cannot b built. Some of the pieces of Sunray can be found with rays that are frosted. The name for th frosted pattern is "Glacier". Tiffin made a similar pattern that they called Spectra.

The oval decanter is more elusive than the rectangular shaped one that is most ofte seen. Also there is a small handled nappy and a square decanter that look similar to Sunray, bu the quality is not as fine. The maker for these items is unknown.

SUNRAY	Crystal
Almond 1.5", footed, flared, sherbet shape, individual, nut	15
Ashtray 2.4", round, individual	10
Ashtray, 3", shallow, 4 cigarette rests, square	14
Bonbon 6.5", shallow, open handled, oblong	16
Bonbon 7", 3-toed, flared	18
Bowl 5", flat, low, flared, fruit	12
Bowl 5", round w/1 open handle	14
Bowl 5", square w/1 open handle	16
Bowl 5", tri-corn w/1 open handle	18
Bowl 6", open handled, 2 sections, oblong, sweetmeat	35
Bowl 9.5", oval, vegetable	40
Bowl 9.5", round deep, slightly flared, vegetable	32
Bowl 11" wide, 13.5" long counting handles, large plume handled, oval, console	58
Bowl 12", deep, cupped, 4.25" high, salad	48
Bowl 13", rolled edge, 3.5" high, console	48
Butter or cheese w/cover 6", base w/tab plume handles, rectangular, 3.4" wide, lid w/tab finial	38
Candelabra 2-lite 6.5", center circle w/bobeches &, prisms, 8" spread, pair	185
Candlestick 1-lite 3", round base, wafer stem, pair	40
Candlestick 1-lite 5.5", round base, fancy concave stem, pair	55
Candlestick 2-lite 6.5", center circle, rays on arms, 7" spread, pair	85
Candy w/cover 4", tab handled; lid w/finial (also a onion soup)	55
Candy w/cover 7.75", footed, no stem, tab handled, .5 lb.; lid w/finial	65
Cigarette box w/cover 4.75" #2510 1/2, rectangle, 3.4" wide	65
Cigarette jar w/cover 3.9", cylinder shape, lid w/finial	50
Coaster 4", six raised rays	8
Comport 4.25", fancy concave stem, flared, 5" wide	20
Comport 6", flared, jelly, 7.25" wide	24
Cream soup & liner: cup 4.75", tab handled, 10 oz.; saucer w/indent 7.5"	38
Creamer 3.4", footed, trophy shaped handle, individual, 4.5 oz.	10
Creamer 4", footed, trophy shaped handle, regular, 8 oz.	12
Cruet w/stopper 4.75", open handle, oil bottle, 3 oz.	48
Cup & saucer, coffee: cup 2.6", collar footed, 6 oz.; saucer w/indent 6"	12
Decanter w/flat, round stopper 8.25", oval liquor, 18 oz.	95
Decanter w/stopper 9.1" #2510 1/2, rectangle bottle, 26 oz.; square stopper	125
Frozen dessert 2.25" high, flat, deep, custard shape	15
Goblet 3.25", fruit cocktail, 3.5 oz.	12
Goblet 3", cone shaped, oyster cocktail, 4 oz.	14
Goblet 4.9", claret, 4.5 oz.	24
Goblet 3.5", sherbet, 5.5 oz.	10
Goblet 5.75", water, 9 oz.	20
Ice bucket 4.25", flat, 6.15" wide, chrome handle	85
Jelly w/cover 7.25", footed, fancy concave stem; lid w/finial	45
Mayonnaise 3 piece: bowl 5.5", round; liner w/indent 7.1"; ladle	58
Mustard 3 piece: 3.75" collar footed jar; cover w/finial; spoon	48
Pitcher 5", collar foot, cereal w/o ice lip, 16 oz.	45
Pitcher 7.5", water jug w/ice lip, 64 oz.	100
Pitcher 8.5", water jug w/o ice lip, 64 oz.	75
Plate 6", bread & butter	6
Plate 6", flat, round, 1 open handle, lemon server	12
Plate 7.25", salad or dessert	10
Plate 8.5", lunch	14
Plate 9.5", dinner	32
Plate 11", small center, cupped up edge, chop/torte	35
Plate 12", flat w/small center, sandwich	38
Plate 15", small center, cupped up edge, chop/torte	50
Plate 16", flat w/small center, deep salad bowl liner	65
Relish 6", open handled, oblong, pickle	22
Relish 6.5", 3 open handles, 3 equal sections	28
Relish 8", 2 open handles, 4 equal sections	30
Relish 8", 4 open handles, 4 equal sections	32
Relish 10", open handled, oblong, celery	34
Relish 10", open handled, oblong, 2 sections	36
Salt dip 1.75", flat, triangular	18
Shaker 2.25" #2510 1/2, flat base, individual, pair	45

aker 4", flat, rounded base, pair	50
gar 2.75", trophy shaped handles, individual, 4.5 oz.	10
gar 3.75", footed, trophy shaped handles, regular, 8 oz.	12
ay 6.5", rectangle, tab plume handled, individual cream/sugar	15
ay 7", flat, open handled, oblong	24
ay 8.5", tab plume handled, elongated clover leaf shape, condiment	50
ay 10", square	48
ay 10.5", rectangle (holds liquor decanter & 6 whiskeys)	65
mbler 2.25", flat, straight sided, whiskey, 2 oz.	16
mbler, 3.5", flat, straight sided, juice, 5 oz.	14
mbler 4.6", footed, juice, 5 oz.	16
mbler, 3.5", flat, straight sided, old fashion, 6 oz.	16
mbler 4.1", flat, straight sided, water, 9 oz.	22
mbler 4.75", footed, water, 9 oz.	22
mbler 5.1", flat, straight sided, beverage, 13 oz.	25
mbler 5.25", footed, beverage, 13 oz.	25
se 3.25", small collar foot, round rose bowl	35
se 5", small collar foot, round rose bowl	40
se 5.25", squat, straight sided, crimped, sweet pea shape	42
se 6", flat, straight sided, crimped	48
se 7", flat, straight sided, flared	55
se 9", square footed, short concave stem, slightly flared	60
se 9", squat, straight sided, crimped, sweet pea shape	70

Left: Ice bucket 4.25", flat, 6.15" wide, chrome handle. **Right:** Decanter w/stopper 9.1" #2510 1/2, rectangle bottle, 26 oz.; square stopper.

eft: Candy w/cover 7.75", footed, no stem, tab handled, .5 lb.; lid w/finial. **Center:** andlestick 1-lite 3", round base, wafer stem. **Right:** Goblet 5.75", water, 9 oz., Glacier.

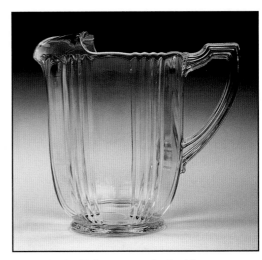

Pitcher 7.5", water jug w/ice lip, 64 oz.

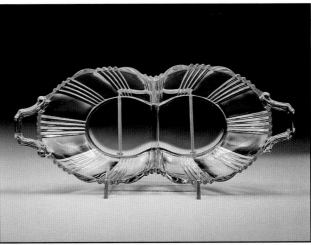

Relish 10", open handled, oblong, celery.

eft: Salt dip 1.75", flat, triangular. **Center:** Candy w/cover 4", tab handled; lid w/finial (also n onion soup). **Right:** Ashtray 2.4", round, individual.

Pattern Detail, Sunrise Medallion.

Left: Goblet 7.5" #7664, braided stem, cafe parfait, 5 oz., Rose (pink).
Center: Goblet 6.25" #7630, lady leg stem, saucer champagne, 6.5 oz., Crystal. **Right:** Goblet 7.8" #7630, lady leg stem, water, 9 oz., Crystal.

Blue grouping: **Left:** Goblet 2.5" #2941, collar foot (no stem) oyster cocktail, 3.5 oz. **Center:** Goblet 5.1" #7630, lady leg stem, cordial, 1.5 oz. **Right:** Goblet 5" #7630, lady leg stem, sherbet, 5.5 oz.

SUNRISE MEDALLION

Morgantown Glass Works   Etching #758   1930s
Colors: Blue, Crystal, Green, and Rose (pink)

Sunrise Medallion features a girl dancing inside a medallion and looks like she is reachin for something. The Queen Anne, #7664 stem is the most attractive of all of the stems a features a braided effect. The #7654 1/2 Lorna goblet has a flat-bottomed bowl with a ri tapering up and out. The stem has a spiral twist to it. The #7665 1/2 Laura goblet has a f bottom, cone-shaped bowl with also a twist to the stem. The lady leg stem is on blank #763 Morgantown also made a sister etched pattern called Saranac Sunrise. This features the sam girl in an irregular oval that is surrounded by leaves.

Blue seems to be the most sought-after color. A hard item to find is the pitcher. The mo common items are the sherbets & water goblets.

SUNRISE MEDALLION

	Crystal	Green Rose (pink)	Blue
Creamer 4" #48, flat, upright (tall) rib optic, low applied handle, 6 oz.	85	165	225+
Finger bowl & liner: bowl 4.4" #2940, flat; plate w/indent 6.5"			95
Goblet 5.1" #7630, lady leg stem, cordial, 1.5 oz.	65	135	175
Goblet #7654 1/2, spiral/ribbed/spiral stem, cordial, 1.5 oz.	95		
Goblet 5" #7664, braided stem, cordial, 1.5 oz.	85	165	275
Goblet #7630, lady leg stem, wine, 2.75 oz.	28	58	75
Goblet #7654 1/2, spiral/ribbed/spiral stem, wine, 2.75 oz.	40		
Goblet #7664, braided stem, wine, 2.75 oz.	38	75	95
Goblet #7630, lady leg stem, liquor cocktail, 3 oz.	26	50	65
Goblet 2.5" #2941, collar foot (no stem) oyster cocktail, 3.5 oz.			125
Goblet #7654 1/2, spiral/ribbed/spiral stem, cocktail, 3.5 oz.	35		
Goblet 5.5" #7664, braided stem, liquor cocktail, 3.5 oz.	30	60	80
Goblet #7665 1/2, spiral/ribbed/spiral stem, cocktail, 3.5 oz.	35		
Goblet #7630, lady leg stem, cafe parfait, 5 oz.	46	92	120
Goblet 7.5" #7664, braided stem, cafe parfait, 5 oz.	58	115	150
Goblet 5" #7630, lady leg stem, sherbet, 5.5 oz.	26	50	68
Goblet #7665 1/2, spiral/ribbed/spiral stem, sherbet, 5.5 oz.	35		
Goblet #7665 1/2, spiral/ribbed/spiral stem, saucer champagne, 5.5 oz.	40		
Goblet #7654 1/2, spiral/ribbed/spiral stem, sherbet, 6.5 oz.	35		
Goblet 5.25" #7664, braided stem, sherbet, 6.5 oz.	30	60	80
Goblet 6.25" #7630, lady leg stem, saucer champagne, 6.5 oz.	28	62	75
Goblet #7654 1/2, spiral/ribbed/spiral stem, sau champagne, 6.5 oz.	42		
Goblet 6.75" #7664, braided stem, saucer champagne, 6.5 oz.	35	70	95
Goblet 8" #7664, braided stem, tall champagne, 6.5 oz.	38	72	98
Goblet 2.75" #7664, collar foot (no stem) flared seafood, 7 oz.	42	85	110
Goblet 7.8" #7630, lady leg stem, water, 9 oz.	52	98	135
Goblet #7665 1/2, spiral/ribbed/spiral stem, water, 9 oz.	60		
Goblet #7654 1/2, spiral/ribbed/spiral stem, water, 10 oz.	62		
Goblet 8.5" #7664, braided stem, water, 10 oz.	42	82	110
Mug #9069, footed (deep bell shaped) low applied handle, 9 oz.	55	115	145
Mug #9069, footed (deep bell shaped) low applied handle, 12 oz.	62	125	160
Pitcher 9" #37, footed, cone shape w/o ice lip, applied handle, 48 oz.	215	395	550
Plate 6.5" #1511, bread & butter	5	15	20
Plate 7.5" #1511, salad	10	24	32
Plate 8.5" #1511, lunch	12	26	35
Plate 10.5" #1511, dinner	72	145	195
Sugar 2.5" #48, flat, squat, rib optic, low applied handles, 6 oz.	85	165	225+
Tumbler 3.4" #9074, footed, cone (green foot) whiskey, 2.5 oz.	125		
Tumbler 4.25" #9074, footed, cone (green foot) juice, 6 oz.	62		
Tumbler 4.6" #9074, footed, cone (green foot) lunch, 8 oz.	72		
Tumbler 4.25" #7606, flat, 2 (pink) stacked disc base, rib optic	200		
Tumbler 4.25" #7664, flat, slight tapering out to flared top	68		175
Tumbler #9069, footed (deep bell shaped) water, 9 oz.	28	60	72
Tumbler 5.4" #9074, bell footed, cone (green foot) ice tea, 11 oz.	82		
Tumbler #9069, footed (deep bell shaped) ice tea, 12 oz.	30	62	80
Vase 6" #7602, flip shape, rib optic	100	225	275
Vase 8" #45, footed, flared top, bud vase	70	145	
Vase 10" #45, footed, spiral optic, flared top, bud vase	82	165	
Vase 10" #24, footed, necked in, crimped top, bud vase	72	145	190
Vase 10" #36, footed, short stem, tapering in, flared top, bud vase	72	145	190
Vase 10" #36, footed, short stem, tapering in, crimped top, bud vase	75	150	195
Vase 10" #53, footed, cone bottom, tall concave sides, flared top		110	148
Vase 10" #53, footed, cone bottom, tall concave sides, crimped top		120	160

TALLY HO

Cambridge Glass Company **Blank #1402** **1932-40s**

Main Colors: Amethyst, Carmen, Cobalt, and Emerald Green
Other Colors: Amber and Crystal

Tally Ho features a cluster of tight rings. This is a fairly heavy pattern. There are two very distinctive types of stems for this pattern, even though they have the same number. The pressed goblets have concentric rings coming up from the bottom of the bowl. On the blown goblets, there are wafers on the stem that surround an oval disk. Imperial Hunt Scene is a favorite etch on the pressed goblets, while Elaine is found on the blown goblets. Note, Amber & Crystal are priced at 50% of the Emerald Green listed price. Blown stemware seems to be more of a challenge for collectors than the pressed ones.

This is another pattern that can be mixed with other collections to set a very attractive table. Many collectors are using pieces from this pattern to compliment their etched pattern. Crystal dinner plates are great to use with the Elaine pattern and a whole lot cheaper. Favorite items of collectors are: the three section bowl, cocktail shaker, cookie jar, punch bowl, tankard, and vase.

Carmen (ruby) grouping: **Left:** Mug #78, flat, punch or Tom & Jerry, 6 oz. **Center:** Punch bowl 13" #77, terraced footed, large, deep. **Right:** Mug #78, flat, punch or Tom & Jerry, 6 oz.

Hat 10" #139, topper w/2 sides turned down, Cobalt.

TALLY HO	Amethyst Green	Carmen Cobalt
Ashtray 4", flat, round w/4 rests	18	28
Ashtray 4", round, center handled w/4 rests	28	45
Ashtray base 4", round w/ashtray (makes 2 piece ash well)	38	60
Bowl 4.5" #30, footed, shallow, fruit	16	24
Bowl 6" #89, handled	18	26
Bowl 6.25", open handled, flared	16	24
Bowl 6.5" #32, flared, rim grapefruit	18	28
Bowl 6.5", footed, cereal	15	20
Bowl 6.5", open handled, sweetmeat	28	32
Bowl 8", cupped, vegetable	30	42
Bowl 8.5" #131, deep, 3 equal sections	55	72
Bowl 9", cupped, vegetable	32	45
Bowl 9", shallow (pan shape) cupped	35	48
Bowl 10", shallow, fruit	32	52
Bowl 10", shallow (pan shape) cupped	30	50
Bowl 10.25", very shallow (pan shape) open handled	32	52
Bowl 10.4" #122, deep, 3 equal sections	65	85
Bowl 10.5" #70, flat, deep, salad	38	55
Bowl 10.5" #64, footed, shallow, fruit	35	48
Bowl 10.5" #128, fruit or salad	38	55
Bowl 11" #88, flared, shallow, salad	42	60
Bowl 12.5" #125, flat, rim fruit	45	68
Bowl 12.5" #127, flared, rim fruit	45	68
Bowl 13.5" #132, flat, shallow, salad	40	58
Bowl 17", shallow (pan shape) cupped	45	60
Candelabra 1-lite 6.5" #81, fancy stem, bobeche & prisms, pair	165	200
Candlestick 1-lite 5" #76, square base, pair	65	85
Candlestick 1-lite 6.5" #80, fancy stem, pair	75	98
Cheese & cracker: comport #124, short stem, cupped, 5.5" wide; plate 11.5", handled	55	75
Cheese & cracker: comport #101, short stem, 9" wide; plate 13.5"	75	95
Cigarette holder, footed, oval	42	60
Coaster 4" #47, round, 8 raised rays	14	18
Cocktail shaker w/stopper, footed, handled, chrome top, 50 oz.	125	195
Cocktail shaker w/stopper, footed, no handle, chrome top, 50 oz.	100	165
Comport 3.6", short stem, cupped, 4.4" wide	24	35
Comport #66, fancy stem, flared, 6" wide	32	45
Comport #67, cupped, 6.5" wide	34	48
Comport, short stem (deep bowl) 7" wide	38	56
Comport, short stem (deep bowl) 8" wide	42	60
Cookie jar w/cover, (or pretzel jar) w/chrome handle	125	195
Creamer #33, footed, regular, 6 oz.	16	24
Cup 2.4" #140, flat, handled punch, 5 oz.	16	24
Cup & saucer, coffee: cup 2.5" #19, footed, 7 oz.; saucer w/indent 5.9"	18	28
Decanter w/stopper 9.25" #38, flat, cylindrical, no handle, 34 oz.	65	85
Decanter w/stopper 9.25" #39, flat, cylindrical, handled, 34 oz.	75	98
Finger bowl & liner: bowl 5" #14, deep; plate w/indent 6.5"	24	32
Frappe cocktail 5", low footed w/liner	22	32
Frappe cocktail, high footed w/liner	25	36
Goblet #13 (pressed), cordial, 1 oz.	35	50
Goblet (blown), cordial, 1 oz.	42	60
Goblet #12 (pressed), wine, 2.5 oz.	22	32
Goblet (blown), wine, 2.5 oz.	28	40
Goblet #10 (pressed), high liquor cocktail, 3 oz.	18	24
Goblet 6" (blown), liquor cocktail, 4 oz.	25	36
Goblet #11 (pressed) oyster cocktail, 4 oz.	14	20
Goblet #9 (pressed), claret, 4.5 oz.	20	28
Goblet (blown), claret, 4.5 oz.	28	40
Goblet (blown), oyster cocktail, 4.5 oz.	15	22
Goblet #20 (pressed), belled sherbet, 4.5 oz.	12	18

Pitcher 9.6" #50, tankard, straight sided, 74 oz., Amethyst.

Ice bucket 5.8" #52, chrome handle, Emerald Green.

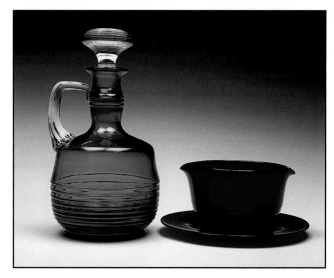

Left side: Shaker 3.25" #116, flat, clear glass top, pair, Cobalt. **Back row:** Bowl 10.25", very shallow (pan shape) open handled, Emerald Green. **Front center left:** Mug 2", flat, handled, barrel shape, whiskey, 2.5 oz., Amethyst. **Front center right:** Goblet 3.75" (pressed), short stem, ice cream, 8 oz., Carmen (ruby). **Front right:** Cup & saucer, coffee: cup 2.5" #19, footed, 7 oz.; saucer w/indent 5.9", Cobalt.

Left: Goblet 3.75" (pressed), short stem, ice cream, 8 oz., Carmen (ruby). **Center:** Goblet 6" (blown), liquor cocktail, 4 oz., Crystal stem/foot & Amber bowl. **Right:** Goblet 6.5" (blown), saucer champagne, 8 oz., Crystal stem/foot & Amber bowl.

Left: Decanter w/stopper 9.25" #39, flat, cylindrical, handled, 34 oz., Emerald Green & Crystal handle/stopper. **Right:** Mayonnaise 2 piece: bowl 4.5" #16, two spouted; #17 liner w/indent 7", Cobalt.

Goblet #8 (pressed), low tomato/orange juice, 5 oz.	18	24
Goblet #7 (pressed), tall tomato/orange juice, 6 oz.	20	28
Goblet (blown), sherbet, 6 oz.	12	18
Goblet #6 (pressed), sherbet, 6.5 oz.	14	20
Goblet #5 (pressed), saucer champagne, 7.5 oz.	18	24
Goblet 6.5" (blown), saucer champagne, 8 oz.	20	28
Goblet 3.75" (pressed), short stem, ice cream, 8 oz.	18	24
Goblet #4 (pressed), lunch water, 10 oz.	22	32
Goblet 6.3" #3 (pressed), dinner water, 10 oz.	22	32
Goblet (blown), water, 10 oz.	24	34
Goblet 6.25" #2 (pressed), ice tea, 14 oz.	28	40
Goblet 6.9" #1 (pressed), jumbo, 18 oz.	35	50
Hat 10" #139, topper w/2 sides turned down	150	225
Ice bucket 5.8" #52, chrome handle	65	85
Iced fruit 6", or salad service w/liner	30	42
Iced fruit 7", or salad service w/liner	32	45
Ladle #111, side spouted punch	65	85
Mayonnaise 2 piece: bowl 4.5" #16, two spouted; #17 liner w/indent 7"	48	65
Mayonnaise bowl #96, footed, salad dressing, use w/Sunday nite supper 18" plate	75	115
Mayonnaise 2 piece #133: bowl 4.75" flat, salad dressing, 5.75" wide; liner w/indent	58	82
Mayonnaise 2 piece: bowl #137, 2 spouted, salad dressing; liner w/indent	58	78
Mayonnaise bowl 5.75" #95, footed, salad dressing	35	50
Mug 2", flat, handled, barrel shape, whiskey, 2.5 oz.	22	32
Mug #78, flat, punch or Tom & Jerry, 6 oz.	20	28
Mug #35, handled, straight sided, stein, 12 oz.	32	45
Mug #36, convex sided, applied handle, stein, 14 oz.	35	50
Pitcher 9.6" #50, tankard, straight sided, 74 oz.	185	245
Pitcher 9", water jug, 88 oz.	225	285
Plate 6" #21, bread & butter	10	16
Plate 7" #99, handled, lemon server	18	28
Plate 7" #138, dessert or salad	14	20
Plate 8" #23, salad	16	24
Plate 9.5" #24, lunch or small dinner	35	50
Plate 10.5" #25, large dinner	45	60
Plate 11.5" #34, handled, sandwich	40	58
Plate 13" #126, small center, turned up edge, cabaret	42	60
Plate 14" #104, w/4" indent in center	40	58
Plate 14" #26, chop plate	42	60
Plate 17.5" #102, small center, turned up edge, cabaret	48	70
Plate 18" #119, footed, week end supper	50	75
Punch bowl 13" #77, terraced footed, large, deep	195	400
Punch bowl liner 17.5" #29, or Sunday nite supper plate	55	75
Relish 6" #90, handled, 2 sections	20	28
Relish 8" #91, 2-handled, 3 sections	30	38
Relish 10" #92, handled, 4 sections	32	42
Relish 12" #94, oval, scalloped, celery	30	38
Shaker 3.25" #116, flat, clear glass top, pair	65	85
Sugar #33, footed, regular, 6 oz.	16	24
Tray 6", footed, low, mint	20	28
Tray 6", footed, high, mint	22	32
Tumbler #40 (pressed), flat, whiskey, 2.5 oz.	34	48
Tumbler (blown), footed, wine, 3 oz.	22	32
Tumbler #41 (pressed), flat, juice, 5 oz.	30	40
Tumbler (blown), footed, juice, 5 oz.	24	34
Tumbler #42 (pressed), flat, old fashion, 7 oz.	30	40
Tumbler #46 (pressed), flat, table water, 10 oz.	32	42
Tumbler #43 (pressed), flat, tall water, 10 oz.	34	45
Tumbler (blown), footed, ice tea (low bowl) 12 oz.	30	40
Tumbler (blown), footed, ice tea (tall bowl) 12 oz.	30	40
Tumbler (blown), footed, beverage, 16 oz.	34	45
Tumbler (blown), brandy inhaler (low bowl)	36	50
Tumbler (blown), brandy inhaler (tall bowl)	45	60
Vase 12", footed, shouldered & flared	145	185

Mayonnaise bowl 4.75" #133: flat, salad dressing, 5.75" wide, Emerald Green.

Duncan & Miller Glass Co.   Blank #301   1930s-55

Main Color: Crystal
Other Colors: Crystal with colored handles

Tear Drop utilized miniature hobnails as the basis for the design. It is reminiscent of early American pressed glass, but yet has the brilliance of elegant glassware. This is fire polished crystal with attention to detail by the third generation Duncan family artisans. This was another extensive pattern for Duncan & Miller, with many different serving pieces made. Time stands still for this pattern, as it fits with any fashion or time period perfectly. The pattern was designed by Robert A. May. The pattern was only made in Crystal. Considering that most pieces are reasonably priced, it is a fine choice for a beginning collector. If you put stemware & some table pieces with a china pattern, this would let you set a very elegant table. A few items can be found with transparent colored handles. An unlisted pitcher was discovered and is pictured here.

The #5300 & #5301 are the numbers given to the lead blown stemware for this pattern. The small divided relish and stemware seem to be abundant in this pattern. We finally had the opportunity to photograph the elusive icer.

Note that the round, divided relish has been reproduced by Gillinder Glass Company in an Alexandrite-like color and several other colors. It is only marked with a paper label.

EAR DROP	Crystal
Ashtray 3.25" #85, individual, 3 cigarette holes on edge w/1 rest	6
Ashtray 5" #86, oblong, beaded top edge w/2-tab cigarette rests	8
Basket 10", bowl, ball handles, turned up	48
Basket 11.5", applied handle, crimped, add $50 for colored handle	85
Basket 12", applied handle, oval, 9.25" tall, add $50 for colored handle	95
Bonbon 6" #90, four - graduated ball tab handles	15
Bowl 5" #87, shallow fruit	8
Bowl 5" #89, one - ball tab handle	10
Bowl 5.5", ball tab handled, oval, candy	20
Bowl 5.5", ball tab handled, star crimped, sweetmeat	24
Bowl 6" #88, shallow fruit	10
Bowl 7", cereal	12
Bowl 7", ball tab handled	12
Bowl 7", ball tab handled, star crimped, sweetmeat	35
Bowl 7.5", ball tab handled, oval, candy basket	18
Bowl 7.5" #91, one - ball tab handle, heart shape, candy	20
Bowl 9" #103, flat, deep, salad	32
Bowl 9.5", ball tab handled, vegetable	28
Bowl 10" #104, flared, fruit	30
Bowl 10", ball tab handled, 3 styles (diamond, square, & star crimped)	38
Bowl 10.5" #105, flat, deep, salad (touraine shape)	48
Bowl 11", collar footed, deep, salad	54
Bowl 11", pedestal footed, cupped, fruit	55
Bowl 11.5" #106, crimped, 4.25" high, fruit or flower	45
Bowl 11.5" #107, flared, 3" high, fruit or flower	38
Bowl 11.5", pedestal footed, deep, flared, fruit	45
Bowl 12" #108, shallow, 2" high, 4 - ball tab handles	48
Bowl 12" #113, flared, console	42
Bowl 12", footed w/short stem, star crimped, 5" high, fruit (comport shaped)	50
Bowl 12", leaf & ball tab handled, oval, console	60
Bowl 12" #110, shallow, salad	45
Bowl 13" #111, very shallow, turned up edge, gardenia	38
Butter w/cover 6" #81: oblong base, ball tab handled, .25 lb.; lid - round open beaded finial	35
Cake salver 13", pedestal footed, short stem, 3.5" high	60
Candelabra 2-lite 7", beaded edge on arms, large ball center, bobeches & prisms, pair	175
Candelabra 2-lite 7" #123, curled arms w/beaded circle center, bobeches & prisms, pair	195
Candlestick 1-lite 4", bell footed, ball candle cup, pair	32
Candlestick 1-lite 4" #121, ball stem, 3 balls on each side, pair	45
Candlestick 2-lite 6", beaded edge on arms, large ball center, 9" spread, pair	75
Candlestick 2-lite 6" #122, curled arms w/beaded circle center, 9" spread, pair	95
Candy w/cover 7", round, flat, ball tab handled, ball finial	50
Candy w/cover 7", round, flat, ball tab handled, 2 sections, ball finial	60
Candy w/cover 8" #92: 3 ball tab handled, 3 section; lid w/ball finial	65
Coaster 3" #38, round, 6 raised rays	8
Cheese & cracker #: comport 3.5", short ball stem, 5.5" wide; plate 11", ball tab handled	48
Comport 4", bell footed, leaf & ball tab handles, 6" wide	30
Comport 4.25", ball stem, cupped, 4.75" wide	16
Creamer 2.75" #63, footed, individual, 3 oz.	8
Creamer 4" #66, footed, regular, 6 oz.	8
Cruet w/stopper 4.75", flat oil, 3 oz.	25
Cup & saucer, after dinner #: cup 2.75", footed w/leaf & ring handle, 2.5 oz.; saucer w/indent 4.5"	12
Cup 2.25", flat, punch w/leaf & ring handle, 5 oz.	8
Cup & saucer, coffee #35: cup 2.75", footed w/beaded handle, 6 oz.; saucer w/indent 5.5"	8

Left to right: Marmalade 2 piece #5301-84: jar w/lipped top; cover notched for spoon w/ball finial; Goblet 4.75" #5301-4 (blown), tall stem, wine, 3 oz.; Goblet 4.25" #5301-8 (blown), tall stem, cordial, 1 oz.; Goblet 5" #5301-2 (blown), tall stem, saucer champagne, 5 oz.; Tumbler 3.25" #5300-14, flat, straight sided, old fashion, 7 oz.; Goblet 7" #5301-1 (blown), tall stem, dinner water, 9 oz.

Basket 11.5", applied handle, crimped, applied cobalt handle, 9.25" tall.

Candy w/cover 8" #301-92: 3-ball tab handled, 3 sections; lid w/ball finial – shown w/lid off.

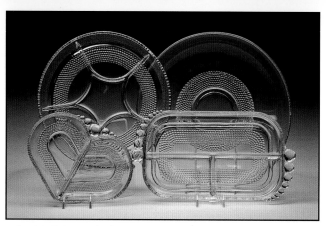

Back left: Relish 10" #301-57, 5 equal sections & a star shaped center. **Back right:** Bowl 13" #301-111, very shallow, turned up edge, gardenia. **Front left:** Relish 7.5" #301-91, 1-ball tab handle, 2 sections, heart shape. **Front right:** Relish 12" #301-51, rectangular, graduated ball tab handled, 2 equal sections & celery section.

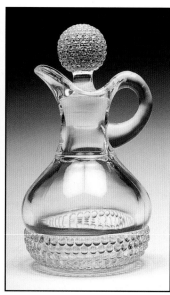

Cruet w/stopper 4.75" #301-, flat oil, 3 oz.

Decanter w/stopper 12" #301-, bar bottle, straight sided; ball shape stopper.

Back row: Plate 8" #301-, ball tab handled. **Front left:** Shaker 3.5" #301-69, flat, spherical base w/short neck, chrome top, pair. **Front right:** Ash tray 3.25" #301-85, individual, 3 cigarette holes on edge w/1 rest.

Cup & saucer, tea #: cup 2.75", footed w/leaf & ring handle, 6 oz.; saucer w/indent 6"	10
Decanter w/stopper 12", bar bottle, straight sided; ball stopper	135
Finger bowl 4.25" #5301- (blown), deep, 2.25" high	8
Goblet 4.25" #5301-8 (blown), tall stem, cordial, 1 oz.	25
Goblet 4.5" #5301-11 (blown), tall stem, sherry, 1.75 oz.	24
Goblet 4.75" #5301-4 (blown), tall stem, wine, 3 oz.	15
Goblet 2.75" #5301-6 (blown), no stem, oyster cocktail, 3.5 oz.	7
Goblet 4.5" #5301-3 (blown), tall stem, liquor cocktail, 3.5 oz.	10
Goblet 5.5" #5301-7 (blown), tall stem, claret, 4 oz.	16
Goblet 2.5" #5301-5 (blown), no stem, sherbet, 5 oz.	6
Goblet 3.5" #5301-10 (blown), short stem, ice cream, 5 oz.	7
Goblet 5" #5301-2 (blown), tall stem, saucer champagne, 5 oz.	10
Goblet 6.25" #5301-12 (blown), short stem, ale, 8 oz.	16
Goblet 5.75" #5301-9 (blown), short stem, lunch water, 9 oz.	14
Goblet 7" #5301-1 (blown), tall stem, dinner water, 9 oz.	16
Ice bucket 6.5", collar footed, graduated ball handles, 5.5" wide	70
Icer 2 piece, clam & shrimp #: 6" bowl 1" tall; lipped divided cover insert (indents for clams) 6.25"	95
Icer 2 piece, oyster cocktail #: 7" bowl w/center indent; cocktail insert, flat, flared, 3 oz.	65
Marmalade 4 piece #5301-84: jar w/lipped top; cover notched for spoon w/ball finial; liner w/indent 4"; spoon	55
Mayonnaise comport 4.5", footed, ball stem, 4.5" wide	18
Mayonnaise 2 piece #45: bowl 4.5", footed, w/2 leaf & ball tab handles; liner w/indent 6"	38
Mayonnaise 2 piece #44: bowl 4.5", bell footed, w/leaf & ball tab handles, salad dressing; liner w/indent 6"	45
Mug #5301- (blown), applied handled, punch, concave sides, add $10 for colored handle	18
Mustard w/cover 4.25", lipped top (also used for catsup)	45
Pitcher 5" #5301-, footed, upright w/o ice lip, 16 oz.	68
Pitcher 8.5" #5301-82, flat, ball jug w/ice lip, 64 oz.	125
Pitcher 8.5" #5301-82, flat, ball jug w/ice lip, 64 oz., add $50 for colored handle	135
Plate 6" #25, bread & butter	5
Plate 6", ball tab handled	8
Plate 6", round canape/off center indent, for footed 4 oz. cocktail (no pattern)	12
Plate 6", round canape (no indent)	14
Plate 7" #33, four - ball tab handled, lemon server	16
Plate 7.5" #26, salad	6
Plate 8", ball tab handled	10
Plate 8.5" #27, lunch	8
Plate 10.5" #28, dinner	48
Plate 11" #34, ball tab handled	30
Plate 13", flat edge, torte	28
Plate 13" #29, four - ball tab handled, sandwich	40
Plate 13" #30, small center, slightly turned up edge, cabaret or salad bowl liner	30
Plate 14" #31, flat edge, torte	34
Plate 14" #32, small center, slightly turned up edge, cabaret	36
Plate 18", flat edge, torte	45
Plate 18", small center, slightly turned up edge, cabaret or punch bowl liner	50
Punch bowl 15.5" wide, 7.75" deep, flared, 2.5 gallon	125
Relish 5", ball tab handled, oval, olive (bowl like)	12
Relish 5.75", ball tab handled, round, 2 equal sections, nut	16
Relish 6" #46, ball tab handled, oblong, pickle	16
Relish 6", bell footed, w/leaf & ball tab handles, 2 sections	32
Relish 6" #48, ball tab handled, 2 sections, oval	20
Relish 7" #49, ball tab handled, 2 sections, 2 styles (diamond or oval)	22
Relish 7.5" #49, ball tab handled, 2 sections, 2 styles (star or square)	24
Relish 7.5" #91, one - ball tab handle, 2 sections, heart shape	24
Relish 8", round, 3 sections, applied handle	20
Relish 9" #55, ball tab handled, 4 sections	28
Relish 9" #50, 3-ball tab handled, 3 sections	28
Relish 10" #56, 4 equal sections & celery section	30
Relish 10" #57, 5 equal sections & a star shaped center	40
Relish 10.9" #47, wide counting ball tab handles, oblong, celery	30
Relish 11", ball tab handled, oblong, 2 sections, radish/celery (divided 1/3 & 2/3)	32
Relish 11", ball tab handled, oblong, 3 sections w/curved dividers	35
Relish 12" #50, oval, 2 equal sections & celery section	32
Relish 12" #51, rectangular, graduated ball tab handled, 2 equal sections & celery section	35
Relish 12" #52, four - ball tab handled, 4 sections	40
Relish 12" #53, round, 4 equal sections & celery section	38
Relish 12" #54, round, 5 equal half circle sections & star shaped center	48
Shaker 3.5" #69, flat, spherical base w/short neck, glass or chrome top, pair	26
Shaker 5" #68, flat, spherical base w/long neck, glass or chrome top, pair	28
Sugar 2.6" #63, footed, individual, 3 oz.	8
Sugar 3.25" #66, footed, regular, 8 oz.	8
Tray 6", oval w/2 indents for cruets or mustard/catsup, plume center handle	18

Tray 6" #69, ball tab handled, oval for s & p 12
Tray 6.5" #70, center heart handled, sweetmeat or lemon server 28
Tray 8" #71, ball tab handled, oval for individual cream/sugar or 2 cruets 16
Tray 9" #72, ball tab handled, for s & p w/2 cruets 16
Tray 10" #66, ball tab handled, for regular cream/sugar 18
Tumbler 2.25" #5300-9, flat, straight sided, whiskey, 2 oz. 18
Tumbler 2.75" #5301-14, footed, whiskey, 2 oz. 16
Tumbler 3" #5301-15, footed, whiskey, 3 oz. 16
Tumbler 3.25" #5300-10, flat, straight sided, juice, 3.5 oz. 8
Tumbler 4" #5301-6, footed, juice, 4.5 oz. 10
Tumbler 3.5" #5300-13, flat, straight sided, juice, 5 oz. 10
Tumbler 3.25" #5300-14, flat, straight sided, old fashion, 7 oz. 12
Tumbler 4.5" #5300-16, flat, straight sided, split, 8 oz. 12
Tumbler 5" #5301-8, footed, party glass, 8 oz. 12
Tumbler 4.25" #5300-17, flat, straight sided, water, 9 oz. 12
Tumbler 4.5" #5301-9, footed, table water, 9 oz. 14
Tumbler 4" #5300-18, flat, straight sided, double old fashioned, 10 oz. 12
Tumbler 6" #5300-12, flat, straight sided, water, 10 oz. 12
Tumbler 5.25" #530015-, flat, straight sided, ice tea, 12 oz. 14
Tumbler 5.5" #5301-7, footed, hi ball, 12 oz. 16
Tumbler 5.75" #5300-11, flat, straight sided, ice tea, 14 oz. 16
Tumbler 6" #5300-5, footed, ice tea, 14 oz. 18
Urn w/cover 9" #108: footed, graduated ball handles; dome lid w/ball finial 145
Vase 9" #109, footed, round, graduated ball handles 35
Vase 9" #10, footed, fan shape, graduated ball handles 45

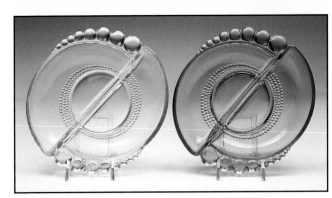

Left: Relish 5.75" #301-, ball tab handled, round, 2 equal sections, nut, Crystal. **Right:** Relish 5.75" #301-, ball tab handled, round, 2 equal sections, nut. Note! Reproduction made by Gillinder Glass, Pink.

Pitcher 8.5" #5301-82, flat, ball jug w/ice lip, 64 oz., shown w/ Amber handle, add $50 for colored handle.

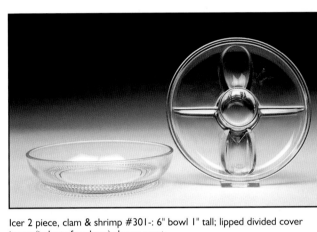

Icer 2 piece, clam & shrimp #301-: 6" bowl 1" tall; lipped divided cover insert (indents for clams) shown apart.

Plate 7" #301-33, 4-ball tab handled, lemon server, Crystal – shown w/silver overlay decoration.

Icer 2 piece, clam & shrimp #301-: 6" bowl 1" tall; lipped divided cover insert (indents for clams).

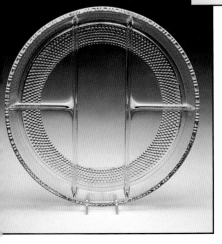

Relish 12" #301-53, round, 4 equal sections & celery section.

Back left: Plate 9", square, lunch, Crystal. **Front left:** Tumbler 4", flat, water, 9 oz., Amber. **Front center left:** Tumbler 3.5", flat, juice, 4 oz., Cobalt. **Front center right:** Tumbler 2.25", flat, whiskey, 1.5 oz., Ruby. **Front right:** Relish 9", round, 2-tab handled, 4 equal sections, Ruby.

Candlestick 1-lite 4", footed, terrace stem, pair, Cobalt.

Back row: Relish 10.5", 2-tab handled, round, 4 equal sections & round center, Crystal. **Front left:** Mayonnaise bowl 6", collar footed, flared, salad dressing, Cobalt. **Front right:** Creamer & sugar, collar footed, wing handled, regular, 10 oz., Cobalt.

TERRACE
Duncan & Miller Glass Co.   **Blank #111**   **1935-55**
Colors: Amber, Cobalt, Crystal, and Ruby

    The futuristic style of this glassware brought rave reviews when it was first introduced i[n] 1935. With the clean Art Deco style of this pattern, collectors seem to favor the square rathe[r] than round when given a choice. This was a favorite blank to use with the First Love etching.

    This is one of the patterns where the plates and bowls must not be stacked because of th[e] chance of damage. If stacking is necessary, place protectors between each item. The tw[o] stemware numbers are #111 (having a tiered or stacked stem) and #5111 1/2 (this one ha[s] balls on the stem). The footed urn with cover is something missing from most collections.

    Not all items were made in all of the colors. Amber is usually priced less than crystal. A[t] this time, though, there seems to be very little interest in the amber pieces. Cobalt and Rub[y] items are very exquisite items. They are usually priced as much as 300% more than the crysta[l.]

TERRACE	Crystal
Ashtray, 4.75" square	12
Basket 6", bowl, 2-tab handles pulled up	28
Bowl 5", round, shallow, fruit	12
Bowl 5.5", shallow, square	14
Bowl 6", tab handled	18
Bowl 7", shallow, square	16
Bowl 8.5", shallow, square crimped	34
Bowl 9", deep, salad	38
Bowl 10", collar foot, deep, flared, fruit	48
Bowl 10", flared, fruit	45
Bowl 10", tab handled, round, fruit	30
Bowl 11", shallow, cupped, salad	45
Bowl 11.25", flared, flower	45
Bowl 12", deep, salad	48
Bowl 12", collar footed, shallow, cupped, console	60
Cake salver 13", collar foot (clear plate colored foot)	85
Candlestick 1-lite 4", footed, terrace stem, pair	48
Candy w/cover 7.5", flat, shallow, 2-tab handled; ribbed cylinder finial	65
Cheese & cracker: comport 3", short stem, 5.25" wide; plate 10.75", round, tab handled	48
Cocktail mixer 9", flat, martini	100
Comport 3.25", short stem, cupped, 5" wide	24
Creamer 3", collar footed, wing handle, regular, 10 oz.	14
Cup & saucer, after dinner: cup 2.6", long handle, footed, 2.5 oz.; square saucer w/indent	24
Cup & saucer, coffee: cup 2.5", footed, wing handle, 6 oz.; square saucer w/indent	16
Finger bowl 4.25" #5111 1/2 (blown), flat	30
Goblet 3.75" #5111 1/2, 1 ball stem, cordial, 1 oz.	42
Goblet 5.25" #5111 1/2, 3 ball stem, wine, 3 oz.	32
Goblet 4.5" #5111 1/2, 3 ball stem, liquor cocktail, 3.5 oz.	24
Goblet 3.75" #5111 1/2, 1 ball stem, oyster cocktail, 4.5 oz.	16
Goblet 6" #5111 1/2, 3 ball stem, claret, 4.5 oz.	45
Goblet 4" #5111 1/2, 1 ball stem, sherbet or ice cream, 5 oz.	12
Goblet 5" #5111 1/2, 3 ball stem, saucer champagne, 5 oz.	14
Goblet 6.75" #5111 1/2, 3 ball stem, water, 10 oz.	28
Ice Bucket, footed, tab handled, straight sided	58
Mayonnaise 3 piece: bowl 5.5", collar foot, wing handled; liner w/indent 7.5", tab handled; ladle	60
Mayonnaise 3 piece: bowl 6", collar footed, flared, salad dressing; 2 ladles	58
Pitcher, spherical base, applied handle, ice lip	245
Plate 5", round, 2-tab handled, lemon server	14
Plate 6", round, bread & butter	12
Plate 6", square, bread & butter	15
Plate 6", round, tab handled, lemon server	18
Plate 7", round, dessert/salad	14
Plate 7.5", square, salad	16
Plate 8.5", round, lunch	20
Plate 9", square, lunch	24
Plate 10.75", round, 2-tab handled, sandwich, small center	28
Plate 13", flat, round, torte	32
Plate 13", round, small center, turned up edge, cabaret	35
Plate 18", round, small center, turned up edge, cabaret	45
Relish 6", round, 2-tab handled, 2 equal sections	24
Relish 6", tab handled, 2 sections, diamond or square shape	28
Relish 8", tab handled, oblong, celery	22
Relish 9", round, 2-tab handled, 4 equal sections	32
Relish 10.5", 2-tab handled, round, 4 equal sections & round center	65
Sugar w/cover 2.8" collar footed, regular, wing handled, 10 oz.	25
Tumbler 2.25", flat, whiskey, 1.5 oz.	30
Tumbler 4.5" #5111 1/2, footed, 1 ball stem, whiskey, 3 oz.	24
Tumbler 3.5", flat, juice, 4 oz.	14
Tumbler 5.25" #5111 1/2, footed, 1 ball stem, juice, 5 oz.	16
Tumbler 4", flat, water, 9 oz.	30
Tumbler 5.75" #5111 1/2, footed, 1 ball stem, lunch water, 10 oz.	28
Tumbler 6.5" #5111 1/2, footed, 1 ball stem, ice tea, 12 oz.	30
Tumbler 6.75" #5111 1/2, footed, 1 ball stem, beverage, 14 oz.	32
Urn w/cover 10.25", footed, tab handled	95
Vase 10", footed, large w/terrace stem, flared	65

TROJAN
Fostoria Glass Company   Etching #280   1929-44
Colors: Rose (pink) and Topaz (yellow)

Trojan features a heart shaped leaf in the design. This etched pattern is most often found in Topaz but the Rose makes an outstanding place setting on a table. It just will take more patience to accumulate Rose pieces. The Fairfax #2375 is the blank on which the majority of this etched pattern is found. Stemware was produced on the #5099 blank, with a Crystal foot & stem with a Rose or Topaz bowl. Hard to find pieces are the cruet, footed candy jar, and pitcher. It was nice to get the accurate information about the exceedingly rare decanter.

Like other Fostoria etched patterns, collectors seem to want the following: candy, cruet, decanter, sauce boat with liner, scroll handled console bowl, shakers, sugar pail, and vase.

Pattern detail, Trojan.

TROJAN	Topaz	Rose
Ashtray 3.75" #2350, small, individual	18	28
Ashtray 5" #2350, large, round, flared edge	26	32
Bonbon 6.75" #2375 Fairfax, 2 style of handles, both turned up	24	28
Bottle w/rounded top stopper 7" #2375 Fairfax, flat, salad dressing, 4.75 oz.	395	
Bowl 5.1" #2375 Fairfax, flat, flared, fruit	28	32
Bowl 5.4" #2375 Fairfax, 2 style of handles, sweetmeat	30	35
Bowl 6" #2375 Fairfax, flat, flared, cereal	38	48
Bowl 7" #2375 Fairfax, flat, flared, soup	98	110
Bowl 8.5" #2375 Fairfax, handled, dessert	85	95
Bowl 9.25" #2375 Fairfax, oval, vegetable	85	95
Bowl 10" #2395, oval, large scroll handles, console	125	160
Bowl 12" #2375 Fairfax, 3-toed, flared, console	70	85
Bowl 12" #2394, flared, 3-footed, "A" shape	85	100
Bowl #2415, oval, combination (candle holder handles)	195	225
Cake plate 9.75" #2375 Fairfax, small center, open handled	65	75
Candle bowl 1-lite 2" #2394, 3-footed, flared, pair	38	45
Candlestick 1-lite 3.25" #2375 Fairfax, pair	50	60
Candlestick 1-lite 5" #2395 1/2, 2 high scroll handles, pair	110	145
Candy jar w/cover 6" #2394, 3-footed, .5 lb., 6.75" wide	275	325
Cheese & cracker #2375 Fairfax: comport 2.4", short stem, 5.25" wide; liner w/indent, 2 style handles 9.75"	95	110
Cheese & cracker #2368: comport 2.9", short stem, cupped w/o optic, 5" wide; handled plate w/o optic, 11"	85	98
Comport 4.5" #2400, low lady leg stem, flared, 6" wide	65	80
Comport 5" #5099 (or 5299), flared, 6" wide	68	85
Cream soup & liner #2375 Fairfax: bowl 6", footed, handled & flared, 10 oz.; saucer w/indent 7.4"	65	75
Creamer, 3" #2375 1/2 Fairfax, footed, individual, 3.25 oz.	40	48
Creamer 3.3" #2375 1/2 Fairfax, footed, regular, 6.75 oz.	24	28
Cruet/stopper 9.25" #2375 Fairfax, footed, handled, 5 oz.	275	395
Cup & saucer, after dinner #2375 Fairfax: cup 2.75", footed, 2.5 oz.; saucer w/indent 4.75"	58	68
Cup & saucer, bouillon #2375 Fairfax: cup 2.5", footed, handled, 5 oz., 4" wide; saucer w/indent 5.75"	35	45
Cup & saucer, coffee #2375 Fairfax: cup 2.5" footed, 6 oz.; saucer w/indent 5.75"	24	28
Decanter w/stopper 10.75" #2439, flat, reverse cone shape, 30 oz.	1,000+	1,500+
Finger bowl & liner: bowl 4" #869; plate w/indent (#2283 optic) 6"	48	55
Goblet 3.9" #5099, cordial, .75 oz.	80	98
Goblet 5.5" #5099, wine, 2.5 oz.	45	60
Goblet 5.1" #5099, cocktail, 3 oz.	32	30
Goblet 6" #5099, claret, 4 oz.	80	90
Goblet 3.5" #5099, oyster cocktail, 4.5 oz.	24	28
Goblet 6.1" #5099, parfait, 5.5 oz.	60	70
Goblet 4.25" #5099, sherbet, 6 oz.	18	22
Goblet 6.1" #5099, saucer champagne, 6 oz.	22	25
Goblet 8.25" #5099, dinner water, 9 oz.	40	45
Grapefruit #5282 1/2, footed, bowl (large sherbet shape)	75	85
Grapefruit insert #945 1/2, small version of grapefruit (non-etched)	30	35
Ice bucket 6" #2375 Fairfax, chrome handle, 5.15" wide	125	145
Ice dish 2.75" #2451, bowl w/3-tabs hold liners, 4.8" wide	50	60
Ice dish liner 2.75" #2451, crab meat, 4 oz.	30	35
Ice dish liner 1.9" #2451, fruit cocktail, 5 oz.	35	40
Ice dish liner 3.5" #2451, tomato juice, 5 oz.	24	34
Ice dish plate 7" #2451, plain w/indent	16	18
Mayonnaise 2 piece #2375 Fairfax: bowl 5.6", footed, flared; plate w/indent 7.4"	80	95
Pitcher 9.75" #5000, footed, applied handle, water w/o ice lip, 48 oz.	395	595
Plate 6" #2283, optic	8	10
Plate 6.25" #2375 Fairfax, bread & butter	8	10
Plate 6.25" #2375 Fairfax, canape w/offset indent	30	45
Plate 6.8" #2375 Fairfax, open handled, lemon server	28	35
Plate 7.35" #2375 Fairfax, salad or dessert	12	14
Plate 8.6" #2375 Fairfax, lunch	16	18
Plate 9.25" #2375 Fairfax, small dinner	30	40

Topaz (yellow) grouping: **Back left:** Plate 6.25" #2375 Fairfax, bread & butter. **Back center:** Plate 9.25" #2375 Fairfax, small dinner. **Front left:** Sugar 3.1" #2375 1/2 Fairfax, footed, regular 6.75 oz. **Front center:** Creamer 3.3" #2375 1/2 Fairfax, footed, regular, 6.75 oz. **Front right:** Cup & saucer, coffee #2375 Fairfax: cup 2.5" footed, 6 oz.; saucer w/indent 5.75".

Topaz (yellow) bowl & Crystal stem/foot grouping: **Left:** Tumbler 4.5" #5099, footed, juice, 5 oz. **Center left:** Goblet 6.1" #5099, parfait, 5.5 oz. **Center right:** Goblet 4.25" #5099, sherbet, 6 oz. **Right:** Goblet 6.1" #5099, saucer champagne, 6 oz.

Bowl 12" #2375 Fairfax, 3-toed, flared, console, Rose (pink).

Topaz (yellow) grouping: **Left:** Goblet 3.5" #5099, oyster cocktail, 4.5 oz. **Center left:** Goblet 5.1" #5099, cocktail, 3 oz. **Center:** Goblet 4.25" #5099, sherbet, 6 oz. **Center right:** Goblet 6.1" #5099, saucer champagne, 6 oz. **Right:** Goblet 8.25" #5099, dinner water, 9 oz.

Plate 10.25" #2375 Fairfax, divided, grill	85	95
Plate 10.25" #2375 Fairfax, large dinner	75	90
Plate 13.75" #2375 Fairfax, large center, chop or torte	100	125
Platter 12.25" #2375 Fairfax, oval	125	145
Platter 15" #2375 Fairfax, oval	175	225
Relish 8.5" #2375 Fairfax, oval, pickle	38	48
Relish 10.75" #2375 Fairfax, oval, celery	60	85
Relish #2350, round, 3 sections	45	55
Sandwich server 11" #2375 Fairfax, center "fleur-de-lis" handle	85	95
Sauce 2 piece #2375 Fairfax: bowl 6.75", oval 2 spouted, 3.5" wide; oval liner w/indent 8"	195	245
Shaker 3.25" #2375 Fairfax, footed w/chrome top, pair	150	175
Sugar 2.75" #2375 1/2 Fairfax, footed, individual, 3 oz.	40	48
Sugar 3.1" #2375 1/2 Fairfax, footed, regular 6.75 oz.	24	28
Sugar pail 3.75" #2378, chrome handle	250	325
Tray 6" #2394, 3-footed, mint	30	35
Tray 12" #2429 Fairfax, oblong service or cordial tray, 7" wide	98	125
Tray 12" #2429 Fairfax, oblong service, 2 piece w/lemon insert (plain not etched)	265	295
Tumbler 3" #5099, footed, whiskey, 2.5 oz.	40	46
Tumbler 4.5" #5099, footed, juice, 5 oz.	28	32
Tumbler 5.4" #5099, footed, water, 9 oz.	24	28
Tumbler 5.9" #5099, footed, ice tea, 12 oz.	45	55
Vase 8" #4105, flat, shouldered w/optic	225	275
Vase 8" #2417	200	245
Whip cream bowl 5.5" #2375 Fairfax, handled	36	42
Whip cream pail 4.5" #2378, chrome handle, 2.5" tall	175	200

Vase 8" #4105, flat, shouldered w/optic, Topaz (yellow).

Topaz (yellow) grouping: **Back left:** Cake plate 9.75" #2375 Fairfax, small center, open handled. **Back right:** Bowl 12" #2394, flared, 3-footed, "A" shape. **Center left:** Whip cream pail 4.5" #2378, chrome handle, 2.5" tall. **Front left:** Bowl 5.4" #2375 Fairfax, 2 style of handles, sweetmeat. **Front right:** Bonbon 6.75" #2375 Fairfax, 2 style of handles, both turned up.

Topaz (yellow) grouping: **Top:** Sugar pail 3.75" #2378, chrome handle. **Bottom Left:** Whip cream pail 4.5" #2378, chrome handle, 2.5" tall. **Right:** Ice bucket 6" #2375 Fairfax, gold handle, 5.15" wide – Golden Anniversary issue 1935 only.

Topaz (yellow) grouping: **Top:** Candle bowl 1-lite 2" #2394, 3-footed, flared. **Bottom:** Bowl #2415, oval, combination (candle holder handles).

Topaz (yellow) grouping: **Left:** Sugar 3.1" #2375 1/2 Fairfax, footed, regular 6.75 oz. **Right:** Creamer 3.3" #2375 1/2 Fairfax, footed, regular, 6.75 oz. **Bottom:** Tray 12" #2429 Fairfax, oblong service, 2 piece w/lemon insert (plain not etched).

Topaz (yellow) grouping: **Left:** Candy jar w/cover 6" #2394, 3-footed, .5 lb., 6.75" wide. **Right:** Cruet/stopper 9.25" #2375 Fairfax, footed, handled, 5 oz.

Topaz (yellow) grouping: **Left:** Candlestick 1-lite 5" #2395 1/2, 2 high scroll handles. **Right:** Bowl 10" #2395, oval, large scroll handles, console.

Sauce 2 piece #2375 Fairfax: bowl 6.75", oval 2 spouted, 3.5" wide; oval liner w/ indent 8", Rose (pink).

Topaz (yellow) grouping: **Back:** Plate 8.6" #2375 Fairfax, lunch. **Front:** Bowl 9.25" #2375 Fairfax, oval, vegetable.

Left: Candlestick 1-lite 3.25" #2375 Fairfax, Topaz (yellow). **Center:** Cup, bouillon #2375 Fairfax: cup 2.5", footed, handled, 5 oz., Topaz (yellow). **Right:** Bowl 9.25" #2375 Fairfax, oval, vegetable, Rose (pink).

Moongleam (green) grouping: **Back left:** Creamer 4.25", footed, lightning handles, regular, 9 oz. **Center:** Goblet 7", 2 block stem, dinner water, 10 oz. **Front left:** Relish 7", oblong, leaf shaped, pickle. **Right:** Cup & saucer, coffee: cup 2.5", lightning handle, 7 oz.; saucer w/indent 5.8".

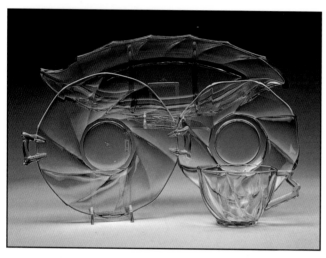

Flamingo (pink) grouping: **Back row:** Relish 13", oblong, leaf shaped, 3 section. **Front left:** Plate 6.75", 2 open handles (U shape) lemon server. **Front right:** Cup & saucer, coffee: cup 2.5", lightning handle, 7 oz.; saucer w/indent 5.8".

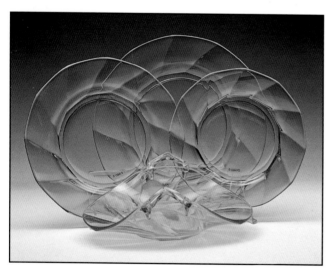

Marigold grouping: **Back center:** Plate 8", lunch. **Center row left:** Plate 7", salad. **Center row right:** Plate 6", bread & butter. **Front center:** Bonbon 6.75", 2 triangular handles turned up, mint.

TWIST

A. H. Heisey & Company   **Blank #1252**   **1928-38**

Colors: Crystal, Flamingo (pink), Marigold, Moongleam (green), and Sahara (yellow)
Other Colors: Alexandrite and Hawthorne (lilac)

Twist was a unique modernistic pattern when it was introduced. The different spiral twist effect combined with triangular or lightning style handles and the stacked block stems give this pattern its own rich quality. This popular Heisey pattern, designed by T. Clarence Heisey, offered an extensive table line. The number of panels on each piece are always even numbers, but remember they will vary in total number. Goblets can have a foot with two square graduated stacking flat blocks or two inverted pyramid shaped blocks.

On the cups it is interesting to note that you can find two different styles of lighting handles, one has a point at the top that protrudes out more than the other style. We would guess that the longer handle was hard to remove from the mould and it was shortened to make the production process simpler.

Marigold was Heisey's first attempt at making a yellow color. Unfortunately, Marigold proved to an unstable color causing all sorts of problems in production. It was a very short-lived color. Many Marigold items will be found with a blistered look. Those with this blistering effect will usually continue to deteriorate.

On occasion, you can find some Twist items in either Alexandrite or Hawthorne.

TWIST

	Crystal	Moongleam Flamingo Sahara	Marigold
Almond 2.5", footed, 1 ball stem, slightly turned up handles, 4.75" wide	30	60	80
Bonbon 3.25", 2 triangular handles turned up	24	45	70
Bonbon 6.75", 2 triangular handles turned up, mint	18	28	30
Bottle w/stopper 7.5", flat, 2 spouted, French dressing, 8 oz.	50	110	150
Bowl 3.3", 2 triangular handles, individual nut, 1.2" high	20	48	60
Bowl 4", deep, slightly flared	10	25	35
Bowl 4.5", 2 triangular handles	12		
Bowl 5.25", deep, triangular handled	20	32	40
Bowl 6", 2 triangular handles, jelly	22	35	45
Bowl 8", deep, slightly flared	28	60	85
Bowl 8", 4-tab triangle footed, round, deep, cupped, nasturtium	45	95	145
Bowl 8.25", footed, short stem, flared	30	75	95
Bowl 9", oval, rim vegetable	30	60	
Bowl 9.25", deep, flared, floral centerpiece	35	75	125
Bowl 9.25", deep, rolled edge, floral centerpiece	40	85	125
Bowl 10", 4-footed, oval, deep, cupped, nasturtium	60	125	175
Bowl 12.25", 4-tab triangular feet, round, flared, floral	50	100	130
Bowl 12.5", 4-tab triangular feet, oval, flared, floral	55	110	145
Candlestick 1-lite 2", footed, mushroom shape, pair	50	100	175
Candy w/cover 6.6" #1253, 3 cornered (mint & cover)	65	85	110
Candy w/cover 6.6", flat, triangle shaped, 3 (U shaped) handles	55	80	100
Comport 5.75", tall stem 2 stacked balls at base) flared, 7.4" wide	40	95	165
Cocktail shaker 8", square footed, threaded top		1,000+	
Cream soup or bouillon & liner: cup 4.6", flat, lightning handles, 10 oz.; saucer w/indent 6.5"	32	55	85
Creamer 2.5", footed, 1 ball stem, U shaped handle, individual, 3 oz.	30	60	80
Creamer 2.5", flat, lightning handle, regular, 7 oz.	50	85	110
Creamer 4.25", footed, lightning handles, regular, 9 oz.	35	65	85
Creamer 4.1", flat, spherical, Hotel w/high spout	30	60	80
Cruet w/stopper 4.25", flat, lightning handle, oil, 2.5 oz.	95	160	195
Cruet w/stopper 4.75", flat, lightning handle, oil, 4 oz.	85	145	165
Cup & saucer, coffee: cup 2.5", lightning handle, 7 oz.; saucer w/indent 5.8" (flat or slightly cupped)	20	45	60
Cup & saucer, coffee: cup 2.6" #1252 1/2, footed, loop & plumage handle, 7 oz.; saucer w/indent 5.25", round, edge with .75" plain rim	35	75	95
Goblet 5", 2 block stem, wine, 2.5 oz.	28	60	85
Goblet 3.5", no stem, oyster cocktail, 3 oz.	12	28	35
Goblet 4.6", 2 block stem, cocktail, 3 oz.	14	45	60
Goblet 5.75", 2 block stem, claret, 4 oz.	16	50	75
Goblet 3.75", 1 block stem, sherbet, 5 oz.	14	28	45
Goblet 4.75", 2 block stem, saucer champagne, 5 oz.	15	38	50
Goblet 3.75", short plain stem, grapefruit (large sherbet shape)	16	30	65
Goblet 6.5", 1 block stem, lunch water, 9 oz.	30	65	85
Goblet 7", 2 block stem, dinner water, 10 oz.	35	75	95
Ice bucket 5.4", oval w/chrome handle (held on w/nut) 8.75" wide	95	195	250
Mayonnaise 5.5", square footed, short stem, flared w/ handles, 4.6" high	35	75	95
Mayonnaise 5.5", round footed, short stem, flared w/ handles, 3.5" high	30	65	85
Mustard w/cover 3.5", flat, straight sided	60	125	145
Mustard spoon 4" #5, fits into cut out part of mustard cover	35	95	125

Pitcher 6", flat squat (convex sided) w/o ice lip, 48 oz.	95	195	265
Plate 4.5",	15	30	45
Plate 6", bread & butter	6	12	24
Plate 6.75", 2 open handles (U or triangle shape) lemon server	18	28	35
Plate 7", salad	7	14	30
Plate 8", lunch	9	16	35
Plate 8.25", rectangular indent in center, Kraft cheese	24	65	85
Plate 9", small dinner	28	60	70
Plate 10", 3 small feet (looks like shallow bowl) utility	45	90	110
Plate 10.75", large dinner	54	145	195
Plate 12", handled, sandwich	24	45	60
Plate 12", torte	30	55	85
Platter 12", oval	28	65	90
Platter 15", oval	40	95	125
Relish 7", oblong, leaf shaped, pickle	18	32	50
Relish 8.25", 2 oval sections w/open scroll handles	32	65	
Relish 10", oblong, leaf shaped, celery	30	60	85
Relish 13", oblong, leaf shaped, celery	35	75	95
Relish 13", oblong, leaf shaped, 3 sections	38	80	100
Shaker 3.5", footed square base, glass top, pair	100	150	245
Shaker 3.8", flat squat cylindrical, chrome top, pair	50	75	145
Sugar 2.5", footed, 1 ball stem, slightly turned up handles, 4.75" wide, individual, 3 oz. (same as almond)	30	60	80
Sugar w/cover 3.5", flat, lightning handles, regular, 7 oz.	50	85	110
Sugar 4.4", footed, lightning handles, regular, 9 oz.	35	65	85
Sugar 3", flat, spherical, squat Hotel	30	60	80
Tray 6", 2 triangular handles, cheese	15	28	35
Tray 12", 2 handles turned up, muffin	33	75	85
Tumbler 4", flat, straight sided, soda, 5 oz.	25	50	75
Tumbler 4", flat, straight sided, flared top, soda, 5 oz.	25	50	75
Tumbler 4.5", footed, no stem, cone shaped, soda, 5 oz.	35	50	75
Tumbler 3.8", flat, straight sided, high ball, 8 oz. (base 2.5")	24	45	65
Tumbler 3.8", flat, straight sided with 8 panels, soda, 8 oz. (base 2.25")	20	40	60
Tumbler 3.8", flat, straight sided with 6 panels, flared top, soda, 8 oz. (base 2.25")	22	50	60
Tumbler 5.5", footed, no stem, cone shaped, soda, 9 oz.	24	50	70
Tumbler 5.25", flat, straight sided, ice tea/soda, 12 oz.	30	55	75
Tumbler 5.25", flat, straight sided, flared top, ice tea/soda, 12 oz.	30	55	75
Tumbler 6.25", footed, no stem, cone shaped, ice tea, 12 oz.	35	60	80

Flamingo (pink) grouping: **Top left:** Bowl 9.25", deep, flared, floral centerpiece. **Top right:** Bowl 12.25", 4-tab triangular feet, round, flared, floral. **Bottom left:** Bowl 6", 2 triangular handles, jelly; Cruet w/stopper 4.25", flat, lightning handle, oil, 2.5 oz. **Bottom right:** Bowl 12.5", 4-tab triangular feet, oval, flared, floral.

Top row: Relish 10", oblong, leaf shaped, celery, Crystal – shown w/ cutting. **Front left:** Mayonnaise 5.5", round footed, short stem, flared w/ handles, 3.5" high, Sahara (yellow). **Front right:** Cruet w/stopper 4.75", flat, lightning handle, oil, 4 oz., Sahara (yellow).

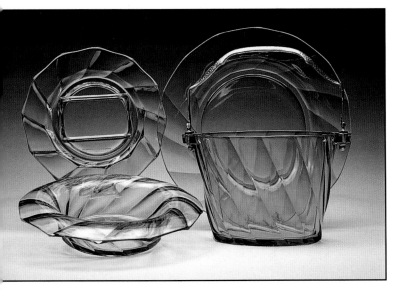

Moongleam (green) grouping: **Back left:** Plate 8.25", rectangular indent in center, Kraft cheese. **Back right:** Plate 10.75", large dinner. **Front left:** Bowl 9.25", deep, rolled edge, floral centerpiece. **Front right:** Ice bucket 5.4", oval w/chrome handle (held on w/nut) 8.75" wide.

Back row: Relish 10", oblong, leaf shaped, celery, Sahara (yellow). **Center left:** Bowl 3.3", 2 triangular handles, individual nut, 1.2" high, Moongleam (green). **Center right:** Plate 6.75", 2 open handles (triangle shape) lemon server, Moongleam (green). **Front left:** Bowl 5.25", deep, triangular handled, Moongleam (green). **Front right:** Almond 2.5", footed, 1 ball stem, slightly turned up handles, 4.75" wide, Sahara (yellow).

Pattern detail, Vernon.

Orchid grouping: **Back**: Plate 10.25" #2375 Fairfax, large dinner. **Center left**: Plate 7.35" #2375 Fairfax, salad or dessert. **Front left**: Candlestick 1-lite 3.25" #2375 Fairfax. **Center**: Creamer 3.3" #2375 1/2 Fairfax, footed, regular, 6.75 oz. **Right**: Cup & saucer, coffee #2375 Fairfax: cup 2.5" footed, 6 oz.; saucer w/indent 5.75".

Bowl 3 piece, 13" #2375 1/2 Fairfax, oval, mushroom shaped, centerpiece; w/crystal insert for frog; frog, Orchid.

Orchid grouping: **Left**: Cup & saucer, bouillon #2375 Fairfax: cup 2.5", footed, handled, 5 oz., 4" wide; saucer w/indent 5.75". **Right**: Grapefruit 5.5" wide, 5.6" tall, #877, with #945 1/2 liner.

VERNON
Fostoria Glass Company   **Etching #277**   **1927-34**
Colors: Amber, Azure (blue), Green, and Orchid
Other Color: Crystal

Vernon is another Fostoria etching we are listing here for the first time. The etching #27? features two flowers hanging from scroll work surrounded by tendrils. This etched pattern wa introduced in 1927 and discontinued in 1934. The Fairfax blank, #2375, was used mainly fo this etched pattern. The stemware is found on the #877 blank that uses a paneled optic.

The colors of Azure, Amber, Green, & Crystal were all made for most of the length of th pattern. Orchid was used only from 1927-28 and makes all of the items in that color in ver short supply. Crystal can only be found on the stemware, tumblers, and a few other pieces.

VERNON	Amber	Green	Azure	Orchid
Ashtray 3.75" #2350, individual	15	17	20	28
Bonbon 6.75" #2375 Fairfax, 2 style of handles, both turned up	17	19	24	
Bowl 5.1" #2375 Fairfax, flared, fruit	14	16	18	26
Bowl 5.4" #2375 Fairfax, 2 style of handles, sweetmeat	20	22	26	35
Bowl 6" #2375 Fairfax, flared, cereal	22	24	28	40
Bowl 7" #2375 Fairfax, flared, soup	32	34	38	60
Bowl 9.25" #2375 Fairfax, oval, vegetable	40	45	54	95
Bowl 12" #2375 Fairfax, 3-toed, flared, console	56	62	75	110
Bowl 12" #2394, flared, 3 spade footed	56	62	75	110
Bowl 3 piece, 13" #2375 1/2 Fairfax, oval, mushroom-shaped, centerpiece; w/crystal insert for frog; frog	235	250	295	365
Candlestick 1-lite 2" #2394, pair	42	48	58	78
Candlestick 1-lite, 2.75" #2375 1/2 Fairfax, mushroom-shaped, pair	70	75	95	135
Candlestick 1-lite 3.25" #2375 Fairfax, pair	48	54	65	90
Candy box w/cover 7" #2331, 3 equal sections, "fleur-de-lis" finial	74	80	95	175
Cheese & cracker: compote 2.9" #2368, short stem, cupped, w/o optic, 5" wide; plate, 11"	60	68	80	125
Comport 6" #2375 Fairfax, lady leg stem, flared, 6.75" wide	32	36	42	65
Comport 7.5" #2400, high, lady leg stem, flared, 8" wide	34	38	45	69
Cream soup & liner #2375 Fairfax: bowl 6", footed, handled & flared, 10 oz.; saucer w/indent 7.4"	35	42	54	78
Creamer, 3" #2375 1/2 Fairfax, footed, individual, 3.25 oz.	10	12	15	24
Creamer 3.3" #2375 1/2 Fairfax, footed, regular, 6.75 oz.	14	16	20	36
Cruet w/stopper 9.25" #2375 Fairfax, footed, 5 oz.	90	98	125	
Cup & saucer, after dinner #2375 Fairfax: cup 2.75", footed, 2.5 oz.; saucer w/indent 4.75"	24	26	30	48
Cup & saucer, bouillon #2375 Fairfax: cup 2.5", footed, handled, 5 oz., 4" wide; saucer w/indent 5.75"	20	22	28	38
Cup & saucer, coffee #2375 Fairfax: cup 2.5" footed, 6 oz.; saucer w/indent 5.75"	20	22	28	38
Finger bowl & liner: bowl 4.6" #869, blown, 8 oz.; #2283 liner w/indent 6"	26	28	35	48
Goblet 4" #877, cordial w/optic, .75 oz.	32	36	45	85
Goblet 5" #877, cocktail w/optic, 3.5 oz.	14	16	20	30
Goblet 4" #877, claret w/optic, 4 oz.	24	27	32	48
Goblet, 3.5" #877, oyster cocktail w/optic, 4.5 oz.	12	14	18	26
Goblet 4" #877, low sherbet w/optic, 6 oz.	14	16	20	30
Goblet 6.1" #877, saucer champagne w/optic, 6 oz.	18	20	24	38
Goblet 7.9" #877, water w/optic, 10 oz.	25	28	34	58
Grapefruit 5.5" wide, 5.6" tall, #877, with #945 1/2 liner	55	62	75	125
Ice bucket 6" #2375 Fairfax, chrome handle, 5.15" wide	90	98	125	
Ice bucket 6" #2378, flat, cylindrical chrome handle	90	100	125	185
Mayonnaise 2 piece #2375 Fairfax: bowl 5.6", footed, flared; plate w/indent 7.4"	45	50	60	95
Pitcher 9.75" #5000, footed, water, without ice lips, 48 oz.	245	265	325	450
Plate 6.25" #2375 Fairfax, bread & butter	5	6	8	12
Plate 6.8" #2375, handled, lemon server	16	18	22	35
Plate 7.35" #2375 Fairfax, salad or dessert	7	8	10	18
Plate 8.6" #2375 Fairfax, lunch	9	10	14	24
Plate 9.25" #2375 Fairfax, small dinner	16	18	24	38
Plate 10.25" #2375 Fairfax, large dinner	40	45	52	80
Plate 13.75" #2375 Fairfax, large center, chop or torte	38	42	48	75

Item				
Platter 12.25" #2375 Fairfax, oval	58	64	75	125
Platter 15" #2375 Fairfax, oval	70	80	95	
Relish 8.5" #2375 Fairfax, oval, 2 equal sections	25	28	35	48
Relish 11.5" #2375 Fairfax, oval, celery	24	26	30	45
Sandwich server 11" #2375 Fairfax, center "fleur-de-lis" handle	42	48	60	95
Sauce 2 piece #2375 Fairfax: bowl 6.75", oval 2 spouted, 3.5" wide; oval liner w/indent 8"	78	84	95	
Shaker, 3.25" #2375 Fairfax, footed, w/chrome or glass top, pair	78	84	95	
Shaker #5000, footed ball shape	72	80		135
Sugar 2.75" #2375 1/2 Fairfax, footed, individual, 3 oz.	10	12	15	24
Sugar 3.1" #2375 1/2 Fairfax, footed, regular 6.75 oz.	14	16	20	36
Sugar bowl cover #2375 1/2 Fairfax, lid	42	48	60	95
Tumbler 2.75" #877, footed, whiskey w/optic, 2.5 oz.	25	28	34	48
Tumbler 4.25" #877, footed, juice w/optic, 5 oz.	16	18	24	36
Tumbler 5.25" #877, footed, parfait w/optic, 5 oz.	25	30	35	58
Tumbler 5.25" #877, footed, water w/optic, 9 oz.	16	18	24	45
Tumbler 6" #877, footed, ice tea w/optic, 12 oz.	20	22	28	50
Whip cream bowl 5.5" #2375 Fairfax, handled	38	42	52	

Candy box w/cover 7" #2331, 3 equal sections, "fleur-de-lis" finial, Orchid.

Orchid grouping: **Left:** Goblet 4" #877, low sherbet w/optic, 6 oz. **Center left:** Goblet 5" #877, cocktail w/optic, 3.5 oz. **Center right:** Goblet 6.1" #877, saucer champagne w/optic. **Right:** 7.9" #877, water w/optic, 10 oz.

Orchid grouping: **Left:** Tumbler 4.25" #877, footed, juice w/optic, 5 oz. **Center:** Tumbler 5.25" #877, footed, parfait w/optic, 5 oz. **Right:** Tumbler 6" #877, footed, ice tea w/optic, 12 oz.

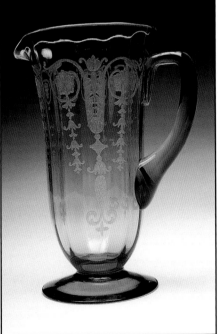

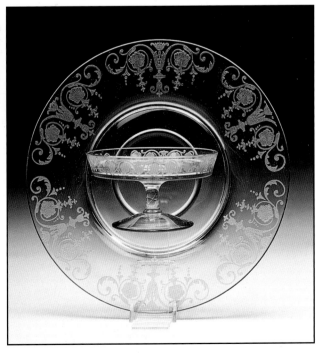

Ice bucket 6" #2375 Fairfax, chrome handle, 5.15" wide w/tongs and metal insert, Orchid.

Pitcher 9.75" #5000, footed, water, without ice lips, 48 oz., Orchid.

Cheese & cracker: compote 2.9" #2368, short stem, cupped, w/o optic, 5" wide; plate, 11", Orchid.

Pattern detail, Versailles.

Rose (pink) grouping: **Back left:** Plate 6.25" #2375 Fairfax, bread & butter. **Back center:** Plate 10.25" #2375 Fairfax, large dinner. **Back right:** Plate 9.25" #2375 Fairfax, small dinner. **Front left:** Tumbler 4.4" #5098 & #5099, footed, juice, 5 oz. **Front center:** Goblet 6" #5098 & #5099, saucer champagne, 6 oz. **Front right:** Goblet 4.1" #5098 & #5099, sherbet, 6 oz.

Azure (blue) grouping: **Back:** Plate 10.25" #2375 Fairfax, large dinner. **Center Left:** Plate 8.6" #2375 Fairfax, lunch. **Center:** Creamer 3.3" #2375 1/2 Fairfax, footed, regular, 6.75 oz. **Front left:** Candlestick 1-lite 5" #2395 1/2, 2 high scroll handles. **Front center:** Sugar 3.1" #2375 1/2 Fairfax, footed, regular 6.75 oz. **Front right:** Cup & saucer, coffee #2375 Fairfax: cup 2.5" footed, 6 oz.; saucer w/indent 5.75".

VERSAILLES

Fostoria Glass Company   **Etching #278**   **1928-44**

Colors: Azure (blue), Green, Rose (pink), and Topaz (yellow)

Versailles is a pretty etched pattern that incorporates a shell shaped fan surrounded by lots of scrolls & curlicues. The prices of Green goblets have really escalated in the last few years. Collectors buy all that they can find. This is a strong shift from the once popular blue color. The Fairfax #2375 is the blank on which most of this etched pattern is found. Stemware was produced on the #5098 & #5099 blanks. Note, #5098 stemware has a Crystal foot & stem with an Azure, Green, or Rose colored bowl, and the #5099 stemware has a Crystal foot & stem with a Topaz colored bowl.

New collectors are being attracted to the yellow color, which runs cheaper than the other colors. We need to get many younger collectors into this market. There is so much more available at shows than the import stuff sitting on the shelves of department stores.

Collectors seem to want the following: cereal bowl, sauce boat w/liner, salad dressing bottle, shakers, sugar pail, and vase.

VERSAILLES

	Topaz	Green Rose	Azure
Ashtray 3.75" #2350, individual	24	28	38
Bonbon 6.75" #2375 Fairfax, handles turned up	24	28	38
Bottle w/rounded top stopper 7" #2375 Fairfax, flat, salad dressing, 4.75 oz.	575	675	950
Bowl 5.1" #2375 Fairfax, flared, fruit	28	34	38
Bowl 5.4" #2375 Fairfax, handled, sweetmeat	24	30	40
Bowl 6" #2375 Fairfax, flared, cereal	50	75	85
Bowl 6" #2394, footed, flared	45		
Bowl 7" #2375 Fairfax, flared, soup	100	125	160
Bowl 8.5" #2375 Fairfax, handled, dessert	95	110	145
Bowl 9.25" #2375 Fairfax, oval, vegetable	90	100	160
Bowl 10.4" #2395, oval, 2 curled handles	100	115	150
Bowl 12" #2375 Fairfax, 3-toed, flared, console	78	90	125
Bowl 12" #2375 1/2 Fairfax, mushroom-shaped, console	95	110	145
Bowl 12" #2394, flared, 3-footed, "A" shape	78	90	125
Cake plate 10" #2375 Fairfax, handled	45	55	75
Candle bowl 1-lite 2" #2394, 3-footed, flared, pair	60	72	95
Candlestick 1-lite, 2.75" #2375 1/2 Fairfax, mushroom-shaped, pair	78	90	125
Candlestick 1-lite 5" #2395 1/2, 2 high scroll handles, pair	95	110	145
Candy jar w/cover 6" #2394, 3-footed, w/dome lid, .5 lb.	225		
Candy w/cover 7" #2331, 3 equal sections, "fleur-de-lis" finial		245	285
Cheese & cracker #2375 Fairfax: comport 2.4", short stem, 5.25" wide; liner w/indent, 2 style handles 9.75"	95	110	125
Cheese & cracker #2368: comport 2.9", short stem, cupped w/o optic, 5" wide; handled plate w/o optic, 11"	85	95	110
Comport 4.5" #2400, low lady leg stem, flared, 6" wide	68	80	85
Comport 5" #5098 & #5099, tall stem, 6" wide	75	85	95
Comport 6" #2375 Fairfax, lady leg stem, flared, 6.75" wide	65	85	110
Cream soup & liner #2375 Fairfax: bowl 6", footed, handled & flared, 10 oz.; saucer w/indent 7.4"	65	75	85
Creamer, 3" #2375 1/2 Fairfax, footed, individual, 3.25 oz.	30	40	55
Creamer 3.3" #2375 1/2 Fairfax, footed, regular, 6.75 oz.	20	22	26
Cruet w/stopper 9.25" #2375 Fairfax, footed, handled, 5 oz.	375	450	600
Cup & saucer, after dinner #2375 Fairfax: cup 2.75", footed, 2.5 oz.; saucer w/indent 4.75"	54	65	80
Cup & saucer, bouillon #2375 Fairfax: cup 2.5", footed, handled, 5 oz., 4" wide; saucer w/indent 5.75"	50	60	80
Cup & saucer, coffee #2375 Fairfax: cup 2.5" footed, 6 oz.; saucer w/indent 5.75"	24	30	35
Decanter w/stopper 10.75" #2439, flat, reverse cone shape, 30 oz.	925+	1,200+	1,800+
Finger bowl & liner: bowl 4.6" #869, blown, 8 oz.; plate w/indent 6"	50	60	85
Goblet 3.9" #5098 & #5099, cordial, .75 oz.	98	125	160
Goblet 5.9" #5098 & #5099, wine, 2.5 oz.	70	85	120
Goblet 5.1" #5098 & #5099, liquor cocktail, 3 oz.	30	40	48
Goblet 6" #5098 & #5099, claret, 4 oz.	90	110	150
Goblet 3.75" #5098 & #5099, oyster cocktail, 5 oz.	24	34	45
Goblet 6.1" #5098 & #5099, parfait, 6 oz.	65	85	100
Goblet 4.1" #5098 & #5099, sherbet, 6 oz.	22	28	36
Goblet 6" #5098 & #5099, saucer champagne, 6 oz.	25	32	40
Goblet 8.25" #5098 & #5099, water, 9 oz.	55	80	90
Grapefruit bowl #5082 1/2, large sherbet shape	40	48	68
Grapefruit insert #945 1/2, small version of grapefruit (non-etched)	20	24	30
Ice bucket 6" #2375 Fairfax, chrome handle, 5.15" wide	110	145	185
Ice dish 2.75" #2451, bowl w/3-tabs hold liners, 4.8" wide	50	58	75
Ice dish liner 2.75" #2451, crab meat, 4 oz.	30	35	40
Ice dish liner 1.9" #2451, fruit cocktail, 5 oz.	35	40	45

e dish liner 3.5" #2451, tomato juice, 5 oz.	24	28	34
e dish plate 7" #2451, plain w/indent	18	20	20
ayonnaise 2 piece #2375 Fairfax: bowl 5.6", footed, flared;			
olate w/indent 7.4"	65	75	95
tcher 9.75" #5000, footed, applied handle, water			
w/o ice lip, 48 oz.	400	475	650
ate 6.25" #2375 Fairfax, bread & butter	8	10	12
ate 6.8" #2375 Fairfax, open handled, lemon server	20	25	32
ate 7.35" #2375 Fairfax, salad or dessert	14	16	20
ate 8.6" #2375 Fairfax, lunch	16	20	26
ate 9.25" #2375 Fairfax, small dinner	34	40	55
ate 10.25" #2375 Fairfax, large dinner	78	90	125
ate 13.75" #2375 Fairfax, large center, chop or torte	70	85	100
atter 12.25" #2375 Fairfax, oval	95	110	145
atter 15" #2375 Fairfax, oval	150	180	250
elish 8.5" #2375 Fairfax, oval, pickle	24	30	38
elish 8.5" #2375 Fairfax, oval, 2 equal sections	26	32	40
elish 10.75" #2375 Fairfax, oval, celery	78	90	125
andwich server 11" #2375 Fairfax, center "fleur-de-lis" handle	60	75	90
auce 2 piece #2375 Fairfax: bowl 6.75", oval 2 spouted,			
3.5" wide; oval liner w/indent 8"	195	250	350
haker 3.25" #2375 Fairfax, footed, chrome top, pair	120	140	198
ugar 2.75" #2375 1/2 Fairfax, footed, individual, 3 oz.	30	40	55
ugar 3.1" #2375 1/2 Fairfax, footed, regular 6.75 oz.	20	22	26
ugar bowl cover #2375 1/2 Fairfax, lid	100	125	160
ugar pail 3.75" #2378, chrome handle	185	235	325
ay 6" #2394, 3-footed, mint	20	25	32
ay 12" #2429 Fairfax, oblong service or cordial tray, 7" wide	110	125	165
ay 12" #2429 Fairfax, oblong service, 2 piece w/			
lemon insert (plain not etched)	265	295	395
umbler 2.9" #5098 & #5099, footed, whiskey, 2.5 oz.	60	85	100
umbler 4.4" #5098 & #5099, footed, juice, 5 oz.	34	38	45
umbler 5.25" #5098 & #5099, footed, water, 9 oz.	30	42	50
umbler 6" #5098 & #5099, footed, ice tea, 12 oz.	48	58	75
ase 8" #4100 & #2417, straight sided, flip shape	225	275	350
Vhip cream bowl 5.5" #2375 Fairfax, handled	24	30	40
Vhip cream pail 4.5" #2378, chrome handle, 2.5" tall	200	250	325

Topaz (yellow) grouping: **Front left:** Creamer 3.3" #2375 1/2 Fairfax, footed, regular, 6.75 oz. **Back left:** Sugar 3.1" #2375 1/2 Fairfax, footed, regular 6.75 oz. **Right:** Cream soup & liner #2375 Fairfax: bowl 6", footed, handled & flared, 10 oz.; saucer w/indent 7.4".

Rose (pink) grouping: **Back left:** Bowl 6" #2375 Fairfax, flared, cereal. **Back right:** Plate 6.8" #2375 Fairfax, open handled, lemon server. **Front left:** Bowl 5.1" #2375 Fairfax, flared, fruit. **Front right:** Finger bowl & liner: bowl 4.6" #869, blown, 8 oz.; plate w/indent 6".

.eft: Cup & saucer, after dinner #2375 Fairfax: cup 2.75", footed, 2.5 oz.; saucer w/indent .75", Topaz (yellow). **Right:** Cup & saucer, coffee #2375 Fairfax: cup 2.5" footed, 6 oz.; aucer w/indent 5.75", Rose (pink).

Green grouping: **Back left:** Candy w/cover 7" #2331, 3 equal sections, "fleur-de-lis" finial. **Back right:** Ice bucket 6" #2375 Fairfax, chrome handle, 5.15" wide. **Front center:** Candle bowl 1-lite 2" #2394, 3-footed, flared, pair

Topaz (yellow) & Crystal stem/foot grouping: **Left:** Tumbler 5.25" #5099, footed, water, 9 oz. **Center:** Goblet 3.75" #5099, oyster cocktail, 5 oz. **Right:** Goblet 6.1" #5099, parfait, 6 oz.

Azure (blue) & Crystal stem/foot grouping: **Left:** Tumbler 5.25" #5098, footed, water, 9 oz. **Center:** Tumbler 6" #5098, footed, ice tea, 12 oz. **Right:** Goblet 8.25" #5098, water, 9 oz.

Comport 6" #2375 Fairfax, lady leg stem, flared, 6.75" wide, Rose (pink).

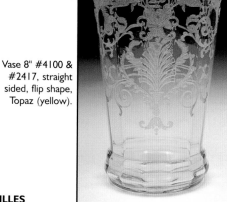

Vase 8" #4100 & #2417, straight sided, flip shape, Topaz (yellow).

Azure (blue) grouping: **Back left:** Platter 15" #2375 Fairfax, oval. **Back right:** Sandwich serve 11" #2375 Fair, center "fleur-de-lis" handle. **Front center:** Candle stick 1-lite 5" #2395 1/2, 2 h, scroll handles, p

Topaz (yellow) grouping: **Left:** Candle bowl 1-2" #2394, 3-footed, flared, p **Center:** Bowl #2394, flared, footed, "A" shape **Right:** Candle bowl 1-lite 2" #2394, 3-footed flared, pair.

Rose (pink) grouping: **Back left:** Vase 8" #4 & #2417, straig sided, flip shape **Back center:** Sugar pail 3.75" #2378, chrome handle. **Back right:** Pitcher 9. #5000, footed, applied handle, water w/o ice lip 48 oz. **Front center:** Creame sugar #2375 1/2 Fairfax, footed, individual, 3.25 c

Back left: Ice bucket 6" #237 Fairfax, chrome handle, 5.15" wi Green. **Back center:** Ice buck 6" #2375 Fairfax chrome handle, 5.15" wide, Azu (blue). **Back rig** Ice bucket 6" #2375 Fairfax, chrome handle, 5.15" wide, Rose (pink). **Front:** Ornate metal drainer and tong

WILDFLOWER

Cambridge Glass Company   **1940-58**

Main Color: Crystal

Other Colors: Amber, Ebony (black), Emerald Green, and Gold Krystol (yellow)

Collecting this etched pattern reminds you of being in the middle of a field of wildflowers in the summer time. A very gorgeous mix of flowers prevail on this etched pattern. Like several other Cambridge etched patterns, this has an extremely large listing of items made. What makes this etched pattern different from other Cambridge etchings is that only one stem blank was predominately used. Other etched patterns can have up to six different stems. Hard to find items include: pitcher, nite set, cheese dish, and hurricane lamp. The average collector always needs more dinner plates. For the gold encrusted Crystal pieces, add 25% for mint condition. Worn items will bring less than Crystal.

Colored pieces in this etched pattern have shown up, but not enough to give the fair market value.

Pattern detail, Wildflower.

WILDFLOWER	Crystal
Basket 5.75" #3500/55 Gadroon, footed, 2-handled, crimped, 3.5" tall	36
Basket 6.25" #3400/1182, 2 handles turned up	40
Basket 7" #119, flared, applied handle	395
Bell 6" #3650, dinner (bowl is cocktail size)	125
Bonbon 5.6" #3400/1179, low, flared, open handled	32
Bonbon 6" #3500/54 Gadroon, footed, handled	34
Bottle w/stopper 6.5" #1263, flat, French dressing, 8 oz.	245
Bottle w/stopper 7.25" #1261, footed, French dressing, 8 oz.	265
Bowl 5" #1534 Pristine, blown, cupped, fruit	56
Bowl 5" #3400/74, 4-footed, tab handled, mint	40
Bowl 5.25" #3400/1180, handled, sweetmeat	32
Bowl 5.25" #3400/74, 4-toed, tab handled, mint	35
Bowl 5.75" #3900/130, footed, tab handled, sweetmeat	26
Bowl 5.8" #3400/13, 4-toed, tab handled, flared	34
Bowl 6" #1402/89 Tally Ho, handled, sweetmeat	32
Bowl 6" #3400/136, 4-toed, deep, fancy crimped	85
Bowl 7.5" #435 Pristine, deco tab handled, sweetmeat	65
Bowl 8.5" #381, rim soup	135
Bowl 8.5" #1402/131 Tally Ho, deep, 3 equal sections	150
Bowl 9.5" #225 Pristine, blown, 2 sections	295
Bowl 9.5" #3400/34, open handled, vegetable	65
Bowl 9.75" #3500/16 Gadroon, collar footed, tab handled, flared	70
Bowl 10" #3400/1185, deep, open handled	70
Bowl 10" #3500/28 Gadroon, footed, handled, flared	70
Bowl 10" #3900/54, 4-footed, flared	58
Bowl 10.25" #3900/34, handled, flared	70
Bowl 10.4" #1402/122 Tally Ho, deep, 3 equal sections	175
Bowl 10.5" #1359 Pristine, tab footed, flared smooth edge	70
Bowl 10.5" #3400/168, flat, flared	65
Bowl 11" #1399, deep salad, scalloped edge	110
Bowl 11" #3400/45, 4-footed, square crimped	75
Bowl 11" #3500/16 Gadroon, collar footed, tab handled, flared	75
Bowl 10.5" #3900/28, footed, tab handled, flared	70
Bowl 11.5" #3900/62, 4-footed, flared	60
Bowl 12" #933 Pristine, tab footed, flared smooth edge	68
Bowl 12" #1349 Pristine, tab footed, flared crimped edge	72
Bowl 12" #3400/4, square, 4-footed, flared edge	68
Bowl 12" #3400/160, 4-footed, oblong, crimped	68
Bowl 12" #3900/65, 4-footed, oval, handled	85
Bowl 12.6" #3400/1240, 4-footed, oval, refractory	100
Bowl 13" #1398, shallow, fruit/salad	110
Butter w/cover 5.5" #506, round, tab handled	135
Butter w/cover 5.5" #3400/52, round, 2 open handles; dome lid w/fancy ball finial	165
Butter w/cover 7.5" #3900/52 Corinth, rectangle, 2.75" tall, 3.25" wide, .25 pound	285
Cake plate 11.75" #3500/35 Gadroon, handled	80
Cake salver 13" #170 Martha, footed	175
Canape set #693/3000, plate/cocktail, use #3000 footed cocktail, 3.5 oz. or 5 oz.	150
Candelabra 1-lite 6.25" #3400/648, keyhole stem, etched bobeches &, prisms, pair	230
Candelabra 1-lite 7.5" #3121, fancy stem w/etched bobeches & prisms, pair	275
Candelabra 2-lite 6.5" #3400/1268, keyhole stem bobeches & prisms, pair	245
Candelabra 2-lite 6.5" #496 Martha, #19 bobeches & #1 prisms, pair	275
Candelabra 3-lite 5.5" #1545, w/1 #19 bobeche on center cup & prisms, pair	285
Candlestick 1-lite 3.5" #628 Pristine, wafer stem, pair	65
Candlestick 1-lite 4.4" #3900/68, bell footed, skirted, pair	80
Candlestick 1-lite 5" #3900/67, skirted, pair	95
Candlestick 1-lite 5.25" #3400/646, keyhole stem, pair	80
Candlestick 1-lite 7" #3121, fancy stem, pair	125
Candlestick 2-lite 5.75" #495 Martha, plume arms & ball center, 8.25" spread, pair	175
Candlestick 2-lite 6" #3400/647, keyhole stem, 7.75" spread, pair	125
Candlestick 2-lite 6" #3900/72, pair	95
Candlestick 3-lite 5.5" #1545, bell footed, pair	135
Candlestick 3-lite #1307, pair	85
Candlestick 3-lite 6" #3900/74, pair	100

Back left: Bowl 9.75" #3500/16 Gadroon, collar footed, tab handled, flared. **Back right:** Cake plate 11.75" #3500/35 Gadroon, handled. **Front left:** Bowl 12.6" #3400/1240, 4-footed, oval, refractory, Crystal w/Gold encrusted. **Front right:** Basket 5.75" #3500/55 Gadroon, footed, 2 handled, crimped, Crystal w/Gold encrusted.

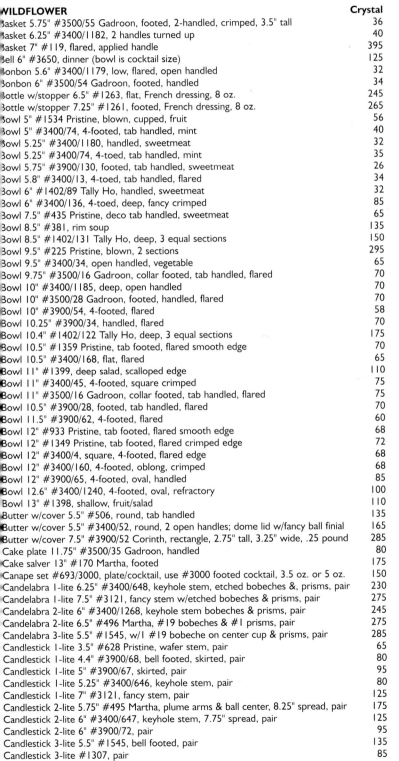

Butter w/cover 7.5" #3900/52 Corinth, rectangle, 2.75" tall, 3.25" wide, 1/4 pound.

Relish 9.5" #477 Pristine, oblong w/tab feet, oval pickle or corn.

Top left: Butter w/cover 5.5" #3400/52, round, 2 open handles; dome lid w/fancy ball finial. **Top right:** Candy w/cover 5.5" #300 Pristine, 3-footed, low, Crystal w/Carmen (ruby) rose finial. **Bottom left:** Candy w/cover 7" #500 Pristine, 3-footed, knob finial, Ebony (black) w/Gold encrusted. **Bottom right:** Candy w/cover 8" #3500/57 Gadroon, 3 open handled, 3 equal sections, Amber.

Left to right: Tumbler 7.5" #3121, footed, ice tea, 12 oz.; Goblet 5.25" #3725, sherbet, 6 oz.; Goblet 4.4" #3121, oyster cocktail, 4.75 oz.; Goblet 6.5" #3725, water, 10 oz.; Goblet 6.4" #3121, saucer champagne, 6.75 oz.; Goblet 8.25" #3121, dinner water, 11 oz.

Left: Comport 6.1" #3121/2 (blown), tall stem, 5.4" wide. **Center left:** Mayonnaise 2 piece #1532 Pristine: bowl 4.5" (blown), spherical, 3" high; liner w/indent 6.75". **Center right:** Shaker 3.75" #3400/77, footed, glass top, pair. **Right:** Comport 7.5" #3400/14, fancy wafer stem, flared, 7" wide.

Bowl 11.5" #3900/62, 4-footed, flared, Amber w/Gold encrusted ($175 – we found it priced this).

Candlestick 3-lite 7" #3400/638, keyhole stem, pair	135
Candy w/cover 5.4" #1066/4, blown w/fancy ball stem, plain finial	195
Candy w/cover 5.4" #3121/4, low, blown	145
Candy w/cover 5.4" #3121/3, tall, blown	150
Candy w/cover 5.4" #3500/103 Gadroon, blown	160
Candy w/cover 5.5" #313, flat, wafer finial	195
Candy (open) 5.5" #3500/47 Gadroon, handled	35
Candy w/cover 5.5" #300 Pristine, 3-footed, low, rose finial	275
Candy w/cover 7" #500 Pristine, 3-footed, knob finial	195
Candy w/cover 7" #500 Pristine, 3-footed, rose finial	275
Candy w/cover 6.5" #3400/9, 4-footed, tab handled, 7" wide; dome lid w/finial	125
Candy w/cover 7" #3900/165, round	115
Candy w/cover 8" #3500/57 Gadroon, 3 open handled, 3 equal sections	75
Cheese & cracker: comport 3" #3400/7, short stem, flared, 5.3" wide; plate 10.5" or 11.5", tab handled	85
Cheese dish w/cover 5" #980, flat, pointed finial	375
Cocktail mixer #1395, chrome lid & spoon, 28 oz.	225
Cocktail shaker #97, small #9 chrome lid	265
Cocktail shaker #98, large #10 chrome lid	145
Cocktail shaker #99, sham base, chrome lid	160
Cocktail shaker #3400/175, w/large #10 chrome lid	145
Cocktail icer 4.2" #187 Pristine, footed, 2 piece, non-etched insert	115
Cocktail icer 4.2" #3600, footed, 2 piece, non-etched insert	68
Cocktail icer 4.6" #968, footed, 2 piece, non-etched insert	72
Comport 5.3" #3400/28, keyhole stem, 7.25" wide	65
Comport 6.1" #3121/2 (blown), tall stem, 5.4" wide	68
Comport 7" #3500/148 Gadroon, high fancy stem, 6" wide	48
Comport 7.5" #3400/14, fancy wafer stem, flared, 7" wide	65
Comport 7.5" #3900/136, scalloped edge, 7.25" wide	52
Creamer 2.5" #3500/15 Gadroon, footed, individual, 3 oz.	22
Creamer 2.6" #3900/40, footed, individual, 3.5 oz.	24
Creamer 3.8" #3400/68, scalloped foot, regular, 4.75 oz.	26
Creamer 3" #3900/41, footed, regular, 6 oz.	22
Cruet w/stopper #3400/161, footed, handled, 6 oz.	175
Cruet w/stopper #3400/193, flat, 6 oz.	100
Cruet w/ball stopper 4.4" #3400/99, tilt ball, 6 oz.	125
Cruet w/stopper 6" #3900/100, flat, spherical, 6 oz.	125
Cup 2.5" #488 Martha, punch w/fancy handle, 5 oz.	30
Cup & saucer, coffee #3900/17: cup 2.5", 7 oz.; saucer w/indent 5.5"	28
Decanter w/stopper 13.25" #1372, flat, slim bottle shape, 28 oz.	600+
Epergne 4 piece #645, etched 3-light candlestick w/plain arm & 2 non-etched vases	135
Epergne 5 piece #654, etched keyhole w/plain bobeche-prisms & 2 non-etched vases	125
Goblet 5.25" #3121, cordial, 1 oz.	68
Goblet 6" #3121, liquor cocktail, 3 oz.	28
Goblet 5.8" #3121, wine, 3.5 oz.	52
Goblet 6.25" #3121, claret, 4.25 oz.	60
Goblet 4.4" #3121, oyster cocktail, 4.75 oz.	18
Goblet 5.25" #3725, sherbet, 6 oz.	20
Goblet 4.75" #3121, sherbet, 6.75 oz.	22
Goblet 6.4" #3121, saucer champagne, 6.75 oz.	24
Goblet 6.5" #3725, water, 10 oz.	36
Goblet 8.25" #3121, dinner water, 11 oz.	40
Hurricane lamp 8" #1601, short stem, bobeche w/prisms & etched chimney, each	225
Hurricane lamp 9.3" #1617, skirted w/etched chimney, each	225
Hurricane lamp 10.25" #1603, keyhole stem, bobeche w/prisms & etched chimney, each	245
Ice bucket 5.75" #3400/851, scalloped top, chrome handle	125
Ice bucket 5.75" #3900/671, chrome handle	135
Icer Fruit #188, scalloped edge fits in pristine #427 deep salad	300
Lamp 11" (glass only) #278, large footed, no stem, flared top w/metal parts	300
Marmalade w/cover 5.4" #147 Pristine, flat, blown, 8 oz.	125
Mayonnaise 2 piece #1402/137 Tally Ho: salad dressing, 2 spouted; liner w/indent	115
Mayonnaise bowl (Tally Ho) #1402/96, footed, salad dressing; liner w/indent 17.5"	165
Mayonnaise bowl 4" #3900/19, footed, ball shape, 4.1" high	54
Mayonnaise 2 piece #1532 Pristine: bowl 4.5" (blown), spherical, 3" high; liner w/indent 6.75"	80
Mayonnaise 2 piece #3900: #127 bowl 5", flared; #128 liner w/indent 6.5"	58
Mayonnaise 2 piece #3900/111: bowl 5.25", salad dressing; liner w/indent 6.75"	60
Mayonnaise 2 piece #1490 Pristine: bowl 5.5", cupped, salad dressing; use #1491 liner w/indent 6.4"	90
Mayonnaise 2 piece #1491 Pristine: bowl 5.5", flared, salad dressing; liner w/indent 6.4"	90
Mayonnaise bowl 5.75" #1402/95 Tally Ho, footed, salad dressing; liner w/indent	85
Mayonnaise 2 piece #3400: #13 bowl 5.8", 4-toed, flared, tab handled; #11 liner w/indent 5"	68
Mustard w/cover 3" #151 Pristine, blown, spherical, 3 oz.	125
Nite set #103, flat, handled jug & flat tumbler w/flared base	600+
Pitcher #1408, cocktail churn, metal plunger, 60 oz.	1,000+

Pitcher #3400/100, high w/ice lip, 76 oz. — 195
Pitcher 9.25" #3400/152, Doulton style w/o ice lip, 76 oz. — 345
Pitcher 8.1" #3400/141, water jug w/o ice lip, 80 oz. — 245
Pitcher 9" #3400/38, ball jug w/ice lip, 80 oz. — 225
Pitcher #119, flat, high w/ice lip, 83 oz. — 450
Pitcher #1561, flat, ball w/ice lip, 86 oz. — 275
Plate 6" #3400/60, bread & butter (6 sided) — 12
Plate 6" #3400/1181, handled, lemon server — 20
Plate 6.5" #3900/20, bread & butter — 14
Plate 7" #1402/99 Tally Ho, handled, lemon server — 24
Plate 7" #131 Pristine, (blown) salad/coupe — 75
Plate 7.5" #555, dessert — 15
Plate 7.5" #3400/176, square, salad or dessert — 15
Plate 8" #3900/22, salad or lunch — 20
Plate 8" #3900/131, handled, lemon server — 26
Plate 8.5" #3400/62, lunch (6 sided) — 22
Plate 9.5" #485, crescent salad — 175
Plate 10.25" #3900/24, dinner — 100
Plate 10.5" #3400/64, large dinner — 120
Plate 11" #3400/35, open handled, sandwich — 48
Plate 12" #3900/26, 4-footed, service/torte — 58
Plate 12.5" #3400/1186, oblong, open handled sandwich — 60
Plate 13" #3900/33, 4-footed, rolled edge, torte — 65
Plate 13.5" #1396 Pristine, flat, torte/service — 58
Plate 13.5" #1397 Pristine, small center, turned up edge, cabaret — 60
Plate 14" #130 Pristine, flat, blown, torte — 150
Plate 14" #3400/65, chop, large center — 120
Plate 14" #3900/166, torte — 62
Plate 17.5" #1402/29, Sunday nite supper — 120
Plate 18" #1402/28, Sunday nite supper — 125
Punch bowl 15" #478 Martha, 2.5 gallon — 3,000+
Punch bowl liner 18" #129, scalloped edge — 400
Relish 5.5" #3500/60 Gadroon, 2 sections, one handle — 34
Relish 6" #1402/90, handled, 2 sections — 35
Relish 6.25" #3500/69 Gadroon, 3 equal sections, scalloped edge — 34
Relish 6.5" #3500/61 Gadroon, scalloped edge, 3 sections, loop handle — 48
Relish 6.5" #3400/90, 2 open handles, 2 equal sections — 32
Relish 7" #3900/123, 4-toed, tab scroll handled, oblong pickle — 34
Relish 7" #3900/124, 4-toed, tab scroll handled, 2 equal sections, oblong — 36
Relish 8" #3500/57 Gadroon, 3 equal sections, 3 handled (candy bottom) — 35
Relish 8.75" #3400/88, 2 open handled, oblong, 2 equal sections — 52
Relish 9" #3900/125, handled, oval, 2 equal sections & celery section — 48
Relish 9.5" #464 Pristine, crescent salad shape, 3 sections — 135
Relish 9.5" #477 Pristine, oblong w/tab feet, oval pickle or corn — 68
Relish 10" #3500/64 Gadroon, 4-toed, handled, 2 equal sections & celery section — 52
Relish 11" #3400/200, handled, 4-toed, curved divider, 2 equal sections & celery section — 58
Relish 11" #3400/652, oblong, celery — 48
Relish 12" #3500/67 Gadroon, round, 6 piece (5 inserts & tray) scalloped edge — 195
Relish 12" #3900/120, oblong, 4 equal sections & celery section — 65
Relish 12" #3900/126, handled, oval, 2 equal sections & celery section — 56
Sandwich server 10.5" #3400/10, center keyhole handle — 90
Shaker 2.25" #1468, egg shaped, square glass base, pair — 100
Shaker #1470, ball shaped, individual, square glass base, pair — 90
Shaker #1471, ball shaped, regular, square glass base, pair — 95
Shaker 3.5" #3900/1177, flat, chrome or glass top, pair — 48
Shaker 3.75" #3400/77, footed, glass top, pair — 50
Sugar 2.4" #3500/15 Gadroon, footed, individual, 3 oz. — 22
Sugar 2.4" #3900/40, footed, individual, 3.5 oz. — 24
Sugar 3" #3400/68, scalloped foot, regular, 5 oz. — 26
Sugar 2.75" #3900/41, regular footed, 6 oz. — 22
Toast or cheese cover 4.5" #1533, blown, ball finial — 400+
Tray 8.25" #3500/161 Gadroon, footed, shallow, round, handled — 28
Tumbler #321, sham base, whiskey, 2 oz. — 90
Tumbler #498, flat, cut flute, straight sided, whiskey, 2 oz. — 60
Tumbler #321, sham base, tapered juice, 5 oz. — 65
Tumbler #498, flat, cut flute, straight sided, juice, 5 oz. — 40
Tumbler 5.75" #3121, footed, juice, 5 oz. — 38
Tumbler #3400/38, flat, juice, 5 oz. — 28
Tumbler #7801, footed, juice, 5 oz. — 30
Tumbler #321, sham base, old fashion, 8 oz. — 50
Tumbler #498, flat, cut flute, straight sided, 8 oz. — 35
Tumbler 4.9" #497, sham, cut flute, straight sided, 9 oz. — 38
Tumbler #498, flat, cut flute, straight sided, 10 oz. — 38
Tumbler 7" #3121, footed, water, 10 oz. — 38
Tumbler (cut flute) #497, sham, straight sided, 11 oz. — 40
Tumbler #498, flat, cut flute, straight sided, 12 oz. — 40
Tumbler 7.5" #3121, footed, ice tea, 12 oz. — 42
Tumbler #3400/38, flat, ice tea, 12 oz. — 50

Top left: Tray 8.25" #3500/161 Gadroon, footed, shallow, round, handled. **Top right:** Cheese & cracker: comport 3" #3400/7, short stem, flared, 5.3" wide; plate 10.5" or 11.5", tab handled. **Bottom left:** Butter w/cover 5.5" #3400/52, round, 2 open handles; dome lid w/fancy ball finial. **Bottom right:** Relish 8.75" #3400/88, 2 open handled, oblong, 2 equal sections.

Left: Pitcher 8.1" #3400/141, water jug w/o ice lip, 80 oz. **Right:** Pitcher 9.25" #3400/152, Doulton style w/o ice lip, 76 oz.

Left: Hurricane lamp 9.3" #1617, skirted w/etched chimney. **Right:** Hurricane lamp 10.25" #1603, keyhole stem, bobeche w/prisms & etched chimney.

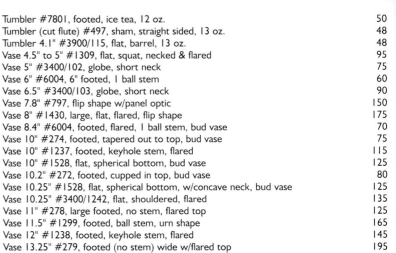

Tumbler #7801, footed, ice tea, 12 oz.	50
Tumbler (cut flute) #497, sham, straight sided, 13 oz.	48
Tumbler 4.1" #3900/115, flat, barrel, 13 oz.	48
Vase 4.5" to 5" #1309, flat, squat, necked & flared	95
Vase 5" #3400/102, globe, short neck	75
Vase 6" #6004, 6" footed, 1 ball stem	60
Vase 6.5" #3400/103, globe, short neck	90
Vase 7.8" #797, flip shape w/panel optic	150
Vase 8" #1430, large, flat, flared, flip shape	175
Vase 8.4" #6004, footed, flared, 1 ball stem, bud vase	70
Vase 10" #274, footed, tapered out to top, bud vase	75
Vase 10" #1237, footed, keyhole stem, flared	115
Vase 10" #1528, flat, spherical bottom, bud vase	125
Vase 10.2" #272, footed, cupped in top, bud vase	80
Vase 10.25" #1528, flat, spherical bottom, w/concave neck, bud vase	125
Vase 10.25" #3400/1242, flat, shouldered, flared	135
Vase 11" #278, large footed, no stem, flared top	125
Vase 11.5" #1299, footed, ball stem, urn shape	165
Vase 12" #1238, footed, keyhole stem, flared	145
Vase 13.25" #279, footed (no stem) wide w/flared top	195

Back left: Bowl 8.5" #1402/131 Tally Ho, deep, 3 equal sections. **Back right:** Relish 9.5" #477 Pristine, oblong w/tab feet, oval pickle or corn. **Front center:** Relish 12" #3500/67 Gadroon, round, 6 piece (5 inserts & tray) scalloped edge.

Top left: Comport 5.3" #3400/28, keyhole stem, 7.25" wide. **Right:** Sandwich server 10.5" #3400/10, center keyhole handle. **Bottom left:** Relish 6.25" #3500/69 Gadroon, 3 equal sections, scalloped edge, Crystal w/Gold encrusted.

Top row: Vase 5" #3400/102, globe, short neck, Crystal. **Bottom row left to right:** Vase 7.8" #797, flip shape w/panel optic, Crystal w/Gold encrusted; Vase 8.4" #6004, footed, flared, 1 ball stem, bud vase, Crystal w/Gold encrusted; Vase 10" #1237, footed, keyhole stem, flared, Crystal w/Gold encrusted; Vase 10.2" #272, footed, cupped in top, bud vase, Dianthus (pink) w/Gold encrusted; Vase 10.25" #1528, flat, spherical bottom w/concave neck, bud vase, Crystal; Vase 10" #274, footed, tapered out to top, bud vase, Crystal; Vase 10.25" #3400/1242, flat, shouldered, flared, Amber.

Left: Vase 12" #1238, footed, keyhole stem, flared, w/Gold encrusted. **Center:** Vase 8" #1430, large, flat, flared, flip shape. **Right:** Vase 11" #278, large footed, no stem, flared top.

Left: Candlestick 1-lite 5.25" #3400/646, keyhole stem. Center: Bowl 11.5" #3900/62, 4-footed, flared. Right: Candlestick 1-lite 5.25" #3400/646, keyhole stem; Amethyst w/Gold encrusted ($1,600 set – we found it priced this).

Cake salver 13" #170 Martha, footed.

Bonbon 6" #3500/54 Gadroon, footed, handled w/Gold trim edge.

Vase 6.5" #3400/103, globe, short neck, Gold Krystol ($395 – we found it priced this).

Vase 4.5" #1309, flat, squat, necked & flared.

Pattern detail, Willowmere.

Back left: Plate 6", #2560 Coronet, bread & butter. **Back center:** Plate 8.5", #2560 Coronet, lunch. **Front left:** Creamer 3.25", #2560 Coronet, footed, individual, 3.5 oz. **Front center:** Sugar 3", #2560 Coronet, footed, individual, 4 oz. **Front right:** Cup & saucer, coffee: cup 2.75", #2560 Coronet, footed, 5.5 oz.; saucer w/indent 5.75".

Back: Bowl 12.75", #2560 Coronet, shallow, flared, fruit. **Front:** Bowl 12", #2560 Coronet, deep, crimped, fruit.

WILLOWMERE
Fostoria Glass Company   Etching #333   1939-71
Color: Crystal

Willowmere is another of Fostoria's many rose etched patterns. Two roses are close together and linked by an intertwining branch of leaves. New collectors may confuse this etched pattern with Midnight Rose. Take a close look at the etched pattern detail to study the differences between the two. Willowmere is found on the Coronet #2560 blank. Accessory pieces and the stemware was produced on the Cellini #6024 blank.

The candlesticks are hard to spot, because the cascade part of the pattern is only found on the drip edge of the candle cup. This may cause you to overlook them.

Two-lite candlesticks, ice bucket, five section celery, pitcher, and vase are all items which collectors are always happy to find. Willowmere is still reasonably priced to attract new collectors. The pieces of Coronet can be mixed with the etching to stretch the budget even more and add variety to the table.

WILLOWMERE	Crystal
Bonbon 6.25" #2560 Coronet, flat, tab plume handles turned up	20
Bonbon 7.25", #2560 Coronet, 3-toed, flared	28
Bowl 5", #2560 Coronet, rim fruit	18
Bowl 5.5" #2560 Coronet, flat, tab plume handled, sweetmeat	22
Bowl 6", #2560 Coronet, flared, rim cereal	28
Bowl 8.5" #2560 Coronet, flat, tab plume handled, vegetable	36
Bowl 10", #2560 Coronet, deep, salad	58
Bowl 11", #2560 Coronet, plume handled, flared	65
Bowl 12", #2560 Coronet, deep, crimped, fruit	55
Bowl 12", #2560 Coronet, round, flared	48
Bowl 12.75", #2560 Coronet, shallow, flared, fruit	54
Cake plate 10.5" #2560 Coronet, tab plume handled	48
Candlestick 1-lite 4" #2560 1/2, tapered column stem, w/drip ring on candle cup, pair	60
Candlestick 1-lite 4.25" #2560 Coronet, graduated plume handled, pair	68
Candlestick 2-lite 5.1", #2560 Coronet, plume center, 9" spread, pair	95
Cheese & cracker: comport 2.8", #2560 Coronet, short stem, 5.25" wide; plate 11"	75
Comport 4.6", #2560 Coronet, plain stem, flared, 6" wide	48
Creamer 3.25", #2560 Coronet, footed, individual, 3.5 oz.	24
Creamer 4.1", #2560 Coronet, footed, regular, 7 oz.	20
Cruet w/stopper 4.5" #2560 Coronet, footed, oil, 3 oz.	110
Cup & saucer, coffee: cup 2.75", #2560 Coronet, footed, 5.5 oz.; saucer w/indent 5.75"	24
Finger bowl & liner: bowl 4.6" #869, blown, 8 oz.; plate w/indent 6"	28
Goblet 3.75" #6024 Cellini, cordial, 1 oz.	48
Goblet 4.75" #6024 Cellini, liquor cocktail, 3.5 oz.	22
Goblet 5.4" #6024 Cellini, wine, 3.5 oz.	28
Goblet 5.25" #6024 Cellini, claret, 4 oz.	30
Goblet 3.5" #6024 Cellini, oyster cocktail, 4.5 oz.	16
Goblet 4.35" #6024 Cellini, sherbet, 6 oz.	18
Goblet 5.75" #6024 Cellini, saucer champagne, 6 oz.	22
Goblet 7.25" #6024 Cellini, water, 10 oz.	30
Ice bucket 4.9", #2560 Coronet, footed, chrome handle	115
Mayonnaise 3 piece #2560 Coronet: bowl 5.5", footed, 3.25" high; liner w/indent 7.1"; ladle 5.75"	68
Mayonnaise 4 piece #2560 Coronet: bowl 6.75", footed, salad dressing, 3.5" high; liner w/indent 7.1"; 2 ladles 5.75"	85
Pitcher 6.9" #2666 Contour, flat, applied handle, ice lip, 32 oz.	295
Pitcher 9.75" #5000, footed, applied handle, water w/o ice lip, 48 oz.	325
Plate 6", #2560 Coronet, bread & butter	6
Plate 7.5", #2560 Coronet, salad or dessert	10
Plate 8.5", #2560 Coronet, lunch	14
Plate 9.5", #2560 Coronet, dinner	45
Plate 14", #2560 Coronet, torte or salad bowl liner	42
Relish 6.5", #2560 Coronet, flat, tab plume handled, 2 sections	28
Relish 6.75", #2560 Coronet, oval, olive	24
Relish 8.75", #2560 Coronet, oval, pickle	28
Relish 10", #2560 Coronet, tab plume handled, 2 equal sections & celery section	38
Relish 10", #2560 Coronet, tab plume handled, 3 equal sections & celery section	48
Relish 11", #2560 Coronet, oval, celery	34
Relish 13.25", #2560 Coronet, oval, 4 equal sections & celery section	75
Sandwich server 11.25" #2560 Coronet, center "question mark shape" handle	65
Shaker 2.9" #2560 Coronet, footed, chrome top, pair	85
Sugar 3", #2560 Coronet, footed, individual, 4 oz.	24
Sugar 3.5", #2560 Coronet, footed, regular, 7 oz.	20
Tray 7.5", #2560 Coronet, rectangle, for individual cream/sugar	26
Tray 10" #2560 Coronet, tab plume handles turned up, muffin	60
Tumbler 4.6" #6024 Cellini, footed, juice, 5 oz.	20
Tumbler 5.25" #6024 Cellini, footed, water, 9 oz.	26
Tumbler 5.75" #6024 Cellini, footed, ice tea, 12 oz.	30
Vase 7.5" #2567, square base, short stem, flared	75
Vase 9" #2568, square base, short stem, flared	85
Vase 9.5" #2470, footed, w/fancy 3 scroll stem, flared	175
Vase 10" #5100, round footed, flared large	160
Whip cream bowl 5" #2560 Coronet, flat, tab plume handled	32

Left: Goblet 4.35" #6024 Cellini, sherbet, 6 oz. Center left: Goblet 5.25" #6024 Cellini, claret, 4 oz. Center: Goblet 5.75" #6024 Cellini, saucer champagne, 6 oz. Center right: Goblet 7.25" #6024 Cellini, water, 10 oz. Right: Tumbler 5.75" #6024 Cellini, footed, ice tea, 12 oz.

Pitcher 9.75" #5000, footed, applied handle, water w/o ice lip, 48 oz.

Relish 13.25", #2560 Coronet, oval, 4 equal sections & celery section.

Back center: Cake plate 10.5" #2560 Coronet, tab plume handled. Front left: Sugar 3.5", #2560 Coronet, footed, regular, 7 oz. Front right: Creamer 4.1", #2560 Coronet, footed, regular, 7 oz.

Top left: Relish 10", #2560 Coronet, tab plume handled, 3 equal sections & celery section. Right: Sandwich server 11.25" #2560 Coronet, center "question mark shape" handle. Bottom left: Bonbon 7.25", #2560 Coronet, 3-toed, flared.

Collector Organizations

No matter what pattern you collect, we encourage you to belong to a non-profit organization that works to preserve the history of the American glass-making industry. These organizations enable you to gather more information on a particular glass company. All of the national organizations listed below provide information by publishing an educational newsletter, doing study guides, reprinting of company catalogs, doing seminars, holding a convention, having a museum, and presenting other educational activities.

Fostoria Glass Society
P.O. Box 826, Moundsville, WV 26041 304-845-9188
$16/year 8 newsletters a year
www.fostoriaglass.org

Glasstown USA
Attention: JR Schonscheck
5216 63rd Street
Kenosha, WI 53142 262-652-9749 or 262-358-0801
$12/year 6 newsletters a year
glasstown_usa@yahoo.com

Heisey Collectors of America
169 West Church Street, Newark, OH 43055 740-345-2932
$22/year 12 newsletters a year
www.heiseymuseum.org

National Cambridge Collectors
P.O. Box 416, Cambridge, OH 43725-0416
$17/year 12 newsletters a year
www.cambridgeglass.org

National Duncan Glass Society
P.O. Box 965, Washington, PA 15301 724-225-9950
$15/year 4 newsletters a year
http://duncan-glass.com

National Imperial Glass Collectors Society
P.O. Box 534, Bellaire, OH 43906 410-995-1254
$15/year 4 newsletters a year
www.imperialglass.org

Old Morgantown Collectors Guild
Box 849, Morgantown, WV 26505 304-599-2750
$15/year 4 newsletters
www.oldmorgantown.org

Pacific NW Fenton Association
P.O. Box 881, Tillamook, OR 97141 503-842-4815
$23/year 4 newsletters & exclusive piece of Fenton glass
www.glasscastle.com/pnwfa.htm

Paden City Glass Collectors Guild
P.O. Box 139, Paden City, WV 26159 304-337-9257
$15/year 4 newsletters
pcglasssociety@mailcity.com

Tiffin Glass Collectors
P.O. Box 554, Tiffin, OH 44883 419-447-5505
$15/year 4 newsletters
www.tiffinglass.org

West Virginia Museum of American Glass
P.O. Box 574, Weston, WV 26452
$25/year 4 newsletters

Replacing Items

Many times in our collections we have items that get damaged or broken. The best way to try to find a replacement is to contact dealers in your area to assist you. Go to every glass show and related convention you can. Many dealers will put you on their mailing list for locating items. Belong to an organization that specializes in the glass you collect. Another way is to contact Replacements. They have a huge data base and a large staff geared towards matching up your requests.

Replacements
P.O. Box 26029 or 1089 Knox Road, Greensboro, NC 27420
1-800-737-5223
Web Site: www.replacements.com

Glass Museums

To further enhance our education, it is extremely worth while to visit many glass museums to see other fine examples of American glass. It is really important to support all of their various activities so more examples can be acquired for us to view. The following is list of several museums we recommend visiting.

All American Museum of Glass, 748 Hwy 99 W Lafayette, OR (located inside the antique mall) 503-864-2720
Cambridge Glass Museum, Cambridge, OH ; 740-432-4245
Corning Museum of Glass, Corning, N Y; 607-937-5371
Duncan Glass Museum, Washington, PA;
Fenton Art Glass Museum, 700 Elizabeth St., Williamstown, WV (located inside factory) 304-375-7772
Heisey Glass Museum, 169 W. Church St., Newark, OH; 740-345-2932
Imperial Glass Museum, Bellaire, OH
Museum of American Glass at Wheaton Village; Millville, NJ; 800-998-4552
Museum of Glass, Tacoma, WA; 866-468-7386
Oglebay Institute Glass Museum, Wheeling, WV; 304-242-7272
Sandwich Glass Museum, Sandwich, MA; 508-888-1251
West Virginia Museum of American Glass, Weston, WV; 304-269-5006

Bibliography

A. H. Heisey & Co. *Company Brochures*. Newark, Ohio: A. H. Heisey & Company, 1940s.

Archer, Margaret & Douglas. *Collector's Encyclopedia of Glass Candlesticks*. Paducah, Kentucky: Collector Books, 1983.

Barnett, Jerry. *Paden City The Color Co*. Astoria, Illinois: Stevens Publishing, 1978.

Bickenheuser, Fred. *Tiffin Glass Masters Volume I*. Grove City, Ohio: Glass Masters Publication, 1979.

_____. *Tiffin Glass Masters Volume II*. Grove City, Ohio: Glass Masters Publication, 1981.

_____. *Tiffin Glass Masters Volume III*. Grove City, Ohio: Glass Masters Publication, 1985.

Bones, Frances. *Duncan Glass*. Des Moines, Iowa: Wallace Homestead Book Company, 1973.

_____. *Fostoria Glassware 1887-1982*. Paducah, Kentucky: Collector Books, 1999.

Bones, Frances & Lee R. Fisher. *Standard Encyclopedia of American Silverplate*. Paducah, Kentucky: Collector Books, 1998.

Bradley, S. & C. & R. Ryan. *Heisey Stemware*. Newark, Ohio: Spencer Walker Press, 1979.

Bredehoft, Neila. *Collectors Encyclopedia of Heisey Glass*. Paducah, Kentucky: Collector Books, 1986.

_____. *Heisey's Orchid Etching*. Newark, Ohio: Heisey Collectors of America, 1983.

_____. *Heisey Rose*. Newark, Ohio: Heisey Collectors of America, 1983.

Bredehoft, Neila & Thomas. *Fifty Years of Collectible Glass 1920-70 Volume I*. Dubuque, Iowa: Antique Trader Books, 1997.

_____. *Fifty Years of Collectible Glass 1920-70 Volume II*. Dubuque, Iowa: Antique Trader Books, 2000.

_____. *Heisey Glass 1896-1957*. Paducah, Kentucky: Collector Books, 2001.

Bredehoft, Neila & Thomas & Louise Ream. *Encyclopedia of Heisey Glassware Volume I Etchings & Carvings*. Newark, Ohio: Heisey Collectors of America, 1977.

Bredehoft, Neila & Dean Six. *Paden City Glass The Lost Plates*. Weston, West Virginia: West Virginia Museum of American Glass, 2000.

Brown, O. O. *Paden City Catalog Reprints 1920s*. Marietta, Ohio: Antique Publications, 2000.

Burns, Mary Louise. *Heisey's Glassware of Distinction*. Grants Pass, Oregon: Mary Louise Burns, 1983.

Cambridge Glass Co. *Company Catalogs*. Cambridge, Ohio: Cambridge Glass Company, 1930s-'50s.

Conder, Lyle. *Collectors Guide to Heisey's Glassware For Your Table*. Gas City, Indiana: L-W Books, 1984.

Corning Glass Museum. *Archival material and microfiche*. Corning, New York: Corning Glass Museum, 2000.

Cudd, Viola. *Heisey Glassware*. Brenham, Texas: Herrmann Print Shop, 1969.

Dolan, Maryanne. *American Sterling Silver*. Florence, Alabama: Books Americana, 1993.

Duncan & Miller Glass Company. *Company Catalog #93*. Washington, Pennsylvania: The Duncan & Miller Glass Company, 1955.

_____. *Company Catalog #89*. Washington, Pennsylvania: The Duncan & Miller Glass Company, 1950.

_____. *Highest Quality Glass*. Washington, Pennsylvania: The Duncan & Miller Glass Company.

Duncan & Miller Glass Society. *Duncan Glass*. Washington, Pennsylvania: The Duncan & Miller Glass Society, 1997.

_____. *Company Brochures*. Washington, Pennsylvania: The Duncan & Miller Glass Society, 1930s-'50s.

Ezell, Elaine and George Newhouse. *Cruets, Cruets, Cruets Volume I*. Marietta, Ohio: Antique Publications, 1991.

Felt, Tom. *Heisey's Lariat & Athena Patterns*. Newark, Ohio: Heisey Collectors of America, 1986.

Felt, Tom & Bob O'Grady. *Heisey Candlesticks, Candelabra, & Lamps*. Newark, Ohio: Heisey Collectors of America, 1984.

Felt, Tom and Elaine & Rich Stoer. *Glass Candlestick Book Volume 1*. Paduch, Kentucky: Collector Books, 2003.

_____. *Glass Candlestick Book Volume 2*. Paduch, Kentucky: Collector Books, 2003.

Fenton Art Glass Co. *Company Catalogs*. Williamstown, West Virginia: Fenton Art Glass Co., 1958-90s.

Fenton, Frank M. *Personal correspondence*. Williamstown, West Virginia: Fenton Art Glass Company, 2000.

Florence, Gene. *Elegant Glassware of the Depression Era*. Paducah, Kentucky: Collector Books, 1999.

_____. *Collectors Encyclopedia of Depression Era Glass*. Paducah, Kentucky: Collector Books, 2000.

_____. *Collectible Glassware from the 40s, 50s, 60s*. Paducah, Kentucky: Collector Books, 2003.

Fostoria Glass Company. *Company Catalogs*. Moundsville, West Virginia: Fostoria Glass Co., 1930-80s.

Fostoria Glass Society. *Fostoria #2412*. Colony, Ohio: Fostoria Glass Society, 1990.

_____. *Facets of Fostoria newsletters*. Moundsville, West Virginia: Fostoria Glass Society, 1970s-'90s.

Gallagher, Jerry. *Handbook of Old Morgantown Glass*. Minneapolis, Minnesota: Merit Printing, 1995.

Gammon, Don. *Heisey Orchid Etched Glassware*. Cape Girardeau, Missouri: Don Gammon, 1975.

Garrison, Myrna & Bob. *Candlewick: The Crystal Line*. Atglen, Pennsylvania: Schiffer Publications, 2003.

_____. *Imperials Boudoir, Etcetera*. Marceline, Missouri: Walsworth Publishing, 1996.

_____. *Imperial Cape Cod*. Arlington, Texas: Myrna & Bob Garrison, 1991.

Goshe, Ed, Ruth Hemninger, & Leslie Piña. *'40s, '50s, & '60s Stemware by Tiffin*. Atglen, Pennsylvania: Schiffer Publications, 1999.

_____. *Depression Era Stems & Tableware Tiffin*. Atglen, Pennsylvania: Schiffer Publications, 1998.

Heacock, Bill. *Fenton Glass The First Twenty-five Years*. Marietta, Ohio: O-Val Advertising Corporation, 1978.

_____. *Fenton Glass The Second Twenty-five Years*. Marietta, Ohio: O-Val Advertising Corporation, 1980.

_____. *Fenton Glass The Third Twenty-five Years*. Marietta, Ohio: O-Val Advertising Corporation, 1989.

Heisey Collectors of America. *Heisey Catalog & Price List #32*. Newberg, Oregon: Headrick Buchdruckerei, 1994.

_____. *Heisey News newsletters*. Newark, Ohio: Heisey Collectors of America, 1970s-'90s.

Hildreth, Melanie, Therese Ujfalusi, Irene Gardner, & Gary Schneider. *Navarre Master Etching*. Walnut, California: Past Reflections, 1998.

Imperial Glass Corporation. *Company Brochure*. Bellaire, Ohio: Imperial Glass Corporation, 1947.

_____. *Company Brochures*. Bellaire, Ohio: Imperial Glass Corporation, 1950s.

Jones, Jim & Vince Sparacia. *Heisey's Classic Ridgeleigh Glassware*. Newark, Ohio: Heisey Collectors of America, 1987.

Krause, Gail. *Duncan Glass*. Smithtown, New York: Exposition Press, 1976.

Kerr, Ann. *Fostoria*. Paducah, Kentucky: Collector Books, 1994.

_____. *Fostoria Vol. II*. Paducah, Kentucky: Collector Books, 1997.

Kovar, Lorraine. *Westmoreland Glass 1950-84*. Marietta, Ohio: Antique Publications, 1991.

Krumme, Michael. *Paden City Party Line Newsletters*. Westminster, California: Michael Krumme, 1980s.

L. G. Wright Glass Company. *Company Catalogs*. New Martinsville, West Virginia: L. G. Wright Glass Company, 1960-70s.

Long, Milbra & Emily Seate. *Fostoria Useful & Ornamental*. Paducah, Kentucky: Collector Books, 2000.

_____. *Fostoria Stemware*. Paducah, Kentucky: Collector Books, 1995.

_____. *Fostoria Tableware 1924-43*. Paducah, Kentucky: Collector Books, 1999.

_____. *Fostoria Tableware 1944-86*. Paducah, Kentucky: Collector Books, 1999.

Mauzy, Barbara & Jim. *Mauzy's Depression Glass*. Atglen, Pennsylvania: Schiffer Publications, 2003.

McGrain, Patrick H. *Fostoria the Popular Years*. Frederick, Maryland: McGrain Publications, 1982.

Measell, James. *Imperial Glass Encyclopedia Volume I*. Marietta, Ohio: The Glass Press, 1995.

_____. *Imperial Glass Encyclopedia Volume II*. Marietta, Ohio: The Glass Press, 1997.

_____. *New Martinsville Glass 1900-44*. Marietta, Ohio: Antique Publications, 1994.

Measell, James & Berry Wiggins. *Great American Glass Volume 1*. Marietta, Ohio: Antique Publications, 1998.

_____. *Great American Glass Volume 2*. Marietta, Ohio: Antique Publications, 2000.

Miami Valley Cambridge Study Group. *Etchings by Cambridge Volume I*. Brookville, Ohio: Brookville Publishing, 1997.

Miller, Everett & Addie. *The New Martinsville Glass Story*. Marietta, Ohio: Richardson Publishing Co., 1972.

Mitchell, Dale. *Fuchsia*. San Jose, California: Dale Mitchell, 1998.

National Cambridge Collectors. *Cambridge Glass Co. 1949-53*. Paducah, Kentucky: Collector Books, 1978.

_____. *Cambridge Glass Co. 1930-34*. Paducah, Kentucky: Collector Books, 1976.

_____. *Crystal Ball newsletters*. Cambridge, Ohio: National Cambridge Collectors, 1970s-'90s.

National Duncan Glass Society. *Duncan Glass Journals*. Washington, Pennsylvania: National Duncan Glass Society, 1970s-'90s.

National Imperial Glass Collectors Society. *Imperial Glass Catalog #66A*. Marietta, Ohio: Richardson Printing Corporation, 1991.

_____. *Imperial Collectors Gazettes*. Bellaire, Ohio: National Imperial Glass Collectors, 1970s-'90s.

Nye, Mark A. *Cambridge Stemware*. Miami, Florida: Mark Nye, 1994.

_____. *Candlelight*. Cambridge, Ohio: National Cambridge Collectors, 2000.

_____. *Caprice*. Cambridge, Ohio: National Cambridge Collectors, 1994.

_____. *Chantilly*. Cambridge, Ohio: National Cambridge Collectors, 2000.

_____. *Personal Correspondence*. Brooklyn, Michigan, 2000.

_____. *Rose Point*. Cambridge, Ohio: National Cambridge Collectors, 1989.

Old Morgantown Collectors Guild. *Morgantown newsletters*. Morgantown, West Virginia: Old Morgantown Collectors Guild, 1990s.

Pacific NW Fenton Association. *Nor'Wester newsletters*. Tillamook, Oregon: Pacific NW Fenton Association, 1990s.

Paden City Glass Collectors Guild. *Paden City newsletters*. Paden City, West Virginia: Paden City Glass Collectors Guild, 1990s.

Pendergrass, Paula and Sherry Riggs. *Glass Candleholders*. Atglen, Pennsylvania: Schiffer Publications, 2001.

Pendergrass, Paula and Sherry Riggs. *Elegant Glass Candleholders*. Atglen, Pennsylvania: Schiffer Publications, 2002.

Piña, Leslie. *Depression Era Glass by Duncan*. Atglen, Pennsylvania: Schiffer Publications, 1999.

_____. *Fostoria American Line 2056*. Atglen, Pennsylvania: Schiffer Publications, 1999.

Piña, Leslie and Jerry Gallagher. *Tiffin Glass 1914-40*. Atglen, Pennsylvania: Schiffer Publications, 1996.

Piña, Leslie and Paula Ockner. *Depression Era Art Deco Glass*. Atglen, Pennsylvania: Schiffer Publications, 1999.

Roberts, Mary Ann. *Heather Plate Etching No. 343*. Chatsworth, California: Fostoria Glass Society of Southern California, 1993.

Seligson, Sidney. *Fostoria American A Complete Guide*. Wichita Falls, Texas: Sidney Seligson, 1994.

Six, Dean. *Viking Glass 1944-1970*. Atglen, Pennsylvania: Schiffer Publications, 2003.

Smith, Bill & Phyllis. *Cambridge Glass 1927-29*. Springfield, Ohio: Bill & Phyllis Smith, 1986.

Snyder, Jeffrey B. *Morgantown Glass From Depression Glass Through the 1960s*. Atglen, Pennsylvania: Schiffer Publications, 1998.

Stout, Sandra. *Heisey on Parade*. Lombard, Illinois: Wallace Homestead Book Co., 1985.

Tiffin Glass Collectors. *Tiffin newsletters*. Tiffin, Ohio: Tiffin Glass Collectors, 1980s-'90s.

Walk, John. *Big Book of Fenton Milk Glass*. Atglen, Pennsylvania: Schiffer Publications, 2002.

_____. *Fenton Glass Compendium 1940 - 1970*. Atglen, Pennsylvania: Schiffer Publications, 2001.

West Virginia Museum of American Glass. *Archival material*. Weston, West Virginia: West Virginia Museum of American Glass, 2001-'03.

_____. *Glory Hole newsletters*. Weston, West Virginia: West Virginia Museum of American Glass, 1990s.

_____. *L.G. Wright Glass*. Atglen, Pennsylvania: Schiffer Publications, 2003.

Viking Glass Co. *Company Catalogs*. New Martinsville, West Virginia: Viking Glass Co., 1960-80s.

Vogel, Clarence. *Heisey's Early & Late Years*. Galion, Ohio: Fisher Printing, 1971.

_____. *Heisey's Art & Colored Glass*. Galion, Ohio: Fisher Printing, 1970.

Washburn, Kent. *Price Survey*. San Antonio, Texas: Kent Washburn Antiques, 1994.

Weatherman, Hazel Marie. *Fostoria the First 50 Years*. Springfield, Missouri: The Weathermans, 1972.

_____. *Colored Glassware of the Depression Era 2*. Springfield, Missouri: Weatherman Glass Books, 1974.

Welker, Mary, Lyle & Lynn. *Cambridge Glass Company Catalogs I*. Cambridge, Ohio: Lynn Welker, 1970.

_____. *Cambridge Glass Company Catalogs II*. Cambridge, Ohio: Lynn Welker, 1970.

Westmoreland Glass Co. *Della Robbia Catalog*. Grapeville, Pennsylvania: Westmoreland Glass Company, 1940.

Wetzel-Tomalka, Mary M. *Candlewick The Jewel of Imperial Book II*. Marceline, Missouri: Walsworth Publishing Company, 1995.

Whitmyer, Kenn & Margaret. *Fenton Art Glass Patterns 1939-80*. Paducah, Kentucky: Collector Books, 1999.

_____. *Fenton Art Glass 1907-39*. Paducah, Kentucky: Collector Books, 1999.

Williams, Juaninta. *Fostoria Glass: Scarce, Unique and Whimseys*. Atglen, Pennsylvania: Schiffer Publications, 2004.

_____. *Fostoria the Glass of Fashion*. Jacksonville, Oregon: Juanita L. Williams, 1997.

Williams, Juanita L. & Christopher George. *Chintz*. Jacksonville, Oregon: Juanita L. Williams, 1996.

_____. *Fostoria Popular Plate Etchings*. Jacksonville, Oregon: Juanita L. Williams, 1998.

_____. *Fostoria By Ye Candlelight*. Jacksonville, Oregon: Juanita L. Williams, 1996.

Williams, Juanita L. & Jonathan. *Fostoria Glass Co. Study Guide to Patterns*. Jacksonville, Oregon: Juanita L. Williams, 1996.

Williams, Juanita, Therese McIlrath, & Maryanne Roberts. *Fostoria Master Etchings 1936-72*. Chatsworth, California: Fostoria Glass Society of Southern California, 1993.

Wilson, Jack. *Phoenix & Consolidated Glass*. Marietta, Ohio: Antique Publications, 1989.

Yeakley, Virginia & Loren. *Heisey Glass in Color*. Marietta, Ohio: Richardson Printing Corporation, 1978.

Glossary

There are many different terms that are used throughout this book. We have tried to use original company terms as much as possible. To help the collector understand different terminology, we are providing this reference page.

after dinner cup & saucer - footed small size used for cappuccino also referred to as demitasse

baked apple - round bowl that has a flat rim, which is parallel to the table, around the edge of the bowl (smaller than a rim soup bowl)

baker - term once used by glass companies for an oval vegetable bowl (note: not meant for oven use)

banana split - an oblong serving dish, with one handle, for the traditional banana split dessert

banana stand - footed oval dish with 2 sides turned up, used as a center piece by placing the bananas with the curled end down and radiating out forming a fan shape

banquet size - refers to large size of tall figural stem made by Cambridge

barrel - term used to describe even convex shape, used on tumblers

basket - refers to either conventional handled basket, or a 2-handled bowl with the handles turned up (usually these are footed)

bellied - term used to describe uneven convex shape

beverage - tumbler: flat, no stem or a short stem, usually holding more than 13 oz.

biscuit jar - cylindrical container with metal bail (handle) and metal cover, smaller than a cookie jar

bitters - flat spherical bottom with narrow short or long neck; looks like a small barber bottle but was used for spirits or liquor

black out lamp - candle holder with a cylindrical glass shade, produced and used during WWII during black outs, to give a soft light enabling movement around the house

bobeche - a piece of glass that has prisms attached to it by a wire hook, which can be attached, set on or part of the candle holder itself changing it into a candelabra

bonbon - flat small dish with two handles turned up, usually 5" to 6" diameter

bouillon cup - 2-handled bowl for serving soup;smaller than a cream soup

brandy - goblet having a tall stem, usually holding .75 to 1.25 oz.

brandy inhaler - goblet having a short stem, usually holding 12 to 40 oz.

bread & butter plate - plate usually around 6" diameter

cabaret - flat plate larger than a dinner plate, used for serving finger food (have small center) turned or cupped up on the edge

cake plate - flat plate with two opposing handles, used for serving cake, from 9.75" to 11.75"

cake salver - short footed plate used for serving cake or desserts

cake stand - tall footed plate used for serving cake or desserts

California butter - short butter dish, looking like a .25 lb. covered butter, only smaller

candelabra - candle holder with bobeche and prisms

candle bowl - bowl made into a candle holder

candle lamp - candle holder with glass shade also referred to as a hurricane lamp

celery - oval or rectangular shaped relish dish designed to accommodate celery sticks

celery radish relish - oval or rectangular shaped relish dish designed to accommodate radishes and celery, by being two sections (one section 1/3 and one section 2/3 of length of piece)

celery relish - oval or rectangular shaped relish dish designed to accommodate pickles, olives and celery, by three or five sections divided (note one section is long for celery and other sections are equal)

celery vase - flat cylindrical straight sided; used to serve celery

center handled server tray - used in serving cut up sandwiches, also referred to as a sandwich server or lunch tray

cereal bowl - round, larger than a fruit, but smaller than a soup

cheese comport - low footed dish, bowl or plate with a stem used to serve cheese and made to fit into the center indent of a cracker plate as a two piece serving set

cigarette box - flat rectangular or cylindrical(upright or on side) covered container for holding cigarettes (old cigarettes were shorter), usually had individual ash trays to form a smoking set

cigarette holder - flat or footed, open container that is rectangular or oval open for holding cigarettes (old cigarettes were shorter)

claret - goblet having a tall stem, usually holding 4 to 4.5 oz.

club plate - name for divided plate with usually three sections, also referred to as grill plate

coaster - round plate with indent or recessed center, usually having raised rays or pattern in the bottom to keep moisture from building up on bottom of glass (table protection)

cocktail - goblet having a tall stem, usually holding 3 to 3.5 oz.

cocktail icer - a deep sherbet that holds a liner; liner is a small lipped finger bowl that sits on the ice

cocktail mixer - flat or footed cylindrical vessel with metal or glass lid, with or without a handle, also referred to as a cocktail shaker

cocktail shaker - flat or footed cylindrical vessel with metal or glass lid, with or without a handle, also referred to as a cocktail mixer

comport - footed dish, bowl or plate with a stem also referred to as compote in some sales material

confectionery box - flat covered container for use in holding chocolates

console bowl - large(several shapes, footed or flat) used as a center piece

console set - large bowl (several shapes, footed or flat) used with two candle holders to form a three piece center piece

cookie jar - cylindrical covered container also referred to as cracker or pretzel jar

cordial - goblet having a tall stem, usually holding .75 to 1.25 oz.

cornucopia - flat open center piece arranger also can be a footed short stem tapered from wide opening down to a pointed tail (sometimes with a ball on the end)

coupe salad - plate usually around 6.5" to 7.5" diameter cupped or turned up on edge

crab meat insert - cylindrical vessel slightly flared at top used to keep the juice from mixing with the ice that would keep it chilled, usually 4 oz.

cracked ice - extra large ice tub holding .5 gallon of ice; used by hotels

cracker jar - cylindrical covered container also referred to as pretzel or cookie jar

cracker plate - a with or without handled plate with indent, used to serve crackers with a cheese comport setting on the center of it, forming a two piece serving set

cream soup - 2-handled bowl for serving soup, larger than a bouillon cup

creme de menthe - goblet having a tall stem, usually holding 1.75 to 2 oz.

crescent salad - kidney shaped side plate, resembling a bone dish but larger

crimped - top edge will be reworked by the glass artisan to create several different finishes, such as ruffle, pie crimped, tri-corner, etc.

cruet - bottle with a stopper, most often handled, also referred to as oil or vinegar bottle

crushed fruit - covered cylindrical vessel used to hold and serve a fruit dessert

crushed fruit spoon - long handled spoon used with a crushed fruit to serve a fruit dessert

cut flute - refers to the panels on a stem the appear to have been cut away to form the pattern

dessert plate - plate usually around 7" to 8.5" diameter (small center)

dinner plate - ranges from 9" to 9.5" diameter for small size dinner and 10" to 10.5" for large size dinner plate (large flat center)

dinner water - goblet having a tall stem, usually holding 8 to 10 oz.

Doulton - Cambridge pitcher having a handle rising above the rim

drip-cut - name used for the Sani-cut type of metal syrup pitcher cover (spring loaded thumb operated cover)

epergne - center piece item with multiple horns for flowers or sometimes multiple vases or bowls for serving finger foods

ferrule - a metal ring (holds a mirror) that has a shaft

finger bowl - flat, flared out (looks like a large custard cup) usually blown

flip vase - flat, straight sides that taper out to the top (top wider than the base) named for a 1920s popular drink that was served in this shape tumbler

floating garden - usually oval straight sided bowl or center piece flower arranger, used to float flowers in

flower block - used in bottom of a bowl to arrange flowers or at the top of some vases for arranging flowers also referred to as a flower frog

flower frog - used in bottom of a bowl to arrange flowers or at the top of some vases for arranging flowers also referred to as a flower block

French salad dressing bottle - flat or footed bottle with stopper, usually concave sided, rolled lip and spouted, 7-8 oz.

fruit bowl - round flat bowl, smaller than a cereal bowl

fruit cocktail - goblet having a short stem, usually holding 5 to 5.5 oz.

fruit cocktail insert - cylindrical vessel flaring out wide from almost the bottom of the piece used to keep the fruit cocktail from mixing with the ice that would keep it chilled, 5 oz.

gardenia bowl - shallow bowl, used for floating cut gardenias as a center piece

globe vase - spherical or ball shaped

glove box - covered container for holding ladies dress gloves, sometimes used as part of a dresser set or vanity set

grapefruit icer - flat bowl with three raised rays to hold insert, to keep it from separated from the ice that would keep it chilled

gravy boat - spouted bowl, usually handled and oval; can be round, even with an attached liner

grill plate - name for divided plate with usually three sections, also referred to as a club plate

guest set - spherical water vessel with/with out a handle which has a tumbler placed on top, used to hold water for use at night also referred to as a nite set or tumble up

G. W. W. - Gone with the Wind Lamp

hair receiver - covered container for holding ladies hair, when saved up could be used as a added adornment for hair styling

handkerchief box - covered container for holding ladies handkerchiefs, sometimes used as part of a dresser set or vanity set

hollow stem - goblet having a tall stem that is hollow all the way down to the foot

honey jar - flat covered jar

horseradish bottle - flat or footed small covered container, usually having a spoon that fits through the slot in the lid

humidor - flat cylindrical covered container, used for tobacco or cigars, usually lid was metal

hurricane lamp - candle holder with glass shade also referred to as a candle lamp

ice bucket - flat cylindrical container for ice with tab handles or metal bail (handle) also referred to as ice tub

ice cream - low footed dish also referred to as a sherbet or sundae

ice dish - flat bowl with three raised rays to hold liners and ice, to keep food chilled

ice dish liner - the special shaped vessel that is put inside the ice dish

ice dish plate - small plate used under the ice dish, usually 6"

ice tea - tumbler: flat, or a short stem, usually holding 11 to 13 oz.

ice tub - flat cylindrical container for ice with tab handles or metal bail (handle) also referred to ice bucket

ivy ball - footed with a stem, cylindrical or ball shaped vase

J. I. P. - jack in pulpit

jack in pulpit - vase, has top edge pulled down and back pulled up to look like a tulip. Also called tulip vase.

jelly - flat or footed dish, smaller than a candy, it also can be covered

jewel box - covered small size container for holding ladies jewelry

jug - large flat or footed handled vessel for serving water also referred to as a water pitcher

juice - tumbler: flat, or a short stem, usually holding 4 to 5 oz.

keyhole - refers to a stem or finial that was produced by Cambridge & Paden City that looks like the keyhole cover which used old skeleton keys

lady leg - shape of stem on goblets that resemble a lady's leg

lemon dish - flat shallow covered dish with two handles

lemon plate - flat small dish with two handles, usually 5" to 6" diameter

lily pond - shallow bowl, cupped in at the edge for floating flowers

liner - under plate for a serving vessel or term used for the insert that would hold item being served keeping it from mixing with the ice that would keep it chilled

liquor cocktail - goblet having a tall stem, usually holding 3 to 3.5 oz.

lunch plate - plate usually around 8" to 9" diameter (large flat center)

lunch tray - center handled server tray for use in serving cut up sandwiches, also can sometimes be referring to a 2-handled serving tray or sandwich server

lunch water - goblet having a short stem, usually holding 8 to 10 oz.

mantle lustre - large vase with attached prisms, originally placed on a fireplace mantle for decoration

marmalade - flat small covered container, usually blown with necked in lip at the top

martini cocktail - goblet having a tall stem, usually holding 3 to 3.5 oz.

mayonnaise - bowl for serving mayonnaise, many shapes: flared, cupped, rolled edge, round, heart, oval, handled and square

mint dish - flat flared dish with two handles

muffin - flat plate with two turned up handles (looks like a large bonbon), usually 12" or larger

mushroom shape - shape found on bowls and also candle holders, resembling a mushroom

mustard - flat or footed small covered container, usually having a mustard spoon that fits through the slot in the lid

nappy - another name for bowl, many shapes and with handle or with out

nite set - spherical water vessel with/with out a handle which has a tumbler placed on top, used to hold water for use at night also referred to as a guest set or tumble up

oil bottle - bottle with a stopper, most often handled, but not always, also referred to as cruet

old fashion - tumbler, flat, or a short stem, usually holding 6 to 8 oz.

olive - oval or rectangular shaped relish dish designed to accommodate olives

optic - technique of using the varying thickness of glass to form an interior pattern

oval vegetable bowl - serving bowl usually flared at top or with a rim used for vegetables or other foods also referred to as a baker by glass companies

oyster cocktail - goblet, no stem or a short stem, usually holding 4 to 4.5 oz.

parfait - goblet having a short stem and tall bowl, usually holding 4.5 to 6.5 oz.

pansy vase - footed, small rose bowl, usually under 4"

pickle - oval or rectangular shaped relish dish designed to accommodate pickles, cut lengthwise

pin tray - open oval or rectangular shaped dish, sometimes used as part of a dresser set or vanity set

platter - flat oval serving plate

Pokal - Imperial's term for a covered urn

pomade box - covered small size container for holding ladies cosmetics

porch vase - vase slightly swung by the glass artisan, using centrifugal force to pull the vase into a short fat swung vase (some distorting of the pattern in the center)

powder box - covered container for holding ladies facial powder, used as part of a dresser set or vanity set also referred to a puff box

preserve - open or covered handled dish, usually smaller than a candy

pretzel jar - cylindrical covered container also referred to as a cracker or cookie jar

puff box - covered container for holding ladies facial powder, used as part of a dresser set or vanity set also referred to a powder box

refractory - oval, four footed bowl, that is cupped

Rhine wine - goblet having a extra tall stem, usually holding 4 to 4.5 oz.

rim - refers to the flat rim which is parallel to the table, that can be found on certain pieces

rim soup - bowl for soup that has a flat rim which is parallel to the table, around the edge of the bowl

rose bowl - flat spherical or ball shaped vase

salad dressing bottle - flat or footed bottle with stopper, usually concave sided, rolled lip and spouted, 7 to 8 oz.; also called French salad dressing

salad dressing bowl - divided for serving two types of sauce, many shapes: flared, cupped, rolled edge, round, heart, oval, handled and square

salad plate - plate usually around 7" to 8.5" diameter

salt dip - flat individual open salt, usually less that 2" diameter

sandwich plate - round 2-handled, usually 11" to 14"

sandwich server - center handled server tray for use in serving cut up sandwiches also can sometimes be referring to a 2-handled serving tray or lunch tray

Sani-cut - name used for the drip-cut type of metal syrup pitcher cover (spring loaded thumb operated cover)

saucer champagne - goblet having a tall stem, usually holding 5 to 6.5 oz. also referred to as a high or tall sherbet

service plate - plate usually larger than 11" diameter (small center)

sham - refers to the base of a vessel, denotes that it is weighted (thick like bar ware)

sherbet - goblet having a short stem, usually holding 5 to 6.5 oz. also referred to as a low sherbet, ice cream or sundae

sherry - goblet having a tall stem, usually holding 1.5 to 2 oz.

shrimp & dip - large bowl with indent in center to hold small sauce dish

spooner - flat, cylindrical straight sided, made to hold spoons

straw jar - flat cylindrical straight sided covered jar, tall enough to hold drinking straws

sugar cuber - flat cylindrical straight sided container with sugar tongs built into the chrome plated lid, used for serving sugar cubes

sundae - goblet low footed no stem, usually holding 5 to 6.5 oz. also referred to as a ice cream or sherbet

sweet pea vase - flat wide flared, looks like a deep flared bowl

sweetmeat - flat small deep flared dish with two handles, usually 5" to 6" diameter

swung vase - any vase swung by the glass artisan, using centrifugal force to pull the vase into a longer form than it came out of the mould (distorts the pattern in the center)

syrup - flat handled pitcher, usually with cover

table goblet - water short stem, usually holding 8 to 10 oz.

table tumbler - water: flat, or a short stem, usually holding 8 to 10 oz.

tidbit - two plates or two bowls with a metal center handle to hold them apart for serving finger food

Tom & Jerry - footed, small sized punch bowl

tomato juice insert - cylindrical vessel slightly flared at top used to keep the juice from mixing with the ice that would keep it chilled, usually 5 oz.

toothpick - flat or footed cylindrical vessel designed to hold toothpicks, for table use

torte plate - flat plate larger than a dinner plate used for serving (have small center)

trophy bowl - flat or footed bowl with two large handles that extend above the edge of the bowl (a classic trophy shape)

tumble up - spherical water vessel with/with out a handle which has a tumbler placed on top, used to hold water for use at night also referred to as a guest set or nite set

urn - footed tall covered container, usually twice the size of a footed candy jar

utility - bowls or trays, 9" to 10", used for serving multiple kinds of foods

vegetable bowl - round or oval serving bowl usually flared at top or with a rim used for vegetables or other foods

vinegar bottle - bottle with a stopper, most often handled but not always, also referred to as cruet

violet vase - flat or footed (no stem) cylindrical or ball shaped vase (smaller than a rose bowl)

wedding box - pedestal covered square container

whiskey - tumbler: flat, no stem or a short stem, usually holding 2 to 2.5 oz.

wine - goblet having a tall stem, usually holding 3 to 4 oz.

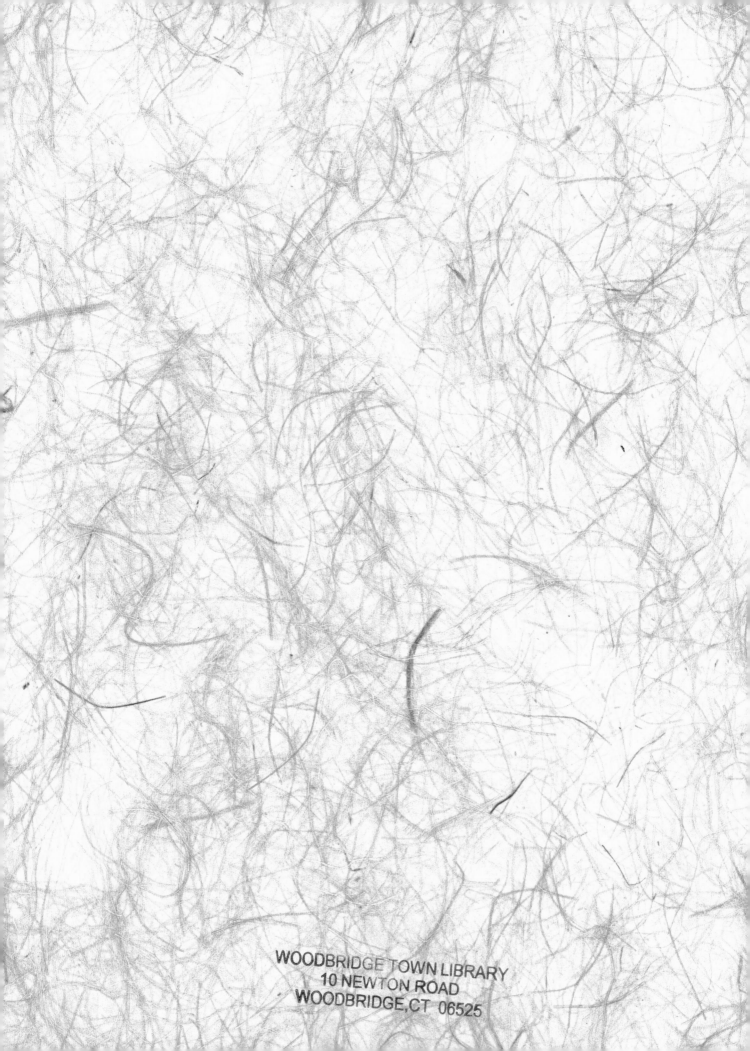